CONTENTS

ACT III: THE WAR YEARS

Appendices

The springs of song have died, the age of glory is done.
Never again have such poets arisen
Never again have such songs been sung.

Judah Alharisi (c. 1165—1225)

PRELUDE

What makes a popular song a standard? By what magic is a seemingly inconsequential collection of words and music converted into an enduring national treasure. Surely it isn't quality alone; in this book there are some marvelously inventive songs, but many perfectly ordinary ones as well. These 546 songs of the 1920s, '30s, and '40s have only one thing in common: somewhere along the line they hit a chord with the public, a resounding chord that is still ringing.

A few of us grew up with these songs, others came along later. But all of us, no matter of what generation, have had some contact with them, whether we realize it or not. How many know, for example, that the theme song of the Harlem Globetrotters ("Sweet Georgia Brown") was written in 1925; or that an increasing number of television commercials feature such old standards as "Blue Skies", written in 1927; "Makin' Whoopee", the hit song of 1928; or "Falling in Love Again (Can't Help It)", introduced to American audiences by Marlene Dietrich in the 1930 film, *The Blue Angel*?

This book is a celebration of standards from what has been dubbed the Golden Age of American popular song, the years from 1920 through 1945, a time when composers and lyricists were at the peak of their powers and the public eagerly ready to receive their creations. In it, I hope to capture the essence of these lasting songs and. to that end, have endeavored to examine each one of them in an early edition. I am indebted to the following institutions for making their extensive collections available to me: the Sarasota Music Archive, in Sarasota, Florida; the Atheneum in La Jolla, California; and the Archive of Popular American Music at the University of California, Los Angeles Music Library Special Collections. In particular, I wish to thank Timothy F. Edwards, Head of Operations at the UCLA Music Library Special Collections, for making available his vast and extraordinary collection of over 650,000 copies of sheet music, with the able assistance of Laura Osweiler and Ben Angeles.

Special thanks go to Professor Hermine W. Williams of Hamilton College, who looked over the manuscript with her usual sharp editorial eye. At Two Bytes Publishing, Ltd., Elizabeth F. Clark has been a steadfast supporter of the project from its inception; her familiarity with the wily ways of the computer has proved invaluable and her encouragement has never lapsed. I also want to thank Walt Matis of Two Bytes for his warm enthusiasm and critical suggestions, and Steve Paymer, David Paymer, Liz Georges, Madalene Kesner, Byron Kesner, Jonathan Lach, and Sally Sarsfield for their technical support and advice, without which the project might never have been realized. As always, an *auszeichnung* goes to my wife, Edye, for her constant support and encouragement during this four-year endeavor.

And a special tribute goes to the working instrumentalists and vocalists who have kept these songs alive for more than half a century.

OVERTURE

The years between 1920 and 1945 were of supreme importance in the history of popular song in America. These twenty-five golden years saw the rise of musical comedy, radio, the big bands, recordings, and the film musical; the eminence of such songwriters as Jerome Kern, Irving Berlin, George and Ira Gershwin, Cole Porter, Vincent Youmans, Richard Rodgers, Lorenz Hart, Oscar Hammerstein II, Harold Arlen, and Johnny Mercer; the creation of the seminal musical plays *Show Boat* in 1927 and *Oklahoma!* in 1943 and the opera *Porgy and Bess* in 1935. They also spawned and nurtured some of the most innovative music and lyrics ever written in the field of popular music, songs that are a distinctive American cultural heritage.

Hundreds of thousands of songs were published during this period. Of this immense outpouring, only a minute fraction is regularly heard today. The 546 songs portrayed in the following pages are known as standards. They are fondly remembered as songs that have lasted for half a century and more and seem to be in a state of perpetual revivification, heard constantly in recordings, on the radio, on television, or in movies. They jingle in our ears while we're shopping in the supermarket, riding an elevator, or waiting while the telephone is on hold. They are played and sung at dances and wedding receptions. They form the backbone of the repertoires of jazz singers and instrumentalists. They are indeed survivors, firmly etched in the memories of those who grew up with them as well as those who didn't.

Inevitably, the selection process will leave out somebody's favorite song. But our central criterion for inclusion remains: Is the song heard today? With that in mind, we have endeavored to include all significant standards, judging from record sales; radio, television, and film performances; wire service playings; utilization by musicians; and just plain familiarity to the general public.

We limit ourselves to the quarter century beginning in 1920 simply because the vast majority of innovative and lasting standards were written during those years. Act I, "The Roaring Twenties", covers the years from 1920 to 1929; Act II, "The Depression Years", those from 1930 to 1939, and Act III, "The War Years", those from 1940 to 1945. Each act begins with a Prologue, giving an overview and general description of the songs of that period. Every annual listing starts with a look at the songs and the background against which they were written: the political, economic, social, and artistic events of that year, followed by the songs themselves, listed alphabetically.

Each song portrait begins with its writer(s) and where, when, and by whom it was introduced. The body of each entry tells us more about the song: what makes it special, how it was created, something about its background. It also includes a brief characterization of the music and lyrics, along with early recordings and a summary of films that used the song. The entry closes with the song's vital statistics: its initial publisher(s); the presence or absence of a *verse*; the lengths of verse and *refrain*; and the *key*, starting note, first chord after the *pickup*, and *form* of the refrain.[1]

The Popular Song Index

Inasmuch as some songs are more familiar or unusual than others, we have devised a Popular Song Index to distinguish ordinary songs from those that are either better known or more innovative, as follows:

* * * * Classic songs, familiar to almost everyone
* * *   Well-known songs, often performed as jazz standards
* *   Very familiar songs
*   Songs of more than average familiarity
!   Unusual or innovative songs that break away from the ordinary

Eighteen Superstandards

The eighteen four-star songs in this book transcend the popularity of ordinary standards. These are superstandards: truly the classics of popular song, heard so often that they have become part of the collective consciousness. They are part of our heritage, uniting and defining us as Americans. Although full information about each of these songs may be found under its appropriate year, we list them here chronologically, for the reader's convenience.

---

1.   Explanation of the words in italics and of other technical terms may be found in the "Glossary".

18. *White Christmas* (1942), p. 435
   Berlin's seasonal perennial

These superstandards share several characteristics. All were produced between the years 1924 and 1942. Most were written in the 1930s, a decade which coincided with the Great Depression: a time of poverty, despair, and, paradoxically, of musical masterworks. The majority are romantic ballads. Most are by composers of stature: four by George Gershwin, three by Irving Berlin, two each by Cole Porter and Jerome Kern, and one each by Harold Arlen, Hoagy Carmichael, Vernon Duke, and Vincent Youmans. Lyricists represented (besides Berlin and Porter, who wrote their own words), are Ira Gershwin, with three songs, and E. Y. "Yip" Harburg, with two.

Musically, these classics run the gamut from simple ("White Christmas") to complex ("All the Things You Are"), from banal ("As Time Goes By") to sophisticated ("April in Paris"), from light-hearted ("Tea for Two") to serious ("God Bless America"), from the rhythm of the waltz ("Always") to that of the beguine ("Begin the Beguine"). It is interesting to note that we have categorized thirteen of the eighteen, those with exclamation points, as innovative or unusual. But innovative or not, each of these eighteen songs is a masterpiece in its own right. Collectively, they are living testaments to the artistic vitality of American popular music during its greatest flowering.

The Entries

As much information about each song is given as limited space will allow. To this end, every entry begins with the following information:

> Line 1: Name(s) of lyricist(s) and composer(s)
> Line 2: Date and place of the song's premiere, with number of
>   performances in parentheses
> Line 3: Name(s) of the person(s) who introduced the song

– and closes with the following information:

> Line 1: Type of song (ballad, foxtrot, waltz, rhythm song, etc.)
>   and length in bars of the verse (if present) and refrain
> Line 2: Original publisher(s)
> Line 3: Original key, starting note, first chord after pickup
>   (in parentheses), and form of the refrain

To indicate starting notes and other notes in the text, a commonly-used shorthand is used. Middle C of the piano keyboard is shown as c'. Notes below middle C are un-primed; those an octave and more above middle C are double-primed. Thus the full compass of notes can be shown as follows:

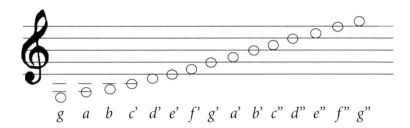

Form is illustrated in the conventional manner: "A" for first theme, "B" for second, and "C" for third. Thus, the most popular song form, "AABA", denotes a primary theme (A), its exact repetition (A), a new idea (B) in the middle section (also known as release or bridge), and a return to the first theme (A). Subsequent modifications to themes are shown by single or multiple primes (A' or A").

Thus the entry for a well-known song might begin:

SENTIMENTAL JOURNEY ✷ ✷ ✷
WORDS AND MUSIC: Bud Green, Les Brown, and Ben Homer
INTRODUCED BY: Les Brown and his Orchestra, vocal by Doris Day in a Columbia recording

The subsequent paragraphs of the entry (see page 464) tell us more about "Sentimental Journey": how it came to be, how it was introduced, who popularized it, when and by whom it was revived, the style characteristics of its music and lyrics, and if it was used in films. The entry then concludes with more technical information:

Very slow rhythm song with verse (8) and refrain (32)
PUBLISHER: Edwin H. Morris Company, Inc.
KEY: C maj., *STARTS*: e' (C maj.), *FORM:* AABA

≈≈≈≈≈≈≈≈≈≈≈≈≈≈≈≈≈≈

In other words, each song in this book poses for an intimate portrait. Words, of course, can never do full justice to any music. Nevertheless, we have endeavored to capture in words the essence of all the songs in this book. Needless to say, their true value can only be realized by hearing them "in person".

1920-1929

ACT I: THE ROARING TWENTIES

Prologue

Wait a minute! You ain't heard nuthin' yet.

– Al Jolson
The Jazz Singer

It would be inaccurate to think of the history of music as a continuum, gradually evolving from there to here. Like life itself, there have been peaks and valleys. So it was with popular song in the early years of the twentieth century. When Franz Lehár's operetta, *The Merry Widow,* opened at the New Amsterdam Theatre in New York on October 21, 1907, it had an enormous impact and launched a new era in the American musical theater; its influence extends to the present day. But that operetta's centerpiece is the waltz, a dance that had been around since the 1780s.

By the second decade of the new century, the waltz was still king in American popular music – it had been since the 1890s. But new sounds were stirring: ragtime, blues, and jazz. Songwriters soon capitalized on these new ideas. Although Irving Berlin's "Alexander's Ragtime Band" was a runaway hit in 1911 and W. C. Handy's "St. Louis Blues" was a sensation in 1914, they were neither ragtime nor pure blues (one section of "St. Louis Blues" is a tango). Yet most songs were still written in the old-fashioned way: simple in melody and harmony; light and cheerful in spirit. For the most part, they avoided the subject of romantic love, although there were a few exceptions such as "My Melancholy Baby" in 1912, and "You Made Me Love You (I Didn't Want to Do It)" in 1913.

That all changed when a musical play called *The Girl from Utah* opened at the Knickerbocker Theatre in New York on August 24, 1914. The hit of the show was an interpolated song with music by a young composer named Jerome Kern. "They Didn't Believe Me" became a model for all future writing for the musical stage. It is a ballad in 4/4 time on the subject of love, with a soaring melody and sophisticated harmonies. Still considered one of the most perfect songs ever written, it was way ahead of its time. Only in the 1930s were songs its equal in quality being produced.

The first jazz recordings were made in 1917 by The Original Dixieland Jass (sic) Band, which introduced two new songs that year: "The Darktown Strutters' Ball" and "Back Home Again in Indiana". So by 1920, jazz was definitely in the air. In fact, so pervasive did it become that it gave its name to the entire decade: The Jazz Age. Although the period has also been called The Roaring Twenties, the sobriquet, The Jazz Age, does properly summon up images of flappers, speakeasies, flaming youth, and bathtub gin. Still, The Roaring Twenties is probably more accurate, since the music of the 1920s was not consistently jazz-oriented. Immortal love songs, such as "The Man I Love" (1924) and "Someone to Watch Over Me" (1926) first saw the light of day. The landmark musical play, *Show Boat,* with a remarkable score by Oscar Hammerstein II and Jerome Kern, was produced in 1927. Both quality and quantity of songs improved as the decade progressed, paving the way for the remarkable output of the thirties.

What are the songs of the twenties like?

Most of them are foxtrots, a dance that had been introduced in 1913 by a vaudeville entertainer named Harry Fox, who glided around the stage with female partners in something called "Mr. Fox's Trot". The famous dance team of Vernon and Irene Castle made it the social dance of choice a few years later. There are many different types of foxtrots: slow, medium, and fast. Some are happy, some are sad, but all are either in 4/4 or 2/4 meter. Many of them are lively, echoing the spirit of the time. Each year has at least one fast-moving number: "Margie" (1920), "The Sheik of Araby" (1921), "Toot Toot Tootsie (Goo' Bye)" (1922), "Charleston" (1923), "California, Here I Come!" (1924), "Five Foot Two, Eyes of Blue (Has Anybody Seen My Girl?)" (1925), "Bye Bye Blackbird" (1926), "The Best Things In Life Are Free" (1927), "Button Up Your Overcoat" (1928), "Happy Days Are Here Again" (1929).

There also are a few ballads, a genre that developed out of the torch song. Although the ballad will not come into its own until the thirties, some beautiful ones, such as "Why Do I Love You? (1927), "More Than You Know" (1929), and the giant of them all, "Star Dust" (1929), stem from the twenties.

For good measure, the ubiquitous waltz of earlier days never really disappears. It keeps popping up at unexpected times. In the midst of the jazz mania, Irving Berlin manages to have two waltz hits in 1924, "All Alone" and "What'll I Do?" and two more in the following year, "Always" and "Remember". Adding spice to the mix are the novelties; 1923 is a big year for them, with "Barney Google", "Charleston", and "Yes! We Have No Bananas".

Like the times, most songs move along at a fast clip. Most foxtrots are in medium to fast tempo, from Moderato to Allegro. Even the ballads and waltzes are marked "Moderato" rather than "Slow". A few songs, like "The Sheik of Araby" (1921), are written to be performed in very fast tempo (Presto), as accompaniment to a gliding dance called The Peabody.

Virtually every song of the twenties is divided into two sections: verse and refrain. In the early years, more often than not, there are two verses. This is a holdover from the 1890s, when songs customarily had four or five verses that told a story. By 1924, one verse and one refrain is *de rigueur* and as time goes on, the refrain will become by far the most important part of the song.

In most songs, lyricist and composer are credited separately for words and music. But a few songwriters, notably the already established Irving Berlin, and the rising talents of Cole Porter and Noël Coward, write both words and music. One of the star composers is Vincent Youmans, who brings forth such hits as "Tea for Two" in 1924 and "Sometimes I'm Happy" in 1927. Several collaborations are particularly fruitful during the decade: those of Ira and George Gershwin, Lorenz Hart and Richard Rodgers, and Oscar Hammerstein II and Jerome Kern. There are also the prolific songwriting teams of Buddy De Sylva, Lew Brown, and Ray Henderson; and Dorothy Fields and Jimmy McHugh.

The vast majority of songs emanate from New York, although Hollywood gets an increasing share of the market with the advent of talking pictures in 1927. More specifically, most songs are spawned in Tin Pan Alley, the center of the popular music industry in New York. In the early twenties that legendary street is located on West 28th Street between Broadway and Sixth Avenue. As the decade progresses, however, many publishers move their offices uptown to the Times Square area, around Broadway and Seventh Avenue between 42nd and 50th Streets.

Song pluggers are active throughout the twenties, peddling their wares in beer gardens and department stores. Both George Gershwin and Jerome Kern begin their careers in this way. In the early twenties, vaudeville remains the favored method of introducing a new song. But as the decade progresses, more and more songs come to be introduced in revues and musical comedies. Technology begins to have an impact on the industry with the proliferation of record-players, radios, and motion picture palaces.

Subjects of the songs are varied, but they usually look at life through rose-colored glasses; "I'm Looking Over a Four Leaf Clover" is quite representative of the decade. There are the usual array of name songs like "Margie", "Dinah", and "Bill"; and place songs like "Chicago", "California, Here I Come!", and "Manhattan". Relatively few songs are about love, but even these are usually light-hearted, on the order of "Somebody Loves Me", "'S Wonderful", and "I Can't Give You Anything But Love (Baby)". With few exceptions, the romantic ballad does not come into its own until the thirties.

The year 1924 is a watershed in the history of American popular music. Before that time, refrains are somewhat amorphous in form and not always clearly structured. Very often the initial theme, "A", is simply repeated and elaborated upon, as in "Whispering": AA'AA. At other times, new themes are brought in, seemingly at random, as in "Margie":

ABA'C. There is no set pattern. This all changes in 1924, however, when one form comes to predominate, AABA, where "B" is the release or bridge. George Gershwin is a pioneer in using this form; three of his songs of that year are based on it: "Oh, Lady Be Good!", "The Man I Love", and "Somebody Loves Me". The thirty-two-bar refrain in AABA form comes to be the dominant one until well into the fifties. The wonders performed by composers working within the strictures of this simple form are comparable to those of classical composers of the 1780s, such as Haydn and Mozart, constrained to write within the boundaries of sonata form.

Of all the elements of music, rhythm dominates in the 1920s. Most songs, like the times, are upbeat. Off-the-beaten-path experiments produce such syncopated mavericks as "Charleston", "Fascinating Rhyhm", and "Crazy Rhythm". Melody is often relegated to second place, as in the simplistic pattern of thirds in "Carolina in the Morning" or the repeated broken chords of "Happy Days Are Here Again". Yet soaring melodies do appear, created for the theater by such masters as Sigmund Romberg ("Lover, Come Back to Me"), Richard Rodgers ("With a Song in My Heart"), and Jerome Kern ("Ol' Man River"). Harmonies are often simple, as in "I Want to Be Happy"; sometimes subtle, as in "Tea for Two"; and occasionally take surprising turns, as in "There'll Be Some Changes Made" and "Sweet Georgia Brown". But in general, they have not reached the level of sophistication they will reach in the thirties.

When all is said and done, the Roaring Twenties is an astonishing decade, a time when an art form takes root, flourishes, and branches out in many directions, foreseeing its flowering in the years to come.

1920

A GENTLE NOSTALGIA

1920

Remember somewhere the sun is shining.

B. G. (Buddy) De Sylva
"Look for the Silver Lining"

This is a year of gentle songs, nostalgic songs about love; with the onset of peace, the world seems to be taking a breather. Popular songs either look backward to the quiet years before the "War to End All Wars", when the waltz reigned supreme, or forward to a time when they can "travel on to Avalon". There are romantic waltzes ("I'll Be With You in Apple Blossom Time"), gentle lullabies ("The Japanese Sandman"), gliding foxtrots ("Whispering"), and occasionally an upstart from the new world of jazz ("Margie"). New currents are in the wind. Jazz is emerging from the throes of Dixieland and finding its way from New Orleans to New York, by way of Chicago. Paul Whiteman is the self-appointed King of Jazz, and his band pays a visit to Europe, bringing along a rage for *le jazz hot*. The raucous saxophone is beginning to replace the romantic violin.

It is, literally speaking, a sobering year on this side of the Atlantic. The nation is now officially dry, in fancy if not in fact. Women at last have the right to vote and are beginning to assert their independence. Hemlines are now nine inches above the ground, dresses are growing flimsier, and the flapper is about to be born (see 1925). Popular novels are F. Scott Fitzgerald's *This Side of Paradise,* D. H. Lawrence's *Women in Love,* and Edith Wharton's *The Age of Innocence.*

Radio is beginning to become something of a national obsession. Two radio stations claim to inaugurate regular broadcasting: WWJ in Detroit and KDKA in Pittsburgh. The latter begins broadcasting on 2 November, just in time to carry the Harding-Cox election returns (Harding is the winner). Other new stations as well as radio "hams" are broadcasting throughout the land, with amateur wireless sets being offered for sale for ten dollars. The craze will accelerate; by the end of the decade, radio will be the single most important means of dissemination of popular song.

On the silent screen, audiences can see Lillian Gish in *Way Down East*, Jackie Coogan in *The Kid*, and John Barrymore in *Dr. Jekyll and Mr. Hyde*. Two hit plays by Eugene O'Neill grace the Broadway boards: *Beyond the Horizon* and *The Emperor Jones*. Also opening on Broadway are the musical comedy *Sally*, with lyrics by B. G. De Sylva and music by Jerome Kern; and the revue *The Greenwich Village Follies*.

SONGS OF 1920

     Avalon **
     I'll Be with You in Apple Blossom Time
     The Japanese Sandman
     Look for the Silver Lining *!
     Margie **
     When My Baby Smiles at Me
     Whispering *

AVALON * *

WORDS and MUSIC: Al Jolson and Vincent Rose
PREMIERE: Interpolated in the musical show, *Sinbad*
New York: Winter Garden Theatre, 4 Feb.1918 (388 perf.)
INTRODUCED BY: Al Jolson

"Avalon" is the most celebrated example in American popular music of alleged plagiarism from the classics. It was charged that its melody was taken directly from the famous tenor aria, "*É lucevan le stelle*", from Giacomo Puccini's opera, *Tosca* (1900). The only evidence for this assumption is the similarity in pitch of the first ten tones of the refrain of "Avalon" to the opening tones of the aria. But even here, the shoe doesn't fit. The mode of the song is major, while the aria is in minor and the melodic rhythms of the two works are markedly different: smooth in the song, disjunct in the aria. Nevertheless, Puccini's publishers in Milan, G. Ricordi & Co., instituted a lawsuit claiming copyright infringement. They won, and Puccini and his publishers were awarded $25,000 in damages and all future royalties. The recording company that initially put out the song was forced out of business.

"Avalon" was designed as a vehicle for Al Jolson to sing in his exuberant fashion in the Broadway extravaganza, *Sinbad*. Over the long run of that show, Jolson had captivated audiences with other interpolated songs, including "Rock-a-Bye Your Baby with a Dixie Melody", "Mammy", and "Swanee" (George Gershwin's first hit). With this song (for which Jolson shared author's credits) he hit pay dirt. It is interesting to note that some editions of "Avalon" give the credit for words to Al Jolson and B. G. De Sylva and for music to Vincent Rose. In any case, it is known that Jolson made it a practice to attach his name as songwriter to any song he introduced. The first recording was by Harry Reser and the Cliquot Club Eskimos, and the song has been recorded numerous times since, most notably in the 1937 Victor recording by The Benny Goodman Quartet.

"Avalon" shows every sign of having been put together in a hurry: the verses are mundane, beginning in vaudeville style, with the direction: "Vamp till ready", The title does not refer to the mystical land of Arthurian legend, but rather to the resort city on Santa Catalina Island off the California coast. The lyrics describe the place as "beside the bay" and end with the enticing line: "I'll travel on / To Avalon". The music is simple, a rare instance of monothematicism in popular music. The entire refrain may be divided into four sections, each of twelve notes, The last three sections are variations of the first. Harmonies are mostly tonic and dominant, with a brief excursion in the third section to A minor.

It has been featured in at least five films: *Cairo* (1942, sung by Jeanette MacDonald and Robert Young); *The Jolson Story* (1946, sung by Al Jolson and lip-synched by Larry Parks); *Margie* (1946); *The Benny Goodman Story* (1956); and *The Helen Morgan Story* (1957, sung by Gogi Grant, dubbing for Ann Blyth, and the De Castro Sisters). Because of its simplicity and slow harmonic changes, "Avalon" has long been favored by jazz performers as a vehicle for improvisation.

Moderate foxtrot with two verses (16) and refrain (32)
PUBLISHER: Jerome H. Remick & Co.
KEY: G maj., *STARTS:* d' (D7), *FORM:* A A' A" A'''

≈≈≈≈≈≈≈≈≈≈≈≈≈≈≈≈≈≈≈≈

I'LL BE WITH YOU IN APPLE BLOSSOM TIME *

WORDS: Neville Fleeson, *MUSIC:* Albert Von Tilzer
INTRODUCED BY: Nora Bayes

Nora Bayes (née Dora Goldberg), the popular entertainer of vaudeville, Broadway, and London, introduced and recorded this romantic waltz. Albert Von Tilzer, the prolific composer of such hits as "Take Me Out to the Ball Game" (1908) and "Put Your Arms Around Me, Honey (Hold Me Tight)", wrote the music. With this song, he reverted to the old fashioned waltz that had been so popular around the turn of the century.

The song remained very popular, although something of an anachronism in three-quarter time, until 1941, when it enjoyed a renaissance. Sung by the Andrews Sisters in a jazzy 4/4 arrangement in the Abbott and Costello film *Buck Privates* and sparked by the sensational success of their Decca recording, "Apple Blossom Time" had a spectacular revival. A contributing factor to the song's universal appeal at that time was without doubt the forced wartime separation of many couples, hoping to be together in some future "apple blossom time". Later hit recordings were by Tab Hunter (1959) and Wayne Newton (1965).

As originally written, the waltz could have just as easily stemmed from 1890 as 1920. The melody alternates stepwise motion in the "A" sections with upward leaps in the "B" section. Harmonically, the song ends traditionally with a tour through the circle of fifths: E7- A7- D7- G7- C. The lyrics tell the story of a marriage to come, but they don't always exactly rhyme, as in: "Church bells will chime / You will be mine".

"I'll Be With You in Apple Blossom Time" received a repeat performance by the Andrews Sisters in the 1944 film *Follow the Boys*. While its origin as a waltz is often forgotten, the song is frequently performed today as a jazz tune in 4/4 meter.

Slow waltz with verse (32) and refrain (32)
PUBLISHER: Albert Von Tilzer & Co.
KEY: C maj., *STARTS:* c" (C maj.), *FORM:* ABA'B'

≈≈≈≈≈≈≈≈≈≈≈≈≈≈≈≈≈≈≈

THE JAPANESE SANDMAN

WORDS: Raymond B. Egan, *MUSIC:* Richard A. Whiting
INTRODUCED: in vaudeville by Nora Bayes

Although originally conceived as a sweet and gentle lullaby, "The Japanese Sandman" has most often through the years been performed fast and loud. Nora Bayes introduced the song in vaudeville, but it was Paul Whiteman's Victor recording (with "Whispering" on the other side) that brought it instant fame; two million copes of the recording were sold in its first year.

For Richard A. Whiting, its composer, this was his first big hit. He went on to co-write such standards as "Sleepy Time Gal" in 1925, "She's Funny That Way" in 1928, and "Too Marvelous for Words" in 1937. Whiting's daughter Margaret, a talented singer, kept this and many other of her father's songs alive over the years.

The music is innovative for its day. The verse is dark and mysterious, moving from F minor to A-flat major and back to F minor again. Its sonorous ninth chords evoke exotic images of far-away places. The prevailing motive of the refrain, undoubtedly chosen for its "Oriental" flavor, is the minor third (c"-a') carried monothematically throughout over changing harmonies. An unexpected change to c-sharp" in the second section of the song heralds a harmonic change to A major. The last two sections are unusual as well, moving first to the lowest and then to the highest points of the song. Raymond B. Egan's lyrics are also far from ordinary, as in: "Just an old second-hand man / Trading new days for old".

Benny Goodman and His Orchestra had a hit Victor recording of the song in 1935. Like other things referring to the Japanese, it had a long hiatus in popularity after Pearl Harbor. But after World War II, it slowly but surely regained its status as a jazz standard.

Moderate foxtrot with verse (20) and refrain (32)
PUBLISHER: Jerome H. Remick & Co.
KEY: F maj., *STARTS*: c" (F6), *FORM*: AA'A"A"'

≈≈≈≈≈≈≈≈≈≈≈≈≈≈≈≈≈≈≈

LOOK FOR THE SILVER LINING *!

WORDS: B. G. (Buddy) De Sylva, *MUSIC*: Jerome Kern
PREMIERE: Musical comedy, *Sally*
New York: New Amsterdam Theatre, 21 December 1920 (570 perf.)
INTRODUCED BY: Marilyn Miller and Irving Fisher

This lovely ballad was written for an earlier Kern musical, *Zip Goes a Million*, but was dropped from the show during rehearsals in 1919. The show itself folded before it reached New York – the only Kern show ever to do so. But within a year "Look for the Silver Lining" found a new home in the Ziegfeld musical, *Sally*. This Cinderella tale was designed as a showcase for Florenz Ziegfeld's latest discovery, Marilyn Miller, a talented dancer (the dance music was composed by no less a personage than Victor Herbert). It is built around the rags-to-riches story of a waif who starts out washing dishes at the Alley Inn in Greenwich Village and ends up marrying a duke, played by a fumbling Leon Erroll.

"Look for the Silver Lining" is Kern at his most purely melodic, free from harmonic constraints. Its hymn-like quality was remarked upon by Kern himself, who confessed a love for hymns. The mostly stepwise melodic movement is contradicted in two places by dotted quarter notes and eighth notes a step apart: in the introduction and at the end of the "B" section. The harmonies are hymn-like as well: tonic, dominant, and subdominant, except for a brief excursion to the dominant of the dominant (F7) near the song's end. The philosophical concept of looking on the bright side of things, for the silver lining, "when e'er a cloud appears in the blue", adds immeasurably to the song's appeal. So do De Sylva's heartfelt lyrics.

"Look for the Silver Lining" became an international hit when *Sally* went to London, where it was produced at the Winter Garden Theatre and ran for 387 performances. The first recording was by Marion Harris, one of the foremost popular singers of the 1920s. In 1942 *Sally* was revived in London as *Wild Rose*, with Jesse Matthews in the starring role. Several films have featured the song: the screen version of *Sally* (1929), in which it was sung by Marilyn Miller and Alexander Gray; the 1936 film *The Great Ziegfeld*, sung by William Demarest and William Powell; the Kern biography *Till the Clouds Roll By* (1946), sung by Judy Garland; and the

Marilyn Miller biography *Look for the Silver Lining* (1949), sung by June Haver and Gordon MacRae.

> Moderate ballad with two verses (9) and refrain (32)
> *PUBLISHER*: T. B. Harms Company
> *KEY:* E-flat maj., *STARTS:* g' (E-flat maj.), *FORM:* ABA'C

≈≈≈≈≈≈≈≈≈≈≈≈≈≈≈≈≈≈≈

MARGIE * *

> *WORDS:* Benny Davis, *MUSIC:* Con Conrad and J. Russel Robinson
> *INTRODUCED*: in a Victor recording by the Original Dixieland Band

Eddie Cantor made this sprightly song popular; he featured it throughout his long career as comedian, singer, and dancer. But it was the Original Dixieland Band that introduced it. This ground-breaking group began in Chicago as Stein's Dixie Jass (sic) Band, and changed its name to the Famous Original Dixieland Jazz Band for its engagement at Reisenweber's Restaurant in New York. In London, J. Russel Robinson, co-composer of "Margie", became the band's pianist. His collaborator, Con Conrad (né Conred K. Dober), went on to a distinguished composing career: among his credits are "Ma! He's Making Eyes at Me", "The Continental", and "Prisoner of Love". Early recordings of "Margie" were by Gene Rodemich and his Orchestra, Eddie Cantor, Ted Lewis, and Frank Crumit. Jimmy Lunceford and his Orchestra had a popular recording in 1937.

Both words and music are simple, almost to the point of ingenuousness. The refrain begins with a pickup consisting of a threefold repetition of the opening note. Whole notes spaced a third apart are favored for the title. The "B" section is lightly syncopated and is invariably performed with a break at the words "home and ring and ev'rything".

"Margie" was sung by Tom Brown, and reprised by Joy Hodges, in a 1940 film of the same name. Betty Hutton sang it in the 1945 film *Incendiary Blonde*; In 1946, it was featured in still another film titled *Margie*, starring Jeanne Crain. It was also heard in the 1949 biographical film *The Eddie Cantor Story*, with Cantor dubbing for its star, Keefe Brasselle. "Margie" is one of a number of songs of the twenties known more for its nostalgic properties than for its integral quality.

Moderate foxtrot with two verses (16) and refrain (32)
PUBLISHER: Waterman, Berlin & Snyder Co.; assigned to Mills Music Inc.
KEY: F maj., *STARTS:* c" (F maj.), *FORM:* ABA'C

≈≈≈≈≈≈≈≈≈≈≈≈≈≈≈≈≈≈

WHEN MY BABY SMILES AT ME

WORDS: Andrew Sterling and Ted Lewis, *MUSIC*: Bill Munro
PREMIERE: Revue, *Greenwich Village Follies, 1920 Edition*
New York: Nora Bayes Theatre, 30 August 1920 (192 perf.)
INTRODUCED BY: Ted Lewis and His Orchestra

When one hears "When My Baby Smiles at Me", one immediately thinks of Ted Lewis, the clarinetist, singer, and band leader who co-wrote it, introduced it, and used it as his theme song throughout his long career. Lewis, born Theodore Leopold Friedman in Circleville, Ohio, went on to become internationally known as "The High-Hat Tragedian of Song". His Columbia recording was a big hit: "When My Baby Smiles at Me", wailed on his clarinet, became his signature song. Along with his trademark expression "Is ev'rybody happy?", the song contributed mightily to Lewis's long-lasting success: he performed well into the 1960s.

In the refrain, the most interesting aspect of the music is the startling blue note (in this case, a flatted sixth) on the first syllable of the word "Baby", immediately after the three-note pickup "For when my..." This e-flat' gives the song a "jazzy" feel it would not otherwise have. In all other respects the music is conventional, characterized by simple harmonies, discrete chromaticism, long notes, and lack of syncopation.

"When My Baby Smiles at Me" has been featured in several films. The Ritz Brothers sang it in *Sing Baby Sing* (1936), Lewis himself sang it in *Hold That Ghost* (1941). It was featured in *Behind the Eight Ball* (1942), and used as the title song of the 1948 film biography of Lewis, *When My Baby Smiles at Me*, starring Dan Dailey and Betty Grable.

Moderate foxtrot with two verses (16) and refrain (32)
PUBLISHER: Harry Von Tilzer Music Publishing Co.
KEY: G maj., *STARTS:* d' (E-flat maj.), *FORM:* A A' A" B

≈≈≈≈≈≈≈≈≈≈≈≈≈≈≈≈≈≈

WHISPERING *

> *WORDS and MUSIC*: John Schonberger, Richard Coburn and
> Vincent Rose
> *INTRODUCED BY*: Paul Whiteman and His Orchestra

Paul Whiteman's Victor recording of this standard, with "The Japanese Sandman" on its flip side, sold two million copies in its first year. It was Whiteman's first hit recording and took the country by storm. Whiteman had conceived the idea of "symphonic jazz" just the year before, while he was performing at the Fairmount Hotel in San Francisco with singer Morton Downey. "Whispering" was revived in 1954, with a Capitol recording by guitarist Les Paul.

The languid melody of the refrain describes a downward curve in long notes. The harmonies change slowly too, each new one lasting a full two bars. But they are striking harmonies, especially the chromatic movement to the B seventh in Bar 3. The lyrics are undistinguished, with such simplistic rhymes as "While you cuddle near me" and "So no one can hear me".

"Whispering" has shown up in numerous films, among them *Ziegfeld Girl* (1941, sung by a male trio), *Greenwich Village* (1944, sung by Vivian Blaine), Vincente Minnelli's *The Clock* (1945, sung by a chorus). It was also featured in *Belles On Their Toes* (1952), and played by Carmen Cavallaro on the soundtrack of *The Eddy Duchin Story* (1956). It remains popular more than three-quarters of a century after it was written.

> Moderate foxtrot with two verses (16) and refrain (32)
> *PUBLISHER*: Miller Music Corporation
> *KEY*: C maj., *STARTS*: c" (C maj.), *FORM*: AA'AA"

≈≈≈≈≈≈≈≈≈≈≈≈≈≈≈≈≈≈≈≈≈

1921

JAZZ AND SPEAKEASIES

1921

I'm gonna change the way I strut my stuff

Billy Higgins
"There'll Be Some Changes Made"

Jazz takes off with a vengeance this year, with such sprightly songs as "I'm Just Wild About Harry", "The Sheik of Araby", and "There'll Be Some Changes Made". These songs, and others, are popularized in the thousands of speakeasies that are cropping up everywhere, supplied by speedboats smuggling liquor from outside the three-mile limit. Despite this surface hilarity, the nation has slipped into an economic depression. Things are not quite as bright as they seem when Warren Harding takes over from an ailing Woodrow Wilson on 4 March.

But the public's thirst for entertainment has not abated. Al Jolson brings the house down nightly in *Bombo*; the first all-black revue, *Shuffle Along*, has moved from Harlem to Broadway; and Irving Berlin and Sam H. Harris open their new jewel of a theater, The Music Box, starting a tradition of intimate revues. Radio is gaining in popularity. Vincent Lopez is the first bandleader to broadcast, on WJZ in New York, starting a trend that is to flourish in the thirties. The bathing beauty comes into her own with the first Beauty Pageant at Atlantic City, New Jersey. Best selling books are Sinclair Lewis's *Main Street* and H. G. Wells's *The Outline of History*. Rudolph Valentino creates a sensation in his first two films, *Four Horsemen of the Apocalypse* and *The Sheik*. Jack Dempsey knocks out Georges Carpentier in the first million-dollar fight. Two hit plays on Broadway are Somerset Maugham's *Rain* (with a scratchy phonograph playing "Wabash Blues" throughout) and Eugene O'Neill's *The Emperor Jones*. But even in this year of jazz and speakeasies, there is room for nostalgic songs like "Say It with Music" and "Three O' Clock in the Morning".

SONGS OF 1921

Ain't We Got Fun
April Showers **
I'm Just Wild About Harry *
Ma! (He's Making Eyes at Me)
Say It with Music
The Sheik of Araby **
There'll Be Some Changes Made *!
Three O'Clock in the Morning

AIN'T WE GOT FUN

WORDS: Gus Kahn and Raymond B. Egan, *MUSIC*: Richard A. Whiting
INTRODUCED: in vaudeville by George Watts

The vaudeville team of Van and Schenck popularized this bubbly song in their vaudeville act and in a Columbia recording. The song sold over a million copies of sheet music and became symbolic of the spirit of the Roaring Twenties. But it was conceived as a song of the ongoing post-war Depression, with more than a touch of irony in such expressions as: "The rich get richer and the poor get children".

The jaunty melody of the refrain starts with the upward leap of a major sixth and is replete with repeated quarter notes, intervals of the minor second, and octave jumps. There are three sets of lyrics for both verse and refrain.

"Ain't We Got Fun" was sung by Doris Day, Danny Thomas, and a chorus in the 1951 biographical film of lyricist Gus Kahn, *I'll See You In My Dreams*; and by Doris Day, Gordon MacRae, and Russell Arms in the 1953 film musical, *By the Light of the Silvery Moon*.

Moderate foxtrot with three verses (16) and 3 refrains (32)
PUBLISHER: Jerome H. Remick & Co.
KEY: E-flat maj., *STARTS*: b-flat (E-flat maj.), *FORM*: ABAC

≈≈≈≈≈≈≈≈≈≈≈≈≈≈≈≈≈≈≈

APRIL SHOWERS * *

WORDS: B. G. De Sylva, *MUSIC*: Louis Silvers
PREMIERE: Musical comedy, *Bombo*
New York: Jolson Theatre, 6 October 1921
INTRODUCED BY: Al Jolson

This enduring song was not on the opening night program of the Jolson extravaganza *Bombo*; like "Toot, Toot Tootsie Goo' Bye" and "California Here I Come", it was a later interpolation. Performed by the master of interpolations, Al Jolson, it stole the show. With its "look-for-the-silver-lining" sentiments the song was perfectly attuned to the uncertain economic times. Its tuneful melody sent theater-goers happily humming their way home. Recordings by Jolson (on Columbia), Paul Whiteman and his Orchestra, Ernie Hare, Charles Harrison, and Ernie Fields brought the song universal fame. A new recording by Jolson on Decca sold over a million copies in 1946, and Guy Lombardo and his Royal Canadians had a hit recording in 1947.

B. G. De Sylva's lyrics are unforgettable, with their allusions to "raining violets" and "crowds of daffodils". Louis Silvers's music is equally entrancing. His device of increasing intervals always returning to the same melodic pattern was used five years later by Richard Rodgers in his "Blue Room".

Among films featuring "April Showers" are *The Singing Kid*, in which it was sung by Jolson; and *The Jolson Story* (1946) and *Jolson Sings Again* (1949), sung by Jolson dubbing for Larry Parks. It was also dubbed in by Carmen Cavallaro in the 1956 film *The Eddy Duchin Story*, starring Tyrone Power and Kim Novak; and sung by Jack Carson and Ann Sothern in the 1948 film, *April Showers*. It is in every respect a sunny and delightful song.

Moderate foxtrot with verse (16) and refrain (32)
PUBLISHER: Warner Brothers Music
KEY: G maj., *STARTS*: d' (D7), *FORM*: ABAC

≈≈≈≈≈≈≈≈≈≈≈≈≈≈≈≈≈≈≈≈

I'M JUST WILD ABOUT HARRY *

WORDS and MUSIC: Noble Sissle and Eubie Blake
PREMIERE: Musical comedy, *Shuffle Along*
New York: 63rd Street Theatre, 23 May 1921 (504 perf.)
INTRODUCED BY: Lottie Gee

This rousing song enjoyed its greatest spurt of popularity twenty-seven years after it was written, when it became the theme song of Harry Truman's campaign for the presidency in 1948. Appropriately enough, it was written as a campaign song; in the musical, *Shuffle Along*, it was the theme song of a candidate named Harry Walton, who was running for the mayoralty of New York. *Shuffle Along* was a smash hit, but the song about "Harry" is its only survivor.

It's hard to realize that "I'm Just Wild About Harry" was originally written as a waltz; it has all the earmarks of a ragtime song. Its over-the-bar syncopation is intoxicating. So are its references to "choc'late candy" and "honey from the bee". Also adding to the song's appeal is the three-fold repetition forming a coda, to the words, "And he's just wild about, cannot do without, he's just wild about me".

"I'm Just Wild About Harry" was popularized by Marion Harris and Florence Mills, among others. It was recorded by Vincent Lopez and his Orchestra. It has also been featured in more than its share of motion pictures. It was sung by Judy Garland, Mickey Rooney, and a chorus in the

1939 film, *Babes in Arms*; by Alice Faye, with Louis Prima and his Orchestra, in *Rose of Washington Square* (also 1939); in the 1942 George Raft gangster film, *Broadway*; by Ted Lewis in *Is Everybody Happy?* (1943); and by Al Jolson, dubbing for Larry Parks, in *Jolson Sings Again* (1949). Along with "Margie", it remains one of the classic "name" songs.

> Fast rhythm song with two verses (16) and refrain (36)
> *PUBLISHER*: M. Witmark & Sons
> *KEY*: C maj., *STARTS*: d' (C maj.), *FORM*: ABAC'

≈≈≈≈≈≈≈≈≈≈≈≈≈≈≈≈≈≈≈≈

MA! (HE'S MAKING EYES AT ME)

> *WORDS*: Sidney Clark, *MUSIC:* Con Conrad
> *PREMIERE*: Revue, *The Midnight Rounders*
> New York: Century Theatre, 12 July 1921
> *INTRODUCED BY*: Eddie Cantor

The Midnight Rounders was actually a cabaret that presented a summer revue, produced by the Shubert brothers, on the roof of the Century Theatre in New York. It was there, on a hot July night, that Eddie Cantor introduced this hardy perennial. The song has two sets of lyrics: one for each sex. Cantor's version, of course, was "Ma! (She's Making Eyes At Me)", but the female version is by far the more popular. The sheet music equivocates regarding sex, calling the song simply "Ma!". Cantor's recording was a best seller and there have been others: by Dick Robertson in 1940 and by Lena Zavaroni in 1974.

The melody outlines simple chords in long notes. But this process is accelerated in the "C" section, where shorter notes are used very effectively leading up to the climactic words: "Ma! He's kissing me".

A film titled *Ma! He's Making Eyes at Me"*, with Tim Brown and Constance Moore, was made in 1940. The song was sung by Judy Canova in the 1946 movie, *Singin' in the Corn*; and by Eddie Cantor, dubbing for Keefe Brasselle in *The Eddie Cantor Story* (1953).

> Moderate foxtrot with two verses (16) and two refrains (32)
> *PUBLISHER*: Fred Fisher, Inc.
> *KEY*: E-flat maj., *STARTS*: e-flat" (E-flat maj.), *FORM*: ABA'C

≈≈≈≈≈≈≈≈≈≈≈≈≈≈≈≈≈≈≈≈

SAY IT WITH MUSIC

WORDS and MUSIC: Irving Berlin
PREMIERE: Revue, *Music Box Revue 1921-1922*
New York: Music Box Theatre, 22 September 1921 (328 perf.)
INTRODUCED BY: Wilda Bennett and Joe Santley

Irving Berlin and his partner, Sam H. Harris, spent $947,000 to build their new jewel box of a theater, the Music Box. It was the first theater ever built in America to highlight a single songwriter's work. For the opening revue they spared no expense, spending an unprecedented $187,613 to produce the lavish *Music Box Revue 1921-1922*. Most of this cost went into production numbers, but the highlight of the show was this little ballad, performed in a simple setting by Wilda Bennett and Joe Santley. The song did not receive particular attention at first, but eventually was the only one to survive. Popularized in a Victor recording by Paul Whiteman and his Orchestra, "Say It With Music" stayed a hit for seventy-five weeks, selling 374,408 copies of sheet music, 102,127 piano rolls, and 1,223,905 records.

The song itself is very understated. There is a paucity of notes – only fifty-two in the entire refrain. Deliberately written in the style of Berlin's own 1919 hit "A Pretty Girl Is Like a Melody", it features long-held tones, chiefly whole and half notes, interspersed with some light syncopation. Written for the revue as a duet, there are two verses, for male and female. Musical allusions spot the lyrics, as in "a melody mellow played by a cello" and "to the strains of Chopin or Liszt".

"Say It With Music" became the theme song of all the subsequent *Music Box Revues*. In 1938, Ethel Merman sang it in the film, *Alexander's Ragtime Band*

Moderate ballad with two verses (16) and refrain (32)
PUBLISHER: Irving Berlin, Inc.
KEY: E-flat maj., *STARTS*: e-flat' (E-flat maj.), *FORM*: ABAC

≈≈≈≈≈≈≈≈≈≈≈≈≈≈≈≈≈≈≈

THE SHEIK OF ARABY * *

WORDS: Harry B. Smith and Francis Wheeler, *MUSIC*: Ted Snyder
PREMIERE: Revue, *Make It Snappy*
New York: Winter Garden Theatre, 19 April 1922
INTRODUCED BY: Eddie Cantor

This jaunty tune was Tin Pan Alley's response to the mass hysteria resulting from Rudolph Valentino's appearance in the silent film, *The Sheik*. Music publishers were quick to capitalize on this object of millions of womens' fantasies: "The Sheik of Araby" soon became a great hit. On the sheet music, the song is called a "Fox-Trot and Shimmy", but in reality it became one of the preferred accompaniments to a frantic contemporary dance known as The Peabody. First popularized by The Club Royal Orchestra, "The Sheik of Araby" has been periodically revived over the decades. Jack Teagarden and his Orchestra had a best-selling record in 1939 and Spike Jones and his Orchestra recorded one of its renowned satirical versions in 1943.

True to its exotic, Middle-Eastern inspiration, the verse, in B-flat minor, has a decidedly oriental sound. The refrain, in contrast, is pure exuberance in a major key, without a trace of exoticism. The melody line beats out a persistent long-short rhythm of dotted half and a quarter, interspersed with occasional long-held notes of six beats. The melody itself is sparse, with a preponderance of the notes f' and g'. The lyrics seem made-to-order for the Valentino hysteria, including the phrase "into your tent I'll creep".

"The Sheik of Araby" was sung by Alice Faye, Betty Grable, Billy Gilbert, and a chorus in the 1940 film musical, *Tin Pan Alley*. As a jazz standard, it is usually performed in ultra-fast tempo.

Moderate rhythm song with two verses (24) and refrain (32)
PUBLISHER: Ted Snyder Music Publishing Co.
KEY: B-flat maj., *STARTS*: f' (B-flat maj.), *FORM*: ABA'C

≈≈≈≈≈≈≈≈≈≈≈≈≈≈≈≈≈≈≈

THERE'LL BE SOME CHANGES MADE *!

WORDS: Billy Higgins, *MUSIC*: W. Benton Overstreet
INTRODUCED BY: Billy Higgins

This revolutionary little song heralded a new era in songwriting, free from the compositional restraints of Tin Pan Alley. Through the years it has remained a musicians' favorite, due to its refreshing harmonic changes, relaxed rhythm, and unusual form. Introduced by its co-lyricist, the singer Billy Higgins, the song universally known as "Changes" was popularized in a Black Swan recording by the incomparable Ethel Waters. Many artists have recorded it, from Mildred Bailey to Vaughn Monroe, and there have been a number of revivals. Hit recordings were made by Sophie Tucker (1928), Benny Goodman and his Orchestra (1941), and Ted Weems and his Orchestra (1947). In 1976, it was featured in the all-black revue, *Bubbling Brown Sugar*.

True to its title, the song's most striking aspect is its "changes": its harmonic changes – that is. There is no verse. The first half of the short refrain starts with two bars of G ninth harmony, then two bars of C ninth. Then, it quickly moves through the circle of fifths: from D seventh to G seventh, to C ninth, to F seventh. In the second half of the refrain, the same sequence of harmonies is repeated. Finally, the repetition of the last phrase forms a short coda. Over the years, the second set of lyrics has been contemporaneously updated, as in "even Jack Benny has been changing jokes".

In motion pictures, "There'll Be Some Changes Made" was sung by Ida Lupino in *Road House* (1948); by Joan Blondell in *The Blue Veil* (1951); by Dolores Gray in *Designing Woman* (1957); and by Ann Reinking in *All That Jazz* (1979).

Moderate rhythm song with two refrains (18)
PUBLISHER: Edward B. Marks Music Company
KEY: B-flat maj., *STARTS*: c' (G9), *FORM*: ABAB'

≈≈≈≈≈≈≈≈≈≈≈≈≈≈≈≈≈≈≈

THREE O' CLOCK IN THE MORNING

WORDS: Dorothy Terriss, *MUSIC*: Julian Robledo
PREMIERE: Revue, *Greenwich Village Follies of 1921*
New York: Shubert Theatre, 31 August 1921 (167 perf.)
INTRODUCED BY: Richard Bold and Rosalind Fuller

This "Waltz Song with Chimes" – "The Sensational Hit of Two Continents" – has had an interesting history. It began as a piano solo – written by Julian Robledo, an Argentine composer born in Spain– which was published in New Orleans in 1919. In 1920 it was published, still without words, in both England and Germany. Only in 1921 did Dorothy Terriss (whose real name was Theodora Morse, wife of composer Theodore Morse) supply it with words. The song created a sensation when it was interpolated in the seventh edition of the *Greenwich Village Follies*. Sung by Richard Bold and Rosalind Fuller, it was also presented in an elaborate ballet featuring two chime-ringers. Frank Crumit recorded it for Columbia. Paul Whiteman's Victor recording sold over three-and-a-half million copies. The waltz has since been periodically revived, with recordings by Monty Kelly and his Orchestra (1953), Bert Kaempfert and his Orchestra, and Lou Rauls (1965).

"Three O'Clock in the Morning" is strongly reminiscent of waltzes written thirty years before its time, although its subject is romantic love rather than sections of the city ("The Bowery") or means of transportation ("On a Bicycle Built for Two"), both written in 1892. The opening words of the refrain tell it all: "It's Three O' Clock in the Morning, We danced the whole night through". Musically, it features the unusually wide range of an octave and a sixth, all in the first seven notes of the refrain. Most striking of all is the song's incorporation of the historic Westminster Chimes, composed for London's Big Ben in 1793.

"Three O'Clock in the Morning" was sung by Judy Garland in the film, *Presenting Lily Mars* (1943), was featured in an ice-skating sequence in *Margie* (1946); and was sung by J. Carrol Naish in *That Midnight Kiss* (1949). It was also featured in the movies, *Belles on Their Toes* (1952) and *The Eddy Duchin Story* (1956).

Slow waltz with two refrains (32) and interlude (28)
PUBLISHER: West's, Ltd. (London), assigned to Leo Feist, Inc.
KEY: C maj., *STARTS*: g' (C maj.), *FORM*: ABA'C

≈≈≈≈≈≈≈≈≈≈≈≈≈≈≈≈≈≈≈

1922

FARAWAY PLACES

1922

I'm going to get there at any price

B. G De Sylva and Ira Gershwin
"I'll Build a Stairway to Paradise"

In this generally listless year for American popular song, some songs yearn for far-away places, such as Carolina, Chicago, New Orleans, London, or even Paradise. Others lament the passing of a fallen comrade, as in "My Buddy" – or meditate about "Trees". But even in this bleak year, there are bright spots on the horizon. A young composer named George Gershwin brings a fresh new sound, a blue sound, to the musical theater with "I'll Build a Stairway to Paradise". Other experimental songs this year include Zez Confrey's "Stumbling" and that old New York standby "'Way Down Yonder in New Orleans".

As the economy shows signs of recovery, radio becomes a national craze, with sales of radios and accessories exceeding $60 million. The first radio commercial is heard on Station WEAF in New York; the charge for ten minutes of air time is $50 in the afternoon and $100 at night. Ed Wynn does the first comedy broadcast on Station WJZ in New York. It lays an egg, but picks up with the added laughter of a studio audience. The Hall-Mills murder case near New Brunswick, New Jersey, creates a national sensation. Best-selling books include Hendrik Willem Van Loon's *Story of Mankind* and J. Arthur Thomson's *Outline of Science*. T. S. Eliot's *The Waste Land* and A. E. Housman's *Last Poems* are published this year. The musical theater in New York has a lackluster year, although a little non-musical play called *Abie's Irish Rose* begins a phenomenal run of 2,327 performances on Broadway. In Hollywood, the first *Our Gang* comedies are produced by Hal Roach.

And even in a listless year, there are compensations: the cocktail makes its début, and a brand new game called mah-jongg, imported from China, starts yet another national craze.

SONGS OF 1922

Carolina in the Morning *
Chicago **
China Boy *
Do It Again
I'll Build a Stairway to Paradise!
Limehouse Blues **
My Buddy
Stumbling!
Toot Toot Tootsie (Goo' Bye) **
Trees
Way Down Yonder in New Orleans **!

CAROLINA IN THE MORNING *

WORDS: Gus Kahn, *MUSIC*: Walter Donaldson
INTRODUCED: in vaudeville by William Frawley

This delightful patter song was first introduced in vaudeville by William Frawley but did not become a hit until it was interpolated in *The Passing Show of 1922*, which opened at the Winter Garden Theatre in New York on 20 September 1922. The highlight of that show was "Carolina's" harmonization by the team of Willie and Eugene Howard. Soon the vaudeville team of Van and Schenck had a No. 1 Chart Record. The recording by Paul Whiteman and his Orchestra also reached the top of the charts.

"Carolina in the Morning" shows lyricist, Gus Kahn, at the peak of his form, using such evocative expressions as "Butterflies all flutter up and kiss each little buttercup" and "If I had Aladdin's lamp for only a day". He also is a master of inner rhymes, as witness "No-one could be sweeter than my sweetie when I meet her", or "Strolling with my girlie where the dew is pearly early in the morning". The music is a perfect counterfoil to these sentiments, setting forth a sixteen-fold repetition of two notes a minor third apart in each "A" section: first g' and e' and then a' and f'. The rhythmic pattern of dotted-eighth and sixteenth adds to the song's appeal and makes it ideal for tap-dancing. The closing "C" section of the refrain is in two parts: first presenting entirely new material, then recapitulating the opening idea.

In the movies, Betty Grable sang "Carolina in the Morning" in *The Dolly Sisters* (1945). Robert Alda and Ann Sothern did it in *April Showers* (1948). Al Jolson dubbed it in for Larry Parks in *Jolson Sings Again* (1949), and Patrice Wymore sang it in the Gus Kahn biographical film, *I'll See You in My Dreams* (1951).

Moderate foxtrot with two verses (12) and refrain (32)
PUBLISHER: Jerome H. Remick & Co.
KEY: C maj., *STARTS*: g' (C maj.), *FORM*: ABAC

≈≈≈≈≈≈≈≈≈≈≈≈≈≈≈≈≈≈≈≈≈

CHICAGO * *

WORDS and MUSIC: Fred Fisher
INTRODUCED BY: Ben Selvin and his Orchestra

Songs about cities have always occupied a special niche of their own. As subjects, New York and Paris have had more than their share of songs, as in "Autumn in New York: and "April in Paris", both written in

1932. But America's "second city" did not fare so well. Until "My Kind of Town" came out in 1964, only this song, often known from its first words as "Chicago (That Toddlin' Town)", represented Carl Sandburg's "hog butcher of the world". Still it evokes the vibrant energy of that burgeoning city on Lake Michigan in the early 1920s. Fred Fisher, its author and publisher later went out to Hollywood on the invitation of Irving Thalberg. When asked to write a symphony, Fisher agreed and stayed on the Metro Goldwyn Mayer payroll. However, he never delivered the goods (although he did eventually write songs for the movies). Blossom Sealey, the celebrated vaudeville entertainer, did much to popularize "Chicago" in the 1920s, as did Paul Whiteman and his Orchestra, in a Victor recording. The song also enjoyed several revivals: in 1939 and again in 1957, with a recording by Frank Sinatra.

"Chicago" lacks a verse. Its most striking musical feature is its persistent anticipation of the third beat, later to be known as the "Charleston beat" (after the song "Charleston", which, however, did not come out until the following year). Other forms of syncopation abound throughout the song, giving it a distinctively ragtime feel. As befits a pseudo-anthem, the lyrics are highly singable: "On State Street, that great street".

"Chicago" had its innings in films. It was sung by a chorus, and danced to by Fred Astaire and Ginger Rogers, in *The Story of Vernon and Irene Castle* (1939). June Haver sang it in the Fred Fisher biography, *Oh, You Beautiful Doll* (1949). Jane Froman dubbed it in for Susan Hayward in the 1957 Froman biography, *With a Song in My Heart*. And Frank Sinatra sang it in *The Joker is Wild* (1957). To this day, whenever "city songs" are performed, "Chicago" is high on the list.

Moderate rhythm song with two verses (16) and refrain (32)
PUBLISHER: Fred Fisher, Inc.
KEY: C maj., *STARTS*: c" (C maj. 7), *FORM*: ABA'C

≈≈≈≈≈≈≈≈≈≈≈≈≈≈≈≈≈≈≈≈≈

CHINA BOY *

    WORDS and MUSIC: Dick Winfree and Phil Boutelje
    POPULARIZED BY: Paul Whiteman and his Orchestra

This enduring jazz standard was recorded by both Paul Whiteman and his Orchestra (on Victor) and Red Nichols and his Five Pennies. In 1936, The Benny Goodman Trio revived it with a hit Victor recording. In search of an oriental motive, the melody plays around the intervals of the third: first, a' to c"; and then f' to a'. Notes are in short supply and there are few harmonic changes, except for a brief excursion to A-flat major in the "C" section. The Benny Goodman Trio performed it in the 1956 screen biography, *The Benny Goodman Story*. Often played in very fast tempo, "China Boy" offers the jazz instrumentalist a blank canvas, making it fertile ground for imaginative improvisation.

>Bright rhythm song with verse (12) and refrain (32)
>*PUBLISHER*: Leo Feist, Inc.
>*KEY*: F maj., *STARTS*: a' (F maj.), *FORM*: ABCA'

≈≈≈≈≈≈≈≈≈≈≈≈≈≈≈≈≈≈≈

DO IT AGAIN

>*WORDS*: B. G. De Sylva, *MUSIC*: George Gershwin
>*PREMIERE*: Revue, *The French Doll*, New York, 1922
>*INTRODUCED BY*: Irene Bordoni

In this, one of George Gershwin's earliest published ballads, the young composer is finding his way towards his mature style. The song has many of the earmarks of the great Gershwin ballads to follow: the understatement, the winsome melody, the plaintive harmonies. It remained one of Gershwin's favorites for the rest of his life. Introduced by the vivacious French entertainer Irene Bordoni in a revue called *The French Doll*, it was also featured in a London revue, *Mayfair and Montmartre*, sung by Alice Delysia. Paul Whiteman and his Orchestra had a popular Victor recording.

"Do It Again" was long banned from radio, because of its highly seductive lyrics, containing such passages as "Do it lightly / So politely". Gershwin's music complements them perfectly, using the favorite Gershwin device of repeating a motive over changing harmonies. The simple main motive consists of five notes descending scalewise, with constant harmonic shifts from F major to D minor.

"Do It Again" was sung by Gogi Grant, dubbing in for Ann Blyth, in the 1957 film, *The Helen Morgan Story* (known in Britain as *Both Ends of the Candle*). Carol Channing sang it (seductively) in *Thoroughly Modern Millie* (1967).

>Moderate ballad with verse (16) and refrain (32)
>*PUBLISHER*: New World Music Corp., assigned to Harms, Inc.
>*KEY*: F maj., *STARTS*: a' (F maj.), *FORM*: ABAB'

≈≈≈≈≈≈≈≈≈≈≈≈≈≈≈≈≈

I'LL BUILD A STAIRWAY TO PARADISE   !

WORDS: B. G. De Sylva and Arthur Francis (Ira Gershwin),
MUSIC: George Gershwin
PREMIERE: Revue, *George White's Scandals of 1922*
New York: Globe Theatre, 8 August 1922 (88 perf.)
INTRODUCED BY: Winnie Lightner, Pearl Regay and the cast,
accompanied by Paul Whiteman and the Palais Royal Orchestra

With this important song, a new voice was heard in the American musical theater. Although George Gershwin had been writing songs for Broadway since 1916, "I'll Build a Stairway to Paradise" was written in an entirely new style, making free use of the blues. The lyrics were a collaboration between George's brother Ira (who used the pseudonym Arthur Francis, after their siblings Arthur and Frances Gershwin) and B. G. (Buddy) De Sylva. It was George's first solid hit since "Swanee" in 1919. Presented as a spectacular production number closing the first act of *George White's Scandals of 1922*, it featured fifty beautiful showgirls dressed in black patent leather marching up two circular staircases. Accompanied by the pit band of Paul Whiteman and his Palais Royal Orchestra, the setting was a vision in black and white.

The title was originally "A New Step Every Day", a phrase which indeed remains in the lyrics. The song is striking in its originality. The verse alone breaks new ground, consisting of four repeated notes moving chromatically up the scale from g' to d-flat", accompanied by an array of chromatic harmonies all avoiding the C major tonality until the ultimate G dominant seventh chord. The refrain is shorter than the verse: only sixteen bars. Opening with an upward leap of an octave, it is replete with blue notes, both flatted sevenths and flatted thirds. The starting four-bar phrase in E-flat is quickly followed by its transposition a fourth higher, in A-flat. New material is introduced in the release (B), followed by a shortened restatement of the first theme. In practice, the final two bars is often repeated as a coda.

"I'll Build a Stairway to Paradise" was featured in the 1945 film biography of Gershwin, *Rhapsody in Blue*. In 1951, Georges Guetary sang it in the memorable film featuring Gershwin's music, *An American in Paris*. It remains an exciting song, one of the first great standards to employ the blues idiom.

Moderate rhythm song with verse (24) and refrain (16)
PUBLISHER: New World Music Corporation
KEY: C maj., *STARTS*: c' (C maj.), *FORM*: ABA"

≈≈≈≈≈≈≈≈≈≈≈≈≈≈≈≈≈≈≈≈≈

LIMEHOUSE BLUES * *

WORDS: Douglas Ferber, *MUSIC*: Philip Braham
PREMIERE: André Charlot's London Revue of 1924
New York: Times Square Theatre, 9 January 1924 (298 perf.)
INTRODUCED BY: Gertrude Lawrence, Robert Hobbs, and Fred Leslie

A provocative English import, "Limehouse Blues" was interpolated in a London revue of 1921, called *A to Z*, in which it was sung by Teddie Gerrard. It came to America with another British revue, *André Charlot's London Revue of 1924*. Gertrude Lawrence, who was in both revues, adopted the song and used it as her theme thereafter. Paul Whiteman and his Orchestra brought it to national attention; it was one of the numbers performed at his historic concert of 12 February 1924 at Aeolian Hall in New York which introduced George Gershwin's *Rhapsody in Blue*.

There is little connection of the song with either Limehouse, the one-time Chinese district of London's East End, or the blues. The verse, in F major and thirty-two bar AABA form, is almost a song in itself; it offers a touch of orientalism with its clanging E-flat major chords. In the refrain, in A-flat major, the main thematic material consists of three repeated notes: f', g', a-flat', in a syncopated rhythmic pattern. The harmonies are unusually meandering for the time, starting with the opening chords of D-flat seventh and B-flat seventh, each held for four bars, and rarely touching on the home chord of A-flat major.

"Limehouse Blues" was sung by Harriet Lee in the 1946 film *Ziegfeld Follies*, and by Julie Andrews and a chorus in the 1968 film, *Star!* As a jazz standard, it is usually performed in fast tempo.

Moderate rhythm song with verse (32) and refrain (32)
KEY: A-flat maj., *STARTS*: f' (D-flat 7), *FORM*: ABA'C

≈≈≈≈≈≈≈≈≈≈≈≈≈≈≈≈≈≈≈

MY BUDDY

WORDS: Gus Kahn, *MUSIC*: Walter Donaldson
INTRODUCED: in vaudeville by Al Jolson

This old-fashioned waltz could just as well have been written in the 1890s as in the Jazz Age. It was the first collaborative effort of Gus Kahn and Walter Donaldson, a prolific team that went on to write many endearing standards. Its subject matter – a fallen comrade of World War I – was a complete reversion to the tear-jerking songs of the past. Al Jolson was first to popularize the song. It was later recorded by Ben Bernie and his Orchestra and, in 1942, by Sammy Kaye and his Orchestra.

The verse, in 6/8 meter, is in recitative style. The refrain is marked "rubato", indicating that the song was not originally meant for dancing. The form of the refrain is like a hymn, consisting of two almost identical sixteen-bar segments. A pleasant touch is afforded by the juxtaposition of G major and E dominant-seventh harmonies.

An arrangement of "My Buddy" was written for pianists to perform, as accompaniment to the silent film, *Wings* (1927). It also served as the title song of the 1944 film, *My Buddy*, sung by Donald Barry. Doris Day sang it in the 1951 Gus Kahn screen biography, *I'll See You In My Dreams*.

Moderate waltz with two verses (8, in 6/8 meter) and refrain (32)
PUBLISHER: Jerome H. Remick & Co.
KEY: G maj.,*STARTS*: d" (G maj.), *FORM*: ABAB'

≈≈≈≈≈≈≈≈≈≈≈≈≈≈≈≈≈≈≈

STUMBLING !

WORDS and MUSIC: Zez Confrey
INTRODUCED: as a piano solo by Zez Confrey

Zez (Edward Elzear) Confrey was a pianist, drummer, composer, and bandleader, known for such virtuoso pieces as "Kitten on the Keys" (1921) and "Dizzy Fingers" (1923). He wrote and introduced "Stumbling" midway between those two dazzling pieces and two years before he was featured, along with George Gershwin, in the legendary concert at Aeolian Hall on 12 February 1924 that introduced *Rhapsody in Blue*. Confrey was noted for his offbeat placement of accents – a device Gershwin used two years later in his "Fascinating Rhythm" – and "Stumbling" is no exception. It was popularized both by Confrey's own band and in a Victor recording by Paul Whiteman and his Orchestra.

The refrain is built upon the notes of the pentatonic scale, which coincide with the black keys of the piano. These are the same notes used by Irving Berlin (noted for his preference for black keys) in his "Always" (1925). The five tones are played three times in each "A" section. But far more striking in these sections are the displaced accents, falling on the first and fourth beats of the first bar and the third beat of the second. These passages could just as well have been written as two bars in 3/4 meter and one in 2/4. But either way, they convey a dizzy feeling. So do Confrey's clever lyrics about a clumsy dancer: "I stepped right on her toes, and when she bumped my nose..."

The trio of Mona Freeman, Lee Patrick, and Chick Chandler sang "Stumbling" in the 1947 film, *Mother Wore Tights*. The duo of Julie Andrews and Mary Tyler Moore sang it in *Thoroughly Modern Millie* (1967).

Moderate novelty song with two verses (8) and refrain (32)
PUBLISHER: Leo Feist, Inc.
KEY: G maj., *STARTS:* d' (G maj.), *FORM:* ABAC

≈≈≈≈≈≈≈≈≈≈≈≈≈≈≈≈≈≈≈≈

TOOT TOOT TOOTSIE (GOO' BYE) * *

WORDS and MUSIC: Gus Kahn, Ernie Erdman, Dan Russo and Ted Fiorito
PREMIERE: Musical comedy, *Bombo*
New York: The Jolson Theatre, 6 October 1921
INTRODUCED BY: Al Jolson

The Sigmund Romberg musical, *Bombo*, featured Al Jolson as a black seaman who helps Christopher Columbus discover America. But the show soon discarded the impossible plot, using three interpolated numbers by Jolson that went on to become standards: "April Showers" (1921), "California, Here I Come" (1924), and "Toot Toot Tootsie (Goo' Bye)". Two of the four writers credited with the latter song were bandleaders Ted Fiorito and Dan Russo. The other two were the prolific lyricist, Gus Kahn, and the former pianist of the Original New Orleans Jazz Band, Ernie Erdman. Jolson had a hit recording on Columbia.

The bird-like melody is easy to remember, beginning with repeated thirds at two different levels (e-flat" - c" and b-flat' - g'). The length and structure of the refrain are somewhat unusual, forty bars in rondo form, but otherwise the song is simplicity itself. The deliberately silly lyrics have a punch line: "If you don't get a letter / Then you'll know I'm in jail".

The song's long history in talking pictures began in 1927 when Jolson sang it in the first movie musical, *The Jazz Singer*. Jolson also sang it in three other films: *Rose of Washington Square* (1939), *The Jolson Story* (1946), and *Jolson Sings Again* (1949); in the latter two he dubbed it on the soundtrack for Larry Parks. Doris Day sang the song in the Gus Kahn biography, *I'll See You in My Dreams* (1951); June Allyson and Van Johnson sang it in the 1953 film, *Remains to be Seen*; and Linda Sue Risk did it in *The Trouble with Girls* (1969). Usually performed in brisk tempo, "Toot Toot Tootsie (Goo' Bye)" brings something of the frantic spirit of the Roaring Twenties to the present.

Moderate rhythm song with two verses (16) and refrain (40)
PUBLISHER: Leo Feist, Inc.
KEY: E-flat maj., *STARTS*: e-flat" (E-flat maj.), *FORM*: ABA'CA"

≈≈≈≈≈≈≈≈≈≈≈≈≈≈≈≈≈≈≈≈

TREES

WORDS: Joyce Kilmer, *MUSIC*: Oscar Rasbach

The poet, Joyce Kilmer, wrote these poignant words in 1913. He was said to have been inspired by an old oak tree that stood near his home at the corner of Route 1 and Ryder's Lane in New Brunswick, New Jersey. Kilmer went off to France during World War I and died there in 1918 as a sergeant in the United States Army. Four years later, Rasbach set the words to music. The result is an American classic. Its popularity was enhanced by the Victor recordings of Paul Robeson, Nelson Eddy and John Charles Thomas. In 1931, Isham Jones and his Orchestra recorded it for Brunswick. "Trees" has been performed in all sorts of settings: for solo voice, duet, chorus and in an array of instrumental versions from solo piano and organ to orchestra and concert band.

Since there is no verse, the opening six tones of the refrain (b', b', a', a', f-sharp', f-sharp') also act as introduction, interlude, and coda. The form of the song itself essentially alternates an "A" section of four bars with a "B" section of eight bars, and then repeats itself. With its wide range (b-flat to f-sharp") and frequent upward leaps, it is more an art song than a typical popular song. Not only does it accelerate and then retard, but it has a held note (fermata) at the word "God" in the famous final line: "Poems are made by fools like me, But only God can make a tree".

"Trees" was sung by Donald Novis in the 1932 film, *The Big Broadcast,* and performed by Fred Waring's Pennsylvanians in the film, *Melody Time* (1948).

Art song with refrain (30)
PUBLISHER: G. Schirmer, Inc.
KEY: D maj., *STARTS*: b' (D6), *FORM*: ABAB'

≈≈≈≈≈≈≈≈≈≈≈≈≈≈≈≈≈≈≈

'WAY DOWN YONDER IN NEW ORLEANS * *!

WORDS and MUSIC: Henry Creamer and J. Turner Layton
PREMIERE: Revue, *Spice of 1922*
New York: Winter Garden Theatre, 6 July 1922 (65 perf.)
INTRODUCED BY: Henry Creamer and J. Turner Layton

Ironically, this Dixieland standard paying homage to the Southland, never saw the light of day south of Staten Island. A pure product of New York, "'Way Down Yonder in New Orleans" was written for the all-black revue, *Strut Miss Lizzie*. The show, with songs by Henry Creamer and J. Turner Layton, opened at the Times Square Theatre on 19 June 1922, but without the song. A few weeks later, however, it was interpolated and sung by its writers in another black revue, *Spice of 1922*. Blossom Sealey popularized it in vaudeville and with a Columbia recording. Paul Whiteman and his Orchestra recorded it for Victor. Freddy Cannon revived it in 1960 with a hit recording on Swan.

Despite its many repeated notes, there is an air of originality about the refrain. It departs from the norm both in length (28 bars) and form (ABACDA). Most striking of all is the complete caesura at the word "Stop!" at the thirteenth bar and again at the seventeenth. There is also more than a hint of ragtime and early jazz in the preponderance of dotted notes and syncopation.

In films, "'Way Down Yonder in New Orleans" was sung by a chorus and danced to by Fred Astaire and Ginger Rogers in *The Story of Vernon and Irene Castle* (1939). Bob Haymes sang it in the 1943 Ted Lewis biography, *Is Everybody Happy?* Betty Hutton and a chorus delivered it in *Somebody Loves Me* (1952). And Gene Krupa and his Orchestra performed it in the drummer's 1960 screen biography, *The Gene Krupa Story*. With its infectious rhythm, the happy-go-lucky song is a standby of the Dixieland repertoire.

Moderate rhythm song with two verses (16) and refrain (28)
PUBLISHER: Shapiro, Bernstein & Co., Inc.
KEY: F maj., *STARTS*: c" (C7), *FORM*: ABACDA

≈≈≈≈≈≈≈≈≈≈≈≈≈≈≈≈≈≈≈≈

1923

IN SEARCH OF NOVELTY

1923

Ev'ry step you do / Leads to something new

Cecil Mack and Jimmy Johnston
"Charleston"

This is a year of novelty. In their search for something new, people embrace a new dance called The Charleston or entertain outlandish ideas for songs. Thus, we have a sensational new song to go along with the dance ("Charleston"), a comic strip character with "Goo Goo Googly Eyes" ("Barney Google"), and a Greek fruit and vegetable peddler who mixes up his affirmatives and negatives ("Yes! We Have No Bananas"). But amidst all this novelty there is still room for a few old-fashioned waltzes like "Mexicali Rose" and "Wonderful One". Radio is still a novelty, but the medium is growing in leaps and bounds. The A & P Gypsies begin broadcasting over station WEAF in New York, starring Harry Horlick's Orchestra with tenor Frank Parker, and sponsored by the Great Atlantic and Pacific Tea Company. Each broadcast begins with the Russian folk song "Two Guitars".

It is a time of new beginnings. President Warren Gamaliel Harding dies unexpectedly in his suite at the Palace Hotel in San Francisco. In Plymouth Notch, Vermont, Calvin Coolidge is administered the oath of office as the nation's thirtieth president by his father, a notary public. The economy begins to explode. Automobile sales reach a new high; half of all new cars sold are Fords. Babe Ruth hits a three-run homer in his first season for the New York Yankees at Yankee Stadium. The public, in its search for novelty, welcomes comics Stan Laurel and Oliver Hardy, Harold Lloyd, Buster Keaton, and Ben Turpin to Hollywood; and Eddie Cantor, Fannie Brice, W. C. Fields, and Frank Fay to Broadway. Also in New York, the all-black musical comedy, *Runnin' Wild*, opens, featuring a dance and novelty song destined to sweep the country and symbolize the entire decade, The Charleston.

SONGS OF 1923

Barney Google
Charleston ***
I Cried for You (Now It's Your Turn to
      Cry Over Me)
I Love You
It Ain't Gonna Rain No Mo'
Linger Awhile
Mexicali Rose
Nobody's Sweetheart *
Swingin' Down the Lane
Who's Sorry Now? *
Wonderful One *
Yes! We Have No Bananas

BARNEY GOOGLE

> *WORDS and MUSIC:* Billy Rose and Con Conrad
> *INTRODUCED:* in vaudeville by Eddie Cantor

Based on the popular cartoon character, "Barney Google" is a prime example of the humorous novelty song so popular in the twenties. Billy Rose, its co-writer, also had a hand in the 1924 hit "Does the Spearmint Lose Its Flavor on the Bedpost Over Night?".

Eddie Cantor introduced "Barney Google" in vaudeville, but it was the madcap comic team of Olsen and Johnson that popularized it. In their skit, they played the front and rear ends of a horse prancing around the stage, while another actor made up to look like Barney Google played a jockey. Popular recordings of the song were made by the entertainer Georgie Price and the comic team of Jones and Hare.

The music is harmonically simple, in the novelty tradition, with an emphasis on tonic and dominant. It is also short; each refrain is only sixteen bars long. The lyrics refer to "Barney Google with his Goo Goo Googly Eyes" – very appropriate for Cantor who was called Banjo Eyes. Each refrain has a one-liner joke about horse racing and there are numerous contemporary references to Mister Hughes, Douglas Fairbanks (Sr.), and Rudolf Valentino.

> Moderate novelty song with two verses (16) and two refrains (16)
> *PUBLISHER:* Jerome H. Remick & Co.
> *KEY:* C major, *STARTS:* c" (C maj.), *FORM:* AA'AA"

≈≈≈≈≈≈≈≈≈≈≈≈≈≈≈≈≈≈≈

CHARLESTON * * *

> *WORDS and MUSIC:* Cecil Mack (Richard D. Mc Pherson) and
> James P. Johnson
> *PREMIERE:* Musical comedy, *Runnin' Wild*
> New York: Colonial Theatre, 29 October 1923
> *INTRODUCED BY:* Elisabeth Welch

If any one song epitomizes the twenties, it is "Charleston", the song that gave its name to the high-stepping dance known as The Charleston. Introduced in the all-black musical comedy, *Runnin' Wild*, both song and dance became instant sensations. Paul Whiteman and his Orchestra soon had a hit recording. The writers were James P. Johnson, known as the king of stride piano, and James P. McPherson, who went under the *nom de plume* of Cecil Mack. The Charleston dance craze lasted through the twenties, inspiring a host of spin-off songs from "Charleston Crazy", in 1923, to "Charleston Is the Best Dance After All", in 1928.

The verse, in G minor, tells the story about a song of the city (Charleston, South Carolina) and of a new dance that has come from there. The most striking musical feature of the refrain is the back beat, or anticipated third beat, that permeates it. This persistent syncopation contributes to the song's animation and, of course, inspires the quirky gyrations of the dance. The harmonies are also of interest, gliding through the circle of fifths from D seventh to G seventh to C seventh to F seventh and back to B-flat major, There is a brief excursion to D minor in the second section (A'), but the final section (B) forthrightly proclaims its B-flat major tonality.

"Charleston" was danced by Dan Dailey and Ann Baxter in the 1949 film, *You're My Everything* and by Billy De Wolfe and Patrice Wymore in the 1950 film *Tea for Two*. It was the theme song of the vivacious dancer, Ann Pennington. As a symbol of the Jazz Age, it is very much alive today.

Moderately fast rhythm song with verse (16) and refrain (32)
PUBLISHER: Harms, Inc.
KEY: B-flat maj., *STARTS*: f' (B-flat maj.), *FORM*: AA'AB

≈≈≈≈≈≈≈≈≈≈≈≈≈≈≈≈≈≈≈≈≈

I CRIED FOR YOU (NOW IT'S YOUR TURN TO CRY OVER ME)

WORDS and MUSIC: Arthur Freed, Gus Arnheim, and Abe Lyman
INTRODUCED BY: Abe Lyman and his Orchestra

This song about unrequited love and subsequent revenge was written by eminent band leader Abe Lyman; his pianist, Gus Arnheim (who later went on to lead a band of his own); and a lyricist, Arthur Freed, who later became a movie producer. It was initially popularized by its co-writer, Abe Lyman, and by Cliff Edwards, known as Ukelele Ike. Half-forgotten, the song had a remarkable comeback in the late thirties, with best-selling records by Bunny Berigan and his Orchestra in 1938, by Glen Gray and The Casa Loma Orchestra (sung by Kenny Sargent) and Bing Crosby in 1939, and by Harry James and his Orchestra (sung by Helen Forrest) in 1942.

Apart from its subject of love and revenge, the refrain is unusual in several respects. The melody is far-reaching, jumping first up a fifth (from a' to e") and then down an octave (from e" to e'). The length (40 bars) and form (rondo) are seldom found in songs of the period. Most interesting of all are the harmonic changes in each "A" section. Moving from F major to E seventh, and then through the circle of fifths: A seventh, D seventh, G seventh, C seventh, and finally back to F major.

"I Cried for You" has been sung in a number of movies: by Judy Garland in *Babes in Arms* (1939), by Helen Forrest in *Bathing Beauty* (1944), by Ralph Meeker in *Somebody Loves Me* (1952), by Frank Sinatra in *The Joker is Wild* (1957), and by Diana Ross in *Lady Sings the Blues* (1972). It has a special place in history as a song of the early twenties that is off the beaten path.

Moderate foxtrot with two verses (16) and refrain (40)
PUBLISHER: Sherman, Clay & Co. (San Francisco)
KEY: F maj., *STARTS*: a' (F maj.), *FORM*: ABA'CA"

≈≈≈≈≈≈≈≈≈≈≈≈≈≈≈≈≈≈≈

I LOVE YOU

WORDS: Harlan Thompson, *MUSIC*: Harry Archer
PREMIERE: Musical comedy, *Little Jessie James*
New York: Longacre Theatre, 15 August 1923
INTRODUCED BY: Nan Halperin and Jay Velie

This enchanting song was simultaneously published as "Je t'aime", with French lyrics by Paul Combis. It is one of many songs with the same title written over the years, including Cole Porter's very different "I Love You" of 1944. The 1923 song was greatly popularized by Paul Whiteman and his Orchestra in a Victor recording, and enjoyed the distinction of being one of the songs Whiteman performed in his historic concert at New York's Aeolian Hall on 12 February 1924 along with the world premiere of George Gershwin's *Rhapsody in Blue*.

The particular poignancy of Archer's music lies in the opening gesture of its refrain: the downward leap of an octave followed by a rising whole step: c" - c' - d'. This three-note module is repeated at different pitch levels throughout the refrain. The melody sweeps broadly along with an enticing bit of syncopation just before the end.

"I Love You" enjoyed a brief revival in 1928. It was also featured in the 1957 film version of Ernest Hemingway's *The Sun Also Rises*, starring Errol Flynn, Ava Gardner, and Tyrone Power.

Moderate foxtrot with two verses (16) and refrain (32)
PUBLISHER: Leo Feist, Inc.
KEY: F maj., *STARTS*: c" (F maj.), *FORM*: AA'A"B

≈≈≈≈≈≈≈≈≈≈≈≈≈≈≈≈≈≈≈

IT AIN'T GONNA RAIN NO MO'

WORDS and MUSIC: Wendell Hall
PREMIERE: Revue, *The Punch Bowl*, 1923
INTRODUCED BY: Wendell Hall

Singer Wendell Hall, known on early radio as "The Red-Headed Music Maker", wrote and introduced this folk-like ditty, accompanying himself on the four-stringed Hawaiian ukelele, an instrument which he also did much to popularize. The song is based on a Kentucky folk song originating before the 1870s. Hall's Victor recording sold over two million copies in 1923 alone and five million copies over all.

Boasting a string of five verses (expanded on the sheet music by an additional twenty-four), each alternating with a refrain (with five different lyrics), the song carries a note of unrestrained optimism. The music of the refrain is in the folk-song tradition of simplicity, using only two harmonies – tonic and dominant – with a range of less than an octave. Much of the enjoyment of the song rises in the long-held opening note of each refrain: the d" on the word "Oh!", held by a sustained note or fermata.

"It Ain't Gonna Rain No Mo' was republished in 1942 with a string of "Victory Verses" designed to elevate the morale of civilians and servicemen during the War Years. It was interpolated in a 1953 film about the twenties, *Has Anybody Seen My Gal*, starring Rock Hudson, Piper Laurie, and Charles Coburn.

Moderate novelty song with five verses (8) and five refrains (8)
PUBLISHER: Forster Music Publisher, Inc.
KEY: B-flat maj., *STARTS*: d" (B-flat maj.), *FORM*: AB

≈≈≈≈≈≈≈≈≈≈≈≈≈≈≈≈≈≈≈≈

LINGER AWHILE

WORDS: Harry Owens, *MUSIC*: Vincent Rose
INTRODUCED BY: Jack Shildkret

This gliding foxtrot rode the wave of popularity of Paul Whiteman and his Orchestra, sparked by the banjo playing of diminutive virtuoso, Mike Pingatore, in a Victor recording that sold over two million copies. Ted Lewis had a successful cover recording.

"Linger Awhile" is unusual in its sheer minimalism; there are only forty-four notes in the entire refrain. Many of these are half notes occurring on the second and third beats of the measure, giving the music a syncopated effect. The harmonies stay close to tonic and dominant, except for the "B" section, which briefly goes to D minor. The rising melodic line of each "A" section creates a natural crescendo, which adds to the overall exhilarating effect of the refrain. In the movies, the song was performed by the Whiteman band in *King of Jazz* (1940), and featured in *Give My Regards to Broadway* (1948) and *Belles On Their Toes* (1952).

> Moderate foxtrot with verse (16) and refrain (32)
> *PUBLISHER*: Leo Feist, Inc.
> *KEY*" F maj., *STARTS*: c' (F maj.), *FORM*: AA'BA"

≈≈≈≈≈≈≈≈≈≈≈≈≈≈≈≈≈≈≈

MEXICALI ROSE

> *WORDS*: Helen Stone, *MUSIC*: Jack B. Jenney
> *INTRODUCED ON RADIO BY*: The Cliquot Club Eskimos

The Cliquot Club Eskimos was one of a number of ensembles in early radio bearing merchandising names; another was Harry Horlick and the A & P Gypsies. Both played "Mexicali Rose" over the airwaves in the 1920s. But it was not until 1938, fifteen years after it was written, that this little waltz became famous: Bing Crosby's Decca recording, accompanied by John Scott Trotter's Orchestra, was a phenomenal success.

It is a simple country song, almost monothematic in nature. The same stepwise motive, repeated at different levels, permeates both verse and refrain. The song's only exoticism is its title, referring to the border city in Mexico, near California.

"Mexicali Rose" has been featured in a number of films, including two bearing its title: *Mexcali Rose* (1929, starring a miscast Barbara Stanwyck as a Mexican senorita) and *Mexicali Rose* (1939, in which it is sung by screen cowboy Gene Autry). In 1936 Bing Crosby sang it to Martha Raye in *Rhythm on the Range*. Autry sang it again in 1952 in *Barbed Wire*. Another cowboy, Roy Rogers, sang it in *Song of Texas*. But it is the rich, booming voice of Crosby that always comes to mind whenever this enduring waltz is heard.

> Slow waltz with two verses (32) and refrain (32)
> *PUBLISHER*: W. A. Quincke, assigned to M. M. Cole Publishing Co.
> *KEY*: C Maj., *STARTS*: e' (C maj.), *FORM*: ABA'C

≈≈≈≈≈≈≈≈≈≈≈≈≈≈≈≈≈≈≈

NOBODY'S SWEETHEART *

WORDS and MUSIC: Gus Kahn, Ernie Erdman, Billy Meyers, and
Elmer Schoebel
PREMIERE: Revue, The Passing Show of 1923
New York: Winter Garden Theatre, 14 June 1923
INTRODUCED BY: Ted Lewis

Interpolated in the rather weak revue, The Passing Show of 1923,
and introduced by bandleader Ted Lewis ("Is everybody happy?"), this
hoary standard was popularized by Isham Jones and his Orchestra. One of
its four writers was Elmer Schoebel, pianist and arranger with the New
Orleans Rhythm Kings. Red Nichols and his band recorded the song in
1928, Cab Calloway in 1931, and The Mills Brothers in 1932.

The forty-bar refrain (in the manner of "Toot Toot Tootsie (Goo'
Bye)", written the previous year), has a minimum of notes. The harmonies
of the "A" sections move reassuringly through the circle of fifths: from G
major, to E seventh, A seventh, and then to D seventh. The lyrics tell the
heart-rending tale of a fallen woman, with "Painted lips, painted eyes /
Wearing a bird of paradise".

A number of films have used the song, They include The Vagabond
Lover (1929, sung by Rudy Vallee and his Connecticut Yankees), The Cuban
Love Song (1931 sung by Constance Moore), Hit Parade of 1943; Stormy
Weather (1943, sung by Ernest Whitman), Atlantic City (1944, sung by
Belle Baker), and I'll See You in My Dreams (1951, sung by Doris Day and
Danny Thomas). Its slowly wandering chord changes make it a favorite
vehicle for jazz improvisation.

Moderate foxtrot with two verses (24) and refrain (40)
PUBLISHER: Mills Music, Inc.
KEY: G maj., STARTS: d' (G maj.), FORM: ABACA'

≈≈≈≈≈≈≈≈≈≈≈≈≈≈≈≈≈≈≈≈

SWINGIN' DOWN THE LANE

WORDS: Gus Kahn, MUSIC: Isham Jones
INTRODUCED: in vaudeville by Cliff Edwards (Ukelele Ike)

Captioned on its sheet music as "An Old-Fashioned Song With a
Fox Trot Swing", "Swingin' Down the Lane" lives up to its billing. Popular
bandleader, Isham Jones (its composer), went on to write three standards
in the following year: "I'll See You in My Dreams", "It Had to Be You", and
"The One I Love (Belongs to Somebody Else)". Gus Kahn, the lyricist was

one of the most prolific in the business, with songs too numerous to mention here. Introduced by vaudeville star, Cliff Edwards (Ukelele Ike), "Swingin' Down the Lane" was popularized in a Brunswick recording by Jones and his Orchestra and by Ben Bernie and his Orchestra on Vocalion.

It is indeed an old-fashioned song in the sense of its turn-of-the-century form (ABAC) and its simple harmonies leisurely moving through the circle of fifths (E seventh, A seventh, D seventh, G major). The one modern note, literally speaking, is the lowered seventh, the blue note f'-natural', in Bar Twenty-five. The four-note pickup of eighth notes that begins the refrain acts as a rhythmical leitmotiv, appearing twelve times throughout. Kahn's lyrics are folksy in their use of contractions and archaisms, as in: "When the moon is on the wane / Still I'm waitin' all in vain".

"Swingin" Down the Lane" was performed in the 1944 film, *Greenwich Village*; Mona Freeman sang it with a chorus in the 1947 film, *Mother Wore Tights*; and Danny Thomas, Doris Day and a chorus of children performed it in the Gus Kahn biographical film, *I'll See You In My Dreams* (1951).

Moderate foxtrot with two verses (16) and refrain (32)
PUBLISHER: Leo Feist, Inc.
KEY: G maj., *STARTS*: g' (G maj. 6), *FORM*: ABAC

≈≈≈≈≈≈≈≈≈≈≈≈≈≈≈≈≈≈≈

WHO'S SORRY NOW? *

WORDS: Bert Kalmar and Harry Ruby, *MUSIC*: Ted Snyder
INTRODUCED: in vaudeville by Van and Schenck

This tearful waltz has most often been performed over the years in 4/4 time, and indeed the sheet music has a foxtrot chorus. As such, the song remains a jazz standard, although its origin as a waltz is forgotten. Its writers all had illustrious careers. With this song, Bert Kalmar and Harry Ruby, who collaborated on the lyrics, had their first solid hit; they went on to have many more. Ted Snyder, responsible for the music, was Irving Berlin's first publisher, and later his business partner. The popular singing duo of Van and Schenck introduced "Who's Sorry Now? in their vaudeville act. Early recordings were made by singer Marion Harris and by Isham Jones and his Orchestra.

It's not hard to understand the song's attraction to jazz musicians. Its unhurried tour through the circle of fifths – from B-flat major to D seventh to G seventh to C seventh to F seventh, and then back to B-flat major – makes it a perfect vehicle for improvisation. Also a contributing factor is the slow harmonic rhythm: each harmonic change lasts for two measures.

"Who's Sorry Now?" enjoyed a revival in 1957, sparked by a successful Metro Goldwyn Mayer recording by Connie Francis. It has also been featured in several films: sung by Lisette Verea and a chorus in the Marx Brothers picture, *A Night in Casablanca* (1946); by Gloria De Haven in the 1950 biographical film of songwriters Bert Kalmar and Harry Ruby, *Three Little Words*; by Connie Francis in *National Lampoon's Animal House* (1978); and by a chorus in *All That Jazz* (1979).

Moderate waltz with two verses (16) and refrain (32)
PUBLISHER: Waterson, Berlin & Snyder Co.
KEY: B-flat maj., *STARTS*: d' (B-flat maj.), *FORM*: ABAC

≈≈≈≈≈≈≈≈≈≈≈≈≈≈≈≈≈≈≈

WONDERFUL ONE *

WORDS: Dorothy Terriss, *MUSIC:* Paul Whiteman and Ferdie Grofe; adapted from a theme by Marshall Neilan
INTRODUCED BY: Paul Whiteman and his Orchestra

This lovely waltz is usually known by its opening words: "My Wonderful One". Its creators were illustrious: Marshall Neilan, successful actor and director of silent films, conceived the theme; conductor Paul Whiteman, "The King of Jazz", and his talented arranger, Ferdie Grofe, adapted it; Dorothy Terriss, the lyricist, was a pseudonym for Mrs. Theodora Morse, wife of Theodore Morse, who wrote "Hail, Hail, the Gang's All Here" and many other turn-of-the-century hits. She herself wrote the lyrics of many songs, including "Three O'Clock in the Morning" (1922) and "Siboney" (1929). But it was Whiteman, riding the crest of his popularity, who made the song a hit in a Victor recording with his orchestra. Tenor Morton Downey, singing with the Whiteman band, also helped popularize the song. It was accurately billed on the sheet music cover as "Paul Whiteman's Sensational Waltz Hit".

The refrain has a haunting melody, with each "A" section descending in half and whole steps. The starting harmony of C minor is itself unusual in popular songs of the day. There is no verse, but rather an interlude, of equal length to the refrain, in D major.

"Wonderful One" was featured in the 1946 period musical, *Margie*, which starred Jeanne Crain as a shy adolescent growing up in the 1920s.

Moderate waltz with refrain (32) and interlude (32)
PUBLISHER: Leo Feist Inc.
KEY: G maj. or A-flat maj., *STARTS*: b' (C min.) or c" (D-flat min.),
FORM: AA'AB

≈≈≈≈≈≈≈≈≈≈≈≈≈≈≈≈≈

YES! WE HAVE NO BANANAS

WORDS and MUSIC: Frank Silver and Irving Cohn
INTRODUCED: in vaudeville and on radio by Frank Silver's
Music Masters

By far the biggest novelty hit of the twenties, this nonsense song achieved instant popularity when it was interpolated by Eddie Cantor in the revue, *Make It Snappy*, which had opened in New York at the Winter Garden Theatre 13 April 1922. Cantor's Victor recording was a rousing success. The silly title inspired spin-offs such as "I've Got the Yes! We've Got No Bananas Blues" and a parody of the sextet from *Lucia di Lammermoor* in Irving Berlin's *Music Box Revue of 1923*. At the historic Aeolian Hall concert of 12 February 1924, which introduced George Gershwin's *Rhapsody in Blue*, it was presented as an example of humor in popular music. It was there that its borrowings were pointed out: from the "Hallelujah Chorus" of Handel's *Messiah* to "My Bonnie Lies Over the Ocean" and "I Dreamt That I Dwelt in Marble Halls", among others. In fact, the publishers of *Messiah* won a lawsuit for plagiarism against the writers of the popular number. It has been suggested by Sigmund Spaeth (*A History of Popular Music in America*, 1946) that more accurate lyrics would be:

"Hallelujah, Bananas! Oh, bring back my bonnie to me.
I dreamt that I dwelt in marble halls – the kind that you seldom see.
I was seeing Nellie home, to an old-fashioned garden; but, Hallelujah,
Bananas! Oh, bring back my Bonnie to me!"

The song is indeed a crazy quilt of fragments from various sources, but the fragments are almost too small to be recognizable. The chief absurdity lies in the initial yes/no idea. Everything else is secondary, but adds to the hilarity: the exaggerated dialect ("string beans and HONions"), the slightly skewed pronunciation ("Long Island PoTAHto), and the nine extra choruses of lyrics.

"Yes! We Have No "Bananas" was recorded on the Emerson label by the Pennsylvanian Syncopators and on Vocalion by Billy Jones. In 1950, it was satirized in a Victor recording by Spike Jones and his City Slickers. Al

Jolson sang a parody of it (with extra lyrics by Irving Berlin) in the early film, *Mammy* (1930). The Pied Pipers sang it in the 1948 film, *Luxury Liner*, and Eddie Cantor did the dubbing for Keefe Brasselle in *The Eddie Cantor Story* (1953). In retrospect, the song has become a symbol of a zany year in a zany decade.

Moderate novelty song with two verses (16) and refrain (32)
PUBLISHER: Skidmore Music Co., Inc.
KEY: C maj., *STARTS*: c" (C maj.), F ORM: ABCA

≈≈≈≈≈≈≈≈≈≈≈≈≈≈≈≈≈≈≈≈≈

BIRTH OF THE MODERN SONG

1924

Fascinating Rhythm / You've got me on the go!

Ira Gershwin
"Fascinating Rhythm"

If any year qualifies as the birthdate of American popular music in the modern style, it is this one: a strong contender for the starting point of what has been called the "golden age" of American popular song. George and Ira Gershwin are well-represented this year, with such innovative songs as "Fascinating Rhythm", "The Man I Love", and "Oh, Lady, Be Good!" It is the first year to have nine well-known standards, including "California, Here I Come" and "It Had To Be You"; and the only one of the entire decade to boast two four-star standards: "The Man I Love" and "Tea for Two".

With Calvin Coolidge reelected by a landslide and with more than half the population now living in cities, interests have turned from the rural to the urban, from the sedate to the lively, from operetta to musical comedy, from the waltz to jazz. Crossword puzzles and dance marathons are the rage. On the silent screen, audiences flock to see an elegant John Barrymore as Beau Brummel and a dashing Douglas Fairbanks as The Thief of Bagdad. And jazz has become respectable since Paul Whiteman's historic concert, "An Experiment in Modern Music", presented at New York's Aeolian Hall on 12 February. The featured work, the twenty-second on that memorable program, is George Gershwin's *Rhapsody in Blue*. With the composer at the piano and Whiteman leading his thirty-two piece orchestra, the audience is electrified from the opening wail of Russ Gorman's clarinet glissando to the momentous conclusion. Jazz has come of age. It is not just something to dance to, but is worthy of serious consideration.

This is a boisterous year for the musical theater, with two hit operettas of the old school, *Rose Marie* and *The Student Prince*, vying against two musical comedies of the new school: *Lady, Be Good!* And *No,*

No, Nanette. The songs of 1924 reflect that dichotomy, with two old-fashioned waltzes by Irving Berlin, "All Alone" and "What'll I Do", contrasting with a dazzling array of Gershwin songs, such as "Fascinating Rhythm" and "Somebody Loves Me", using devices of jazz and the blues. A most important year, 1924, a watershed in the history of American popular song.

SONGS OF 1924

All Alone *
Amapola (Pretty Little Poppy) *
California, Here I Come ***
Deep in My Heart, Dear
Fascinating Rhythm *!
I Want to Be Happy *
I'll See You in My Dreams ***
Indian Love Call *
It Had to Be You ***
Jealous
The Man I Love ****!
Oh, Lady Be Good! ***
The One I Love Belongs to Somebody Else
Rose-Marie
Serenade *
Somebody Loves Me **
Tea for Two ****
What'll I Do?

ALL ALONE *

WORDS and MUSIC: Irving Berlin
INTRODUCED: on network radio by John McCormick, January, 1924

Irving Berlin wrote this lament to loneliness while he was staying at the Ritz Hotel in Atlantic City, New Jersey, where he had retreated to rest on the beach each day and write songs by night. In it, he expressed his sadness at the recent passing of his mother, Lena, as well as his loneliness since the passing of his first wife. Spurred by the singing of Metropolitan Opera star John McCormick over network radio – a performance that reached over eight million listeners – "All Alone" was soon recorded on Brunswick by Al Jolson, on Victor by Paul Whiteman and his Orchestra and John McCormick, and by Abe Lyman and his Orchestra. The waltz eventually sold over a million recordings and a million copies of sheet music. Already popular, it was then interpolated in Berlin's *Music Box Revue of 1924-1925*, which opened at the Music Box Theatre on 1 December 1924 and lasted for 186 performances. In that revue, Grace Moore – bathed in spotlights – sang the song into a telephone on one side of a darkened stage to Oscar Shaw, holding a phone at the other side.

The song is deceptive in its apparent simplicity. The melody unfolds with a rhythmic motive of three notes, short-short-long, placed at different pitch levels, at first ascending and then descending. The form is unusual for a popular song, and more appropriate for a German *lied*. It is, in fact, through composed, with a gently curving melodic line that never repeats itself. The lyrics, thoroughly integrated with the music, tell how one can be lonely while sitting by a new-fangled telephone. They even include the high-tech expression "ring a ting-a-ling".

In the movies, Alice Faye sang "All Alone" in the Berlin extravaganza, *Alexander's Ragtime Band*.

Moderate waltz with two verses (18) and refrain (32)
PUBLISHER: Irving Berlin, Inc.
KEY: F maj., *STARTS*: f' (F maj.), *FORM*: ABCD

≈≈≈≈≈≈≈≈≈≈≈≈≈≈≈≈≈≈

AMAPOLA (PRETTY LITTLE POPPY) *

ENGLISH WORDS: Albert Gamse, *MUSIC*: Joseph M. Lacalle
INTRODUCED BY: The Castillians

One of the last of many tangos imported into the United States from Europe and Latin America since the 1910s, "Amapola (Pretty Little

Poppy)" rested in tranquillity for sixteen years after its first stateside publication this year. Only in 1940 was it rescued from oblivion in a magical recording by Jimmy Dorsey and his Orchestra with vocals by Helen O'Connell and Bob Eberly. The rollicking swing arrangement on Decca #3629 became a sensational hit and put "Amapola" on radio's *Your Hit Parade* for nineteen weeks. To this day, the erstwhile tango is almost always performed with a solid swing beat.

The verse, in G minor, is in some ways more interesting than the refrain, which is notable for its static harmony, staying as much as six measures without harmonic change. The melodic line, in typical tango fashion, juxtaposes long notes with passages of eight notes.

Deanna Durbin sang "Amapola" in the film musical, *First Love* (1939).

Tango with two verses (16) and refrain (32)
PUBLISHER: Edward B. Marks Corporation
KEY: B-flat maj., *STARTS*: d' (B-flat maj.), *FORM*: ABA'C

≈≈≈≈≈≈≈≈≈≈≈≈≈≈≈≈≈≈≈

CALIFORNIA, HERE I COME * * *

WORDS and MUSIC: Al Jolson, Bud De Sylva, and Joseph Meyer
PREMIERE: Road show of the musical comedy, *Bombo*.
New York: Jolson Theatre, 6 October 1921
INTRODUCED BY: Al Jolson

The Jolson extravaganza, *Bombo,* ran for years, featuring such interpolations as "April Showers" and "Toot, Toot, Tootsie!" One of the last interpolations was this lively song. It met with such success that it was soon interpolated in another Jolson musical, *Big Boy*, which opened at the Winter Garden Theatre on 7 January 1925. In the fashion of the time, Jolson was credited as one of the writers. This time, he deserved it; more than anyone, he was responsible for the song's immense popularity, spurred on by his Brunswick recording. Later on, it became the theme song of Abe Lyman and his Californians.

Both verse and refrain are built around repeated half notes: six in the verse, four in the refrain. The verse, in E minor, could be a song in itself. It consists of thirty-two bars in AABA form, with its "B" section giving a preview of the main theme of the refrain. That theme is a joyful one, almost a shout, with just a touch of syncopation. The climax, and highest point, of the refrain occurs in the "C" section at the words: "Open up that Golden Gate".

So closely is Jolson identified with "California, Here I Come", that he sang it in four films: *The Singing Kid* (1936), *Rose of Washington Square* (1939), *The Jolson Story* (1946), and *Jolson Sings Again* (1949); in the last two, he dubbed it in for Larry Parks. Jane Froman also sang it for Susan Hayward in the 1952 film, *With a Song In My Heart*. It remains the California song – *par excellence*.

Moderate foxtrot with two verses (32) and refrain (32)
PUBLISHER: M. Witmark & Sons
KEY: C maj., *STARTS*: c" (C maj.), *FORM*: ABAC

≈≈≈≈≈≈≈≈≈≈≈≈≈≈≈≈≈≈

DEEP IN MY HEART, DEAR

WORDS: Dorothy Donnelly, *MUSIC*: Sigmund Romberg
PREMIERE: Operetta, *The Student Prince*
New York: Jolson Theatre, 2 December 1924 (608 perf.)
INTRODUCED BY: Howard Marsh and Ilse Marvenga

The operetta, *The Student Prince*, originally called *The Student Prince in Heidelberg*, was a phenomenal success, touring America constantly for decades, despite (or maybe because of) its Viennese-style score by Sigmund Romberg and its male chorus of thirty-six men (no women). In this beautiful duet, Prince Karl Franz and his favorite waitress, Kathie, swear their eternal love for each other.

It is a waltz, very much in the operetta tradition, with long notes, a wide range (an octave and a sixth), and impassioned harmonies. The changes in the first four measures of the refrain are particularly enticing, moving from F major to A seventh and then to D minor and G seventh. The highest point is reached just before the end, with a high a" held by a fermata, at the word "dear".

"Deep In My Heart, Dear" was featured in two films of 1954. One was the Romberg biographical film, *Deep in My Heart*, in which it was sung by a chorus. The other was the film version of *The Student Prince*. In that, it was sung by Ann Blyth and Mario Lanza, dubbing in for Edward Purdom. Lanza also had a successful Victor recording.

Slow waltz with verse (8) and refrain (32)
PUBLISHER: Harms, Inc., with M. Witmark & Sons
KEY: F maj., *STARTS*: a' (F maj.), *FORM*: AA'BA"

≈≈≈≈≈≈≈≈≈≈≈≈≈≈≈≈≈≈

FASCINATING RHYTHM *!

WORDS: Ira Gershwin, *MUSIC*: George Gershwin
PREMIERE: Musical comedy, *Lady, Be Good!*
New York: Liberty Theatre, 1 December 1924 (330 perf.)
INTRODUCED BY: Fred and Adele Astaire and Cliff Edwards

The aptly named "Fascinating Rhythm" is one of the most fascinating songs to emanate from Broadway. Initially heard in the first all-Gershwin musical comedy, *Lady, Be Good!*, it brought immediate attention because of its unusual rhythm. But more than that, it inaugurated a new era of experimentation in show tunes. The earliest recording was by Cliff Edwards (Ukelele Ike) who had introduced the song on stage along with Fred and Adele Astaire.

The song's principal fascination lies in its clashing rhythms: the irregular one of the melody against the steady one of the bass. The upper line is particularly distinctive because of its accents on off-beats, with the theme starting at varying places within the bar. Against these contrasting rhythms, all played staccato, are almost constantly changing harmonies. In contrast, the "B" sections offer some respite from rhythmic and harmonic change. Ira Gershwin made a valiant effort to force his lyrics into the constraining matrix of George's music, and to some extent he succeeded, with such rhymes as "I'm all aquiver" and "Just like a flivver".

"Fascinating Rhythm" was the big finale of the 1941 film, *Lady Be Good*, performed by Connie Russell and The Berry Brothers, and danced to by Eleanor Powell. Tommy Dorsey and his Orchestra did it in the 1943 film, *Girl Crazy*. It was also played by pianist Hazel Scott in the 1945 Gershwin biographical film, *Rhapsody in Blue*.

Moderate rhythm song with verse (16) and refrain (32)
PUBLISHER: New World Music Corporation
KEY: E-flat maj., *STARTS*: f' (B-flat 7), *FORM*: ABAB'A

≈≈≈≈≈≈≈≈≈≈≈≈≈≈≈≈≈≈≈

I WANT TO BE HAPPY *

WORDS: Irving Caesar, *MUSIC*: Vincent Youmans
PREMIERE: Musical comedy, *No, No, Nanette.*
New York: Globe Theatre, 16 September 1925 (321 perf.)
INTRODUCED BY: Charles Winniger, Louise Groody, and chorus

The musical comedy, *No, No, Nanette,* had a bumpy road to Broadway. It got very poor reviews at its opening in Detroit in 1924. The show was freshened up considerably in Chicago where it ran for a year. It was there that two songs were added that became the show's biggest hits: "Tea for Two" and "I Want to Be Happy". By the time *No, No Nanette* came to New York, in the fall of 1925, it was a smash hit, aided by the growing popularity of its two major songs. Early recordings of "I Want to Be Happy" were by Vincent Lopez and his Orchestra and Jan Garber and his Orchestra. Benny Goodman and his Orchestra recorded it in swing style in 1937. In 1971, *No, No Nanette* became a smash hit all over again with its revival at the Forty-Sixth Street Theatre in New York. This time, "I Want to Be Happy" was sung by Jack Gilford and Susan Watson and danced to by Ruby Keeler and a chorus; that revival lasted for an astronomical 861 performances. In 1981. Lena Horne sang it as a waltz in her Broadway revue, *Lena Horne: The Lady and Her Music.*

The song is a duet, sung by the characters Nanette and Jimmy. It is charming in its simplicity. The melody is almost child-like, emulating scales in the verse and playing around intervals of the major third and second in the refrain.

"I Want to Be Happy" was featured in three Hollywood versions of *No, No, Nanette,* neatly spaced at the beginnings of three decades: Bernice Claire and Alexander Gray sang it in *No, No, Nanette* (1930); Anna Neagle and Richard Carlson did it in *No, No, Nanette* (1940); and Doris Day and Gordon MacRae performed it in the retitled *Tea for Two* (1950). One of the most versatile of popular tunes, it has been performed as foxtrot, waltz, swing tune, jazz standard, and cha cha.

Moderate foxtrot with two verses (16) and refrain (32)
PUBLISHER: Harms, Inc.
KEY: C Maj., *STARTS*: e'(Cmaj.), *FORM*: AABA

≈≈≈≈≈≈≈≈≈≈≈≈≈≈≈≈≈≈≈

I'LL SEE YOU IN MY DREAMS * * *

WORDS: Gus Kahn, *MUSIC*: Isham Jones
INTRODUCED BY: Isham Jones and his Orchestra

Isham Jones was not only a very popular bandleader – he had a long engagement at the College Inn in Chicago – but also a remarkable composer. In the year 1924 alone, he managed to have three hits: "It Had to Be You", "The One I Love Belongs to Somebody Else", and this one, "I'll See You in My Dreams". Gus Kahn was the lyricist of all three. Besides being a lovely ballad, "I'll See You in My Dreams", has the distinction of being one of the most popular good-night songs, often played at the end of dances.

Jones had a hit Brunswick recording; a cover record was made by Lewis James. Pat Boone revived it in 1962.

There are only fifty notes of melody in the entire refrain, most of them half notes. The slowly-rising melody and opening chords of B-flat major and B-flat minor give the song a nostalgic, dream-like quality. A touch of pathos is added with the slight syncopation in the "B" section and the blue note (e-flat") in the "C" section.

In the movies, Jeanette MacDonald sang it in *Follow the Boys* (1924); Bob Crosby in *Pardon My Rhythm* (1944); Jeanne Crain in *Margie (1946);* and Doris Day, Danny Thomas, and a chorus in the Gus Kahn biography built around the title of the song, *I'll See You In My Dreams* (1951). It remains one of America's favorite ballads and a lovely way to end an evening.

> Moderate foxtrot with two verses (16) and refrain (32)
> *PUBLISHER:* Leo Feist, Inc.
> *KEY*: F maj., *STARTS*: c' (B-flat maj.), *FORM*: ABAC

≈≈≈≈≈≈≈≈≈≈≈≈≈≈≈≈≈≈≈

INDIAN LOVE CALL *

> *WORDS*: Otto Harbach and Oscar Hammerstein II, *MUSIC*: Rudolf Friml
> *PREMIERE*: Operetta, *Rose-Marie.*
> New York: Imperial Theatre, 2 September 1924 (557 perf.)
> *INTRODUCED BY*: Mary Ellis and Dennis King

The biggest musical of the decade, *Rose-Marie,* had a long run on Broadway and even longer runs in London and Paris (851 and 1250 performances respectively). In addition, there were four road companies touring the United States. The main reason for the operetta's overwhelming success was the magnificent score by Czech-born Rudolf Friml. A mélange of Viennese operetta and Indian tom-toms in a north-woods setting, *Rose-Marie* had something for everyone. A highlight is the striking duet for Rose-Marie and Jim, "Indian Love Call". In 1938, the song enjoyed an impressive revival in an entirely different context, as a swing tune, in a hit Bluebird recording by Artie Shaw and his Orchestra, with vocal by Tony Pastor, on the flip side of Shaw's famous version of "Begin the Beguine" (see 1935) In its original form, "Indian Love Call" was the favorite song of President Dwight D. Eisenhower. Country singer Slim Whitman did a revival with a hit Imperial recording in 1952.

The verse is extremely complex, in four sections. The first brings a touch of the principal theme of the refrain; the second, *poco più animato,* has chromatic harmonies; the third is in F minor; while the fourth has an abundance of augmented chords. In contrast, the melody of the refrain, in F major, is sunny, with simple harmonies. The opening notes are famous with a four-note pickup stretching over the interval of a ninth, from c' to d". The Indian tom-toms appear as accompaniment in the "B" section. The range of the song is extreme, even for operetta: stretching an octave and a sixth, from c' to a".

"Indian Love Call" was sung by Grace Moore in the 1934 film musical, *One Night of Love*. It was also featured in the two screen versions of the operetta: sung by Jeanette MacDonald and Nelson Eddy in the 1936 *Rose Marie*, and by Ann Blyth and Fernando Lamas in the 1954 version. It survives as a song with two faces: a somewhat corny, but reliable, semi-classical concert piece, and a swing tune.

> Slow art song with verse (40) and refrain (32)
> *PUBLISHER*: Harms Inc.
> *KEY*: F maj., *STARTS*: c' (C9), *FORM*: ABA'C

≈≈≈≈≈≈≈≈≈≈≈≈≈≈≈≈≈≈≈≈≈

IT HAD TO BE YOU * * *

WORDS: Gus Kahn, *MUSIC:* Isham Jones
INTRODUCED BY: Isham Jones and his Orchestra

Isham Jones was a famous bandleader of the day and also an outstanding composer. Together with prolific lyricist Gus Kahn, he wrote two great standards in 1924: I'll See You in My Dreams" and "It Had to Be You". The latter was immediately picked up in recordings on Perfect by Cliff Edwards (Ukelele Ike) and on Victor by Paul Whiteman and his Orchestra, among many others. It has enjoyed a number of revivals over the years: in 1941, by Artie Shaw and his Orchestra, and in 1944, by singers Helen Forrest and Dick Haymes. Singers have embraced "It Had to Be You", and so has the public. And for good reason: it is a perfect blend of words and music.

Its musical premise is simple enough: a five-note pickup leading to the major seventh and then repeated at differing pitch levels. But interesting harmonic changes, moving through the circle of fifths, give the music a quality of inevitability. Most of all, Kahn's lyrics, wedded to the music, are a strong contributing factor to the song's lasting success. They are inherently sincere, as in "With all your faults, I love you still".

True to its status as a world-class standard, "It Had to Be You" has been featured in a remarkable number of films. They include *Casablanca*

(1942), in which it was sung by Dooley Wilson, along with the better-known "As Time Goes By"; *Is Everybody Happy?* and *Nobody's Darling,* both in 1943; *Show Business* in 1944, sung by Eddie Cantor, George Murphy and Constance Moore; *Incendiary Blonde* (1945), sung by Betty Hutton; *Living in a Big Way* (1947), danced to by Gene Kelly and Marie McDonald; *I'll See You in My Dreams* (1951, the Gus Kahn biography), sung by Doris Day and Danny Thomas; and Annie Hall (1977), sung by Diane Keaton. After three-quarters of a century, it remains one of the most beloved of American ballads.

Moderate ballad with two verses (16) and refrain (32)
PUBLISHER: Jerome H. Remick & Co.
KEY: G maj., *STARTS*: d' (G maj. 7), *FORM*: ABAC

≈≈≈≈≈≈≈≈≈≈≈≈≈≈≈≈≈≈≈

JEALOUS

WORDS: Tommy Malie and Dick Finch, *MUSIC*: Jack Little
INTRODUCED: on radio by Little Jack Little

This teasing song was composed and introduced on radio by pianist and singer Little Jack Little, who later went on to form his own big band. Singer Marion Harris had an early Brunswick recording. The Andrews Sisters brought about a revival with their 1941 recording on Decca.

The melodic line of the refrain simply goes up the chromatic scale: twice in each "A" section and once again at the end. Dotted rhythm prevails and harmonies are mostly tonic and dominant. Appropriately, "Jealous" was featured in two films about jealousy: *The Feminine Touch* in 1941 and *Don't Trust Your Husband* (first called *An Innocent Affair*) in 1948. In the 1952 film, *Somebody Loves Me*, Betty Hutton and Pat Morgan (dubbing in for Ralph Meeker) sang it. The song's dotted rhythms make it eminently suitable for tap dancing.

Moderate foxtrot with two verses (24) and refrain (32)
PUBLISHER: Mills Music, Inc.
KEY: G maj., *STARTS*: c-sharp' (D7), *FORM*: ABAC

≈≈≈≈≈≈≈≈≈≈≈≈≈≈≈≈≈≈≈

THE MAN I LOVE * * * *!

WORDS: Ira Gershwin, *MUSIC*: George Gershwin
INTRODUCED BY: Adele Astaire in the Philadelphia tryouts of *Lady, Be Good!*, Autumn, 1924

It is a curious fact that one of the most familiar show tunes, "The Man I Love", was never heard in a Broadway show. The song was written for the musical comedy, *Lady, Be Good!*, and introduced by Adele Astaire in the Philadelphia tryouts. However, the powers that be decided that it slowed down the action and "The Man I Love" was dropped from the show before it reached New York. It was tried out again in the 1927 Gershwin show, *Strike Up the Band*; this time tenor, Morton Downey, sang it as "The Girl I Love". But the show only played two weeks. Then, in 1928, Marilyn Miller sang it in the tryouts of the musical, *Rosalie*, but somehow the song never reached the boards in New York. Finally, "The Man I Love" was published as an individual number. Lady Mountbatten, a friend of George Gershwin, brought the song to England, and it became very popular throughout Britain and France. Then it recrossed the ocean and slowly grew in popularity in the United States over the years, aided by the recordings of Marion Harris, Helen Morgan, and many others. The Benny Goodman Trio had a hit recording in 1937.

The melody is a spin-off from the *Rhapsody in Blue*, written earlier the same year; the initial motive of the refrain is almost identical to that of the first entrance of the solo piano in *Rhapsody*. The essence of the song is, of course, the blue note: here, it is the flatted seventh, conspicuously displayed in the first three bars of each "A" section. Pungent harmonies add greatly to the song's emotional power. The release, in C minor, is particularly effective, with wandering harmonies cadencing first on G seventh and then on B-flat seventh. Ira Gershwin's tender lyrics add a plaintive touch, as in the famous line: "Maybe Tuesday will be my good news day".

"The Man I Love" has been heard in a string of motion pictures: played by pianist Hazel Scott in the Gershwin biography, *Rhapsody in Blue* (1945); *Young Man with a Horn* (1950, sung by Doris Day); *Sincerely Yours* (1955); *The Eddy Duchin Story* (1956); *The Helen Morgan Story*, known in Britain as *Both Ends of the Candle* (1957, with Gogi Grant dubbing in for Ann Blyth); *Lady Sings the Blues* (1972, sung by Diana Ross); and *New York, New York* (1977, sung by Liza Minnelli). It occupies a very special place in the history of American popular music, as one of the first truly dramatic songs.

Slow ballad with verse (16) and refrain (32)
PUBLISHER: New World Music Corp.
KEY: E-flat maj., *STARTS*: b-flat' (E-flat maj.), *FORM*: AA'BA'

≈≈≈≈≈≈≈≈≈≈≈≈≈≈≈≈≈≈≈

OH, LADY BE GOOD! ★ ★ ★

WORDS: Ira Gershwin, *MUSIC*: George Gershwin
PREMIERE: Musical comedy, *Lady, Be Good!*
New York: Liberty Theatre, 1 December 1924 (330 perf.)
INTRODUCED BY: Walter Catlett (sung to Adele Astaire)

The title song of the musical comedy, *Lady, Be Good!*, begins with the supplication, "Oh", for good reason. The character, Watty Watkins (played by Walter Catlett), is trying to entice the character, Susie (Adele Astaire), into impersonating a Mexican heiress. At the same time, he would not be averse to a little personal attention from her. Hence the pleading tone of the ballad, the verse of which begins: "Listen to my tale of woe".

The verse, in E minor, is in recitative style, with many repeated notes. The refrain, on the other hand, has a particularly mobile melody, with broken chords in triplets each time the words "Lady, Be Good!" are stated. The melody is notable for its economy of means, spelling out chords with a minimum of notes. The only blues quality in the song lies in the harmonization in the second bar of each "A" section: the b-flat' in the C seventh chord. But that is enough to give the song a feeling of the blues, despite its otherwise simple tonic and dominant harmonies.

"Oh, Lady Be Good!" was sung by Ann Sothern, Robert Young, Red Skelton, Virginia O'Brien, John Carroll, and a chorus in the 1941 film version of the show, *Lady, Be Good*. It was also sung by Joan Leslie in the 1945 Gershwin biographical film, *Rhapsody in Blue*. To this day, the song is almost always performed as an up-tempo jazz standard, with a strong beat. Its origin as a plaintive ballad, in slow tempo, is forgotten.

Slow ballad with two verses (16) and two refrains (32)
PUBLISHER: New World Music Corp.
KEY: G maj., *STARTS*: d" (G maj.), *FORM*: AABA

≈≈≈≈≈≈≈≈≈≈≈≈≈≈≈≈≈≈

THE ONE I LOVE BELONGS TO SOMEBODY ELSE *

WORDS: Gus Kahn, *MUSIC*: Isham Jones
INTRODUCED BY: Isham Jones and his Orchestra

Another hit by the songwriting team of Gus Kahn and Isham Jones, this torch song had early recordings by Jones and his Orchestra (Brunswick), Al Jolson (Brunswick), and Sophie Tucker (Okeh). It was revived in 1938, with a recording by Tommy Dorsey and his Orchestra. Both Bing Crosby and Ella Fitzgerald recorded it for Decca.

The simple melody is built around the repeated rhythm of the dotted quarter and eighth note. Emphasis is placed on the sixth and fifth degrees of the scale (e' and d') and later the third and second degrees (b' and a'). In contrast to the sprightly music, the lyrics are sad, telling a tale of unrequited love in true torch song tradition: "It's tough to be alone on the shelf / It's worse to fall in love by yourself".

In the movies, Judy Garland sang it in *Everybody Sing* (1938); Doris Day and Danny Thomas sang it in the Gus Kahn biographical film, *I'll See You in My Dreams* (1951); and Gogi Grant dubbed it in for Ann Blyth in *The Helen Morgan Story* (known in Britain as *Both Ends of the Candle, 1957*). In practice, the song's origin as a torch song is often forgotten; it is usually performed as an uptempo jazz tune.

Moderate torch song with two verses (16) and refrain (32)
PUBLISHER: Milton Weil Music Co., Inc., Chicago
KEY: G maj., *STARTS*: d' (G 6), *FORM*: ABA'C

≈≈≈≈≈≈≈≈≈≈≈≈≈≈≈≈≈≈≈

ROSE-MARIE

WORDS: Otto Harbach and Oscar Hammerstein II, *MUSIC*: Rudolf Friml
PREMIERE: Operetta, *Rose-Marie*.
New York: Imperial Theatre, 2 September 1924 (557 perf.)
INTRODUCED BY: Dennis King

The title song of the hit operetta, *Rose-Marie,* bears reminiscences of European operetta of the turn of the century. It is sung in the show by Jim (originally played by Dennis King) and tells of his undying love for Rose-Marie. The broad melody of the refrain has the range of a tenth, reaching its highest notes in the second half. Grace notes are frequent and there are careful performance annotations. Traces of Rose-Marie's Indian heritage are indicated by the occasional dotted rhythm. Nelson Eddy sang "Rose-Marie" in the unhyphenated 1934 film version, *Rose Marie*. Howard Keel did it in the second film version of *Rose Marie* (1954).

Moderate ballad with two verses (24) and refrain (32)
PUBLISHER: Harms, Inc.
KEY: E-flat maj., *STARTS*: b-flat' (E-flat maj.), *FORM*: ABA'C

≈≈≈≈≈≈≈≈≈≈≈≈≈≈≈≈≈≈≈

SERENADE *

WORDS: Dorothy Donnelly, *MUSIC*: Sigmund Romberg
PREMIERE: Operetta, *The Student Prince*
New York: Jolson Theatre, 2 December 1924 (608 perf.)
INTRODUCED BY: Ed Howard Marsh, Raymond Marlowe,
Frederic Wolff, Paul Kleeman, and chorus

In this beautiful song from *The Student Prince*, Prince Karl Franz
swears his eternal love to his favorite waitress, Kathie. The operetta has
been periodically revived over the years, and for many this flowing melody
is its high point. A Victor recording was made by violinist Efrem Zimbalist.

With a range of almost two octaves, from c' to a-flat", "Serenade"
requires an exceptionally strong voice. The striking melody consists of
broken chords, outlined in the outer sections, contrasting with mostly
stepwise movement in the inner. In its original arrangement, there is a
sixteen-measure refrain, followed by a ten-measure interlude, and then a
return to the refrain: forty-two measures in all.

"Serenade" was sung in two 1954 films: by William Olvis in the
Romberg biography, *Deep in My Heart*; and by Mario Lanza, dubbing for
Edward Purdom, in the screen version of *The Student Prince*.

Moderate art song with two refrains (16) and interlude (10)
PUBLISHER: Harms Inc.
KEY: E-flat maj., *STARTS*: g' (E-flat maj.), *FORM*: ABCA'

≈≈≈≈≈≈≈≈≈≈≈≈≈≈≈≈≈≈≈

SOMEBODY LOVES ME * *

WORDS: B. G. De Sylva and Ballard MacDonald
MUSIC: George Gershwin
PREMIERE: Revue, *George White's Scandals of 1924*
New York: Apollo Theatre, 30 June 1924 (192 perf.)
INTRODUCED BY: Winnie Lightner

The only standard to emerge from the lackluster revue, *George
White's Scandals of 1924*, "Somebody Loves Me" was sung by Winnie
Lightner to an imaginary cast of characters including Marc Antony,

Romeo, and Harold Lloyd. At the time, George Gershwin was earning $125 a week plus royalties as pianist for the show. When he asked White for a raise, he was turned down and Gershwin went on to other pursuits. The show didn't last long any way, but the song did. Originally popularized by Paul Whiteman and his Orchestra, it was revived in 1952 by The Four Lads.

The verse is simple enough, modulating from E minor to G major. But it is the refrain that captivates. Again Gershwin resorts to the blue note, this time the b-flat' in Bars Four and Six, accompanied by chords of the C seventh. The song is lifted from the mundane by an unexpected modulation to B minor in the second "A" section. The release meanders amid neighboring tones in mostly stepwise motion, while the closing section leads happily to a cadence at the words "Maybe it's you". Curiously, although the song was written for a female, the lyrics are meant for a male to sing, as in "I wonder who she can be". In practice, however, "Somebody Loves Me" is sung by both sexes.

"Somebody Loves Me" has been featured in a number of films. Lena Horne sang it in *Broadway Rhythm* (1944); Tom Patricola in *Rhapsody in Blue* (1945); Doris Day and Gene Nelson in *Lullaby of Broadway* (1951); Betty Hutton and Pat Morgan, dubbing for Ralph Meeker, in *Somebody Loves Me* (1952, a biography of Blossom Seeley and Benny Fields); Peggy Lee in *Pete Kelly's Blues* (1955); and Gogi Grant, dubbing for Ann Blyth in *The Helen Morgan Story* (1957). Over the years, the song has made the transformation from coy ballad to one of the brightest of jazz standards.

> Moderate foxtrot with verse (20) and refrain (32)
> *PUBLISHER*: New World Music Corp.
> *KEY*: G maj., *STARTS*: d' (G maj.), *FORM*: AA'BA"

≈≈≈≈≈≈≈≈≈≈≈≈≈≈≈≈≈≈≈≈

TEA FOR TWO * * * *

> *WORDS*: Irving Caesar, *MUSIC*: Vincent Youmans
> *PREMIERE*: Musical comedy, *No, No, Nanette*
> New York: Globe Theatre,16 September 1925 (321 perf.)
> *INTRODUCED BY*: Louise Groody, John Barker, and chorus

When Vincent Youmans was asked to write a duet for a situation in the musical comedy, *No, No, Nanette*, he came up with this charming tune, which he scribbled down while he was on lunch break. His partner, Irving Caesar, supplied a set of "dummy lyrics", in order to indicate stressed and unstressed syllables. So delightful was this first draft that it became the permanent version. "Tea for Two,' initially popularized in a Brunswick recording by singer Marion Harris, was soon recorded by almost every major artist. At the height of the cha cha craze, in 1958, a takeoff called "Tea for Two Cha Cha", played by Warren Covington and his Orchestra, was an instant hit on Decca. The versatile song became immensely popular all over again in 1971, when it was sung by Susan Watson and Roger Rathburn in the revival of *No, No, Nanette*, which ran for 861 performances.

The lyrics are immediately compelling, picturing a dream house in the country for two people alone together, but intent on raising a family: "a boy for you, a girl for me". The verse is replete with such inner rhymes as "hide in", "side by side in", and "abide in", while its melody rambles up and down the scale in a most pleasant way. As for the refrain, it is built around a seemingly endlessly – repeated rhythmic motive of dotted quarter and eighth note. Two variations – both in the "B" section – save it from monotony: the tonal movement from A-flat major to C major, and the syncopated change in the basic rhythm to quarter, dotted eighth, and sixteenth.

In films, "Tea for Two" was sung by Bernice Claire in the 1930 version of *No, No Nanette*; by Anna Neagle in the 1940 version; by Doris Day, Gordon MacRae, and chorus in *Tea for Two* (1950); by Doris Day in *Young Man with a Horn* (1950); and by Jane Froman dubbing for Susan Hayward in *With a Song in My Heart* (1952). It was also featured in the 1955 film, *Sincerely Yours*. A perfect union of words and music, "Tea for Two" has been called the most often-performed song of the twentieth century. That may be. Certainly, in its feeling of coziness and charm it is without parallel. To this day, it is performed as ballad, jazz standard, and cha cha.

Moderate rhythm song with two verses (16) and refrain (32)
PUBLISHER: Harms Inc.
KEY: A-flat maj., *STARTS*: a-flat' (B-flat min. 7), *FORM*: ABA'C

≈≈≈≈≈≈≈≈≈≈≈≈≈≈≈≈≈≈≈

WHAT'LL I DO? *

WORDS and MUSIC: Irving Berlin
PREMIERE: *The Music Box Revue 1923-1924*
New York: Music Box Theatre, 22 September 1923
INTRODUCED BY: Grace Moore and John Steel

This little waltz was supposedly written by Irving Berlin under the influence of champagne while he was attending a birthday party in November, 1923. Published in early 1924, it was popularized in a Victor recording by Paul Whiteman and his Orchestra, and went on to sell over a million copies of sheet music and a million records. Interpolated in *The Music Box Revue of 1923-1924* early in 1924, the song became even more popular. At the time, Berlin was wooing Ellen Mackay against her father's wishes. "What'll I Do?" expresses its author's loneliness during his forced separation from his beloved. Many other recordings have been made over the years, notably by Frank Sinatra, Nat "King" Cole and Linda Ronstadt.

The melody effectively conveys sadness by being placed in the lower register in the "A" sections. As in "Tea for Two", the refrain is built around a prevailing rhythmic motive; this time it is a tied half note and eighth note. The range of each "A" section is very narrow: only a major sixth. However, it widens out to a ninth in the release. Also notable are the eighth-note triplets, occurring seven times in the course of the refrain; and the plaintive flatted sixth of the melody in the second bar of each "A" section.

In the movies, "What'll I Do?" was sung by a chorus in *Alexander's Ragtime Band* (1938) and by Danny Thomas in *The Big City* (1948).

Moderate waltz with two verses (16) and refrain (32)
PUBLISHER: Irving Berlin, Inc.
KEY: E-flat maj., *STARTS*: e-flat' (E-flat maj.), *FORM*: AABA

≈≈≈≈≈≈≈≈≈≈≈≈≈≈≈≈≈≈≈

1925

FLAPPERS AND FLOOZIES

1925

There's none so classy as this fair lassy.

B. G. De Sylva and Joseph Meyer
"If You Knew Susie (Like I Know Susie)"

Reflecting the transitional nature of the times, songs this year are a curious mixture of the old and the new; a balance between waltzes ("Always") and jazz tunes ("Dinah"); between reminiscences from the past ("Remember") and portents of the future ("Manhattan"). But, as is so often the case, the songs tell the times; the emphasis is on the here and now. If one looks for a common denominator in the songs of 1925, it is the present and, in particular, the flapper. Whether she's named "Cecilia", "Dinah", "Susie", Or simply called "My Baby"; whether she's "Five Foot Two, Eyes of Blue", going "Collegiate", or carrying a hip flask ("Show Me the Way to Go Home"); this is the year of the flapper.

What, exactly, is a flapper? This phenomenon has been described by H. L. Mencken as "a somewhat foolish girl, full of wild surmises and inclined to revolt against the precepts and admonitions of her elders". This revolt often entailed strange apparel, like short shifts, rolled-down hose, and galoshes with buckles that flap – hence the name. The drawings of John Held, Jr. and writings of F. Scott Fitzgerald best depict these flat-chested, hipless beauties who smoked, drank, danced, partied, petted, sometimes acted like floozies, and generally made the Twenties roar.

In this year of Coolidge prosperity, people buy up real estate in Florida in a frenzy of speculation, hoping for a quick killing or, at least, a place in the sun. The Florida land boom reaches a peak this year – next year will see the bust. There are plenty of diversions, from dance marathons to crossword puzzles, from flagpole sitting to mah-jongg. The sounds of jazz emanate from thousands of speakeasies. This is a year of good times.

In the spirit of the times, the United States Senate declares itself a raise from $7,500 to $10,000 a year, while the Vice President's salary jumps from $12,000 to $15,000. In sports, Henry Louis Gehrig plays the first of 2,130 consecutive games for the New York Yankees, while Red Grange makes his début in professional football with the Chicago Bears.

Books published this year include Theodore Dreiser's *An American Tragedy*, John Dos Passos's *Manhattan Transfer*, Francis Scott Key Fitzgerald's *The Great Gatsby* (hinting at dark clouds on the horizon), and Sinclair Lewis's Arrowsmith. The first edition of *The New Yorker* appears, edited by Harry Ross, formerly of *Stars and Stripes*"; it is thirty-two pages long and costs fifteen cents. With witty commentary by such contributors as George S. Kaufman, Alexander Woolcott, and Dorothy Parker and whimsical cartoons by Peter Arno and Helen Hokinson, it brings a new dimension to sophisticated reading.

Two delightful musicals open on Broadway: *The Garrick Gaieties*, a sparkling revue with lyrics by Lorenz Hart and music by Richard Rodgers; and *Sunny*, a rousing musical comedy with book and lyrics by Otto Harbach and Oscar Hammerstein II and music by Jerome Kern. Two classic silent films emerge from Hollywood: Charles Chaplin's whimsical *The Gold Rush*, pitting The Little Tramp against the wilds of the Yukon; and the spectacular $4 million production of *Ben-Hur*, starring Ramon Novarro and Francis X. Bushman and featuring an exciting chariot race.

SONGS OF 1925

Alabamy Bound
Always ****
Collegiate
Dinah **
Does Your Mother Know You're Out, Cecilia?
Five Foot Two, Eyes of Blue
    (Has Anybody Seen My Gal?)
I Never Knew
If You Knew Susie (Like I Know Susie)
I'm Sitting On Top of the World **
Manhattan ***!
Moonlight and Roses (Bring Mem'ries of You)
Remember
Show Me the Way to Go Home
Sleepy Time Gal *
Sweet Georgia Brown ***!
Who? *!
Yes Sir, That's My Baby

ALABAMY BOUND

WORDS: B. G. De Sylva and Bud Green, *MUSIC*: Ray Henderson
PUBLISHER: Shapiro, Bernstein & Co., Inc.
INTRODUCED: in vaudeville by Al Jolson

Two great entertainers, Al Jolson and Eddie Cantor, had much to do with popularizing this vintage train song. Although Jolson introduced it, Cantor's interpolation of it in the long-running Zeigfeld musical *Kid Boots* made it famous. Early recordings were by Blossom Seeley and Isham Jones and his Orchestra. Years later, in 1954, The Mulcays had a hit recording.

The verse could be considered a song in itself; and indeed has all the credentials: thirty-two bars, AABA form, and a key of its own, D minor. Both verse and refrain are heavily syncopated. The emphasis in the refrain, in F major, is on the fourth beat, which is anticipated and then tied over. Most striking of all, and in the spirit of a train whistle, is the opening chord of the refrain, a B-flat ninth.

"Alabamy Bound" has been featured in a number of films. The Ink Spots sang it in *The Great American Broadcast* (1941). It was heard in *Babes on Broadway* and *Broadway* (both produced in 1942) and *Is Everybody Happy?* (1943). Eddie Cantor sang it in *Show Business* (1944), and it was sung by a chorus in the Jane Froman biographical film, *With a Song in My Heart* (1952). As a song of the rails, it resounds with the propulsive spirit of the Roaring Twenties.

Moderate rhythm song with two verses (32) and refrain (32)
KEY: F maj., *STARTS:* a (B-flat 9), *FORM:* ABAB'

≈≈≈≈≈≈≈≈≈≈≈≈≈≈≈≈≈≈≈≈

ALWAYS * * * *

WORDS and MUSIC: Irving Berlin
PUBLISHER: Irving Berlin, Inc.
INTRODUC ED: in vaudeville by Gladys Clark and Henry Bergman

As is the case with many of Irving Berlin's creations, the idea for "Always" came long before the song was written. The story goes that Berlin's musical secretary, Arthur Johnston, was something of a ladies' man and that one of Johnston's "ladies", named Mona, once asked Berlin to write a song about her. The master obliged with a ditty called "I'll Be Loving You, Mona". In 1925, while the composer was collaborating with George S. Kaufman on a new show called *The Cocoanuts*, featuring the four

Marx Brothers, "Mona" was reborn as "Always", keeping the first four words of the refrain. The sardonic Kaufman, notoriously unimpressed by music, insisted that a more realistic opening line might be "I'll be loving you Thursday". Although *The Cocoanuts* was a huge success, "Always" did not stay in it. Introduced by the vaudeville team of Gladys Clark and Henry Bergman, it became an immediate hit, sparked by early recordings by Vincent Lopez and his Orchestra (Okeh), George Olson and his Orchestra (Victor), and Nick Lucas (Brunswick). In the 1940s hit recordings were made by the bands of Benny Goodman, Gordon Jenkins, Sammy Kaye, and Guy Lombardo.

"Always" was written at a tempestuous time in Berlin's life, while he was romancing his second wife, Ellin Mackay, daughter of telegraph magnate Clarence Mackay. This on-again, off-again romance coincided with a number of other Berlin waltzes that may be considered vaguely autobiographical in subject matter: "All Alone", "What'll I Do", and "Remember". But best known of all is "Always".

The song deserves its international celebrity. Words and music are inseparable. The prevailing five-note rhythmic motive at the words "I'll be loving you" occurs ten times in the refrain at varying degrees of the scale. The most striking harmonic change occurs in the "B" section: from F major to A major. The first five notes themselves form the pentatonic scale. As is well known, this was a favorite of the composer since it could be formed on the black keys of the piano. Berlin had a special piano with a lever capable of transposing to any key from the key of F-sharp. The first notes of "Always" fill this prescription admirably: in F-sharp major they would be: c-sharp', d-sharp', f-sharp', g-sharp', a'-sharp'. The lyrics, in themselves, are masterful. Heartfelt and sincere, they perfectly mirror the feelings of a person in love. It is interesting to note that the word "Always" occurs seven times in the refrain.

In early films, "Always" was sung by Betty Avery in *The Pride of the Yankees* (1942), by Deanna Durbin in *Christmas Holiday* (1944), and by a chorus in the Berlin biographical film, *Blue Skies* (1946). Almost three quarters of a century after it was written, it remains one of America's most performed romantic songs.

Moderate waltz with two verses (24) and refrain (32)
KEY: F major, *STARTS:* c' (F maj.), ***FORM:*** ABA'C

≈≈≈≈≈≈≈≈≈≈≈≈≈≈≈≈≈≈

COLLEGIATE

WORDS and MUSIC: Moe Jaffe and Nat Bonx
INTRODUCED: in vaudeville and on a Victor recording by Fred Waring's
Pennsylvanians

The quintessential flapper song, "Collegiate" was introduced by Fred Waring's Pennsylvanians on the college circuit, but did not achieve notoriety until it was interpolated in the revue, *Gay Paree*, which opened at the Shubert Theatre in New York on 18 August 1925. Carl Fenton and his Orchestra had an early recording.

The lyrics are redolent of the Roaring Twenties, with a host of contemporary allusions in the two sets of verses and three sets of refrains. For instance, the second set of lyrics covers Greek letters (Alpha, Beta, Delta), while the third is about universities (Harvard, Princeton, Yale, Cornell, Virginia). Both close with nonsense lines ("Milkshake", "S'lami", "P'strami", "B'loni"). Contractions are an integral part of the song; the opening word of the refrain is "C'llegiate". At times things get a little racy: "Garters are things we never wear". As opposed to all this verbiage, the music is almost simplistic, spelling out in each "A" section first the F major chord and then the C dominant seventh.

"Collegiate" was featured in two early films: *The Time, the Place and the Girl* (1929) and *Animal Crackers* (1930), as well as in the 1946 film about the twenties, *Margie*. It survives as a bit of nostalgia from the flapper era.

Moderate novelty song with two verses (16) and three refrains (32)
PUBLISHER: Shapiro, Bernstein & Co., Inc.
KEY: F maj., *STARTS:* f' (F maj.), *FORM:* AABA'

≈≈≈≈≈≈≈≈≈≈≈≈≈≈≈≈≈≈≈

DINAH * *

WORDS: Sam M. Lewis and Joe Young, *MUSIC:* Harry Akst
PREMIERE: *Plantation Revue*
New York: Plantation Club, Summer 1925
INTRODUCED BY: Ethel Waters

The Plantation Club, in midtown New York at 50th Street and Broadway, was a nightclub geared to high society. Harry Akst, who composed the songs for the floor show, had served as accompanist to both Nora Bayes and Al Jolson. His words were supplied by one of the few long-term collaborations between lyric writers, the team of Sam M. Lewis and

Joe Young. Shortly after young Ethel Waters replaced Florence Mills at the club, Waters's career took off with a vengeance. One of her first hits there was "Dinah", sung in her inimitable style. The song was soon interpolated by Eddie Cantor in his hit show, *Kid Boots*, which was still running on Broadway. Waters later sang "Dinah" in the revues, *Africana*, in 1927 and *Blackbirds of 1930*. Among early recordings were those of Waters, Cantor, Louis Armstrong, Cliff Edwards and Fletcher Henderson and his Orchestra. In 1932 Bing Crosby had a No. 1 Chart Record. Best selling records were also made by The Mills Brothers in 1932, The Boswell Sisters in1935, and Fats Waller in 1936. Throughout her long career, singer Dinah Shore used it as her theme song.

The song is deceptively simple both melodically and harmonically. In the "A" sections of the refrain, only five tones are outlined over the space of an octave. The only departure from tonic and dominant harmony is in the release, in E minor; this release also features a moving bass line that is a favorite of jazz artists. The words are attractive, rhyming "Dinah" with "finer", "Carolina", and "China". There is an enticing pun in the release: "Dinah might". At the end of the song, Dinah's last name is at last revealed; it is "Lee".

Many movies have featured the song. Bing Crosby sang it in *The Big Broadcast* of 1932; Jeanette MacDonald in *Rose Marie* (1936); George Raft and Janet Blair in *Broadway* (1942); and Eddie Cantor, George Murphy, Constance Moore, and Joan Davis in *Show Business* (1944). The relatively blank musical canvas afforded by "Dinah", has made it a particular favorite of jazz instrumentalists, who use it as a background for all sorts of imaginative improvisations.

Moderate rhythm song with two verses (16) and refrain (32)
PUBLISHER: Mills Music, Inc.
KEY: G major or A-flat maj., *STARTS:* d' (G maj.) or e-flat' (A-flat maj.),
FORM: AA'BA

≈≈≈≈≈≈≈≈≈≈≈≈≈≈≈≈≈≈≈

DOES YOUR MOTHER KNOW YOU'RE OUT, CECILIA?

WORDS: Herman Ruby, *MUSIC:* Dave Dreyer
INTRODUCED: on radio and a Victor recording, by Whispering Jack Smith

Dave Dreyer was a pianist who accompanied two of the greatest entertainers of the twenties, Al Jolson and Sophie Tucker. This song, usually simply known as "Cecilia", was his big first big hit. He went on to compose others, among them "Me and My Shadow" and "Back In Your

Own Backyard". In 1940, "Cecilia" enjoyed a revival with a Vocalion recording by Dick Jurgens and his Orchestra, with vocal by Ronnie Kemper.

The music of the refrain is almost a parody of itself, juxtaposing staccato and legato: dotted notes (quarters and eighths) and sustained (whole) notes. In the style of a patter song, a bit of the opening motive recurs at the close. The rhyming is sometimes careless, pairing the title with the line "Does she know that I'm about to steal you". It also turns out that "little Miss Cecilia" is just a "little over Sweet Sixteen", making that kind of theft a federal offense.

"Does Your Mother Know You're Out, Cecilia" was sung by Michael Dees in the 1981 film, *Buddy Buddy*.

Slow patter song with two verses (16) and refrain (32)
PUBLISHER: ABC Music Corp.
KEY: C maj., *STARTS:* g' (C maj.), *FORM:* ABA'C

≈≈≈≈≈≈≈≈≈≈≈≈≈≈≈≈≈≈≈≈

FIVE FOOT TWO, EYES OF BLUE * *
(HAS ANYBODY SEEN MY GAL?)

WORDS: Joe Young and Sam M. Lewis, *MUSIC:* Ray Henderson
INTRODUCED: in vaudeville and a Victor recording by Gene Austin

With one of the longest titles in popular song, "Five Foot Two, Eyes of Blue (Has Anybody Seen My Gal?)" was another hit by the lyric-writing team of Sam M. Lewis and Joe Young, this time with music by Ray Henderson. The song started out as a glorification of the flapper but took on a new life as a jazz standard in 1948, with a hit Metro Goldwyn Mayer recording by Art Mooney and his Band.

There are two verses, one for a male and one for a female. The refrain is in conventional thirty-two bar AABA form, but is distinguished by the harmonic change in the second bar of each "A" section from C major to E seventh. The harmonies then slowly return to the tonic through the circle of fifths: A seventh, D seventh, G seventh. The lyrics describe a flapper, with "turned-up nose" and "turned-down hose".

The subtitle of the song itself became a film title in the 1952 movie *Has Anybody Seen My Gal?*, starring Rock Hudson and James Coburn. "Five Foot Two" was also in the 1974 film *The Great Gatsby*, sung by Nick Lucas.

Fast rhythm song with two verses (16) and two refrains (32)
PUBLISHER: Leo Feist, Inc.
KEY: C maj., **STARTS:** e'(C Maj.), **FORM:** AABA

≈≈≈≈≈≈≈≈≈≈≈≈≈≈≈≈≈≈≈

I NEVER KNEW

WORDS: Gus Kahn, **MUSIC:** Ted Fiorito
INTRODUCED BY: Ted Fiorito and his Orchestra

Written as a love ballad, this song is often referred to by its first line, "I Never Knew That Roses Grew", in order to distinguish it from the 1920 hit "I Never Knew I Could Love Anybody". Composed by pianist Ted Fiorito (who in these years spelled his last name, Fio Rito), it was introduced by his own sweet band, which featured temple blocks and a Hammond organ. Among early recordings were those of Vincent Lopez and his Orchestra (Okeh) and Gene Austin (Victor). Over the years, it has evolved from love ballad to jazz standard, usually improvised in bright tempo. The flowing melodic line uses very few notes. The song is saved from banality by the C minor harmony in the second bar of each "A" section and by the move to B minor in the release. Gus Kahn's lyrics are not among his best: "I never knew what love could do / Until I met you today". Doris Day sang "I Never Knew" in the 1951 Gus Kahn biographical film, *I'll See You In My Dreams*. Peggy Lee sang it in *Pete Kelly's Blues* (1955).

Moderate foxtrot with two verses (16) and refrain (32)
PUBLISHER: Bourne, Inc.
KEY: G maj., **STARTS:** d' (G maj.), **FORM:** AABA

≈≈≈≈≈≈≈≈≈≈≈≈≈≈≈≈≈≈

IF YOU KNEW SUSIE (LIKE I KNOW SUSIE)*

WORDS and MUSIC: B. G. De Sylva and Joseph Meyer
INTRODUCED BY: Al Jolson

Almost always identified with Eddie Cantor, this song was actually tried out by Al Jolson, to be used in his free-wheeling show, *Big Boy.* However, Jolson decided not to use it and passed it on to Cantor. The latter interpolated it in his long-running show, *Kid Boots,* to great acclaim. It served as Cantor's signature song thereafter. Cliff Edwards (Ukelele Ike) had an early hit recording.

"Susie" is in some ways an old-fashioned type of song, but it is at the same time a paean to the modern-day flapper. The lyrics set the tone, with "Oh! Oh! Oh! What a girl". In the style of ragtime, one lightly-syncopated rhythmical motive appears throughout the refrain.

The song has had a lengthy movie career. Buddy Doyle sang it in *The Great Ziegfeld* (1936). It was in two films in 1945: sung by Frank Sinatra and Gene Kelly in *Anchors Aweigh*; and by George Brent, Dennis O'Keefe, Don De Fore, Rita Johnson, and Walter Abel in *The Affairs of Susan*. Eddie Cantor sang it under the credits in the namesake film, *If You Knew Susie* (1948), and dubbed it in for Keefe Brasselle in *The Eddie Cantor Story*. It was heard in *The Benny Goodman Story* (1955). In 1966, Dean Martin sang it in *The Silencers*. And in 1981, Dudley Moore sang it in *Arthur*.

Fast rhythm song with two verses (16) and two refrains (32)
PUBLISHER: Shapiro, Bernstein & Co.
KEY: B-flat maj., *STARTS:* f' (B-flat maj.), *FORM:* AA'BA"

≈≈≈≈≈≈≈≈≈≈≈≈≈≈≈≈≈≈≈

I'M SITTING ON TOP OF THE WORLD **

WORDS: Sam M. Lewis and Joe Young, *MUSIC:* Ray Henderson
INTRODUCED and RECORDED: on Brunswick by Al Jolson

One of the most optimistic songs ever written, "I'm Sitting On Top of the World" was a natural for Al Jolson. He sang it extensively on the stage before bringing it to a wider audience three years later in *The Singing Fool*, Jolson's second "part-talkie, part-singie" for Warner Brothers. It was the third hit of 1925 for the lyric-writing team of Sam M. Lewis and Joe Young, and their second with music by Ray Henderson. It was revived in 1953, with a best-selling record on Capitol by Les Paul and Mary Ford.

Both lyrics and music jump with joy: the lyrics with such picturesque expressions as "Just rolling along" and "Just like Humpty-Dumpty, I'm going to fall"; and the music with its jumpy melodic lines and simple harmonies.

Besides Jolson's rendition in *The Singing Fool* (1928), "I'm Sitting On Top of the World" was sung again by Jolson (this time dubbing in for Larry Parks) in the biographical *Al Jolson Story* of 1946. In 1955 it was featured in two films: sung by Susan Hayward in *I'll Cry Tomorrow* and by Doris Day in *Love Me or Leave Me*. It is still used as an ideal vehicle for upbeat jazz improvisation.

Moderate rhythm song with two verses (16) and refrain (32)
PUBLISHER: Leo Feist, Inc.
KEY: F major, *STARTS:* c" (F maj.), *FORM:* AABA

≈≈≈≈≈≈≈≈≈≈≈≈≈≈≈≈≈≈≈

MANHATTAN * * *!

WORDS: Lorenz Hart, *MUSIC:* Richard Rodgers
PREMIERE: Revue, *The Garrick Gaieties (First Edition)*
New York: Garrick Theatre, 17 May 1925 (211 perf.)
INTRODUCED BY: Sterling Holloway and June Cochrane

Produced by junior members of the Theatre Guild, the first edition of *The Garrick Gaieties* was a fund-raiser in order to purchase drapes for the Guild's new theater on Fifty-Second Street. Scheduled to run over the weekend, it ran for twenty-five weeks. *The Garrick Gaieties* was the first big success of the young songwriting team of Lorenz Hart and Richard Rodgers, fresh out of Columbia University. Audiences could not get enough of the hit song of the show, "Manhattan". Each night, they cheered it, demanded encores, and left the theater humming. Initially popularized by Ben Selvin and his Orchestra, the song was kept alive in intimate nightclubs and has had a broad resurgence of popularity in recent years.

Notable for its four sets of evocative lyrics and its stunning use of inner rhyme, "Manhattan" also boasts a charming melody. The verse features the favorite Rodgers device of an ascending scale. But it is the refrain, with its five-note motive, that immediately captivates. This catchy gesture (c", b', c", e", d") is quickly echoed a seventh below. Starting off the beat and with dotted rhythm, it appears eight times in the refrain. But it is Hart's lyrics that really make "Manhattan" shine. They offer a catalogue of New York attractions: The Bronx, Staten Island, the Zoo, Delancey Street, the subway, Mott Street, Greenwich Village, Bowling Green, Brighton Beach, Jamaica Bay, Canarsie, Yonkers, Child's Restaurant, Coney Island, Central Park, Fifth Avenue, and Flatbush. Especially captivating are the inner rhymes, as in "And tell me what street compares with Mott Street in July". And Hart does not hesitate to stretch his rhyming a little for comic effect, pairing "onyx" with "Bronnix" and "never spoil" with "boy and goil".

"Manhattan" was sung by Mickey Rooney, Tom Drake, and Marshall Thompson in the 1948 Rodgers and Hart biographical film, *Words and Music*; played on the piano by Carmen Cavallaro in *The Eddy Duchin Story* (1957); and sung by Bob Hope and Vera Miles in *Beau James* (1957). More than three-quarter of a century after its début, it remains one of the most delightful songs in the repertoire, as fresh as the day it was written.

Moderate rhythm song with verse (16) and four refrains (32)
PUBLISHER: Edward B. Marks Music Corporation
KEY: F maj., *STARTS:* c" (F maj.), *FORM:* AA'AB

≈≈≈≈≈≈≈≈≈≈≈≈≈≈≈≈≈≈≈≈

MOONLIGHT AND ROSES (BRING MEM'RIES OF YOU)

WORDS and MUSIC: Edwin H. Lemare, Ben Black, and Neil Morét (Charles N. Daniels)
INTRODUCED: on radio and in a Victor recording, by John McCormack

Originally composed for organ in 1892 by the British-American organist and composer Edwin Henry Lemare, and called "Andantino in D-flat", this piece acquired wide popularity more than thirty years after it was written as "Moonlight and Roses". Lemare had the post of municipal organist in San Francisco, and it was there the song was published. Introduced by the famous Irish tenor John McCormack, it later went on to become popular singer Lanny Ross's theme song on radio. There were several revivals: in 1928; in 1940; and again in 1954, with a recording by The Three Suns. The refrain features a broad, majestic melody, mostly stepwise in motion. The jump to the high note, f", at the beginning of the last section is particularly effective. Despite lyrics that are sometimes strained, as in "My heart reposes", the flowing, cantabile melody has made the song a particular favorite of tenors. In the movies, it was sung by Betty Grable in *Tin Pan Alley* (1940), by Gloria Jean in *Mr. Big*, (1943) and by Roy Rogers in *Song of Texas* (1943).

Moderate ballad with two verses (16) and refrain (32)
PUBLISHER: Villa Morét (San Francisco),
assigned to Chappell & Co., Inc.
KEY: A-flat maj., *STARTS:* c" (A-flat maj.), *FORM:* ABA'C

≈≈≈≈≈≈≈≈≈≈≈≈≈≈≈≈≈≈≈≈

REMEMBER

WORDS and MUSIC: Irving Berlin

In order to put a damper on the budding romance between his daughter, Ellin, and brash young composer Irving Berlin, Clarence Mackay bribed her with a trip abroad. Berlin expressed his unhappiness over the forced separation with this self-pitying waltz, originally titled "You Forgot to Remember", There was some uncertainty among his cohorts about the wisdom of publishing the song, but Berlin insisted and had his way. It took several months of song-plugging to turn "Remember" into a hit. But, with the help of recordings by Isham Jones and his Orchestra, Jean Goldkette and his Orchestra, and singer Ruth Etting, a hit it did become.

In the style of "Always", "Remember" is built on a five-note scale, compatible with Berlin's preference for the five black keys in each octave of the piano. Each section of the refrain begins with the chord of the subdominant (B-flat major) and slowly wends its way to the tonic (F major). The lyrics are rather mundane, but there is a nice twist at the end with the inner rhyming of "forget me not" with "you forgot".

In the movies, "Remember" was sung by Alice Faye in *Alexander's Ragtime Band* (1938); by Kathryn Grayson in *So This Is Love* (known in Britain as *The Grace Moore Story*, 1953); and by Ethel Merman, Dan Dailey, and a chorus in *There's No Business Like Show Business* (1954).

Moderate waltz with two verses (24) and refrain (32)
PUBLISHER: Irving Berlin, Inc.
KEY: F maj., *STARTS:* c' (B-flat maj.), *FORM:* AABA'

≈≈≈≈≈≈≈≈≈≈≈≈≈≈≈≈≈≈≈≈≈

SHOW ME THE WAY TO GO HOME

WORDS and MUSIC: Irving King (Reginald Connelly and Jimmy Campbell)
INTRODUCED BY: The Hal Swain Princess Toronto Orchestra

Ironically, this anthem of the American Prohibition years was written by an English songwriting team: Reginald Connelly and Jimmy Campbell, who also wrote such hits as "Goodnight, Sweetheart", "If I Had You", and "Try a Little Tenderness". But, in this case, they went under the fictitious pseudonym of "Irving King". The idea was not original; a song with the title "Show Me the Way to Go Home, Babe", had been published way back in 1901. But its music bore no resemblance to this simple ditty, which was popularized in the United States by Billy Jones and Ernie Hare, who were known as The Happiness Boys; and by Vincent Lopez and his Orchestra.

The short refrain consists of four sections, each of four measures, and has one of the narrowest ranges of any popular song: only a fourth (from g' to c"). The lyrics are, of course, the main attraction. In the age of rotgut liquor, many imbibers could identify with the concept: "I had a little drink about an hour ago and it went right to my head". No wonder the song was so popular an expression of its times.

Moderate patter song with two verses (16) and refrain (16)
PUBLISHER: Campbell, Connelly & Co. (London), assigned to Harms, Inc.
KEY: G maj., *STARTS:* b' (G maj.), *FORM:* ABAC

≋≋≋≋≋≋≋≋≋≋≋≋≋≋≋≋≋≋≋≋

SLEEPY TIME GAL*

WORDS: Joseph R. Aldan and Raymond B. Egan
MUSIC: Ange Lorenzo and Richard A. Whiting
INTRODUCED: in a Victor recording by Ben Bernie and his Orchestra

Billed on its sheet music as "A Wide Awake Fox Trot Song", "Sleepy Time Gal" is best played in a lazy shuffle rhythm. Ben Bernie, who introduced it with his orchestra, was known as "The Old Maestro", and closed his radio broadcasts reciting: "Au Revoir. Pleasant dreams. Think of us when requesting your themes". "Sleepy Time Gal" was one of his first hits. Other early recordings were made by singers Gene Austin and Nick Lucas. There were revivals in the 1940s, with recordings by the orchestras of Harry James, Buddy Cole, Art Lund and Paul Weston.

The song has a multiplicity of notes, with a jazzy verse and a refrain full of dotted quarters and eighths. Perhaps its most distinctive feature is the break near the end of the "B" section", at the words "It's gettin' late and, dear, your pillow's waitin'".

"Sleepy Time Gal" was sung by Judy Canova in the 1942 namesake film, *Sleepytime Gal,* and by Frances Langford in the 1943 film *Never a Dull Moment.*

Moderate foxtrot with two verses (16) and refrain (32)
PUBLISHER: Leo Feist, Inc.
KEY: G maj., *STARTS:* b' (G maj.), *FORM:* ABAC

≋≋≋≋≋≋≋≋≋≋≋≋≋≋≋≋≋≋

SWEET GEORGIA BROWN * * *!

WORDS and MUSIC: Ben Bernie, Maceo Pinkard, and Kenneth Casey
INTRODUCED BY: Ben Bernie and his Orchestra

A spinoff from "Charleston", written two years before, "Sweet Georgia Brown" is a jazz performer's delight. Its intoxicating Charleston rhythm and chord-based structure have inspired all sorts of imaginative improvisations. It started out as something of a race song and, indeed, the verse refers to "colored folks" and "brownskin gals". In fact, it was written and performed by blacks: Maceo Pinkard, who was probably responsible for the music, was one of the most successful black songwriters of the twenties; Ethel Waters, who popularized it, was perhaps the best-known black singer. The orchestras of Ben Bernie (credited as one of the writers) and Isham Jones had early recordings. In 1932 Bing Crosby had a hit record. So did The Brothers Bones in 1949. The song was also featured in the all-black revue, *Bubbling Brown Sugar*, in 1976. The traveling basketball team, The Harlem Globetrotters, used it as their theme song in exhibition games and on television.

Most striking are the wide-ranging harmonies of the seventh. Written in the key of G major, the opening chord of the refrain is an unprecedented E seventh, held for four bars; followed by four bars of A seventh; four of D seventh; and then finally, G major. The last half of the refrain starts out in the same way, but then moves unexpectedly to E minor, with an entirely new theme of repeated notes. There is a brief reminiscence of the opening theme at the end of the refrain. It is interesting to observe that the main theme of the verse is identical to that of the E minor strain. The backbeat Charleston rhythm, anticipating the third beat of the measure, permeates both verse and refrain.

"Sweet Georgia Brown" was featured in the 1942 George Raft film, *Broadway*. It was sung by Cara Williams in the 1957 film, *The Helen Morgan Story*, and by Anne Bancroft and Mel Brooks in *To Be or Not to Be* (1983). The song remains a staple of the jazz repertoire.

Moderate rhythm song with two verses (20) and refrain (32)
PUBLISHER: Jerome H. Remick & Co.
KEY: G or A-flat maj., *STARTS:* e' (E7) or f' (F7), *FORM:* ABAC

≈≈≈≈≈≈≈≈≈≈≈≈≈≈≈≈≈≈≈≈

WHO? *!

WORDS: Otto Harbach and Oscar Hammerstein II, *MUSIC:* Jerome Kern
PREMIERE: Musical Comedy, *Sunny*
New York: New Amsterdam Theatre, 22 September 1925 (517 perf.)
INTRODUCED BY: Marilyn Miller and Paul Frawley

Sunny was the first collaborative effort of Jerome Kern and the rising young lyricist, Oscar Hammerstein II. The story about an English circus performer who falls in love with an American tourist, it starred

Marilyn Miller (then at the peak of her fame), Jack Donahue, Clifton Webb, Cliff Edwards (Ukelele Ike), and George Olsen and his Orchestra. The hit song of the show was "Who?" Although Otto Harbach collaborated on book and lyrics of the show with Hammerstein, it is the latter who is credited with the inspired idea of supplying the sustained note, b' – held for two-and-a-quarter measures – with the word "who?" The Victor recording by George Olsen and his Orchestra, with vocal by the trio of Fran Frey, Bob Rice, and Jack Fulton, sold over a million copies.

Written as a duet, this charming song has two verses in the key of D minor. They are in jaunty operetta style. But it is the refrain in D major that captivates. The long-held (nine-beat) first note is repeated five times at differing levels of pitch during its course: at the sixth, the fifth, the ninth, the sixth, and the fifth. The form itself is difficult to analyze; it could be called through-composed, except for the recurrence of the sustained note throughout, which acts as a unifying motive.

"Who?" was sung by Marilyn Miller and Lawrence Gray in the first movie version of *Sunny* (1930); by Anna Neagle and Ray Bolger in the second movie version of *Sunny* (1941); and by Judy Garland, Lucille Bremer, and a chorus in *Till the Clouds Roll By* (1946). It was also danced to by Ray Bolger in a memorable tap-dancing sequence in the 1939 film, *Look for the Silver Lining.*

> Moderate foxtrot with two verses (16) and refrain (32)
> *PUBLISHER:* T. B. Harms Co.
> *KEY:* D or E-flat maj., *STARTS:* b' (D6) or c" (E-flat 6), *FORM:* ABCD

≈≈≈≈≈≈≈≈≈≈≈≈≈≈≈≈≈≈≈≈

YES SIR, THAT'S MY BABY

WORDS: Gus Kahn, *MUSIC:* Walter Donaldson
INTRODUCED BY: Eddie Cantor

Still another song about the flapper, "Yes Sir, That's My Baby" had its origin at Eddie Cantor's home in Great Neck, Long Island. While visiting the Cantors one day, Gus Kahn played with a mechanical pig belonging to one of their daughters. The opening line of the song, to the jerky rhythm of the toy, came to Kahn in a flash. Walter Donaldson supplied the music, and the song became an instant success, aided by the recordings of Cantor, Lillian Roth, Gene Austin, and Ben Bernie and his Orchestra.

The music would delight a minimalist. Each "A" section of the refrain mainly plays around only two notes – b-flat' and c", in alternating quarter and half notes – which are repeated incessantly. Harmonies are also the simplest, chiefly tonic and dominant. Only the release offers some contrast, with long notes and a turn to the subdominant (A-flat). The words are also simple and repetitive. It is interesting to note that there is no syncopation at all in the song, although it is almost always performed in a syncopated manner.

"Yes Sir, That's My Baby" was featured in the 1942 film, *Broadway*. It became the title song of a movie called *Yes Sir That's My Baby* in which it was sung by Donald O'Connor, Gloria De Haven, Charles Coburn, Joshua Shelley, and Barbara Brown. Doris Day, Danny Thomas and a chorus of children sang it in the 1951 Gus Kahn biography, *I'll See You in My Dreams*. A year later, Eddie Cantor dubbed it in for Keefe Brasselle in Cantor's biographical film, *The Eddie Cantor Story*. Finally, Jason Robards, Jr. sang it in the 1965 movie, *A Thousand Clowns*.

Moderate foxtrot with two verses (16) and two refrains (32)
PUBLISHER: Irving Berlin, Inc.
KEY: E-flat maj., *STARTS*: b-flat' (E-flat maj.), *FORM:* AABA

≈≈≈≈≈≈≈≈≈≈≈≈≈≈≈≈≈≈≈

FRIVOLOUS PURSUITS

1926

"*Pack up all your cares and woes*"

Mort Dixon
"*Bye Bye Blackbird*"

In this year of good times and often frivolous pursuits, songwriters seem to strive for something different. There are numerous experiments in rhythm: offbeat accents in "Clap Yo' Hands", the beat of the Charleston in *Black Bottom* and *The Girl Friend*, the broad syncopation of "I Know That You Know", and the dotted notes and triplets of "Gimme a Little Kiss, Will Ya, Huh?" Only one great ballad emerges, the beguiling "Someone to Watch Over Me", but even that begins life as an up-tempo rhythm song.

Things are quiet in Washington, with silent Calvin Coolidge snugly ensconced in the White House. Since there is an isolationist attitude toward the rest of the world, Americans look inward for excitement. They wonder over the disappearance of evangelist Aimee Semple MacPherson (she turns up alive, well, and married). Over 100,000 of them line the streets of New York to watch the funeral procession of silent film star Rudolph Valentino, who dies unexpectedly at age thirty-one. New Yorkers give the biggest ticker-tape parade in history to honor Gertrude Ederle, the first woman to swim the English Channel. People speculate whether escape artist Harry Houdini will return from the dead after he is dispatched by four blows to the stomach delivered by an admirer. They discuss the marriage of songwriter Irving Berlin and Postal Telegraph heiress Ellin Mackay. And many of them lose money when the Florida land boom dissolves with a huge hurricane.

For diversion, many go to the movies; there are 19,500 theaters throughout the land and over 400 silent films are produced this year. Many flock to see the war film, *What Price Glory?*, or Ronald Colman in *Beau Geste*. And more and more listen to the radio. The National Broadcasting Company is founded this year, and Eddie Cantor is one of the first to sign up. A radio program called Sam and Henry originates on Station WGN in Chicago; two years later, it is renamed Amos 'n' Andy. Broadway has its attractions, too, from Sigmund Romberg's operetta, *The Desert Song*, to the Gershwins' musical comedy, *Oh, Kay!*; from De Sylva, Brown, and Henderson's enticing score for *George White's Scandals of 1926* to Rodgers and Hart's sparkling music for *The Girl Friend* and *Garrick Gaieties of 1926*. In short, one can say that 1926 is a prosperous year, reflected in the carefree rhythms of its songs.

SONGS OF 1926

    Baby Face **
    The Birth of the Blues *
    Black Bottom **
    Blue Room **
    Bye Bye Blackbird ***
    Charmaine
    Clap Yo' Hands *!
    Deed I Do
    Do, Do, Do
    Gimme a Little Kiss, Will
        Ya, Huh?
    The Girl Friend
    I Can't Believe That You're
        in Love with Me
    I Know That You Know **!
    Lucky Day
    Mountain Greenery *!
    Muskrat Ramble *
    One Alone
    Someone to Watch Over Me ***!
    What Can I Say After I Say I'm Sorry?
    When Day Is Done
    When the Red, Red Robin Comes Bob, Bob Bobbin'
        Along

BABY FACE * *

WORDS and MUSIC: Benny Davis and Harry Akst
INTRODUCED: in a Victor recording by Jan Garber and his Orchestra, vocal by Benny Davis

This rousing song was written by two denizens of Tin Pan Alley, Benny Davis and Harry Akst. It quickly became a favorite on the vaudeville circuit, sung by Eddie Cantor, Al Jolson, and many other high-powered singers. Besides Jan Garber's Victor recording (sung by co-writer Benny Davis), early recordings were by Ben Selvin and his Orchestra and Whispering Jack Smith. A Metro Goldwyn Mayer recording by Art Mooney and his Orchestra brought about a revival in 1948. Later recordings were by Little Richard (1958) and Bobby Darin (1962).

The song is very much in the English music-hall tradition of easy-to-remember words and music. The melody of the refrain outlines the minor third (g'-e'-g'), followed by a descending scale starting on c", with each note repeated; this pattern is then repeated a step below.

In the movies, "Baby Face" was sung by Mary Eaton in Florenz Zeigfeld's 1930 spectacle, *Glorifying the American Girl*. Al Jolson dubbed it in for Larry Parks in *Jolson Sings Again* (1949); and Julie Andrews sang it in *Thoroughly Modern Millie* (1967). Along with "Toot Toot Tootsie (Goo' Bye)" (1922) and "I'm Looking Over a Four Leaf Clover" (1927), it is a mainstay at sing-alongs.

Moderate foxtrot with two verses (20) and refrain (32)
PUBLISHER: Jerome H. Remick & Co.
KEY: C maj., *STARTS*: g' (C maj.), *FORM*: ABA'C

≈≈≈≈≈≈≈≈≈≈≈≈≈≈≈≈≈≈≈

THE BIRTH OF THE BLUES *

WORDS: B. G. De Sylva and Lew Brown, *MUSIC*: Ray Henderson
PREMIERE: Revue, *George White's Scandals of 1926*
New York: Apollo Theatre, 14 June 1926 (424 perf.)
INTRODUCED BY: Harry Richman, danced to by Ann Pennington

This dramatic and powerful song was first sung by Harry Richman in the revue, *George White's Scandals of 1926*. Richman presented it on center stage, surrounded by a circular staircase filled with showgirls dressed as angels, representing the opposing forces of classical and contemporary music. Fittingly, the conflict was resolved with a quotation from George Gershwin's *Rhapsody in Blue*. Off-stage, "The Birth of the

Blues" was recorded on Victor by Richman, as well as by Paul Whiteman and his Orchestra. The Revelers recorded it, and, in 1952, Frank Sinatra had a hit Capitol record.

Although the sheet music includes the performance direction "Tempo di Blues", this is not a blues song. It is rather a traditional thirty-two bar song in AABA form. The only blue notes are the lowered thirds (e-flat') in the verse, which begins strikingly with a C dominant seventh chord. The refrain has a three-note pickup of quarter notes descending chromatically. The intriguing melodic idea in the "A" section consists of two scales ascending in tandem: one starting on a', the other on e'. There are only two harmonies in the release: E dominant seventh and A dominant seventh, each held for four measures. The clever lyrics – "and so they nursed it, rehearsed it…" – actually try to tell the story about the birth of the blues.

A movie called *The Birth of the Blues* came out in 1941, in which Bing Crosby sang the title song. In 1948, Ted Lewis and his Orchestra did it in *When My Baby Smiles At Me*. Lucille Norman sang it in the 1951 film, *Painting the Clouds with Sunshine*. Danny Thomas sang it in the 1953 version of *The Jazz Singer*. And Gordon MacRae sang it in the De Sylva-Brown-Henderson biographical film, *The Best Things in Life Are Free* (1956).

Slow rhythm song with verse (16) and refrain (32)
PUBLISHER: Harms, Inc.
KEY: C maj., *STARTS*: g' (C maj.), *FORM*: AABA

≈≈≈≈≈≈≈≈≈≈≈≈≈≈≈≈≈≈≈

BLACK BOTTOM *

WORDS: B. G. De Sylva and Lew Brown, *MUSIC*: Ray Henderson
PREMIERE: Revue, *George White's Scandals of 1926*
New York: Apollo Theatre, 14 June 1926 (424 perf.)
INTRODUCED BY: Ann Pennington, The McCarthy Sisters,
Frances Wilson, and Tom Patricola

The Black Bottom was fashioned as a dance craze to compete with the still very popular Charleston. Like the Charleston, it became symbolic of flaming youth, flappers, the lost generation and bathtub gin. Also like the Charleston, the song outlasted the dance. "Black Bottom" was recorded by Johnny Hamp and his Orchestra. Ann Pennington, who introduced it in *George White's Scandals of 1926*, used it as her theme song.

As in "Charleston" the music emphasizes the back beat, or anticipated third beat. Harmonies are not as interesting, however, mostly tonic and dominant, although a little harmonic variety is offered in the release, which moves through the circle of fifths: G seventh - C minor - F seventh - B-flat seventh.

Judy Garland sang "Black Bottom" in *A Star Is Born* (1954). Sheree North, Jacques D'Amboise and a chorus did it in *The Best Things In Life Are Free* (1956). It is still played at dances as a bit of nostalgia from the twenties.

Fast rhythm song with verse (240 and refrain (32)
PUBLISHER: Harms, Inc.
KEY: E-flat maj., *STARTS*: e-flat' (E-flat maj.), *FORM*: AA'BA'

≋≋≋≋≋≋≋≋≋≋≋≋≋≋≋≋≋≋≋

BLUE ROOM * *

WORDS: Lorenz Hart, *MUSIC*: Richard Rodgers
PREMIERE: Musical comedy, *The Girl Friend*
New York: Vanderbilt Theatre, 17 March 1926 (c. 300 perf.)
INTRODUCED BY: Eva Puck and Sammy White

A delightful Rodgers and Hart song, "Blue Room" is often referred to with the definite article, as "The Blue Room". Perhaps this is because the show in which it was introduced and its title song are titled *The Girl Friend*. However, the sheet music is entitled "Blue Room", and the word "the" does not even appear in the refrain. In any case, "Blue Room" is credited with keeping the show – with its very thin plot – alive for nine months. In the show, it was sung by the romantic leads, Eva Puck and Sammy White. But the song soon took on a life of its own. Recordings were made by Sam Lanin and his Orchestra, The Melodic Sheiks, and The Revelers. Perry Como recorded it in 1949.

The verse, in AABA' form, is a miniature song in itself, consisting of a simple motive in dotted rhythm, repeated on offbeats. There are two sets of lyrics, designated "He" and "She". The romantic refrain employs the favorite Rodgers device of a rising scale, this time starting on f', and always returning to the same two lower notes: d' and c'. The release is again a rising scale, but without interruption and beginning on e'; it is followed by a fragmented, descending scale. Hart's tender lyrics paint an almost cloying picture of domestic happiness, as in: "With Mister and Missus / On little blue chairs".

Perry Como and Cyd Charisse sang "Blue Room" in the 1948 biographical film of Rodgers and Hart, *Words and Music*. It was featured in *Young Man with a Horn* (1950), and dubbed in by Carmen Cavallaro in *The Eddy Duchin Story* (1956). The song has taken its place as both a dance tune and a jazz standard, usually performed in moderate to fast tempo.

Slow ballad with two verses (16) and refrain (32)
PUBLISHER: Harms, Inc.
KEY: F maj., *STARTS*: c' (F maj.), *FORM*: AA'BA"

≈≈≈≈≈≈≈≈≈≈≈≈≈≈≈≈≈≈≈

BYE BYE BLACKBIRD   * * *

WORDS: Mort Dixon, *MUSIC*: Ray Henderson
POPULARIZED: in vaudeville by Eddie Cantor and The Duncan Sisters

Beginning with the provocative words: "Pack up all your cares and woes", this eminently singable standard is a favorite at sing-alongs, together with such rousing songs as "Toot Toot Tootsie, Goo' Bye" (1922) and "I'm Looking Over a Four Leaf Clover" (1927). Early recordings were by Eddie Cantor, Gene Austin, Nick Lucas, George Olsen and his Orchestra, and Leo Reisman and his Orchestra. Georgie Price used it as his theme song in vaudeville. It was recorded in 1938 by Russ Morgan and his Orchestra.

The song's attraction to amateur singers is easy to understand. The melody of the refrain is full of repeated notes and moves mostly stepwise within a very narrow range of only a major seventh. The carefree, optimistic nature of both words and music serve to chase the blues away.

It has been performed in a number of films. Frankie Lane sang it in *Rainbow 'Round my Shoulder* (1952). Eddie Cantor dubbed it in for Keefe Brasselle in *The Eddie Cantor Story* (1953). Marilyn Monroe sang it in the 1954 film, *River of No Return*. Peggy Lee sang it in *Pete Kelly's Blues* (1955), In 1963, Ty Hardin and Jerry Van Dyke sang it in *Palm Springs Weekend*. And Jason Robards sang it in the 1980 film, *Melvin and Howard*. The song may also have inspired an entire series of revues called *Blackbirds*, produced by Lew Leslie, featuring black entertainers and running from 1926 to 1939.

Moderate rhythm song with two verses (32) and refrain (32)
PUBLISHER: Jerome H. Remick & Co.
KEY: G maj., *STARTS*: b' (G maj.), *FORM*: ABCA'

≈≈≈≈≈≈≈≈≈≈≈≈≈≈≈≈≈≈≈≈

CHARMAINE

WORDS and MUSIC: Lew Pollack and Erno Rapee
PREMIERE: Silent film, *What Price Glory?*, soundtrack theme, 1927.
Played by piano and orchestra

Erno Rapee wrote this sentimental waltz in 1913 while he was still living in Hungary. Thirteen years later, he used it as part of the musical background of the film, *What Price Glory?* Given words by Lew Pollack, it became "Charmaine", the forerunner of many other songs to be developed out of cinema scores. In their first recording for Columbia, Guy Lombardo and his Royal Canadians, had a solid hit. The song was revived in 1952, with a hit London recording by Mantovani and his Orchestra, coinciding with the remake of *What Price Glory?* There have been numerous jazz recordings, in 4/4 meter, by Neal Heftie, Jimmy Lunceford, Billy May, and others.

The romantic melody of the refrain, in AA'A"B form, outlines the pentatonic scale in the first three sections. The last section, pausing at the high point, brings the range to an octave and a sixth, more suitable for an operatic aria than a popular song.

In other films, Harry James and his Orchestra performed "Charmaine" in *Two Girls and a Sailor* (1944). It was also heard in *Margie* (1946) and *Thoroughly Modern Millie* (1967). Historically significant as the first important song to emanate from the movies, it is also a jazz standard.

Moderate waltz with two verses (24) and two refrains (32)
PUBLISHER: United Artists Music
KEY: E-flat maj., *STARTS*: B-flat' (E-flat maj.), *FORM*: AA'A"B

≈≈≈≈≈≈≈≈≈≈≈≈≈≈≈≈≈≈≈≈

CLAP YO' HANDS *!

WORDS: Ira Gershwin, *MUSIC*: George Gershwin
PREMIERE: Musical comedy, *Oh, Kay!*
New York: Imperial Theatre, 8 November 1926 (256 perf.)
INTRODUCED BY: Harland Dixon, Betty Compton, Paulette Winston, Constance Carpenter, and Janette Gilmore

This revival-type number was one of the big hits of the Gershwin show, *Oh, Kay!*, a rum-runners' romp that starred Victor Moore and Gertrude Lawrence. The title never appears as "Clap Yo' Hands" in the song, it is written "Clap-a yo' hands", to go along with the music of two eighth notes and two quarter notes. The song was popularized by Roger Wolfe Kahn and his Orchestra.

The verse, in D minor, resembles a spiritual. With a call to "Gather around, you children", it exhorts participants to come to the Jubilee. The refrain, in F major, is noteworthy for its shifting accents as well as for its pentatonic theme (also common in other songs from *Oh, Kay!*). There are also attractive blue notes (lowered thirds and sevenths) throughout. Ira's words in the release, "On the sands of time you are only a pebble", were criticized at the time. But a trip to the beach convinced disbelievers that there are indeed pebbles in the sand.

"Clap Yo' Hands" was featured in the Gershwin biographical film, *Rhapsody in Blue* (1946). Fred Astaire and Kay Thompson sang it in the 1957 film musical, *Funny Face*.

Moderate rhythm song with verse (24) and refrain (32)
PUBLISHER: New World Music Corp.
KEY: F maj., *STARTS*: c' (F maj.), *FORM*: AABA'

≈≈≈≈≈≈≈≈≈≈≈≈≈≈≈≈≈≈≈

'DEED I DO

WORDS: Walter Hirsch, *MUSIC*: Fred Rose

Initially popularized with recordings by Ruth Etting and Ben Bernie and his Orchestra, this erstwhile sentimental foxtrot has become a jazz standard, often performed in very fast tempo. Popular recordings were by Tommy Dorsey and his Orchestra (Victor), Charlie Barnet and his Orchestra (Bluebird), and Lena Horne (Metro Goldwyn Mayer). In the refrain, the lyrics ask the question answered by the title: "Do I want you?" with a minimum of notes and slow-moving harmonies. The song's chief attribute is its prevailing rhythmic motive of a dotted quarter, followed by an eighth note tied to a half note. The open harmonies offer a clean slate for imaginative improvisation.

Moderate foxtrot with two verses (16) and refrain (32)
PUBLISHER: The Herald Square Music Company
KEY: E-flat maj., *STARTS*: c" (E-flat maj.), *FORM*: AA'BA'

≈≈≈≈≈≈≈≈≈≈≈≈≈≈≈≈≈≈≈

DO, DO, DO

WORDS: Ira Gershwin, *MUSIC*: George Gershwin
PREMIERE: Musical comedy, *Oh, Kay!*
New York: Imperial Theatre, 8 November 1926 (256 perf.)
INTRODUCED BY: Gertrude Lawrence and Oscar Shaw

According to Ira Gershwin, this charming song was completed in half an hour, before going to dinner with his fiancée and brother, George. Introduced in *Oh, Kay!*, it was first recorded for Victor by George Olsen and his Orchestra with the vocal by Gertrude Lawrence.

Like many other songs from *Oh, Kay!*, it is built around the pentatonic scale. The melodic rhythm consists of quarter notes with an occasional dotted quarter and eighth on the fourth beat. The three-fold pattern of the lyrics is continued throughout, as in: "I know, know, know what a beau, beau, beau should do". There also is excessive use of the word "baby".

In the movies, it was sung by Doris Day and Gordon MacRae in *Tea for Two* (1950). Gogi Grant dubbed it in for Ann Blyth in the 1957 film, *The Helen Morgan Story*. And in 1968, Julie Andrews sang it in the Lawrence biography, *Star!*

Moderate foxtrot with two verses (16) and two refrains (32)
PUBLISHER: New World Music Corp.
KEY: E-flat maj., *STARTS*: b-flat' (E-flat maj.), *FORM*: ABA'C

≈≈≈≈≈≈≈≈≈≈≈≈≈≈≈≈≈≈≈≈

GIMME A LITTLE KISS, WILL YA, HUH?

WORDS and MUSIC: Roy Turk, Jack Smith, and Maceo Pinkard
INTRODUCED: in a Victor recording by Whispering Jack Smith

Maceo Pinkard was one of the most successful black songwriters of the twenties; "Sweet Georgia Brown" (1925) was his biggest hit. He wrote this tap-dancer's delight along with lyricist Roy Turk. Whispering Jack Smith – also credited as one of the writers – had a hit Victor record. A quarter of a century later, in 1951, it was recorded for RCA Victor, by April Stevens.

The refrain, only twenty bars long, has varying rhythms: eighth-note triplets followed by dotted quarters and eighths. The form is modified rondo, consisting of five sections of four bars each: ABA'CA". The "C" section can leave singers breathless with its continuous succession of dotted notes. The closing words sum up the song's frolicsome nature: "And I'll give it right back to you".

Deanna Durbin sang it in the 1945 film, *Lady On a Train*.

Slow foxtrot with two verses (16) and three refrains (20)
PUBLISHER: Irving Berlin, Inc.
KEY: C maj., *STARTS*: e' (C maj.), *FORM*: ABA'CA"

≈≈≈≈≈≈≈≈≈≈≈≈≈≈≈≈≈≈≈

THE GIRL FRIEND

WORDS: Lorenz Hart, *MUSIC*: Richard Rodgers
PREMIERE: Musical comedy, *The Girl Friend*
New York: Vanderbilt Theatre, 17 March 1926 (c. 300 perf.)
INTRODUCED BY: Eva Puck and Sammy White

The title song of the hit show, *The Girl Friend*, makes free use of the back-beat rhythm popularized in "Charleston" (1923) and in this year's "Black Bottom". George Olsen and his Orchestra had a hit Victor record.

There are two verses and two refrains: for "He" and "She". The verse moves from C major to E major, with many dotted eighths and sixteenths. The refrain accents nearly every third beat in the style of "Charleston". It also is highly syncopated and has a profusion of notes. The release starts out in E minor, but quickly modulates back to C major. Hart's clever lyrics stand out for their inner rhymes, as in "She's gentle and mentally nearly complete" and "A look at this vision will cause a collision".

"The Girl Friend" was danced to by Cyd Charisse in the 1946 Rodgers and Hart film biography, *Words and Music*.

Fast rhythm song with two verses (16) and two refrains (32)
PUBLISHER: Harms, Inc.
KEY: C maj., *STARTS*: g' (C maj.), *FORM*: AABA

≈≈≈≈≈≈≈≈≈≈≈≈≈≈≈≈≈≈≈

I CAN'T BELIEVE THAT YOU'RE IN LOVE WITH ME

WORDS and MUSIC: Clarence Gaskill and Jimmy McHugh
PREMIERE: Revue, *Gay Paree*
New York: Winter Garden Theatre, 9 November 1926 (175 perf.)
INTRODUCED BY: Winnie Lightner

This moderate foxtrot was popularized with a Victor recording by Roger Wolfe Kahn and his Orchestra. It was revived in 1953, with an RCA Victor recording by The Ames Brothers. The music of the refrain is characterized by persistent dotted rhythms and slowly changing harmonies beginning, unusually, on the subdominant (E-flat major). In the release, harmonies move abruptly to D dominant seventh and then through the circle of fifths: G seventh - C seventh - F seventh - and back to B-flat major. In films, Claudia Drake sang it in *Detour* (1945), May Wynn in *The Caine Mutiny* (1954), Connie Francis in *Looking for Love* (1964), and it was featured in *Thoroughly Modern Millie* (1967).

Moderate foxtrot with verse (16) and refrain (32)
PUBLISHER: Mills Music, Inc.
KEY: B-flat maj., *STARTS*: b-flat' (E-flat maj.), *FORM*: AA'BA'

≈≈≈≈≈≈≈≈≈≈≈≈≈≈≈≈≈≈≈

I KNOW THAT YOU KNOW * *!

WORDS: Ann Caldwell, *MUSIC*: Vincent Youmans
PREMIERE: Musical comedy, *Oh, Please!*
New York: Fulton Theatre, 17 December 1926
INTRODUCED BY: Beatrice Lillie and Charles Purcell

This rousing theater piece is the only survivor from a disappointing show called *Oh, Please!* Over the years, it has done double duty as a curtain-opener or -closer and as a jazz standard. Among many recordings are those of Benny Goodman and his Orchestra (Victor) and Nat "King" Cole (Capitol).

Its musical premise is simple enough. As in many Vincent Youmans songs – "Tea for Two" (1924), for example – there is a persistent rhythmic motive throughout, rescued from monotony by changing harmonies. In this case, it is an accented quarter note on the fourth beat tied over to a dotted half note. A simple ascending diatonic scale interrupts the pattern at the close of each half.

In films, "I Know That You Know" was featured in the 1929 screen version of *Hit the Deck* and in *Powers Girl* (1943). Doris Day, Gordon MacRae, and Gene Nelson performed it in the 1950 film, *Tea for Two*. Jane Powell and Vic Damone sang it in the 1955 remake of *Hit the Deck*.

Fast rhythm song with verse (32) and refrain (32)
PUBLISHER: Harms, Inc.
KEY: C maj., *STARTS*: e' (D9), *FORM*: ABA'C

≈≈≈≈≈≈≈≈≈≈≈≈≈≈≈≈≈≈≈

LUCKY DAY

WORDS: B.G. De Sylva and Lew Brown, *MUSIC*: Ray Henderson
PREMIERE: Revue, *George White's Scandals of 1926*
New York: Apollo Theatre, 14 June 1926 (424 perf.)
INTRODUCED BY: Harry Richman and chorus

Best known as the theme of *Your Hit Parade*, broadcast over network radio every Saturday night and sponsored by Lucky Strike Cigarettes, "Lucky Day" was another hit from the revue, *George White's Scandals of 1926*. Introduced in the show by entertainer, Harry Richman, its first recording was by George Olsen and his Orchestra. The song is easy to remember, with a simple, march-like melody playing around three notes: e', d', and c'. One can imagine many in the audience humming it as they left the theater. Maurice Chevalier sang it in the 1930 film, *The Big Pond*, and Dan Dailey performed it in the 1956 film biography of De Sylva, Brown, and Henderson, *The Best Things in Life Are Free*.

Fast rhythm song with verse (16) and refrain (32)
PUBLISHER: Harms, Inc.
KEY: C maj., *STARTS*: e' (C maj.), *FORM*: AABA

≈≈≈≈≈≈≈≈≈≈≈≈≈≈≈≈≈≈≈

MOUNTAIN GREENERY *!

WORDS: Lorenz Hart, *MUSIC*: Richard Rodgers
PREMIERE: Revue, *The Garrick Gaieties of 1926*
New York: Garrick Theatre, 10 May 1926 (174 perf.)
INTRODUCED BY: Sterling Holloway and Bobbie Perkins

The second edition of Rodgers and Hart's *The Garrick Gaieties* brought forth this joyful song, their second great hit after "Manhattan" in the first edition (1925). Early recordings were by Roger Wolfe Kahn and his Orchestra and Frank Crumit (both on Victor). Suffused with youthfulness and vigor, the song's popularity has hardly waned over the years.

Both words and music are carefully wrought. The verse is very melodic and charming in itself. The refrain, marked "Cheerfully", is built around the simple device of three repeated notes, themselves repeated at different octave levels: c", c", c"; then c', c', c'; then back to c", c", c". The release also makes use of repeated notes, with three identical phrases descending from c" to d' over changing harmonies. There is also a most unusual "trio-patter" of forty-eighth bars, with many repeated notes. Hart's lyrics are extremely witty, rhyming such disparate words as "beanery", "machinery", and, of course, "greenery".

It was sung by Perry Como and Allyn McLerie in the 1948 film biography of Rodgers and Hart, *Words and Music*. As a model of youthful exuberance in the Roaring Twenties, the song is in a class by itself.

> Moderate rhythm song with two verses (16), two refrains (32) and trio-patter (48)
> *PUBLISHER*: Harms, Inc.
> *KEY*: C maj., *STARTS:* c" (C maj.), *FORM*: AABA'

≈≈≈≈≈≈≈≈≈≈≈≈≈≈≈≈≈≈≈

MUSKRAT RAMBLE *

WORDS: Ray Gilbert, *MUSIC*: Edward "Kid" Ory
INTRODUCED: in an Okeh recording by Louis Armstrong and his Hot Five

A Dixieland classic, "Muskrat Ramble" was composed as an instrumental by Edward "Kid" Ory, the famous New Orleans "tailgate" trombonist, so-called because he customarily played his trombone at the very edge of the musicians' wagon, the better to maneuver his slide. Introduced by Louis Armstrong and his Hot Five in 1926, it was revived in 1937, and again in 1954, with a recording by The McGuire Sisters.

Ray Gilbert's lyrics were added in 1950, but they are seldom heard. The piece is almost always played by jazz instrumentalists in the order in which it was first presented: verse, refrain, then a "sneeze" chorus with harmonies derived from the verse, a return to the verse, and a brief coda. The verse is lightly syncopated, featuring broken chords in the style of ragtime. The refrain is somewhat more syncopated, with a rollicking melody and subtle use of chromaticism.

> Fast rhythm song with two verses (16) and two refrains (16)
> KEY: A-flat maj., STARTS: f'(B-flat 7),
> FORM (Overall): AA'BB'CC'A'A

≈≈≈≈≈≈≈≈≈≈≈≈≈≈≈≈≈≈≈

ONE ALONE

WORDS: Otto Harbach and Oscar Hammerstein II
MUSIC: Sigmund Romberg
PREMIERE: Operetta, *The Desert Song*
New York: Casino Theatre, 30 November 1926 (471 perf.)
INTRODUCED BY: Robert Halliday, reprised by Robert Halliday and
Vivienne Segal

The big ballad from *The Desert Song*, "One Alone" was sung by Robert Halliday in the Broadway production. Three years later, John Boles sang it the film version of *The Desert Song*; it was the first operetta to be brought to the screen.

The verse, in 2/4 meter, begins: "Lonely as a desert breeze". The soaring melody of the refrain is accompanied by harmonies going through the circle of fifths: C seventh, F seventh, B-flat seventh, and E-flat seventh – each lasting for two bars.

Other movies featuring the song besides the 1929 film version were *The Desert Song* of 1943 (sung by Dennis Morgan and Irene Manning), *The Desert Song* of 1953 (sung by Kathryn Grayson and Gordon MacRae), and the Romberg biographical film, *Deep in My Heart* of 1954 (danced to by Cyd Charisse and James Mitchell). A romantic song with a spacious melody, it is still a singer's delight.

Slow ballad with verse (8) and refrain (16)
PUBLISHER: Harms, Inc.
KEY: A-flat maj., *STARTS*: c' (A-flat maj.), *FORM:* ABAC'

≈≈≈≈≈≈≈≈≈≈≈≈≈≈≈≈≈≈≈≈

SOMEONE TO WATCH OVER ME * * *!

WORDS: Ira Gershwin, *MUSIC:* George Gershwin
PREMIERE: Musical comedy, *Oh, Kay!*
New York: Imperial Theatre, 8 November 1926 (256 perf.)
INTRODUCED BY: Gertrude Lawrence

A plaintive song and George and Ira Gershwin's second big ballad after "The Man I Love" (1924), "Someone to Watch Over Me" was not originally conceived as a ballad, as its marking "Scherzando" implies. George wrote it originally as a jazzy tune to be played in fast tempo. One day, however, he happened to play the music in slower tempo, and both he and his brother realized that it would make a touching ballad. So it was given to Gertrude Lawrence to sing in the musical comedy, *Oh, Kay!* – her first show in America. Lawrence played Kay, who alone on the stage and dressed as a cook, wistfully sings the ballad to a rag doll (George had found the doll in a Philadelphia toy shop during the tryouts). The song was an immediate hit and remains one of the Gershwins' best-loved and best-known creations.

The verse, in three sections: AAB, is particularly appealing; unlike many other verses, it is often performed. Its lyrics tell a story about seeking someone, and contains the evocative line: "I'd like to add his initial to my monogram". As in other songs from *Oh, Kay!*, the melody of the refrain makes use of the pentatonic scale, first rising and then gently subsiding in each "A" section. The release begins with an A-flat major chord and then modulates to C major before returning to E-flat major.

"Someone to Watch Over Me" has had a lengthy screen history. In 1955, Frank Sinatra sang it in *Young at Heart*, and Marge and Gower Champion danced to it in *Three for the Show*. In 1957, Vera Miles sang it in *Beau James* and Gogi Grant dubbed it in for Ann Blyth in *The Helen Morgan Story*, known in Britain as *Both Ends of the Candle*. Julie Andrews sang it in *Star!* (1968), and Dinah Shore in *A Safe Place* (1971). The song also became the title of a 1987 dramatic film starring Tom Berenger and Mimi Rogers. After more than seventy years, it remains as fresh and heartfelt as the day it was written.

Moderate ballad with verse (24) and refrain (32)
PUBLISHER: New World Music Corp.
KEY: E-flat maj., *STARTS*: e-flat', *FORM:* AA'BA'

≈≈≈≈≈≈≈≈≈≈≈≈≈≈≈≈≈≈

WHAT CAN I SAY AFTER I SAY I'M SORRY?

WORDS and MUSIC: Walter Donaldson and Abe Lyman
INTRODUCED: in a recording on Brunswick by Abe Lyman and his Orchestra

Bandleader Abe Lyman introduced this bland and sentimental foxtrot, which he co-wrote with Walter Donaldson. Both verse and refrain are rather ordinary. The main theme combines major thirds with repeated notes in a steady dotted rhythm. In the lyrics, the word "Dear" is inserted after "Say" in the title, in order to maintain the rhythm. The climax of the song and its highest point is in the "C" section", at the words "I'm so sorry, dear". Peggy Lee sang the song in the 1955 film, *Pete Kelly's Blues*.

Moderate foxtrot with verse (16) and refrain (32)
PUBLISHER: Leo Feist, Inc.
KEY: G maj., *STARTS*: b' (G maj.), *FORM*: ABAC

≋≋≋≋≋≋≋≋≋≋≋≋≋≋≋≋≋≋≋≋

WHEN DAY IS DONE

WORDS: B. G. De Sylva, *MUSIC*: Dr. Robert Katscher
POPULARIZED: in the United States by Paul Whiteman and his Orchestra,
with trumpet solo by Henry Busse

An import from Austria, "When Day Is Done" began life in a Viennese revue of 1924 called *Kusse um Mitternacht*, with German words and music by Dr. Robert Katscher; the song was titled "Madonna, Du Bist Schöner als der Sonnen schein!" Two years later, with English lyrics by B. G. De Sylva, it became a hit in the United States, sparked by Henry Busse's muted trumpet in a Victor recording by Paul Whiteman and his Orchestra. This recording single-handedly launched a vogue for sweet jazz. Busse later used it as his theme song, when he organized his own band.

The music is in the Viennese operetta tradition of Franz Lehár and Emmerich Kálmán, with a dramatic verse in the parallel minor and a mellifluous refrain in major. The "A" sections consist of repeated notes falling sequentially. The highest point (g") is reached in the "C" section. The English lyrics complement the music perfectly in such sequential passages as "That yearning returning" and "Although I miss your tender kiss".

Slow ballad with two verses (16) and refrain (32)
PUBLISHER: Wiener Boheme Verlag (Vienna, 1924),
assigned to Harms, Inc.
KEY: B-flat major, *STARTS*: f' (B-flat maj.), *FORM*: ABA'C

≋≋≋≋≋≋≋≋≋≋≋≋≋≋≋≋≋≋≋≋

WHEN THE RED, RED ROBIN COMES BOB, BOB BOBBIN' ALONG

WORDS and MUSIC: Harry Woods
INTRODUCED: in vaudeville by Sophie Tucker
CHICAGO: Woods Theatre

This happy-go-lucky song, introduced by Sophie Tucker, was also a favorite of Al Jolson and Lillian Roth. It is one of two popular "bird songs" to come out this year – the other is "Bye, Bye Blackbird". The melody of the refrain is full of repeated notes and dotted rhythms. Birdcalls are imitated in the "B" section by repeated thirds, starting at the words "Wake up, wake up you sleepy head". Al Jolson dubbed in the song for Larry Parks in two films: *The Jolson Story* (1946) and *Jolson Sings Again* (1949). Susan Hayward sang it in *I'll Cry Tomorrow* (1955)

Moderate foxtrot with two verses (16) and refrain (32)
PUBLISHER: Bourne, Inc. (Irving Berlin, Inc.)
KEY: G maj., *STARTS*: g' (G maj.), *FORM*: ABAC/A

≈≈≈≈≈≈≈≈≈≈≈≈≈≈≈≈≈≈≈

1927

THE PLAY'S THE THING

1927

Hear the cymbals ring! Calling one and all...

Ira Gershwin,
"Strike Up the Band"

This is a boom year for all sorts of popular entertainment: theater, film, radio, and song. Broadway has more openings than at any time before or since: 280 shows. Many of them are hits, including the greatest hit of all, *Show Boat*. This landmark musical, the first to integrate book and score, is the outstanding achievement of the twenties. It is the first American musical play, the forerunner of such giants as *Oklahoma!*, *Carousel*, and *West Side Story*. As if to emphasize showmanship this year, Flo Ziefeld's own Ziegfeld Theatre, a masterpiece of art-deco style, opens in New York on 2 February. Its first show is *Rio Rita*, a smash hit; followed on 27 December by the immortal *Show Boat*. Other hit musicals of the year include *Hit the Deck!*, *Good News*, *A Connecticut Yankee*, and *Funny Face*. Among non-musical plays are *Burlesque*, starring Barbara Stanwyck; and *The Barker*, with Walter Huston and Claudette Colbert. The popular songs of 1927 reflect this great proliferation of entertainment. Many of them are show tunes of higher quality than the more mundane songs originating in Tin Pan Alley. They include such innovative songs as "Hallelujah!", "Ol' Man River", "'S Wonderful", "Strike Up the Band", and "Thou Swell".

This is also the year that talkies come of age. The first sound film, the part-talking *The Jazz Singer* opens on 6 October in New York. In it, Al Jolson sings a number of songs, including "Blue Skies", written this year by Irving Berlin. Also this year, the first Academy Awards are given: to Emil Jannings as best actor, Janet Gaynor as best actress, and *Wings* as best picture.

The first car radios appear. As broadcasting continues to expand, the Columbia Broadcasting System is established. Among early sponsored radio shows on the National Broadcasting Company's Red and Blue Networks are: *The Cities Service Orchestra*, *The General Motors Family*

Party, The Ipana Troubadours, The Palmolive Hour, and *The Atwater Kent Hour.*

Even current events convey a feeling of showmanship. Charles Lindbergh's daring flight on 19 May from Roosevelt Field in New York to Le Bourget Airport in Paris, – 3,610 miles in 33 hours – captures the world's imagination and makes the young aviator a folk hero. The laconic Calvin Coolidge passes an eight-word note to reporters, saying "I do not choose to run in 1928". Babe Ruth hits his sixtieth home run of the season, a world record. Gene Tunney beats Jack Dempsey after taking the longest count of eight on record. Indeed, in this year of good times, the play's the thing.

SONGS OF 1927

Ain't She Sweet *
Among My Souvenirs
At Sundown (Love Is Calling Me Home)
The Best Things in Life Are Free **
Bill *
Blue Skies **
Can't Help Lovin' Dat Man **!
Diane (I'm in Heaven When I See You Smile)
Girl of My Dreams
Hallelujah!
How Long Has This Been Going On?!
I'm Looking Over a Four Leaf Clover **
Just a Memory!
Make Believe **
Me and My Shadow
My Blue Heaven **
My Heart Stood Still **
Ol' Man River ***!
Sometimes I'm Happy **
Stouthearted Men
Strike Up the Band *
Sugar
'S Wonderful ***
Thou Swell **
Why Do I Love You? **

AIN'T SHE SWEET *

WORDS: Jack Yellen, *MUSIC*: Milton Ager
INTRODUCED BY: Paul Ash and his Orchestra

A creation of Tin Pan Alley, "Ain't She Sweet" only reached Broadway more than half a century after it was written, when it was featured in the 1979 musical comedy, *The 1940's Radio Hour*. Back in the twenties, Gene Austin and Paul Whiteman's Rhythm Boys recorded it for Victor, while Ben Bernie and his Orchestra recorded it for Brunswick. Jimmy Lunceford and his Orchestra recorded it in 1939, and The Beatles in 1964.

The song has all the earmarks of the Roaring Twenties: the frantic rhythm, the flapper "walking down the street", the hummable melody, the repetition, the thirty-two bar AABA form. It even has Charleston rhythm in its verse. The main theme of the refrain features three chromatically-lowered half notes (a', a-flat', g'), immediately doubled in quarter notes. There are also many repeated notes in the release.

"Ain't She Sweet" was featured in the film, *Margie* (1946). In the 1948 film, *You Were Meant for Me*, it was sung by Dan Dailey, Jeanne Crain, Barbara Lawrence, and a chorus. Dan Dailey also sang it in *You're My Everything* (1949). A chorus sang it in *Picnic* (1955), and Carmen Cavallaro dubbed it in on the piano in *The Eddy Duchin Story* (1956).

Moderate foxtrot with two verses (16) and refrain (32)
PUBLISHER: Advanced Music Corp.
KEY: C maj., *STARTS*: a' (C maj.), *FORM*: AABA

≈≈≈≈≈≈≈≈≈≈≈≈≈≈≈≈≈≈≈≈

AMONG MY SOUVENIRS

WORDS: Edgar Leslie, *MUSIC*: Horatio Nicholls (pseudonym for Lawrence Wright))
INTRODUCED: in the United States by Paul Whiteman and his Orchestra

This charming ballad has a somewhat obscure creative history. It is alleged that the title and lyrics were written by Al Dubin – who later went on to a fruitful collaboration in Hollywood with Harry Warren – and sold to Edgar Leslie for $25. Supposedly, Dubin needed the money as stakes in a poker game. The credited composer, Horatio Nicholls, is actually a pseudonym for the English publisher and songwriter, Lawrence Wright. The song was first popularized in England by Jack Hylton and his Orchestra, and later in the United States by Paul Whiteman and his

Orchestra, in a Victor recording. Other early recordings were by Ben Selvin and his Orchestra, Roger Wolfe Kahn and his Orchestra, and The Revelers. In 1959, Connie Francis recorded it and, in 1976, Marty Robbins.

The refrain is a study in minimalism, with a scale-wise melody of few notes, each repeated once. There are, in fact, only six different pitches in each "A" section, with a range of only a minor sixth. The total range of the refrain is a mere seventh. Yet it is this very paucity of notes that makes the song so effective. Still, "Among My Souvenirs" is not quite as simple as it sounds. The last two sections of the refrain are each of nine measures, making the total length an unusual thirty-four bars.

Hoagy Carmichael sang it in the 1946 film, *The Best Years of Our Lives.*

Moderate ballad with two verses (8) and refrain (34)
PUBLISHER: Lawrence Wright Music Co. (London); De Sylva, Brown and Henderson (New York)
KEY: E-flat maj., *STARTS*: g' (E-flat maj.), *FORM*: AABA

≈≈≈≈≈≈≈≈≈≈≈≈≈≈≈≈≈≈

AT SUNDOWN (LOVE IS CALLING ME HOME)

WORDS and MUSIC: Walter Donaldson
INTRODUCED BY: Cliff Edwards (Ukelele Ike)
New York: The Palace Theatre

"At Sundown" is one of several songs with both words and music by Walter Donaldson, the prolific composer best known for his collaboration with lyricist Gus Kahn. Introduced by Cliff Edwards, it was popularized in a hit record by George Olsen and his Orchestra. Recordings by these and other performers sold more than two million copies in the song's first year.

It is a perky little song, distinguished by its four-note pickup at the words "Ev'ry little", and by its endearing four-bar phrases descending in skips and steps. In contrast, the "B" sections broaden out considerably, with long notes outlining chords of the ninth. A bit of the main theme returns to close out the refrain. The seldom-used subtitle emanates from the closing words: "When night is falling and love is calling me home".

"At Sundown" has been featured in an unusually long line of films. It was in Florenz Ziegfeld's *Glorifying the American Girl* (1930). Marsha Hunt sang it in *Music for Millions* (1944). It was featured in the films, *This Is the Life* (1944) and *Margie* (1946). The unlikely trio of Tommy Dorsey, Jimmy Dorsey, and Paul Whiteman sang it in the 1947 film, *The Fabulous*

Dorseys. Doris Day sang it in the 1955 biographical film of Ruth Etting, *Love Me or Leave Me*. Frank Sinatra sang it in *The Joker Is Wild* (1957). It was also featured in *The Rat Race* (1960). With its light syncopation, dotted rhythm, and jaunty melody, "At Sundown" is a tap-dancer's delight.

>Moderate foxtrot with verse (16) and refrain (32
>*PUBLISHER:* Leo Feist, Inc.
>*KEY:* F maj., *STARTS:* c" (G min.), *FORM:* ABAB'

≈≈≈≈≈≈≈≈≈≈≈≈≈≈≈≈≈≈≈

THE BEST THINGS IN LIFE ARE FREE * *

>*WORDS and MUSIC*: B. G.De Sylva, Lew Brown, and Ray Henderson
>*PREMIERE*: Musical comedy, *Good News*
>New York: 46th Street Theatre, 6 September 1927 (557 perf.)
>*INTRODUCED BY*: Mary Lawlor and John Price Jones

The musical comedy, *Good News,* had a collegiate motif. Even the ushers were dressed in college jerseys. So were George Olsen and his band, who rushed down the aisles into the orchestra pit. *Good News* epitomized the twenties, with its brassy sounds, its jazzy music, and its general air of hilarity. There were five hit songs by the team of De Sylva, Brown, and Henderson in the show, of which "The Best Things in Life Are Free" is the most enduring. The song's first recording was by George Olsen and his Orchestra, on Victor. It was revived in 1948, with recordings by Dinah Shore and Jo Stafford.

The broad melody of the refrain outlines first the C major and then the D minor chord in half notes. In contrast, the release features shorter notes and jazzy syncopation.

"The Best Things in Life Are Free" was performed by Mary Lawlor and Stanley Smith in the first film version of *Good News* (1930). In the second screen version (1947), it was sung by June Allison, Peter Lawford, and Mel Tormé. In the 1956 movie based on the lives of De Sylva, Brown, and Henderson, using the song title, *The Best Things In Life Are Free*, the quartet of Gordon MacRae, Ernest Borgnine, Sheree North, and Dan Dailey sang the rousing and boisterous song.

>Moderate rhythm song with verse (8) and refrain (32)
>*PUBLISHER:* Crawford Music Corporation
>*KEY*: C maj., *STARTS:* g' (C maj.), *FORM:* ABCA'

≈≈≈≈≈≈≈≈≈≈≈≈≈≈≈≈≈≈≈

BILL

WORDS: P. G. Wodehouse and Oscar Hammerstein II
MUSIC: Jerome Kern
PREMIERE: Musical play, *Show Boat*
New York: Ziegfeld Theatre, 27 December 1927 (572 perf.)

"Bill" has a long and interesting history. Written in 1918 by P. G Wodehouse and Jerome Kern for the Princess Theatre production of *Oh, Lady, Lady!*, it was dropped before the first performance. The song was tried again, this time as a vehicle for Marilyn Miller, in the 1920 show, *Sally*, but again was deemed unsuitable. It finally found a home as an interpolation to be sung by torch singer Helen Morgan in the first musical play, *Show Boat*. Hammerstein, who wrote the lyrics for most of the songs in that immortal show, is often credited as co-lyricist of "Bill". However, he himself always insisted that the lyrics for this song were written solely by Wodehouse. Although perhaps not as popular as the other great songs from *Show Boat*, "Bill" is a favorite of female singers; many include it in their repertoires, including Morgan herself, who recorded it for Victor and used it as her theme song throughout her career.

Wodehouse's lyrics are immediately striking. The verse tells a tale of looking for a perfect lover, "a God-like" kind of man. The refrain, on the contrary, says that Bill is "an ordinary boy" who is "not that type at all". This is one of those songs where music and words form a perfect marriage: one could not be conceived of without the other. Kern's poignant drop of a sixth at the beginning of each "A" section and in the final "C" section gives a special note of pathos to the haunting melody.

Helen Morgan sang "Bill" in both the 1929 and 1936 film versions of *Show Boat*. In the 1951 version, Annette Warren dubbed it in for Ava Gardner. Gogi Grant dubbed it for Ann Blyth in *The Helen Morgan Story* (1957), known in Britain as *Both Ends of the Candle*.

Slow ballad with two verses (16) and two refrains (16)
PUBLISHER: T. B. Harms Company
KEY: B-flat maj., *STARTS*: f' (B-flat maj.), *FORM*: ABA'C

≈≈≈≈≈≈≈≈≈≈≈≈≈≈≈≈≈≈≈≈

BLUE SKIES * *

WORDS and MUSIC: Irving Berlin
PREMIERE: Musical comedy, *Betsy*
New York: New Amsterdam Theatre, 28 December 1926 (39 perf.)
INTRODUCED BY: Belle Baker

The Ziegfeld show, *Betsy,* boasted a score by Rodgers and Hart and the singing talents of Belle Baker. Nevertheless, it was a dismal failure. But near the end of the show, Baker sang an interpolated song that was written expressly for her, an Irving Berlin number called "Blue Skies". The audience went wild and asked for and got twenty-four encores, the last of which she did together with Berlin, who was sitting in the first row. Recordings soon followed: by George Olsen and his Orchestra, Vincent Lopez and his Orchestra, and Harry Richman. Ben Selvin and his Orchestra had a No. 1 Chart Record. "Blue Skies" received an even wider audience when Al Jolson sang it in the first sound film, *The Jazz Singer* (1927). Over the years, the song's popularity never waned. Johnny Long and his Orchestra had a hit recording in 1941. The swing arrangement recorded by Benny Goodman and his Orchestra incited Berlin's wrath. No lover of jazz or swing, the composer commented to Goodman, somewhat ambiguously: "That was the most incredible playing I've ever heard". But then he added: "Never do that again!"

"Blue Skies" is one of Berlin's most likable songs. In conventional AABA form, each "A" section begins in E minor and modulates to G major. The release, in C minor, is reminiscent of Russian folk music out of Berlin's past. In the song, the word "blue" has different shades of meaning: a color, a feeling, or even a bird. And throughout the song, words and music form a perfect unity.

"Blue Skies" has had an illustrious film career. Besides *The Jazz Singer,* it was sung by Eddie Cantor in Florenz Ziegfeld's *Glorifying the American Girl* (1930). Alice Faye and Ethel Merman did it in *Alexander's Ragtime Band* (1938). Bing Crosby sang it in the film musical built around its title, *Blue Skies* (1946). Finally, Bing Crosby and Danny Kaye sang it in *White Christmas* (1954). Perhaps because of its interesting minor-major tonality, it remains one of the most-performed jazz standards.

> Moderate foxtrot with two verses (16) and refrain (32)
> *PUBLISHER*: Irving Berlin Music Corporation
> *KEY*: G maj., *STARTS*: e' (E min.), *FORM*: AABA

≈≈≈≈≈≈≈≈≈≈≈≈≈≈≈≈≈≈≈

CAN'T HELP LOVIN' DAT MAN * *!

> *WORDS*: Oscar Hammerstein II, *MUSIC*: Jerome Kern
> *PREMIERE*: Musical play, *Show Boat*
> New York: Ziegfeld Theatre, 27 December 1927 (572 perf.)
> *INTRODUCED BY:* Helen Morgan, Tess Gardella, Norma Terris,
> Allan Campbell, and Jules Bledsoe

In the first act of *Show Boat*, Julie (originally played by Helen Morgan) sings this showstopper, together with other characters playing Queenie, Magnolia, Joe, and Windy. An unusually powerful song, it was greatly popularized by Morgan.

The sheet music begins with a curious performance direction: "Tempo di Blues". And, indeed, the verse consists of two sections in twelve-bar blues form and is replete with flatted blue notes. The lyrics and the title are in dialect, using such colloquialisms as "It must be sumpin'" and "De chimbly's smokin'"; the opening words of the refrain are especially famous: "Fish got to swim and birds got to fly". The music of the refrain is much more conventional: thirty-two bars in AABA form. The only blue notes occur at the words "lovin' dat man" – the flatted sixth and third. Unusually for Kern, there is syncopation in the "A" section. The release is more characteristic of his style: it is more lyrical, using repeated notes rising inexorably to the song's highest note, at the word "fine" (f ").

"Can't Help Lovin' Dat Man" was performed in all three screen versions of *Show Boat*: in 1929, 1936 and 1951. Morgan sang it in 1929. In the 1936 version it was sung by Helen Morgan, Irene Dunne, Hattie McDaniel, Paul Robeson, and a chorus. In 1951, it was sung by Kathryn Grayson, and Annette Warren dubbing in for Ava Gardner. Lena Horne sang it in the Kern biographical film, *Till the Clouds Roll By* (1946). Gogi Grant dubbed it in for Ann Blyth in *The Helen Morgan Story*, known in Britain as *Both Ends of the Candle* (1957). It is a favorite of torch singers to this day.

Slow torch song with verse (24) and refrain (32)
PUBLISHER: T. B. Harms Company
KEY: E-flat maj., *STARTS*: b-flat' (E-flat maj.), *FORM*: AABA

≈≈≈≈≈≈≈≈≈≈≈≈≈≈≈≈≈≈≈

DIANE (I'M IN HEAVEN WHEN I SEE YOU SMILE)

WORDS and MUSIC: Erno Rapee and Lew Pollack
PREMIERE: Film, *Seventh Heaven*; William Fox, 1927

Written by the same songwriting team that produced "Charmaine" in 1926, "Diane" is very similar; it is a sentimental waltz with a soaring melody, simple harmonies, and a wide range. Billed as the "Love Waltz", it dominates the soundtrack of the movie, *Seventh Heaven*, starring Janet Gaynor and Charles Farrell. Gaynor won the first Academy Award for Best Actress for her role in that film about love in a garret in Paris. "Diane", like "Charmaine" before it, became a standard waltz. The first hit recording was by Nat Shilkret and his Orchestra (Victor). Mantovani and his Orchestra revived it with a hit recording in 1955; so did The Bachelors in 1964.

The music, by the Hungarian-born Erno Rapee, is in the style of early twentieth-century operetta. The refrain has only one theme, albeit a powerful one. The melody rises first stepwise and then by leaps, soaring to a range of an octave and a fourth in only four bars. Harmonies are mostly tonic and dominant, except for a brief excursion to A major at the end of the second section. The song survives as a romantic memory.

Moderate waltz with two verses (24) and refrain (32)
PUBLISHER: Sherman, Clay & Co. (San Francisco)
KEY: F maj., *STARTS*: c' (C7), *FORM*: AA'AA"

≈≈≈≈≈≈≈≈≈≈≈≈≈≈≈≈≈≈

GIRL OF MY DREAMS

WORDS and MUSIC: Sunny Clapp
INTRODUCED: as a Victor recording by Blue Steele and his Orchestra

An old fashioned waltz, "Girl of My Dreams" was popularized by singer Gene Austin, in a Victor recording, and later by Perry Como. Words and music hold few surprises. The melody of the refrain begins with eighth-note triplets going up the chromatic scale. There is some chromaticism in the main theme as well: the b-flat' and a-flat'. The release goes through the circle of fifths, from E seventh to A minor, and then from D seventh to G seventh. Lyrics are heartfelt and sincere: "Honest, I do". It is still a popular first dance at weddings.

Moderate waltz with two verses (16) and refrain (32)
PUBLISHER: Mills Music, Inc.
KEY: C maj., *STARTS*: e' (C maj.), *FORM*: AA'BA

≈≈≈≈≈≈≈≈≈≈≈≈≈≈≈≈≈≈

HALLELUJAH!

WORDS: Leo Robin and Clifford Grey, *MUSIC*: Vincent Youmans
PREMIERE: Musical Comedy, *Hit the Deck!*
New York: Belasco Theatre, 25 April 1927 (352 perf.)
INTRODUCED BY: Stella Mayhew and a chorus

During World War I, a young sailor named Vincent Youmans was stationed at the Great Lakes Naval Station in Illinois. It was there, in 1917, that he wrote a march that became a favorite of navy bands and, soon after, of John Philip Sousa, the greatest bandmaster of them all. Ten years later, in preparing songs for *Hit the Deck!* (a show about sailors), that march was given words and became "Hallelujah!". "Strutted rather than sung" by Stella Mayhew and a chorus of sailors, it stopped the show with each performance. "Hallelujah!" was criticized when *Hit the Deck!* reached London – it was thought that the use of the words meaning "Praise the Lord" in a popular song was sacrilegious. Nevertheless, the march's popularity never waned, aided by a recording by Nat Shilkret and his Orchestra.

The thirty-six bar verse could be a song in itself; it is in E-flat minor and has its own middle section. The song's instrumental origin is made apparent by its wide range (an octave and a half) and skipping melody (first outlining the E-flat major chord and then jumping a fifth, from b-flat to f", at the word "Hallelujah"). The release is especially interesting harmonically, descending by whole tones every two bars. But most striking of all is the offbeat syncopation in the "A" sections. Undoubtedly, that is what made the march so attractive to military and concert bands.

There were two screen versions of *Hit the Deck!* Marguerite Padula sang "Hallelujah!" in the 1929 one; Jane Powell, Tony Martin, Kay Armen, Vic Damone, Ross Tambly, and The Jubalaires sang it in the 1955 version.

Fast march with verse (36) and refrain (32)
PUBLISHER: Harms, Inc.
KEY: E-flat maj., *STARTS*: B-flat' (E-flat maj.), *FORM*: AABA

≈≈≈≈≈≈≈≈≈≈≈≈≈≈≈≈≈≈≈≈

HOW LONG HAS THIS BEEN GOING ON?   !

WORDS: Ira Gershwin, *MUSIC:* George Gershwin
PREMIERE: Operetta, *Rosalie*
New York: New Amsterdam Theatre, 10 January 1928 (335 perf.)
INTRODUCED BY: Bobbe Arnst

The operetta, *Rosalie*, produced by Florenz Ziegfeld, boasted two illustrious composers, Sigmund Romberg and George Gershwin. Of its many songs, this sentimental ballad by George and Ira Gershwin is the only survivor. It had been written as a duet for Adele Astaire and Jack Buchanan in *Funny Face*, but was discarded. It is reported that Ziegfeld was so taken with the song that he insisted it be used as a solo number in *Rosalie*. The song did not take on at first, but became a standard in the thirties after Peggy Lee recorded it with Benny Goodman and his Orchestra. Over the years, its sheer quality has kept the song alive.

Although designated "moderato" in the music, the song is usually performed in very slow tempo. The refrain shows George's propensity for the fifth and sixth degrees of the scale; it revolves largely around the notes d" and e", with an occasional blue note (b-flat') thrown in. Harmonies are innovative, starting with the dominant seventh and diminished seventh and moving to the C seventh and C minor. The release offers some light syncopation, and vacillates between the C major seventh and B minor. Ira's clever lyrics offer such contemporary delights as "What a break!" and "For Heaven's sake!"

Audrey Hepburn sang "How Long Has This Been Going On?" in the 1957 film musical, *Funny Face*. So it came about that this lovely ballad at last returned to the place of its origin.

Moderate ballad with two verses (24) and two refrains (32)
PUBLISHER: New World Music Corp.
KEY: G maj., *STARTS:* d" (D7), *FORM:* AABA

≈≈≈≈≈≈≈≈≈≈≈≈≈≈≈≈≈≈≈≈

I'M LOOKING OVER A FOUR LEAF CLOVER * *

WORDS: Mort Dixon, *MUSIC*: Harry Woods

This happy-go-lucky song was a pure product of Tin Pan Alley. It was popularized in recordings by Nick Lucas, Ben Bernie and his Orchestra, and virtually every other popular entertainer of the day, from Al Jolson to Eddie Cantor. It became popular all over again in 1948, when an Metro Goldwyn Mayer recording by Art Mooney and his Orchestra – featuring a rousing banjo solo by Mike Pingatore – sold over a million copies. At that time, the vintage song stayed on radio's *Your Hit Parade* for fourteen weeks.

It is an old-fashioned sort of song, in ABAC form. The verse is in G minor, while the refrain is in B-flat major. The simple melody outlines simple chords, making it very easy to sing.

Al Jolson dubbed it in for Larry Parks in the film, *Jolson Sings Again* (1953). Danny Thomas sang it in the 1953 remake of *The Jazz Singer*. Because of its blithe spirit and congeniality to the human voice, "I'm Looking Over a Four Leaf Clover" is especially favored at sing-alongs.

Moderate rhythm song with verse (16) and refrain (32)
PUBLISHER: Jerome H. Remick & Co.
KEY: B-flat maj., *STARTS*: b-flat' (B-flat maj.), *FORM:* ABAC

≈≈≈≈≈≈≈≈≈≈≈≈≈≈≈≈≈≈≈≈

JUST A MEMORY !

WORDS: B. G. De Sylva and Lew Brown, *MUSIC*: Ray Henderson
PREMIERE: Musical comedy, *Manhattan Mary*
New York: Apollo Theatre, 26 September 1927 (c. 256 perf.)
POPULARIZED BY: Paul Whiteman and his Orchestra

This haunting ballad came from a forgotten show called *Manhattan Mary*, which starred the irrepressible comic, Ed Wynn, playing a waiter named Crickets. It was popularized in recordings by the bands of Paul Whiteman (Victor) and Vincent Lopez (Brunswick).

The song has several interesting aspects. The verse is in 4/4 meter, while the refrain, with the unusual length of forty-seven bars, is in 2/4. Each of the "A" sections is eleven bars in length, while the release is fourteen. The melody of the refrain is built around a rising scale, with repeated notes going first to a-flat' and then to a' natural, accompanied first by a D-flat major chord and then by an F major. The release, in B-flat major, uses similar melodic material. The total effect is one of nostalgia; a perfect complement to the lyrics.

"Just a Memory" was featured in the 1949 film, *Look For the Silver Lining*. Eileen Wilson dubbed it in for Sheree North, who sang it with a chorus in the 1956 film, *The Best Things in Life Are Free*. And Gogi Grant dubbed it in for Ann Blyth in *The Helen Morgan Story* (1957), known in Britain as *Both Ends of the Candle*.

Slow ballad with verse (8) and refrain (47)
PUBLISHER: Harms, Inc.
KEY: F maj., *STARTS*: c' (F maj.), *FORM*: AABA'

≈≈≈≈≈≈≈≈≈≈≈≈≈≈≈≈≈≈≈

MAKE BELIEVE * *

WORDS: Oscar Hammerstein II, *MUSIC*: Jerome Kern
PREMIERE: Musical play, *Show Boat*
New York: Ziegfeld Theatre, 27 December 1927 (572 perf.)
INTRODUCED BY: Howard Marsh and Norma Terris

In *Show Boat*, the riverboat gambler, Gaylord Ravenal, professes his love for Magnolia, the Captain's daughter, in this touching duet, originally titled "Only Make Believe". It remains one of the most popular songs to emanate from that landmark musical.

Both verse and refrain are of melodic interest; the former using repeated phrasing, the latter with a beautiful, soaring melody. In the verse, two notes are often sung to only one syllable, a practice acceptable in operetta, but rare in popular songs of the day. The refrain begins with a held note (fermata) on a diminished chord and then proceeds with a pickup of dotted quarter and eighth. This rhythmic motive reappears throughout the refrain. The range is wide (an octave and a fourth) and there are numerous jumps of the fifth and octave. The postlude, which is rarely performed, is a little waltz in which the singer begs pardon for presuming to "make believe" they're in love. The lyrics splendidly portray the game of "just supposing".

Irene Dunne and Allan Jones sang "Make Believe" in the second film version of *Show Boat* (1936). Kathryn Grayson and Tony Martin sang it in the 1946 Kern biographical film, *Till the Clouds Roll By.* Grayson and Howard Keel performed it in the third screen version of *Show Boat* (1951).

Slow ballad with verse (17), refrain (32), and postlude (16)
PUBLISHER: T. B. Harms Company
KEY: C maj., *STARTS*: g' (G7), *FORM*: ABAC/A'

≈≈≈≈≈≈≈≈≈≈≈≈≈≈≈≈≈≈≈

ME AND MY SHADOW

WORDS: Billy Rose, *MUSIC*: Al Jolson and Dave Dreyer
PREMIERE: Revue, *Delmar's Revels*
New York: Shubert Theatre, 28 November 1927 (c. 112 perf.)
INTRODUCED BY: Frank Fay

Ted Lewis popularized this soft-shoe number in vaudeville, along with his "shadow", played by Eddie Chester, who imitated his every movement and gesture. It was always a sure audience-pleaser. Among many recordings over the years are those of Pearl Bailey and the duo of Frank Sinatra and Sammy Davis, Jr.

The refrain begins with a whole note and two halves, spelling out the E-flat major triad, and moves unexpectedly to b natural' before sliding to c" – a bit of teasing chromaticism. The lyrics include the debonair phrase, "strolling down the avenue".

In the movies, Ted Lewis sang it in *Hold That Ghost* (1941), Donald O'Connor in *Feudin', Fussin', and A-Fightin'* (1948), and James Caan in *Funny Lady* (1975).

Moderate foxtrot with two verses (16) and refrain (32)
PUBLISHER: Irving Berlin, Inc. (Bourne, Inc.)
KEY: E-flat maj., *STARTS*: e-flat' (E-flat maj.), *FORM*: AA'BA

≈≈≈≈≈≈≈≈≈≈≈≈≈≈≈≈≈≈≈

MY BLUE HEAVEN * *

WORDS: George Whiting, *MUSIC*: Walter Donaldson
INTRODUCED: in vaudeville by George Whiting

It is reported that the celebrated standard "My Blue Heaven" was conceived by its composer, Walter Donaldson, in 1924, while he was waiting for a game of billiards at the Friars Club in New York. It was first performed by its lyricist, George Whiting, as part of his vaudeville act. It was also performed on radio by singer Tommy Lyman, who kept it as his theme song. Three years later, it was interpolated in *Ziegfeld Follies of 1927*, with Eddie Cantor singing it in blackface and white gloves. A year later, a Victor record by singer Gene Austin sold over five million copies; Austin used it as his theme song thereafter. It was revived in 1939, with a recording by Jimmy Lunceford and his Orchestra.

The lyrics are rather old-fashioned: "When whippoorwills call / And evening is nigh". As in "Tea for Two" (1924), they paint a picture of domestic tranquillity, with "Just Molly and me / And baby makes three". The melody is simple, outlining chords of the E-flat sixth and two of its inversions. The release is based on two descending scales, with each note repeated. Of such simple ingredients is a great standard made.

"My Blue Heaven" has been heard in many movies. Frances Langford sang it in *Never a Dull Moment* (1943). Gene Austin repeated his success with the song in 1944 in *Moon Over Las Vegas*. It was the title of a film, *My Blue Heaven*, in 1950, in which it was sung by Betty Grable and Dan Dailey. Doris Day did it in *Love Me or Leave Me*, in 1955. Bob Crosby sang it in the 1959 film, *The Five Pennies*. In 1972, Peter O'Toole and Carolyn Seymour performed it in the British film, *The Ruling Class*. And Fats Domino did it in the 1973 film, *Let the Good Times Roll*. It is regularly performed to this day, both as a ballad and as an up-tempo jazz standard.

Moderate ballad with two verses (16) and refrain (32)
PUBLISHER: Leo Feist, Inc.
KEY: E-flat maj., *STARTS*: g' (E-flat maj.), *FORM*: AABA

≈≈≈≈≈≈≈≈≈≈≈≈≈≈≈≈≈≈≈

MY HEART STOOD STILL * *

WORDS: Lorenz Hart, *MUSIC*: Richard Rodgers
PREMIERE: Musical comedy, *A Connecticut Yankee*
New York: Vanderbilt Theatre, 3 November 1927 (418 perf.)
INTRODUCED BY: William Gaxton and Constance Carpenter

It is said that the title of this tender ballad came from the mouth of a female passenger in a Parisian taxicab; after a near-accident, she loudly exclaimed: "My heart stood still". Richard Rodgers duly wrote the phrase down and set it to music. Lorenz Hart's lyrics followed soon after. Back in London, the Prince of Wales was charmed by the song and requested it from the Teddy Brown Orchestra. After it was interpolated in the London revue, *One Dam Thing After Another* (sung by Jessie Matthews and Richard Dolman), the song created a sensation in Britain. Wanting to use it in the American production of *A Connecticut Yankee*, Rodgers and Hart were required to buy back the rights to the song from the London revue's producer. This they did, and a hit was born, popularized by the recordings of George Olsen and his Orchestra and Ben Selvin and his Orchestra. The song became popular again in 1943, with a revival of *A Connecticut Yankee* in New York.

The verse, in male and female versions, is harmonically complex, moving stepwise from F major to E-flat major to D-flat major, and then to A major and C major. In contrast, the harmonies of the refrain are simple, staying in F major except for a brief diversion to F minor in the release. The melody is a model of stepwise procedure, moving downward in almost childlike patterns of three notes, starting respectively on f', g', a', b-flat', and c". The climax of the song, and its highest point occurs in the last section: the d" at the word "thrill".

"My Heart Stood Still" was heard in the 1931 film, *A Connecticut Yankee*, as well as in the Rodgers and Hart biographical film, *Words and Music* of 1948, in which it underscored the depiction of Hart's untimely death five years before.

Slow ballad with two verses (16) and refrain (32)
PUBLISHER: Harms, Inc.
KEY: F maj., *STARTS*: f' (F maj.), *FORM*: AA'BA'

≈≈≈≈≈≈≈≈≈≈≈≈≈≈≈≈≈≈≈

OL' MAN RIVER * * *!

WORDS: Oscar Hammerstein II, *MUSIC*: Jerome Kern
PREMIERE: Musical play, *Show Boat*
New York: Ziegfeld Theatre, 27 December 1927 (572 perf.)
INTRODUCED BY: Jules Bledsoe and the Jubilee Singers

The big song from the epochal *Show Boat*, and certainly its best known, is this powerful ballad. It was sung in the original production by Jules Bledsoe, but it was the bass-baritone Paul Robeson who made it famous. The latter's Victor recording, with Paul Whiteman and his Orchestra, brought the song national attention (Whiteman had previously recorded it with Bing Crosby). Robeson also sang it in the 1932 revival of *Show Boat*, the first of many to come. The melody of "Ol' Man River" was the subject of a plagiarism suit in 1928, claiming similarity to "Long-Haired Mamma", by Maury Madison, published in 1927. However, nothing more was heard about the suit.

It is an extraordinarily emotional song, propelled by Hammerstein's forceful lyrics and Kern's dramatic music. The lyrics are in dialect – acceptable at the time – with plenty of "dem"s and "dats"s. The verse is almost always performed along with the refrain; in fact, the verse's secondary theme, in G minor, is identical to the theme of the release. It is hard to say why the song has so much impact. The lyrics certainly have a lot to do with it. So does the melody's inexorable rise from its lowest point (b-flat') to its highest (g"). Like its mighty subject, the Mississippi River, the music can only be described as majestic.

Jules Bledsoe again sang "Ol' Man River", with a chorus, in the 1929 film version of *Show Boat*. Paul Robeson and a chorus did it in the 1936 version. Caleb Peterson and a chorus sang it, and Frank Sinatra reprised it, in the 1946 Kern biographical film, *Till the Clouds Roll By*. Finally, William Warfield and a chorus did it in the 1951 film version of *Show Boat*.

Slow ballad with verse (25) and refrain (32)
PUBLISHER: T. B. Harms Company
KEY: E-flat maj., *STARTS*: b-flat (E-flat maj.), *FORM*: AA'BA"

≈≈≈≈≈≈≈≈≈≈≈≈≈≈≈≈≈

SOMETIMES I'M HAPPY

WORDS: Irving Caesar, *MUSIC:* Vincent Youmans
PREMIERE: Musical Comedy, *Hit the Deck!*
New York: Belasco Theatre, 25 April 1927 (352 perf.)
INTRODUCED BY: Charles King and Louise Groody

Vincent Youmans's melody for this sprightly song was first used in 1923, for a song provocatively called "Come On and Pet Me", written for a show called *Mary Jane McKane* but dropped before the show opened. Two years later, with new lyrics by Irving Caesar, it became "Sometimes I'm Happy", written for a show called *A Night Out*, which never reached Broadway. Finally, four years after its birth, the song found a home in the musical comedy, *Hit the Deck!* The song was revived in 1935, with a hit Victor record by Benny Goodman and his Orchestra.

The melody of the refrain is rather eccentric, built around a chromatic motive: g-sharp' - a' - a' - a' - b- flat'. The words "blue" and "you" are each given two musical notes: a' and g'. In the "B" sections, a blue note, the lowered seventh, is emphasized.

Polly Walker and Jack Oakie sang "Sometimes I'm Happy" in the first screen version of *Hit the Deck!* (1930). Jane Powell and Vic Damone sang it in the second screen version (1955). Although written as a love song to be played in slow tempo, the song is almost always played in moderate to fast tempo and is a favorite subject for jazz improvisation.

Slow ballad with two verses (24) and refrain (32)
PUBLISHER: Harms, Inc.
KEY: F maj., *STARTS*: g-sharp' (E maj.), *FORM*: ABAB'

≈≈≈≈≈≈≈≈≈≈≈≈≈≈≈≈≈≈≈

STOUTHEARTED MEN

WORDS: Oscar Hammerstein II, *MUSIC*: Sigmund Romberg
PREMIERE: Operetta, *The New Moon*
New York: Imperial Theatre, 19 September 1927 (509 perf.)
INTRODUCED BY: Robert Halliday, William O'Neal, and The Male Chorus

This stirring march, originally called "Shoulder to Shoulder", was a highlight of the operetta, *The New Moon*. That show, which had opened and closed at the beginning of 1927, was extensively revised and recast. "Stouthearted Men" was the only song to survive from the original production. Robust singers like Lawrence Tibbett and Nelson Eddy did much to popularize the song, and it has lasted through the years. Barbara Streisand recorded it as a ballad in 1967, and in 1978 it was featured in the Bob Fosse revue, *Dancin'*.

Both verse and refrain are integral parts of the march. The verse, in F minor, is like a clarion call with the answering accompaniment of eighth-note triplets. The refrain, in dotted rhythm, chiefly plays around three notes: f', e', and d'. In contrast to the two "A" sections in common time, the two "B" sections are in 2/4 meter.

Lawrence Tibbett and a chorus sang "Stouthearted Men" in the first film version of *The New Moon* in 1930. Nelson Eddy and a chorus sang it in the second film version (1940). Helen Traubel sang it in the Sigmund Romberg biographical film, *Deep in My Heart* (1954).

Moderate march with verse (20) and refrain (28)
PUBLISHER: Harms, Inc.
KEY: F maj., *STARTS*: f' (F maj.), *FORM*: AABB'

≈≈≈≈≈≈≈≈≈≈≈≈≈≈≈≈≈≈≈

STRIKE UP THE BAND *

WORDS: Ira Gershwin, *MUSIC*: George Gershwin
PREMIERE: Musical play, *Strike Up the Band*
Philadelphia: 5 September 1927
New York: Times Square Theatre, 14 January 1930
INTRODUCED BY: Jim Townsend, Jerry Goff and Chorus, with Red Nichols and his Orchestra

A majestic march, with its refrain proudly beginning "Let the drums roll out!", "Strike Up the Band" did not become popular until three years after it was written. The first production of the show, *Strike Up the Band,* died in Philadelphia in 1927. It took almost three years for a greatly revised show to reach New York. When it did, both the show and its title song became hits. In the orchestra pit in the 1930 production, the Red Nichols band had a formidable array of musicians, including Benny Goodman, Gene Krupa, Jimmy Dorsey, Jack Teagarden, and Glenn Miller. More than half a century later, the song "Strike Up the Band" was again featured on Broadway in the retrospective Gershwin revue, *My One and Only* (1983).

The verse, in recitative style, has many repeated notes. The refrain, like a military flourish, consists of a motive of dotted notes, each last note of which goes up a half step for the entire first half of the song, from g' to e-flat". Slowly descending in the "C" section, the refrain ends with a paraphrase of the beginning motive.

Judy Garland and Mickey Rooney sang "Strike Up the Band" as the finale of the 1940 film of the same name. Judy Garland sang it solo in the 1942 film, *For Me and My Gal.*

Slow march with verse (26) and two refrains (32)
PUBLISHER: New World Music Corp.
KEY: B-flat maj., *STARTS*: f' (B-flat maj.), *FORM*: ABCA'

≈≈≈≈≈≈≈≈≈≈≈≈≈≈≈≈≈≈≈

SUGAR

WORDS and MUSIC: Sidney Mitchell, Edna Alexander, and Maceo Pinkard
POPULARIZED BY: Ethel Waters

Alternatively known as "That Sugar Baby o' Mine", this catchy song is still favored by jazz groups. Originally recorded by Ethel Waters (Columbia), there have been many recordings over the years, including those of Louis Armstrong, Count Basie, Teddy Wilson, and Bix Beiderbecke. The lyrics are sprinkled with all kinds of sweet words, ranging from "she's granulated" and "so confectionery" to "tutti frutti". The syncopated verse has the same rhythm as "Charleston" (1923). In the more subdued refrain, dotted quarters and eighths predominate. "Sugar" enjoyed a revival in 1955 after Peggy Lee performed it in the film *Pete Kelly's Blues.*

Moderate rhythm song with two verses (16) and refrain (32)
PUBLISHER: W. C. Handy Music Publisher
KEY: G maj., *STARTS*: b' (G maj.), *FORM*: AA'BA"

≈≈≈≈≈≈≈≈≈≈≈≈≈≈≈≈≈≈≈

'S WONDERFUL * * *

WORDS: Ira Gershwin, *MUSIC*: George Gershwin
PREMIERE: Musical comedy, *Funny Face*
New York: Alvin Theatre, 22 November 1927 (244 perf.)
INTRODUCED BY: Adele Astaire and Allen Kearns

The musical comedy, *Funny Face,* started out in Philadelphia as *Smarty.* When it reached Broadway as *Funny Face,* it was a showplace of fine songs by the Gershwins, of which this one is best known. The first recording was by Frank Crumit. In 1983, "'S Wonderful" returned to

Broadway in the Gershwin retrospective, *My One and Only*, sung and danced to by Tommy Tune and Twiggy.

The song's most striking characteristic lies in its lyrics, with their manifold contraction of "it's" to "'s". The music of the refrain plays around two notes a minor third apart, b-flat' and g', repeated each time to different harmonies. The release, in G major, has a plethora of repeated d"s. Despite the seeming monotony and simplicity of the melody, the song is rescued by its charming rhythm and subtle harmonic changes.

In the movies, Louise Hogan dubbed it in for Joan Leslie in the 1945 Gershwin biography, *Rhapsody in Blue*. In 1951, Doris Day sang it in *Starlift*, and Georges Guetary and Gene Kelly performed it, unforgettably, in *An American in Paris*. Fred Astaire and Audrey Hepburn sang it in the 1957 film production of *Funny Face*. The overall effect of this sparkling standard and its endurance over the years can be summed up in three syllables: "'S Wonderful".

> Moderate foxtrot with two verses (24) and refrain (32)
> *PUBLISHER*: New World Music Corp.
> *KEY*: E-flat maj., *STARTS*: b-flat' (E-flat maj.), *FORM*: AA'BA"

≈≈≈≈≈≈≈≈≈≈≈≈≈≈≈≈≈≈≈

THOU SWELL * *

> *WORDS*: Lorenz Hart, *MUSIC*: Richard Rodgers
> *PREMIERE*: Musical comedy, *A Connecticut Yankee*
> New York: Vanderbilt Theatre, 3 November 1927 (418 perf.)
> *INTRODUCED BY:* William Gaxton and Constance Carpenter

Marked "In a jolly tempo", this bubbly song is another survivor from *A Connecticut Yankee*, the long-running show that was inspired by Mark Twain's book, *A Connecticut Yankee in King Arthur's Court*.

Lorenz Hart's lyrics are a delightful mix of contemporary and Arthurian allusions, such as "Wouldst kiss me pretty?", "Hear me holler", and of course "Thou swell". Richard Rodgers's music is most inventive. The verse is strongly syncopated, with a jagged melody containing many skips of the sixth. Skipping and syncopation also characterize the refrain; especially effective is the downward jump of a fifth at the words "witty" and "pretty" and the ragtime-like syncopation at the words, "I choose a sweet lollapaloosa in thee".

"Thou Swell" was featured in the 1931 screen version of *A Connecticut Yankee*. June Allyson and The Blackburn Twins sang it in the

1948 Rodgers and Hart biographical film, *Words and Music*. It is often performed as a jazz standard in fast tempo.

> Moderate rhythm song with two verses (24) and refrain (32)
> *PUBLISHER*: Harms, Inc.
> *KEY*: E-flat maj., *STARTS*: g' (B-flat 7), *FORM*: ABAB'/A

≈≈≈≈≈≈≈≈≈≈≈≈≈≈≈≈≈≈

WHY DO I LOVE YOU? * *

> *WORDS*: Oscar Hammerstein II, *MUSIC*: Jerome Kern
> *PREMIERE*: Musical play, *Show Boat*
> New York: Ziegfeld Theatre, 27 December 1927 (572 perf.)
> *INTRODUCED BY:* Norma Terris, Howard Marsh, Edna May Oliver, and Charles Winninger

Still another lasting song from the epochal *Show Boat*, this ingratiating ballad was reportedly written during the show's tryout in Pittsburgh. Norma Terris, who played Magnolia, had asked for a comfortable song to sing in Act II. At rehearsal the next morning, Jerome Kern and Oscar Hammerstein II handed her the sheet music saying, "We sat up all night writing this".

Marked "tenderly", the refrain is indeed tender in both words and music: uncomplicated in melody, harmony, rhythm, and wording. Kern's melody repeats such five-note phrases as "Why do I love you?", "Why do you love me", and "How can any two?" The net effect is one of charming simplicity.

Allen Jones and Irene Dunne sang "Why Do I Love You" in the 1936 film version of *Show Boat*. Howard Keel and Kathryn Grayson performed it in the 1951 screen version.

> Moderate ballad with verse (4) and refrain (32)
> *PUBLISHER*: T. B. Harms Company
> *KEY*: A-flat maj., *STARTS*: a-flat' (A-flat maj.), *FORM*: ABAB'

≈≈≈≈≈≈≈≈≈≈≈≈≈≈≈≈≈≈

1928

MAKING WHOOPEE

1928

"People say, in Boston, even beans do it".

Cole Porter
"Let's Do It (Let's Fall in Love)"

In this year of wonderful prosperity, songs reflect the times in their uninhibited gleefulness. Some of the most frenetic standards erupt this year, a litany of songs that radiate happiness to this day: "Button Up Your Overcoat", "Crazy Rhythm", "I Can't Give You Anything But Love (Baby)", "Sweet Lorraine", and, of course, "Makin' Whoopee". Amid all this frivolity, there is little call for love ballads. Nevertheless, there are a few: the poignant "I'll Get By (As Long As I Have You)", the wrenching "Love Me or Leave Me", and the sentimental "Lover, Come Back to Me!" Still, the main idea in this year of plentiful bootleg hooch seems to be to keep the beat rolling and the skirts swirling to the rhythms of songs like "Sweet Sue", "When You're Smiling (The Whole World Smiles with You)", and "You're the Cream in My Coffee".

With stock prices soaring ever higher, it is not surprising that Herbert Hoover, the Republican, is elected President over Alfred E. Smith, the Democratic governor of New York; the people always vote for prosperity. But it is a nasty and divisive campaign, pitting urban vs. rural, wet vs. dry, Catholic vs. Protestant, North and East vs. South and West. Elsewhere, there is little news: just the economy booming away and Amelia Earhart becoming the first woman to fly the Atlantic.

Radio is still the great diversion. Amos 'n' Andy begin their regular broadcasting on NBC, sponsored by Pepsodent, every weekday night from 7:00 to 7:15 PM. And new-fangled talking pictures are slowly spreading their wings. A little rodent named Mickey Mouse does his first talkie: a cartoon called *Steamboat Willie*, using the voice of his master, Walt Disney. Every major studio rushes to make talking pictures, although this year they produce little more than Al Jolson's *The Singing Fool* and Fanny Brice's *My Man*.

Broadway is another story: it is flourishing. There is Eugene O'Neill's long play *Strange Interlude*, which wins the Pulitzer Prize; Mae West in *Diamond Lil* (she and her entire cast make a well-publicized trip to the lockup); and Charles MacArthur and Ben Hecht's hit play, *Front Page*, starring Lee Tracy. If one seeks comedy, one can enjoy the four Marx Brothers in *Animal Crackers*, W. C. Fields in *Vanities*, Victor Moore and Bert Lahr in *Hold Everything*, or Will Rogers in *Three Cheers*. Musicals are in abundance, too, with the all-black revue, *Blackbirds of 1928*, and Eddie Cantor's *Whoopee* for starters. There is even an old-fashioned operetta, a reminder of the golden days, *The New Moon*, with romantic music by Sigmund Romberg and Oscar Hammerstein II. But in this roaring year of 1928, that lovely reminiscence of times past can hardly be heard above the brassy and strident sounds of a populace making whoopee.

SONGS OF 1928

Basin Street Blues
Button Up Your Overcoat *
Crazy Rhythm **
Honey
I Can't Give You Anything But Love (Baby) ***
If I Had You **
I'll Get By (As Long As I Have You) **
Let's Do It (Let's Fall in Love) ***!
Love Me or Leave Me
Lover, Come Back to Me! *
Makin' Whoopee! ***
Marie
One Kiss
(I Got a Woman Crazy for Me)
    She's Funny That Way *
Sonny Boy
Sweet Lorraine **
Sweet Sue – Just You *
Together
When You're Smiling
    (The Whole World Smiles with You)
You Took Advantage of Me
You're the Cream in My Coffee

BASIN STREET BLUES

WORDS and MUSIC: Spencer Williams
INTRODUCED: in a Vocalion recording by trumpeter and vocalist,
Louis Armstrong, accompanied by pianist Earl "Fatha" Hines and
drummer Zutty Singleton

This jazz standard about the famous street in New Orleans seems much older than it really is. One of many written by Spencer Williams (with the uncredited assistance of Glenn Miller on the verse), it was introduced by Louis Armstrong and popularized in a Columbia recording by a group known as The Charleston Chasers, led by Benny Goodman, with vocal by trombonist Jack Teagarden. Goodman and his Orchestra recorded it in 1934, and Bing Crosby and Connee Boswell in 1937.

Both verse are refrain are integral parts of the song. Despite its title, the song is not in twelve-bar blues form, but rather in two sections of sixteen bars each. Prominent in the verse are blue notes (flatted sevenths). The melody of the refrain consists of many repeated notes over the familiar harmonic progression of the circle of fifths: D seventh, G seventh, C seventh, F seventh, B-flat major.

Louis Armstrong played and sang "Basin Street Blues" in three films: *New Orleans* (1947), *The Strip* (1951), and *The Glenn Miller Story* (1951).

Moderate rhythm song with verse (16) and refrain (16)
PUBLISHER: Edwin H. Morris & Company, Inc.
KEY: B-flat maj., *STARTS*: d' (B-flat maj.), *FORM* (Overall): AABB'

≈≈≈≈≈≈≈≈≈≈≈≈≈≈≈≈≈≈≈≈≈

BUTTON UP YOUR OVERCOAT *

WORDS: B. G. De Sylva and Lew Brown, *MUSIC*: Ray Henderson
PREMIERE: Musical comedy, *Follow Thru.*
New York: Forty-Sixth Street Theatre, 9 January 1929 (403 perf.)
INTRODUCED BY: Jack Haley and Zelma O'Neal

Follow Thru was a show about golfing that punningly advertised itself as "a musical slice of country club life". This lively song, sung by Jack Haley (in his first important comic role) and Zelma O'Neal, was a show-stopper. Since the show opened in the dead of winter, the very idea of buttoning up against the cold was heart-warming. "Button Up Your Overcoat" was an immediate hit, with early recordings by Paul Whiteman and his Orchestra (Victor), Helen Kane (Victor), Ruth Etting Columbia), and Fred Waring's Pennsylvanians. In later years, the song enjoyed a long run on television in commercials for Contac cold medication.

The lyrics are simple but striking, admonishing the loved one to "take good care of yourself / You belong to me". Prohibition also gets its innings, as in "Keep away from bootleg hooch / When you're on a spree". The release, too, has its share of cuteness with the threefold use of the exclamation "Oo-oo!" – particularly effective in the recording of Helen Kane, the original "Boop-oop-a-doop" girl. The melody is a perfect match in cuteness, moving daintily down the scale and then suddenly rising an octave.

Jack Haley and Zelma O'Neal repeated their success with the song in the 1930 film version of *Follow Thru*. In 1956, the unlikely quartet of Gordon MacRae, Ernest Borgnine, Sheree North and Dan Dailey sang it in the De Sylva, Brown, and Henderson film biography, *The Best Things in Life Are Free*.

> Moderate foxtrot with two verses (16) and two refrains (32)
> *PUBLISHER*: De Sylva, Brown and Henderson, Inc.
> *KEY*: G maj., *STARTS*: d" (G maj.), *FORM*: AABA

≋≋≋≋≋≋≋≋≋≋≋≋≋≋≋≋≋

CRAZY RHYTHM * *

> *WORDS*: Irving Caesar, *MUSIC*: Joseph Meyer and Roger Wolfe Kahn
> *PREMIERE*: Musical comedy, *Here's Howe*
> New York: Broadhurst Theatre, May 1928 (c. 64 perf.)
> *INTRODUCED BY*: Ben Bernie, Peggy Chamberlain, and June O'Dea

The musical comedy, *Here's Howe*, boasted a score by Irving Caesar, Joseph Meyer, and Roger Wolfe Kahn – the latter, son of banker and Metropolitan Opera benefactor, Otto Kahn. Although the show was not a success, it had one song that took the audience by storm, "Crazy Rhythm". Later the same year, the song was interpolated in another musical, *Luckee Girl*, which was also a failure. However, Roger Wolfe Kahn, who led his own band, had a popular Victor recording which helped make the song a hit, as did Ben Bernie and his Orchestra with a Brunswick recording.

The riff-like music of the refrain consists of a single two-bar syncopated motive, playing around the notes a', g', and f-sharp', that is endlessly repeated. Different pitches are introduced in the release and at the very end of the refrain, but the "crazy rhythm" stays the same throughout. The words bear a striking resemblance to dummy lyrics: "What's the use of Prohibition / You provide the same condition".

In the movies, Dan Dailey sang "Crazy Rhythm" in *You Were Meant for Me* (1948) and Patrice Wymore and Gene Nelson in *Tea for Two* (1950). Its infectious rhythmic pattern and unchanging harmonies make it a natural for jazz improvisation, often in upbeat tempo.

Moderate rhythm song with two verses (16) and refrain (32)
PUBLISHER: Harms, Inc.
KEY: G maj., *STARTS:* e" (G maj.), *FORM:* AABA'

≋≋≋≋≋≋≋≋≋≋≋≋≋≋≋≋≋≋≋

HONEY

WORDS and MUSIC: Seymour Simons, Haven Gillespie, and Richard A. Whiting
POPULARIZED: in a Victor recording by Rudy Vallee and his Orchestra

Rudy Vallee's Victor recording of this bouncy little song was a hit; and "Honey" eventually sold over a million copies of sheet music. The sixteen-bar refrain consists almost entirely of dotted quarters and eighths. The harmonically-derived melody outlines simple chords (F major sixth, G dominant seventh, C dominant seventh, F major...), each lasting for two measures. "Honey" was featured in the 1945 film, *Her Highness and the Bellboy*, starring Hedy Lamarr, Robert Walker, and June Allyson.

Moderate foxtrot with two verses (16) and refrain (16)
PUBLISHER: Leo Feist, Inc.
KEY: F maj., *STARTS:* c' (F6), *FORM:* ABA'C

≋≋≋≋≋≋≋≋≋≋≋≋≋≋≋≋≋≋≋

I CAN'T GIVE YOU ANYTHING BUT LOVE (BABY) * * *

WORDS: Dorothy Fields, *MUSIC:* Jimmy McHugh
PREMIERE: Revue, *Lew Leslie's Blackbirds of 1928*
New York: Liberty Theatre, 9 May 1928 (518 perf.)
INTRODUCED BY: Aida Ward and Willard McLean

This sturdy standard was written for Patsy Kelly to sing in the 1927 revue, *Harry Delmar's Revels,* but was dropped from the show. It was originally titled "I Can't Give You Anything But Love, Lindy". Retrieved for the all-black revue, *Lew Leslie's Blackbirds of 1928*, it was an immediate hit. The song was said to have been inspired by a bit of eavesdropping by its creators, Dorothy Fields and Jimmy McHugh, who overheard a poor couple's conversation as they were gazing at the treasures in Tiffany's window. Ironically, such complaints were to become commonplace after the crash, little more than a year later. The song quickly caught on, with hit recordings by Cliff Edwards and Gene Austin. Over the years it has seen a multitude of recordings, including a notable one by Billie Holiday and Teddy Wilson in 1936. In 1948, Rose Murphy recorded it for Majestic, substituting "che-chee" for "baby". Fifty years after it was written, it was presented as a Fats Waller song in the retrospective revue, *Ain't Misbehavin'*, which opened at the Longacre Theatre in New York 9 May 1978. According to the producers, Waller wrote the music to this as well as "On the Sunny Side of the Street" (1930) and sold them to Jimmy McHugh – a common practice at the time. A year later, the song was performed by Ann Miller and Mickey Rooney in the revue, *Sugar Babies*, which opened at the Mark Hellinger Theatre 8 October 1979 and had an astounding run of 1,208 performances.

Despite all that background, it is a very simple song. The verse, starting with the words; "Gee, but it's tough to be broke", is heavily syncopated. In contrast, the refrain consists mostly of quarter notes, with syncopated slurs occurring each time the word "baby" is intoned. There is a break at the close of the "B" section. Fields's words are provocative, with such contemporary references as "Diamond bracelets Woolworth doesn't sell, baby".

As befits a world-class standard, there are an astounding number of screen credits. Cary Grant and Katherine Hepburn sang it in *Bringing Up Baby* (1938). In 1940, it was featured in the film, *I Can't Give You Anything But Love,* and Marlene Dietrich sang it in *Seven Sinners*. It was heard in *True to the Army* in 1942 and, in 1943, Lena Horne and Bill Robinson sang it in *Stormy Weather*. Louis Armstrong sang it in *Jam Session* in 1944 and Judy Holliday in *Born Yesterday* in 1950. Gloria De Haven did it in *So This Is Paris* (1954), and Gogi Grant dubbed it in for Ann Blyth in *The Helen Morgan Story* (1957)– known as *Both Sides of the Candle* in Britain. Rudy Vallee sang it in *The Grissom Gang* (1971). And finally, Ethel Waters belted out her version in the 1984 film, *The Cotton Club*. A very adaptable song, this erstwhile ballad is usually performed as a jazz standard, in moderate to fast tempo.

Moderate foxtrot with two verses (16) and refrain (32)
PUBLISHER: Jack Mills, Inc.
KEY: G maj. or A-flat maj., *STARTS*: g' (G maj.) or a-flat' (A-flat maj),
FORM: ABA'C

≈≈≈≈≈≈≈≈≈≈≈≈≈≈≈≈≈≈≈≈

IF I HAD YOU * *

WORDS and MUSIC: Ted Shapiro, Jimmy Campbell, and Reg Connelly
POPULARIZED: on radio and recording by Rudy Vallee and his Connecticut Yankees

An English import, "If I Had You" was advertised as "The Prince of Wales' Favourite Fox-Trot". Stateside, it was one of Rudy Vallee's first recordings (Harmony), performed with his Connecticut Yankees – newly named after the Rodgers and Hart show of 1927. Art Bowlly also had a popular recording on Brunswick. The melody is repetitive, with the chromatic passage d"-d"-d-flat"-c" heard twelve times in the refrain – three times in each "A" section. The release, in D minor, affords some harmonic variety. Dan Dailey performed the song in the 1948 film, *You Were Meant for Me*.

Moderate foxtrot with two verses (8) and refrain (32)
PUBLISHER: Campbell, Connelly & Co. (London), assigned to Robbins Music Corporation
KEY: B-flat maj., **STARTS**: d' (B-flat maj.), **FORM**: AA'BA'

≈≈≈≈≈≈≈≈≈≈≈≈≈≈≈≈≈≈≈≈

I'LL GET BY (AS LONG AS I HAVE YOU) * *

WORDS: Roy Turk, **MUSIC**: Fred E. Ahlert
POPULARIZED: in recordings and night clubs by Ruth Etting

With early recordings by Nick Lucas, Ruth Etting, and Gus Arnheim and his Orchestra, this poignant ballad attained even greater popularity after Irene Dunne sang it to Spencer Tracy in the 1943 film, *A Guy Named Joe*. In 1944, a Columbia recording by Harry James and his Orchestra, with vocal by Dick Haymes, made the song a hit all over again, and it remained an impressive twenty-two weeks on *Your Hit Parade*. In 1960, Billy Williams revived it yet again, with a hit recording.

The song is interesting in several respects. The long verse moves to E major before modulating back to C major. The twenty-eight-bar refrain is unusual in length and phrasing: alternating two six-bar "A" sections with two eight-bar "B" sections. The soaring melody of long notes outlining major sevenths has a romantic quality that is most effective.

In addition to *A Guy Named Joe*, "I'll Get By" has been featured in a remarkable number of films. Harry Richman sang it in *Puttin' On the Ritz* (1930); Dinah Shore did it in *Follow the Boys* (1944). Dan Dailey sang it in

You Were Meant for Me (1948). In 1950, the trio of Dennis Day, June Haver, and Gloria De Haven sang it in the inevitable namesake movie, *I'll Get By*. And in 1957 Gogi Grant dubbed it in for Ann Blyth in *The Helen Morgan Story* (known as *Both Sides of the Candle* in Britain).

> Moderate ballad with two verses (24) and refrain (28)
> *PUBLISHER*: Cromwell Music Inc., Fred E. Ahlert Music Corp.,and
> Pencil Mark Music, Inc.
> *KEY*: C maj., *STARTS*: c' (C maj.), *FORM*: ABAB'

≈≈≈≈≈≈≈≈≈≈≈≈≈≈≈≈≈≈≈

LET'S DO IT (LET'S FALL IN LOVE) * * *!

> *WORDS and MUSIC:* Cole Porter
> *PREMIERE*: Play with songs, *Paris*
> New York: Music Box Theatre, 8 October 1928 (195 perf.)
> *INTRODUCED BY*: Irene Bordoni and Arthur Margetson

Cole Porter's first big hit, this song is also one of his wittiest. It was written for a "naughty" new play called *Paris*, starring Irene Bordoni, the celebrated French singer and comedienne, who happened at the time to be married to E. Roy Goetz, the show's producer. A year later, "Let's Do It" was interpolated in the English revue, *Wake Up and Dream*, which had its London premiere at the Pavilion Theatre, 27 March 1929 and its New York premiere at the Selwyn Theatre, 30 December 1929. Popularized by Paul Whiteman and his Orchestra, "Let's Do It" enjoyed a revival with Frank Sinatra's recording in 1960. It also was used for a time in a commercial television campaign for Rheingold Beer.

A catalogue song, "Let's Do It" presents a seemingly endless array of creatures (from moths to giraffes) and nationalities (from Siamese to Letts) that "do it". The lyrics are very clever indeed, containing such fascinating lines as: "Electric eels do it / Though it shocks them I know", and "In shallow shoals / English soles do it". But the music is more than a match for this onslaught of wittiness. The melody of the refrain plays around three notes: g', g-flat', and f', with the chromatic g-flat' accented. The release, starting in G minor, has a similar theme.

Jane Wyman sang it in the Cole Porter biographical film, *Night and Day* (1946), while Frank Sinatra and Shirley MacLaine performed it in *Can-Can* (1960). The song is a marvelous *tour de force* and a testament to the mighty talents of its creator.

Moderate foxtrot with verse (16) and five refrains (32)
PUBLISHER: Harms, Inc.
KEY: B-flat maj., *STARTS*: g' (B-flat 6), *FORM*: AA'BA"

≈≈≈≈≈≈≈≈≈≈≈≈≈≈≈≈≈≈≈≈

LOVE ME OR LEAVE ME

WORDS: Gus Kahn, *MUSIC*: Walter Donaldson
PREMIERE: Musical comedy, *Whoopee*
New York: New Amsterdam Theatre, 4 December 1928 (379 perf.)
INTRODUCED BY: Ruth Etting

So closely is this torch song identified with Ruth Etting that its title was given to her 1955 screen biography, *Love Me or Leave Me*. Etting herself introduced the song in the hit 1928 musical comedy, *Whoopee*; she recorded it for Columbia and it became her signature song. It was interpolated in the otherwise Rodgers-and-Hart musical, *Simple Simon*, in 1930 – again sung by Etting. In the 1930s, Benny Goodman and his Orchestra made two hit recordings for Columbia. Among the many other recordings were those of Sammy Davis Jr. and Lena Horne.

The music has more than a touch of dramatic pathos. Each "A" section begins in F minor with a descending jump of an octave, with each note repeated. This motive is then repeated in A-flat major. The release is more syncopated, beginning with an F dominant seventh chord and then moving to B-flat minor.

Film credits for "Love Me or Leave Me" include *Tell It to a Star* (1945), sung by Ruth Terry; *The Flame* (1947), sung by Constance Dowling; *I'll See You in My Dreams* (1951), sung by Patrice Wymore; and *Love Me or Leave Me* (1955), sung by Doris Day.

Slow torch song with verse (16) and refrain (32)
PUBLISHER: Bregman, Vocco & Conn, Inc.
KEY: A-flat maj., *STARTS*: c" (F min.), *FORM*: AABA

≈≈≈≈≈≈≈≈≈≈≈≈≈≈≈≈≈≈≈≈

LOVER, COME BACK TO ME!   *

WORDS: Oscar Hammerstein II, *MUSIC*: Sigmund Romberg
PREMIERE: Operetta, *The New Moon*
New York: Imperial Theatre, 19 September 1928 (509 perf.)
INTRODUCED BY: Evelyn Herbert

The New Moon was not only Sigmund Romberg's last operetta, but also the last great American operetta in the European tradition. This melodious song was its big, romantic ballad. However, the original score for *The New Moon* written eight months before the premiere, did not include it. Inserted in the operetta at the last moment, "Lover, Come Back to Me!" was an immediate hit popularized by Rudy Vallee and his Connecticut Yankees. In 1953, Nat "King" Cole revived it.

Strongly in the tradition of operetta, "Lover, Come Back to Me!" has a broad melody of long notes and a wide range (an octave and a fourth). The expansive melody underlines the pleading nature of the lyrics. The clearly-defined harmonies – in the first four bars: E-flat major, G dominant seventh, C minor, F dominant seventh – bring emotional depth. The melody of the release, in C minor, is strongly reminiscent of Tchaikovsky's "June Bacarolle", from *The Seasons*.

On the screen, Grace Moore, Lawrence Tibbett, Roland Young, and Adolph Menjou sang it in the first film version, *New Moon*, in 1930. Jeanette MacDonald and Nelson Eddy sang it in the second film version (1940). Tony Martin and Joan Weldon performed it in the 1954 Romberg film biography, *Deep in My Heart*. Seldom done in its original fashion, the song is favored by jazz combos, who play it in medium to fast tempo.

Moderate ballad with verse (12) and refrain (32)
PUBLISHER: Harms, Inc.
KEY: E-flat maj., *STARTS*: e-flat' (E-flat maj.), *FORM*: AABA

≈≈≈≈≈≈≈≈≈≈≈≈≈≈≈≈≈≈≈

MAKIN' WHOOPEE! * * *

WORDS: Gus Kahn, *MUSIC*: Walter Donaldson
PREMIERE: Musical comedy, *Whoopee*
New York: New Amsterdam Theatre, 4 December 1928 (379 perf.)
INTRODUCED BY: Eddie Cantor

The pungent expression "making whoopee" allegedly first appeared in Walter Winchell's chatty gossip column in *The New York Daily Mirror*. But this song and the show it came from made the expression part of the contemporary idiom. "Makin' Whoopee!" became Eddie Cantor's signature song, requested whenever he performed with his trademark goggly eyes; he recorded it for Victor, Ben Bernie and his Orchestra had a best-selling Brunswick recording, and Ray Charles recorded it in 1965.

The music of the refrain is charmingly understated, from the dotted-note pickup to the slowly rising melodic line, to the occasional blue note, to the jazzy syncopation of the release. The lyrics tell the story of a hasty wedding and its consequences: "He washes dishes and baby clothes. He's so ambitious he even sews". They give a picture of domestic bliss straight out of "Tea for Two" (1924).

Cantor sang it in two films, the 1930 screen version of *Whoopee!* and *Show Business* (1944). Doris Day and Danny Thomas did it in the 1951 screen biography of Gus Kahn, *I'll See You in My Dreams*. Cantor dubbed it in for Keefe Braselle in Cantor's film biography, *The Eddie Cantor Story* (1953). "Makin' Whoopee!" is a very versatile song responsive to all sorts of treatment: from sad to comic, from romantic to jazz, from symphonic to bebop.

> Moderate rhythm song with verse (12) and two refrains (32)
> *PUBLISHER*: Donaldson, Douglas & Gumble, Inc.
> *KEY*: G maj., *STARTS*: d' (G maj.), *FORM*: AABA

≈≈≈≈≈≈≈≈≈≈≈≈≈≈≈≈≈≈

MARIE

> *WORDS and MUSIC*: Irving Berlin
> *PREMIERE*: Film, *The Awakening*, 1928: theme song
> *INTRODUCED:* off-screen by an unnamed female vocalist

This innocent little waltz was specially composed by Irving Berlin for one of the first talking pictures, *The Awakening*, starring Vilma Banky. Early recordings were by Nat Shilkret and his Orchestra and Rudy Vallee and his Connecticut Yankees. But the song's real fame began nine years later, in 1937, when it was recorded for Victor in duple time by Tommy Dorsey and his Orchestra, with vocals by Jack Leonard and a chorus of musicians, and a trumpet solo by Bunny Berigan. It was Dorsey's first big hit. Owing to the resounding success of that swinging arrangement, the song's origin as a waltz has largely been forgotten. Almost always performed as a swing tune, "Marie" was revived in 1965, with a recording by The Bachelors. The most unusual aspect of the refrain is its opening on the subdominant (B-flat major). Otherwise, the melody and harmonies are of the utmost simplicity.

Besides *The Awakening*, "Marie" has been performed in film by a chorus in *Alexander's Ragtime Band* (1938); by Janet Blair, Stuart Foster, and a chorus in *The Fabulous Dorseys* (1947); and by a chorus in *There's No Business Like Show Business* (1954).

Moderate waltz with verse (16) and refrain (32)
PUBLISHER: Irving Berlin, Inc.
KEY: F maj., *STARTS*: d" (B-flat maj.), *FORM*: ABAB'

≈≈≈≈≈≈≈≈≈≈≈≈≈≈≈≈≈≈

ONE KISS

WORDS: Oscar Hammerstein II, *MUSIC*: Sigmund Romberg
PREMIERE: Operetta, *The New Moon*
New York: Imperial Theatre, 19 September 1928 (509 perf.)
INTRODUCED BY: Evelyn Herbert

Another enduring song written for the completely revised and recast operetta, *The New Moon*, "One Kiss" was not in the original production which had opened and closed eight months before. It is an old-fashioned waltz in the Viennese tradition. With an interesting verse in 2/4 meter and a rather long interlude in C major, the refrain is literally the song's centerpiece.

The principal charm of the refrain lies in its second note, the g-sharp', which falls uncharacteristically on a strong beat and is accompanied by an F major chord. This quickly-resolving discord adds a touch of piquancy to the melody, which skips around and has a wide range of an octave and a fourth.

Grace Moore sang "One Kiss" in the 1930 screen version, *New Moon* (omitting the definite article). Jeanette MacDonald performed it in the 1940 *New Moon*.

Moderate waltz with verse (24), refrain (32), and interlude (40)
PUBLISHER: Harms, Inc.
KEY: F maj., *STARTS*: a' (F maj. + g-sharp'), *FORM*: ABA'C

≈≈≈≈≈≈≈≈≈≈≈≈≈≈≈≈≈≈

SHE'S FUNNY THAT WAY (I GOT A WOMAN CRAZY FOR ME) *

WORDS: Richard A. Whiting, *MUSIC*: Neil Morét (Charles N. Daniels)
INTRODUCED: in a Victor recording by Gene Austin

The refrain of this poignant song begins with the self-effacing words: "I'm not much to look at, nothin' to see". There were many early recordings, including those of Gene Austin, Ted Lewis, Connie Haines, and

Martha Stewart; but Frank Sinatra had the most popular recording of all in the fifties.

The music is curiously emotional; its essence is repetition. The verse is scale-like, with each note repeated. In the refrain, the same rhythmical motive appears six times in each "A" section, at differing pitch levels. The release, consisting mostly of dotted quarters and eighths, has two ascending, partly-modal scales. The overall effect of this repetitive music is hypnotic.

The song's most effective use in film was in *The Postman Always Rings Twice* (1946). In that memorable picture, starring Lana Turner and John Garfield, the character played by Cecil Kellaway sang it as an anthem to his own destruction. In 1952 it was in two films: Frank Sinatra sang it in *Meet Danny Wilson* and Frankie Laine and Billy Daniels in *Rainbow 'Round My Shoulder*.

Slow torch song with two verses (16) and refrain (32)
PUBLISHER: Villa Morét, Inc.
KEY: E-flat maj., *STARTS*: b-flat' (E-flat 6), *FORM*: AABA

≈≈≈≈≈≈≈≈≈≈≈≈≈≈≈≈≈≈≈≈

SONNY BOY

WORDS and MUSIC: Al Jolson, B. G. De Sylva, Lew Brown, and Ray Henderson
PREMIERE: Film musical, *The Singing Fool*, Warner Brothers, 1928
INTRODUCED BY: Al Jolson

This tear-jerker was allegedly written as a jest in a single night by the team of De Sylva, Brown, and Henderson. They were in Atlantic City, New Jersey, preparing a new show, when Jolson, who was in California, called them, urgently requesting a new song for his second film, *The Singing Fool*. They wrote the song with tongue-in-cheek, but Jolson's performance in the film at his character's three-year-old son's deathbed brought it instant fame. Jolson's Brunswick recording sold over three million copies; over a million copies of sheet music were sold.

The verse ("Climb upon my knee",) is in C minor, while the chorus ("When there are gray skies") is in C major. The broad melody of the refrain outlines the underlying harmonies: C major, A seventh. D minor, G seventh.

Al Jolson repeated his success with "Sonny Boy" in the films, *Big Boy* (1930) and *The Singing Kid* (1936). He also dubbed it in for Larry Parks in *The Jolson Story* (1946) and *Jolson Sings Again* (1949). Norman

Brooks sang it as Jolson in the De Sylva, Brown, and Henderson film biography, *The Best Things in Life Are Free* (1956).

Slow ballad with two verses (8) and refrain (32)
PUBLISHER: De Sylva, Brown and Henderson, Inc.
KEY: C maj., *STARTS*: c" (C maj.), *FORM*: AA'BA'

≈≈≈≈≈≈≈≈≈≈≈≈≈≈≈≈≈≈≈

SWEET LORRAINE * *

WORDS: Mitchell Parish, *MUSIC*: Cliff Burwell
INTRODUCED: in a Victor recording by Rudy Vallee and his Connecticut Yankees

Composed by Rudy Vallee's pianist, Cliff Burwell, this jazz standard was recorded for Victor by Vallee and his Connecticut Yankees. Its true jazz potential was realized by clarinetist Jimmy Noone, who had an early recording. But it was Nat "King" Cole who made the song universally popular; it was one of the first songs that the erstwhile pianist sang in public. Frank Sinatra's recording was also a best-seller.

The song's appeal to musicians lies in its congenial, sequential melody over ever-changing harmonies, with an average of two different chords in each bar. For example, in the first four bars of the "A" sections alone the following harmonies appear: G maj., E seventh, A seventh, D seventh, E minor, C seventh, and B seventh. The release also has interesting harmonies, starting in C major and moving to A minor. The song stands supreme as a vehicle for jazz improvisation in slow tempo.

Slow rhythm song with two verses (16) and refrain (32)
PUBLISHER: Mills Music, Inc.
KEY: G maj., *STARTS*: a-sharp' (G maj.), *FORM*: AA'BA'

≈≈≈≈≈≈≈≈≈≈≈≈≈≈≈≈≈≈≈

SWEET SUE – JUST YOU *

WORDS: Will J. Harris, *MUSIC*: Victor Young
INTRODUCED: Bennie Kreuger and his Orchestra

A simple little song with an easily-remembered melody of very few notes, "Sweet Sue – Just You" immediately caught on with the public. The song is dedicated to film actress, Sue Carol, who became Mrs. Alan Ladd – her photograph graces the sheet music cover. First popularized by Ben Pollack and his Orchestra, the song has had a number of revivals: it was recorded in 1932 by The Mills Brothers, in 1939 by Tommy Dorsey and his Orchestra, and in 1949 by Johnny Long and his Orchestra.

The music, written by Victor Young, who went on to a distinguished career in Hollywood, is almost childlike in its ingenuousness. Melody, harmony, and rhythm are of the simplest, with only the release offering some harmonic digression from tonic and dominant. The lyrics share this simplicity: "Ev'ry star above knows the one I love".

In films, Artie Shaw and his Orchestra performed the song in *Second Chorus* (1941), The Mills Brothers sang it in *Rhythm Parade* (1942), and in 1956 Carmen Cavallaro played it on the piano in *The Eddy Duchin Story*.

Moderate foxtrot with two verses (16) and refrain (32)
PUBLISHER: Shapiro, Bernstein & Co., Inc.
KEY: G maj., *STARTS*: d' (A min. 7), *FORM*: AABA'

≋≋≋≋≋≋≋≋≋≋≋≋≋≋≋≋≋

TOGETHER

WORDS and MUSIC: B.G. De Sylva, Lew Brown, and Ray Henderson

The celebrated songwriting and publishing team of De Sylva, Brown, and Henderson, famous for some of the jazziest tunes of the Roaring Twenties, wrote this old-fashioned waltz in 1928. It was moderately successful, popularized on radio and in recordings by Nick Lucas, Cliff Edwards (Ukelele Ike), and Paul Whiteman and his Orchestra. But the song realized its full potential sixteen years later, in 1944, when it was interpolated in *Since You Went Away*, a film about the home-front during World War II, with a stellar and variegated cast including Claudette Colbert, Jennifer Jones, Joseph Cotton, Robert Walker, Lionel Barrymore, Shirley Temple, and Hattie McDaniel. Connie Francis recorded it in 1961.

The plaintive melody outlines several different chords: F major, C major, D major, and finally E major. The lyrics are straightforwardly sentimental: "You've gone from me / But in my memory / We always will be together".

Dan Dailey and Phyllis Avery sang "Together" in the De Sylva, Brown, and Henderson biographical film, *The Best Things in Life Are Free* (1956).

Moderate waltz with two verses (16) and refrain (32)
PUBLISHER: De Sylva, Brown and Henderson, Inc.
KEY: F maj., *STARTS*: c' (F maj.), *FORM*: ABA'C

≋≋≋≋≋≋≋≋≋≋≋≋≋≋≋≋≋≋≋

WHEN YOU'RE SMILING (THE WHOLE WORLD SMILES WITH YOU) *

WORDS and MUSIC: Mark Fisher, Joe Goodwin, and Larry Shay

The very idea of this song, expressed in its title, has made it a winner. Initially popularized by Seger Ellis, a 1929 Okeh recording by Louis Armstrong brought it immense popularity during the Depression, when smiles were in short supply and desperately needed. Many other recordings followed.

The melody of the first four bars of the refrain spells out its harmonies: B-flat major, B-flat major seventh, G seventh, and C minor. The second section repeats the same progression a step higher. The release ("But when you're crying you bring on the rain") offers darker harmonies and some chromaticism. But sunny harmonies prevail in the last section, to give the song a happy ending.

"When You're Smiling" has been featured in at least five films. The King's Men sang it in *You're a Lucky Fellow, Mr. Smith* (1943). The song gave it's title to *When You're Smiling* (1950); Frank Sinatra sang it in *Meet Danny Wilson* (1952); Roberta Flack in *$(Dollars)* (1972); and Louis Armstrong (posthumously) in *The Cotton Club* (1984).

Moderate foxtrot with two verses (16) and refrain (32)
PUBLISHER: Mills Music, Inc.
KEY: B-flat maj., *STARTS*: d' (B-flat maj.), *FORM*: AA'BA"

≋≋≋≋≋≋≋≋≋≋≋≋≋≋≋≋≋≋≋

YOU TOOK ADVANTAGE OF ME

WORDS: Lorenz Hart, *MUSIC*: Richard Rodgers
PREMIERE: Musical comedy, *Present Arms*
New York: Mansfield Theatre, 26 April 1928 (c. 160 perf.)
INTRODUCED BY: Busby Berkeley, Joyce Barber, and a chorus

This sparkling song is aptly marked both "gracefully" and "liltingly". Busby Berkeley, who introduced it along with Joyce Barber, also created the dances for *Present Arms*, which were so much off the floor that one critic called them "aerial formations". "You Took Advantage of Me", the only hit from the show, has survived as a favorite of cabaret singers.

Most captivating of all are Lorenz Hart's lyrics, with such marvelous rhymes as "So what's the use, you've cooked my goose" and "Lock the doors and call me yours". The melody of the refrain consists mostly of dotted quarters and eighths. Harmonies are fast-changing, with many diminished chords. They change particularly rapidly in the release, which begins in E-flat major and passes through the circle of fifths (D seventh, G seventh, C seventh, F seventh, B-flat seventh, E-flat major) all in the space of four bars. The entire progression is then repeated in the next four bars.

"You Took Advantage of Me" was sung by Lilyan Tashman and Fred Santley in the 1930 film version of *Present Arms*, called *Leathernecking*. Judy Garland sang it in the 1954 film, *A Star Is Born*.

Moderate rhythm song with two verses (16) and refrain (32)
PUBLISHER: Harms, Inc.
KEY: E-flat maj., *STARTS:* b-flat' (E-flat maj.), *FORM*: AABA

≈≈≈≈≈≈≈≈≈≈≈≈≈≈≈≈≈≈≈

YOU'RE THE CREAM IN MY COFFEE

WORDS and MUSIC: B. G. De Sylva, Lew Brown, and Ray Henderson
PREMIERE: Musical comedy, *Hold Everything!*
New York: Broadhurst Theatre, 10 October 1928
INTRODUCED BY: Jack Whiting and Ona Munson

"You're the Cream in My Coffee" is the only song to survive from the short-lived show, *Hold Everything!*, about a punch-drunk prize fighter (played to perfection by comedian Bert Lahr). It demonstrates the song-writing ability of that most dynamic team of the twenties: De Sylva, Brown, and Henderson. Early recordings included those of Ruth Etting and Ben Selvin and his Orchestra (both Columbia), and Ted Weems and his Orchestra (Victor).

There are separate verses for a boy and a girl. The refrain, in straight AABA form, starts unusually on the major ninth (f"). It is heavily syncopated, especially in the release, which also utilizes the chromatic scale. The lyrics are exceedingly clever, offering a catalogue of good pairings: "the salt in my stew", the starch in my collar", "the lace in my shoe". There is also the intriguing internal rhyming of "So this is clear, dear" with "You're my Worcestshire, dear".

"You're the Cream in My Coffee" was featured in one of the earliest sound films, *The Cock-Eyed World* (1929).

Moderate foxtrot with two verses (16) and two refrains (32)
PUBLISHER: De Sylva, Brown and Henderson, Inc.
KEY: E-flat maj., *STARTS*: f" (E-flat maj. 9), *FORM*: AABA

≈≈≈≈≈≈≈≈≈≈≈≈≈≈≈≈≈≈≈

WHAT GOES UP MUST COME DOWN

1929

I tried to reach the moon but when I got there / All that I could get was the air

Howard Dietz
"I Guess I'll Have to Change My Plan"

This eventful year sees a dichotomy among popular songs. On the one hand are those frolicsome tunes still exploring the hedonistic delights of the Roaring Twenties, such as "Happy Days Are Here Again" and "Ain't Misbehavin'". On the other hand are the great ballads that give a foretaste of things to come, like "Star Dust" and "What is This Thing Called Love?". Songs of desperation ("Why Was I Born?") appear alongside songs of unmitigated joy ("Singin' in the Rain").

And indeed, desperation does come for many on 29 October, when the stock market crashes with a bang, dropping by some $50 billion, ending the great bull market of the twenties, and initiating the worst depression in United States history. But earlier this year things are normal enough. Prohibition is at its peak, speakeasies abound, and gangsters are running rampant, as exemplified by the St. Valentine's Day massacre in Chicago, allegedly instigated by Al Capone, who is now Public Enemy No. 1.

Hollywood offers a way to get away from all these troubles; this year alone, there are 110 million paid admissions to movie houses. And more and more theaters are converting to talking pictures. Film musicals are the rage, starting with *The Broadway Melody*: the first "all-singing, all-talking, all-dancing" motion picture. Songs are beginning to come from these films, including "Sonny Boy", from *The Singing Fool;* "Singin' in the Rain", from *Hollywood Revue of 1929*; "Tip-Toe Through the Tulips with Me", from *Gold Diggers of Broadway*; and "You Were Meant for Me", from *The Broadway Melody*. Many screen actors talk for the first time: The Marx Brothers in *The Coconuts*, Gloria Swanson in *The Trespasser,* Joan

Crawford in *Untamed*, George Arliss in *Disraeli*, and Mary Pickford in *Coquette*.

Broadway suffers by comparison: the majority of theaters are converting to sound pictures. However, Elmer Rice's *Street Scene* wins the Pulitzer Prize, and several distinguished musicals do open, including Rodgers and Hart's *Spring Is Here*, Noël Coward's *Bitter Sweet*, and the boisterous revues, *Connie's Hot Chocolates* and *The Little Show*.

Radio is still a national obsession, and Amos 'n' Andy still the No. 1 program. This year, Kate Smith and Arthur Godfrey make their debuts on the air, Bing Crosby is touring with Paul Whiteman and his Orchestra, and Rudy Vallee and Russ Columbo are becoming nationally known as "crooners". On a more serious note are the novels, *All Quiet on the Western Front*, by Erich Maria Remarque; *Look Homeward, Angel*, by Thomas Wolfe, and *The Sound and the Fury*, by William Faulkner. Like the economy, all the media seem to be having their ups and downs in this topsy-turvy year of 1929.

SONGS OF 1929

Ain't Misbehavin' ***
Am I Blue? *
(I'm a Dreamer) Aren't We All
Can't We Be Friends?
Don't Ever Leave Me!
Great Day
Happy Days Are Here Again **
Honeysuckle Rose **
I Guess I'll Have to Change My Plan
    (The Blue Pajama Song)
I May Be Wrong, But I Think You're Wonderful!
I'll See You Again **
Just You, Just Me *
Liza (All the Clouds'll Roll Away *
Louise
Mean to Me *
More Than You Know *
Siboney
Singin' in the Rain ***
Star Dust ****!
Tip-Toe Thru the Tulips with Me

What Is This Thing Called Love? **!
Why Was I Born? *
With a Song in My Heart *
Without a Song
You Do Something to Me **
You Were Meant for Me
Zigeuner!

AIN'T MISBEHAVIN' ***

WORDS: Andy Razaf, *MUSIC*: Thomas "Fats" Waller and Harry Brooks
PREMIERE: Revue, *Connie's Hot Chocolates*
New York: Connie's Inn, 20 June 1929
INTRODUCED BY: Margaret Simms, Paul Bass, and Russell Wooding's
Hallelujah Singers

This jaunty jazz standard is most often associated with its co-composer, Thomas "Fats" Waller, talented pianist, singer, and songwriter who popularized the song as his theme until his premature death in 1943 at age thirty-nine. It was first heard in Harlem in the all-black revue, *Connie's Hot Chocolates*, performed by Louis Armstrong during the intermissions. Early recordings were by Waller (on Victor), Ruth Etting (Columbia), and Leo Reisman and his Orchestra (Victor). The song gained renewed popularity in 1978 as the title song of another all-black revue – this time written for Broadway – itself entitled *Ain't Misbehavin'*.

It is well known that popular composers frequently turn to the classics for inspiration. In a reversal of this common practice, a melody similar to that of "Ain't Misbehavin'" was used by Dmitri Shostakovich as the third theme of the first movement of his *Symphony No. 7,* Op. 60 written in 1945. Although the rhythmical configurations of the two melodies differ, their outlines bear similarities. Perhaps this may be attributed to coincidence or perhaps to unconscious borrowing; it was certainly not intentional.

The song's universal appeal is not hard to understand. The refrain is decidedly keyboard-oriented, with more than a hint of ragtime influence. The initial melodic idea of rising fifths ascending sequentially gives the melody an air of optimism. In contrast, the middle section features descending thirds repeated over changing harmonies.

In the 1943 film, *Stormy Weather*, Waller's rendition, along with Ada Brown, was a show-stopper. The song was also sung by Mary Beth Hughes in *Follow the Band*; by Louis Armstrong in *Atlantic City* (1944); by Fred Kohlmar, dubbing in for Dan Dailey in *You Were Meant for Me* (1948); by Mickey Rooney and Louis Armstrong in *The Strip* (1951); and by Jane Russell, Anita Ellis (dubbing in for Jeanne Crain), and Alan Young in *Gentlemen Marry Brunettes* (1955). It was the title song of a 1955 film, *Ain't Misbehavin'*, and was sung by Burt Reynolds in *Lucky Lady* (1975). "Ain't Misbehavin'" remains today a staple of the jazz musician's repertoire.

Moderate rhythm song with two verses (16) and refrain (32)
PUBLISHER: Mills Music, Inc.
KEY: E-flat maj., *STARTS*: e-flat' (E-flat maj.), *FORM*: AABA

≈≈≈≈≈≈≈≈≈≈≈≈≈≈≈≈≈≈≈

AM I BLUE? *

WORDS: Grant Clarke, *MUSIC*: Harry Akst
PREMIERE: Film musical, *On With the Show* (1929)
INTRODUCED BY: Ethel Waters and the Harmony Four Quartet

Like "Sonny Boy" the year before, "Am I Blue?" had its inception in the early days of the screen musical. Harry Akst, the song's composer, had served as accompanist to Nora Bayes, the celebrated vaudeville entertainer and had been associated with Irving Berlin during World War I. Later, during World War II and the Korean War, he toured overseas as Al Jolson's accompanist. In 1929, when asked for a torch song for Ethel Waters to sing in the now-forgotten film *On With the Show*, Akst and lyricist Grant Clarke came up with this gem. It was recorded by Waters on Columbia as well as by torch singer Libby Holman.

The title is somewhat misleading: "Am I Blue?" is not a blues song. Its only connection to the blues is its liberal use of blue notes (in this case, flatted thirds) at the closing cadences of each "A" section. Otherwise, the song is simplicity itself: thirty-two bars in straightforward AABA form. Perhaps its only distinctive feature is its ascending melodic line, reaching up to three notes (a', b-flat', c") and always returning to two lower notes (c', d'). This was by no means an original idea, having been done by Richard Rodgers three years earlier in "The Blue Room" (1926). The only harmonic contrast lies in the middle section, in A minor. The lyrics, written in what passed for southern dialect at the time, make opulent use of such colloquialisms as "done fell through" and "Lawdy".

The song has been featured in a number of films since *On With the Show*, including *So Long Letty* (1930), *The Hard Way* (1942, starring Ida Lupino and Joan Leslie), and *Is Everybody Happy?* (1943, with Ted Lewis and Larry Parks). It was sung by Andy Williams (dubbing for Lauren Bacall) and Hoagy Carmichael in Bacall's debut film with Humphrey Bogart, *To Have and Have Not* (1944). It was played by Carmen Cavallaro in *The Eddy Duchin Story* (1956, starring Tyrone Power and Kim Novak), sung by Barbara Streisand in the 1975 film *Funny Lady,* and sung again by Ethel Waters in *The Cotton Club* (1984).

It remains a favorite of jazz singers and instrumentalists alike.

Moderate torch song with two verses (16) and refrain (32)
PUBLISHER: M. Witmark & Sons
KEY: F maj., *STARTS*: c' (F maj.), *FORM*: AABA

≈≈≈≈≈≈≈≈≈≈≈≈≈≈≈≈≈≈

(I'M A DREAMER) AREN'T WE ALL

WORDS and MUSIC: B. G. De Sylva, Lew Brown, and Ray Henderson
PREMIERE: Film musical, *Sunny Side Up* (1929)
INTRODUCED BY: Janet Gaynor

Sunny Side Up was one of the most innovative film musicals of 1929. The story of a poor girl from Yorkville (Janet Gaynor) who falls in love with a young millionaire from Long Island (Charles Farrell), it features girls, a production number, and an entertainment sequence in two colors. It also features the demure Miss Gaynor singing this tender song to her own accompaniment on a zither. Usually known by the first words of the refrain, "I'm a Dreamer", the song is actually titled "Aren't We All", the last words of the refrain. It became immensely popular after performances and a recording by Paul Whiteman and his Orchestra.

The music of the refrain is organized symmetrically. Each "A" section consists of four major harmonies descending chromatically: C, B, B-flat, A; while each "B" section has a rising sequence of dotted quarter and eighth notes. The lyrics are somewhat self-deprecating, ending: "And I'm a fool! But Aren't We All!"

Along with a host of other songs by the trio, the ballad was featured in the 1956 biopic of De Sylva, Brown, and Henderson, *The Best Things in Life Are Free*, starring Gordon MacRae, Dan Dailey, and Ernest Borgnine as the three tunesmiths.

Moderate ballad with two verses (24) and refrain (32)
PUBLISHER: De Sylva, Brown and Henderson, Inc.
KEY: C maj., *STARTS*: c" (C maj.), *FORM*: ABAB'

≈≈≈≈≈≈≈≈≈≈≈≈≈≈≈≈≈≈

CAN'T WE BE FRIENDS?

WORDS: Paul James (pseudonym for James Warburg)
MUSIC: Kay Swift
PREMIERE: Revue, *The Little Show* (First Edition).
New York: Music Box Theatre, 30 April 1929 (321 perf.)
INTRODUCED BY: Libby Holman

Libby Holman, the quintessential torch singer, introduced this ballad in the historic first edition of *The Little Show*, which also brought forth such diverse talents as Fred Allen, Clifton Webb, George S. Kaufman, Arthur Schwartz, Howard Dietz, and Ralph Rainger. That revue also introduced Holman's signature song, "Moanin' Low" and Schwartz and Dietz's erstwhile camp song, "I Guess I'll Have to Change My Plan".

Kay Swift, the song's talented composer, wrote the music in collaboration with her husband, James Warburg, who wrote under the pen name of Paul James. The same team wrote "Fine and Dandy" a year later.

The verse, in F minor, is off the beaten path, in the style of a Russian gypsy ballad. The refrain, on the other hand, is conventional: thirty-two bars in AABA form. What makes the refrain distinctive is its "jazzy" feel, occasioned by its unusual starting chord (G9) and use of the Neapolitan sixth (D-flat 7). In true torch song tradition the lyrics proclaim" a self-fulfilling prophecy: He's goin' to turn me down and say 'Can't We Be Friends?'.

"Can't We Be Friends" has been favored by jazz trumpeters ever since it was played by Harry James on the soundtrack of the 1950 film, *Young Man with a Horn*, in which Kirk Douglas played the part of a trumpet player who neglected his women (played by Doris Day and Lauren Bacall). Despite an occasional dated colloquialism like "What a bust!", it also remains in the repertoire of jazz vocalists.

Moderate torch song with verse (12) and two refrains (32)
PUBLISHER: Harms, Inc.
KEY: F maj., *STARTS*: a' (G9), *FORM*: AABA

≈≈≈≈≈≈≈≈≈≈≈≈≈≈≈≈≈≈≈≈

DON'T EVER LEAVE ME!

WORDS: Oscar Hammerstein II, *MUSIC*: Jerome Kern
PREMIERE: Musical comedy, *Sweet Adeline*
New York: Hammerstein's Theatre, 3 September 1929 (234 perf.)
INTRODUCED BY: Helen Morgan and Robert Chisholm

Sweet Adeline was a period piece set in Hoboken and New York in the 1890s, in which Helen Morgan introduced two beautiful Kern-Hammerstein ballads that were destined to become standards: "Why Was I Born? and "Don't Ever Leave Me". The latter has a refrain of only sixteen bars but is most often performed as thirty-two bars in double time. The wistful melodic line of each "A" section forms a sinuous curve, first descending from c" to f' to c', then back again to f' and c". There is some harmonic contrast in the middle section, in A minor. But the most interesting harmonic change occurs in the verse, in which Kern, master of modulation, moves from F major to A major and then back to F again.

"Don't Ever Leave Me" was sung by Irene Dunne in the 1935 film *Sweet Adeline*. In the 1957 film, *The Helen Morgan Story* (known in Great Britain as *Both Ends of the Candle*), Gogi Grant dubbed it in for Ann Blyth. With its light syncopation and emphasis on fourths and fifths, it remains one of Kern and Hammerstein's most moving creations.

Moderate ballad with verse (12) and refrain (16)
PUBLISHER: T. B. Harms Company
KEY: F maj., *STARTS*: c" (F maj.), *FORM*: AA'BA'

≈≈≈≈≈≈≈≈≈≈≈≈≈≈≈≈≈≈≈

GREAT DAY

WORDS: William Rose and Edward Eliscu, *MUSIC*: Vincent Youmans
PREMIERE: Musical play, *Great Day!*
New York: Cosmopolitan Theatre 17 October 1929 (36 perf.)
INTRODUCED BY: Lois Deppe and the Russell Wooding Jubilee Singers

The ambitious musical *Great Day!* did not have a great day in New York. Twelve days after its opening, the financial world crumbled, and the show folded in short order. The idea of setting the story on a plantation outside New Orleans belonged to Vincent Youmans, the show's composer. But the musical suffered from a weak book, in addition to bad timing, in spite of which it did produce three great standards: the title song, "More Than You Know", and "Without a Song". Paul Whiteman and his Orchestra recorded it on the Victor label, with vocal by Bing Crosby. Nearly half a century later, John Raitt sang "Great Day" in the retrospective revue, *A Musical Jubilee* (1975).

"Great Day" is a stirring song, sharply evoking an image of the Southland. The expressive verse is the same length as the refrain and could easily be a song in itself. It is written as a march in the style of a fanfare, outlining the E-flat major chord. The lyrics are gospel-oriented and in the nature of a sermon, punctuated liberally with the ubiquitous "Amen". The melody of the refrain starts with a simple rhythmical motive, very much in the Youmans style: see "More Than You Know", "Sometimes I'm Happy", "Time On My Hands", "Tea for Two", and "Without a Song". In this case it is intoxicating, because of its syncopation carried over the barline. For contrast, the "C" section resorts to an upward moving scale followed by martial, fanfare-like passages, before returning to the initial theme. The whole effect is immensely soul-stirring, aided by the lyrics' assurance that "There's gonna be a Great Day".

The song is a favorite of female singers. Barbra Streisand sang it with a chorus in the 1975 film biography of Fanny Brice, *Funny Lady.*

Moderate foxtrot with verse (32) and refrain (32)
PUBLISHER: Miller Music, Inc. and Vincent Youmans, Inc.
KEY: E-flat maj., *STARTS:* g' (E-flat 6), *FORM:* ABCA

≈≈≈≈≈≈≈≈≈≈≈≈≈≈≈≈≈≈≈

HAPPY DAYS ARE HERE AGAIN * *

WORDS: Jack Yellen, *MUSIC:* Milton Ager
PREMIERE: Musical film, *Chasing Rainbows,* starring Bessie Love and Charles King, 1929
INTRODUCED BY: Charles King, Bessie Love, and The Ensemble

Ineradicably identified with the Great Depression, "Happy Days Are Here Again" was born at its very beginning. It was introduced in the film musical, *Chasing Rainbows,* which featured Jack Benny and Eddie Phillips as well as Bessie Love and Charles King. Although the film was not released until early 1930, the song is copyrighted 1929 and was popularized that year by George Olsen and his Orchestra. Its fame has far transcended that of the film, which is forgotten, and really skyrocketed when "Happy Days Are Here Again" became the campaign song of Franklin D. Roosevelt in the 1932 election.

The melody of the refrain is familiar to almost everyone. It outlines the C major triad, first rising, then falling and then outlining the G dominant seventh chord. For emphasis, as if to accentuate the positive, each note is repeated. There is no mistaking the sunny message of this refrain. In contrast, the verse is in C minor with descending chords and lyrics exhorting the "sad times" and "bad times" to go away.

The refrain's unusual length of 56 bars is a consequence of three "A" sections of 16 bars and a "B" section of 8 bars: 16+16+8+16. This disparity in length enhances the song's bite, which is further enhanced by the pervading syncopation and profusion of accented notes. The lyrics are simple enough, rhyming "here again" with "clear again" and "cheer again". They are identical in the first and last sections of the refrain.

"Happy Days Are Here Again" has been featured in a number of films since *Chasing Rainbows.* It was sung by Joe Cook in the 1930 film, *Rain or Shine;* by Fred Allen, Raymon Walburn, Andrew Tombes, and a chorus in the 1935 film, *Thanks a Million;* and by a chorus in *The Night of the Iguana* (1964). It was sensationally revived by Barbara Streisand in a 1963 recording, ironically set in a lugubriously slow tempo. It is a particular favorite on New Year's Eve and other happy occasions.

Fast foxtrot with verse (16) and refrain (56)
PUBLISHER: Ager, Yellen & Bornstein
KEY: C maj., *STARTS*: c' (C maj.), *FORM*: AABA

≈≈≈≈≈≈≈≈≈≈≈≈≈≈≈≈≈≈≈

HONEYSUCKLE ROSE * *

WORDS and MUSIC: Andy Razaf and Thomas "Fats" Waller
PREMIERE: Revue, *Load of Coal*
New York: Connie's Inn, 1929
INTRODUCED BY: Louis Armstrong, with Carroll Dickerson and his Orchestra

This happy-go-lucky jazz standard originated as a dance number at Connie's Inn, located at the corner of Seventh Avenue and 131st Street in Harlem. Carroll Dickerson's band from Chicago was there, fronted by a young trumpeter named Louis Armstrong. The song gained a much wider audience when Paul Whiteman and his Orchestra introduced it on radio. Many recordings followed: by the bands of Benny Goodman, the Dorsey Brothers, Red Norvo, Bunny Berigan, and Fletcher Henderson; and by vocalists including Lena Horne and Thomas "Fats" Waller.

Waller, who wrote the music, was renowned not only as a fine pianist and organist, but also as a tremendous showman (something of a clown) and prolific composer. Perpetually in debt and grossly overweight, alcoholism and overindulgence contributed to his death in 1943 at age thirty-nine. He also composed "Ain't Misbehavin'" this year and is rumored to have ghost-written others – including "I Can't Give You Anything but Love" (1928) and "On the Sunny Side of the Street" (1930) – and to have sold them for ready cash. Honeysuckle Rose" was featured in two retrospective revues of the seventies: *Bubbling Brown Sugar* (1976) and *Ain't Misbehavin'* (1978). Willie Nelson had a Columbia recording in 1980.

The music is simple but quietly effective. The pentatonic melody plays the same five-note pattern three times in each "A" section. Harmonies are repetitive as well, alternating between dominant (four bars) and tonic (four bars). Some contrast is offered by the release: two ascending scales over sequential harmonies: F seventh to B-flat, and G seventh to C seventh.

Films featuring the song include *Tin Pan Alley* (1940) in which it was sung by Betty Grable and a chorus; *Thousands Cheer* (1943), sung by

Lena Horne; *Walking My Baby Back Home* (1953), sung by Donald O'Connor and Paula Kelly, dubbing for Janet Leigh; and *New York, New York* (1977), sung by Diahann Abbott. Simple in structure (AABA), melody, and harmony, Honeysuckle Rose" cries out for improvisation and has been part of every jazz musician's repertoire for more than six decades.

> Moderate rhythm song with verse (12) and refrain (32)
> *PUBLISHER*: Santley Brothers, Inc.
> *KEY*: F maj., *STARTS*: c" (C7), *FORM*: AABA

≋≋≋≋≋≋≋≋≋≋≋≋≋≋≋≋≋≋≋

I GUESS I'LL HAVE TO CHANGE MY PLAN
(THE BLUE PAJAMA SONG)

WORDS: Howard Dietz, *MUSIC*: Arthur Schwartz
PREMIERE: Revue, *The Little Show* (First Edition)
New York: Selwyn Theatre, 30 April 1929 (321 perf.)
INTRODUCED BY: Clifton Webb

A surprising number of popular songs had their beginnings with words and ideas far different from the finished product. A case in point is "I Guess I'll Have to Change My Plan". This jaunty tune first came into being in 1924 when Arthur Schwartz, a counselor at a boys' summer camp, joined forces with Lorenz Hart, who was a counselor at a nearby camp. This collaboration resulted in the official "Brandt Lake Camp Song", which began with the words:

> *I love to lie awake in bed.*
> *Right after Taps*
> *I pull the flaps*
> *Above my head.*

This early example of Hart's lyrical prowess illustrates his penchant for inner rhymes in such passages as: "And tears are born within the corner of my eye". But the song was never popular outside the environs of Brandt Lake.

Five years later, when Howard Dietz asked Schwartz to collaborate with him on songs for the first edition of *The Little Show*, Schwartz dug up the old camp song. Dietz supplied it with a new set of lyrics and the result was "I Guess I'll Have to Change My Plan". Dietz's lyrics turned the song into a lament about wearing blue pajamas "before the big affair began". So closely did these words come to identify the song that it became known at home and abroad as "The Blue Pajama Song".

Three years later, when the song was being prepared for wider dissemination, Dietz wrote a second set of lyrics, this time leaving out the blue pajamas. To this day, both sets of lyrics are used, with the later version preferred. Early recordings were by Rudy Vallee and his Connecticut Yankees (Columbia) and Guy Lombardo and his Royal Canadians (Brunswick). In 1975 Dick Shawn sang it in *An American Jubilee*.

"I Guess I'll Have to Change My Plan" is a catchy tune, with an infectious profusion of dotted quarter notes. It is tailor-made for soft-shoe and tap dancing and is often performed for those purposes. The music of the refrain is simplicity itself, consisting of a gently falling and then rising melodic line over basic harmonies. The only departures from the norm are the song's twenty-bar length and five-section form.

In 1953, long after the run of *The Little Show*, the song was sung and danced to by Fred Astaire and Jack Buchanan in the Schwartz-Dietz biographical film, *The Band Wagon*. In 1981, it was sung by Kristy McNichol and Marsha Mason in the Neil Simon film, *Only When I Laugh*.

Moderate foxtrot with verse (16) and two refrains (20)
PUBLISHER: Harms, Inc.
KEY: C maj., *STARTS*: e" (C maj.), *FORM*: ABA'CA"

≈≈≈≈≈≈≈≈≈≈≈≈≈≈≈≈≈≈≈

I MAY BE WRONG, BUT I THINK YOU'RE WONDERFUL! *

WORDS: Harry Ruskin, *MUSIC*: Henry Sullivan
PREMIERE: Revue, *Murray Anderson's Almanac*
New York: Erlanger Theatre, 14 August 1929.
INTRODUCED BY: Trixie Friganza and Jimmy Savo

This enduring jazz standard began life as a spoof of sentimental ballads, sung by the two stars of a failed revue, *Murray Anderson's Almanac*. Anderson had more luck with his revues before and after under his full name, John Murray Anderson.

The melody is replete with repeated notes: eleven on the first b-flat' followed by five on the g' a minor third below. In each "A" section, it describes half a descending scale from b-flat' to e-flat'. As if in compensation for this paucity of invention, the middle section acts as a true release, with triplets and interesting harmonic changes, including one as far distant from the home key as D seventh. There are two complete sets of lyrics for male and female singers.

"I May Be Wrong" has been featured in a number of films. It was performed in *Swingtime Johnny* (1943), starring the Andrews Sisters and Harriet Hilliard; in *Wallflower* (1948), with Janis Paige and Joyce Reynolds; and in *You're My Everything* (1949), with Dan Dailey and Ann Baxter. It was sung by Doris Day in the 1950 film, *Young Man with a Horn*; by Jane Wyman in *Starlift* (1951); and by Frankie Lane in the 1951 film, *Sunny Side of the Street.*

It remains a mainstay of the jazzman's (and -woman's) repertoire.

Moderate foxtrot with two verses (16) and two refrains (32)
PUBLISHER: Advanced Music Corporation
KEY: E-flat maj., *STARTS:* b-flat' (E-flat maj.), *FORM*: AABA

≈≈≈≈≈≈≈≈≈≈≈≈≈≈≈≈≈≈

I'LL SEE YOU AGAIN * *

WORDS and MUSIC: Noël Coward
PREMIERE: Operetta, *Bitter Sweet*
London: His Majesty's Theatre, 1 July 1929 (697 perf.);
New York: Ziegfeld Theatre, 5 November 1929 (159 perf.).
INTRODUCED BY: Peggy Wood and George Metaxa (London);
Evelyn Laye and Gerald Nodin (New York)

"I'll See You Again" is truly an American song, despite the fact that both its creator and premiere were British. According to Noël Coward, the melody came to him in its entirety while he was in a taxi in New York, being driven across town for his obligatory rest between performances of *This Year of Grace.* Traffic came to a halt, horns were blowing, but Coward kept the melody in his head. When he reached home, he was unable to write down the tune (he was unschooled in music), but fixed it in his memory by playing it over and over again on the piano.

The song is conceived as a romantic duet for the protagonists of the operetta, Sarah and Carl. The verse, in 4/4 time and notable for its extraordinary length, begins with Carl, the music teacher, asking Sarah to sing a scale, first in C major, then in E-flat major. The two then sing an impassioned duet of love and remembrance. The refrain is a beautiful waltz, solidly in the tradition of Viennese operetta as epitomized by Franz Lehár and Emmerich Kálmán. The enchanting melody is characterized by rising fourths in the "A" sections contrasting with descending quarter notes in the "B" section and descending eighth notes in the "C" section. The result is marvelously romantic.

Bitter Sweet had a reincarnation as a British film in 1933, in which "I'll See You Again" was sung by Anna Neagle and Fernand Gravet. In 1940, the operetta was made into an American film and the duet sung by Jeanette MacDonald and Nelson Eddy. Coward had a special affinity for "I'll See You Again". Throughout his multi-faceted career as playwright, composer, librettist, entertainer, actor and director, he used it as his theme song.

Slow waltz with verse (60) and refrain (32)
PUBLISHER: Chappell & Co. Ltd., assigned to Harms, Inc.
KEY: C maj., *STARTS*: e' (C maj.), *FORM*: ABA'C

≈≈≈≈≈≈≈≈≈≈≈≈≈≈≈≈≈≈≈≈

JUST YOU, JUST ME *

WORDS: Raymond Klages, *MUSIC*: Jesse Greer
PREMIERE: Film musical, *Marianne*, 1929
INTRODUCED BY: Marion Davies and Lawrence Gray

This rhythmical song first saw the light of day as a love duet, written for the Metro-Goldwyn-Mayer film musical, *Marianne*, in which Marion Davies, William Randolph Hearst's celebrated paramour, plays a French girl courted by American soldiers during World War I. Its first recording was by Cliff Edwards (Ukelele Ike), who also appeared in the film. By a strange turn of circumstance, the erstwhile love song went on to become a jazz standard, starting with the release of its recording by Benny Goodman and his Orchestra in 1935. Another famous recording was by the duo of Ray Charles and Betty Carter.

The attraction of "Just You, Just Me" to jazz musicians is not hard to fathom. The music of the refrain is characterized by strong offbeats moving contrapuntally against a descending bass line. By contrast, the lyrics are unbearably cute, and underline the song's original function by the use of such expressions as "To cuddle and coo" and "Use your imagination".

The song was featured in the 1959 film, *This Could Be the Night*, with Jean Simmons, Anthony Franciosa, and Paul Douglas. It was also sung by Liza Minnelli in the 1975 film, *New York, New York*. As a jazz standard, it is usually performed in fast tempo.

Moderate rhythm song with verse (16) and refrain (32)
PUBLISHER: Robbins Music Corporation
KEY: E-flat maj., *STARTS*: b-flat' (E-flat maj.), *FORM*: AABA

≈≈≈≈≈≈≈≈≈≈≈≈≈≈≈≈≈≈≈≈

LIZA (ALL THE CLOUDS'LL ROLL AWAY) *

WORDS: Ira Gershwin and Gus Kahn, *MUSIC*: George Gershwin
PREMIERE: Musical comedy, *Show Girl*
New York: Ziegfeld Theatre, 2 July 1929 (111 perf.)
INTRODUCED BY: Nick Lucas, danced to by Ruby Keeler

The Gershwin brothers had only two weeks to write a complete musical score for Florenz Ziegfeld. To aid them, Ziegfeld assigned the seasoned lyricist, Gus Kahn. No expense was spared. Besides Ruby Keeler, *Show Girl* featured Jimmy Durante, Eddy Foy, Jr., and one hundred (count-'em) beautiful girls. Duke Ellington was in charge of the pit band. Despite this array of talent, the show was not an outstanding success.

Only one song survived: "Liza (All the Clouds'll Roll Away)". It was designed as a minstrel song for the second act, to be sung by Nick Lucas and danced to by Keeler and the one hundred beautiful girls. One night, Keeler's newly-acquired husband, Al Jolson, came to the theatre and sang "Liza" from the audience. He went on to popularize it himself, and it became an important part of his repertoire for the remainder of his career.

Most striking in the refrain is the sonority of the opening chords over a chromatic bass line rising from E-flat to B-flat. Also of interest are the riff endings of each "A" section, at the words "All the clouds'll roll away" and the whole notes in the middle section. Opposed to this musical sophistication are the lyrics, written in the minstrel tradition, as witness: "We should make a date with Parson Brown".

Among films featuring "Liza" are *Rhapsody in Blue*, the 1945 Gershwin biography, with Robert Alda, Alexis Smith, and Oscar Levant; *George White's Scandals* (1945), played by Ethel Smith on the organ; the 1946 film, *The Man I Love*, with Ida Lupino and Robert Alda; *The Jolson Story*, also 1946, with Jolson dubbing for Larry Parks and Evelyn Keyes and a chorus; *An American in Paris* in 1951, with Gene Kelly and Leslie Caron; and *Starlift* (1951), starring Doris Day and Gordon MacRae, in which it was sung by Patrice Wymore. Liberace performed it on the piano in *Sincerely Yours* (1955).

Moderate foxtrot with verse (18) and refrain (32)
PUBLISHER: New World Music Corporation
KEY: E-flat maj., *STARTS*: b-flat' (E-flat maj.), *FORM*: AABA

≈≈≈≈≈≈≈≈≈≈≈≈≈≈≈≈≈≈≈≈≈≈

LOUISE

WORDS: Leo Robin, *MUSIC*: Richard A. Whiting
PREMIERE: Film musical, *Innocents of Paris*, Paramount, 1929
INTRODUCED BY: Maurice Chevalier

This bouncing ballad became Maurice Chevalier's signature song after he introduced it in one of the earliest talking pictures, *Innocents of Paris;* it was his first full-length American film. Chevalier had a hit Victor recording, as did Paul Whiteman's Rhythm Boys (the trio of Harry Barris, Bing Crosby, and Al Rinker). The music has a distinctly French air about it, with its dotted quarters and eighth notes merrily playing around three tones: f', g', and a'. In other films, Johnny Johnson and Betty Jane Rhodes sang "Louise" in *You Can't Ration Love* (1944), Dean Martin and Jerry Lewis clowned through it in *The Stooge* (1953), Chevalier revived it in *A New Kind of Love* (1963), and Neal Diamond performed it in the third screen version of *The Jazz Singer* (1980).

Moderate ballad with verse (8) and refrain (32)
PUBLISHER: Famous Music Corp.
KEY: F maj., *STARTS:* c' (F maj.), *FORM:* A A' B A'

≈≈≈≈≈≈≈≈≈≈≈≈≈≈≈≈≈≈≈≈

MEAN TO ME *

WORDS and MUSIC: Fred E. Ahlert and Roy Turk
INTRODUCED BY: Ruth Etting

Like several other popular songwriters, Fred E. Ahlert originally intended to be a lawyer. But that soon changed when he got involved with music as entertainer, arranger, and composer. He had a big hit with "I'll Get By" in 1928, "Mean to Me" followed a year later, and he went on to write such infectious tunes as "Walkin' My Baby Back Home" in 1930 and "I'm Gonna Sit Right Down and Write Myself a Letter", in 1935.

The somewhat wistful lyrics of "Mean to Me" fall within the torch song tradition of unrequited love, but the music is too light-hearted to properly belong. Nevertheless, two torch singers contributed to its early success: Ruth Etting and Helen Morgan. Billie Holiday and Teddy Wilson made a memorable recording in 1937. More than forty years later, Nell Carter sang it in the Broadway revue, *Ain't Misbehavin'*. Perhaps the most striking characteristic of the refrain is the prolonged pickup note a-sharp' on the contraction "You're". In other respects – melody, harmony, rhythm, form – the music holds no surprises. It is characterized by light syncopation and a gradually rising melodic line in each "A" section of traditional AABA form in thirty-two bars.

Doris Day sang "Mean to Me" in the 1955 biographical film of Ruth Etting, *Love Me or Leave Me*. Diana Ross did it in the 1972 biographical film of Billie Holiday, *Lady Sings the Blues*. It was also featured on Broadway in the 1978 revue, *Ain't Misbehavin'*.

Moderate torch song with two verses (16) and refrain (32)
PUBLISHER: Fred Ahlert Music Co., assigned to Cromwell Music, Inc.
KEY: G maj., *STARTS*: a-sharp' (G maj.), *FORM*: AABA'

≋≋≋≋≋≋≋≋≋≋≋≋≋≋≋≋≋≋

MORE THAN YOU KNOW *

WORDS: William Rose and Edward Eliscu, *MUSIC*: Vincent Youmans
PREMIERE: Musical play, *Great Day!*
New York: Cosmopolitan Theatre, 17 October 1929 (36 perf.)
INTRODUCED BY: Mayo Methot

Another song from the ill-fated musical, *Great Day!*, "More Than You Know" is one of Vincent Youmans's loveliest ballads. Lacking the liveliness and syncopation of such spirited songs as "Hallelujah!", "I Know That You Know", and "Carioca", it is a slow and tender love song. Its beauty was quickly recognized by many singers. The song was first popularized by Jane Froman. Later, Mildred Bailey and then Perry Como recorded it, followed by many others.

Like most of Youmans's creations ("Tea for Two" is a good example), the refrain is built around a rhythmical motive that is endlessly repeated. The pervading rhythm in this case consists of a quarter-note triplet followed by a half note. First occurring as a pickup, this rhythmical motive is repeated fifteen times in the refrain, each time with the triplets rising chromatically. Despite this economy of means, the music never gets cloying. Indeed, the rhythmic repetition on different pitches lends it a hypnotic effect. In addition, there are other dimensions to the song. The verse, in E-flat minor, is almost a song in itself. The middle section affords welcome relief from the pervasive triplets with its descending melodic line, and its modulation fron G minor to B-flat major.

Several films have featured "More Than You Know", including the first screen version of *Hit the Deck* in 1930 and the British film, *Encore* in 1952. Tony Martin sang it in the 1955 screen version of *Hit the Deck*. In 1957, Gogi Grant sang it for Ann Blyth in *The Helen Morgan Story* (known in Britain as *Both Ends of the Candle*). Finally, Barbra Streisand sang it in *Funny Lady*, the 1975 film biography of Fanny Brice.

Slow ballad with verse (16) and refrain (32)
PUBLISHER: Miller Music, Inc. and Vincent Youmans, Inc.
KEY: E-flat maj., *STARTS*: b-flat' (E-flat maj.), *FORM*: AA'BA"

≈≈≈≈≈≈≈≈≈≈≈≈≈≈≈≈≈≈≈

SIBONEY

ENGLISH WORDS: Dolly Morse, *MUSIC*: Ernesto Lecuona
INTRODUCED BY: Don Azpiazú and his Havana Casino Orchestra

Ernesto Lecuona, Cuba's most renowned composer, was a child prodigy, born in 1896, who appeared at New York's Aeolian Hall at the age of seventeen. Dolly Morse, the English lyricist, held something of a record for *noms de plumes;* she also wrote under the names: Theodora Morse, D. A. Esrom (a not-so-clever disguise), and Dorothy Terriss. Furthermore, way back in 1917, she had co-authored "Hail, Hail, the Gang's All Here", with her husband, Theodore Morse.

Originally written with Spanish words by the composer, it was called "Canto Siboney". Published in New York in 1929 as a "Danzon Cubano" and advertised as "That Quaint Melody That All Havana Dances To", the song road the wave of popularity of Cuban music in the United States that began a year later, with the phenomenal success of Don Azpiazú's recording of "The Peanut Vendor" for RCA Victor. "Siboney" was soon further popularized by the orchestras of Xavier Cugat and Enric Madriguera. Since then, it has been recorded many times and in many ways. One of the most extraordinary recordings was made in 1953, by a jazz quartet featuring Dizzy Gillespie and Stan Getz.

The verse is an integral part of the song, and both verse and refrain are usually played together. The music is an artful juxtaposition of major and minor tonality. The verse sets the tone, with a striking melody outlining the C minor triad. The refrain has a similar, but higher pitched, melody outlining the C major chord, while the coda returns again to C minor. Thus the overall tonality is minor-major-minor.

"Siboney" has also had its day in films. Don Azpiazú featured it in a 1931 film short; Grace Moore sang it in *When You're in Love* (1937); it was sung by a chorus in *Vogues of 1938*, later titled *All This and Glamour Too*; and by Gloria Jean in *Get Hep to Love* (1942), known in Britain as *It Comes Up Love*.

Moderate rumba with verse (28) and refrain (40)
PUBLISHER: Leo Feist, Inc.
KEY: C maj., *STARTS*: e' (C maj.), *FORM*: AA'AA'B

≈≈≈≈≈≈≈≈≈≈≈≈≈≈≈≈≈≈≈

SINGIN' IN THE RAIN ＊＊＊

WORDS: Arthur Freed, *MUSIC*: Nacio Herb Brown
PREMIERE: Musical film, *Hollywood Revue of 1929*
INTRODUCED BY: Cliff Edwards, The Rounders, and The Brox Sisters

"Singin' in the Rain" is a pure product of Hollywood. Inseparably identified with Gene Kelly since his unforgettable song and dance routine in the 1952 film, *Singin' in the Rain*, its Hollywood credentials began long before that. The song was written by two studio writers for one of the first musical films, *Hollywood Revue of 1929*. This concoction, one of the few screen revues, had an all-star cast including Jack Benny, Joan Crawford, Buster Keaton, John Gilbert, Norma Shearer, Marion Davies, and Laurel and Hardy. Cliff Edwards, who introduced the song, along with The Rounders and The Brox Sisters, was a country-style entertainer better known as 'Ukelele Ike.' Unmistakably a West Coast song, "Singin' in the Rain" was first recorded by Gus Arnheim and his Orchestra at the famous Cocoanut Grove in Los Angeles. Illustrating the song's longevity, a stage production using the song's title and based on the 1952 film, *Singin' in the Rain*, opened at the Gershwin Theatre in New York 2 July 1985.

With its dotted rhythms, "Singin' in the Rain" is a natural for singing and dancing in a nonchalant way. Adding to its appeal is its quasi-pentatonic melody, which skips merrily from note to note while staying within a range of exactly one octave. There is no verse, but an interesting patter built around the E-flat seventh chord.

The song went on to a long and distinguished career in cinema. Jimmy Durante sang it in the 1932 film *Speak Easily*. Judy Garland sang it in *Little Nellie Kelly* (1940). In 1944, the song was one of many in the film, *Hi, Beautiful*. Then it was Gene Kelly's turn, an astounding five-minute production number, in the Metro Goldwyn Mayer blockbuster, *Singin' in the Rain* (1952), in which he co-starred with Debbie Reynolds and Donald O'Connor. Kelly reprised the song, along with Malcolm McDowell, in a violent song and dance scene in Stanley Kubrick's 1971 film, *A Clockwork Orange*. Finally, this venerable and beloved song of the twenties was featured in the 1973 Metro Goldwyn Mayer compendium, *That's Entertainment*. And whenever the song is heard, it evokes memories of Kelly dancin' and singin' in the rain.

Moderate foxtrot with refrain (32) and patter (24)
PUBLISHER: Metro Goldwyn Mayer Corporation, assigned to
Robbins Music Corporation
KEY: G maj., *STARTS*: d' (G maj.), *FORM*: ABA'B'

≈≈≈≈≈≈≈≈≈≈≈≈≈≈≈≈≈≈≈≈

STAR DUST ＊＊＊＊!

WORDS: Mitchell Parish, *MUSIC*: Hoagy Carmichael
INTRODUCED: at the Cotton Club in Harlem, New York

One of the most popular ballads ever written, "Star Dust" is in reality two songs. Either verse or chorus could stand alone. Indeed, both portions of the song have been recorded on their own, by Frank Sinatra and others.

"Star Dust" began in 1927 as a "lazy rag", an instrumental ragtime piece for piano, entitled "Barnyard Shuffle". Later the same year, it was recorded on Gannett Records as an instrumental called "Stomp", featuring a group called Hoagy Carmichael and his Pals.

The composer was a young law-school graduate named Howard Hoagland Carmichael, who wrote the tune while he was visiting his alma mater, Indiana University. According to Carmichael, the melody came to him while he was sitting on the so-called "spooning wall", and remembering a girl named Dorothy whom he had loved and lost.

Two years later, publisher Irving Mills in New York persuaded Carmichael to slow down the tempo. He also had a young lyricist who was working for him, named Mitchell Parish, supply the lyrics. The title came from a classmate of Carmichael's, Stuart Gorrell, who likened the melody to stars slowly falling from the sky.

"Star Dust" is in many ways an unusual song. The melody, consisting of wide leaps and unexpected turns from major to minor, is more suitable for instruments than for voices. Indeed, it was conceived that way. Very often, the melody outlines the harmonies, which are jazz-oriented, with a plenitude of sevenths, ninths, and thirteenths. Starting with a minor chord on the second degree of the scale was very daring in its day; the same idea was taken up by Johnny Green a year later, in his "Body and Soul".

Unlike most standards, "Star Dust" did not originate in a show or film. It is a pure product of Tin Pan Alley. It was introduced at the Cotton Club in New York's Harlem and later the same year was popularized in a recording by Isham Jones and his Orchestra, which was a best seller. Jones further contributed to the song's success by playing it in concert form on a nationwide radio broadcast.

Over the years, "Star Dust" has been recorded hundreds of times, by Bing Crosby, Louis Armstrong, Frank Sinatra, Nat "King" Cole, and by virtually every other singer imaginable. It was recorded by the big bands of Wayne King, Jimmy Lunceford, Benny Goodman, Tommy Dorsey, and Glenn Miller, to mention just a few. Artie Shaw's Victor recording of 1941 sold over two million copies. It has crossed the threshold into rock, in recordings by Billy Ward and his Dominoes in 1957 and by Nino Tempo and April Stevens in 1964.

In the movies, "Star Dust" has had an equally impressive career. It was sung by Mary Healy in the 1940 film *Star Dust*, by David Essex in the British film, *Stardust* (1975); by Nat "King" Cole in *My Favorite Year* (1952); and by Rob Wasserman and Aaron Neville in *Rain Man* (1988). It was dubbed in on the piano by Carmen Cavallaro in *The Eddy Duchin Story* (1956, with Tyrone Power and Kim Novak) and was featured in *Sleepless in Seattle* (1994, with Tom Hanks and Meg Ryan).

One of the all-time classics of American popular song, "Star Dust" has been translated into at least forty different languages, was selected for ASCAP's All-Time Hit Parade, and was chosen for *Variety*'s Golden 100.

Slow ballad with verse (16) and refrain (32)
PUBLISHER: Mills Music, Inc.
KEY: C maj. or D-flat maj., *STARTS*: b' (D min.) or c'' (E-flat min.),
FORM: ABAC

≈≈≈≈≈≈≈≈≈≈≈≈≈≈≈≈≈≈≈

TIP-TOE THRU THE TULIPS WITH ME

WORDS: Al Dubin, *MUSIC*: Joe Burke
PREMIERE: Film musical, *Gold Diggers of Broadway* (1929)
INTRODUCED BY: Nick Lucas

Produced by Warner Brothers, *Gold Diggers of Broadway* was built around the familiar plot of three girls and three wealthy admirers. It had all the necessary ingredients for a hit: Technicolor, girls, comedy, music, dancing, and production numbers. But only one of its many songs has retained its popularity: "Tip-Toe Thru the Tulips With Me". Still, the idea of gold diggers took root and many more Gold Digger films followed in the thirties. Early recordings were by Nick Lucas (Brunswick) and Jean

Goldkette and his Orchestra (Victor). There have been several revivals, notably that of 1968, sparked by Tiny Tim's famous recording on Reprise.

The song is a natural for tap dancing. It also is noted for its excessive, almost campy, cuteness. Each "A" section has an ascending line of repeated notes and dotted rhythms. In abrupt contrast, there are drops of an octave in the middle section, at the words "Knee-deep" and "We'll keep".

The song was featured in the 1945 film, *Confidential Agent*, starring Charles Boyer, Lauren Bacall, and Peter Lorre. In the 1951 film, *Painting the Clouds with Sunshine*, it was sung by Gene Nelson, Lucille Norman, Virginia Mayo, and Virginia Gibson. As a period piece, it was again sung by Nick Lucas in the 1974 film, *The Great Gatsby*.

Moderate foxtrot with two verses (16) and refrain (32)
PUBLISHER: M. Witmark & Sons
KEY: E-flat maj., *STARTS*: g' (E-flat maj.), *FORM*: AABA

≈≈≈≈≈≈≈≈≈≈≈≈≈≈≈≈≈≈≈≈

WHAT IS THIS THING CALLED LOVE? * *!

WORDS and MUSIC: Cole Porter
PREMIERE: Revue, *Wake Up and Dream*
New York: Selwyn Theatre, 30 December 1929 (136 perf.)
INTRODUCED BY: Frances Shelley, danced by Tilly Losch and chorus

One of Cole Porter's most inventive songs, "What Is This Thing Called Love?" was also one of the last songs to come out in the twenties. It was first heard in New York the night before New Year's Eve, with the opening of the English revue, *Wake Up and Dream*. In that revue, Tilly Losch danced it exotically to the incessant beat of tom-toms in front of an African idol. Although *Wake Up and Dream* had had a profitable run in London ((263 performances), it suffered from mixed revues on this side of the Atlantic. However, columnist Walter Winchell especially liked this song and favorably reported on it. It became a hit and was revived in 1942.

The refrain is marked "Slow (in the manner of a "Blues)". Although not in fact a blues song, the emphasis throughout is the blue note: in this case the flatted seventh (b-flat') and flatted sixth (a-flat'). The opening chord of the refrain, the C seventh, is rare in popular music, as is the immediate modulation to F minor. The melody of the release is similar to the main theme, but a fourth higher, with harmonies moving from F seventh to B-flat, and then stepwise to A-flat and G.

In film, "What Is This Thing Called Love?" was sung by The King's Men in *You're a Lucky Fellow, Mr. Smith* (1943), by Peg La Centra in *Humoresque* (1946), by Ginny Simms in *Night and Day* (1946), and played by Harry James and his Orchestra in *Young Man with a Horn* (1950). Lucille Norman and Gordon MacRae sang it in the 1953 film, *Starlift,* and it was featured in the 1956 film, *The Eddy Duchin Story.* Rarely performed as a ballad, this innovative song survives as a jazz standard, often performed in moderate to fast tempo.

Slow ballad with verse (18) and refrain (32)
PUBLISHER: Harms, Inc.
KEY: C maj., *STARTS*: b-flat' (C7), *FORM*: AA'BA"

≈≈≈≈≈≈≈≈≈≈≈≈≈≈≈≈≈≈≈

WHY WAS I BORN?

WORDS: Oscar Hammerstein II, *MUSIC*: Jerome Kern
PREMIERE: Musical comedy, *Sweet Adeline*
New York: Hammerstein's Theatre, 3 September 1929 (234 perf.)
INTRODUCED BY: Helen Morgan

From *Sweet Adeline*, the same show that brought forth "Don't Ever Leave Me", this song is a cry of loneliness and despair. It was introduced by Helen Morgan, the consummate torch singer, who went on to popularize the song over the years, performing it from her trademark perch atop a grand piano. "Why Was I Born?" was not an immediate favorite with the New York theatre critics. Percy Hammond of the *New York Herald-Tribune* called it "Kern's wailing obbligato". The critic at *Theatre Magazine* characterized it as "rather lugubrious". Almost half a century later, Patrice Munsel sang it in the 1975 revue, *A Musical Jubilee.*

The song is a perfect marriage of words and music, an artful concoction blending Hammerstein's lamentful words with Kern's moving music. The key to the song's perfection lies in its rhythmic subtleties. The words "Why Was I Born?" perfectly fit the framework of the first four e-flat"s, pitched at the highest point of the refrain in the rhythmic pattern: short-short-short-long. This pattern is repeated in each "A" section, in contrast to the "B" sections in entirely different rhythmical configurations beginning with two eighth notes (the only eighth notes in the refrain). Another rhythmic subtlety is the alternation of line endings between single- and double-note cadences. Thus, phrases ending with the words "born" and "get" alternate with those ending with "living" and "giving". As in a number of his other works, Kern uses material from the refrain in the verse: in this case, echoing the rhythmic pattern of the "B" sections.

"Why Was I Born?" has been featured in several films, including the 1935 screen version of *Sweet Adeline*, sung by Irene Dunne; and two films of 1946: *Till the Clouds Roll By*, sung by Lena Horne; and *The Man I Love*, sung by Ida Lupino. Gogi Grant dubbed it in for Ann Blyth in the 1957 film, *The Helen Morgan Story*, known in Great Britain as *Both Ends of the Candle*.

Moderate torch song with verse (20) and refrain (32)
PUBLISHER: T. B. Harms Company
KEY: E-flat maj., *STARTS*: e-flat" (E-flat maj.), *FORM*: ABAB'

≈≈≈≈≈≈≈≈≈≈≈≈≈≈≈≈≈≈≈≈

WITH A SONG IN MY HEART *

WORDS: Lorenz Hart, *MUSIC*: Richard Rodgers
PREMIERE: Musical comedy, *Spring Is Here*
New York: Alvin Theatre, 11 March 1929 (104 perf.)
INTRODUCED BY: Lillian Taiz and John Hundley

This romantic ballad was written for *Spring Is Here*, a show that did not outlast the spring season of 1929. The song did, however. With its bravura melody, straightforward harmonies, and lack of syncopation, it remains a favorite with popular as well as classical singers. Concert artists such as Placido Domingo and Luciano Pavarotti feature it in their repertoires.

Both words and music contribute to the song's charm. Hart, master of rhyming, has such lovely pairings as "your adorable face" and "a hymn to your grace"; while Rodgers plays around three neighboring tones, b-flat', a', and c", and carries them along in sequence. Although the first five notes of the refrain, to the words "With a song in my...," feel like a pickup, they are not. Rather, with an opening rest, they constitute the first bar.

"With a Song In My Heart" has been featured in many films. Alexander Gray and Bernice Claire sang it in the 1930 screen version of *Spring Is Here*. In 1944, Susana Foster and Donald O'Connor sang it in *This Is the Life*. Perry Como did the honors in the 1948 Rodgers-Hart biopic *Words and Music*. Doris Day did it in the 1950 film, *Young Man with a Horn*, known in Britain as *Young Man of Music*. In *Painting the Clouds with Sunshine* (1951), it was sung by Dennis Morgan and Lucille Norman. Finally, in 1952, the song was used as the title of the Jane Froman biographical film, *With a Song in My Heart*, and dubbed in by Jane Froman herself for Susan Hayward.

Slow ballad with two verses (16) and refrain (32)
PUBLISHER: Harms, Inc.
KEY: E-flat maj., *STARTS*: b-flat' (E-flat maj.), *FORM*: ABAB'

≈≈≈≈≈≈≈≈≈≈≈≈≈≈≈≈≈≈≈

WITHOUT A SONG

WORDS: William Rose and Edward Eliscu, *MUSIC*: Vincent Youmans
PREMIERE: Musical play, *Great Day!*
New York: Cosmopolitan Theatre, 17 October 1929 (36 perf.)
INTRODUCED BY: Lois Deppe and The Russell Wooding Jubilee Singers

This powerful song has been closely identified with the Metropolitan Opera baritone Lawrence Tibbett, who featured it in the 1931 Metro Goldwyn Mayer film *The Prodigal* and recorded it for Victor. He then used it as his theme song throughout his career. There have been numerous other recordings, by Nelson Eddy, Perry Como, and Frank Sinatra, to name a few. Lacking a verse, the song's great effectiveness comes from several factors: its use of the pentatonic scale, its wide range, its outlining of chords with repeated notes, and its groups of three quarter-note pickups. Welcome harmonic contrast is offered by the release, which begins in A-flat major and modulates to G minor before returning to the tonic of E-flat major. Like "With a Song in My Heart", it is favored by concert singers as part of their "semi-classical" repertoire.

Slow ballad with refrain (32)
PUBLISHER: Vincent Youmans, Inc.
KEY: E-flat maj., *STARTS*: b-flat' (E-flat maj. 7), *FORM*: AABA

≈≈≈≈≈≈≈≈≈≈≈≈≈≈≈≈≈≈≈

YOU DO SOMETHING TO ME * *

WORDS and MUSIC: Cole Porter
PREMIERE: Musical comedy, *Fifty Million Frenchmen*
New York: Lyric Theatre, 27 November 1929 (254 perf.)
INTRODUCED BY: William Gaxton

As with many Cole Porter creations, this enticing song began life as a slow ballad but is most often played uptempo, with a beat. In *Fifty Million Frenchmen*, William Gaxton sang it to a French girl he was wooing while he was masquerading as a guide taking her on a tour of Paris. In spite of the stock market crash, the musical was a success and so was the song. Early recordings were by Marlene Dietrich (Brunswick), Leo Reisman and his Orchestra (Victor), and Marion Harris (Brunswick).

With its long-held notes, reaching ever higher and higher, the first three sections of the refrain give it an air of optimism. The peak is reached at the end of the third section, where words and music coalesce at the syncopated passage: "Do do that voodoo that you do so well". As usual with Porter, his lyrics carry a special cachet, as in the rhyming of "mystifies me" with "hypnotize me".

Numerous films have featured the song. Gaxton sang it again in the 1931 film version of *Fifty Million Frenchmen*. Joan Crawford and Peg La Centra sang it in *Humoresque* (1946). That same year, Jane Wyman and a chorus sang it in *Night and Day*, the Porter biography. Doris Day did it in *Starlift* (1951), and Mario Lanza and Doretta Morrow in *Because You're Mine* (1952). Gogi Grant sang it for Ann Blyth in *The Helen Morgan Story* (1957), while Louis Jourdan sang it in the 1960 film musical *Can-Can*.

Endowed with sparkling lyrics and music, "You Do Something to Me" is one of Cole Porter's most admired creations.

Slow ballad with verse (16) and refrain (32)
PUBLISHER: Harms, Inc.
KEY: E-flat maj., *STARTS*: e-flat' (E-flat maj.), *FORM*: A A'BA"

≈≈≈≈≈≈≈≈≈≈≈≈≈≈≈≈≈≈≈

YOU WERE MEANT FOR ME

WORDS: Arthur Freed, *MUSIC*: Nacio Herb Brown
PREMIERE: Film musical, *The Broadway Melody*. Metro Goldwyn Mayer
Hollywood: Grauman's Chinese Theatre, 1 February 1929;
New York: Astor Theatre, 8 February 1929
INTRODUCED BY: Charles King

This historic ballad was part of the first musical score written specifically for a motion picture: *The Broadway Melody*, the first all-talking, all-singing, all-dancing screen spectacular, and the forerunner of many to come. The song's composer, Nacio Herb Brown, had a most distinguished career as a songwriter for films. Its lyricist, Arthur Freed, went on to become Metro Goldwyn Mayer's top producer of film musicals. This ballad, also featured in two other films this year alone, launched a new and fertile venue for the introduction of songs: the silver screen.

Freed's words, "You're like a plaintive melody /That never lets me free", sets the tone of the song. The melody is indeed plaintive, using an economy of means. Each "A" section consists of only four half notes leading to a tied whole note, with the five notes then repeated.

True to its Hollywood origins, "You Were Meant for Me" has been featured in a number of films in addition to *The Broadway Melody*, in which it was sung by Charles King. King dubbed it in for Conrad Nagel in *The Hollywood Revue of 1929*. Winnie Lightner and Bull Montana performed it in *The Show of Shows* (also 1929). In 1940 Frank Morgan sang it in *Hullabaloo* and a chorus performed it in *Forty Little Mothers*. It was the title of the 1948 film, *You Were Meant for Me*, in which it was sung by Dan Dailey. And in 1952, Gene Kelly sang it in the immortal *Singin' in the Rain*.

Moderate ballad with verse (16) and refrain (32)
PUBLISHER: Robbins Music Corporation
KEY: F maj., *STARTS*: d" (G min. 6), *FORM*: ABAC/A'

≈≈≈≈≈≈≈≈≈≈≈≈≈≈≈≈≈≈

ZIGEUNER!

WORDS and MUSIC: Noël Coward
PREMIERE: Operetta, *Bitter Sweet*
London: His Majesty's Theatre, 1 July 1929 (697 perf.);
New York: Ziegfeld Theatre, 5 November 1929 (159 perf.)
INTRODUCED BY: Peggy Wood (London), Evelyn Laye (New York)

This sentimental Gypsy air fits in handsomely with the nostalgic plot of *Bitter Sweet*, the tale of an elderly lady who, in advising her niece whether to marry for love or money, remembers her own marriage for love. Although the times were against the operetta's success in New York, this song has managed to survive, along with another from the same operetta, "I'll See You Again". It is an enchanting waltz and a far cry from Noël Coward's usual output. Very much in the Viennese tradition, it is melodious and rampant with chromatic harmonies. The verse by itself – with its scales cascading downwards – would make a magnificent song. The refrain brings forth a new dimension in its chromaticism, especially the voluptuous harmonic movement from c-flat ninth to b-flat seventh at the first two utterings of the word "Zigeuner" in the "A" sections. In practice, most of the scalewise passages of eighth notes in both verse and refrain are usually performed in parallel thirds. Anna Neagle sang "Zigeuner" in the 1933 film version of *Bitter Sweet* and Jeanette MacDonald sang it in the 1940 screen version. It remains a light classic, especially favored by violinists, pianists, and string ensembles.

Slow waltz with two verses (16) and refrain (32)
PUBLISHER: Chappell & Co. Ltd.
KEY: E-flat maj., *STARTS*: f-sharp' (E-flat maj.)

≈≈≈≈≈≈≈≈≈≈≈≈≈≈≈≈≈≈≈

1930-1939

ACT II: THE DEPRESSION YEARS

Prologue

> *It was the best of times, it was the worst of times,.*
> *it was the spring of hope, it was the winter of despair...*
>
> Charles Dickens,
> *A Tale of Two Cities*

It is ironic to observe that The Great Depression, a time of much heart-rending despair, was also the incubator for some of the most inventive and lasting songs ever written. The 1930s saw the birth of a multitude of memorable standards, a rich legacy of songs that remain American icons more than half a century after they were written.

A striking feature of many of these songs is their individuality. Innovative standards like "Body and Soul" (1930) and "All the Things You Are" stand as masterpieces in miniature, a seamless wedding of music and lyrics. But even more ordinary songs, such as "As Time Goes By" (1931) and "I Only Have Eyes for You". have a strong feeling of singularity. They also share with their more adventurous brethren the characteristic of endurance.

The Depression was above all an era of experimentation. As if to compensate for the dreariness of much everyday life, many songs seem deliberately designed to be different, to get away from commonplace harmony and from the tyranny of thirty-two bar, AABA form. Some of them, such as "Begin the Beguine" and "Lullaby of Broadway" (both 1935), are vastly extended in length. Others, like "April in Paris" (1932) and "Sophisticated Lady" (1933), have complex, impressionistic harmonies. But even such conventional songs as "Memories of You" (1930) and "These Foolish Things Remind Me of You" (1936) share a quality of originality that has contributed to their endurance.

The romantic ballad stands supreme in this decade, in lockstep with the decline of the foxtrot of the twenties. Expressions of love such as "Embraceable You" (1930) and "Love Is Here to Stay" (1938) are at the forefront. Almost all ballads are in common time, emphasizing melody and harmony at the expense of rhythm. In general, tempos have slowed down drastically from those of the fast-paced twenties. Moderato is the tempo of choice, except for a few leftover torch songs in slow tempo, like "Body and Soul" and "But Not for Me" (both 1930). Rhythm songs are in short supply, only emerging at decade's end with the rise of swing and the big bands. There are still a few lingering waltzes, remnants of the previous century, most of them from the pen of Richard Rodgers who brings a new dimension to the genre in songs like "Lover" (1933) and "Falling in Love with Love (1938)." From Latin America comes an exciting new rhythm, the rumba, introduced to New York in 1931 with "The Peanut Vendor". a Cuban sensation. A craze for things south of the border ensues, with Mexican imports such as "Magic Is the Moonlight" (1930) and "What a Diff'rence a Day Made" (1934).

The two verse/chorus format so prevalent in the twenties is now rarely seen. Most songs consist simply of verse and refrain. However, an increasing number do away with the verse altogether. This is especially true in the case of Jerome Kern who disposes with verses entirely in such gems as "Smoke Gets in Your Eyes" (1933) and "The Way You Look Tonight" (1936).

Most songs give separate credits for words and music, although an increasing number are marked "Words and Music By..." George and Ira Gershwin are at the peak of their powers, producing the political satire, *Of Thee I Sing*, in 1931 and the opera, *Porgy and Bess*, in 1935; their collaboration comes to a sudden end with George's death in 1937. Jerome Kern is also at his peak, writing with a succession of lyric writers including Otto Harbach, Oscar Hammerstein II and Dorothy Fields. Lorenz Hart and Richard Rodgers are among the top echelon of songwriters, producing a myriad of delightfully fresh creations. Irving Berlin is at his most original in his work in Hollywood, notably in *Top Hat* (1935). And a bright, new comet appears on the horizon with the incomparable words and music of Cole Porter. Among other composers active in the thirties are: Harold Arlen, Harry Warren, Jimmy McHugh, Nacio Herb Brown, Duke Ellington, Hoagy Carmichael, Arthur Schwartz, Vernon Duke, and Johnny Green. Lyricists include Oscar Hammerstein II, Johnny Mercer, Al Dubin, Harold Dietz, and E. Y. "Yip" Harburg.

The center of gravity of the nation's songs has shifted from Tin Pan Alley to somewhere between Broadway and Hollywood. Indeed, by the end of the decade, many writers are firmly entrenched on the West Coast. The number of inventive songs emanating from the movies reaches a crescendo in the last half of the decade, with such classics as "Cheek to Cheek" (1935), "I've Got You Under My Skin" (1936), and "A Foggy Day" (1937). Also in the late thirties, the proliferating big bands and emerging crooners make their contribution by disseminating these songs nation-wide on radio and in recordings.

The subject of choice is clearly romantic love; in strong contrast to the twenties, there are very few "name" songs and hardly any "place" songs. Although thirty-two bar refrains in AABA form still predominate, there are a number of other structural patterns, as for example in Porter's works, "Night and Day" (1932) – ABA'BCB' – and "Begin the Beguine" (1935) – AA'BA"CC'. With a surfeit of beautiful melodies, increasingly sophisticated harmonies and carefully wrought lyrics, there is no doubt that the art of the popular song has reached its apogee in America during the Depression years of the thirties.

1930

A CORNUCOPIA OF STANDARDS

1930

Stocks can go down, business slow down
But the milk and honey flow down.

Ira Gershwin and Billy Rose
"Cheerful Little Earful"

The first full year of the Great Depression is a banner year for standards. Thirty-five of them come out this year, including some of the most popular songs ever written: "Body and Soul", "Embraceable You", "Georgia on My Mind", "I Got Rhythm", and "On the Sunny Side of the Street". Although most of them emanate from Broadway, an increasing number originate in films. These songs are a varied lot, ranging from the lugubrious "But Not for Me" to the exuberant "Fine and Dandy"; from the waltz, "When Your Hair Has Turned to Silver, I Will Love You Just the Same", to the foxtrot, "Exactly Like You"; from the ordinary "Walkin' My Baby Back Home" to the strikingly original "Love for Sale".

This proliferation of standards is hard to understand in face of the terrible times. By late spring, unemployment rises and the country sinks into deep Depression. Over 1,000 banks close their doors, including the prestigious Bank of the United States. And to make matters worse, a severe drought scorches the Midwest. Spurred on by credit given them by the International Apple Shippers' Association, thousands of unemployed men take to the streets to sell apples.

But there are diversions aplenty. Bathtub gin parties, flaunting Prohibition, become the rage; so do miniature golf and tree-sitting. The public flocks to the movies to see the newfangled talking pictures. Spurred on by advertisements reading "Garbo Talks!", they rush to see the Swedish star in her first talkie, *Anna Christie*, and relish her first words on screen: "Gif me a viskey, and don't be stingy, baby." Other films introduce Jean Harlow in *Hell's Angels*, Lew Ayres in *All Quiet on the Western Front*, and Marlene Dietrich in the German film, *The Blue Angel*.

Broadway suffers, by comparison, with fewer shows and fewer live theaters. But there are several productive musicals, including the revue, *Three's a Crowd,* and the Gershwins' *Strike Up the Band* and *Girl Crazy* – the latter introducing two new stars, Ethel Merman and Ginger Rogers. Non-musical plays include *Once in a Lifetime* by Moss Hart and George S. Kaufman and Vicki Baum's *Grand Hotel.* Marc Connelly's *The Green Pastures* wins the Pulitzer Prize.

With less money available, people can't afford to buy records. They spend more and more time at home listening to their favorite songs on the radio. Perhaps that explains why there is such an abundance of standards in this *annus horribilis.*

SONGS OF 1930

    Beyond the Blue Horizon
    Bidin' My Time *
    Body and Soul * * * *!
    But Not for Me *
    Bye Bye Blues
    Cheerful Little Earful
    Confessin' (That I Love You)
    A Cottage for Sale
    Dancing on the Ceiling * *
    Embraceable You * * * *
    Exactly Like You * *
    Falling in Love Again (Can't Help It)
    Fine and Dandy
    For You
    Georgia on My Mind * * *
    Get Happy
    I Got Rhythm * * *
    I'm Yours
    I've Got a Crush on You *!
    Just a Gigolo
    Little White Lies
    Love for Sale *!
    Magic Is the Moonlight
    Memories of You * *
    On the Sunny Side of the Street * * *

Please Don't Talk About Me When I'm Gone
Puttin' on the Ritz
Something to Remember You By *
Them There Eyes
Three Little Words *
Time on My Hands *
Walkin' My Baby Back Home
When Your Hair Has Turned to Silver
    (I Will Love You Just the Same)
You Brought a New Kind of Love to Me
You're Driving Me Crazy (What Did I Do?)

BEYOND THE BLUE HORIZON

WORDS: Leo Robin, *MUSIC*: Richard A.Whiting and W. Franke Harling
PREMIERE: Film musical, *Monte Carlo*, 1930
INTRODUCED BY: Jeanette MacDonald and chorus of "peasants"

In one of the most memorable sequences in cinematic history, Jeanette MacDonald sings this rollicking train song as the character she portrays, a countess, speeds from Paris to Monte Carlo aboard the famed Blue Express, to the accompaniment of rolling wheels, hissing steam, and rhythmic pistons. Peasants abandon their work in the fields to sing the second refrain. Shortly after its momentous introduction, "Beyond the Blue Horizon" was popularized by George Olsen and his Orchestra. It was revived in 1951 in a popular recording by Hugo Winterhalter and his Orchestra.

This splendid song is an early example of art music written specifically for the screen. The idea for the striking melody came from the symphonic and operatic composer, W. Franke Harling; it was adapted by the established popular composer, Richard A. Whiting. The dramatic verse beginning with the words "On, on, from darkness unto dawn" is in the key of C minor contrasting with that of the refrain in A-flat major. The jagged melody of the refrain, with its chromaticism and frequent intervals of the sixth, is most appealing.

Jeanette MacDonald reprised "Beyond the Blue Horizon" in the 1944 film, *Follow the Boys*. Lou Christie sang it in *Rain Man* (1988).

Moderate foxtrot with verse (35) and refrain (32)
PUBLISHER: Famous Music Corporation
KEY: A-flat maj., *STARTS*: e-flat' (A-flat maj.), *FORM*: ABAB'

≈≈≈≈≈≈≈≈≈≈≈≈≈≈≈≈≈≈≈

BIDIN' MY TIME *

WORDS: Ira Gershwin, *MUSIC*: George Gershwin
PREMIERE: Musical comedy, *Girl Crazy*
New York: Alvin Theatre, 14 October 1930 (272 perf.)
INTRODUCED BY: The Foursome

The musical comedy, *Girl Crazy,* brought forth a surprising array of major talents, among them Ethel Merman, Ginger Rogers, and Willie Howard. In the pit was the Red Nichols Orchestra, with such illustrious sidemen as Benny Goodman, Jimmy Dorsey, Glenn Miller, Gene Krupa, and Jack Teagarden. The show also brought forth a ravishing score by the

Gershwin brothers, including such future standards as "Embraceable You," "I Got Rhythm," "But Not For Me" and "Bidin' My Time." The last-named song was introduced in the show by four cowboys, played by a vocal group called The Foursome. In one of the show's most memorable sequences, they not only sang the ditty while sitting on a fence but played it in perfect harmony on their respective instruments: harmonica, jew's harp, ocarina, and tin flute.

The song's most unusual feature is its three-part form: ABA. It lacks repeat of the first "A" section, almost routine in popular songs of the day. It was originally written in traditional thirty-two-bar AABA form, but both Ira and George felt that the song dragged too much at this length. They accordingly cut it down to twenty-four bars. Aside from this departure from convention, the melody is simple enough, moving step-wise except for descending intervals of the fourth at the words "I'm" and "time" in the evocative passage "I'm Bidin' My Time / 'Cause that's the kinda guy I'm." It is notable that the first two bars of the refrain bear a marked resemblance to the famous slow theme of George's own *Rhapsody in Blue*, written six years earlier. In keeping with the rustic nature of the piece, harmonies are mostly tonic and dominant except for a brief excursion to C major in the first half of the release. A touch of humor is injected in the first verse by clever quotations, both verbal and musical, from four popular songs of the day: "Tip Toe Through the Tulips," "Singin' in the Rain," "Painting the Clouds with Sunshine", and Swingin' Down the Lane."

"Bidin' My Time" was featured in the first Hollywood treatment of *Girl Crazy* in 1932. Judy Garland sang it in the second *Girl Crazy* film in 1943. The song also appeared in the Gershwin biographical film, *Rhapsody in Blue* (1945). A male quartet sang it in *The Glenn Miller Story* (1954). Finally, Herman's Hermits sang it in a 1965 Hollywood remake of *Girl Crazy* called *When the Boys Meet the Girls*. Over the years, it has evolved from a rustic patter song into a jazz standard.

Moderate patter song with two verses (16) and two refrains (24)
PUBLISHER: New World Music Corporation
KEY: E-flat maj., *STARTS*: g' (E-flat maj.), *FORM*: ABA

≈≈≈≈≈≈≈≈≈≈≈≈≈≈≈≈≈≈≈≈

BODY AND SOUL * * * *!

WORDS: Edward Heyman, Robert Sour, and Frank Eyton
MUSIC: Johnny Green
PREMIERE: Revue, *Three's a Crowd*
New York: Selwyn Theatre, 15 October 1930 (272 perf.)
INTRODUCED BY: Libby Holman

"Body and Soul" is a very special song, beloved by singers, instrumentalists and jazz aficionados alike. Its Bluebird recording in 1939 by Coleman Hawkins brought a new dimension to jazz with the tenor saxophonist's improvisational daring, thus preparing the way for the new wave of modern jazz to come in the 1940s. Musicians, intrigued by the song's complex harmonies, interesting modulations, and instrumentally-oriented melody, have embraced "Body and Soul" whole-heartedly. Johnny Green, who wrote the music, later went on to an illustrious career as composer of film scores, arranger, and concert conductor. The song was first published in London, 18 February 1930, sung by Gertrude Lawrence over BBC radio and recorded in England by Bert Ambrose and his Orchestra. In October, it was brought to New York to be interpolated in the revue, *Three's a Crowd*, which starred Fred MacMurray, Fred Allen, and Alan Jones. The song was introduced there by the notorious torch singer, Libby Holman, along with another future standard, "Something to Remember You By."

The music of "Body and Soul" is most unusual for its time, especially in its key relationships. All told, there are six changes of key signature throughout the song including two in the release alone (five flats and four sharps, in the key of C major). The melody is unconventional as well, characterized by unexpected skips, altered notes and sudden changes of intonation. The very first chord of the refrain (D minor in the key of C major) is built on the second degree of the scale but in the minor mode (an idea anticipated in "Star Dust" the year before). Both length and form of the refrain are conventional, AABA in thirty-two bars, with each "A" section closing on a blue note, the lowered third. The lyrics are at times rather awkward (even though it took three collaborators, two Americans and one Englishman, to write them), as witness: "My life a wreck you're making."

The first American recording of "Body and Soul" was by Leo Reisman and his Orchestra, with Eddy Duchin at the piano. Paul Whiteman and his Orchestra had a hit record on Columbia with a vocal by Jack Fulton. Other early recordings were by Ruth Etting, Helen Morgan, Ozzie Nelson and his Orchestra, Louis Armstrong, and the Benny Goodman Trio. Then there was Coleman Hawkins's monumental recording of 1939. The song has been featured in many films, including *The Man I Love*, sung by Ida Lupino (1946); the prize-fighting film, *Body and Soul*, starring John Garfield and Lilli Palmer (1947); and *The Eddy Duchin Story*, starring Tyrone Power and Kim Novak (1956). Gogi Grant dubbed it in for Ann Blyth in the 1957 film, *The Helen Morgan Story*.

More than sixty-five years after it was written, "Body and Soul" remains a jazz classic, one of the most widely-used subjects for improvisation. It is a song beloved by singers and instrumentalists alike.

> Slow torch song with verse (16) and refrain (32)
> *PUBLISHERS*: Chappell & Co., Ltd. and Harms, Inc.
> *KEY*: C maj. or D-flat maj., *STARTS*: d' (D min.) or e-flat' (E-flat min.)
> *FORM*: AABA

≈≈≈≈≈≈≈≈≈≈≈≈≈≈≈≈≈≈≈

BUT NOT FOR ME *

> *WORDS*: Ira Gershwin, *MUSIC*: George Gershwin
> *PREMIERE*: Musical comedy, *Girl Crazy*
> New York: Alvin Theatre, 19 October 1930 (272 perf.)
> *INTRODUCED BY*: Ginger Rogers, reprised by Willie Howard

This poignant ballad is one of very few Gershwin songs about unrequited love. Sung by Ginger Rogers in *Girl Crazy*, it has become a staple of torch singers. Contributing to the song's popularity was the 1942 Columbia recording by Harry James and his Orchestra, with vocal by Helen Forrest. Other recordings were by Judy Garland (Decca) and Teddy Wilson (Columbia).

Musically, "But Not For Me" stands out for its economy of means; the refrain particularly is a minimalist's delight. The form involves only two themes: ABAB'. The melody in the "A" sections plays around only three notes: f', g', and e-flat'. The "B" sections, in contrast, have upward leaps of the third, the fourth, and the fifth. The verse, marked "pessimistically," is in recitative style, with many repeated notes. Harmonically, it is somewhat more complex, with chromatic changes and tonal shifts from E-flat major to G major and then back to E-flat. But most remarkable of all are Ira Gershwin's lyrics. In the refrain, they are full of clichés: "a lucky star", "clouds of gray", "a fool to fall", "a feller needs a friend". Ira's fondness for wordplay reaches a climax at the close of the second refrain with his glorious pun about a marriage knot: "And there's no knot for me".

"But Not For Me" was featured in three films based on *Girl Crazy*. It was in the 1932 film of that name, which starred Bert Wheeler and Robert

Woolsey. Judy Garland and Rags Ragland sang it in the 1943 version. And in 1965, Harve Presnell and Connie Francis sang it in the film remake, *When the Boys Meet the Girls*. Ella Fitzgerald sang it in the 1959 film based on the song's title, *But Not for Me*.

> Slow torch song with verse (24) and two refrains (32)
> *PUBLISHER*: New World Music Corporation
> *KEY*: E-flat maj., *STARTS*: f' (E-flat maj,), *FORM*: ABAB'

≈≈≈≈≈≈≈≈≈≈≈≈≈≈≈≈≈≈≈≈

BYE BYE BLUES

> *WORDS and MUSIC*: Fred Hamm, Dave Bennett, Bert Lown, and Chauncey Gray
> *INTRODUCED BY*: Bert Lown and his Hotel Biltmore Orchestra in New York

This favorite of soft-shoe and tap dancers became the signature song of Bert Lown and his Hotel Biltmore Orchestra in New York. Lown's recording in 1930, with an excellent trombone solo by Al (Tex) Philburn, made the song a hit. Other bands followed suit. Soon, Leo Reisman and his Orchestra had a hit recording. So did Cab Calloway and his Orchestra in 1941. Other hit recordings over the years were by Les Paul and Mary Ford in 1953, and Bert Kaempfert and his Orchestra in 1965.

The origin of "Bye Bye Blues" is somewhat obscure. It apparently was written by Fred Hamm and Dave Bennett as far back as 1925; it was recorded by Hamm in that year. The names of Bert Lown, the band leader, and Chauncey Gray, his pianist, were only added as collaborators after the song was recorded in July, 1930. But the song may go back even further than that. Two songs that may have inspired it were "The Star", written by James H. Rogers in 1912; and "Good-bye Boys", written by Andrew B. Sterling and William Jerome in 1913.

The main musical idea in the refrain consists of three whole notes – e", g', a-flat' – the last of which is held over for an additional bar. The beginning of this motive is then repeated, but this time ending on a'-natural. Thus, in keeping with the lyrics, the blue note (a-flat') has gone "bye-bye" and become a natural'. The range of the refrain is extremely narrow (only a major sixth). Like "But Not For Me", "Bye Bye Blues" belongs to the minimalist tradition, characterized by very few notes and the simplest of harmonies.

Moderate foxtrot with verse (16) and refrain (32)
PUBLISHER: Irving Berlin, Inc.
KEY: C maj., *STARTS*: e" (C maj.), *FORM*: ABAB'

≈≈≈≈≈≈≈≈≈≈≈≈≈≈≈≈≈≈≈

CHEERFUL LITTLE EARFUL

> *WORDS*: Ira Gershwin and Billy Rose, *MUSIC*: Harry Warren
> *PREMIERE*: Revue, *Sweet and Low*
> New York,: 46th Street Theatre, 17 November 1930 (184 perf.)
> *INTRODUCED BY*: Hannah Williams and Jerry Norris

A forgotten revue produced by impresario Billy Rose as a showcase for his wife, Fanny Brice, *Sweet and Low* also featured George Jessel, James Burton, and Arthur Treacher. Two Harry Warren songs became hits of the day: "Cheerful Little Earful" and "Would You Like To Take a Walk", both crediting Rose as co-lyricist, with Ira Gershwin and Mort Dixon respectively. Of these songs, only the first has survived. Ben Selvin and his Orchestra had an early Columbia recording. The song's hallmark is its cuteness, both in words and music. The "earful" referred to is "the well-known I love you". The lyrics do not show Ira Gershwin's usual adroitness and occasional resort to nonsense, as in "Poo-pa-roo-it, soft and cu-it." But they are contemporaneous: "Stocks can go down, bus'ness slow down". The "A" sections are appropriately cute, alternating high and low groups of notes. The release is more inventive, bringing in a strong new theme.

> Moderate foxtrot with verse (16) and refrain (32)
> *PUBLISHER*: Remick Music Corp.
> *KEY*: E-flat maj., *STARTS*: b-flat' (B-flat 7), *FORM*: AABA

≈≈≈≈≈≈≈≈≈≈≈≈≈≈≈≈≈≈≈

CONFESSIN' (THAT I LOVE YOU)

> *WORDS*: Al J. Neiberg, *MUSIC*: Doc Dougherty and Ellis Reynolds
> *INTRODUCED BY*: Rudy Vallee and his Orchestra on radio and in recording

This popular ballad is often known by the first line of its refrain: "I'm Confessin' That I Love You." A pure product of Tin Pan Alley, it has not been associated with any stage or film production. The most popular recording was Louis Armstrong's, on Okeh.

The music holds no surprises, with a conventional thirty-two bar refrain in AABA form. The melody moves mostly stepwise. Harmonies glide leisurely through the circle of fifths. Despite its general lack of distinction, "Confessin'" is still performed, more for its dreaminess and the air of nostalgia it conveys than for its quality.

Moderate ballad with two verses (16) and refrain (32)
PUBLISHER: General Music Publishers, assigned to Irving Berlin, Inc.
KEY: G maj., *STARTS*: d' (G maj.), *FORM*: AABA

≈≈≈≈≈≈≈≈≈≈≈≈≈≈≈≈≈≈≈

A COTTAGE FOR SALE

WORDS: Larry Conley, *MUSIC*: Willard Robison
INTRODUCED BY: Willard Robison and his Deep River Orchestra

The composer of this gentle song, Willard Robison, was much admired by such artists and creators as Mildred Bailey and Johnny Mercer. Robison himself, with his Deep River Orchestra – organized since his college days – introduced it. Words were by his trombonist, Larry Conley. The song was popularized in a Columbia recording by Guy Lombardo and his Royal Canadians. Billy Eckstine made a memorable recording in 1945. But the most popular recording of all was that of Frank Sinatra.

"A Cottage for Sale" is uncompromisingly sad. The lyrics tell the story of "a bungalow empty and still" with "ev'ry dream gone." In keeping with this tale of woe, the melody line of the refrain drifts slowly downwards, oftentimes chromatically, in sequence. Harmonies are interesting, moving largely through the circle of fifths from E-flat to G seventh to C seventh.

In 1987, the song was performed by Chuck Berry in the documentary film, *Chuck Berry: Hail! Hail! Rock 'n' Roll*. It remains a ballad much admired for its poignancy.

Slow ballad with two verses (8) and refrain (32)
PUBLISHER: Crawford Music Corporation, a division of De Sylva, Brown and Henderson, Inc.
KEY: E-flat maj., *STARTS*: b-flat' (E-flat maj.), *FORM*: AABA

≈≈≈≈≈≈≈≈≈≈≈≈≈≈≈≈≈≈≈

DANCING ON THE CEILING * *

WORDS: Lorenz Hart, *MUSIC*: Richard Rodgers
PREMIERE: Musical comedy, *Ever Green*
London: Adelphi Theatre, 3 December 1930 (254 perf.)
INTRODUCED BY: Jessie Matthews and Sonnie Hale

Rodgers and Hart wrote this lilting tune for the show, *Simple Simon*, which opened at the Ziegfeld Theatre in New York 18 February 1930. However, Flo Ziegfeld thought it unsuitable and the song never appeared in that show. Later the same year, however, it found a home in the London production of the musical comedy, *Ever Green*. The setting was an upside-down room with an inverted chandelier in center stage. Jessie Matthews's memorable performance, with her real-life husband, Sonnie Hale, brought down the house. She repeated it in the 1934 film version, *Evergreen*. The song was popularized in Britain by Jack Hylton and his Orchestra and soon found its way to the United States with the group's Victor recording.

The verse is in the style of recitative, with many repeated notes over changing harmonies. The refrain is charming, revealing Rodger's penchant for scalewise passages (in the "A" sections) and repeated notes (in the "B" section). Against this simple backdrop, Hart's romantic lyrics are resplendent, as in the passage: "I try to hide in vain / Underneath my counterpane.". Often they seem to mirror the music, ascending at the words "He dances overhead" (Bars 1 and 2), jumping upwards a seventh at the words "near my bed." This is no accident, since in this case the music was written before the words.

"Dancing on the Ceiling" is most often played either in moderately fast "society tempo" or as a jazz standard.

Moderate foxtrot with verse (20) and refrain (32)
PUBLISHER: Rodart Music Corporation
KEY: F maj., *STARTS*: c' (F maj.), *FORM*: AABA

≈≈≈≈≈≈≈≈≈≈≈≈≈≈≈≈≈≈≈≈

EMBRACEABLE YOU * * * *

WORDS: Ira Gershwin, *MUSIC*: George Gershwin
PREMIERE: Musical comedy, *Girl Crazy*
New York: Alvin Theatre, 14 October 1930 (272 perf.)
INTRODUCED BY: Ginger Rogers and Allan Kearns

This classic, one of the most popular Gershwin ballads, was written in 1928 for an ill-fated operetta, *East Is West*, which never got off the ground. Florenz Ziegfeld abandoned the project and the song in order to do *Show Girl*. Two years later, "Embraceable You" found a home in *Girl Crazy*. Red Nichols, the leader of the pit band, had one of the earliest recordings, along with his Five Pennies.

Originally written as a duet, the song represents an enchanting marriage of words and music. Male and female verses set the scene, each giving its own version of the perils and pitfalls of falling in love, and ending with a series of ten repeated notes to the words "listen to the rhythm of my heartbeat". The refrain bears similarities to that of "The Man I Love". Each begins with a rest, filled in by harmonies in the accompaniment, and in each case the initial motive is immediately repeated over changing harmonies. But the resemblance stops there. Unlike "The Man I Love", "Embraceable You" has only one blue note: the poignant use of the flatted e' at the syllable "-brace" at the end of the refrain. Otherwise, it is one of the most romantic of Gershwin ballads, with a soaring melody combining steps and skips. This is one of Ira Gershwin's few songs with four-syllable rhymes such as "embraceable / irreplaceable", "tipsy in me / gypsy in me", and "the many charms about you / I want my arms about you". The best moment of all comes in the "C" section, with the famous repeated notes at the words "Come to papa, come to papa do!" It is reported that the Gershwins' father, Morris, thought until his dying day that this phrase was a direct reference to himself.

As befits a world-class standard, "Embraceable You" has been featured in many movies. It was sung by Eddie Quillan and Dorothy Lee in the 1932 film version of *Girl Crazy*. Judy Garland and a chorus sang it in the 1943 film version. Joan Leslie sang it in *Rhapsody in Blue* (1945). Leslie Caron danced to it in *An American in Paris* (1951). Robert Wagner and Jane Froman, dubbing in for Susan Hayward, sang it in *With a Song in My Heart* (1952). In 1954, Peg La Centra sang it in *Humoresque*. Liberace played it in *Sincerely Yours* (1955). It was also sung by Harve Presnell and Connie Francis in the 1965 film version of *Girl Crazy*, called *When the Boys Meet the Girls*. Internationally known, it is among the most beloved standards.

Moderate ballad with two verses (20) and three refrains (32)
PUBLISHER: New World Music Corporation
KEY: G maj., *STARTS*: e' (G maj,), *FORM*: ABAC

≈≈≈≈≈≈≈≈≈≈≈≈≈≈≈≈≈≈≈≈

EXACTLY LIKE YOU * *

WORDS: Dorothy Fields, *MUSIC*: Jimmy McHugh
PREMIERE: *The International Revue*
New York: Majestic Theatre, 25 February 1930 (95 perf.)
INTRODUCED BY: Gertrude Lawrence and Harry Richman

Impresario Lew Leslie spared no expense in his lavish production, *The International Revue*, which reportedly cost over $200,000 and featured a star-studded cast that included Harry Richman, Gertrude Lawrence, and Jack Pearl. But the revue was a flop nonetheless; one critic called it "dirty and dull". Still it brought forth two songs destined to become jazz standards: "On the Sunny Side of the Street" and "Exactly Like You". The latter was popularized in recordings by Harry Richman and Ruth Etting. Benny Goodman recorded it in 1936. Almost forty years after it was written, Anita Morris brought it back to Broadway in the smash hit, *Sugar Babies*, which opened at the Mark Hellinger Theatre on 8 October 1979, ran for 1,208 performances, and then went on the road until 1986.

The most striking aspects of the music of the refrain are its wide range (an octave and a half), its disjunct melody (moving mostly in fourths), and the octave drop each time the title is proclaimed ("Ex-act-ly Like You"). The release is in the style of ragtime and has a profusion of words, leaving little time for the vocalist to take a breath. Precisely for these reasons, the song has become a favorite of jazz instrumentalists rather than vocalists. It was featured in the 1956 film, *The Eddy Duchin Story*, starring Tyrone Power and Kim Novak.

Moderate rhythm song with verse (16) and refrain (32)
PUBLISHER: Shapiro, Bernstein & Co., Inc.
KEY: C maj., *STARTS*: e" (C maj.), *FORM*: AABA

≈≈≈≈≈≈≈≈≈≈≈≈≈≈≈≈≈≈≈≈

FALLING IN LOVE AGAIN (CAN'T HELP IT)

WORDS and MUSIC: Frederich Hollander
PREMIERE: Film, *The Blue Angel*, 1930
INTRODUCED BY: Marlene Dietrich

An international waltz favorite, "Falling In Love Again" has always been inseparably associated with the German actress and singer, Marlene Dietrich. She introduced it in her drawling style in the film, *The Blue Angel*, which also starred Emil Jannings as a love-sick professor who falls for a night-club singer. In the film's last reprise of the song, Dietrich sings it astride a chair which she ultimately tosses at the audience. The song was

187

written with German words and music by Frederich Hollander, who went on to write many film scores both in Germany and the United States. Although Hollander is given credit for both words and music on the original American sheet music, the English lyrics have been variously ascribed to Reginald Connelly and Sammy Lerner in other sources.

It is a tender waltz, tailored to Dietrich's limited vocal ability. The melody of the "A" sections only spans half an octave, slowly drifting downwards stepwise, but broadening out in the release to a full octave. Rhythmically, the first beat is often emphasized by splitting it into eighth notes. Harmonies are simple, except for a brief diversion to C minor in the release. The English lyrics seem rather simplistic ("Never wanted to, What am I to do?"), but aided by Dietrich's sultry, husky delivery, the song became a solid international hit. May Britt sang it in the 1959 remake of the film, *The Blue Angel*, which also starred Curt Jurgens.

Slow waltz with verse (16) and refrain (32)
PUBLISHERS: Ufaton-Verlag (Berlin), assigned to Famous Music Corp.
KEY: E-flat maj., *STARTS*: g' (E-flat maj.)), *FORM*: AABA

≈≈≈≈≈≈≈≈≈≈≈≈≈≈≈≈≈≈≈

FINE AND DANDY

WORDS: Paul James, *MUSIC*: Kay Swift
PREMIERE: Musical comedy, *Fine and Dandy*
New York: Erlanger Theatre. 23 September 1930 (255 perf.)
INTRODUCED BY: Joe Cook and Alice Boulden

This happy song – the refrain is marked "Gaily" – was the title song of a show that thumbed its nose at the deepening depression. *Fine and Dandy* featured comedian Joe Cook's clowning, juggling, and crazy inventions à la Rube Goldberg. It also featured a vivacious tap dancer named Eleanor Powell. But best of all was the score by the husband-and-wife team of Kay Swift and James Paul Warburg (pseudonym Paul James). At the time, Warburg was a Wall Street broker, scion of a banking family. A few years later, Swift was to become one of George Gershwin's closest confidantes.

The lyrics have both contemporary and historical references, from Amos 'n' Andy and Schmeling and Sharkey to Napoleon and Josephine. But it is the music of the refrain that carries the day. Its persistent syncopation, constant anticipation of the fourth beat, jumpy melody, and profusion of seventh and diminished chords, all convey a feeling of optimism: an antidote to the desperate times. Usually played in fast tempo, "Fine and

Dandy" has enjoyed a long run as the brassy opener and closer of entertainers' acts.

Moderate rhythm song with verse (32) and four refrains (32)
PUBLISHER: Harms, Inc.
KEY: F maj., *STARTS*: e' (F maj.), *FORM*: ABAC

≈≈≈≈≈≈≈≈≈≈≈≈≈≈≈≈≈≈≈

FOR YOU

WORDS: Al Dubin, *MUSIC*: Joe Burke
PREMIERE: Film, *A Holy Terror*, 1931

This sentimental waltz was written by two Hollywood tunesmiths for an early Humphrey Bogart film, *A Holy Terror*, also starring James Kirkwood. It was lifted out of obscurity by Glen Gray and The Casa Loma Orchestra, who used it as one of their signature songs, along with "It's the Talk of the Town" and "Under a Blanket of Blue". The group's Brunswick recording, with vocal by Kenny Sargent, swept the country. Years later, It was recorded by Nat "King" Cole and Rosemary Clooney. In 1964, a Decca record by Rick Nelson reached the Top Ten. The refrain marked "dreamily", is very simple melodically and harmonically, distinguished by two upward jumps in each "A" section at the words "for you": first a fourth and then a minor third. The predominant C major tonality is relieved in the release, which moves briefly to E minor. Although written as a waltz, "For You" is often performed in duple time, either as a ballad or uptempo, and sometimes with a strong beat.

Moderate waltz with two verses (16) and refrain (32)
PUBLISHER: M. Witmark & Sons
KEY: C maj., *STARTS*: g' (C maj.), *FORM*: AABA

≈≈≈≈≈≈≈≈≈≈≈≈≈≈≈≈≈≈≈

GEORGIA ON MY MIND * * *

WORDS: Stuart Gorrell, *MUSIC*: Hoagy Carmichael
INTRODUCED BY: Mildred Bailey

A hardy jazz standard, this is not the first song about the Peach State ever written. As far back as 1915, Spencer Williams wrote "Georgia Grind." There was a fairly popular song of 1922, simply called "Georgia," with words by Howard Johnson and music by Walter Donaldson. But when one thinks about the state, this is certainly the song that pops into mind.

And unlike many other standards, it has withstood all kinds of treatment and stayed popular through the age of rock and beyond. With music by the incomparable Hoagy Carmichael and lyrics by his classmate, Stuart Gorrell (coiner of the title "Star Dust"), "Georgia On My Mind" was not written for a show or a movie. It achieved its popularity solely through the medium of recordings. First there were Carmichael's and Mildred Bailey's (both on Victor). Three decades later, in 1960, Ray Charles's version sold over a million copies and won a Grammy award. Successful recordings were also made by the Righteous Brothers in 1966, Wes Montgomery in 1968, and Willie Nelson in 1978 (also a Grammy), to mention but a few.

At first glance, this is a modest-appearing song in conventional 32-bar, AABA form. But the melody of the refrain bears Carmichael's unmistakable stamp. In the key of F major, it plays around a focal point of only two notes: a' and g'. The harmonic changes are interesting as well, in particular the change in the second bar from F major to A dominant seventh. Then too, the release, in D minor, is unusual, with a modal quality brought about by the use of b' rather than the expected b-flat'. All the above factors, along with the poignant and nostalgic lyrics, account for the song's popularity.

Ray Charles sang it in the 1966 film, *The Big TNT Show*. With its appealing changes, "Georgia On My Mind" remains one of the great subjects for jazz improvisation.

> Moderate rhythm song with verse (16) and refrain (32)
> *PUBLISHER*: Peer International Corporation
> *KEY*: F maj., *STARTS*: a' (F maj.), *FORM*: AABA

≈≈≈≈≈≈≈≈≈≈≈≈≈≈≈≈≈≈≈≈

GET HAPPY

> *WORDS*: Ted Koehler, *MUSIC*: Harold Arlen
> *PREMIERE*: Revue, *Nine-Fifteen Revue*
> New York: George M. Cohan Theatre, 11 February 1930 (7 perf.)
> *INTRODUCED BY:* Ruth Etting

Harold Arlen's first published song is also one of his most inventive. The tune evolved as a vamp while Arlen was working as a rehearsal pianist for the show, *Great Day!* It was introduced by Ruth Etting as the first-act finale of a now-forgotten theater piece, *Nine-Fifteen Revue*, which closed in a week despite the contributions of such illustrious composers as George Gershwin, Vincent Youmans, Victor Herbert, Rudolf Friml, and

Kay Swift. "Get Happy" was the only song to survive. It was first recorded by Nat Shilkret and his Orchestra.

The music of the refrain is strikingly original. In unusual ABCA form, its hallmark is jazzy syncopation. The opening gesture outlines the E-flat major triad in the second inversion, with emphasis on the repeated note b-flat'. The "B" section, in turn, outlines the A-flat major triad in its second inversion, emphasizing the repeated note, "e-flat". The "C" section acts as a release, introducing new material: a riff-like motive descending stepwise and then repeated.

"Get Happy" was featured in several films of the fifties. It was in *Young Man with a Horn* (1950), known in Britain as *Young Man of Music*; Judy Garland sang it with a chorus in *Summer Stock* (1950), known in Britain as *If You Feel Like Singing*; Jane Froman dubbed it in for Susan Hayward in her 1952 film biography, *With a Sing in My Heart*; and it was in the 1956 film, *Cha-Cha-Cha-Boom*. With its instrumentally-oriented sound, "Get Happy" is a favorite of jazz musicians, who often play it in ultra-fast tempo.

> Moderate rhythm song with verse (25) and refrain (32)
> *PUBLISHER*: Remick Music Corporation
> *KEY*: E-flat major, *STARTS*: b-flat' (E-flat maj.), *FORM*: ABCA

≈≈≈≈≈≈≈≈≈≈≈≈≈≈≈≈≈≈≈

I GOT RHYTHM ***

> *WORDS*: Ira Gershwin, *MUSIC*: George Gershwin
> *PREMIERE*: Musical comedy, *Girl Crazy*
> New York: Alvin Theatre, 14 October 1930 (272 perf.)
> *INTRODUCED BY:* Ethel Merman, the Foursome, and Company

One of the most popular jazz standards, "I Got Rhythm" was the début song of Ethel Merman in *Girl Crazy*; it remained her theme song throughout her long and illustrious career. Her spectacular rendition of the second chorus, holding a high note for sixteen bars, captivated audiences. The musical background supplied by the Red Nichols Orchestra – which included such sidemen as Benny Goodman, Jimmy Dorsey, Jack Teagarden, Glenn Miller, and Gene Krupa – also contributed to the song's success with a Brunswick recording. Cover records were soon made by Ethel Waters and Louis Armstrong. Both George and Ira Gershwin loved the song; in 1933 George composed his '*I Got Rhythm*' *Variations* for piano and orchestra and dedicated it to Ira. Over the years almost every jazz performer has used the song. In 1967 The Happenings had a best-selling record.

Like many of George Gershwin's songs, "I Got Rhythm" is built on the pentatonic scale – in this case f', g', b-flat', c", d". The scale goes upwards at the words "I Got Rhythm" and downwards at "I got music." But it is the syncopation, the anticipation of the second and fourth beats, that lends spice to the refrain. Harmonically, the "A" sections stay close to tonic and dominant, but the release resorts to the time-honored circle of fifths, progressing from D seventh to G and from C seventh to F. The lyrics seem deceptively simple with much repetition and general avoidance of rhyme. But they are well-crafted, a perfect complement to the music. Each "A" section ends with the words "Who could ask for anything more", repeated at the end as a brief, two-bar coda.

In films, "I Got Rhythm" was featured in the 1932 version of *Girl Crazy*. Judy Garland, Mickey Rooney, and a chorus sang it in the 1943 version. It was heard in *Rhapsody in Blue* (1945). In 1951 it was memorably performed by Gene Kelly, Lucien Planzoles, Christian Pasques, and Anthony Mazola in *An American in Paris*. Finally, in 1965 Harve Presnell, Connie Francis, and Louis Armstrong sang it in the *Girl Crazy* remake, *When the Boys Meet the Girls*. Over the years, "I Got Rhythm" has inspired a host of jazz musicians who have used its rather bland harmonies as a basis for all sorts of imaginative improvisation, often leaving out the two-bar coda.

Fast rhythm song with verse (26) and refrain (34)
PUBLISHER: New World Music Corporation
KEY: B-flat maj., *STARTS*: f' (B-flat maj.), *FORM*: AABA

≈≈≈≈≈≈≈≈≈≈≈≈≈≈≈≈≈≈≈

I'M YOURS

WORDS: E. Y. Harburg, *MUSIC*: Johnny Green
PREMIERE: Musical comedy, *Simple Simon*
New York: Ziegfeld Theatre, 18 February 1930 (135 perf.)
INTRODUCED BY: Ruth Etting

This charming ballad was one of a number of songs interpolated in the Rodgers and Hart musical, *Simple Simon*, which starred a bumbling Ed Wynn. Sung in the show by Ruth Etting, it was recorded by her and by Ben Bernie and his Orchestra.

It is a pleasantly relaxed song with few pretensions. The melody of the refrain rambles up and down the scale in dotted eighths and sixteenths.

Harmonies are the simplest, unexpected in composer Johnny Green, who used intricate harmonies for his songs, "Body and Soul" (this year) and "You Came Along (From Out of Nowhere)", in 1931. As for the lyrics, they are a bit awkward, also unexpected in a lyricist of the caliber of E. Y. "Yip" Harburg whose credits include "April in Paris" (1932) and "Over the Rainbow" (1939).

"I'm Yours" was heard in the 1941 film, *Second Chorus*, and Dean Martin sang it in the 1953 Dean Martin and Jerry Lewis film, *The Stooge*.

> Moderate ballad with verse (12) and refrain (32)
> *PUBLISHER*: Famous Music Corporation
> *KEY*: E-flat maj., *STARTS*: e-flat" (E-flat maj.), *FORM*: AA'BA'

≈≈≈≈≈≈≈≈≈≈≈≈≈≈≈≈≈≈≈

I'VE GOT A CRUSH ON YOU *!

WORDS: Ira Gershwin, *MUSIC*: George Gershwin
PREMIERE: Musical comedy, *Treasure Girl*
New York: Alvin Theatre, 8 November 1928 (68 perf.)
INTRODUCED BY: Clifton Webb and Mary Hay

The musical comedy, *Treasure Girl,* was that Gershwin rarity, a flop, despite its illustrious stars: Gertrude Lawrence, Clifton Webb, and Walter Catlett. Nevertheless, one song survived, and a wonderful song it is: "I've Got a Crush on You". Although it didn't create an immediate sensation, it got more attention two years later when it was interpolated by Dorothy Carson and Gordon Smith in the revised version of *Strike Up the Band,* which opened at the Times Square Theatre in New York on 14 January 1930. However the song's real success came years later, after vocalist Lee Wiley recorded it at a much slower tempo, paving the way for the song's most famous recording of all, by Frank Sinatra.

Written as a duet, "I've Got a Crush on You" is one of few songs after 1920 to be written in 2/4 meter. The verse could be a song in itself: equal in length to the refrain, its form is AA'BA". As for the refrain, it immediately captivates the listener with its three-note pickup on the words "I've got a", its perky melody, its light syncopation, and its pungent harmonies.

Sinatra sang it in the 1952 film, *Meet Danny Wilson*. Betty Grable and Jack Lemmon did it as a duet in the 1955 film, *Three for the Show*. Gogi Grant dubbed it in for Ann Blyth in *The Helen Morgan Story* (1957), known in Britain as *Both Ends of the Candle*. And Ellen Burstyn sang it in the 1975 film, *Alice Doesn't Live Here Anymore*. This engaging song shows the Gershwin brothers at the peak of their form.

Moderate foxtrot with verse (32) and refrain (32)
PUBLISHER: New World Music Corporation
KEY: B-flat maj., *STARTS*: f' (B-flat maj. 7), *FORM*: ABA'B'

≋≋≋≋≋≋≋≋≋≋≋≋≋≋≋≋≋≋≋

JUST A GIGOLO

ENGLISH WORDS: Irving Caesar, *MUSIC*: Leonello Casucci
INTRODUCED BY: Irene Bordoni in the United States

"Just a Gigolo" is something of an international oddity. It began life in Vienna as "Schöner Gigolo," composed by Leonello Casucci, with German words by Julius Brammer. The French chanteuse, Irene Bordoni, brought it to America. The British bandleader, Jack Hylton, popularized it with his big band. Early American recordings were by Bing Crosby and the bands of Vincent Lopez and Ted Lewis. There have been several revivals, one by Jaye P. Morgan in 1953, and another by David Lee Roth in 1985. But the greatest revival of all was by trumpeter Louis Prima and his Orchestra, who performed the serious ballad playfully, uptempo, and in shuffle rhythm. That treatment was not as far-fetched as it seems, since the melody itself is playful, moving down the scale in repeated notes starting at different pitch levels. Two held notes, or fermatas, at the words "What will they say about me?" and "life goes on with out me" heighten the dramatic effect.

Moderate ballad with verse(17) and refrain (16)
PUBLISHER: Wiener Bohème Verlag (Vienna), assigned to De Sylva, Brown & Henderson (USA)
KEY: G maj., *STARTS*: b' (G maj.), *FORM*: AA'A"B

≋≋≋≋≋≋≋≋≋≋≋≋≋≋≋≋≋≋≋

LITTLE WHITE LIES

WORDS and MUSIC: Walter Donaldson

This winsome little ballad was popularized with recordings by Guy Lombardo and his Royal Canadians and Fred Waring and his Pennsylvanians. It enjoyed a revival in 1948, sparked by a Decca recording by Dick Haymes, with Four Hits and a Miss. The song, in G major, has a bitonal structure: the last part of the verse has a passage in B major, which anticipates the refrain's release, which starts in B major. In the "A" sections, the melody rises at first, outlining a G major chord resting on the sustained note c", and then descends, resting on a sustained e-flat'. "Little White Lies" was featured in the 1961 film, *Lover Come Back*, starring Doris Day and Rock Hudson.

Moderate ballad with verse (10) and refrain (32)
PUBLISHER: Donaldson, Douglas & Gumble, Inc.
KEY: G maj., *STARTS*: d" (G maj.), *FORM*: AA'BA'

≈≈≈≈≈≈≈≈≈≈≈≈≈≈≈≈≈≈≈≈

LOVE FOR SALE *!

WORDS and MUSIC: Cole Porter
PREMIERE: Musical comedy, *The New Yorkers*
New York: Broadway Theatre, 8 December 1930 (168 perf.)
INTRODUCED BY: Kathryn Crawford, assisted by June Shafer, Ida Pearson, and Arline Judge, accompanied by Fred Waring and his Pennsylvanians

The only song to be banned from radio, "Love for Sale" is unabashedly about prostitution. The opening line of the refrain tells it all: "Love for sale / Appetizing young love for sale." In the musical, *The New Yorkers,* Kathryn Crawford played the role of a young white prostitute, and sang it along with a trio of streetwalkers. At least one member of the press was not amused; Charles Darnton of *The New York World* said that the song was "in the worst possible taste." In an effort to quell the frenzy, the producers quickly changed the song's locale to Harlem and had it sung by a black singer named Elisabeth Welch. (Apparently black prostitutes were more acceptable in 1930). Offstage, the song was popularized by torch singer Libby Holman and by Hal Kemp and his Orchestra. Fred Waring and his Pennsylvanians, the pit band of the show, had a hit record on Victor, as did Libby Holman on Brunswick. But the song was banned from radio for many years.

Subject matter aside, "Love for Sale" is one of the most unusual songs in the popular literature. The verse, marked "Semplice (not fast)," is in the form of a recitative, with repeated notes going down the whole tone scale. The refrain, marked "with swinging rhythm and not fast," is beautifully written. Ninety-eight bars in length, it ambiguously exploits the contrast between major and minor tonality, starting in B-flat major, moving to B-flat minor, and then returning to B-flat major, only to land on a deceptive cadence (an E diminished chord), which finally resolves to B-flat major. There is musical tone painting as well: the melody rises at the words "Follow me and climb the stairs". The refrain ends with a twelve-bar coda, with a vocalize at the final word "love" and a sustained b-flat' at the word "sale." The song's only screen appearance was in the Porter biography, *Night and Day* (1945).

> Moderate foxtrot with verse (20) and refrain (98)
> *PUBLISHER*: Harms, Inc.
> *KEY*: B-flat maj., *STARTS*: b-flat' (E-flat maj.), *FORM*: AA'BA"

≈≈≈≈≈≈≈≈≈≈≈≈≈≈≈≈≈≈

MAGIC IS THE MOONLIGHT

ENGLISH WORDS: Charles Pasquale, *MUSIC*: Maria Grever

This popular rumba was composed and given Spanish words by Maria Grever, who was born of Mexican parents *en route* to Spain. Although never a Mexican citizen, she considered Mexico her homeland. "Magic Is the Moonlight" was originally written as a Spanish cancion entitled "Te Quiero Dijiste." A forerunner of the dance crazes of the thirties, it became popular only in 1944, when it was featured in the Metro Goldwyn Mayer film, *Bathing Beauty*, starring Esther Williams. It was sung in that film by Carlos Ramirez, accompanied by Xavier Cugat and his Orchestra. Shortly after, the bands of Freddy Martin and Art Kassel recorded it.

The music of the refrain is simple, in AABA form, with a broad melody revolving around tonic and dominant harmonies in the "A" sections. A touch of harmonic subtlety is offered in the release, with a brief excursion to the subdominant.

Andy Russell sang "Magic Is the Moonlight" in the 1946 film, *Breakfast in Hollywood*. In the film, *Nancy Goes to Rio* (1950), it was sung by Jane Powell and reprised by Ann Sothern.

> Moderate rumba with refrain (32)
> *PUBLISHER*: Peer International Corporation
> *KEY*: F maj., *STARTS*: c' (F maj.), *FORM*: AABA

≈≈≈≈≈≈≈≈≈≈≈≈≈≈≈≈≈≈

MEMORIES OF YOU * *

> *WORDS*: Andy Razaf, *MUSIC*: Eubie Blake
> *PREMIERE*: Revue, *Lew Leslie's Blackbirds of 1930*
> New York: Royale Theatre, 22 October 1930 (26 perf.)
> *INTRODUCED BY*: Minto Cato

Eubie Blake, composer of this lilting jazz standard, lived to be 100. One of his loveliest creations, it was written for *Lew Leslie's Blackbirds of 1930*, advertised as "the world's fastest revue, glorifying the American Negro". With an unusually wide range, spanning an octave and a half, the song was specially designed for Minto Cato, who performed it sitting in front of a slave's cabin dressed in nineteenth-century slave's costume. Although the show closed in seven weeks, the song took on a life of its own, sparked by the hit Decca recording of Glen Gray and The Casa Loma Orchestra, with a memorable trumpet solo by Sonny Dunham. Other recordings were by Louis Armstrong, The Ink Spots, and the Benny Goodman Sextet. The song was again revived in 1978, when it was featured in the revue, *Eubie!*, which opened at the Ambassador Theatre in New York on 20 September and ran for a year.

The music's most striking feature is its wide range. The melody rises with ever-widening spacing – at intervals of the second, third, and fifth – and then similarly descends.

On the screen, "Memories of You" was played by the Benny Goodman Trio in *The Benny Goodman Story* (1956) and sung by Anita O'Day in *The Gene Krupa Story* (1959) – known in Britain as *Drum Crazy*.

Moderate ballad with two verses (16) and refrain (32)
PUBLISHER: Shapiro, Bernstein & Co., Inc.
KEY: E-flat maj., *STARTS*: b-flat' (E-flat maj.), *FORM*: AABA

≈≈≈≈≈≈≈≈≈≈≈≈≈≈≈≈≈≈≈

ON THE SUNNY SIDE OF THE STREET ✶ ✶ ✶

WORDS: Dorothy Fields, *MUSIC*: Jimmy McHugh
PREMIERE: Revue, *The International Revue*
New York: Majestic Theatre, 25 February 1930 (95 perf.)
INTRODUCED BY: Harry Richman

This jazz classic, like "Exactly Like You," emanated from Lew Leslie's *The International Revue*. It was introduced by Harry Richman and popularized by Ted Lewis. Over the years it has seen many revivals: in 1945, by Tommy Dorsey and his Orchestra; in 1951, by Frankie Lane; and in 1979, when it was featured in the long-running revue, *Sugar Babies*, starring Mickey Rooney and Ann Miller.

The refrain opens with five notes spanning an octave and a third, from c' to e", leading the harmony from C major to E seventh. The interesting release repeats the note c" over changing harmonies. Dorothy

Fields's carefree lyrics are pertinent to the Great Depression: "If I never have a cent / I'll be rich as Rockefeller".

As befits a classic, "On the Sunny Side of the Street" has had a long career in the cinema. In the forties, it was in the films, *Is Everybody Happy?* and *Nobody's Darling* (both 1943); in *Swing Parade of 1946*; in *Two Blondes and a Redhead* (1947); and in *Make Believe Ballroom* (1949). In the fifties, it was in was the title song of *Sunny Side of the Street* (1951) in which it was sung by Frankie Laine; Teddy Wilson did a piano solo in *The Benny Goodman Story (1956)*; and Carmen Cavallaro dubbed it in on the piano for Tyrone Power in *The Eddy Duchin Story* (1956); while Gogi Grant sang it for Ann Blyth in *The Helen Morgan Story* (1957) – known in Britain as *Both Ends of the Candle*. In later years, Dean Martin sang it in *The Silencers* (1966); Frankie Laine (again) in *House* Calls (1978); and Willie Nelson in *Rich and Famous* (1981). It remains one of the most performed of jazz standards, beloved by singers and instrumentalists alike.

Moderate rhythm song with verse (16) and refrain (32)
PUBLISHER: Shapiro, Bernstein & Co., Inc.
KEY: C maj., *STARTS*: e' (C maj.), *FORM*: A A'BA'

≈≈≈≈≈≈≈≈≈≈≈≈≈≈≈≈≈≈≈

PLEASE DON'T TALK ABOUT ME WHEN I'M GONE

WORDS and MUSIC: Sidney Clare, Sam H. Stept, and Bee Palmer
INTRODUCED BY: Bee Palmer

This country-style lament was introduced by co-writer Bee Palmer and popularized on radio by the legendary Kate Smith. Gene Austin had an early recording. In 1953, Johnnie Ray recorded it. It is an unpretentious song, with harmonies moving through the circle of fifths from G seventh to C seventh, F seventh, B-flat seventh, and back to E-flat major in all four sections. The lyrics are homespun, to say the least, as in "Oh, honey, though our friendship ceases from now on". Patricia Neal sang it in the 1950 film, *The Breaking Point*; Doris Day in the 1951 film, *Lullaby of Broadway*.

Moderate foxtrot with two verses (16) and refrain (32)
PUBLISHER: Remick Music corp.
KEY: E-flat maj., *STARTS*: e-flat" (E-flat maj.), *FORM*: AA'BA"

≈≈≈≈≈≈≈≈≈≈≈≈≈≈≈≈≈≈≈

PUTTIN' ON THE RITZ!

WORDS and MUSIC: Irving Berlin
PREMIERE: Film, *Puttin' On the Ritz*. United Artists, 1930
INTRODUCED BY: Harry Richman

Puttin' On the Ritz was Irving Berlin's first movie and this jazzy title song was its highlight, as sung by vaudeville singer, Harry Richman. It became Richman's theme song, and he also recorded it (Brunswick), as well as by Leo Reisman and his Orchestra. The lyrics, as originally written, were those of a "coon song", and spoke condescendingly about Harlem and "high browns". Twenty-five years later, Berlin rewrote them to reflect the changing times, and Lenox Avenue became Park Avenue. The song was revived in 1946, after Fred Astaire sang it in the film, *Blue Skies*; Ella Fitzgerald recorded it (with the new lyrics) in the fifties; and Taco revived it with a Top Ten record on RCA in 1983.

The essence of the song is its singular use of rhythm. The first four bars of each "A" section keep the listener completely off-beat, stressing respectively the first, fourth, third, and second beats of the measure. It only lands again on the first beat in the fifth bar, and decisively so, with a whole note tied to a half. The release, in contrast, brings in the anticipated fourth beat of "Charleston" (1923). Unlike in other Berlin songs, the refrain of "Puttin' On the Ritz" is unequivocally in a minor key: beginning and ending in F minor, with a touch of B-flat minor and A-flat major in the release; the verse, on the other hand, is in F major.

Besides the films, *Puttin' On the Ritz* and *Blue Skies*, the song was memorably sung by Clark Gable and a chorus in the 1939 film, *Idiot's Delight*, a performance reprised in the 1974 film, *That's Entertainment*. In the latter year, Peter Boyle and Gene Wilder sang it in *Young Frankenstein*.

Moderate rhythm song with verse and refrain (32)
PUBLISHER: Irving Berlin, Inc.
KEY: F min., *STARTS*: f' (F min.), *FORM*: AABA

≈≈≈≈≈≈≈≈≈≈≈≈≈≈≈≈≈≈≈≈

SOMETHING TO REMEMBER YOU BY *

WORDS: Howard Dietz, *MUSIC*: Arthur Schwartz
PREMIERE: Revue, *Three's a Crowd*
New York, Selwyn Theatre, 15 October 1930 (272 perf.)
INTRODUCED BY: Libby Holman

Arthur Schwartz wrote the melody of this poignant ballad for a song called "I Have No Way to Say How Much I Love You", with lyrics by Desmond Carter. It was performed as a fast foxtrot in the English musical, *Little Tommy Tucker*. At a much slower tempo, and with a new title and lyrics by Howard Dietz, it became a hit when Libby Holman introduced it as "Something to Remember You By" in the revue, *Three's a Crowd*, singing it to a sailor whose back is to the audience (played by a young Fred MacMurray). Holman's Brunswick recording (with "Body and Soul" on the flip side) was a hit. The song was revived in 1943, with a recording by Dinah Shore.

The flowing verse modulates smoothly from F major to G-flat major, and back again to F major. In the refrain, the melody line is simple but effective, consisting of repeated notes alternating with broken chords of tonic and dominant. There is a brief excursion to A minor in the release. The lyrics are heartfelt, pleading for "Some little something, meaning love cannot die".

In films, Betsy Drake sang it in *Dancing in the Dark* (1949); a chorus performed it in *The Band Wagon* (1953); Gogi Grant dubbed it in for Ann Blyth in *The Helen Morgan Story* (1957, known in Britain as *Both Ends of the Candle*); and Helen Forrest sang it in *A Safe Place* (1972).

Slow ballad with verse (16) and refrain (32)
PUBLISHER: Harms, Inc.
KEY: F maj., *STARTS*: c" (F maj.), *FORM*: AA'BA

≈≈≈≈≈≈≈≈≈≈≈≈≈≈≈≈≈≈≈

THEM THERE EYES

WORDS and MUSIC: Maceo Pinkard, William Tracey, and Doris Tauber
INTRODUCED BY: Gus Arnheim and his Orchestra

A perky favorite of jazz musicians, "Them There Eyes" began as a society foxtrot, introduced by Gus Arnheim and his Orchestra at the Coconut Grove nightclub in Los Angeles, and recorded on Victor. Both Louis Armstrong and Billie Holiday had memorable recordings. Cuteness abounds in both words and music. Dotted eighths and sixteenths predominate in the refrain, along with such near-rhymes as "You're over-workin' 'em / There's danger lurkin' in". Diana Ross sang it in the Billie Holiday biographical film, *Lady Sings the Blues* (1972).

Moderate rhythm song with two verses (8) and refrain (32)
PUBLISHER: Bourne, Inc.
KEY: C maj., *STARTS*: g' (C maj.), *FORM*: ABA'B'

≈≈≈≈≈≈≈≈≈≈≈≈≈≈≈≈≈≈≈

THREE LITTLE WORDS *

WORDS: Bert Kalmar, *MUSIC*: Harry Ruby
INTRODUCED BY: Bing Crosby and The Rhythm Boys, with Duke
Ellington and his Orchestra

This venerable standard was introduced in Amos 'n' Andy's film
début, *Check and Double Check*, by Bing Crosby and The Rhythm Boys,
accompanied by Duke Ellington and his Orchestra. Ellington had a hit
record (Victor), with other recordings by Ethel Waters and Rudy Vallee.
The lightly-syncopated melody outlines the C major sixth chord, with the
addition of the repeated blue note, b-flat'. The lyrics carry a measure of
suspense: only at the very end of the refrain does the listener discover that
the three little words are indeed "I love you". The song's title became that of
a movie in 1950, *Three Little Words*, in which it was sung by Fred Astaire,
Red Skelton, Vera-Ellen, and Phil Regan.

Moderate foxtrot with two verses (24) and refrain (32
PUBLISHER: Harms, Inc.
KEY: C maj., *STARTS*: c" (C maj.), *FORM*: AABA'

≈≈≈≈≈≈≈≈≈≈≈≈≈≈≈≈≈≈≈

TIME ON MY HANDS *

WORDS: Harold Adamson and Mack Gordon, *MUSIC*: Vincent Youmans
PREMIERE: Musical comedy, *Smiles*
New York: Ziegfeld Theatre, 18 November 1930 (63 perf.)
INTRODUCED BY: Paul Gregory

By all accounts the show, *Smiles,* should have been a hit; the lavish
Ziegfeld production had a cast that included Fred and Adele Astaire and
Marilyn Miller. But it was a disaster, leaving behind only this sophisticated
standard. Miller didn't like the song and refused to sing it. But the song
became popular in England and in time gained acceptance on these shores.

The unifying device of the refrain is the quarter-note triplet, which
is present in all sections. In fact, in the last section, there are three sets of
quarter-note triplets, each at a higher pitch level. The haunting melody
principally revolves around the major seventh (e').

In the movies, Ray Bolger, June Haver, and Gordon MacRae sang it in *Look for the Silver Lining* (1949); Kathryn Grayson did it in *So This Is Love* (1953), known in Britain as *The Grace Moore Story.*

Moderate ballad with verse (12) and refrain (32)
PUBLISHER: Vincent Youmans, Inc. Music Publisher
KEY: F maj., *STARTS*: e' (F maj. 7), *FORM*: AABA'

≈≈≈≈≈≈≈≈≈≈≈≈≈≈≈≈≈≈≈

WALKIN' MY BABY BACK HOME

WORDS and MUSIC: Roy Turk, Fred E. Ahlert, and Harry Richman
INTRODUCED BY: Harry Richman in vaudeville

Harry Richman, who introduced this jazzy song, was also given writer's credit, in the fashion of the time. Early recordings were by Louis Armstrong, Nick Lucas, and Maurice Chevalier. The song was revived in 1952, with a hit Columbia recording by Johnnie Ray, and recordings by Nat "King" Cole and Dean Martin. The refrain is characterized by syncopation and dotted eighths and sixteenths. Harmonies adhere to tonic and dominant (E-flat major and B-flat seventh) except in the release, in G minor. Lyrics are casually cute, as in "We go 'long harmonizin' a song"; they tell a cautionary tale about getting "talcum all over my vest". The song's title became a movie in 1953, *Walking My Baby Back Home*, in which it was performed by Donald O'Connor.

Moderate rhythm song with two verses (12) and two refrains (32)
PUBLISHER: De Sylva, Brown and Henderson, Inc.
KEY: E-flat maj., *STARTS*: b-flat' (E-flat maj.), *FORM*: AABA

≈≈≈≈≈≈≈≈≈≈≈≈≈≈≈≈≈≈≈

WHEN YOUR HAIR HAS TURNED TO SILVER (I WILL LOVE YOU JUST THE SAME)

WORDS: Charles Tobias, *MUSIC*: Peter De Rose
INTRODUCED BY: Mildred Hunt on radio

An old-fashioned waltz, this long-titled song was introduced by Mildred Hunt, who was known as "Radio's Sweetheart." Popularized by Tommy Christian and his Orchestra, it was recorded by Russ Morgan and his Orchestra and by Rudy Vallee. The melody is unimaginative, almost entirely in the rhythmic pattern of a half note followed by a quarter note. In AA'BA" form, the first "A" section is followed by a second which restates its melody a step higher. As for the lyrics, they are replete with such romantic allusions as "Through a garden filled with roses / Down the sunset trail we'll stray".

Moderate waltz with two verses (16) and refrain (32)
PUBLISHER: Joe Morris Music Co.
KEY: E-flat maj., *STARTS*: b-flat', *FORM*: AA'BA"

≈≈≈≈≈≈≈≈≈≈≈≈≈≈≈≈≈≈

YOU BROUGHT A NEW KIND OF LOVE TO ME

WORDS and MUSIC: Sammy Fain, Irving Kahal, and Pierre Norman
PREMIERE: Film, *The Big Pond*, Paramount, 1930
INTRODUCED BY: Maurice Chevalier

Maurice Chevalier performed this charming song as the highlight of an otherwise forgettable film, *The Big Pond*, which was filmed in French and English at Paramount's Astoria Studios in Long Island, New York. The perky melody alternates ascending skips of a sixth with a descending chromatic line. Chevalier also sang it behind the camera in the 1931 film, *Monkey Business*, starring the Four Marx Brothers. Frank Sinatra sang it in a 1963 film using part of the song's title, *A New Kind of Love*. And, in 1977, Liza Minnelli belted it out in *New York, New York*.

Moderate foxtrot with verse (16) and refrain (2)
PUBLISHER: Famous Music Corporation
KEY: A-flat maj., *STARTS*: e-flat' (B-flat min. 7), *FORM*: AA'BA'

≈≈≈≈≈≈≈≈≈≈≈≈≈≈≈≈≈≈

YOU'RE DRIVING ME CRAZY! (WHAT DID I DO?)

WORDS and MUSIC: Walter Donaldson
PREMIERE: Musical comedy, *Smiles*
New York: Ziegfeld Theatre, 18 November 1930 (63 perf.)
INTRODUCED BY: Adele Astaire and Eddie Foy, Jr.

Interpolated in the short-lived musical *Smiles*, this lively song was popularized with records by Guy Lombardo and his Royal Canadians (Columbia) and Rudy Vallee and his Connecticut Yankees (Victor). The verse is distinctive, with interesting harmonies. The refrain is somewhat static harmonically in the "A" sections, with few notes, but moves abruptly and unexpectedly from F major to A major in the release, along with a fast-moving, chromatic melodic line. Ava Gardner sang it in the 1951 film,

Pandora and the Flying Dutchman. Jane Russell and Anita Ellis (dubbing for Jeanne Crain) did it in *Gentlemen Marry Brunettes.*

Moderate rhythm song with two verses (16) and refrain (32)
PUBLISHER: Donaldson, Douglas & Gumble, Inc.
KEY: F maj., *STARTS*: c" (F maj.), *FORM*: AA'BA

≈≈≈≈≈≈≈≈≈≈≈≈≈≈≈≈≈≈≈≈

LOOKING FOR THE LIGHT

1931

Who cares what banks fail in Yonkers?

Ira Gershwin
"Who Cares? (So Long as You Care for Me)"

In a year of deepening Depression, many popular songs carry a new element of sophistication. More songs than ever are imported from abroad, from places as diverse as England ("Good Night, Sweetheart", "Someday I'll Find You"), Cuba ("Green Eyes", "The Peanut Vendor)", Austria ("Yours Is My Heart Alone"), and Denmark ("Jealousy"). Even American songs have a certain continental elegance, as in "Dancing in the Dark", "Penthouse Serenade", and "Out of Nowhere".

But there is little to cheer about. The economy seems to be worsening by the moment, even as President Herbert Hoover proclaims that it is "fundamentally sound". People vent their anger on Hoover, blaming him for all their troubles. They call newspapers "Hoover blankets" and shantytowns "Hoovervilles". Hoover tries to bring back the good times, but nothing seems to work; he lacks the charisma to establish confidence in the common man.

Still, this dismal year has a brighter side. The world's tallest office building, the Empire State, opens its doors in New York City on the first of May. The Broadway theater enjoys a brilliant season, with Eugene O'Neill's *Mourning Becomes Electra*, Noël Coward's *Private Lives*, and several outstanding musicals: the political satire, *Of Thee I Sing* – the first musical to receive a Pulitzer Prize, with a fascinating score by George and Ira Gershwin; *The Band Wagon*, with an innovative score by Howard Dietz and Arthur Schwartz; and *The Cat and the Fiddle*, with lyrics by Otto Harbach and music by Jerome Kern.

Gangsters are still in the news; Al Capone is convicted of tax evasion. And, accordingly, Hollywood contributes a rash of gangster films, including *Public Enemy*, with James Cagney; and *Scarface*, with Paul Muni and George Raft. Horror films are also the rage, with Bela

Lugosi scary as *Dracula* and Boris Karloff even scarier as *Frankenstein*'s monster. This is a good year for women. Katherine Cornell produces and acts in *The Barretts of Wimpole Street*; Helen Hayes wins an Oscar for her first film, *The Sin of Madelon Claudet*; Pearl Buck has a runaway best-selling novel with *The Good Earth*; and singer Kate Smith breaks all records at New York's Palace Theatre, extending her run for eleven consecutive weeks.

Two out of every five American homes, more than twelve million, now have radio receivers. This year, Eddie Cantor makes his radio debut, soon to be followed by Jack Benny, Bob Hope, George Burns and Gracie Allen, and Fibber McGee and Molly. It seems that in this desperate year, people are "looking for the light", as put so eloquently by Howard Dietz in "Dancing in the Dark". And no one can fault a year that sees the birth of a song destined to become one of the best known of all standards, "As Time Goes By".

SONGS OF 1931

    All of Me * *
    As Time Goes By * * * *
    Beautiful Love
    Dancing in the Dark * * *!
    Dream a Little Dream of Me *
    Good Night, Sweetheart * *
    Green Eyes (Aquellos Ojos Verdes)
    Heartaches
    Home
    I Don't Know Why (I Just Do) *
    I Found a Million Dollar Baby
        (In a Five and Ten Cent Store) *
    I Surrender, Dear *
    I'm Thru with Love *
    Jealousy (Jalousie)
    Just One More Chance
    Lazy River *
    Love Is Sweeping the Country
    Mood Indigo *
    Of Thee I Sing
    Out of Nowhere * * *!

The Peanut Vendor (El Manisero)
Penthouse Serenade (When We're Alone)
Prisoner of Love
She Didn't Say "Yes"
Someday I'll Find You
Who Cares *!
Yours Is My Heart Alone

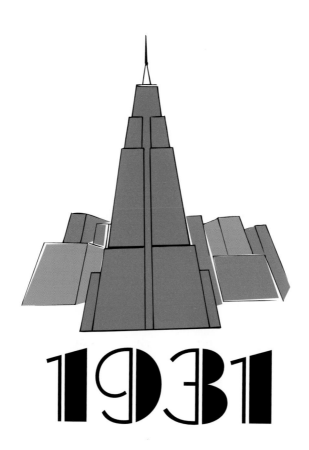

ALL OF ME * *

WORDS AND MUSIC: Seymour Simons and Gerald Marks
INTRODUCED BY: Belle Baker in vaudeville and on radio

Written by two songwriters from Michigan, "All of Me" was introduced by Belle Baker, the celebrated vaudeville singer and comedienne who had introduced Irving Berlin's "Blue Skies" in 1926. Originally designed as a torch song to be sung in slow tempo, "All of Me" has evolved over the years into a jazz standard, usually performed at somewhat faster tempo and in a campy style. Among early recordings were those of Mildred Bailey, Kate Smith, and Billie Holiday. There have been periodic revivals: by Count Basie and his Orchestra in 1943, and by Johnnie Ray in 1952. But the most popular recording of all was made by Frank Sinatra.

The song is old-fashioned in form (ABAC) and style; it could easily have been written in the early twenties. The opening rhythmical motive of a dotted quarter and eighth tied over to a half note gives the refrain a light touch of syncopation. The melody broadly outlines the harmonies, making the song an ideal subject for improvisation. Harmonically, the refrain passes through the circle of fifths three times in succession, moving first from C major to E seventh, A seventh, and D minor; then from E seventh to A minor, D seventh, and G seventh; and then back to the first chord progression. The lyrics, in true torch song character of unrequited love, describe the parts of the singer's body that have been taken away – arms, lips, and heart – and lament: "Why not take all of me?"

In films, "All of Me" was sung by Frank Sinatra in *Meet Danny Wilson* (1952); by Gloria De Haven in *Down Among the Sheltering Palms* (1953); and by Diana Ross as Billie Holiday in *Lady Sings the Blues* (1972). The title was also used in a film, *All of Me*, in 1934 and 1984.

Moderate torch song with verse (12) and refrain (32)
PUBLISHER: Irving Berlin, Inc.
KEY: C maj., *STARTS*: c" (C maj.), *FORM*: ABAC

≈≈≈≈≈≈≈≈≈≈≈≈≈≈≈≈≈≈≈≈

AS TIME GOES BY * * * *

WORDS AND MUSIC: Herman Hupfeld
PREMIERE: Musical comedy, *Everybody's Welcome*
New York: Shubert Theatre, 13 October 1931 (139 perf.)
INTRODUCED BY: Frances Williams

"As Time Goes By" owes its extraordinary popularity to the legendary film, *Casablanca* (1942), in which it was memorably sung by Dooley Wilson. In that screen classic, it was the love song of the characters played by Humphrey Bogart and Ingrid Bergman and formed an integral part of the plot. But actually, "As Time Goes By" was written eleven years earlier and was interpolated in an uninspired musical, *Everybody's Welcome*. Herman Hupfeld, who wrote both words and music, was a man of many talents: violinist, conductor, and pianist, as well as composer and lyricist. His other songs include "Sing Something Simple", "When Yuba Plays the Rumba on the Tuba", and "Let's Put Out the Lights and Go to Sleep". But he is remembered chiefly for "As Time Goes By". After the song appeared in *Everybody's Welcome*, it was popularized by Rudy Vallee in a recording and on radio. There was a tremendous revival in 1942, with the release of *Casablanca*, and the song stayed twenty-one weeks on *Your Hit Parade*. Another revival, in 1952, was sparked by the recording of Ray Anthony and his Orchestra.

The verse, marked to be performed "liltingly", is quite interesting, with such literate expressions as: "We get a trifle weary, with Mr. Einstein's theory". But, of course, it is the refrain that captivates, if only because of its romantic association with *Casablanca*. The music is in the French style, consisting of rising melodic sequences. The opening rhythmical motive occurs four times in each "A" section: ascending first a whole step, then a fourth, and then another whole step. The lyrics are strikingly graphic, referring to "passion, jealousy and hate" and "a case of do or die". More than the rather mundane music, it is probably the lyrics that account for the song's remarkable endurance.

Dooley Wilson again sang "As Time Goes By" in the 1971 film, *A Safe Place*. Barbra Streisand sang it in *What's Up Doc?* (1972). It remains one of the most popular songs in the literature.

Moderate ballad with verse (12) and refrain (32)
PUBLISHER: Harms, Inc.
KEY: E-flat maj, *STARTS*: g' (F min. 7), *FORM*: AA'BA'

≈≈≈≈≈≈≈≈≈≈≈≈≈≈≈≈≈≈≈≈

BEAUTIFUL LOVE

WORDS: Haven Gillespie
MUSIC: Victor Young, Wayne King, and Egbert Van Alstyne
INTRODUCED BY: Wayne King and his Orchestra

An enchanting waltz, "Beautiful Love" was recorded by its co-writer, Wayne King, as well as by singers James Melton and Donald Novis. The song has had a renaissance as a jazz standard, usually in 4/4 meter, and has been recorded by Art Tatum, Dick Hyman, and other pianists. The song's chief attraction to musicians lies in its subtle harmonic changes. The prevailing mode is minor, and harmonies are clearly outlined in the melodic line. Allan Jones sang it as a waltz in the 1944 film, *Sing a Jingle*, known in Britain as *Lucky Days*.

Moderate waltz with two verses (24) and refrain (32)
PUBLISHER: Red Star Music Co., Inc., assigned to Movietone Music Corp.
KEY: D min., *STARTS*: d' (E min. 6, flatted fifth), *FORM*: ABAB'

≈≈≈≈≈≈≈≈≈≈≈≈≈≈≈≈≈≈

DANCING IN THE DARK ✶ ✶ ✶!

WORDS: Howard Dietz, *MUSIC:* Arthur Schwartz
PREMIERE: Revue, *The Band Wagon*
New York: Amsterdam Theatre, 3 June 1931 (260 perf.)
INTRODUCED BY: John Barker; danced to by Tilly Losch

One of the mostly fondly remembered of revues, *The Band Wagon*, boasted a sparkling score by Howard Dietz and Arthur Schwartz and a cast that included Fred and Adele Astaire (their last show together), Helen Broderick, and Frank Morgan. Its most memorable song is "Dancing in the Dark", the quintessential show tune and a seminal influence on other carefully-wrought show tunes to follow. The song was vividly presented in *The Band Wagon*, with Tilly Losch dancing to it on a revolving stage as lights flashed on mirrored floors. It was an instant hit, popularized by recordings by Bing Crosby and Fred Waring's Pennsylvanians. Ten years later, Artie Shaw and his Orchestra had a million-selling Victor recording.

The song is replete with romantic imagery. The poetic lyrics are often alliterative, as in "looking for the light", "waltzing in the wonder", and indeed "Dancing in the Dark". The music itself is a wonder, far removed from the ordinary. Rather than a verse, there is an interlude, sixteen melodramatic bars, first in E-flat minor and then in E-flat major. In the refrain there are many repeated notes; the opening d', for example, is performed five times. Rhythmically, there are numerous dotted quarters and eighths. Blue notes, the flatted seventh (d-flat"), flatted sixth (c-flat"), and flatted third (g-flat'), add a touch of pathos. Above all, it is the harmonies – the many chords of the major, minor, and diminished seventh – that bring the song to life.

In the movies, "Dancing in the Dark" was sung by Betsy Drake in the eponymous *Dancing in the Dark* (1949). Fred Astaire and Cyd Charisse danced to it in the 1953 film version of *The Band Wagon*. It is a song to remember.

Slow ballad with refrain (32) and interlude (16)
PUBLISHER: Harms, Inc.
KEY: E-flat maj., *STARTS*: d' (E-flat maj.), *FORM*: ABAB'

≈≈≈≈≈≈≈≈≈≈≈≈≈≈≈≈≈≈≈

DREAM A LITTLE DREAM OF ME *

WORDS: Gus Kahn, *MUSIC*: Wilbur Schwandt and Fabian André
INTRODUCED BY: Wayne King and his Orchestra, in a Victor recording

The music for this dreamy ballad was written by two specialists in Latin-American music named Wilbur Schwandt and Fabian André. But there is no trace of Latin rhythm in the song; it is a quite ordinary thirty-two bar ballad in AABA form. It was initially popularized by Kate Smith, with a cover record by Jack Owens. However, the song's great popularity came thirty-six years after it was written, in 1968, with a best-selling Dunhill record by Mama Cass Elliott, with the Mamas and the Papas, that is a favorite to this day. It is a simple song, with a stepwise melody, dotted rhythms, and slowly-changing harmonies. In fact, the only unusual aspect of the "Dream a Little Dream of Me" is its release which moves surprisingly to E-flat major with an awkward modulation back to G major at its close. Because of its many dotted notes, the song is often played in shuffle rhythm with a "walking bass".

Slow ballad with two verses (16) and refrain (32)
PUBLISHER: Davis, Coots & Engel, Inc.
KEY: G maj., *STARTS*: g' (G maj.), *FORM*: AA'BA'

≈≈≈≈≈≈≈≈≈≈≈≈≈≈≈≈≈≈≈

GOOD NIGHT, SWEETHEART * *

WORDS AND MUSIC: Ray Noble, Jimmy Campbell, and Reg Connelly
INTRODUCED: in the United States on radio and in a Victor recording by Rudy Vallee

Everybody's favorite way to end an evening, "Good Night, Sweetheart" has been the closing song of ballroom dances for generations. It was written by three Englishmen, introduced in London by Henry Hall's

BBC Orchestra, and advertised as a favorite of the King and Queen of England. Rudy Vallee single-handedly made the song famous in the United States. He also is credited with modifying the lyrics for American consumption. When the song became a No. 1 Chart Record by Guy Lombardo and his Royal Canadians, its popularity positively soared. Wayne King and his Orchestra had a cover record. For a time, the song was interpolated in the revue, *Earl Carroll Vanities*, which opened at the new Earl Carroll Theatre on 27 August 1931; it was sung by Milton Watson and Woods Miller.

The hallmark of the song is its use of chromaticism: in particular, the repeated use of the notes d-sharp' and f sharp'. Otherwise, it is a simple song of the old school, in ABAB' form, which reaches its climactic high point in the final B' section.

On the big screen, "Goodnight, Sweetheart" was sung by composer Ray Noble in *The Big Broadcast of 1936*; by Rudy Vallee in *The Palm Beach Story* (1942); by Gene Autry in *Stardust on the Sage* (1942); by Kenny Baker in *Stage Door Canteen* (1943); and by a chorus in *You Were Meant for Me* (1948). And it still closes public dances everywhere.

Slow ballad with verse and refrain (32)
PUBLISHER: Robbins Music corporation
KEY: C maj., *STARTS*: e' (C maj.), *FORM*: ABAB'

≈≈≈≈≈≈≈≈≈≈≈≈≈≈≈≈≈≈≈

GREEN EYES (AQUELLOS OJOS VERDES) *

ENGLISH WORDS: E. Rivera and E. Woods, *MUSIC*: Nilo Menéndez
INTRODUCED BY: Don Azpiazú and his Havana Casino Orchestra in the United States.

In the vanguard of the Latin invasion of popular music to the United States in the thirties, "Aquellos Ojos Verdes" was published in Cuba in 1929, with music by pianist Nilo Menéndez and Spanish lyrics by Adolfo Utrera. Published in the United States two years later as "Green Eyes", the song was played mostly by Latin orchestras. Recordings by the bands of Don Azpiazú, Enric Madriguera, and Xavier Cugat became popular among aficionados. However, the song's real thrust to fame came ten years later, with a Decca recording by Jimmy Dorsey and his Orchestra, with vocal by Helen O'Connell and Bob Eberly. This No. 1 Chart Record, released in 1941, catapulted "Green Eyes" to international fame. But the Dorsey-band arrangement was purely in swing style; no trace of the song's origin as an innocent cancion bolero remained.

Written as a romantic bolero, the verse is in 6/8 meter, suitable for ad-lib singing. The hallmark of the refrain is the opening gesture: seven notes outlining the E-flat major chord with added sixth and major seventh, ranging over an octave and a fourth. The first five eighth notes act as a pickup. This rhythmical motive, at different pitch levels, permeates the refrain. The highest point, the g", comes in the last section, giving the song an unusually wide range of an octave and a sixth.

In 1947, Helen O'Connell and Bob Eberly reprised the song with the Jimmy Dorsey band in the film, *The Fabulous Dorseys.*

Slow rumba with two verses (16) and refrain (32)
PUBLISHER: Campbell, Connelly & Co. (London), assigned to Robbins Music Corporation
KEY: E-flat maj., *STARTS*: b-flat (E-flat maj.), *FORM*: ABA'C

≈≈≈≈≈≈≈≈≈≈≈≈≈≈≈≈≈≈≈

HEARTACHES

WORDS: John Klenner, *MUSIC*: Al Hoffman
INTRODUCED BY: Guy Lombardo and his Royal Canadians in a Columbia recording

This is a gliding foxtrot of long notes, similar in style to "Linger Awhile" (1923). Initially popularized by Guy Lombardo and his Royal Canadians, it has periodically been revived: by Ted Weems and his Orchestra in 1947 (with a whistling chorus by Elmo Tanner), and by The Marcels in 1961. The refrain begins with four whole notes – e', d', f-sharp', e' – accompanied by harmonies of the G sixth for the first two bars and F-sharp seventh for the second two bars. This mostly stepwise motion, mainly in quarter notes, persists throughout the refrain. The closing line is "My heart aches for you".

Moderate foxtrot with two verses (16) and refrain (32)
PUBLISHER: Leeds Music Corporation
KEY: G maj., *STARTS*: e' (G 6), *FORM*: ABA'B'

≈≈≈≈≈≈≈≈≈≈≈≈≈≈≈≈≈≈≈

HOME

WORDS AND MUSIC: Peter Van Steeden, Harry and Jeff Clarkson
INTRODUCED BY: Peter Van Steeden and his Orchestra, on radio and in a Victor recording

A nostalgic ballad, "Home" is sometimes known by its opening words: "When Shadows Fall". Written by the father-and-son team of Harry and Jeff Clarkson, along with bandleader Peter Van Steeden, the song was introduced by Van Steeden and became his theme song. In 1950 it was revived with a recording by Nat "King" Cole. The melody is harmonically derived, outlining first the E-flat major triad and then the D dominant seventh, F minor, and B-flat dominant seventh chords. The release, which has two sets of lyrics, outlines the A-flat minor chord. The many thirds in the melodic line give the song a hauntingly sweet quality. It was sung by The Andrews Sisters in the 1944 film, *Moonlight and Cactus*.

> Slow ballad with verse (16) and refrain (32)
> *PUBLISHER*: Mills Music, Inc.
> *KEY*: E-flat maj., *STARTS*: b-flat' (E-flat maj.), *FORM*: AA'BA

≈≈≈≈≈≈≈≈≈≈≈≈≈≈≈≈≈≈≈

I DON'T KNOW WHY (I JUST DO) *

WORDS: Roy Turk, *MUSIC*: Fred E. Ahlert

The sheet music cover of this short but snappy song refers to it as a "Ballad-Fox-Trot"; it does in fact lie somewhere between those two genres in tempo and subject matter. Originally popularized by Wayne King and his Orchestra and singer Russ Columbo, the song was revived in 1946 by Tommy Dorsey and his Orchestra. The melody of the sixteen-bar refrain features syncopated repeated notes slowly ascending scalewise. In the release, dotted eighths and sixteenths go through the circle of fifths: D seventh, G seventh, C seventh, F seventh. Very often performed in shuffle rhythm, the song was featured in the 1946 film, *Faithful in My Fashion*, starring Donna Reed and Tom Drake.

> Moderate foxtrot with verse (8) and refrain (16)
> *PUBLISHER*: Leo Feist, Inc.
> *KEY*: B-flat maj., *STARTS*: f' (B-flat maj.), *FORM*: AA'BA"

≈≈≈≈≈≈≈≈≈≈≈≈≈≈≈≈≈≈≈

I FOUND A MILLION DOLLAR BABY (IN A FIVE AND TEN CENT STORE) *

WORDS: Billy Rose and Mort Dixon, *MUSIC:* Harry Warren
PREMIERE: Revue, *Billy Rose's Crazy Quilt*
New York: 44th Street Theatre, 19 May 1931 (79 perf.)
INTRODUCED BY: Fanny Brice, Ted Healy, and Phil Baker

Comedienne Fanny Brice introduced this sprightly song, along with her co-stars Ted Healy and Phil Baker, in the revue, *Billy Rose's Crazy Quilt*; the three of them were dressed in top hat, white tie, and tails. Although the revue only lasted ten weeks, the song soon took on a life of its own: Fred Waring's Pennsylvanians had a No. 1 Chart Record, Bing Crosby and The Boswell Sisters also had hit recordings, singer Ethel Shutta used it as her theme song.

The very idea of mentioning money in a song touched a nerve with the public at a time when money was in short supply. The lyrics tell a story about coming in from the rain and meeting the girl of one's dreams behind a china counter, of then buying china "until the crowd got wise", and of a happy ending in a cottage with the "million dollar baby". Most noticeable in the music is the pervasiveness of dotted eighths and sixteenths.

In 1941, the song was featured in the film, *Million Dollar Baby*, starring Ronald Reagan and Priscilla Lane. In 1975, Barbra Striesand sang it in her screen portrayal of Fanny Brice, *Funny Lady*.

Moderate novelty song with two verses (16) and refrain (32)
PUBLISHER: Remick Music Corp.
KEY: F maj., *STARTS*: c' (F maj.), *FORM*: AA'BA'

≈≈≈≈≈≈≈≈≈≈≈≈≈≈≈≈≈≈≈

I SURRENDER, DEAR *

WORDS: Gordon Clifford, *MUSIC:* Harry Barris
INTRODUCED BY: Gus Arnheim and his Orchestra; vocal by The Three Rhythm Boys, featuring Bing Crosby

Harry Barris, the composer of this song, was a founding member of the Three Rhythm Boys, featured with Paul Whiteman and his Orchestra in the twenties; his partners were Bing Crosby and Al Rinker. Barris went on to compose many songs, including this one, his most popular. At the time of the first recording of this song, Crosby was twenty-four years old. It became his first solid hit. Cover records were made by Earl Bartnett and his Orchestra and by Guy Lombardo and his Royal Canadians.

The melody rises in sequence in the same fashion as "As Time Goes By", also written this year. What lifts "I Surrender, Dear" from the ordinary are its opening harmonies; the verse starts with an A-flat dominant seventh chord, while the refrain begins with a D minor chord. Also unusual are the three consecutive triplets played as accompaniment before each statement of the title – a touch of melodrama not usually adhered to in performance.

A low-budget musical film, *I Surrender, Dear,* was released in 1948. It starred Gloria Jean and David Street and, of course, featured the song.

Slow ballad with verse (16) and refrain (32)
PUBLISHER: Richard J. Powers, Ltd., assigned to Freed & Powers, Ltd.
KEY: C maj., *STARTS*: f' (D min.), *FORM*: AABA

≈≈≈≈≈≈≈≈≈≈≈≈≈≈≈≈≈≈≈

I'M THRU WITH LOVE *

WORDS: Gus Kahn, *MUSIC*: Matt Malneck and Fud Livingston
INTRODUCED BY: Mildred Bailey

This endearing ballad has always been favored by vocalists. It was introduced by Mildred Bailey and popularized in a Brunswick recording by Bing Crosby. Cover records by Paul Whiteman and his Orchestra and by Henry Busse and his Orchestra (played in his famous "shuffle rhythm") added to its popularity. Other popular recordings were by Glen Gray and The Casa Loma Orchestra, vocal by Kenny Sargent (Decca), and Dinah Shore (Bluebird).

Gus Kahn's moving lyrics about love lost are particularly effective, as in "I must have you or no one". So is the music, with its persistent rhythmic pattern of dotted quarter and eighth. The melody rises sequentially in the "A" sections. Some harmonic contrast is offered in the release, which starts out in A minor and then moves to C major.

"I'm Thru with Love" has been featured in a surprising number of films over the years. Harriet Hilliard, accompanied by her husband, Ozzie Nelson, and his orchestra, sang it in the 1943 film, *Honeymoon Lodge.* Jane Froman dubbed it in for Susan Hayward in the Froman biography, *With a Song in My Heart* (1952). Bobby Van sang it in *the Affairs of Dobie Gillis* (1953). Marilyn Monroe sang it in *Some Like It Hot* (1959). Chuck Berry did it in the 1987 film, *Chuck Berry: Hail! Hail! Rock 'n' Roll.* And Woody Allen sang it in *Everybody Says I Love You* (1997).

Moderate ballad with verse (12) and refrain (32)
PUBLISHER: Metro-Goldwyn-Mayer Corp., assigned to Robbins Music
Corporation
KEY: F maj., *STARTS*: f' (F maj.), *FORM*: AABA

≈≈≈≈≈≈≈≈≈≈≈≈≈≈≈≈≈≈≈≈

JEALOUSY (JALOUSIE) *

WORDS: Vera Bloom, *MUSIC*: Jacob Gade

The music of this gypsy tango was published in 1925 as "Jalousie",
by Gade and Warny-Musikforlag in Copenhagen. The composer was a
Danish violinist, composer, and conductor named Jacob Gade. The fiery
music attained international fame and "Jalousie" was published in many
countries, starting with the Paris edition by Charles Brull. The American
edition, with lyrics by Vera Bloom, was published in 1931. In 1938 the song
was popularized in a Victor recording by The Boston Pops Orchestra,
under Arthur Fiedler, as "Tango Tzigane". Other recordings were made by
Harry James and his Orchestra (1947) and Frankie Lane (1951).

Unlike most popular songs, verse and refrain are of equal importance. The verse in C minor, starting with a descending chromatic scale, is
especially effective; it acts as a counterfoil to the romantically melodic
refrain in C major,

Kathryn Grayson sang "Jealousie" in the 1945 film, *Anchors
Aweigh*. Lucille Norman sang it in *Painting the Clouds with Sunshine*
(1951), With its wide range (octave and a fourth) and high tessitura,
"Jealousy" is often performed by trained singers as part of the "semi-
classic" repertoire.

Moderate tango with verse (32) and refrain (32)
PUBLISHER: Harms, Inc.
KEY: C maj. or D maj., *STARTS*: g' (C 6) or a' (D 6), *FORM*: ABAC

≈≈≈≈≈≈≈≈≈≈≈≈≈≈≈≈≈≈≈≈

JUST ONE MORE CHANCE

WORDS and MUSIC: Sam Coslow and Arthur Johnston
*INTRODUCED BY:*Ruth Etting

Crooner Bing Crosby made this song a hit with his Brunswick recording. Recordings by Russ Columbo on Victor and Abe Lyman and his
Orchestra on Brunswick soon followed. The song was revived in 1951, with

a Mercury recording by Les Paul and Mary Ford. The subject is, of course, begging for forgiveness. The opening motive of the refrain outlines the major sixth. Blue notes of the lowered seventh (f') and third (b-flat') contribute to the melancholy sound of the song. Dick Powell sang "Just One More Chance" in the 1933 film, *College Coach* (known in Great Britain as *Football Coach*). Dean Martin sang it in *The Stooge* (1953). It was also featured in the 1958 film, *Country Music Holiday.*

> Moderate torch song with verse (16) and refrain (32)
> *PUBLISHER*: Famous Music Corp.
> *KEY*: G maj., *STARTS*: d' (G maj.), *FORM*: AA'BA

≈≈≈≈≈≈≈≈≈≈≈≈≈≈≈≈≈≈≈

LAZY RIVER *

> *WORDS AND MUSIC*: Hoagy Carmichael and Sidney Arodin
> *INTRODUCED BY*: Hoagy Carmichael and his Orchestra

This winsome song lives up to its title as a "lazy rag" of the thirties. Hoagy Carmichael – the celebrated composer of "Star Dust" (1929) and "Georgia On My Mind" (1930), who was also a pianist, singer, and actor – introduced it with his own band, featuring Benny Goodman, Gene Krupa, Jack Teagarden, and Bix Beiderbecke. The song has seen a number of revivals: in 1941, 1946, 1952, and 1961. The Mills Brothers had a hit Decca record in 1951. The recording by Si Zentner and his Orchestra won a Grammy Award in 1961.

It has one of the widest ranges of any popular song, spanning almost two octaves, from g-sharp to f". It is also one of the most difficult songs to sing; the melody line is in fact idiosyncratic for instruments rather than voices. In the "A" sections, harmonies go through the familiar circle of fifths, starting with D seventh, and then moving at two-bar intervals to G seventh, C seventh, and F seventh. A brief coda rounds out the last section.

Carmichael sang it in the 1946 film, *The Best Years of Our Lives.* Keely Smith, Louis Prima, and a chorus performed it in the 1959 film, *Hey Boy! Hey Girl!* Because of its instrumental orientation and predictable harmonies, it is a favorite of jazz musicians.

> Moderate rhythm song with verse (8) and refrain (20)
> *PUBLISHER*: Peer International Corporation
> *KEY*: F maj., *STARTS*: d' (D 7), *FORM*: ABAC

≈≈≈≈≈≈≈≈≈≈≈≈≈≈≈≈≈≈≈

LOVE IS SWEEPING THE COUNTRY

WORDS: Ira Gershwin, *MUSIC*: George Gershwin
PREMIERE: Musical play, *Of Thee I Sing*
New York: Music Box Theatre, 26 December 1931 (441 perf.)
INTRODUCED BY: George Murphy, June O'Dea, and chorus

The political satire, *Of Thee I Sing,* was the first musical to be awarded a Pulitzer Prize. In it, John P. Wintergreen, who is running for President, needs a platform. What could be better than a platform of love, a love that will sweep the country? That refreshing concept is expressed in this rousing song, presented in the show by Wintergreen's aides at a rally outside Madison Square Garden.

The piece, in 2/4 meter, is a cross between a march and a polka. It combines swinging syncopation with sardonic lyrics ("All the sexes / From Maine to Texas"). The last section vacillates between the notes e-flat' and e-natural', while the next-to-last note is an unexpected blue one, the g-flat'. It is, in every respect, a captivating song.

Moderate two-step with verse (28) and refrain (40)
PUBLISHER: New World Music Corporation
KEY: E-flat maj., *STARTS*: b-flat' (-flat maj.), *FORM*: ABA'C

≈≈≈≈≈≈≈≈≈≈≈≈≈≈≈≈≈≈≈

MOOD INDIGO *

WORDS AND MUSIC: Duke Ellington, Irving Mills, and Albany Bigard
PREMIERE: New York: Cotton Club, 1930
INTRODUCED BY: Duke Ellington and his Orchestra

Duke Ellington wrote this soulful piece together with his clarinet-ist Barney (Leon Albany) Bigard. Designed for orchestral performance, it became the first song to be developed by lyricist and publisher Irving Mills, beginning a long and fruitful relationship with Ellington. It was first introduced by the Ellington band under the title "Dreamy Blues". Mitchell Parish, staff writer at Mills Music, Inc., is reputed to have supplied the lyrics, although he is uncredited. Recordings were made by singer Dinah Shore and the bands of Jimmie Lunceford and Cab Calloway. The Four Freshman recorded a vocal arrangement in 1954.

Although not in twelve-bar blues format, "Mood Indigo" has a blues feeling, imparted by its many blue notes and subtle syncopation. The overall form is unusual, but simple, consisting of three sixteen-bar sections: ABA. The Ellington penchant for Debussian ninth chords is much in evidence. Ellington and his Orchestra performed it in the 1961 film *Paris Blues*.

> Slow rhythm song with refrain (16), verse (16), and refrain (16)
> *PUBLISHER*: Mills Music, Inc.
> *KEY*: A-flat maj., *STARTS*: c" (A-flat maj.), *FORM*: AA'BA

≈≈≈≈≈≈≈≈≈≈≈≈≈≈≈≈≈≈≈

OF THEE I SING

WORDS: Ira Gershwin, *MUSIC*: George Gershwin
PREMIERE: Musical play, *Of Thee I Sing*.
New York: Music Box Theatre, 26 December 1931 (441 perf.)
INTRODUCED BY: William Gaxton, Lois Moran, and chorus

In the Pulitzer-winning play, *Of Thee I Sing*, the title song is also the campaign song of John P. Wintergreen, who sings it to his adoring public on Election Night. It is a powerful song, propelled by the opening notes of its refrain, rising in half steps: g', g-sharp', a'. The verse, with many repeated notes, starts in E-flat major and moves to G major. In the refrain, whole notes alternate with quarter notes, chromatic passages with scalar ones, and archaic words (like "thee") with colloquialisms (such as the ubiquitous "baby").

> Slow anthem with verse (20) and refrain (32)
> *PUBLISHER*: New World Music Corporation
> *KEY*: C maj., *STARTS*: g' (C maj.), *FORM*: ABA'C

≈≈≈≈≈≈≈≈≈≈≈≈≈≈≈≈≈≈≈

OUT OF NOWHERE ＊＊＊!

WORDS: Edward Heyman, *MUSIC*: Johnny W. Green
INTRODUCED BY: Guy Lombardo and his Royal Canadians

The unusual harmonies of this striking ballad have made it a favorite of jazz musicians. Among the myriad recordings were those of singers Bing Crosby and Lena Horne, pianist Teddy Wilson, and the bands of Harry James, Artie Shaw, Guy Lombardo, and Leo Reisman. The song was revived by Helen Forrest in 1945.

In the refrain, the flowing melodic line first outlines the G major seventh chord, leading unexpectedly to an E-flat ninth (on the tone f') in Bar Three and an E-natural ninth (on f-sharp') in Bar Five. Both "B" sections begin with A minor and E seventh harmonies.

The opening words of the refrain became the title of a 1945 movie, *You Came Along* in 1945, in which "Out of Nowhere" was sung by Helen Forrest. Frank Sinatra sang it (with new lyrics by Harry Harris) in the 1957 film, *The Joker Is Wild*. The song was also featured in the films, *The Five Pennies* (1959) and *The Rat Race* (1960). Although written as a wistful ballad, it is very often performed by jazz instrumentalists at ultra-fast tempo.

Moderate ballad with verse (16) and refrain (32)
PUBLISHER: Famous Music Corp.
KEY: G maj., *STARTS*: d' (G maj.), *FORM*: ABAB'

≈≈≈≈≈≈≈≈≈≈≈≈≈≈≈≈≈≈

THE PEANUT VENDOR (EL MANISERO)

ENGLISH WORDS: Marion Sunshine and L. Wolfe Gilbert
MUSIC: Moisés Simons
PREMIERE: New York: Palace Theatre, 1930
INTRODUCED BY: Don Azpiazú and his Havana Casino Orchestra

At New York's Palace Theatre in 1930 the course of Latin music in America was changed forever. It was there that audiences first heard authentic Cuban dance music, played by Don Apiazú's Havana Casino Orchestra; the rumba craze was born in the United States. One of the first Cuban songs to become popular was "The Peanut Vendor (El Manisero)". The song astounded nearly everyone with its novelty, although Guy Lombardo predicted that it would never become popular. Walter Winchell, the celebrated columnist, claimed that the song was based on Ravel's "Boléro", published in 1928. Another reviewer said that "The Peanut Vendor" had a melody like a "plaintive whine". Nevertheless, by 1931 it created a national sensation, sparked by the hit recordings of the bands of Louis Armstrong, Guy Lombardo, Paul Whiteman, and Xavier Cugat.

The music had been written in 1928 by a Cuban pianist and composer named Moisés Simons. New York music publisher Herbert Marks heard the song when he was on his honeymoon in Cuba. He was enthralled and arranged to have his firm publish it with English lyrics. "The Peanut Vendor" created an immediate sensation, and its success was not limited to America. Queen Mary of Britain included it in the music for the Buckingham Palace Ball and also requested it at a Royal Command performance.

The song is unusual structurally, introduced by an insistent vamp using only two chords, tonic and dominant, which soon act as accompaniment to the words "Mani! (Peanuts)". The lively stepwise melody then spins out merrily in rondo form. Finally, the opening cry, "Mani!" is repeated in the coda.

"The Peanut Vendor" was featured in several films. Lawrence Tibbett sang it in *Cuban Love Song* (1931), in which he played a marine on leave in Cuba. It was performed in the 1939 film, *Only Angels Have Wings*, about the lives and loves of pilots in Latin America. Jane Powell sang it, accompanied by Xavier Cugat and his Orchestra, in *Luxury Liner* (1948). And Judy Garland belted it out in *A Star Is Born* (1958). More than any other song, it brought the rumba to America.

Moderate rumba with verse (8), refrain (30), and coda (9)
PUBLISHER: Edward B. Marks Music Co.
KEY: G maj., *STARTS*: b' (G maj.), *FORM* (Overall): ABCBDBA

≈≈≈≈≈≈≈≈≈≈≈≈≈≈≈≈≈≈≈

PENTHOUSE SERENADE (WHEN WE'RE ALONE) *

WORDS AND MUSIC: Will Jason and Val Burton

This urbane ballad is sometimes designated by the closing words of its refrain, "When We're Alone". Initially popularized by singer Ruth Etting, later recordings were by singer Sara Vaughan and pianists Errol Garner and Eddie Heywood. The song has an interesting verse, beginning in D major and moving to G-flat major and then to G major. The refrain is in C major, with a melodic line of quarter-note triplets, descending stepwise. The lyrics are a panegyric to "old Manhattan", referring to "two heavenly hermits in view of the Hudson just over the Drive". "Penthouse Serenade" was featured in the film, *Sweetheart of Sigma Chi* (1946), and performed by Bob Hope, Vera Miles, and a chorus in the 1957 film, *Beau James*.

Moderate ballad with two verses (16) and refrain (32)
PUBLISHER: Famous Music Corporation
KEY: C maj., *STARTS*: g' (C 6), *FORM*: AA'BA'

≈≈≈≈≈≈≈≈≈≈≈≈≈≈≈≈≈≈

PRISONER OF LOVE

WORDS: Leo Robin, *MUSIC*: Russ Columbo and Clarence Gaskill
INTRODUCED BY: Russ Columbo and recorded on Victor

A romantic ballad, "Prisoner of Love" has been a favorite of singers for several generations. It was introduced by its co-composer, Russ Columbo, the most popular singer of his time, and stayed fifteen weeks on *Your Hit Parade*. Perry Como revived it with a recording in 1946, as did James Brown and The Famous Flames in 1963. The broad melody of the refrain outlines chords of the major and minor seventh, repeating each note. In the 1980 film, *Raging Bull*, both Columbo and Como sang it.

Slow ballad with verse (16) and refrain (32)
PUBLISHER: Con Conrad Music Publisher, assigned to Harms, Inc.
KEY: E-flat maj., *STARTS*: e-flat" (F min. 7), *FORM*: AA'BA'

≈≈≈≈≈≈≈≈≈≈≈≈≈≈≈≈≈≈≈

SHE DIDN'T SAY "YES" !

WORDS: Otto Harbach, *MUSIC*: Jerome Kern
PREMIERE: Musical comedy, *The Cat and the Fiddle*
New York: Globe Theatre, 15 October 1931 (395 perf.)
INTRODUCED BY: Bettina Hall

This delightful ditty comes from the quasi-operetta, T*he Cat and the Fiddle*, a piece of fluff set in Brussels. The song's continental flavor is manifest in its sprightly melody of ascending and descending half-steps, its accented fourth beats, its lack of a verse, and its four sets of lyrics. Jerome Kern's penchant for modulation can be seen in the brief diversion from C major to A major in the second section of the five-part refrain, ABA'BA". Jeanette MacDonald sang "She Didn't Say 'Yes'"in the 1934 film version of *The Cat and the Fiddle*. The Wilde twins sang it in the Kern biographical film, *Till the Clouds Roll By* (1946).

Moderate foxtrot with four refrains (20)
PUBLISHER: T. B. Harms Company
KEY: C maj., *STARTS*: g' (C maj.), *FORM*: ABA'BA"

≈≈≈≈≈≈≈≈≈≈≈≈≈≈≈≈≈≈≈

223

SOMEDAY I'LL FIND YOU

WORDS and *MUSIC*: Noël Coward
PREMIERE: Play, *Private Lives*
INTRODUCED BY: Noël Coward and Gertrude Lawrence

In *Private Lives*, Noël Coward's best-known play, the author sang this sentimental waltz along with his co-star, Gertrude Lawrence. Both Lawrence and Coward recorded it. Like many of Coward's melodies, this one is broadly romantic and unabashedly sentimental. It outlines chords, first of E-flat major and then of B-flat augmented, and then repeats the process. The development of the melody is especially praiseworthy considering that Coward could neither read nor write music. In 1968, Julie Andrews sang "Someday I'll Find You" in the film, *Star!*

Moderate waltz with two verses (16) and refrain (32)
PUBLISHER: Chappell-Harms, Inc.
KEY: E-flat maj., *STARTS*: e-flat" (E-flat maj.), *FORM*: ABA'C

≈≈≈≈≈≈≈≈≈≈≈≈≈≈≈≈≈≈≈

WHO CARES? (AS LONG AS YOU CARE FOR ME) * !

WORDS: Ira Gershwin, *MUSIC*: George Gershwin
PREMIERE: Musical play, *Of Thee I Sing*
New York: Music Box Theatre, 26 December 1931 (441 perf.)
INTRODUCED BY: William Gaxton and Lois Moran

This lilting ballad is one of the Gershwins' best songs and also was one of their personal favorites. In the Pulitzer-winning show, *Of Thee I Sing*, it was sung twice in the same scene by the presidential candidate and his wife, first in bright tempo and then slower. Fred Astaire had a hit recording on Columbia, accompanied by Benny Goodman and his Orchestra, in 1940. The lyrics tell of love at a time of economic collapse: "Who cares what banks fail in Yonkers". The verse is a gem, beginning with the words "Let it rain and thunder / Let a million firms go under!", and gives a foretaste of the harmonic complexities to come. In the refrain, the harmonies are unsettling and don't seem to match the broad melody. This very dissonance is germane to the song's theme. There is syncopation, too, and a thrice-played blue note (e-flat") at the climactic words "kiss that conquers". "Who Cares?" was sung by Jack Carson and Betty Oakes in the screen version of *Of Thee I Sing*. The song's harmonic complexities have made it a favorite of jazz musicians.

Moderate ballad with two verses (28) and two refrains (32)
PUBLISHER: New World Music Corporation
KEY: C maj., *STARTS*: g' (C maj. 7), *FORM*: ABA'C'

≈≈≈≈≈≈≈≈≈≈≈≈≈≈≈≈≈≈≈≈

YOURS IS MY HEART ALONE
(DEIN IST MEIN GANZES HERZ) !

ENGLISH WORDS: Harry B. Smith, *MUSIC*: Franz Lehár
PREMIERE: Operetta, *The Land of Smiles*
Longdon: Drury Lane Theatre, 8 May 1931
INTRODUCED BY: Richard Tauber

This magnificent arietta by Franz Lehár has always been associated with the great tenor, Richard Tauber, who originally introduced the song, in German, in the operetta, *Das Land des Lachelns,* at the Metropol Theatre in Berlin on 10 October 1929. As *The Land of Smiles*, with English words by Harry B. Smith, the operetta was presented at the Drury Lane Theatre in London 8 May 1931. A revival of that show, starring Richard Tauber and called *Yours Is My Heart,* opened at the Shubert Theatre in New York 5 September 1946, but closed after a month because Tauber was having problems with his throat. Among recordings were those of singer James Melton and the bands of Leo Reisman and Glenn Miller.

The verse, in 3/4 meter, is based on a pentatonic, quasi-oriental scale. There is an interlude in F minor and then a pedal-point preparation for the refrain on the note A-flat. In the refrain, the broad, legato melody with many sustained notes is custom-made for singing. The song's highest point (a-flat") is reached in the release. "Yours Is My Heart Alone" was Tauber's theme throughout his career.

Slow art song with verse (18) and refrain (16)
KEY: D-flat maj., *STARTS*: d-flat" (D-flat maj.), *FORM*: AA'BA"

≈≈≈≈≈≈≈≈≈≈≈≈≈≈≈≈≈≈≈≈

1932

LOVE IN THE CRUELEST YEAR

1932

Tender words of love, repeat them again I implore you

Bruce Siever,
"Speak to Me of Love (Parlez-Moi d'Amour)"

Paradoxically, in what has been called the Depression's cruelest year, romantic ballads are all the rage. Some of the most romantic love songs are written this year, including such innovative ones as "April in Paris", "Night and Day", and "The Song Is You". And there are other heartfelt expressions of adoration as well, including "How Deep is the Ocean (How High Is the Sky)", "I'm Gettin' Sentimental Over You", and "Isn't It Romantic?" Conspicuous by their absence are the frivolous, upbeat songs of yesteryear. It seems as if people are too worn out to frolic.

And worn out they should be; with as many as seventeen million unemployed, there is little to cheer about. Other news is not so good either; on the first of March, the infant son of aviator and world hero Charles Lindbergh is kidnapped from his crib in New Jersey, initiating what has been called the Crime of the Century. But a ray of sunshine comes in November, with the landmark victory of Franklin Delano Roosevelt over Herbert Hoover.

Those who can afford to, see a play. Many future Hollywood stars are still on Broadway, including Katherine Hepburn, Humphrey Bogart, Leslie Howard, James Stewart, and Basil Rathbone. And in burlesque, stripper Gypsy Rose Lee is getting rave reviews. But it is a lackluster year for musicals, brightened up only in November and December by Jerome Kern's *Music in the Air*, Cole Porter's *Gay Divorce*, and Vernon Duke's *Walk a Little Faster*.

The movies bring escape from reality, seeing the screen débuts of such disparate talents as Shirley Temple (playing herself) and Johnny Weismuller (as Tarzan of the Apes). *Grand Hotel* boasts an all-star cast (including Great Garbo, John and Lionel Barrymore, and Joan Crawford); Fredric March wins an Oscar in *Dr. Jekyll and Mr. Hyde*; while *Rasputin and the Empress* is the only film with all three Barrymores: Ethel, John, and Lionel.

And then there are the cheapest diversions of all, listening to the radio and reading a book. This year sees the débuts of two long-running broadcasts: the soap opera, *One Man's Family,* and Fred Allen's comedy hour (starting with *The Linit Revue*). Two novels are best-sellers: Pearl Buck's *The Good Earth* (which wins the Pulitzer Prize), and Erskine Caldwell's *Tobacco Road*, set in Georgia during the Depression. And so it goes in this strange year of contrasts, of "Brother, Can You Spare a Dime?" and "Speak to Me of Love".

SONGS OF 1932

Alone Together * !
April in Paris * * * * !
Brother, Can You Spare a Dime?
Fascination *
Forty-Second Street
How Deep Is the Ocean (How High Is the Sky)
I Don't Stand a Ghost of a Chance (With You) *
I Gotta Right to Sing the Blues
If I Love Again
I'm Gettin' Sentimental Over You * *
In a Shanty in Old Shanty Town
Isn't It Romantic? *
I've Got the World on a String *
I've Told Ev'ry Little Star
Lover * !
Mimi
My Silent Love
Night and Day * * * * !
Shuffle Off to Buffalo
The Song Is You * !
Speak to Me of Love (Parlez-Moi d'Amour)
Try a Little Tenderness
Willow Weep for Me
You Are Too Beautiful
You're Getting to Be a Habit with Me
Yours (Quiéreme Mucho)

ALONE TOGETHER * !

> *WORDS*: Howard Dietz, *MUSIC*: Arthur Schwartz
> *PREMIERE*: Revue, *Flying Colors*
> New York: Imperial Theatre, 15 September 1932 (188 perf.)
> *INTRODUCED BY:* Jean Sargent, danced by Clifton Webb & Tamara Geva

In the revue, *Flying Colors*, Clifton Webb and Tamara Geva performed a sinuous dance to the strains of this haunting ballad on a specially-designed stage that fell away to the darkness. With money in short supply, the producers were forced to lower the price of admission from a top of $4.40 to a top of $2.20, but were still unable to show a profit. The show did not last long. Only the song survives; recordings by the bands of Leo Reisman and Artie Shaw helped popularize it.

The refrain is in AABA' form. Although very much in the key of D minor, each "A" section ends in D major. The lengths of the sections are out of the ordinary: the first two, fourteen bars each ; the last two, eight bars each. Dramatic intensity increases in the release, with quarter-note triplets reaching the song's highest point on the blue notes e-flat" and d-flat", both held by fermatas. Certainly one of the most interesting songs in the literature, "Alone Together" has long been favored by jazz instrumentalists.

> Moderate ballad with refrain (44)
> *PUBLISHER*: Harms, Inc.
> *KEY*: D min., *STARTS*: d' (D min. 6), *FORM*: AABA'

≈≈≈≈≈≈≈≈≈≈≈≈≈≈≈≈≈≈

APRIL IN PARIS * * * * !

> *WORDS*: E. Y. Harburg, *MUSIC*: Vernon Duke
> *PREMIERE*: Revue, *Walk a Little Faster*
> New York: St. James Theatre, 7 December 1932 (119 perf.)
> *INTRODUCED BY:* Evelyn Hoey

There were two faces to composer Vernon Duke. As Vladimir Dukelsky, he was a Russian-born composer of ballets and concert works for the likes of Serge Diaghilev and Serge Koussevitsky. As Vernon Duke (the pseudonym George Gershwin advised him to use), he wrote beautiful songs for the theater. His first big hit was "April in Paris", written for his first full score for Broadway, that of the intimate revue, *Walk a Little Faster*.

Its title notwithstanding, the song did not have its inception in Paris, but rather on New York's West Side, at Tony Soma's restaurant. According to Duke, it came into being when somebody in his party at the restaurant (variously described as Robert Benchley, Monty Wooley, or Dorothy Parker) off-handedly said: "Oh, to be in Paris now that April's here". Duke immediately seized upon the idea, saying: "What a title! My kingdom for a piano". Fortunately, one was found upstairs, a battered upright, and the music was born. Harburg supplied the lyrics a week later. The ballad was interpolated into the revue during rehearsals and was sung by Evelyn Hoey during the Boston tryout. Hoey died during the run of the show and the song was taken over by John Hundley. Although it met with a cool reception in New York, it slowly but surely gained the success it so richly deserves. The song was first recorded by blues singer Marion Chase. Soon there were recordings by the bands of Henry King and Freddy Martin, and later by singers Doris Day and Vic Damone. But the most important recordings of "April in Paris" were the three made by Count Basie and his Orchestra (on Verve, Dot, and Crest), in a swinging arrangement best known for its twice-repeated coda, prefaced each time by the shouted words: "One more time!"

In the refrain, the most striking feature of the music is the opening gesture of quarter-note triplets of F minor triads over the pedal tones of C and G. These are quickly followed by the clashing suspension of a B major triad over the same pedal tones, resolving to a C major triad. Such sophisticated harmonies were far removed from custom in the popular songs of the day. In spite of these complexities, the melody of "April in Paris" seems to have a life of its own, soaring with seeming abandon to its highest points in the middle section.

"April in Paris" has been featured in several films of the fifties. It was sung by Doris Day in the 1953 film, *April in Paris*; by Gogi Grant, dubbing for Ann Blyth in *The Helen Morgan Story* (1957); and by Bob Hope in *Paris Holiday* (1958). It remains one of the most original and enduring ballads of the Golden Age.

Slow ballad with verse (16) and refrain (32)
PUBLISHER: Harms, Inc.
KEY: C maj., *STARTS*: f' (F min.), *FORM*: AA'BA"

≈≈≈≈≈≈≈≈≈≈≈≈≈≈≈≈≈≈≈

BROTHER, CAN YOU SPARE A DIME?

WORDS: E. Y. Harburg, *MUSIC*: Jay Gorney
PREMIERE: Revue, *New Americana*
New York: Shubert Theatre, 5 October 1932 (77 perf.)
INTRODUCED: by Rex Weber

The revue, *New Americana,* was a mixed bag, consisting of some weak comedy skits, a little stylized dancing, and even a gypsy orchestra playing Strauss waltzes. The show soon faded away, but one of its songs, "Brother, Can You Spare a Dime?", was destined to become the quintessential Depression lament. The song was the first collaboration of E. Y. "Yip" Harburg with Jay Gorney, who at the time was music director for Paramount Pictures at their studio in Astoria, New York. From Gorney Harburg obtained not only some valuable connections, but also Gorney's wife, Edelaine, who became Mrs. Harburg in 1943.

The two songwriters conceived the song as they were walking down Central Park West in New York City. A man in a straw hat, with its brim pulled down over his eyes, approached them and asked: "Buddy, can you spare a dime?" Harburg thought the idea was perfect for *Americana,* and immediately went to work on the lyrics. Gorney's music soon followed. The song, of course, epitomized the times and spawned such imitations as the ad for Lucky Strike cigarettes: "Brother, Can You Spare a Light?" Introduced in the revue by Rex Weber, a comedian who sang it straight, the song was soon recorded by Rudy Vallee, Bing Crosby, and Leo Reisman and his Orchestra.

The lyrics are appropriately dramatic, telling the saga of a man named Al, who once built a railroad and once served his country, but was now reduced to begging. The powerful music of the refrain begins with an ascending C minor scale followed by a descending chromatic melody line. In contrast, the middle section – "Once in khaki suits" – is in C major, with a march-like accompaniment. The climax of the song, both verbally and musically, occurs in the last "A" section, when the melody moves an octave higher at the words: "I'm your pal!"

"Brother, Can You Spare a Dime? was featured in one film of 1934, *Embarrassing Moments,* starring Marian Nixon and Chester Morris. It is remembered to this day as something of a curiosity: the theme song of the Great Depression.

Slow torch song with verse (16) and refrain (32)
PUBLISHER: Harms, Inc.
KEY: C min., *STARTS*: c' (C min.), *FORM*:AABA'

≈≈≈≈≈≈≈≈≈≈≈≈≈≈≈≈≈≈≈

FASCINATION *

WORDS: Dick Manning, **MUSIC**: F. D. Marchetti

A prime example of adaptation from the semi-classics, the waltz "Fascination" was extracted from F. D. Marchetti's "Valse Tsigane" of 1904. As conceived by the composer, the piece was originally a rondo, with the main theme ("A"), in C major, alternating with two other themes ("B" and "C"), in F major. Thus, the overall form is ABACA. In the 1932 publication, with lyrics by Dick Manning, only the "A" section is used, thus doing away with some of the most attractive aspects of the piece.

"Fascination" has been a favorite of violinists and string ensembles throughout the twentieth century, but became hugely popular in its abbreviated version only in 1957. At that time it was prominently featured on the soundtrack of *Love in the Afternoon*, a film starring Audrey Hepburn, Gary Cooper, and Maurice Chevalier. It is the story of a young music student (Hepburn) who falls in love with a much older playboy (Cooper). Much of the romantic background of the film – its ambiance of champagne and violins – comes from its liberal use of "Fascination". Jane Morgan also popularized the song in a million-selling Kapp record; she later reprised it in the 1982 film *Diner*.

A good deal of the waltz's melodic fascination comes from its opening pickup spanning the interval of a ninth: b-c'-e'-g'-c". The song's origin as an instrumental piece is evidenced by its disjunct melody and extreme range. In the vocal version the range is slightly modified at the closing by descending to c-sharp' rather than the original g-sharp. But however it is played, "Fascination" remains a universal romantic favorite.

Moderate waltz with refrain (32)
PUBLISHER: Southern Music Publishing Co., Inc.
KEY: C major, **STARTS**: b' (C maj.), **FORM**: ABAC

≋≋≋≋≋≋≋≋≋≋≋≋≋≋≋≋≋

FORTY-SECOND STREET

WORDS: Al Dubin, **MUSIC**: Harry Warren
PREMIERE: Film musical, *Forty-Second Street*, Warner Brothers
INTRODUCED BY: Ruby Keeler, Dick Powell and chorus

The landmark film musical, *Forty-Second Street,* had it all: newcomers Dick Powell and Ruby Keeler, the songs of Al Dubin and Harry Warren, a bevy of beautiful girls, innovative sets and – above all – the dances of Busby Berkeley. The movie reinvented the somewhat tired genre of the backstage musical that had so captivated audiences since *The Broadway Melody of 1929*. It also brought forth one of the most memorable lines in cinematic history, uttered by Warner Baxter when Keeler is about to replace the ailing leading lady: "Sawyer, you're going out a youngster, but you've got to come back a star!"

The very freshness of the songs helped to brighten up the troublesome times. At least three of them remain standards to this day: "Forty-Second Street", "Shuffle Off to Buffalo", and "You're Getting To Be a Habit with Me". The title song was successfully recorded by Don Bestor and his Orchestra and later by Hal Kemp and his Orchestra.

It is interesting to observe how many songs written in this year of Depression are in minor keys. "Forty-Second Street" is even more unusual in that it is used in a production number, partly danced on top of a New York City taxicab. The refrain is steadfastly in minor; the melody relentlessly grinds out the E minor triad, with numerous repeated notes. The song is also markedly rhythmical, carrying out the thrust of the opening words: "Hear the beat / Of dancing feet".

The song, "Forty-Second Street", was sung by Evelyn Keyes in the 1946 film, *The Jolson Story*. On 25 August 1980, the 1933 film was revived, this time as a stage musical with many added songs which premiered at the Winter Garden Theatre in New York, with the title song performed by Wanda Richert and Lee Roy Reams. Suddenly, the almost-forgotten songs, written almost half a century before, were hits again.

Moderate foxtrot with verse (16) and refrain (32)
PUBLISHER: Harms, Inc.
KEY: E min., *STARTS*: e' (E min.), *FORM*: AABA

≈≈≈≈≈≈≈≈≈≈≈≈≈≈≈≈≈≈≈≈

HOW DEEP IS THE OCEAN (HOW HIGH IS THE SKY)

WORDS and MUSIC: Irving Berlin
INTRODUCED BY: Bing Crosby on radio and in a Brunswick recording

This haunting ballad, like many other Irving Berlin creations, was introduced neither on stage nor screen. Rather, it was a product of Tin Pan Alley, popularized on radio and in recordings by such singers as Bing Crosby, Rudy Vallee, and Ethel Merman. In 1945 Benny Goodman and his Orchestra, with vocalist Peggy Lee, had a hit recording on Columbia.

Similar to Berlin's "Blue Skies" of 1927, the refrain of "How Deep Is the Ocean" starts in a minor key (D minor) and moves to its relative major

(F major). However, it is much more sophisticated musically, characterized by an enchanting descending chromatic bass line. Also notable in the "B" section is the liberal use of the blue note, in this case the a-flat'. The music is yet another outstanding example of how Berlin, the unschooled composer who preferred to play piano only on the black keys, was master of the thirty-two bar form. The lyrics are those of a love song, and are enchanting in their imagery: "How many roses are sprinkled with dew".

In films, "How Deep Is the Ocean" was sung by Bing Crosby and a male quartet in the 1946 Irving Berlin biography, *Blue Skies*, and by Frank Sinatra in *Meet Danny Wilson* (1952).

Moderate ballad with verse (16) and refrain (32)
PUBLISHER: Irving Berlin, Inc.
KEY: F maj., *STARTS*: f' (D min.)), *FORM*: ABAC

≈≈≈≈≈≈≈≈≈≈≈≈≈≈≈≈≈≈≈

I DON'T STAND A GHOST OF A CHANCE WITH YOU *

WORDS: Bing Crosby, Ned Washington, *MUSIC*: Victor Young
INTRODUCED BY: Bing Crosby on radio and in a Brunswick recording

This lovely ballad, often referred to simply as "Ghost of a Chance", was initially recorded by Bing Crosby (who is credited as co-lyricist) and Ted Fiorito and his Orchestra, among others. It was revived in 1939, with recordings by the bands of Lionel Hampton and Will Bradley. Victor Young's music stands out for its economy of means. The melody of the refrain begins with nine repetitions of the note g' on differing harmonies; it then moves up lazily to b-flat', and slides down to a-natural' and a-flat'. At the end of the release, there is a momentary harmonic shift to E-major seventh, quickly resolving to G seventh augmented. Maurice Chevalier sang "Ghost of a Chance" in the 1935 film, *Folies Bergere*.

Slow ballad with verse (8) and refrain (32)
PUBLISHER: American Academy of Music, Inc.
KEY: C maj., *STARTS*: g' (C maj.), *FORM*: AA'BA'

≈≈≈≈≈≈≈≈≈≈≈≈≈≈≈≈≈≈≈

I GOTTA RIGHT TO SING THE BLUES

WORDS: Ted Koehler, *MUSIC*: Harold Arlen
PREMIERE: Revue, *Earl Carroll's Vanities*
New York: Broadway Theatre, 27 September 1932 (87 perf.)
INTRODUCED: by Lillian Shade

Earl Carroll had been delighting audiences with his *Vanities* since 1923. These spectacular annual revues featured scantily-dressed showgirls and off-color humor. This year's edition did not do too well at the box office, notwithstanding its staging by young Vincente Minnelli and the comic antics of young Milton Berle. It featured many songs by a variety of songwriters, but of these only Koehler and Arlen's "I Gotta Right to Sing the Blues" has survived. The song was popularized in myriad recordings, most notably by the bands of Cab Calloway, Louis Armstrong, and Benny Goodman. It also became the theme song of trombonist Jack Teagarden and his Orchestra.

The tempo marking is an interesting amalgam of languages: "Slow tempo di blues". Although the refrain is not characterized by the traditional twelve-bar phrasing of the blues, it has a strong blues feeling due to an abundance of blue notes: flatted thirds and sevenths. Although really a variation on a single theme, the refrain avoids monotony and gains a pungent quality through the liberal use of ninth chords, as in the opening C ninth.

Constance Moore sang "I Gotta Right to Sing the Blues" in the 1946 film, *Earl Carroll Sketchbook*.

Slow blues with verse (16) and refrain (32)
PUBLISHER: Harms, Inc.
KEY: B-flat maj., *STARTS*: d' (C9), *FORM*: AA'AA"

≈≈≈≈≈≈≈≈≈≈≈≈≈≈≈≈≈≈≈

IF I LOVE AGAIN

WORDS: J. P. (Jack) Murray, *MUSIC*: Ben Oakland
PREMIERE: Musical comedy, *Hold Your Horses*
New York: Winter Garden Theatre, 25 September 1933 (88 perf.)
INTRODUCED: by Ona Munsen and Stanley Smith

This lovely ballad didn't find a home on Broadway until a year after it was written. At that time, it was introduced in a short-lived musical, *Hold Your Horses,* which starred zany comedian Joe Cook as the driver of a horse-drawn cab in turn-of-the-century New York. Of the show's many songs, only "If I Love Again" is remembered today. Rudy Vallee popularized it on radio and in a recording.

Ben Oakland, its composer, is also known for the enchanting waltz "I'll Take Romance", written in 1937. The refrain of "If I Love Again" has a haunting quality, in large measure because of its economy of means. The opening phrases are pentatonic, using only the tones F, A, B-flat, C, and D, In contrast, the melody of the verse is diatonic, based on the seven-note scale (the refrain of "I'll Remember April", written nine years later, bears some similarity). But most striking in the refrain of "If I Love Again" is its wide range, disjunct melody, and quasi-symphonic breadth of feeling, so unusual in a popular song.

Barbra Streisand sang "If I Love Again" as Fanny Brice in the film biography, *Funny Lady* (1975).

Moderate ballad with verse (14) and refrain (36)
PUBLISHER: Harms Incorporated
KEY: F maj., *STARTS*: a' (F maj.), *FORM*: ABAB'

≈≈≈≈≈≈≈≈≈≈≈≈≈≈≈≈≈≈

I'M GETTIN' SENTIMENTAL OVER YOU * *

WORDS: Ned Washington, *MUSIC*: George Bassman
INTRODUCED BY: The Dorsey Brothers Orchestra

The smooth, sweet sounds of Tommy Dorsey's trombone have long been associated with this romantic ballad. Originally played by The Dorsey Brothers Orchestra, Tommy Dorsey took it over as his theme when he separated from his brother, Jimmy, and made both his band and the song international favorites. The Ink Spots recorded it in 1940.

The melody of the refrain is idiosyncratic for instruments, moving at odd intervals of the second, minor third, major third, fourth, sixth, and seventh. The opening harmonic progression is attractive in itself, going from F major seventh to E seventh and C minor, and then through the circle of fifths: D seventh, G seventh, C seventh, and back to F major. In the last section, the final phrase is repeated in a brief, two-bar coda.

Carol Bruce sang "I'm Gettin' Sentimental Over You" in the 1941 film, *Keep 'Em Flying*. Tommy Dorsey and his Orchestra performed it in the films, *Du Barry Was a Lady* (1943) and *A Song Is Born* (1948). With its legato sound, the song has long been a favorite of horn soloists.

Very slow ballad with verse (8) and refrain (18)
PUBLISHER: Mills Music, Inc.
KEY: F maj., *STARTS*: e' (F maj. 7), *FORM*: AA'BA"

≈≈≈≈≈≈≈≈≈≈≈≈≈≈≈≈≈≈≈

IN A SHANTY IN OLD SHANTY TOWN

WORDS: Joe Young, *MUSIC*: Little Jack Little and John Siras
INTRODUCED BY: Little Jack Little and his Orchestra and recorded for Columbia

As a waltz on the subject of home, this song is a throwback to the early years of the century. It became a surprise hit in 1932, partly because a lot of people were in fact living in tumble-down shacks "by the old railroad track". Jack Little, who co-wrote the music and introduced the song, was little in name only. Born in London, England in 1900, he had his first hit with "Jealous" in 1924, and thereafter toured the United States with his orchestra, appearing in hotels, nightclubs, and on radio. Rudy Vallee popularized "Shanty" on radio and in a recording. "In a Shanty in Old Shanty Town" was recorded for Columbia by Ted Lewis and his Orchestra and soon reached No. 1 on the charts. But it was the Decca recording by Johnny Long and his Orchestra that brought the song its most lasting fame; here it is performed by the band's glee club in a swinging, syncopated style and in 4/4 time. It is this version that is best-remembered today; the song's origin as a waltz is virtually forgotten.

In its original incarnation as a waltz the music is at least thirty years behind the times, leisurely cruising through the circle of fifths: A7-D7-G7-C7. The lyrics are somewhat graphic: "The roof is so slanty / It touches the ground". But it is Johnny Long's exciting record that has enabled this ordinary song to reach its full potential. In the movies, Doris Day sang it in the backstage musical, *Lullaby of Broadway* (1951).

Moderate waltz with verse (16) and refrain (32)
PUBLISHER: M. Witmark & Sons
KEY: F maj., *STARTS*: c' (F maj.), *FORM*: ABAC

≈≈≈≈≈≈≈≈≈≈≈≈≈≈≈≈≈≈≈

ISN'T IT ROMANTIC? *

WORDS: Lorenz Hart, *MUSIC*: Richard Rodgers
PREMIERE: Film musical, *Love Me Tonight*, Paramount, 1932
INTRODUCED: by Maurice Chevalier, Jeanette MacDonald, Bert Roach,
Rolfe Sedan, Tyler Brooke, and chorus

One of the most brilliant and integrated film musicals ever conceived, *Love Me Tonight* brought the songwriting team of Lorenz Hart and Richard Rodgers on one of its infrequent forays to Hollywood. The opening number, "Isn't It Romantic?, sets the magical tone of the film. Maurice Chevalier, who plays a tailor masquerading as a baron, is first to intone the opening lyrics. The musical strains are then taken up by his companion, played by Bert Roach; then by a taxi driver, who whistles it; and then, in turn, by his passenger, a composer, who writes it down. Soldiers hear the song as they march; a gypsy violinist plays it; and finally it is overheard by Jeanette MacDonald, who plays a Baroness destined to fall in love with Chevalier's character. Thus, the movie's principals are united by this lovely ballad, even before they meet. The song was popularized on radio by Harold Stern and his Orchestra.

"Isn't It Romantic?" is fully worthy of its importance to the plot. Both verse and refrain epitomize romanticism. Most enchanting of all are the six notes, consisting of only three tones (d', e-flat', c'), that open the refrain; this catchy motive appears five times. Contrary to the usual eight-bar phrasing of popular song, this refrain is clearly delineated into eight sections, each of four bars. There are other delightful aspects, most notably the unexpected d-flats" in Bars 8 and 16 and the reprise of the opening motive an octave higher at the very end of the refrain. As for the lyrics, there are two sets: the first, purely poetic "Sweet symbols in the moonlight"; the second, sardonic and chauvinistic: "While I sit around, my love can scrub the floor".

In other films, Mae Questel performed the song in *It's Only Money* (1962) and Michael Dees sang it in *The Day of the Locust* (1975). In 1948, the song begot a film of its own called *Isn't It Romantic?*

Slow ballad with two verses (16) and two refrains (32)
PUBLISHER: Famous Music Corporation (by arrangement with Rodart Music Corporation)
KEY: E-flat maj., *STARTS*: d' (E-flat maj.), *FORM*: ABAB'

≈≈≈≈≈≈≈≈≈≈≈≈≈≈≈≈≈≈≈≈

I'VE GOT THE WORLD ON A STRING *

WORDS: Ted Koehler, *MUSIC*: Harold Arlen
PREMIERE: Revue, *Cotton Club Parade*
New York: Cotton Club, 1932
INTRODUCED BY: Aida Ward

One of Harold Arlen's best, this swinging song was introduced at Harlem's legendary Cotton Club. It was popularized by Cab Calloway and his Orchestra, the house band. Both Bing Crosby and Frank Sinatra had hit records.

Syncopation is at the heart of the music. The first theme of the refrain spans an octave and a fourth. The release, with many repeated notes, goes through the circle of fifths, from A ninth to C thirteenth. June Haver and Gloria de Haven sang "I've Got the World on a String" in the 1950 film, *I'll Get By*. Jazz musicians adore the song whose quirky rhythms and compound harmonies lend themselves well to both instrumentals and vocals.

Moderate rhythm song with verse (16) and refrain (32)
PUBLISHER: Mills Music, Inc.
KEY: F maj., *STARTS*: c' (F maj. 7), *FORM*: AABA

≈≈≈≈≈≈≈≈≈≈≈≈≈≈≈≈≈≈≈

I'VE TOLD EV'RY LITTLE STAR

WORDS: Oscar Hammerstein II, *MUSIC*: Jerome Kern
PREMIERE: Musical comedy, *Music in the Air*
New York: Alvin Theatre, 8 November, 1932 (342 perf.)
London: His Majesty's Theatre, 19 May 1933 (275 perf.)
INTRODUCED BY: Walter Slezak

This delightful song occupied a very special place in Jerome Kern's heart. The composer repeatedly called it his favorite song. Remembering this, as his friend and collaborator lay dying in a New York hospital, Oscar Hammerstein II softly sang it to Kern on 11 November 1945.

Kern's inspiration for the tune was a birdcall, specifically that of a Cape Cod sparrow. While vacationing in Nantucket, Kern, an amateur bird watcher, heard a bird singing in a willow tree outside his window. Next morning, he could not remember the tune. But the following night, the bird repeated its performance, and Kern happily wrote down the melody.

Music in the Air is set in a small Bavarian village. The plot involves two songwriters who have written "I've Told Ev'ry Little Star" and then gone off to Munich to have it published. In the show, young Walter Slezak sang it to his sweetheart, played by Kathryn Carrington. Early recordings of "I've Told Ev'ry little Star" were by Eddy Duchin and his Orchestra, sung by Irene Dunne. The song was revived in 1961, when Linda Scott recorded it, and again in 1975, when Dick Shawn sang it in the revue, *A Musical Jubilee*.

Conventional in both form and harmony, the song's only distinction is in its enchanting middle section in C major with surprising upward jumps of the sixth. This release, repeated, does double duty as the verse. The only evidence of the song's reputed origin as a birdcall is the fourfold repetition of the note a' in Bar 2.

Music in the Air was revived in New York City in 1933 (196 performances) and 1951 (56 performances). "I've Told Ev'ry Little Star" has fared equally well; its popularity has hardly diminished over the years. In the 1934 screen version of *Music in the Air*, it was sung by Gloria Swanson, June Lang, Douglass Montgomery, John Boles, and a chorus. Linda Scott had a hit recording in 1961.

Moderate foxtrot with verse (26) and refrain (32)
PUBLISHER: T. B. Harms Company
KEY: F maj., *STARTS*: f' (F maj.), *FORM*: AABA

≈≈≈≈≈≈≈≈≈≈≈≈≈≈≈≈≈≈≈

LOVER * !

WORDS: Lorenz Hart, *MUSIC*: Richard Rodgers
PREMIERE: Film musical, *Love Me Tonight*, Paramount, 1932
INTRODUCED BY: by Jeanette MacDonald

Another product of the delightful film musical, *Love Me Tonight*, this vivacious waltz was copyrighted a year later in 1933. Like "Isn't It Romantic?", the song is integral to the plot of the film. It is sung in the closing sequence by Jeanette MacDonald, who is on horseback, as she is pursuing her lover played by Maurice Chevalier, who is on a train. Thus, the rhythmic accompaniment of the song is inspired by the combined sounds of hoof-beats and train wheels.

The most striking characteristic of "Lover" is its chromaticism, both melodic and harmonic. In each "A" section, the melody, the harmony (in sevenths), and the bass line descend together chromatically for five half steps, from c" to g'. Also, in keeping with the chase motif, the tempo is doubled, making the refrain 64 bars instead of the usual 32. Another unusual feature of the song is the release, which begins in E major and then modulates to G major.

"Lover" was first popularized by Paul Whiteman and his Orchestra. Other memorable recordings have been made over the years: by Greta Keller in 1933, by Les Paul in 1948, and especially in a million-selling Capitol record by Peggy Lee in 1952. Lee's recording recalled the song's origin: it is in excruciatingly fast tempo, but in duple time. She also sang it in the 1953 version of *The Jazz Singer*.

"Lover" is a maverick, one of the most unusual songs in the popular music canon, but that singularity has in no way detracted from its popularity through the years.

Moderate waltz with verse (32) and two refrains (64)
PUBLISHER: Famous Music Corporation (By arrangement with Rodart Music Corporation)
KEY: C maj., *STARTS*: c" (C maj.), *FORM*: AABA

≈≈≈≈≈≈≈≈≈≈≈≈≈≈≈≈≈≈≈

MIMI

WORDS: Lorenz Hart, *MUSIC*: Richard Rodgers
PREMIERE: Film musical, *Love Me Tonight*, Paramount, 1932
INTRODUCED BY: Maurice Chevalier, C. Aubrey Smith, Charlie Ruggles, Elizabeth Patterson, Ethel Griffies, Blanche Friderici, and Charles Butterworth

"Mimi" is so typically "French" in nature that one is surpised to learn that it is a Rodgers and Hart creation. Its staccato phrasing is strongly reminiscent of the 1926 European favorite, "Valentine". Nevertheless, Rodgers and Hart it is: still another standard written for the film, *Love Me Tonight*. Maurice Chevalier, the French vaudevillian and film star, liked it so much that he made it his signature song.

The refrain's primary motive consists of a note and its repetition (d'-d'). These doubled notes are played on various degrees of the scale (e'-e', a'-a', f-sharp'-f-sharp'). The result is pure delight with an infusion of gallic gaiety.

"Mimi" was featured in the 1957 film, *The Joker Is Wild*. Chevalier later repeated his success with the song in two other films, *Pepi* (1960), and *A New Kind of Love* (1963).

Moderate foxtrot with verse (18) and refrain (32)
PUBLISHER: Famous Music Corporation (By arrangement with Rodart Music Corporation)
KEY: G maj., *STARTS*: d' (G maj.), *FORM*: AA'BA"

≈≈≈≈≈≈≈≈≈≈≈≈≈≈≈≈≈≈≈

MY SILENT LOVE

WORDS: Edward Heyman, *MUSIC*: Dana Suesse

"My Silent Love" is a pure product of Tin Pan Alley; it was not written for the theater or cinema. Dana Suesse, its composer, began as a child prodigy in Kansas City, Missouri. In 1932 she played her own jazz piano concerto at Carnegie Hall in New York. In that same year, together with lyricist Edward Heyman, she adapted this popular ballad from her own piece, "Jazz Nocturne".. Thereafter, she enjoyed a long and distinguished career as composer of both serious and popular music.

"My Silent Love" was Suesse's first published composition. It enjoyed almost immediate success on the radio and in recordings by the bands of Ruby Newman and Isham Jones. There were many other recordings, with Frank Sinatra's the most popular of all.

The refrain is conventional in both length (thirty-two bars) and form (AABA). Its most interesting aspect is the melodic outlining of the B-flat augmented chord in Bar Two of each "A" section. In contrast, the middle section, starting in A-flat major, offers some descending chromatic scales. "My Silent Love" remains today as a slice of romantic nostalgia.

Moderate ballad with verse (16) and refrain (32)
PUBLISHER: Famous Music Corporation
KEY: E-flat maj. , *STARTS*: E-flat (E-flat maj.), *FORM*: AABA

≈≈≈≈≈≈≈≈≈≈≈≈≈≈≈≈≈≈

NIGHT AND DAY ✶ ✶ ✶ ✶ !

WORDS and MUSIC: Cole Porter
PREMIERE: Musical comedy, *The Great Divorce*
New York: Ethel Barrymore Theatre, 29 November 1932 (248 perf.)
INTRODUCED BY: Fred Astaire

"Night and Day" is the song most often associated with Cole Porter, if only because its title also serves as the title of the Porter screen biography. The film, *Night and Day*, released in 1946 is a Hollywood extravaganza bearing little resemblance to Porter's real life, starring Cary Grant as Porter and Alexis Smith as his wife. It also features Monty Wooley, Jane Wyman, Eve Arden, and Mary Martin, singing her celebrated version of "My Heart Belongs to Daddy". Grant and Smith sing "Night and Day" in the film, but the song stands on its own merits as one of the most distinctive love ballads.

Fred Astaire introduced it in the 1932 stage production, *The Great Divorce*, which also featured Grace Moore and Claire Luce. This was Astaire's first solo appearance after his sister Adele's retirement. Two years later "Night and Day" received a much wider audience in the film version of the show, renamed *The Great Divorcée* and starring Astaire, Ginger Rogers, and Edward Everett Horton. A highlight of the film is Astaire's unforgettable rendition of the song to a petulant Rogers. Almost every major singer from Bing Crosby to Frank Sinatra has recorded the song.

Porter, who was notoriously misleading about the sources of his inspiration, once said that "Night and Day" was inspired by the chanting of a muezzin in a call to worship that he heard on a trip to Morocco. On another occasion, however, he declared that the music was put together at the Ritz Carlton and that he wrote the lyrics later, while lying on a beach in Newport. Whatever its provenance, it is an extraordinary song.

Most obvious is the plethora of repeated notes, especially in the verse, where the initial b-flat' is repeated 33 times, followed by the c-flat", repeated 29 times. These repeated notes are accompanied by a startling chromatic array of bass notes. It is said that the resulting dissonance did not please Max Dreyfus of Harms, Inc., who nevertheless published the song. The refrain is equally unusual, with its remarkable harmonies (particularly the C-flat seventh chord that begins it), its unusual length of 48 bars, its asymmetrical form, its many repeated notes, and its descending chromatic melodic line.

"Night and Day" has been featured in a number of films besides *The Gay Divorcée*. It was sung by Sinatra in *Reveille with Beverly* (1934); by Deanna Durbin in *Lady on a Train* (1945); by Cary Grant, Alexis Smith and a chorus in *Night and Day* (1946); and by Katherine Hepburn in *The Desk Set* (1957). It remains a steadfast component of the popular repertoire, performed in a variety of rhythms from beguine to jazz.

Moderate ballad with verse (16) and refrain (48)
PUBLISHER: Harms, Inc.
KEY: E-flat maj., *STARTS*: b-flat' (C-flat maj. 7), *FORM*: ABA'BCB

≈≈≈≈≈≈≈≈≈≈≈≈≈≈≈≈≈≈≈≈

SHUFFLE OFF TO BUFFALO

WORDS: Al Dubin, *MUSIC*: Harry Warren
PREMIERE: Film musical, *Forty-Second Street,* Warner Brothers, 1933
INTRODUCED BY: Ruby Keeler, Clarence Nordstrom, Ginger Rogers,
Una Merkel, and chorus

One of the most memorable scenes in the landmark film musical, *Forty-Second Street,* was set in a Pullman carriage filled with women preparing for bed. In this Busby Berkeley scene, Ginger Rogers and Una Merkel, playing two seasoned veterans of the marital wars, warn a young honeymoon couple (played by Clarence Nordstrom and Ruby Keeler) about the pitfalls of marriage in a production number built around "Shuffle Off to Buffalo". The song was popularized in recordings by the bands of Hal Kemp and Don Bestor. It was also featured in the 1980 stage version of the film.

Both words and music are tailor-made for the scenario. The lyrics are at the same time cynical and suggestive ("When she knows as much as we know / She'll be on her way to Reno; I'll go home and get my panties / You go home and get your scanties"). The music is replete with the rhythm of the rails and chromatic passages simulating train whistles. The melody of the "A" section is repetitive, almost entirely in dotted quarters and eighths. Some tonal contrast is offered by the release, first in F major, then in G major. Appropriately, the song is most often performed in shuffle rhythm.

Moderate foxtrot with verse (12) and refrain (32)
PUBLISHER: M. Witmark & Sons
KEY: C maj., *STARTS*: e' (C maj.), *FORM*: AABA

≈≈≈≈≈≈≈≈≈≈≈≈≈≈≈≈≈≈≈

THE SONG IS YOU * !

WORDS: Oscar Hammerstein II, *MUSIC*: Jerome Kern
PREMIERE: Musical comedy, *Music in the Air*
New York: Alvin Theatre, 8 November 1932 (342 perf.)
London: His Majesty's Theatre, 19 May 1933 (275 perf.)
INTRODUCED BY: Tulio Carminati and Natalie Hall

This musical masterpiece was the big ballad of the quasi-operetta, *Music in the Air,* an anachronism set in the cardboard mountains of Bavaria. *Music in the Air* had all the clichés of old-fashioned operetta: jovial men in lederhosen, lovers at cross-currents with one another, and a pretentious book and lyrics by Oscar Hammerstein II. But it also had

Jerome Kern's music, and that rescued it. Despite the show's shortcomings, it enjoyed considerable success including revivals in New York in 1933 and 1951. Later recordings of "The Song Is You" were by Tommy Dorsey and his Orchestra and Frank Sinatra. John Raitt sang it in the 1975 Broadway revue, *A Musical Jubilee*.

"The Song Is You" is one of the few popular works that can rightfully be called an art song that still remains in the American tradition. Similar to a number of other Kern songs ("Smoke Gets in Your Eyes" and "Yesterdays") it lacks a verse, but the music of the refrain is so extraordinary that the verse is not missed. Kern's harmonic tricks lift the song far above the ordinary. The smoothly-flowing melody of the "A" section is accompanied by fast-changing harmonies. But nothing prepares the listener for the revelation of the middle section: a startling change from C major to E major, and then a masterful modulation through the circle of fifths from G-sharp minor to B seventh. At the words "Why can't I let you know…" this magical chord acts as a leading tone, lifting the entire song up again to C major. As with many other Kern songs ("All the Things You Are", "I Won't Dance") the return to the "A" section becomes a modulatory tour de force.

In the 1934 film version of *Music in the Air*, "The Song Is You" was sung by John Boles. It remains a classic, played both in its original tempo and, because of its exciting harmonic changes, in fast tempo as a jazz standard.

Moderate ballad with refrain (32)
PUBLISHER: T. B. Harms Company
KEY: C maj., *STARTS*: b' (C maj. 7), *FORM*: AABA'

≈≈≈≈≈≈≈≈≈≈≈≈≈≈≈≈≈≈≈≈

SPEAK TO ME OF LOVE (PARLEZ-MOI D'AMOUR)

ENGLISH WORDS: Bruce Siever, *MUSIC*: Jean Lenoir
INTRODUCED BY: Lucienne Boyer

A European favorite, this enchanting waltz has always been associated with Lucienne Boyer, the glamorous French *diseuse* who was the toast of London and Paris. She brought it to America – with French words by the composer, Jean Lenoir – in the intimate revue, *Continental Varieties*, which opened at the Little Theatre in New York 3 October 1934, and ran for ten weeks. Boyer used it as her theme song thereafter. The melodic verse is very often performed, contrasting with the simple refrain, which moves mostly in half steps. The form is truncated, consisting of only three sections, AA'A", in twenty-four bars, with the second section paraphrasing the first a step higher. In the film, *The Helen Morgan Story* (1957, known in Britain as *Both Ends of the Candle*), Gogi Grant dubbed the song in for Ann Blyth.

Moderate waltz with verse (16) and refrain (24)
KEY: G maj., *STARTS*: b' (G maj.), *FORM*: AA'A"

≈≈≈≈≈≈≈≈≈≈≈≈≈≈≈≈≈≈≈

TRY A LITTLE TENDERNESS

WORDS and MUSIC: Harry Woods, Jimmy Campbell, Reginald Connelly

Harry Woods, who collaborated with the English songwriting and publishing team of Jimmy Campbell and Reginald Connelly on this tender ballad, was known for his terrible temper. There is a possibly apocryphal story that once he was in the process of beating up a man in a bar when a woman entered and asked who he was. His friend replied to the astonished woman that he was the writer of "Try a Little Tenderness". First published in England, the song was popularized there by Ray Noble and his Orchestra, and in America by Ruth Etting and Eddy Duchin and his Orchestra. Otis Redding had a Top Forty recording in 1967.

It is a casual sort of song, with a melody sliding up and down the scale. The lyrics reflect the Depression times: "Women do get weary, wearing the same shabby dress". They are also sexist, saying that, with women, "Love is their whole happiness".

With a touch of irony, "Try a Little Tenderness" was heard behind the titles in the anti-nuclear film, *Dr. Strangelove* (1964). Redding sang it again, dubbing for Jon Cryer, in the 1986 film, *Pretty in Pink*. Bennie Wallace and Dr. John did it in *Bull Durham* (1988). Appropriately, "Try a Little Tenderness" was featured on television in the eighties in commercials advertising "Perdue Chicken Parts".

Slow ballad with verse (16) and refrain (32)
PUBLISHER: Campbell, Connelly & Co., Ltd (London), assigned to Leeds Music Corp.
KEY: C maj., *STARTS*: e' (C maj.), *FORM*: AA'BA'

≈≈≈≈≈≈≈≈≈≈≈≈≈≈≈≈≈≈≈

WILLOW WEEP FOR ME

WORDS and MUSIC: Ann Ronell
INTRODUCED BY: Paul Whiteman and his Orchestra, vocal by Irene Taylor, in a Victor recording

This delicate torch song by Ann Ronell is dedicated to her friend George Gershwin. It was introduced and popularized in a Victor recording by Paul Whiteman and his Orchestra, with vocal by Irene Taylor. Ted Fiorito and his Orchestra also recorded it for Brunswick. In 1964 it was revived with a recording by Chad and Jeremy. The lyrics take poetic license, as in "Bend your branches green, along the stream that runs to sea". The dramatic verse combines eighth-note triplets with sustained notes. The melody of the refrain features dotted eighths and sixteenths as well as eighth-note triplets. Very prominent is the blue note, b-flat'. Marion Hutton sang "Willow Weep for Me" in the Marx Brothers' film, *Love Happy* (1949).

Slow torch song with verse (16) and refrain (32)
PUBLISHER: Irving Berlin, Inc.
KEY: G maj., *STARTS*: d" (G maj.), *FORM*: AABA

≈≈≈≈≈≈≈≈≈≈≈≈≈≈≈≈≈≈≈≈≈

YOU ARE TOO BEAUTIFUL

WORDS: Lorenz Hart, *MUSIC*: Richard Rodgers
PREMIERE: Film, *Hallelujah, I'm a Bum,* United Artists, 1933
INTRODUCED: by Al Jolson

Al Jolson was privileged to introduce this lovely ballad in the film, *Hallelujah, I'm a Bum* (called *Hallelujah, I'm a Tramp* in Britain because "Bum" was unacceptable); he sang it remarkably well considering that romantic ballads were not his forte. The movie, about a hobo (played by Jolson) in the Depression, was a flop; audiences of the time preferred escapist spectacle (à la Busby Berkeley) to virtual reality. In 1946 Dick Haymes revived the song with a recording. The tender melody of the refrain unfolds stepwise, emphasizing the blue notes b-flat' and a-flat'. Major and minor chords of the seventh predominate. There is a nostalgic quality to the song that has kept it alive.

Moderate ballad with verse (16) and refrain (32)
PUBLISHER: Rodart Music Corporation
KEY: C maj., *STARTS*: a' (D main. 7), *FORM*: AA'CA'

≈≈≈≈≈≈≈≈≈≈≈≈≈≈≈≈≈≈≈≈≈

YOU'RE GETTING TO BE A HABIT WITH ME

WORDS: Al Dubin, *MUSIC*: Harry Warren
PREMIERE: Film musical, *Forty-Second Street*. Warner Brothers, 1933
INTRODUCED BY: Bebe Daniels and Dick Powell

This lively piece is the closest thing to a ballad in the 1933 backstage musical film *Forty-Second Street*. Bing Crosby popularized it with a Brunswick recording. It was revived in 1980 in the Broadway musical based on the film. Replete with dotted eighths and sixteenths, as well as eighth-note triplets, the song is a tap-dancer's delight. The form is unusual, consisting of five four-bar sections and a final section of six bars, which repeats the last phrase as a coda. A happy sort of song, it was reprised by Doris Day in the 1951 film musical, *Lullaby of Broadway*.

Moderate rhythm song with verse (12) and refrain (26)
PUBLISHER: M. Witmark & Sons
KEY: F maj., *STARTS*: a' (B-flat 6), *FORM*: AA'BB'AC

≈≈≈≈≈≈≈≈≈≈≈≈≈≈≈≈≈≈

YOURS (QUIÉREME MUCHO)

ENGLISH WORDS: Albert Gamse and Jack Sherr, *MUSIC*: Gonzalo Roig
INTRODUCED BY: Dolly Dawn and her Dawn Patrol Boys in the United States

As "Quiéreme Mucho", this Cuban rumba was popularized by Tito Schipa, with Spanish lyrics by Agustin Rodriguez and music by Gonzalo Roig. English words were later supplied by Albert Gamse and Jack Sherr, and the song became "Yours". First popularized by Dolly Dawn and her Dawn Patrol Boys, the song's real popularity began ten years after it was written, with a rousing swing arrangement recorded for Decca by Jimmy Dorsey and his Orchestra, with vocals by Helen O'Connell and Bob Eberly. Other popular recordings were by the bands of Benny Goodman and Vaughn Monroe. British singer Vera Lynn also recorded the song, and it became her theme. The gentle melody of the refrain slides up and down the scale, accompanied by simple harmonies. A touch of syncopation appears in the last section. Gene Autry sang "Yours" in the 1946 film, *Sioux City Sue*.

Moderate rumba with two verses (16) and refrain (32)
PUBLISHER: Edward B. Marks Music Corporation
KEY: D maj., *STARTS*: f-sharp' (D maj.), *FORM*: ABA'C

≈≈≈≈≈≈≈≈≈≈≈≈≈≈≈≈≈≈

1933

A NEW BEGINNING

1933

Life is bare, gloom and mis'ry ev'rywhere....

Ted Koehler
"Stormy Weather (Keeps Rainin' All the Time)"

This year of desperate measures to combat the Depression also sees the birth of some strikingly original music. It sees the cascading harmonies of Duke Ellington's "Sophisticated Lady", the lyrical melodies of Jerome Kern's "Smoke Gets In Your Eyes" and "Yesterdays", the down-home blues feeling of Harold Arlen's "Stormy Weather", the brilliant employment of tango rhythm in Vincent Youmans's "Orchids in the Moonlight", the exotic use of bolero rhythm in Nacio Herb Brown's "Temptation", and the contrapuntal extravagance of George Gershwin's

"Mine". It also sees the origin of some more ordinary songs that are destined to become standards, like "Easter Parade" and "Don't Blame Me".

The year starts out with a bleak winter, but shortly after Franklin Delano Roosevelt's inauguration on 6 March, there is a new feeling of hope in the air. In the first hundred days of his administration, all banks are closed, the United States drops the gold standard, and Congress passes the New Deal, with all sorts of social and economic measures. In short order seventy percent of the banks reopen and people begin to regain their confidence.

Those who can afford it flock to what remains of Broadway; fifty percent of the theaters are dark and many owners are bankrupt. There are plenty of musicals to choose from: Irving Berlin's *As Thousands Cheer*, The Gershwins' *Let 'Em Eat Cake,* a new edition of *Zeigfeld Follies*, and Jerome Kern's *Roberta*, the hit show of the year. They can also empathize with the denizens of Erskine Caldwell's *Tobacco Road*, which begins a monumental run of seven years.

Or for much less money – as little as a quarter – they can go to the movies. They can gaze at the havoc wrought by the great ape, *King Kong*, or forget their troubles by seeing such wonderful film musicals as *Forty-Second Street, Gold Diggers of 1933, Footlight Parade, Dancing Lady*, and *Flying Down to Rio*, the last featuring the newly-created dance team of Fred Astaire and Ginger Rogers. They can also hear Mae West say those immortal words to Cary Grant in the film, *She Done Him Wrong*: "Why don't you come up sometime and see me?"

This is also the year of the world's first drive-in theater, in Camden, New Jersey; these venues are soon to be known as "passion pits". Record sales are at an all-time low, having dropped from $106 million in 1920 to $5.5 million this year. But they begin to pick up with the advent of juke boxes, which begin to turn up everywhere, especially in the newly opened bars and cocktail lounges sprouting up after Prohibition is repealed. It is indeed a year of new beginnings: not only for the nation as a whole but for its music.

SONGS OF 1933

> The Boulevard of Broken Dreams
> Carioca
> Don't Blame Me * *
> Easter Parade * * *
> The Gold Diggers' Song (We're In the Money)

I Cover the Waterfront * *
It's Only a Paper Moon * *
It's the Talk of the Town
Let's Fall in Love *
Maria Elena *
Mine !
One Morning in May !
Orchids in the Moonlight !
Rosetta
Shadow Waltz
Smoke Gets In Your Eyes * * * * !
Sophisticated Lady * * * !
Stormy Weather * * * !
Temptation !
Yesterdays * * * !

THE BOULEVARD OF BROKEN DREAMS

WORDS: Al Dubin, *MUSIC*: Harry Warren
PREMIERE: Film musical, *Moulin Rouge*, Twentieth Century Films, 1934
INTRODUCED BY: Constance Bennett, Russ Columbo, and The Boswell
Sisters

This powerful song, beginning "I walk along the streets of sorrow", came to symbolize the effect of the ongoing Depression on the common man. It was introduced in a lavish production number in the film musical, *Moulin Rouge*, starring Constance Bennett (who played two sisters) and Franchot Tone, and danced to, very effectively, by a Parisian gigolo and gigolette. The song was initially popularized in a Victor record by Jan Garber and his Orchestra, with vocal by Lee Bennett. Many years later, in 1950, it was Tony Bennett's first hit record, on Columbia.

In the true tradition of the tango, the song contrasts the minor mode (in the body of the refrain) with major (in both verse and release). The melody of the refrain, with its seven-note pickups and flatted sixths, is reminiscent of a middle-European or Gypsy tune. Its tone of despair is *à propos* to the desperate times.

Moderate tango with verse (10) and refrain (32)
KEY: D min., *STARTS*: a' (D min.), *FORM*: AABA

≈≈≈≈≈≈≈≈≈≈≈≈≈≈≈≈≈≈≈≈

CARIOCA

WORDS: Gus Kahn and Edward Eliscu, *MUSIC*: Vincent Youmans
PREMIERE: Film musical, *Flying Down to Rio*, RKO, 1933
INTRODUCED BY: Etta Moten; danced to by Fred Astaire & Ginger Rogers

"Carioca" was the studio-invented "dance craze" that made the world realize that Fred Astaire and Ginger Rogers were a dance team beyond compare. In the film, *Flying Down to Rio*, they danced to its inspiring strains on top of seven white grand pianos, played by seven pianists and surrounded by dozens of chorus girls. It was Astaire and Rogers's first film together; Dorothy Jordan, originally slated for Rogers's role, married a producer instead. It was also Vincent Youmans's last score; shortly after the film's release, the composer retired to Denver, with tuberculosis. In 1934, "Carioca" was nominated for an Academy Award, but the prize went to another manufactured dance craze, "The Continental". Among myriad recordings of "Carioca" were those of the orchestras of Enric Madriguera, Xavier Cugat, Artie Shaw, and Harry Sosnik. Les Paul recorded it in 1952.

Musically, this lavish production number is a kaleidoscope of three disparate themes, each repeated, followed by single choruses of the first two themes. Thus, the overall structure is AA'BBCCAB. The first theme ("A"), in E-flat minor, has a seven-note pickup. The second ("B"), in E-flat major, features a broad melody of tied whole notes. The trio is in a style similar to "A". Although "Carioca" never became a dance craze (neither did "The Continental"), it brings back memories of one of the earliest film musicals and of the dancers who made it famous.

Moderate rumba with verse (16), refrain (16), interlude (6), and trio (40)
PUBLISHER: T. B. Harms Co.
KEY: E-flat maj., *STARTS*: g' (E-flat maj), **FORM** (Overall): AA'BBCCAB

≈≈≈≈≈≈≈≈≈≈≈≈≈≈≈≈≈≈≈

DON'T BLAME ME * *

WORDS: Dorothy Fields, *MUSIC*: Jimmy McHugh
PREMIERE: Revue, *Clowns in Clover*, New York, 1933
INTRODUCED BY: Jeanette Leff

Written by the same legendary team that brought forth "Exactly Like You" and "On the Sunny Side of the Street" in 1930, "Don't Blame Me" is the quintessential love ballad of the thirties. Introduced in an obscure New York revue, *Clowns in Clover*, it was popularized in recordings by Ethel Waters and Guy Lombardo and his Royal Canadians. In 1948, Nat

"King" Cole had a hit record. Almost half a century after it was written , the song created a sensation all over again, when it was reprised by Ann Miller and Eddie Pruett in the hit show, *Sugar Babies*: a retrospective revue that opened at the Mark Hellinger Theatre on 8 October, 1979, and ran for an astonishing 1208 performances.

The most striking aspects of the song are Dorothy Fields's touching lyrics ("I'm under your spell / So how can I help it") and Jimmy McHugh's soulful use of quarter-note triplets and of the flatted seventh as a blue note. The harmonic progression from C major to G minor, and then to A major and D minor also raise the song above the ordinary.

A number of films have featured "Don't Blame Me". Among them are *Freddie Steps Out* (1946), sung by Freddie Stewart; *Big City* (1948), sung by Betty Garrett; *The Strip* (1951), sung by Vic Damone; the 1955 film, *Bring Your Smile Along*, sung by Constance Towers; and *Two Weeks in Another Town* (1962), sung by Leslie Uggams. The song's interesting harmonies and abundant blue notes have made it a favorite of jazz musicians from Charlie Parker and Miles Davis to Erroll Garner.

> Slow ballad with two verses (16) and refrain (32)
> *PUBLISHER*: Metro-Goldwym-Mayer Corp., assigned to Robbins Music Corp.
> *KEY*: C maj., *STARTS*: g' (C maj.), *FORM*: AA'BA'

≈≈≈≈≈≈≈≈≈≈≈≈≈≈≈≈≈≈≈

EASTER PARADE * * *

> *WORDS AND MUSIC*: Irving Berlin
> PREMIERE: Revue, *As Thousands Cheer*
> New York: Music Box Theatre, 30 September 1933 (400 perf.)
> *INTRODUCED BY:* Marilyn Miller, Clifton Webb, and company

The music of "Easter Parade" began life way back in 1917, as "Smile and Show Your Dimple". It was written by Irving Berlin during World War I, deliberately fashioned in the style of the hit song, "Pack Up Your Troubles in Your Old Kit Bag". "Smile and Show Your Dimple" never became a hit, but Berlin liked the melody and filed it away in his "trunk". In 1933, he retrieved it as the first act finale of his revue, *As ThousandsCheer*. Inspired by the sepia-toned rotogravure sections then popular in newspapers, the Easter Parade up New York's Fifth Avenue was presented behind a sepia-toned scrim, which, when lifted, brought the song to life. This presentation never failed to bring the house down, and made "Easter Parade" a lasting success. Bing Crosby had a hit record, as did Harry James and his

Orchestra in 1942, Guy Lombardo and his Royal Canadians in 1947, and Liberace in 1954.

As with most Berlin songs, words and music seem to be made for each other. The jaunty melody consists mostly of dotted quarters and eighths and harmonies are of the simple variety. There are two sets of lyrics, one for each sex.

Don Ameche sang "Easter Parade" in the 1938 film, *Alexander's Ragtime Band"*; Bing Crosby did it in *Holiday Inn* (1942); and Judy Garland, Fred Astaire, and a chorus sang it in the film of the same name, *Easter Parade* (1948). It takes a place alongside "White Christmas" (1942), as one of the great holiday songs.

Moderate foxtrot with verse (16) and refrain (32)
PUBLISHER: Irving Berlin Music Corporation
KEY: B-flat maj., *STARTS*: d" (B-flat maj.), *FORM*: AABA

≈≈≈≈≈≈≈≈≈≈≈≈≈≈≈≈≈≈≈

THE GOLD DIGGERS' SONG (WE'RE IN THE MONEY)

WORDS: Al Dubin, *MUSIC*: Harry Warren
PREMIERE: Film musical, *Gold Diggers of 1933*, Warner Brothers, 1933
INTRODUCED BY: Ginger Rogers and chorus

It was a youthful Ginger Rogers who opened the film, *Gold Diggers of 1933*, with this ironic number, clad from head to toe in what looked like silver dollars. At a time when money was in short supply, the song created a sensation, acting as an antidote to the ongoing Depression. Early recordings were by Dick Powell and Leo Reisman and his Orchestra. Along with many other songs by Al Dubin and Harry Warren, it was revived in the hit show, *42nd Street*, which opened at the Winter Garden Theatre in New York 25 August 1980.

The syncopated main theme of the refrain plays around the intervals of the second and third. Real contrast is offered by the release, with a descending scale in E minor, followed by half of a chromatic scale at the words "We can look that guy right in the eye" – referring to the gold diggers' landlord.

"The Gold Diggers' Song" was sung by Evelyn Keyes and a chorus in the 1946 film, *The Jolson Story*. Dennis Morgan and a chorus did it in the 1951 remake of *Gold Diggers of 1933*, renamed *Painting the Clouds with Sunshine*.

Moderate rhythm song with verse (16) and refrain (32)
PUBLISHER: Remick Music Corporation
KEY: C maj., *STARTS*: e' (C maj.), *FORM*: AABA

≈≈≈≈≈≈≈≈≈≈≈≈≈≈≈≈≈≈≈

I COVER THE WATERFRONT * *

WORDS: Edward Heyman, *MUSIC*: Johnny Green
INTRODUCED BY: Ben Bernie and his Orchestra on radio

This lovely ballad was written to promote the similarly-titled movie, starring Claudette Colbert and Ben Lyon. However, the film was finished before the song, which at first was not included in the soundtrack. But soon after Ben Bernie (The Old Maestro) and his Orchestra plugged it on the radio, the song was added to the score of *I Cover the Waterfront*. Eddy Duchin and his Orchestra also had a hit Victor recording and there have been many other recordings over the years, By Billie Holiday, The Ink Spots, and others.

The graceful refrain has a free-flowing melody, supported by harmonies of the major and minor seventh. The release is particularly noteworthy, with quarter-note triplets, octave jumps, and a brief excursion to the tonality of A major. With a languorous air about it, and pungent harmonies, "I Cover the Waterfront has long been favored for jazz improvisation.

Slow ballad with verse (12) and refrain (32)
PUBLISHER: Harms, Inc.
KEY: G maj., *STARTS*: b' (C maj. 7), *FORM*: AA'BA'

≈≈≈≈≈≈≈≈≈≈≈≈≈≈≈≈≈≈≈

IT'S ONLY A PAPER MOON * *

WORDS: Billy Rose and E. Y. Harburg, *MUSIC*: Harold Arlen
PREMIERE: Musical comedy, *The Great Magoo*
New York: December, 1932 (11 perf.)

This joyful tune was written, under the title "If You Believed in Me", for a dismal Broadway entertainment, *The Great Magoo*. That title is still imbedded in the lyrics at the close of each "A" section. Reappearing just a few months later as "It's Only a Paper Moon", the song was the hit of the film, *Take a Chance*, released by Paramount and sung by June Knight, Charles "Buddy" Rogers, and Cliff Edwards (Ukelele Ike). Over the years the song has been popularized by many recording artists, including The Mills Brothers, Ella Fitzgerald, Benny Goodman and his Orchestra, and Nat "King" Cole.

The marvelous lyrics are the main attraction, bearing all the earmarks of E. Y. "Yip" Harburg (even though Billy Rose is co-credited). They evoke magical images, such as "cardboard sky", " honky-tonk parade", "penny arcade", and best of all: "It's a Barnum and Bailey world". Then too, Harold Arlen's music is infectious, showing his fondness for octave jumps and dotted notes.

Apart from the movie *Take a Chance*, the song inspired a film called *Paper Moon* (1973) and was sung by Barbra Streisand, James Caan, and a chorus in the 1975 film biography of Fanny Brice, *Funny Lady*. It remains a jazz-player's (and singer's) delight.

Moderate rhythm song with verse (16) and refrain (32)
PUBLISHER: Harms, Inc.
KEY: G maj., *STARTS*: d' (G maj.), *FORM*: AABA

≈≈≈≈≈≈≈≈≈≈≈≈≈≈≈≈≈≈≈

IT'S THE TALK OF THE TOWN

WORDS: Marty Symes and Al Neiberg, *MUSIC*: Jerry Livingston
INTRODUCED BY: Glen Gray and The Casa Loma Orchestra, vocal by Kenny Sargent and recorded on Brunswick

This sentimental ballad was popularized in a Brunswick recording by Glen Gray and The Casa Loma Orchestra, one of the first of the big bands, and in a Columbia recording by Fletcher Henderson and his Orchestra. Its chief attraction is its central idea of a broken romance that is "the talk of the town". Wedding invitations have been sent to "friends and our relations", and the lyrics desperately ask: "What can I tell them, What can I say?" The simple melody ascends stepwise, two notes at a time, repeating the first note three times: e'-e'-e'-e'- d', f'-f'-f'-f'-e', g'-g'-g'-g'-f', a'-a'-a'-a'-g'. The final strain holds out some hope for a happy ending, imploring: "Let's make up sweetheart".

Slow ballad with verse (8) and refrain (32)
PUBLISHER: Santly Brothers, Inc.
KEY: F maj., *STARTS*: e' (F maj. 7), *FORM*: AA'BA'

≈≈≈≈≈≈≈≈≈≈≈≈≈≈≈≈≈≈≈

LET'S FALL IN LOVE *

WORDS: Ted Koehler, *MUSIC*: Harold Arlen
PREMIERE: Film musical, *Let's Fall in Love*. Columbia, 1934
INTRODUCED BY: Art Jarrett, reprised by Ann Sothern

The title song of the romantic film comedy, *Let's Fall in Love,* is also its most enchanting and best known. "Let's Fall in Love" was popularized by Eddy Duchin and his Orchestra with a No. 1 Chart record. In 1967, it was revived with a recording by Peaches and Herb.

The main theme of the refrain, which is in traditional AABA form, is built around the tones of the C major triad with an added sixth. This theme is played twice in each "A" section. The release begins in A minor, on the high note e"; it then passes through some interesting modulations on the way back to the home key. Also notable is the light syncopation throughout.

True to its Hollywood origin, "Let's Fall in Love" has been featured in many films besides its namesake. Dorothy Lamour sang it in a 1949 remake of *Let's Fall in Love*, called *Slightly French*. Robert Cummings sang it in *Tell It to the Judge*, also in 1949. In 1954, Judy Holliday and Jack Lemmon sang it in *It Should Happen to You*. Carmen Cavallaro dubbed it in on the piano for Tyrone Power in the 1957 film, *The Eddy Duchin Story*. It was featured in *Juke Box Rhythm* in 1959, and Bing Crosby sang it in *Pepe* in 1959. Like many other Harold Arlen tunes, it lends itself well to swinging arrangements.

Moderate foxtrot with verse (16) and refrain (32)
PUBLISHER: Irving Berlin, Inc.
KEY: C maj., *STARTS*: c" (C maj.), *FORM*: AABA

≈≈≈≈≈≈≈≈≈≈≈≈≈≈≈≈≈≈≈

MARIA ELENA *

WORDS: S. K. Russell, *MUSIC*: Lorenzo Barcelata
INTRODUCED: by LawrenceWelk and his Orchestra, in the United States in an Okeh recording

This old-fashioned waltz originated as the title song of a Mexican film, with Spanish words and music by Vera Cruz. The song was dedicated to the wife of the then-President of Mexico, Portes Gil. Like many other Latin-American songs of the twenties and thirties, such as "Amapola" (1924), "Green Eyes" (1931) and "What a Diff'rence a Day Made" (1934), it took part in the great Latin revival of 1941. The Decca record by Jimmy

Dorsey and his Orchestra, with vocal by Bob Eberly, enabled the song to stay twenty-two weeks on *Your Hit Parade*. It is a sentimental waltz, exhibiting not a trace of its Latin heritage. The lyrical melody of the refrain begins with a five-note pickup and the melodic line alternates between steps and skips. The result is a *bel canto* melody that is easy on the ears and hard to forget. "Maria Elena" was heard on the soundtrack of the 1935 film, *Bordertown*, starring Paul Muni.

> Moderate waltz with verse (24) and refrain (32)
> **PUBLISHER**: Southern Music Publishing Co., Ltd., assigned to Peer International Corporation
> *KEY*: C maj., *STARTS*: c" (C maj.), *FORM*: ABA'C

≈≈≈≈≈≈≈≈≈≈≈≈≈≈≈≈≈≈≈

MINE * !

> *WORDS*: Ira Gershwin, *MUSIC*: George Gershwin
> *PREMIERE*: Musical play, *Let 'Em Eat Cake*
> New York: Imperial Theatre, 21 October 1933 (c. 95 perf.)
> *INTRODUCED BY*: William Gaxton, Lois Moran, and ensemble

One of the few instances of counterpoint in popular music, "Mine" is the only surviving song from the Gershwins' score for *Let 'Em Eat Cake*. That show, a political satire, attempted to repeat the resounding success of *Of Thee I Sing* two years before. But its bitter tone alienated audiences at a time of deep Depression in America and growing fascism in Europe. Furthermore, George's contrapuntal score did little to make the music accessible to audiences. Among many recordings over the years is the memorable duet by Bing Crosby and Judy Garland, on Decca.

The verse is a full-fledged *recitativo accompagnato*, with repeated notes punctuated by sharp accompaniment, ending on an ambiguous chord of the B seventh with flatted fifth. It then proceeds to the first refrain, with a melody emphasizing the sixth degree of the scale, the note a'. The second refrain is a duet in counterpoint; a new, patter-like countermelody is introduced, which is sung in tandem with the first theme. The net result is a fresh and original theater piece.

> Slow ballad with verse (19) and two refrains (32)
> **PUBLISHER**: New World Music Corporation
> *KEY*: C maj., *STARTS*: a' (A min. 6), *FORM*: ABA'C

≈≈≈≈≈≈≈≈≈≈≈≈≈≈≈≈≈≈≈

ONE MORNING IN MAY !

WORDS: Mitchell Parish, *MUSIC*: Hoagy Carmichael

With one of the most remarkable melodies in the popular literature, "One Morning in May" was the favorite song of its composer, Hoagy Carmichael. Popular recordings were by the bands of Wayne King and Tommy Dorsey and by vocalists Lanny Ross and Sarah Vaughn. The lengthy refrain (eighty bars) consist of five sections, each sixteen bars in length, in the form AA'BA'C. In the "A" sections, the wide-spaced melody seems to reach ever higher, first to the note b', then to c-natural", and finally to e". The "B" section modulates from D major to F major and back, while the "C" section is in fact a coda, with many repeated notes. But it is the soaring melodic lines of the "A" sections that make the lovely ballad a gem.

Moderate ballad with refrain (80)
PUBLISHER: Mills Music, Inc.
KEY: D maj., *STARTS*: f-sharp' (D maj.), *FORM*: AA'BA'C

≈≈≈≈≈≈≈≈≈≈≈≈≈≈≈≈≈≈≈

ORCHIDS IN THE MOONLIGHT

WORDS: Gus Kahn and Edward Eliscu, *MUSIC*: Vincent Youmans
PREMIERE: Film musical, *Flying Down to Rio*, RKO, 1933
INTRODUCED BY: Raul Roulien, danced to by Fred Astaire and Dolores Del Rio

Vincent Youmans' score for the screen musical, *Flying Down to Rio,* was his last before he retired to Denver with tuberculosis. It includes this delightful tango, which was sung in the movie by Raul Roulien and danced to by Fred Astaire and Dolores Del Rio. Off-screen, the song was popularized in a Victor recording by Rudy Vallee and his Connecticut Yankees and a Brunswick recording by Enric Madriguera and his Orchestra. Both verse and refrain are of equal importance. As in many tangos, they contrast major and minor tonality. In this case, the verse is in F minor, while the refrain is in F major, and the melodies of both are of exceptional beauty. Sixteenth notes predominate in the verse, while sustained notes and chromatic passages characterize the more legato refrain.

Slow tango with verse (16), refrain (16) and verse (16)
PUBLISHER: T. B Harms Company
KEY: F maj., *STARTS*: c' (F maj.), OVERALL *FORM*: AA'BB'AA'

≈≈≈≈≈≈≈≈≈≈≈≈≈≈≈≈≈≈≈

ROSETTA

WORDS AND MUSIC: Earl Hines and Henri Woode
INTRODUCED BY: Earl Hines and his Orchestra in a Brunswick recording

'Fatha" Earl Kenneth Hines, who was one of the most distinguished jazz pianists, co-wrote this jazz standard. He introduced it with his own band, which at various times included in its personnel such eminent musicians as Louis Armstrong, Billy Eckstine, and Charlie Parker. The refrain is minimalist, both in melody and harmony. The "A" sections are indeed pentatonic, containing only the tones a', c", d", e", and f'. Harmonies are correspondingly austere, mainly tonic and dominant. The release begins in A minor and then moves to C major. The song's textural sparseness has made it fair game for improvising jazz instrumentalists, among them pianists Art Tatum, Fats Waller, and Teddy Wilson.

Fast rhythm song with verse (8) and refrain (32)
PUBLISHER: Mayfair Music Corp.
KEY: F maj., *STARTS*: a' (F maj.), *FORM*: AA'BA'

≈≈≈≈≈≈≈≈≈≈≈≈≈≈≈≈≈≈≈≈

SHADOW WALTZ

WORDS: Al Dubin, *MUSIC*: Harry Warren
PREMIERE: Film musical, *Gold Diggers of 1933,* Warner Brothers, 1933
INTRODUCED BY: Dick Powell, Ruby Keeler, and chorus

The sentimental "Shadow Waltz" originated in the film, *Gold Diggers of 1933*, choreographed by Busby Berkeley, where it was danced to by sixty chorus girls who seemed to be playing violins and later formed themselves into a huge violin and bow, shot from above. Bing Crosby had a No. 1 Chart record. Rudy Vallee also recorded it. Almost half a century later, "The Shadow Waltz" was performed by Tammy Grimes and a chorus in the long-running musical comedy, *42nd Street,* which opened at the Winter Garden Theatre in New York 25 August 1980. The melody of the refrain moves stepwise up and down the scale in eighth notes, accompanied by simple harmonies. A new idea is briefly offered in the last section, starting in the subdominant (C major), but the music soon returns to a variation of the original theme, in G major. The song was interpolated in the 1936 film, *Cain and Mabel*, starring Clark Gable and Marion Davies.

Slow waltz with verse (17) and refrain (32)
PUBLISHER: Remick Music Corporation
KEY: G maj., *STARTS*: d' (G maj.), *FORM*: ABA'C/A

≈≈≈≈≈≈≈≈≈≈≈≈≈≈≈≈≈≈≈≈

SMOKE GETS IN YOUR EYES ✶ ✶ ✶ ✶ !

WORDS: Otto Harbach, *MUSIC*: Jerome Kern
PREMIERE: Musical comedy, *Roberta*
New York: New Amsterdam Theatre, 18 Nov. 1933 (295 perf.)
INTRODUCED BY: Tamara Drasin

One of the loveliest of ballads, "Smoke Gets in Your Eyes" began life in 1926, when its melody, composed by Jerome Kern, was used as a musical fragment to be performed in front of the curtain during a scenery change for the then-in-rehearsal *Show Boat*. As originally conceived, the melody was staccato and the tempo was fast. Six years later, Kern used the fragment again as a march that was to be performed as the theme of a proposed radio series for NBC. As it turned out, neither function of the music materialized.

While rummaging through his files in 1933, Kern rediscovered the melody. At that time he was preparing the songs for the show, *Gowns by Roberta* – the title later shortened to *Roberta*. According to Otto Harbach, the song's lyricist, Kern was extremely reluctant to slow down the tempo or to elongate the notes of the melody. It took some powerful persuasion by Harbach to make him change his mind. In later years, the sometimes irascible Kern did not like to be reminded of this matter. Adding coal to the fire, the director of *Roberta* wanted to cut the song from the show altogether. Fortunately, he was overruled by Kern.

"Smoke Gets in Your Eyes" is one of a number of Kern songs lacking a verse, including "A Fine Romance", "She Didn't Say 'Yes'", "The Song Is You", "The Way You Look Tonight", and "Yesterdays". It is also a prime example of a work whose sum is greater than its parts. Both length and form are conventional: thirty-two bars in AA'BA' form. The "A" sections create a sinuous, sequential arc, rising and falling in an isorhythmic pattern of half note and four eighth notes. This pattern is broken only in the release, which begins with a striking unprepared modulation from E-flat major to B major, using the tonic note (E-flat) as a pivot, in its enharmonic equivalent (D-sharp). In sharp contrast to the inventiveness of the music, Harbach's lyrics are rather old-fashioned, bearing such awkward inner rhymes as "chaffed" and "gaily laughed".

Nevertheless, they are effective, and a perfect match to Kern's flowing, somewhat operatic melodic line.

"Smoke Gets in Your Eyes" has been recorded by virtually every popular performer, down to The Platters in 1959 and Blue Haze in 1973. It has been featured in numerous movies, including the film version of *Roberta* (1935, sung by Irene Dunne); the Kern biography, *Till the Clouds Roll By* (1946, sung by a chorus and danced to by Cyd Charisse and Gower Champion); *Lovely to Look At*, a 1952 remake of *Roberta* (sung by Kathryn Grayson, danced to by Marge and Gower Champion); and sung by The Platters in two films of 1973, *American Graffiti* and *That'll Be the Day*. It stands as one of the towering ballads of the twentieth century, and one of the most beloved.

Moderate ballad with refrain (32)
PUBLISHER: T. B. Harms Company
KEY: E-flat maj., *STARTS*: e-flat' (E-flat maj.), *FORM*: AABA

≈≈≈≈≈≈≈≈≈≈≈≈≈≈≈≈≈≈≈

SOPHISTICATED LADY * * * !

WORDS AND MUSIC: Duke Ellington, Irving Mills, and Mitchell Parish
INTRODUCED BY: Duke Ellington & his Orchestra in a Brunswick recording

True to its title, this is one of the most sophisticated songs in the literature. It was published first as an instrumental and later, through the auspices of publisher Irving Mills, supplied with lyrics by Mitchell Parish. The Ellington band recorded it, as did Glen Gray and The Casa Loma Orchestra. In 1948, Billy Eckstine had a hit recording. Many years later, "Sophisticated Lady" was sung by Chip Garnett in the revue, *Bubbling Brown Sugar*, which opened at the ANTA Theatre in New York, 2 March 1976. In 1981, Gregory Hines sang it in the Ellington revue, *Sophisticated Ladies*. It was also featured in the Parish retrospective revue, *Stardust*, which opened at the Biltmore Theatre in New York, 19 February 1987.

Lacking a verse, the song is a study in chromaticism, with Debussy-like parallel seventh chords descending in conjunction with the delicate melody. Elements of new tonality and syncopation are introduced in the release. Played on the soundtrack of the 1961 film, *Paris Blues*, "Sophisticated Lady" was Duke Ellington's signature song and one of his most telling creations.

Slow ballad with refrain (32)
PUBLISHER: Mills Music, Inc.
KEY: A-flat maj., *STARTS*: g-flat' (B-flat min.), *FORM*: AA'BA'

≈≈≈≈≈≈≈≈≈≈≈≈≈≈≈≈≈≈≈

STORMY WEATHER (KEEPS RAININ' ALL THE TIME) * * * !

WORDS: Ted Koehler, *MUSIC*: Harold Arlen
PREMIERE: Revue, *Cotton Club Parade of 1933*
New York: Cotton Club, 1933
INTRODUCED BY: Ethel Waters

This powerful lament about lost love emanated from Harlem's Cotton Club, where it was introduced by that eminent blues singer, Ethel Waters, who used it as her theme. Originally written for Cab Calloway, the song was popularized in a Victor recording by Leo Reisman and his Orchestra, with a vocal by Harold Arlen, its composer. Other early recordings were by the orchestras of Guy Lombardo and Duke Ellington. But the most popular recording of all was by Lena Horne, who has been indelibly associated with the song ever since, and has, like Waters, used it as her theme. Larry Kert sang "Stormy Weather" in the revue, *A Musical Jubilee* (1975), and Horne featured it in *Lena Horne: The Lady and the Music*, which opened 5 December 1981 at the Nederlander Theatre in New York.

Lacking a verse, the song has a blues-like melody which stresses the dominant note, e-flat", and the blue note, b-natural'. Although it is in conventional AA'BA' form, the second and fourth sections are each elongated by two bars, by repeating the last phrase at the words "Keeps rainin' all the time". The release is in gospel style, with only two chords, the subdominant (D-flat major) and the tonic (A-flat major). In sharp contrast to the wailing legato main theme, it is filled with rapid dotted notes and triplets and is very often performed in double time.

Ten years after it was written, the song's title became that of a film, *Stormy Weather* (1943), in which it was sung by Horne and danced to by Katherine Dunham and her troupe. Three years later, Connee Boswell sang it in the film, *Swing Parade of 1946*. "Stormy Weather" was also featured in Federico Fellini's 1973 film, *Amarcord*. It survives as an evocative symbol of hard times in the thirties, weather-driven or not.

Slow torch song with refrain (36)
PUBLISHER: Mills Music, Inc
KEY: A-flat maj., *STARTS*: b' (A-flat maj.), *FORM* AA'BA'

≈≈≈≈≈≈≈≈≈≈≈≈≈≈≈≈≈≈≈

TEMPTATION !

WORDS: Arthur Freed, *MUSIC*: Nacio Herb Brown
PREMIERE: Film musical, *Going Hollywood*. Metro Goldwyn Mayer, 1933
INTRODUCED BY: Bing Crosby

A marvelously out-of-the-ordinary song, "Temptation" illustrates how far Hollywood came in producing film music of quality in just a few years. Written by the preeminent Hollywood lyricist and composer of the time, Arthur Freed and Nacio Herb Brown, it was introduced in the film, *Going Hollywood* by Bing Crosby, who also had a hit Brunswick recording. "Temptation" enjoyed a revival in the mid-forties, with recordings by Artie Shaw and his Orchestra in 1944; Perry Como in 1945; and in a hilarious spoof called "Timtayshun" by Jo Stafford (masquerading as Cinderella G. Stump), with Red Ingle and his Natural Seven, in 1947. The Everly Brothers revived "Temptation" with a hit record in 1961.

The song has a heavily Latin flavor because of its bolero accompaniment in the style of Maurice Ravel's classic orchestral piece *Boléro*, written in 1929. The juxtaposition of C major and D-flat major is reminiscent of Andalusian music in general and of Ernesto Lecuona's *Malaguena* (1928) in particular. The sinuous melodic line has an oriental flavor, with repeated notes, quarter-note triplets, and, at one point, a descending chromatic scale. The refrain is forty-eighth bars in length and in AABA'C form. Its clearest departure from normality is the final "C" section, which starts in F major, and is twice the length of each of the other sections.

In addition to *Going Hollywood*, "Temptation" was played by Xavier Cugat and his Orchestra in the 1948 film, *A Date with Judy*, and sung by Mario Lanzo in the 1958 film, *The Seven Hills of Rome*.

Moderate bolero with refrain (48)
PUBLISHER: Metro-Goldwyn-Mayer Corp., assigned to Robbins Music Corp.
KEY: C maj. ,*STARTS*: c' (C maj.), *FORM*: AABA'C

≈≈≈≈≈≈≈≈≈≈≈≈≈≈≈≈≈≈

YESTERDAYS ＊＊＊!

WORDS: Otto Harbach, *MUSIC*: Jerome Kern
PREMIERE: Musical comedy, *Roberta*
New York: New Amsterdam Theatre, 18 November 1933 (295 perf.)
INTRODUCED BY: Fay Templeton

Jerome Kern's last Broadway score, *Roberta*, brought forth two incomparable ballads, "Smoke Gets in Your Eyes" and "Yesterdays". The latter was originally published under the singular title "Yesterday", while the show was originally called *Gowns by Roberta*.

One of Kern's most beautiful melodies, it is also one of only a few of his songs in a minor key. In C minor and ABAB' form, the harmonic changes in the "B" sections are extraordinary, with a change at every bar, going through the circle of fifths from G seventh to A-flat major. The song ends with the sustained note g', accompanied by varied harmonies and ending, surprisingly, in C major. Otto Harbach's lyrics are sometimes forced, rhyming "truth" with "forsooth" and "sequester'd days" with "yesterdays".

Irene Dunne sang "Yesterdays" in the 1935 film version of *Roberta*. A chorus sang it in the Kern biographical film, *Till the Clouds Roll By* (1946). Finally, Kathryn Grayson sang it and Marge and Gower Champion danced to it in the 1952 remake of *Roberta*, renamed *Lovely to Look At*. The ballad's haunting quality and minor key makes it one of Kern's most evocative and nostalgic songs.

Moderate ballad with refrain (40)
PUBLISHER: T. B. Harms Company
KEY: C min., *STARTS*: g' (C min.), *FORM*: ABAB'

≈≈≈≈≈≈≈≈≈≈≈≈≈≈≈≈≈≈≈

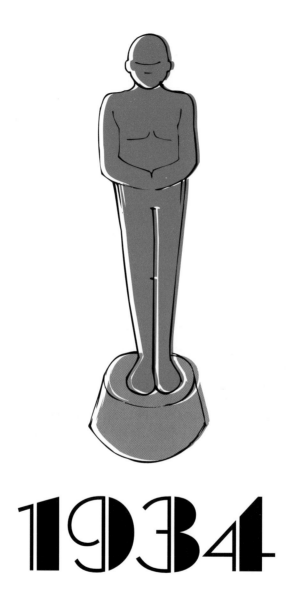

1934

MOBSTERS AND MOVIE HOUSES

1934

With gloom ev'rywhere, I sit and I stare

Duke Ellington, Eddie De Lange, and Irving Mills,
"Solitude"

In this year of generally bad news, songs reflect the cheerlessness of the times. With few exceptions – notably the sparkling score of the musical comedy, *Anything Goes,* and the individual songs, "Autumn in New York" and "The Continental" – they are not a distinguished lot. For the most part they stick to tried-and-true formulas, with thirty-two bar refrains in AABA form and predictable harmonies. Songwriters seem to be treading water in the hope of better things to come. Some of them reach out for new ideas – two Christmas perennials are born this year: "Santa Claus Is Coming to Town" and "Winter Wonderland". Others come from abroad, from England ("The Very Thought of You"), France ("Hands Across the Table"), or Mexico ("What a Diff'rence a Day Made").

The Depression still holds a firm grip on the nation. Unremitting dust storms force thousands of poverty-stricken farm workers to migrate westward in search of fertile land. Gangsters reign supreme, even though a highly-publicized bank robber named John Dillinger is gunned down by the FBI as he is leaving the Biograph Theater in Chicago, accompanied by a lady in red who is acting as a decoy. (The movie he has just seen, *Manhattan Melodrama*, features a song that later will become famous as "Blue Moon").

But all is not doom and gloom; the Dionne Quintuplets are born on a remote farm in Ontario. And there are plenty of diversions to make people forget their troubles. The radio program *Amos 'n' Andy* becomes a national obsession, capturing an audience of millions each weekday between the hours of 7:00 and 7:15 PM. The rip-roaring musical comedy, *Anything Goes,* makes a big splash on Broadway; its score, by Cole Porter, includes four delectable songs destined to become standards. Also on Broadway are Noël Coward's *Conversation Piece*; Lillian Hellman's *The Children's Hour*; and Sinclair Lewis's *Dodsworth*, starring Walter Huston. The best-selling novel of the year is James M. Cain's sensational *The Postman Always Rings Twice.*

Hollywood, too, has a banner year; people can forget their troubles in darkened movie houses, many of which are decked out like Oriental palaces. Frank Capra's comedy, *It Happened One Night*, starring Clark Cable and Claudette Colbert, is awarded five Oscars. The grueling drama, *Of Human Bondage*, stars Betty Davis and Leslie Howard. *The Thin Man* brings together William Powell and Myrna Loy for the first time. And Fred Astaire and Ginger Rogers are co-stars in *The Gay Divorcée*, the first film to win an Academy Award for best song, "The Continental". But the No. 1 box office attraction is a bright-faced little girl named Shirley Temple; she wows Depression audiences in such confections as *Stand Up and Cheer* and *Little Miss Marker* in this year of mobsters and movie houses.

SONGS OF 1934

All Through the Night * !
Anything Goes * * * !
Autumn in New York * !
Blue Moon * * *
Cocktails for Two
The Continental * !
For All We Know
Hands Across the Table
I Get a Kick Out of You * * * !
I Only Have Eyes for You * * *
I'll Follow My Secret Heart
Isle of Capri
Moonglow * *
My Old Flame
The Object of My Affection
Santa Claus Is Coming to Town * * *
Solitude * !
Stars Fell on Alabama *
The Very Thought of You * *
What a Diff'rence a Day Made * * *
Winter Wonderland * * *
You and the Night and the Music !
You're the Top * * !

ALL THROUGH THE NIGHT * !

WORDS and MUSIC: Cole Porter
PREMIERE: Musical comedy, *Anything Goes*
New York: Alvin Theatre, 21 November 1934 (420 perf.)
INTRODUCED BY: William Gaxton (sung to Bettina Hall)

No show captured the spirit of the thirties as well as *Anything Goes*. Not only was it the biggest hit of the year, but with 420 performances, it was Cole Porter's longest running show to date. It was also his only show to produce five hit songs: "Anything Goes", "I Get a Kick Out of You", "Blow, Gabriel, Blow", "You're the Top", and "All Through the Night". The action takes place on the high seas, giving plenty of room for frivolity. The show was a hilarious romp through the mores of the day, with a cast that included Ethel Merman, Victor Moore, William Gaxton, and plenty of chorus girls in bathing suits. But the biggest stars by far were Porter's witty lyrics and imaginative music. "All Through the Night" was the big ballad of the show, otherwise noted for its rhythmical, upbeat music. The first recording was by Paul Whiteman and his Orchestra.

"All Through the Night" was written expressly for Gaxton's voice. He was supposed to sing "Easy to Love", but found that that song did not lay right for his voice – it found a home two years later in the film, *Born to Dance*. Instead, Porter substituted "All Through the Night" – arguably one of the most inventive of his songs. The melody is built around a descending chromatic scale, making it ripe for harmonic change. Harmonies do change quickly, moving in the first sixteen bars from F major to D minor to B-flat major; and then to A-flat major and back to F major. The release is no less innovative, starting in F minor and moving to D-flat major, and then to A-flat major and C major.

"All Through the Night" was heard as background music in the 1936 film version of *Anything Goes*. In the 1956 version, Bing Crosby sang it and Zizi Jeanmaire danced to it, in a dream ballet. With its emphasis on chromaticism and strong romantic harmonies, the song is one of Porter's most evocative creations.

Moderate foxtrot with verse (20) and refrain (64)
PUBLISHER: Harms, Inc.
KEY: F maj., *STARTS*: a' (F maj.), *FORM*: AA'BA

≋≋≋≋≋≋≋≋≋≋≋≋≋≋≋≋≋≋≋

ANYTHING GOES * * * !

WORDS and MUSIC: Cole Porter
PREMIERE: Musical comedy, *Anything Goes*
New York: Alvin Theatre, 21 November 1934 (420 perf.)
INTRODUCED BY: Ethel Merman

The title song of the smash hit, *Anything Goes,* is one of the show's best-known songs. With sparkling lyrics and jazzy music, it epitomizes its times, when almost anything was permitted, from seeing more than a "glimpse of stocking" to using "four-letter words". Paul Whiteman and his Orchestra had the first recording. In 1967 the song was revived with the Warner Brothers recording by Harper's Bizarre.

The verse is in declamatory style, using the favorite Cole Porter device of presenting a theme first in minor and then in major. The heart and soul of the refrain is syncopation, in a most persistent way. The melodic line, with its constant accented offbeats, is reminiscent of ragtime. And the song has further delights. The release emphasizes the first beat of each bar, starting out in E major and then modulating back to C major. As usual, Porter's lyrics are the height of witty sophistication, with some intriguing rhymes, pairing "guys' " with "prize", and "romancer" with "answer".

Ethel Merman reprised the song in the 1936 film version of *Anything Goes*; it was used as background in the Porter biography, *Night and Day* (1946); and Mitzi Gaynor sang it in the 1956 film version of *Anything Goes.*

Moderate rhythm song with verse (16) and refrain (32)
PUBLISHER: Harms, Inc.
KEY: C maj., STARTS: g' (C maj.), FORM: AABA

≈≈≈≈≈≈≈≈≈≈≈≈≈≈≈≈≈≈≈≈

AUTUMN IN NEW YORK * !

WORDS and MUSIC: Vernon Duke
PREMIERE: Revue, *Thumbs Up!*
New York: St. James Theatre, 27 December 1934 (156 perf.)
INTRODUCED BY: J. Harold Murray

Composer Vernon Duke, who wrote classical music under his real name, Vladimir Dukelsky, wrote "Autumn in New York" as a follow-up to his highly successful "April in Paris" of 1932. After all, both songs were about large, romantic cities. "Autumn in New York" was introduced as the grand finale of the John Murray Anderson revue, *Thumbs Up!*, which also brought forth another great standard: "Zing! Went the Strings of My Heart" (see 1935). Many singers made recordings of "Autumn in New York"; Frank Sinatra's was the most popular.

It is a remarkable song in many ways. The verse moves into uncharted territory, with a modicum of blue notes and complicated harmonies. The refrain at first seems more accessible, starting with a lilting motive, consisting mostly of eighth notes. But soon enough, harmonies become more complex, moving in the "B" section to A-flat major and then to C major, while the melody becomes syncopated. The third section of the refrain ("A'") cadences on B-flat minor, while the last section ("C/A'") begins and ends in F minor, with a brief excursion to D-flat major in between. Thus, "Autumn in New York" is one of very few popular songs beginning in major and ending in minor. As a paean to a great city, the song also boasts sophisticated lyrics, written by the composer himself, rhyming "jaded roués" with "gay divorcées". It is known as a musician's song, harmonically one of the most complex in the literature.

Moderate ballad with verse (18) and refrain (32)
PUBLISHER: Harms, Inc.
KEY: F maj., *STARTS*: a' (G min.), **FORM**: ABA'C/A"

≈≈≈≈≈≈≈≈≈≈≈≈≈≈≈≈≈≈≈

BLUE MOON ⋆ ⋆ ⋆

WORDS: Lorenz Hart, *MUSIC*: Richard Rodgers
INTRODUCED BY: by Glen Gray and The Casa Loma Orchestra

"Blue Moon" has one of the most convoluted creative histories in popular song. With the title "Prayer", it was cut from the film it had been written for, *Hollywood Party* (1933), which starred Laurel and Hardy, The Three Stooges, Jimmy Durante, and Mickey Mouse. "Prayer" was to have been sung by Jean Harlow, addressed to the Lord, and ending with Hart's tongue-in-cheek words: "Be nice and make me a star". Hart wrote new lyrics, and in 1934 the song re-emerged as "The Bad in Ev'ry Man", and was sung by Shirley Ross in a film, *Manhattan Melodrama*, (the very film that outlaw John Dillinger was watching just before he was gunned down in Chicago). Finally, Hart wrote yet another set of lyrics and "Blue Moon" was born. It became one of Rodgers and Hart's biggest hits. Glen Gray and The Casa Loma Orchestra had a No. 1 Chart Record. Benny Goodman and his Orchestra had a cover record. Over the years, there have been periodic revivals: by Mel Tormé and Billy Eckstine in 1949, by Elvis Presley and The Marcels in 1961, and in the revue, *The 1940's Radio Hour*, in 1979.

"Blue Moon" is not one of Rodgers and Hart's most distinguished songs. The verse, in C minor, is in the style of recitative. The refrain, in E-flat major, is rather ordinary: thirty-two bars in AABA form. The melody is repetitive, moving sequentially downward in each "A" section, in a range of only a fifth. Harmonies are of the simple variety, using the common ostinato pattern "We Want Cantor": E-flat major - C minor - F minor seventh - B-flat seventh. Nor are the lyrics among Hart's best, with the moon turning to gold when someone whispers "Please adore me".

For a song that did not originate in a show or film, "Blue Moon" has been featured in an amazing string of motion pictures. It was in *Hollywood Hotel* (1937). Harpo Marx played it as a harp solo in *At the Circus* (1939). Mel Tormé sang it in the 1948 Hart-Rodgers film biography, *Words and Music*. Jane Froman dubbed it in for Susan Hayward in her screen biography, *With a Song in My Heart*. India Adams dubbed it in for Joan Crawford in *Torch Song* (1953). It was heard on the soundtrack of *This Could Be the Night* (1957). Mary Kay Place and Robert De Niro sang it in *New York, New York* (1977). Sha Na Na sang it in *Grease* (1978). Dudley Moore sang it in *Arthur*, and The Marcels and Sam Cooke sang it in *An American Werewolf in London* (both 1981). Considering its modest means, "Blue Moon" has had remarkable staying power. Because of its relatively blank pallet of simple harmonies, it is especially admired by jazz musicians as a vehicle for improvisation.

Slow ballad with two verses (16) and refrain (32)
PUBLISHER: Metro-Goldwyn-Mayer Corporation; assigned to Robbins Music Corporation
KEY: E-flat maj., *STARTS*: B-flat' (E-flat maj.), **FORM**: AABA

≈≈≈≈≈≈≈≈≈≈≈≈≈≈≈≈≈≈≈

COCKTAILS FOR TWO

WORDS and MUSIC: Arthur Johnston and Sam Coslow
PREMIERE: Film musical, *Murder at the Vanities,* Paramount, 1934
INTRODUCED BY: Carl Brisson and a chorus

With its newfangled subject of sharing cocktails, this song was the height of sophistication when Carl Brisson introduced it in a film, *Murder at the Vanities*. Initially recorded by Duke Ellington and his Orchestra, the song's real popularity began eleven years after it was written, in a devastating parody recorded on Victor by Spike Jones and his City Slickers. The recording poked fun at the song's many clichés, in a clever fast-tempo arrangement employing cowbells, horns, whistles, and other odd instruments.

Prominent among the song's clichés is the seven-note pickup that begins each "A" section. This rhythmic motive of eighth notes occurs nine times in the refrain. Harmonies are simple and predictable, concentrating on the tonic (C major), dominant (G major), and subdominant (F major).

In films, "Cocktails for Two" was sung by Miriam Hopkins in *She Loves Me Not* (1934), parodied again by Jones and his City Slickers in *Ladies' Man* (1947), and sung by Danny Kaye in *On the Double* (1961).

Moderate foxtrot with verse (15) and refrain (32)
PUBLISHER: Paramount Productions Music Corp., assigned to Famous Music Corp.
KEY: C maj., *STARTS*: c' (C maj.), *FORM*: AABA

≈≈≈≈≈≈≈≈≈≈≈≈≈≈≈≈≈≈≈≈

THE CONTINENTAL (YOU KISS WHILE YOU DANCE) * !

WORDS: Herb Magidson, *MUSIC*: Con Conrad
PREMIERE: Film musical, *The Gay Divorcée*, RKO Radio Pictures, 1934
INTRODUCED BY: Ginger Rogers, danced by Fred Astaire and Ginger Rogers; reprised by Erik Rhodes and Lillian Miles

The first song to win an Academy Award, "The Continental" was written as a production number for Fred Astaire and Ginger Rogers in the film musical, *The Gay Divorcée*. It was one of a number of songs written expressly for the film to replace the Cole Porter score for the Broadway show, *The Gay Divorce*, of 1932 of which only "Night and Day" was retained. "The Continental" is presented in an elaborate Art Deco setting in a scene lasting seventeen minutes – undoubtedly the highlight of the film. The earliest recording was by Leo Reisman and his Orchestra.

"The Continental" is far removed from other popular songs of the day. With 110 measures, it is certainly one of the longest songs written up to that time. It even exceeds the 108-bar "Begin the Beguine", written a year later. Con Conrad's music moves along seamlessly in an arrangement that no one has ever seen fit to change. It begins with a chromatic accompaniment figure at the words "Beautiful music! Dangerous rhythm!" that serves as an introduction. There are two different refrains: the first, lively and with dotted rhythms, in the key of E-flat major; the second, more lyrical and legato, in the key of A-flat major. The introductory figure returns as a coda, this time in A-flat major, again with the opening words.

It is altogether a magnificent number, a fitting recipient of the first Academy Award for best song.

Moderate production number with introduction (12), first refrain (34), and second refrain (60)
PUBLISHER: Harms, Inc.
KEY: first refrain: E-flat maj., second refrain: A-flat maj.
STARTS: first refrain: b-flat' (F min.), second refrain: e-flat' (A-flat maj.),
FORM: first refrain: AABA, second refrain: ABCAD

≈≈≈≈≈≈≈≈≈≈≈≈≈≈≈≈≈≈≈≈

FOR ALL WE KNOW

WORDS: Sam M. Lewis, *MUSIC*: J. Fred Coots
INTRODUCED: on radio and in a recording by Morton Downey

This rather ordinary song is not to be confused with another "For All We Know", written for the film, *Lovers and Other Strangers*, which won the Academy Award for best song of 1970. The 1934 song is a simple, romantic foxtrot, written in the style of the twenties. Popularized by tenor, Morton Downey, it was also recorded by the bands of Hal Kemp and Isham Jones. The Andrew Sisters had a hit Decca record in 1942. The melody consists of long notes gliding upwards at intervals of the fourth and the sixth, with an abundance of quarter-note triplets. It is a song eminently suitable for dreamy dancing.

Moderate foxtrot with two verses (8) and refrain (32)
PUBLISHER: Leo Feist, Inc.
KEY: F maj., *STARTS*: c' (F maj.), *FORM*: ABAB'

≈≈≈≈≈≈≈≈≈≈≈≈≈≈≈≈≈≈≈≈

HANDS ACROSS THE TABLE

WORDS: Mitchell Parish, *MUSIC*: Jean Delettre
PREMIERE: Revue, *Continental Varieties*
New York: Little Theatre, 3 October 1934 (ca. 80 perf.)
INTRODUCED BY: Lucienne Boyer

This bit of Parisian sophistication, with English words by Mitchell Parish, was introduced by the celebrated French chanteuse, Lucienne Boyer, in a short-lived revue, *Continental Varieties*. Recorded for Brunswick by Hal Kemp and his Orchestra, with a vocal by Skinnay Ennis, and for Victor by Eddy Duchin and his Orchestra, the song soon became a favorite dance number of society bands. In 1981, it was revived in the Mitchell Parish revue, *Stardust*, sung by Michele Bautier. The refrain, only sixteen bars in length, has a simple melody revolving about repeated intervals of the minor third: g' to b-flat' and f' to a-flat'. Such mannered simplicity was the essence of French musical style at that time.

> Moderate foxtrot with two verses (8) and refrain (16)
> *PUBLISHER*: Mills Music, Inc.
> *KEY*: E-flat maj., *STARTS*: g' (E-flat maj.), *FORM*: ABAB'

≈≈≈≈≈≈≈≈≈≈≈≈≈≈≈≈≈≈≈

I GET A KICK OUT OF YOU ✳ ✳ ✳ !

> *WORDS and MUSIC*: Cole Porter
> *PREMIERE*: Musical comedy, *Anything Goes*
> New York: Alvin Theatre, 21 November 1034 (420 perf.)
> *INTRODUCED BY:* Ethel Merman and William Gaxton

One of Cole Porter's most celebrated songs, "I Get a Kick Out of You" was originally written for a musical comedy, *Star Dust*. However, that project never got off the ground, and the song was rescued for *Anything Goes*. Popularized by that show's star, Ethel Merman, it became an immediate hit, propelled by its optimistic melody and magical lyrics. Paul Whiteman had an early recording, but the most popular recording of all was by Frank Sinatra.

The opening gesture of the refrain is a rising scale, from c' to b-flat'. In sixty-four bars, twice the normal length, it is replete with half-note triplets. These are seldom performed that way, however; but rather with each triplet as a half note followed by two quarter notes. A subtle touch of syncopation occurs each time the words "I get a kick out of you" are intoned. But most striking of all are the lyrics, which catalogue substances that don't give the protagonist a thrill, or "kick": such as "champagne", "cocaine" (later lamely changed to "a bop type refrain"), or "flying too high in a plane".

A number of films have featured the song. Ethel Merman repeated her triumph in the first screen version of *Anything Goes* in 1936. Ginny Simms sang it in the Porter biography, *Night and Day* (1946). Mitzi Gaynor, Bing Crosby, and Zizi Jeanmaire sang it in the second screen version of *Anything Goes* (1956). Billy Daniels did it in the 1951 film, *Sunny Side of the Street*. And finally, Cybill Shepherd performed it in *At Long Last Love* (1975). It remains one of the most joyful and uninhibited songs in the standard repertoire.

Moderate foxtrot with verse (20) and refrain (64)
PUBLISHER: Harms, Inc.
KEY: E-flat maj., *STARTS*: c' (F min. 7), *FORM*: AA'BA

≈≈≈≈≈≈≈≈≈≈≈≈≈≈≈≈≈≈

I ONLY HAVE EYES FOR YOU * * *

WORDS: Al Dubin, *MUSIC*: Harry Warren
PREMIERE: Film musical, *Dames*, Warner Brothers, 1934
INTRODUCED BY: Dick Powell, Ruby Keeler and chorus

Few songs have been revived as many times as "I Only Have Eyes for You". This winsome ballad was unveiled in the film musical, *Dames*, with a lavish production number choreographed by Busby Berkeley representing a dream Dick Powell is having on a New York subway train. In it, all the chorus girls' faces turn into the face of his sweetheart, Ruby Keeler. At the climax of the dance, the girls – each with a board on her back – bend over, revealing a giant portrait of Keeler. Originally popularized by Eddy Duchin and his Orchestra and by Jane Froman, "I Only Have Eyes for You" was recorded by The Flamingos in 1959, The Lettermen in 1966, Jerry Butler in 1972, and Art Garfunkel in 1975.

The refrain, in AA'BA" form, is very carefully wrought. In each "A" section, the tender melody descends stepwise and then repeats itself, with slight variation. Care for detail is shown in the differing endings of each "A" section: respectively b', c-sharp', and e'. The release also descends stepwise, but changes the note a-natural' to a-flat the second time around. A four-bar coda rounds out the final section. The romantic lyrics ("Are the stars out tonight?") are a perfect foil for the flowing melody.

Besides appearing in *Dames*, "I Only Have Eyes for You" was dubbed in by Al Jolson for Larry Parks in the 1949 film, *Jolson Sings Again*; Virginia Gibson and Gordon MacRae sang it in the 1950 film, *Tea for Two*; it was heard on the soundtrack of *Young Man with a Horn* (1950); and in 1973, The Flamingos sang it in *American Graffiti*. The song is a living testament to the craftsmanship of its writers, working within the confines of conventional AABA form.

Slow ballad with verse and refrain (36)
PUBLISHER: Remick Music Corpoation
KEY: C maj., *STARTS*: d' (D min. 11), *FORM*: AA'BA"

≈≈≈≈≈≈≈≈≈≈≈≈≈≈≈≈≈≈

I'LL FOLLOW MY SECRET HEART

WORDS AND MUSIC: Noël Coward
PREMIERE: Play with music, *Conversation Piece*
New York: 44th Street Theatre, 23 October 1934 (55 perf.)
INTRODUCED BY: Noël Coward and Yvonne Printemps

A lovely waltz in the spirit of Old Vienna, "I'll Follow My Secret Heart" is the only survivor from Noël Coward's not-too-successful play, *Conversation Piece*. It was recorded by singers Hildegarde, Lee Wiley, and many others. In operetta style, the verse is longer than the refrain and very melodic, written in two different keys: C major and D major. The melody of the refrain, in G major, has a haunting quality, made more so by its gentle chromaticism: the second note of each "A" section, following the d', is e-flat'. In every respect, the song is the essence of quiet European elegance and sophistication.

Slow waltz with verse (33) and refrain (32)
PUBLISHER: Chappell & Co., Inc.

≈≈≈≈≈≈≈≈≈≈≈≈≈≈≈≈≈≈

ISLE OF CAPRI

WORDS: Jimmy Kennedy, *MUSIC*: Will Grosz
INTRODUCED BY: Guy Lombardo and his Royal Canadians in the United States

"Isle of Capri" was written in Britain and was introduced there by Lew Stone and his Orchestra. The music was the subject of a copyright dispute in Britain, alleging its similarity to the Viennese tango, "Ich Bin ein Kleiner Armer Strassensänger", which was won by the plaintiff, Paul Reif. Imported to the United States, "Isle of Capri" became a sensational hit after its recording by Guy Lombardo and his Royal Canadians. Cover recordings were made by Wingy Manone and by Xavier Cugat and his Orchestra. A generation later, in 1954, The Gaylords had a hit recording.

The sheet music calls the song, somewhat confusingly, a "Sensational European Tango Fox-Trot". Indeed, in the style of a tango, the verse is in a parallel minor, F minor. However, the resemblance to a tango stops there; the song appears to be a wolf in sheep's clothing, in this case, a fox-trot in the guise of a tango. The music is rather ordinary, with the main theme consisting of broken chords. Harmonies, too, are simple: tonic, dominant, and subdominant (in the release). The lyrics tell a story about meeting someone "beneath the shade of an old walnut tree", about asking her for "a sweet word of love", and then, sadly, about seeing "a plain golden ring on her finger", and saying "goodbye on the Isle of Capri".

> Slow tango with two verses (16) and refrain (32)
> *PUBLISHER*: The Peter Maurice Music Co., Ltd. (London), assigned in the United States to Harms, Inc.
> *KEY*: F maj., *STARTS*: c' (F maj.), *FORM*: AABA

≈≈≈≈≈≈≈≈≈≈≈≈≈≈≈≈≈≈≈

MOONGLOW * *

> *WORDS and MUSIC*: Will Hudson, Eddie DeLange, and Irving Mills
> *PREMIERE*: Revue, *Blackbirds of 1934*
> London: Coliseum Theatre, 25 August 1934
> *INTRODUCED BY:* the Hudson-DeLange Orchestra in the United States

"Moonglow" was the most successful collaboration of composer, Will Hudson, and lyricist, Eddie DeLange. Hudson had written the music as a theme song for his band, then playing at the Graystone Ballroom in Detroit. At the suggestion of publisher Irving Mills, DeLange supplied the instrumental with lyrics, and Mills, as was his custom, also took writer's credit. (He also owned an interest in the newly-formed Hudson-DeLange Orchestra, which introduced the song.) Duke Ellington, closely associated with Mills, also performed it as an instrumental. But the song's real popularity began in London. Among the early recordings were those by the bands of Artie Shaw, Benny Goodman, Guy Lombardo, and Glen Gray. More than twenty years later, in 1956, "Moonglow" achieved even greater fame, when it was used as countermelody to "Theme from *Picnic*", (words by Steve Allen, music by George Duning) in the film, *Picnic* (1956), starring Kim Novak, William Holden, and Rosalind Russell.

The verse of "Moonglow" is in G minor; the refrain in G major. As originally written, the melody of the refrain revolves about only three notes – e', g', and b' – in the "A" sections. However, monotony is avoided by harmonies which change every measure. The release features chords of the seventh descending chromatically.

In the same year as the song's renaissance in *Picnic*, it was featured, in its original manifestation, in the biographical film, *The Benny Goodman Story*, with Steve Allen playing the part of Goodman. Whenever it is heard, it evokes a feeling of tenderness and nostalgia.

Slow ballad with verse (8) and refrain (32)
PUBLISHER: Mills Music, Inc.
KEY: G maj., *STARTS*: e' (C maj.), *FORM*: AABA

≈≈≈≈≈≈≈≈≈≈≈≈≈≈≈≈≈≈≈

MY OLD FLAME

WORDS and MUSIC: Arthur Johnston and Sam Coslow
PREMIERE: Film musical, *Belle of the Nineties*. Paramount, 1934
INTRODUCED BY: Mae West, with Duke Ellington and his Orchestra

In the film, *Belle of the Nineties*, Mae West plays the part of Madame Ruby Carter, who runs a place called the Sensation House in New Orleans. She is a true liberal; as her character says: "I prefer two kinds of men, domestic and foreign". In the film, West sings this lovely ballad accompanied by Duke Ellington and his Orchestra; they later recorded it. Among other recordings were those of Billie Holiday and Benny Goodman and his Orchestra, with vocal by Peggy Lee. Although conventional in length (thirty-two bars) and form (AABA), the refrain has some interesting aspects. The melody stresses blue notes, specifically those of the flatted seventh (f-natural') and sixth (e-flat'). In addition, harmonies have a tendency to stray away from the tonic of G major to the distant reaches of B-flat sixth and E-flat ninth. Indeed, the release begins in B-flat major, which almost acts in the piece as a secondary tonality. The lyrics are effective, offering a number of rhymes for "flame": among them "name", "same", "became", "tame", and (not so successfully) "again".

Moderate ballad with verse (8) and refrain (32)
PUBLISHER: Famous Music Corporation
KEY: G. maj., *STARTS*: b', *FORM*: AA'BA"

≈≈≈≈≈≈≈≈≈≈≈≈≈≈≈≈≈≈≈

THE OBJECT OF MY AFFECTION

WORDS and MUSIC: Pinky Tomlin, Coy Poe, and Jimmie Grier
INTRODUCED BY: Pinky Tomlin, with Jimmy Grier and his Orchestra in a Brunswick recording

In the early and mid-thirties, Jimmy Grier and his Orchestra performed at the famous Cocoanut Grove in Los Angeles. On one of the band's tours. Grier discovered a young college student in Oklahoma, a singer and composer named Pinky Tomlin. He invited him to the West Coast to record some of his own songs. The most famous of these was this happy-go-lucky tune which lends itself well to "rippling rhythm". Other recordings were by The Boswell Sisters and by Jan Garber and his Orchestra, with vocal by Lee Bennett.

Few songs have as many repeated notes as this one, which is also remarkable for its many eighth-note triplets and dotted quarters and eighths. A climax of sorts is reached at the end of the release, with the repeated triplets on the note b-flat' at the words: "go where she wants to go, do what she wants to do".

Pinky Tomlin reprised "The Object of My Affection" in the 1935 film, *Times Square Lady*. Janet Blair sang it in *The Fabulous Dorseys* (1947).

Moderate shuffle song with verse (8) and refrain (32)
PUBLISHER: Bourne, Inc.
KEY: A-flat maj., *STARTS*: b' (A-flat maj.), *FORM*: AABA

≈≈≈≈≈≈≈≈≈≈≈≈≈≈≈≈≈≈≈≈

SANTA CLAUS IS COMIN' TO TOWN * * *

WORDS: Haven Gillespie, *MUSIC*: J. Fred Coots
INTRODUCED BY: George Olsen & his Orch., vocal by Ethel Shutta, on radio

This cheerful song has achieved a certain immortality as a Christmas perennial, returning each season. It was introduced by George Olsen and his Orchestra, with vocal by Olsen's wife, Ethel Shutta. Eddie Cantor also had an early recording. But the song's greatest thrust to fame came with the 1947 Decca record of Bing Crosby and The Andrews Sisters. Bruce Springsteen revived it on Columbia in 1985.

The lyrics are of special importance, with two verses and two refrains – the second of which is called a "Music Box Chorus". The words of course are of special interest to children, referring to "little tin horns and little toy drums". Indeed, some of them have become household words, as in "He's making a list and checking it twice". The simple music is also geared to children, exploiting a single rhythmical motive of two eighth notes followed by two quarter notes. The release offers some contrast with individual quarter notes moving stepwise.

Dudley Moore sang "Santa Claus Is Comin' to Town" in the 1981 film, Arthur. Like Santa Claus himself, it comes back every Christmas.

Moderate novelty song with two verses (16) and refrain (32)
PUBLISHER: Leo Feist, Inc.
KEY: C maj., *STARTS*: g' (C maj.), *FORM*: AABA

≈≈≈≈≈≈≈≈≈≈≈≈≈≈≈≈≈≈≈≈

SOLITUDE * !

WORDS and MUSIC: Duke Ellington, Eddie DeLange, and Irving Mills
INTRODUCED: in two recordings (Brunswick and Victor) by Duke Ellington and his Orchestra

Like many Duke Ellington songs, this beautiful ballad began as an instrumental. Lyrics, by Eddie DeLange, were added later through the auspices of Ellington's publisher Irving Mills – who also received writer's credit. Introduced by the Ellington band, the most popular vocal recording was by Ella Fitzgerald. Lacking a verse, the song has an evocative melody of few notes. Movement is mostly stepwise, with poignant downward jumps of the sixth at the words "haunt me", "taunt me", and "praying". Harmonies demonstrate Ellington's penchant for chords of the major and minor seventh. In conventional AABA form, the song's most unusual aspect is that each "A" section, including the last, ends with a half cadence on the note g'. ASCAP awarded "Solitude" a prize as Best Song of the Year.

Slow ballad with refrain (32)
PUBLISHER: American Academy of Music, Inc.
KEY: E-flat maj., *STARTS*: b-flat' (E-flat maj. 7), *FORM*: AABA

≋≋≋≋≋≋≋≋≋≋≋≋≋≋≋≋≋

STARS FELL ON ALABAMA *

WORDS: Mitchell Parish, *MUSIC*: Frank Perkins

Frank Perkins, composer of this lovely ballad, had a distinguished career as arranger for Fred Waring's Pennsylvanians and later as composer and arranger for Warner Brothers Pictures, Inc. This is his best known song; with lyrics by Mitchell Parish. It was popularized in two recordings (Brunswick and Capitol) by trombonist Jack Teagarden and his Orchestra. The many other recordings include those of the orchestras of Freddy Martin, Guy Lombardo, Woody Herman, and Montovani, as well as instrumentalists Stan Getz and Johnny Guarnieri. In 1987, it was sung by Jim Walton and Maureen Brennan in the Parish retrospective revue, *Stardust*. The evocative melody of the refrain combines chromatic motives with upward and downward skips of the fourth, fifth, and sixth. The striking release starts in F major but moves briefly to E major before returning to the tonic.

Slow ballad with verse (8) and refrain (32)
PUBLISHER: Mills Music, Inc.
KEY: C maj., *STARTS*: e' (C maj.), *FORM*: AA'BA'

≋≋≋≋≋≋≋≋≋≋≋≋≋≋≋≋≋

THE VERY THOUGHT OF YOU ✶✶

WORDS and MUSIC: Ray Noble
INTRODUCED BY: Ray Noble and his Orchestra and recorded on Victor

Ray Noble wrote this tender ballad while he was still in Britain and he recorded it there with his orchestra. The Victor recording became a hit in the United States, and late in 1934 Noble went to the United States himself and, with Glenn Miller's help, organized a new band. "The Very Thought of You" always occupied a special place in the band's repertoire. There were numerous other recordings, but Noble's has always been most popular. The nostalgic melody touches lightly on the intervals of the minor third and fourth, with a modicum of dotted notes. The song was featured in its namesake film of 1944, *The Very Thought of You*, starring Eleanor Parker and Dennis Morgan. In 1950, Doris Day sang it in the film, *Young Man with a Horn*.

Slow ballad with two verses (16) and refrain (32)
PUBLISHER: Campbell, Connelly & Co., Ltd. (London); assigned to
M. Witmark & Sons (North America)
KEY: A-flat maj., *STARTS*: c' (A-flat maj.), *FORM*: ABAB'

≋≋≋≋≋≋≋≋≋≋≋≋≋≋≋≋≋≋≋≋≋

WHAT A DIFF'RENCE A DAY MADE (CUANDO VUELVA A TU LADO) ✶✶✶

ENGLISH WORDS: Stanley Adams, *MUSIC*: Maria Grever

In the early thirties, Mexican lyricist and composer, Maria Grever, wrote the Spanish words and music for a tango called "Cuando Vuelva a tu Lado". As "What a Diff'rence a Day Made", with English lyrics by Stanley Adams, it became one of the most popular of all Latin American imports. Initially popularized in the United States by the Dorsey Brothers Orchestra, with vocal by Bob Crosby, the song has seen a number of revivals: by Benny Carter and his Orchestra (vocal by Maxine Sullivan) in 1941; by Charlie Barnet and his Orchestra (vocal by Kay Starr) in 1944, by Dinah Washington (a Grammy Award) in 1959, and by Little Esther Phillips in 1975.

The broad melody of the refrain is notable for its five-note pickup to the long-held note g' of the B-flat major sixth chord. The refrain is in ABAC form, with the melody moving mostly stepwise in the "A" sections, repeating notes over changing harmonies in the "B" section, and introducing a striking downward sequence in the "C" section. One of the most versatile of songs, this international favorite is equally at home played as a tango, a rumba, a foxtrot, a jazz standard, or a ballad.

Slow rumba / foxtrot with verse (8) and refrain (32)
PUBLISHER: Edward B. Marks Music Corporation
KEY: F maj., *STARTS*: c' (B-flat 6), *FORM*: ABAC

≈≈≈≈≈≈≈≈≈≈≈≈≈≈≈≈≈≈≈≈

WINTER WONDERLAND * * *

WORDS: Dick Smith, *MUSIC*: Felix Bernard

Along with "Santa Claus Is Comin' to Town", also written this year, the charming "Winter Wonderland" reemerges every year at Christmas time. It was initially popularized by Guy Lombardo and his Royal Canadians and revived in 1946 with a recording by The Andrews Sisters. Dotted rhythms of the quarter and eighth prevail throughout the refrain. In the "A" sections, the melody first plays around the interval of the minor third, and then descends stepwise, playing the notes g' and f' four times each. Harmonies are tonic and dominant, except in the release, which begins in G major and then proceeds to B-flat major. The lyrics have a cozy air about them – "Sleigh bells ring / Are you listenin'?"– telling of an impending marriage ceremony by "Parson Brown". The song was featured in the 1944 ice-skating film, *Lake Placid Serenade*.

Moderate novelty song with verse (16) and two refrains (32)
PUBLISHER: Bregman, Vocco and Conn, Inc.
KEY: E-flat maj., *STARTS*: b-flat' (E-flat maj.), *FORM*: AABA

≈≈≈≈≈≈≈≈≈≈≈≈≈≈≈≈≈≈≈≈

YOU AND THE NIGHT AND THE MUSIC !

WORDS: Howard Dietz, *MUSIC*: Arthur Schwartz
PREMIERE: Operetta, *Revenge with Music*
New York: New Amsterdam Theatre, 28 November 1934 (158 perf.)
INTRODUCED BY: Georges Metaxa and Libby Holman

The operetta, *Revenge with Music,* was set in Spain, and was handsomely mounted, but suffered from a poorly-written book. However, it had some lovely songs by Howard Dietz and Arthur Schwartz, including this striking tango-like ballad. Singer Conrad Thibault helped popularize it. Arthur Schwarts's music, originally composed as a theme for the radio serial, *The Gibson Family*, is stirringly Spanish in character, using stepwise harmonies and major-minor contrast. In AABA' form, each "A" section begins in C minor and ends in C major. The release brings back the primary motive a sixth higher, with sonorous harmonies moving downward from B-flat to A-flat, to G. While the music is undeniably beautiful, the lyrics are sometimes poetically out-of-date, as in "Make the best of time ere it has flown". "You and the Night and the Music" was sung by a chorus in the film, *The Band Wagon* (1953).

> Moderate ballad with verse (16) and refrain (32)
> *PUBLISHER*: Harms, Inc.
> *KEY*: C min., *STARTS*: g' (C min.), *FORM*: AABA'

≈≈≈≈≈≈≈≈≈≈≈≈≈≈≈≈≈≈

YOU'RE THE TOP ★★!

WORDS AND MUSIC: Cole Porter
PREMIERE: Musical comedy, *Anything Goes*
New York: Alvin Theatre, 21 November 1934 (420 perf.)
INTRODUCED BY: Ethel Merman and William Gaxton

This frenetic Cole Porter wonder, the tops in catalogue songs, has captivated audiences since Ethel Merman and William Gaxton sang it on opening night of the musical comedy, *Anything Goes*. Both Merman and Porter recorded it: she for Brunswick, he for Victor. Long renowned for the wit-tiness of its lyrics, it boasts a marvelous collection of pairings: "a Bendel bonnet" and "a Shakespeare sonnet"; "a symphony by Strauss" and "Mickey Mouse"; "The Tower of Pisa" and "the Mona Lisa"; not to mention "a Waldorf salad" and a "Berlin ballad", or "the steppes of Russia" and "a Roxy usher".

Which such an abundance of cleverness, it is easy to overlook the music. But the music itself is of great originality, from the syncopated verse to the vibrant refrain. In ABAC form, the refrain starts unusually, with an accompaniment figure on the first two beats of Bar One. The three-note vocal motive begins only after the third beat, and carries over to the first beat of Bar Two. Multi-repeated notes are arrayed at the close of the "B" section (on the note "d") and at the close of the "C" section (on the note e-flat").

Not surprisingly, "You're the Top" has been featured in a number of films. Ethel Merman and Bing Crosby sang it in the 1936 screen treatment of *Anything Goes*. Ginny Simms and Cary Grant performed it in the 1946 Porter screen biography, *Night and Day*. Mitzi Gaynor, Bing Crosby, Donald O'Connor, and Zizi Jeanmaire performed it in the 1956 film version of *Anything Goes*. In 1965, Barbra Streisand and Ryan O'Neal sang it in *What's Up Doc?* Diulio Del Prete and Madeline Kahn presented it in *At*

Long Last Love (1975). And Diana Rigg sang it in the 1982 film, *Evil Under the Sun*. Aptly titled, "You're the Top" is the catalogue song beyond compare, coupling the wittiest of lyrics with music of striking originality.

Moderate rhythm song with two verses (16) and seven refrains (32)
PUBLISHER: Harms, Inc.
KEY: E-flat maj., *STARTS*: a-flat' (B dim.), *FORM*: ABA'C

≈≈≈≈≈≈≈≈≈≈≈≈≈≈≈≈≈≈≈

1935

THE GREAT ESCAPE

1935

And down by the shore an orchestra's playing /
And even the palms seem to be swaying

Cole Porter
"Begin the Beguine"

Escape from reality best describes the songs of this depression year. It is as if songwriters want to reach out to get away from the bleakness of everyday life. And bleak it is for the majority of people; money is in short supply, many banks remain closed, and snow piles up in one of the worst winters on record. But the songs bring some relief from reality. Some of them take us to exotic places; many of them depart from the bounds of convention. This is, after all, the year of America's first opera, *Porgy and Bess,* with a magnificent score by George Gershwin; of songs of unprecedented length, like "Begin the Beguine"; of songs with far-out harmonies, as in "Sophisticated Lady"; and of songs of romance with a European flavor, such as "I Dream Too Much".

In this year of grace, 1935, virtually all the great composers and lyricists are at the peak of their form; Jerome Kern, Oscar Hammerstein II, Irving Berlin, George and Ira Gershwin, Cole Porter, Richard Rodgers, and Lorenz Hart are at their innovative best. But the center of gravity has shifted west, and brought many of the songwriters to Hollywood. Some of their best numbers are introduced in such film musicals as *Top Hat, The Gold Diggers of 1935*, and *The Gay Divorcée.* Audiences go to the movies in droves; after all, they are air conditioned palaces and matinées only cost a quarter. There people can forget their troubles watching the antics of the Marx Brothers in *A Night at the Opera*; or enjoying the singing, mugging, and tap dancing of a seven-year-old named Shirley Temple; or being taken back to eighteenth-century Louisiana in Jeanette MacDonald and Nelson Eddy's classic remake of Victor Herbert's 1910 operetta, *Naughty Marietta.*

But the biggest song hit of the year is less distinguished: "The Music Goes 'Round and Around" blasts forth from millions of radios. Also, on radio are the big band remotes. On any Saturday night, one can listen to broadcasts from hundreds of locations, featuring bands led by Benny Goodman, Glenn Miller, Gene Krupa, Harry James, the Dorsey Brothers (Tommy and Jimmy), and others. Many songs have become standards as a direct result of these repeated hearings by the public.

Although the musical theater does not do as well financially as the movies or radio, it does produce some unforgettable songs, such as "Summertime" (from *Porgy and Bess*") and "Just One of Those Things" (from *Jubilee*). Best-selling books include Sinclair Lewis's *It Can't Happen Here*, Anne Morrow Lindbergh's *North to the Orient*, Vincent Sheehan's *Personal History*, and Clarence Day's *Life with Father.*

Babe Ruth, age 40, finishes his baseball career in typical fashion by hitting three home runs. A new parlor game called Monopoly is introduced by Parker Brothers, with properties named after streets in Atlantic City, New Jersey. It quickly takes the country by storm – another means of escape from harsh reality.

SONGS OF 1935

Begin the Beguine * * * * !
Bess, You Is My Woman Now !
Cheek to Cheek * * * !
East of the Sun (And West of the Moon) *
I Can't Get Started * * * !
I Dream Too Much !
I Got Plenty o' Nuttin' !
I Won't Dance
I'm Gonna Sit Right Down and Write Myself a Letter *
I'm in the Mood for Love * *
Isn't This a Lovely Day (To Be Caught in the Rain?)
It Ain't Necessarily So !
Just One of Those Things * * !
Let's Face the Music and Dance !
Little Girl Blue
Lovely to Look At
Lullaby of Broadway * !
The Most Beautiful Girl in the World !
The Music Goes 'Round and Around
My Man's Gone Now !
My Romance * !
Red Sails in the Sunset *
Summertime * * * * !
Tell Me That You Love Me
These Foolish Things (Remind Me of You)
Top Hat, White Tie and Tails
When I Grow Too Old To Dream
You Are My Lucky Star
Zing! Went the Strings of My Heart

BEGIN THE BEGUINE * * * * !

WORDS and MUSIC: Cole Porter
PREMIERE: Musical comedy, *Jubilee*
New York: Imperial Theatre, 12 October 1935 (169 perf.)
INTRODUCED BY: June Knight, and danced to by her and Charles Walters

While he was living in Paris in the twenties, Cole Porter was very much taken with the rhythm of the beguine, a native dance of people from the island of Martinique who were then living in France. He jotted down "Begin the Beguine" as a good alliterative idea for a song title. Ten years later, while sailing around the world with Moss Hart to put together a new musical, Porter heard a melody played by natives on the island of Kalahabai in the Dutch East Indies. Consolidating the musical idea with the filed-away title, a great song was born. The new musical was *Jubilee*, which despite a lavish production costing an unheard-of $150,000, was not a success, mainly because ticket sales slumped when its star, Mary Boland, returned to Hollywood.

Although two of the songs from the show, "Begin the Beguine" and "Just One of Those Things", became standards, they were slow to catch on. Perhaps this is because they are so unusual that they are better appreciated upon repeated hearings. This is particularly the case with "Begin the Beguine", the lengthiest popular song ever written up to that time. A recording by Xavier Cugat and his Orchestra met with some success. But it was not until 1938 when a new day began for "Begin the Beguine", with the swing recording by Artie Shaw and his Orchestra. This famous Jerry Gray arrangement on Bluebird (B-7746) sold over two million copies; it made Shaw a household name and the song immortal.

Another contributing factor to the song's success was the elaborate dance sequence by Fred Astaire and Eleanor Powell that closes the film, *Broadway Melody of 1940*. Their dancing to the strains of "Begin the Beguine" in various rhythms – flamenco, swing, and tap dance – is a highlight of the film. With sharp contrasts between black and white on a floor of glittering mirrors amid a background of stars, it is one of the most magical dances in cinematic history. Frank Sinatra's recording in 1946 was also a best seller.

Far-removed from most songs of the day, "Begin the Beguine" lacks a verse, has an exotic rhythmic accompaniment, is very long, and is in modified rondo form: AA'BA''CC'. Both words and music conjure up a vision of dancing under the stars in some tropical paradise: the height of romanticism. The melody ebbs and flows, first with simple major harmonies, but later, in the "B" section, with a brief turn to minor and a modulation to A-flat. The highest notes of the song are reached and repeated in the two "C" sections, reaffirming the song's major tonality and bringing it to an emotional climax.

Begin the Beguine" has been featured in several other films besides *Broadway Melody of 1940*, in which it was originally sung by Lois Hodnett and The Music Maids. Deanna Durbin sang it in *Hers to Hold* (1940). Carlos Ramirez and a chorus performed it in the Porter biography, *Night and Day* (1946). Sammy Davis, Jr. did it in the 1988 film, *Moon Over Parador*. One of the most romantic songs ever written, it stands in a class by itself.

Moderate beguine with refrain (108)
PUBLISHER: Harms, Inc.
KEY: C maj., *STARTS*: c' (C maj.), *FORM*: AA'BA"CC'

≈≈≈≈≈≈≈≈≈≈≈≈≈≈≈≈≈≈

BESS, YOU IS MY WOMAN NOW

WORDS: DuBose Heyward, *MUSIC*: George Gershwin
PREMIERE: Opera, *Porgy and Bess*
New York: Alvin Theatre, 10 October 1935 (124 perf.)
INTRODUCED BY: Todd Duncan and Anne Wiggins Brown

Billed as "An American Folk Opera". *Porgy and Bess* brought a new dimension to the American musical theater. Based on DuBose Heyward's novel of 1925 and set in Charleston, South Carolina's Catfish Row, it featured an all-black cast. A tale of stark despair, its tragic theme presented at a time of deep Depression did not attract audiences. However, George Gershwin's beautiful score has made the opera and its magnificent songs part of the American heritage. A highlight of the opera is this emotional duet sung by the two principal characters, Porgy and Bess.

Far removed from the popular canon, "Bess, You Is My Woman Now" is purely an art song. Its centerpiece is the blue note: more specifically the flatted third and flatted seventh, both of which figure prominently throughout. Also notable is the use of modulation: from B-flat major to F-sharp major, and then to D major and beyond. The form is modified rondo, with returns of the three principal themes in several different keys. In the spirit of Catfish Row, the lyrics are in the vernacular, replete with contractions and colloquiums, as in "De real happiness is jes' begun".

"Bess, You Is My Woman Now" was sung by Robert McFerrin (dubbing in for Sidney Poitier) and Adela Addison (for Dorothy Dandridge) in the 1959 film version of *Porgy and Bess*. The opera itself has been revived many times over the years in theaters throughout the world.

This tender duet is one of the most evocative expressions of love in the literature of American song.

Moderate art song with refrain (86)
PUBLISHER: Gershwin Publishing Corporation & Chappell & Co., Inc.
KEYS: B-flat major and D major, **STARTS**: b-flat' (B-flat maj.),
FORM: AA'ABCABC'D

≈≈≈≈≈≈≈≈≈≈≈≈≈≈≈≈≈≈

CHEEK TO CHEEK ✳✳✳!

WORDS and MUSIC: Irving Berlin
PREMIERE: Film musical, *Top Hat*. RKO, 1935
INTRODUCED BY: Fred Astaire, danced to by Fred Astaire and Ginger Rogers

When Irving Berlin went to Hollywood to write the score for a new film, he brought along several songs he had written two years earlier for the revue, *As Thousand Cheer*, but had not used. One of these discards was "Cheek to Cheek" which he is said to have written in a single day. The film, *Top Hat*, was an enormous success sparked by Berlin's remarkable score and by the glorious dancing of Fred Astaire and Ginger Rogers. "Cheek to Cheek" went on to lead a life of its own, first with a No. I Chart Record by Astaire, then with a cover record by Eddy Duchin and his Orchestra, and finally with an Academy Award nomination. To this day, it enjoys a double life as one of the most enduring dance tunes and as a jazz standard.

Lacking a verse, the song is seventy-two bars in length in an unusual form: AABBCA. The opening bars bear a passing resemblance to those of Chopin's "Polonaise in A-Flat". The melody then moves through a charming array of paired notes, first ascending, then descending, with each "A" section consisting of sixteen bars. In contrast, the melody of the two "B" sections outlines the G dominant seventh chord, a total of six times. But the most unusual aspect of the song is the "C" section, also of eight bars which brings still more contrast by means of long notes and the exotic harmonies of C minor and A-flat ninth.

The result is an extraordinary song, which has lasted through the decades, always conjuring up fond memories of Fred and Ginger dressed in their finest and dancing "Cheek to Cheek".

Moderate foxtrot with refrain (72)
PUBLISHER: Irving Berlin, Inc.
KEY: C major, **STARTS**: a' (F major), **FORM**: AABBCA

≈≈≈≈≈≈≈≈≈≈≈≈≈≈≈≈≈≈

EAST OF THE SUN (AND WEST OF THE MOON) *

WORDS and MUSIC: Brooks Bowman
PREMIERE: Princeton University Triangle Club revue, *Stags at Bay,* 1934

This nostalgic ballad was written for the 1934 college production of the revue, *Stags at Bay,* presented by Princeton University's Triangle Club. Brooks Bowman, who wrote both words and music, was offered a Hollywood contract but was killed in an automobile accident on the way to California. Recorded by the orchestras of Tom Coakley, Hal Kemp, and Bob Crosby, "East of the Sun" soon became a hit. Later, helped by the 1941 Bluebird recording by Tommy Dorsey and his Orchestra with vocal by Frank Sinatra, it was elevated to the rank of standard. The prevailing motive in the refrain is the quarter-note triplet of repeated notes leading to varying intervals of the third and fifth. Harmonies tending to sevenths and ninths give the song an ethereal feel, emphasized by poetic lyrics, such as "Living on love and pale moonlight".

Slow ballad with verse (8) and refrain (32)
PUBLISHER: Santly Brothers, Inc.
KEY: G maj., *STARTS*: d' (G maj.), *FORM*: ABAC

≈≈≈≈≈≈≈≈≈≈≈≈≈≈≈≈≈≈≈

I CAN'T GET STARTED * * * !

WORDS: Ira Gershwin, *MUSIC*: Vernon Duke
PREMIERE: Revue, *Ziegfeld Follies of 1936*
New York: Winter Garden Theatre, 30 January 1936 (115 perf.)
INTRODUCED BY: Bob Hope and Eve Arden

The Ziegfeld Follies of 1936 featured a host of talents, including comediennes Fanny Brice, Eve Arden, and Judy Canova; legendary French chanteuse, Josephine Baker; rising young comedian, Bob Hope; and torch singer, Gertrude Niesen. The score was by Ira Gershwin and the Gershwins' friend, Vernon Duke, who wrote classical music under his real name, Vladimir Dukelsky. The hit of the show was a tender love song called "I Can't Get Started". In the show, Hope sang it to Arden, and just as she seemed receptive, he walked away. Duke had written the music several years earlier as "Face the Music with Me", but now, with Gershwin's striking new lyrics, the song came into its own. The first recordings were by Hal Kemp and his Orchestra and by Bunny Berigan and his Orchestra for Vocalion Records. However, it was Bunny Berigan's second recording, for RCA Victor, that made the song famous. Berigan used it as his theme song thereafter, and in 1975 the Victor recording was enshrined in the Recording Academy Hall of Fame.

The lyrics are immediately entrancing, presenting a catalogue of accomplishments from charting the North Pole to selling short in 1929. They are clever and urbane, with such intricate inner rhymes as: "The Astorbilts I visit / But say, what is it with you?" As for the music, the only thing traditional about it is its thirty-two bar AABA form. The melody, outlining major seventh and ninth chords, and the harmonies, with their pungent astringencies, give the song a modern feel. The release is especially interesting, returning to the long note a', each time with a different harmony.

Years after "I Can't Get Started" was written, Gershwin continued to supply it with special lyrics to be used by such singers as Bing Crosby, Frank Sinatra, and Nancy Walker. It remains a jazz classic, beloved by vocalists and instrumentalists alike.

Moderate ballad with verse (16) and two refrains (32)
PUBLISHER: Chappell & Co., Inc.
KEY: C maj., *STARTS*: c' (C maj. 7), *FORM*: AABA

≈≈≈≈≈≈≈≈≈≈≈≈≈≈≈≈≈≈

I DREAM TOO MUCH !

WORDS: Dorothy Fields, *MUSIC*: Jerome Kern
PREMIERE: Film musical, *I Dream Too Much*. RKO, 1935
New York: Radio City Music Hall, 28 November 1935
INTRODUCED BY: Lily Pons

The title song of the RKO film, *I Dream Too Much,* was written expressly for Lily Pons, the diminutive star of the Metropolitan Opera. Also in the movie were Henry Fonda and Lucille Ball. "I Dream Too Much" is an art song with a verse of equal length, and almost equal importance to the refrain. The verse, in fact, is not marked as such in the sheet music. The total effect is that of an especially charming song in the Viennese tradition, with echoes of Franz Léhar. Among the first recordings of the song were those of Pons and Leo Reisman and his Orchestra.

The hallmark of "I Dream Too Much" is chromaticism, both melodic and harmonic. There are also some difficult downward jumps for the singer towards the end: from g" to g-sharp' and from d" to c-sharp'. The verse is most unusual and may be divided into three sections: introduction, modulation, and dominant preparation. At the close of the refrain, a brief reminiscence from the third section of the verse acts as a coda. It is an appealing song, out of the mainstream, and very much in the European tradition.

Moderate waltz with verse (40) and refrain (40)
PUBLISHER: T. B. Harms Company
KEY: F major, *STARTS*: a' (B-flat maj.), *FORM*: ABA'B'

≈≈≈≈≈≈≈≈≈≈≈≈≈≈≈≈≈≈

I GOT PLENTY O' NUTTIN'

WORDS: Ira Gershwin and DuBose Heyward, *MUSIC*: George Gershwin
PREMIERE: Opera, *Porgy and Bess*
New York: Alvin Theatre, 10 October 1935 (124 perf.)
INTRODUCED BY: Todd Duncan

Ira Gershwin collaborated with DuBose Heyward in writing these evocative lyrics, sung by Porgy in Act Two, Scene One of *Porgy and Bess*. It is said that the cheerful melody came to George Gershwin while he was improvising at the piano. Ira said "That's it!," and came up with both the title and its natural following line: "And nuttin's plenty for me". He also improved tremendously on DuBose Heyward's first draft. "I Got Plenty o' Nuttin'" did not immediately catch on with the public. But its carefree melody and saucy lyrics gained it popularity over the years. One of its first recordings was by Leo Reisman and his Orchestra.

I Got Plenty o' Nuttin'" is more complex than first meets the eye. Although it is constructed in AABA form, each section is of a different length: respectively nine bars, eleven bars, ten bars, and sixteen bars. Like most songs in the opera, the emphasis is on the blue note, in this case e-sharp', held for six beats in each of the "A" sections. Harmonic contrast is offered in the release, which starts in B minor and then modulates, with a marked crescendo, to the dominant seventh of G major. As for the lyrics, depression-era audiences could well empathize with such thoughts as "I got no car, I got no mule, I got no misery". Perhaps that expression was a form of sour grapes.

In films, the song was heard on the soundtrack of the Gershwin biography, *Rhapsody in Blue* (1945). In the 1959 screen version of *Porgy and Bess*, it was sung by Robert McFerrin, dubbing in for Sidney Poitier.

Moderate art song with refrain (46)
PUBLISHER: Gershwin Publishing Corporation and Chappell & Co., Inc.
KEY: Gmaj., *STARTS*: d' (G maj.), *FORM*: AA'BA"

≈≈≈≈≈≈≈≈≈≈≈≈≈≈≈≈≈≈

I WON'T DANCE * !

WORDS: Otto Harbach and Oscar Hammerstein II, *MUSIC*: Jerome Kern
PREMIERES: Musical Comedy, *Three Sisters*
London: Drury Lane Theatre, 19 April 1934
INTRODUCED BY: Adele Dixon and Richard Dalman
Film musical, *Roberta*. RKO, 1935
INTRODUCED BY: Fred Astaire and Ginger Rogers

One of Jerome Kern's most sparkling songs, the music of "I Won't Dance" was originally heard, with lyrics by Otto Harbach and Oscar Hammerstein II, in the London production, *Three Sisters*, introduced by Adele Dixon and Richard Dalman. The musical comedy, which opened at the Drury Lane Theatre 19 April 1934, was a dismal flop. But as it happened, Fred Astaire was in London at the time, heard "I Won't Dance", and suggested to RKO that it be used in their forthcoming screen version of *Roberta*. And so it was, with revised lyrics by Dorothy Fields. (In some editions, the lyrics are credited to as many as four individuals: Harbach, Hammerstein, Dorothy Fields, and her ex-partner Jimmy McHugh, but the music is always singularly Jerome Kern's.) Early recordings of "I Won't Dance" were by Eddy Duchin and his Orchestra (No. 1 on the charts) and George Hall and his Orchestra.

The verse is tuneful in itself, and ends with a verbalized vamp: "Not this season! There's a reason!" It leads into the refrain of sixty bars in AA'BA" form, with the first section twelve bars in length, while the others are each sixteen bars long. The principal theme is ordinary enough, with its frequent repeated notes at the words "I Won't Dance!". But it is the release that is most extraordinary. In fact, it is one of the most unusual releases in the literature, along with that of "Have You Met Miss Jones?" (1937). Starting in A-flat major, the harmonies move to D-flat major, and then enharmonically to B major and E seventh, before modulating, in Kern's incomparable way, back to the tonic of C major. The lyrics are delightful, with some charming rhymes, as in "For heaven rest us, I'm not asbestos".

In other films, Van Johnson and Lucille Bremer sang "I Won't Dance" in the Kern biography, *Till the Clouds Roll By* (1946). Marge and Gower Champion danced to its strains in *Lovely to Look At*, the 1952 remake of *Roberta*.

Moderate rhythm song with verse (16) and refrain (60)
PUBLISHER: T. B. Harms Company
KEY: C maj., *STARTS*: g' (C maj.), *FORM*: AA'BA"

≈≈≈≈≈≈≈≈≈≈≈≈≈≈≈≈≈≈≈≈≈

I'M GONNA SIT RIGHT DOWN AND WRITE MYSELF A LETTER *

WORDS: Joe Young, *MUSIC*: Fred E. Ahlert

This perky jump tune has long been associated with Thomas "Fats" Waller, who did much to popularize it with his Victor recording, as did The Boswell Sisters on Decca. It was revived in 1957 with a Coral record by Billy Williams. The song was also sung by Ken Page in the Waller retrospective, *Ain't Misbehavin'*, which opened at the Longacre Theatre in New York 9 May 1978. The very concept of writing oneself a letter has a lot to do with the popularity of the song. The lyrics carry it out with finesse, putting "kisses on the bottom" and "closing 'with love' the way you do". With simple harmonies and a melody primarily of quarter notes. The song cries out for improvisation, and it is indeed a jazz standard.

Moderate rhythm song with verse (16) and refrain (32)
PUBLISHER: Fred Ahlert Music Corp.
KEY: C maj., *STARTS*: f-sharp' (C maj.), *FORM*: ABAC

≈≈≈≈≈≈≈≈≈≈≈≈≈≈≈≈≈≈

I'M IN THE MOOD FOR LOVE * *

WORDS and MUSIC: Jimmy McHugh and Dorothy Fields
PREMIERE: Film musical, *Every Night at Eight*. Twentieth Century Fox, 1935
INTRODUCED BY: Frances Langford

The film musical, *Every Night at Eight*, featured George Raft as an orchestra leader and Alice Faye, Patsy Kelly, and Frances Langford as a vocal trio which performed every night at eight with his orchestra. Sung solo by a sultry Langford in the movie, this song immediately caught on with the public. The recording by Little Jack Little and his Orchestra was a No. 1 Chart Record. Other important recordings were those of Louis Armstrong and, in 1946, Billy Eckstine.

The song's chief attribute is its title, which is of course an attention getter. Otherwise, it is very traditional: thirty-two bars in AABA form, with simple harmonies and a mostly stepwise melodic line. The underlying rhythmical motive is the quarter-note triplet, repeated fifteen times in the course of the refrain.

True to its Hollywood point of origin, "I'm In the Mood for Love" has been featured in a host of films. Langford sang it in two additional films: *Palm Springs* in 1936 and *People Are Funny* in 1946. Gloria De Haven performed it in *Between Two Women* (1944). In 1950, Lizabeth Scott sang it in *Dark City,* and in 1951, Dean Martin crooned it in *That's My Boy.* Shirley Booth put it over in *About Miss Leslie* (1954) and in 1959, a chorus sang it in *Ask Any Girl.*

Moderate ballad with verse (16) and refrain (32)
PUBLISHER: Robbins Music Corporation
KEY: C maj., *STARTS*: e' (C maj.), *FORM*: AABA

≈≈≈≈≈≈≈≈≈≈≈≈≈≈≈≈≈≈

ISN'T THIS A LOVELY DAY (TO BE CAUGHT IN THE RAIN?)

WORDS and MUSIC: Irving Berlin
PREMIERE: Film musical, *Top Hat*. RKO, 1935
INTRODUCED BY: Fred Astaire; danced to by Astaire and Ginger Rogers

In the film classic, *Top Hat*, Fred Astaire sings this nonchalant ballad to Ginger Rogers while they are waiting out a sudden downpour in a gazebo. It was one of the songs that Irving Berlin had taken with him from New York when he was asked to do the score for the movie. It is said that Astaire fooled Berlin into thinking he had unwittingly plagiarized the song but soon admitted that he was only joking. Astaire recorded it for Brunswick, and Phil Ohman and his Orchestra also had a record. The refrain, in ABA'C/A form, has a graceful melody in dotted rhythm, beginning, unusually, on the subdominant. The "B" section has many repeated notes, while the "C" section descends the scale in delicate duplets to the words: "Let the rain pitter-patter, for it really doesn't matter".

Moderate ballad with verse (18) and refrain (32)
PUBLISHER: Irving Berlin, Inc.
KEY: F maj., *STARTS*: d' (B-flat 6), *FORM*: ABA'C/A

≈≈≈≈≈≈≈≈≈≈≈≈≈≈≈≈≈≈

IT AIN'T NECESSARILY SO !

WORDS: Ira Gershwin, *MUSIC*: George Gershwin
PREMIERE: Opera, *Porgy and Bess*
New York: Alvin Theatre, 10 October1935 (124 perf.)
INTRODUCED BY: John W. Bubbles

When the character, Sportin' Life, sings his big number in *Porgy and Bess*, this most unusual song resembles a preacher's sermon, complete with responses by the congregation and a little scat singing – on the order of "Wa-doo, Zim bam boddle-oo" – thrown in. The thrust of the song, of course, is that even if something is written down in the Bible, "it ain't necessarily so". In the original production, John W. Bubbles introduced it. Early recordings were by Paul Robeson and Lawrence Tibbett.

Blue notes abound, especially flatted sevenths and fifths, and minor thirds. There are a number of contradictions about the song. Although it was written as a scherzo and marked "Happily, with humor", it is solidly in a minor key. Although in a minor key throughout, it ends in G major. Although its subject, the Bible, is serious enough, nonsense syllables abound. Its dirge-like melody is accompanied by the most sophisticated of harmonies. Its 4/4 rhythm is counterpoised against a melodic line of quarter note triplets. Its simple rondo form is interrupted by frequent changes of tempo and meter.

"It Ain't Necessarily So" was heard on the soundtrack of the Gershwin biographical film, *Rhapsody in Blue*. Sammy Davis, Jr. and a chorus, gave it their own interpretation in the 1959 film of *Porgy and Bess*. It is still a show-stopper whenever it is performed.

Moderate art song with refrain (86)
PUBLISHER: Gershwin Publishing Corporation and Chappell & Co., Inc.
KEY: G min., *STARTS*: d' (G min.), *FORM*: ABABACAD

≈≈≈≈≈≈≈≈≈≈≈≈≈≈≈≈≈≈

JUST ONE OF THOSE THINGS ＊＊！

WORDS and MUSIC: Cole Porter
PREMIERE: Musical comedy, *Jubilee*
New York: Imperial Theatre, 12 October 1935 (169 perf.)
INTRODUCED BY: June Knight and Charles Walters

Even in this year of inventive songs, "Just One of Those Things stands out in its originality. It is said that Cole Porter wrote this extraordinary song in one day, while he was vacationing in the Ohio country side with Moss Hart, the author of *Jubilee*. It was sung in the show by June Knight (playing an American dancer) and Charles Walters (playing the Prince of a royal family). The song was slow to gain in popularity, helped by a recording by Richard Himber and his Orchestra. In 1952, Peggy Lee had a hit recording, but the most popular recording of all was by Frank Sinatra, in 1955.

"Just One of those Things" is full of surprises. In the verse, the clever lyrics catalogue various ways of saying good-bye, referring to Columbus, Abelard and Eloise, and Romeo and Juliet – not to mention Dorothy

Parker. The lengthy refrain contains marvelous chromatic harmonies, and moves freely between the tonalities of D minor (in which each "A" section begins) and F major (in which it ends). Starting with two held notes (fermatas) on the words "It was...", it is given a lilting character by its accented fourth beats. The release begins in E-flat major and ends in C major. But the most ingratiating aspect of the song are the world-weary lyr-ics, saying, for example, that the duo's love affair "was too hot not to cool down".

As befits a world-class standard, "Just One of Those Things" has been featured in a host of films. Lena Horne sang it in *Panama Hattie* (1942), and Ginny Simms in the 1946 Porter biographical film, *Night and Day*. Doris Day did it in *Lullaby of Broadway* (1951), Peggy Lee in *The Jazz Singer* (1953), and Sinatra in *Young At Heart* (1955). In 1956, it was featured in *The Eddy Duchin Story*. Maurice Chevalier sang it in the 1960 film, *Can-Can*, and Duilio Del Prete, Cybill Shepherd, and Burt Reynolds performed it in *At Long Last Love* (1975). Combining witty words with sparkling music, this marvelous song attains the heights of urban sophistication.

Moderate foxtrot with verse (32) and refrain (64)
PUBLISHER: Harms, Inc.
KEY: F maj., *STARTS*: b-flat' (D min.), *FORM*: AABA'

≈≈≈≈≈≈≈≈≈≈≈≈≈≈≈≈≈≈≈≈

LET'S FACE THE MUSIC AND DANCE !

WORDS and MUSIC: Irving Berlin
PREMIERE: Film musical, *Follow the Fleet*. RKO, 1936
INTRODUCED BY: Fred Astaire, danced to by Fred Astaire and Ginger Rogers

One of Irving Berlin's most innovative numbers, "Let's Face the Music and Dance" was custom-made by Irving Berlin as a production number for Fred Astaire and Ginger Rogers in the film, *Follow the Fleet*. It was popularized in recordings by Astaire, Ray Noble and his Orchestra, and Ted Fiorito and his Orchestra. The song is distinctly unconventional in its lack of a verse, its length (sixty-six bars), and its free movement between major and minor tonality. Although the form seems conventional enough – AA'BA" – each section is of a different length: respectively 14, 16, 8, and 18 bars. Harmonies are also out of the ordinary, moving to G major in the second section and A-flat major in the third. Each "A" section starts in C minor and ends in C major. There is a clamorous ending at the words

"Let's Face the Music", to the repeated notes e" at the song's highest point. Astaire repeated his success with the song in the 1981 film, *Pennies from Heaven*.

Moderate foxtrot with refrain (66)
PUBLISHER: Irving Berlin, Inc.
KEY: C maj., *STARTS*: c' (C min.), *FORM*: AA'BA"

≈≈≈≈≈≈≈≈≈≈≈≈≈≈≈≈≈≈

LITTLE GIRL BLUE !

WORDS: Lorenz Hart, *MUSIC*: Richard Rodgers
PREMIERE: Musical extravaganza, *Jumbo*
New York: Hippodrome Theatre, 16 November 1935 (233 perf.)
INTRODUCED BY: Gloria Grafton

Billy Rose's extravaganza, *Jumbo,* was a much-ballyhooed production, revolving about a circus and starring Jimmy Durante and Paul Whiteman and his Orchestra. In the finale of Act I, a circus-owner's daughter, Mickey (played by Gloria Grafton), dreams that she is a child again, and sings this winsome ballad. Cabaret singer Mabel Mercer popularized it on the nightclub circuit and recorded it for Atlantic.

Richard Rodgers's melody is child-like in its simplicity, mostly cavorting up and down the major scale, but with occasional upward skips of the sixth, fifth, and fourth. The refrain is in three parts, AAB/A, with the last section telescoping the release into the final "A" section. Lorenz Hart's lyrics are also child-like, but with some marvelous inner rhymes in the last section: "surrender", "slender, "send a", and "tender". A dreamy trio in waltz time brings a reminiscence of the circus as it was in bygone days. It ends with repeated notes at the words "Gone are the tinsel and gold". Doris Day sang "Little Girl Blue" in the screen version of the show, *Billy Rose's Jumbo* (1952).

Moderate ballad with refrain (36) and trio (24)
PUBLISHER: T. B. Harms Company
KEY: F maj., *STARTS*: f' (F 6), *FORM*: AAB/A

≈≈≈≈≈≈≈≈≈≈≈≈≈≈≈≈≈≈

LOVELY TO LOOK AT

WORDS: Dorothy Fields and Jimmy McHugh, *MUSIC*: Jerome Kern
PREMIERE: Film musical, *Roberta*. RKO, 1935
INTRODUCED BY: Irene Dunne, and reprised by Fred Astaire, Ginger
Rogers and a chorus

A lilting little ballad, "Lovely to Look At" did not appear in the original Broadway production of *Roberta* in 1933. Just as "I Won't Dance", it was written specifically for the movie version of 1935. Written for a fashion show scene, it is said that when studio executives first heard the song, they pronounced the sixteen-bar refrain too short. However, when Kern responded, "That's all I had to say!", they decided to keep it as it was. The song was nominated for an Academy Award. Eddy Duchin and his Orchestra had a No. 1 Chart record; it was also recorded by Leo Reisman and his Orchestra. The two verses are very melodious; they include an *a cappella* section and a modulation to and from G-flat major. The graceful melody of the short refrain, in ABAB' form, contrasts light syncopation in the "A" sections with dotted notes and triplets in the "B" sections. In 1952, a new screen version of *Roberta* was mounted under the title, *Lovely to Look At*; in it, Howard Keel sang this lovely ballad.

Moderate ballad with two verses (12) and refrain (16)
PUBLISHER: T. B. Harms Company
KEY: E-flat maj., *STARTS*: e-flat' (E-flat maj.), *FORM*: ABAB'

≋≋≋≋≋≋≋≋≋≋≋≋≋≋≋≋≋

LULLABY OF BROADWAY *

WORDS: Al Dubin, *MUSIC*: Harry Warren
PREMIERE: Film musical, *Gold Diggers of Broadway*. Warner Brothers 1935
INTRODUCED BY: Dick Powell, Wini Shaw, and a chorus

The film, *Gold Diggers of 1935* saw renowned choreographer Busby Berkeley at the very peak of his career. The elaborate dance sequence centered around "Lullaby of Broadway" was his own personal favorite. The production number begins with Wini Shaw's face as a minuscule white spot on a black screen, which gradually grows larger and larger; its climax is a frenetic exhibition of precision dancing by a chorus of over a hundred men and women; and its ending shows Shaw's face receding into the black background. The song won the Academy Award for Best Song of 1935. It was recorded by The Dorsey Brothers Orchestra and by Hal Kemp and his Orchestra and reached the No. 1 spot on *Your Hit Parade*. Forty-five years later, Jerry Orbach and a chorus performed it in the Broadway production, *42nd Street.*

The lyrics tell the sad tale of the last day and night of a "Broadway baby" before she is accidentally pushed out of a window. The music, in rondo form (ABACA'C'), is a study in contrast, The "A" theme, in E-flat major, is riff-like, with many repeated and syncopated notes in swing style. The "B" section carries the same theme a fourth higher, in the key of A-flat major. After a short return to the "A" section, the lullaby part appears. It consists of a broad new theme in the key of A-flat major, made up almost entirely of whole notes. The lengthy (72-bar) number concludes with returns to both "A" and "C", followed by a powerful coda.

"Lullaby of Broadway" was featured in three other films besides *Gold Diggers of Broadway.* Evelyn Keyes sang it in *The Jolson Story* (1946); Doris Day in *Young Man with a Horn* (1950); and Doris Day, Gene Nelson, and a chorus in the 1951 namesake movie, *Lullaby of Broadway.*

Moderate rhythm song with refrain (72)
KEY: E-flat maj., *STARTS*: g' (E-flat maj.), *FORM*: ABACA'C'

≈≈≈≈≈≈≈≈≈≈≈≈≈≈≈≈≈≈

THE MOST BEAUTIFUL GIRL IN THE WORLD !

WORDS: Lorenz Hart, *MUSIC*: Richard Rodgers
PREMIERE: Musical extravaganza, *Jumbo*
New York: Hippodrome Theatre, 16 November 1935 (233 perf.)
INTRODUCED BY: Donald Novis and Gloria Grafton

This swinging waltz is another enchanting number from Billy Rose's circus extravaganza, *Jumbo*. Society bandleader, Ted Straeter, used it as his theme. It illustrates Richard Rodgers's propensity for writing American-style waltzes in the Viennese tradition. Equally, it shows Lorenz Hart's captivating way with rhyme: pairing "Dietrich" with "sweet trick", "anywhere" with "platinum hair", and "candy" with "brandy". The lengthy verse is in C major, while the even lengthier refrain is in F major. The melody of the refrain rambles up and down stepwise in repeated groups of three notes; it moves upward to e-flat" in the second and fourth sections and closes with a sprightly eight-bar coda, in which the song reaches its highest point on f". In the 1962 movie version entitled *Billy Rose's Jumbo*, it was sung by Stephen Boyd and reprised by Jimmy Durante.

Moderate waltz with verse (52) and refrain (72)
PUBLISHER: T. B. Harms Company
KEY: F maj., *STARTS*: c' (F maj.), *FORM*: AA'BA"

≈≈≈≈≈≈≈≈≈≈≈≈≈≈≈≈≈≈

THE MUSIC GOES 'ROUND AND AROUND

WORDS: Red Hodgson, *MUSIC*: Ed Farley and Mike Riley
INTRODUCED BY: Riley and Farley and Their Band

The nonsense song of the year, and its biggest seller of sheet music, was this derivative little ditty. It was introduced at New York's Onyx Club on West 52nd Street by its composers, Ed Farley and Mike Riley and their band; their Decca record reached. No. 1 on the charts. Among a multitude of other recordings were those of Tommy Dorsey and his Clambake Seven, Louis Armstrong, and Hal Kemp and his Orchestra. According to Sigmund Spaeth, in his 1948 book, *A History of Popular Music in America*, the music owes allegiance to two works by Gilbert and Sullivan: "If You Want to Know Who We Are", from *The Mikado*; and "I Am the Monarch of the Sea", from *Pinafore*; as well as to an American folk song called "The Fireship".

The silly lyrics, including nonsense syllables, describe how music originates in a three-valve sax horn, goes "'round and around", and comes out at the bell. The melody consists of a proliferation of repeated notes. Harmonies are mostly the tonic and dominant of C major except for a diversion to A minor in the release.

The song caught on like wildfire. It was featured in two films of 1936; sung by Riley and Farley in the similar-titled *The Music Goes Around*, and by The Ritz Brothers in *Sing, Baby, Sing*. It also was heard in *Trocadero* (1944) and *Holiday in Mexico* (1946), and Danny Kaye and Susan Gordon sang it in the 1959 Red Nichols biographical film, *The Five Pennies*.

Moderate novelty song with verse (8) and refrain (32)
PUBLISHER: Select Music Publications, Inc., assigned to Santly-Joy, Inc.
KEY: C maj., *STARTS*: g' (C maj.), *FORM*: AABA

≈≈≈≈≈≈≈≈≈≈≈≈≈≈≈≈≈≈

MY MAN'S GONE NOW

WORDS: DuBose Heyward, *MUSIC*: George Gershwin
PREMIERE: Opera, *Porgy and Bess*
New York: Alvin Theatre, 10 October 1935 (124 perf.)
INTRODUCED BY: Ruby Elzy and a chorus

This haunting aria is one of the most evocative numbers in the opera, *Porgy and Bess*. Although it is in 3/4 meter throughout, it is not a waltz; indeed, most of the normally-accented first beats characteristic of the waltz are here divided into eighth notes. In the opera, it is a dirge sung by Serena, lamenting the passing of her man. The form is unusual, AABB'AC, with each section of a different length. In the key of D minor, there is much melodic and harmonic chromaticism, especially in the "B" sections, which begin with A-flat ninth chords. Harmonies are pungent, with a plethora of major and minor sevenths, ninths, elevenths, and thirteenths. Textural contrast is offered by alternations between soloist and chorus. The aria ends with a wailing upward *glissando* sung by Serena and the chorus, accompanied by a downward chromatic progression of sixth chords. In the 1959 film version of *Porgy and Bess*, "My Man's Gone Now" was sung by Inez Matthews, dubbing for Ruth Attaway, and a chorus. It is arguably one of the most vivid representations of sorrow in the literature.

Moderate art song with refrain (89)
PUBLISHER: Gershwin Publishing Corporation and Chappell & Co., Inc.
KEY: D min., *STARTS*: d" (D min. 7), *FORM*: AABB'AC

≈≈≈≈≈≈≈≈≈≈≈≈≈≈≈≈≈≈

MY ROMANCE !

WORDS: Lorenz Hart, *MUSIC*: Richard Rodgers
PREMIERE: Musical extravaganza, *Jumbo*
New York: Hippodrome Theatre, 16 November 1935 (233 perf.)
INTRODUCED BY: Donald Novis and Gloria Grafton

One of Richard Rodgers and Lorenz Hart's loveliest ballads, "My Romance", is fittingly also one of their most romantic. It is another fine song that emanated from the score of Billy Rose's circus extravaganza, *Jumbo*. Donald Novis, who introduced the song with Gloria Grafton, recorded it for Victor, with Paul Whiteman and his Orchestra. There have been myriad recordings over the years, by performers ranging from singer Morton Downey to pianist Dave Brubeck. Hart's lyrics are enchanting, cataloguing a list of ingredients not needed for this romance: a moon, a blue lagoon, twinkling stars, soft guitars, or "a castle rising in Spain"; all that is necessary is the love object. Rodgers's music is particularly beautiful. The melodic line alternates stepwise movement in the "A" and "C" sections with plaintive downward skips in the "B" section. The refrain ends with repeated notes at its highest point, at the words, "I can make my most fantastic dreams come true". Doris Day sang this tender song in the

1962 film version of the show entitled Billy Rose's *Jumbo*. It is a long-time favorite of cabaret performers.

> Moderate ballad with verse (12) and refrain (32)
> *PUBLISHER*: T. B. Harms Company
> *KEY*: C maj. or D-flat maj., *STARTS*: e' (C maj.) or f' (D-flat maj.),
> *FORM*: A A'BA"

≈≈≈≈≈≈≈≈≈≈≈≈≈≈≈≈≈

RED SAILS IN THE SUNSET *

> *WORDS*: Jimmy Kennedy, *MUSIC*: Hugh Williams (pseud. for Will Grosz)
> *PREMIERE*: Revue, *The Provincetown Follies*
> New York (Greenwich Village): The Provincetown Playhouse, 3 November 1935 (63 perf.)
> *INTRODUCED BY:* Phyllis Austin

An English import, "Red Sails in the Sunset" was brought to American audiences in a British-style revue presented at the Provincetown Playhouse in Greenwich Village, New York. Popularized by Bing Crosby in a Decca record that reached No. 1 on the charts, it quickly took the country by storm. Popular recordings were also made by Ray Noble and his Orchestra and Guy Lombardo and his Royal Canadians, among a host of others. The song was revived in 1951, with a recording by Nat "King" Cole. Lyrics verge on the sentimental: "Oh! carry my loved one / Home safely to me". The simple melody of the refrain is eminently easy to remember, consisting of quarter-note triplets moving downward in sequence. Dean Martin sang the ballad in the 1966 film, *The Silencers*.

> Slow ballad with verse (8) and refrain (32)
> *PUBLISHER*: The Peter Maurice Music, Ltd. (London), assigned to Shapiro, Bernstein & Co., Inc. (New York)
> *KEY*: G maj., *STARTS*: b' (G maj.), *FORM*: AABA

≈≈≈≈≈≈≈≈≈≈≈≈≈≈≈≈≈

SUMMERTIME * * * * !

> *WORDS*: DuBose Heyward, *MUSIC*: George Gershwin
> *PREMIERE*: Opera, *Porgy and Bess*
> New York: Alvin Theatre, 10 October 1935 (124 perf.)
> Introduced by Abbie Mitchell

In the opera, *Porgy and Bess*, a young mother sings this haunting lullaby to the baby in her arms. George Gershwin had tried to fit a number of melodies to DuBose Heyward's lyrics. He finally settled on this one while he was working at the apartment of socialite Kay Halle in the Elysée Hotel in New York City. It soon became the best known song from the opera and has remained so through the decades. Billie Holiday had the first popular record on Vocalion. Bob Crosby used it as his orchestra's theme song. Among other recordings over the years were those of Sam Cooke (1951), Rick Nelson (1962), Billy Stewart (1966), and The Marcels (1971).

Heyward's expressive lyrics contribute to the song's success, with evocative lines such as "Fish are jumpin', an' the cotton is high". But it is Gershwin's seemingly simple music that captivates, transcending a lullaby into an art song. Consisting of two identical sixteen-bar sections, the introduction, accompaniment figures, and coda expand the length of the piece to forty-six bars. In the key of A minor, the melody exploits the intervals of the minor third and fourth. Harmonies are rich and chromatic. Most effective in the accompaniment is the countermelody on the notes f-sharp and g-sharp, in varying octaves.

Anne Brown sang "Summertime" in the 1945 Gershwin biographical film, *Rhapsody in Blue*. Loulie Jean Norman dubbed it in for Diahann Carroll, singing with a chorus in the 1959 film version of *Porgy and Bess*.

Moderate art song with refrain (46)
PUBLISHER: Gershwin Publishing Corporation and Chappell & Co., Inc.
KEY: A. min., *STARTS*: e'' (A min. 6), *FORM*: AA

≈≈≈≈≈≈≈≈≈≈≈≈≈≈≈≈≈≈

TELL ME THAT YOU LOVE ME

WORDS: Al Silverman, *MUSIC*: Cesare A. Bixio
PREMIERE: Stage production, *Lonely Hearts*
New York: Radio City Music Hall, 1935

One of the most famous European songs, "Parlami d'Amore Mariu", with music by Cesare A. Bixio and Italian lyrics by Ennio Neri, was long a favorite of Italian tenors. Given English words by Al Silverman in 1935, it was brought to the United States as "Tell Me That You Love Me", advertised as "The Sensational European Waltz Success". Popularized on radio by tenor Frank Parker (The Jello Program), and recorded by soprano Lily Pons and Freddy Martin and his Orchestra, it became a hit. Both verse and refrain are of equal importance – in fact, they are of the same length. In the verse, in F minor, the melody outlines the underlying harmonies. In the refrain, in F major, the beautiful, cantabile melody moves mostly stepwise.

> Slow waltz with verse (32) and refrain (32)
> *PUBLISHER:* T. B. Harms Co.
> *KEY:* F maj., *STARTS:* c" (G min. 7), *FORM:* ABAB'

≈≈≈≈≈≈≈≈≈≈≈≈≈≈≈≈≈≈≈

THESE FOOLISH THINGS (REMIND ME OF YOU)

WORDS: Holt Marvell (pseud. for Erich Maschwitz)
MUSIC: Jack Strachey and Harry Link

A product of Britain, this nostalgic ballad was written by two established English songwriters, lyricist Erich Maschwitz and composer Jack Strachey, in collaboration with American publisher Harry Link. Introduced in 1936 in William Walker's London revue, *Spread It Abroad*, the audience's favorable reactions to the song soon indeed "spread it abroad" to America, to become one of the most popular ballads of the thirties and forties. Benny Goodman and his Orchestra had a hit Victor recording, with vocal by Helen Ward. Among many subsequent recordings over the years were those of Billy Holiday, with Teddy Wilson at the piano; Gene Krupa and his Orchestra; Lester Young; and The Benny Goodman Sextet.

The lyrics are typical of a catalogue song, effectively listing all sorts of lovable characteristics in its three refrains, including in the first two stanzas the famous lines: "a cigarette that bears a lipstick's traces" and "a tinkling piano in the next apartment". The music of the verse has a romantic quality, as does that of the refrain's release. The main theme, on the other hand, is rather pedestrian, consisting largely of dotted eighths and sixteenths, followed by quarter-note triplets underlining the words of the title.

Helping to keep the song alive during the forties was its presence in several films: *A Yank in the R.A.F.*, starring Tyrone Power and Betty Grable (1941); *Ghost Catchers*, starring Olsen and Johnson and Gloria Jean (1944); and *Tokyo Rose*, starring Humphrey Bogart (1949).

Slow Ballad with verse (2) and three refrains (32)
PUBLISHER: Boosey and Co., Ltd. (London), assigned to Irving Berlin, Inc.
KEY: E-flat maj., *STARTS*: e-flat' (E-flat maj.), *FORM*: AA'BA'

≈≈≈≈≈≈≈≈≈≈≈≈≈≈≈≈≈≈≈

TOP HAT, WHITE TIE AND TAILS

WORDS and MUSIC: Irving Berlin
PREMIERE: Film musical, *Top Hat*. RKO, 1935
INTRODUCED BY: Fred Astaire

Always bringing to mind the debonair singer and dancer, Fred Astaire, this delightful song exudes urban sophistication. Astaire recorded it on Brunswick, with other recordings by The Boswell Sisters and The Dorsey Brothers Orchestra. The form of the refrain is conventional enough, AABA, but the usual eight-bar release is here extended to ten bars, bringing the refrain's total length to thirty-four bars. While the "A" sections are ordinary, contrasting the long-held note on "I'm" with short, dotted notes, the release is most unusual. In the key of E minor, it consists of two heavily-syncopated five-bar phrases. The song is inescapably associated with the image of Astaire in the film putting on his top hat, white tie, and tails in preparation for a night on the town with Ginger Rogers.

Moderate rhythm song with verse (16) and refrain (34)
PUBLISHER: Irving Berlin, Inc.
KEY: C maj., *STARTS*: e' (C maj.), *FORM*: AABA

≈≈≈≈≈≈≈≈≈≈≈≈≈≈≈≈≈≈

WHEN I GROW TOO OLD TO DREAM

WORDS: Oscar Hammerstein II, *MUSIC*: Sigmund Romberg
PREMIERE: Film musical, *The Night Is Young*. Metro Goldwyn Mayer, 1935
INTRODUCED BY: Ramon Novarro and Evelyn Laye

This sentimental waltz is the only survivor from an uninspired movie, *The Night is Young*, which all but ended the careers of its two stars, Ramon Novarro and Evelyn Laye. The song was widely recorded by such singers as Irene Dunne, Nelson Eddy, and Allan Jones. Nat "King" Cole revived it with a Capitol record in 1951. The most interesting aspect of the waltz is its form, ABCB, repeating the second section rather than the first. Lyrics and music suffer from an excess of sweetness. The stepwise melody moves laboriously along in the dactyl rhythm of half-note-quarter note.

Slow waltz with two verses (16) and refrain (32)
PUBLISHER: Robbins Music Corporation
KEY: F maj., *STARTS*: f' (F maj.), *FORM*: ABCB

≈≈≈≈≈≈≈≈≈≈≈≈≈≈≈≈≈≈

YOU ARE MY LUCKY STAR

WORDS: Arthur Freed, *MUSIC*: Nacio Herb Brown
PREMIERE: Film, *Riffraff*. Metro Goldwyn Mayer, 1935
INTRODUCED BY: Jean Harlow and a chorus

This product of Hollywood tunesmiths Arthur Freed and Nacio Herb Brown was written for a melodrama about tuna fishing called *Riffraff*, starring Jean Harlow, Spencer Tracy, and Mickey Rooney; June Harlow sang it in that movie. But the song attained its true popularity a year later, when it was interpolated in the MGM film musical, *Broadway Melody of 1936*, a sequel to *The Broadway Melody* of 1929. Sung in the 1936 *Gold Diggers* by the triumvirate of Eleanor Powell, Frances Langford, and Harry Stockwell, it later appeared in five other movies. Recordings were made by The Dorsey Brothers Orchestra, vocal by Bob Eberly; Eddy Duchin and his Orchestra; and many others.

The lyrics offer a catalogue of lucky stars of the day: "You are my Shearer, Crawford, Hepburn, Harlow and my Garbo". The melody of the refrain is interesting in its exploitation of the octave, taking a cue from Franz Liszt in his famous *Hungarian Rhapsody No. 2*. Written in ABAC/A form, there are seven octave jumps in each "A" section. The "B" and "C" sections, in contrast, are in the lightly-syncopated style of jazz. The refrain ends with a brief return of the main theme that manages to include four octave jumps.

Among the many films besides *Riffraff* and *Broadway Melody of 1936* that feature "You Are My Lucky Star" are *Babes in Arms* (1939, sung by Betty Jaynes), *Born to Sing* (1942), *The Stratton* Story (1949), *Three Little Words* (1950, sung by Phil Regan), *Singin' in the Rain* (1952, sung by Debbie Reynolds and Gene Kelly), *The Boy Friend* (1971, sung by Twiggy), and *New York, New York* (1977, sung by Liza Minnelli).

Moderate ballad with verse (16) and two refrains (32)
PUBLISHER: Metro-Goldwyn-Mayer Corp., assigned to Robbins Music Corp.
KEY: F maj., *STARTS*: c" (F maj.), *FORM*: ABAC/A

≈≈≈≈≈≈≈≈≈≈≈≈≈≈≈≈≈≈

ZING! WENT THE STRINGS OF MY HEART * *

WORDS and MUSIC: James F. Hanley
PREMIERE: Revue, *Thumbs Up!*
New York: St. James Theatre, 27 December 1934 (156 perf.)
INTRODUCED BY: Hal Le Roy and Eunice Healey

This perky standard originated in the revue, *Thumbs Up!*, which also brought forth Vernon Duke's "Autumn in New York". It was the last hit song from the pen of James F. Hanley, whose credits go back to World War I. Judy Garland used it in her successful audition for MGM; she also recorded it for Decca, with Victor Young and his Orchestra. The song differs from the ordinary in the length of its refrain, which consists of three sixteen-bar "A" sections and an eight-bar release. The perkiness comes from the rest before the six-note opening motive, which begins on the second beat and carries over the bar in quarter notes. The same rhythmical motive permeates the refrain at differing pitch levels. In films, Judy Garland sang "Zing!" in *Listen Darling* (1938), it was in the 1943 screen version of *Thumbs Up!*, and Gene Nelson sang and danced to it in *Lullaby of Broadway* (1951).

Moderate ballad with verse and refrain (56)
PUBLISHER: Harms, Inc.
KEY: E-flat maj., *STARTS*: b-flat' (E-flat maj.), *FORM:* AA'BA'

≈≈≈≈≈≈≈≈≈≈≈≈≈≈≈≈≈≈

JITTERBUGS AND JUKE BOXES

1936

You can hear dear Mother Nature murmuring low, "Let yourself go"

Cole Porter,
"It's De-Lovely"

As another election approaches, the Depression wears on, although there is a slight improvement in the economy. Franklin Delano Roosevelt, the incumbent, declares that Alfred Landon's campaign symbol, the sunflower – state flower of Landon's home state, Kansas – is appropriate because it "was yellow, had a black heart, was useful only as parrot food and always died before November". Roosevelt sweeps in by a landslide, even though both William Randolph Hearst and *The Literary Digest* had forecast a Landon victory.

Exciting events are happening in Europe. King Edward VIII abdicates the throne of Britain, saying "I have found it impossible to carry the heavy burden of responsibility and to discharge my duties as king as I would wish to do without the help and support of the woman I love". That woman is the twice-divorced American, Willis Warfield Simpson, who is named by *Time* magazine as Woman of the Year. In Spain, a devastating civil war begins. In Germany, troops occupy the Rhineland.

But the American public's interest lies closer to home. Juke boxes, those ornate, brightly-lit, and baroque machines, are sprouting up everywhere: in ice cream parlors, restaurants, neighborhood bars, and dance halls. And people are dancing, and often jitterbugging, to the music of hundreds of big bands: from Count Basie to Charlie Barnet, from Sammy Kaye to Guy Lombardo, and from Vaughn Monroe to Artie Shaw. Among best sellers at the juke boxes are Bing Crosby and the Andrews Sisters.

A lengthy novel by Margaret Mitchell takes the country by storm; it is called *Gone with the Wind*, and becomes the best selling book of all best sellers. Broadway is thriving, with Claire Booth Luce's *The Women* and Robert Sherwood's *Idiot's Delight*, and such musicals as Cole Porter's *Red, Hot and Blue!*, Noel Cowards's *Tonight at 8:30*, and Rodgers and Hart's *On Your Toes*. From Hollywood comes a host of screen comedies to chase away the Depression blues, including Frank Capra's *Mr. Deeds Goes to Town*, Charlie Chaplin's *Modern Times*, the hilarious *My Man*

Godfrey, and the first Bugs Bunny animated cartoon. There also is a proliferation of film musicals, including two vehicles for Fred Astaire and Ginger Rogers, *Follow the Fleet* and *Swing Time*; *Born to Dance*, with a memorable score by Porter; and a lavish screen treatment of *Show Boat*. And then there is Bing Crosby in *Pennies from Heaven*, advising money-shy people to make sure that their "umbrella is upside down".

And what are this year's songs like? Jitterbugs dance to "Goody-Goody", "Is It True What They Say About Dixie?", and "Stompin' at the Savoy". But there is still room in the juke boxes for beautiful ballads, many from the movies, exemplified by Porter's haunting "Easy to Love" and "I've Got You Under My Skin", and the entrancing "The Way You Look Tonight" (which wins the Academy Award for Best Song of 1936) by Jerome Kern and Dorothy Fields. These lovely creations emerge like spring flowers in the midst of a desert of more humdrum songs like "In the Chapel in the Moonlight" and "It's a Sin to Tell a Lie", in what can only be called a mixed year.

SONGS OF 1936

Easy to Love **!
A Fine Romance *
Glad to Be Unhappy !
The Glory of Love
Goodnight, Irene
Goody-Goody
In the Chapel in the Moonlight
Is It True What They Say About Dixie?
It's a Sin to Tell a Lie *
It's De-Lovely *
I've Got You Under My Skin ***!
The One Rose (That's Left in My Heart)
Pennies from Heaven ***
Poinciana
Say "Si Si"
Stompin' at the Savoy **
There's a Small Hotel *!
The Way You Look Tonight ***!
You Turned the Tables on Me

1936

EASY TO LOVE ★ ★ !

WORDS andMUSIC: Cole Porter
PREMIERE: Film musical, *Born to Dance*. Metro Goldwyn Mayer, 1936
INTRODUCED BY: James Stewart, danced to by Eleanor Powell,
and reprised by Frances Langford

One of Cole Porter's loveliest ballads, "Easy to Love" was dropped from the Broadway show, *Anything Goes,* in 1934 when William Gaxton complained that it did not have the proper range for his voice; he sang "All Through the Night" instead. The ballad was given to an earnest but determined young tenor named James Stewart as a solo in the film musical, *Born to Dance*, starring Eleanor Powell. It was one of the two hit songs of the movie – the other was "I've Got You Under My Skin". Many recordings followed, including those of Langford and the bands of Hal Kemp, Dick Jurgens, and Shep Fields.

The verse is in the key of B-flat major, with an enchanting modulation to G major, the key of the refrain. In ABA'C form, the song has a wide range (an octave and a half), but is so beautifully designed that this fact is scarcely noted. The flowing melodic line moves upward sequentially in the "A" sections. Repeated notes punctuate the "B" section. Most interesting of all are the harmonies, many of which are minor, including the opening chord of A minor.

In addition to *Born to Dance*, "Easy to Love" was sung by a chorus in the Cole Porter biographical film, *Night and Day"* (1946), by Lauritz Melchior in *This Time for Keeps* (1947), and by Tony Martin in the song's namesake film *Easy to Love* (1953). It remains popular both as a show tune and a jazz standard.

Slow ballad with verse (16) and refrain (32)
PUBLISHER: Chappell & Co., Inc.
KEY: G maj., or A-flat maj., STARTS: e' (A min.) or f' (B-flat min.),
FORM: ABA'C

≈≈≈≈≈≈≈≈≈≈≈≈≈≈≈≈≈≈≈≈≈

A FINE ROMANCE

WORDS: Dorothy Fields, MUSIC: Jerome Kern
PREMIERE: Film musical, *Swing Time*. RKO.
New York, Radio City Music Hall, 27 August 1936
INTRODUCED BY: Fred Astaire and Ginger Rogers

A duet to be "sung with sarcasm", this graceful song with no verse and four refrains was introduced by Fred Astaire and Ginger Rogers in a memorable scene from the film musical, *Swing Time*. The first two refrains are sung by Rogers to an aloof Astaire while snow is falling; the last two refrains are Astaire's answer to her. Astaire had a No. 1 Chart Record of "A Fine Romance"; cover records were made by Guy Lombardo and his Royal Canadians, by Bing Crosby and his wife Dixie Lee, and by Billie Holiday.

Kern's most interesting melodic device occurs in the "A" sections. It consists of long notes, with the melody skipping upwards two notes at a time: a'-g', b'-a', d"-c", and e"-d". In contrast, the "B" sections move downwards, with some chromaticism and syncopation. But most effective of all are Fields's clever lyrics, with references to "hot tomatoes" and "yesterday's mashed potatoes". They are the height of sophisticated cynicism, as in "You're just as hard to land as the *Ile de France!*"

"A Fine Romance" was sung by Virginia O'Brien in the 1946 Kern film biography, *Till the Clouds Roll By*.

Moderate rhythm song with four refrains (32)
PUBLISHER: T. B. Harms Company
KEY: C maj., *STARTS*: e' (C maj.), *FORM*: ABAB'

≈≈≈≈≈≈≈≈≈≈≈≈≈≈≈≈≈≈

GLAD TO BE UNHAPPY !

WORDS: Lorenz Hart, *MUSIC*: Richard Rodgers
PREMIERE: Musical comedy, *On Your Toes*
New York: Imperial Theatre, 11 April 1936 (315 perf.)
INTRODUCED BY: Doris Carson and David Morris

A wistful ballad, "Glad to Be Unhappy" has long been a favorite of such cabaret singers as Mabel Mercer and Bobby Short. A standout in the hit Broadway show, *On Your Toes*, it was recorded by Lena Horne, Lee Wiley, and, in 1967, by The Mamas and the Papas. The song's chief attraction are the clever lyrics by Lorenz Hart, playing around the concept of the title with such words as "it's a pleasure to be sad" and whimsically declaring: "with no mammy and no pappy, I'm so unhappy". Richard Rodgers's music is most unusual in form; the refrain is basically tripartite. Only twenty-four bars in length, it nevertheless seems complete. Opening with the melodic interval of a fifth and a harmony of G minor seventh, it has a most appealing quality. "Glad to Be Unhappy" is indeed a maverick among songs.

Slow ballad with verse (16) and refrain (24)
PUBLISHER: Chappell & Co., Inc.
KEY: F maj., *STARTS*: d' (G min. 7), *FORM*: AA'BBA"

≈≈≈≈≈≈≈≈≈≈≈≈≈≈≈≈≈≈≈≈

THE GLORY OF LOVE

WORDS and MUSIC: Billy Hill
INTRODUCED BY: Rudy Vallee and his Orchestra, on radio and in a Mellotone recording

This rhythmical, but otherwise conventional song was popularized in a Victor recording by Benny Goodman and his Orchestra, with vocal by Helen Ward, in a swinging Spud Murphy arrangement that made it No. 1 on the charts. With its dotted quarters and eighth notes and moderate syncopation, the song lends itself naturally to swing. Bing Crosby also helped to popularize it. In 1951, The Five Keys had a hit record for Victor.

"The Glory of Love" is very much a creature of its times; it is thirty-two bars in length, in AABA form, and it swings. It bears the burden of numerous swing-time clichés: repetition, a riff-like melody, and simple harmonies. There is some contrast in the release, which moves from C major to C minor. As for the lyrics, the most interesting idea is the opening line of the refrain: "You've got to give a little, take a little . . ".

It has been used at least twice in films. Dean Martin sang it in *The Silencers* (1966). A year later, Jacqueline Fontaine and a chorus sang it in *Guess Who's Coming to Dinner*. Bette Midler sang it in *Beaches* in 1988.

Moderate swing tune with verse (24) and refrain (32)
PUBLISHER: Shapiro, Bernstein & Co.
KEY: G maj., *STARTS*: d' (G Maj.), *FORM*: AABA

≈≈≈≈≈≈≈≈≈≈≈≈≈≈≈≈≈≈≈≈

GOODNIGHT, IRENE

WORDS and MUSIC: Huddie Ledbetter ; arranged by John Lomax and Alan Lomax (1950)
INTRODUCED BY: Leadbelly (Huddie Ledbetter)

An early predecessor of the folk-song revival of the 1960s, "Goodnight, Irene" was first recorded by guitarist and singer Leadbelly (Huddie Ledbetter) while he was serving time in a Louisiana prison. It was later arranged by John and Alan Lomax and became a hit in 1950, when it was recorded on Decca by The Weavers, with Gordon Jenkins and his Orchestra: a No. 1 Chart record. Recordings by Gordon MacRae, Jo

Stafford, and Frank Sinatra (all on Capitol) soon followed. The three verses tell the story of a man who parts from his wife and wants to jump into the river and drown, but vows to stop his "ramblin' and gamblin' " and go home to his wife and family. The music is related in simple country fashion, with stepwise melodic progression, and mostly tonic and dominant harmonies, and a verse that is a variation of the refrain.

Moderate waltz with refrain (16), three verses (16), and refrain (16)
PUBLISHER: Spencer Music Corp.
KEY: G maj., *STARTS*: g' (G maj.), *OVERALL FORM*: ABABABA

~~~~~~~~~~~~~~~~~~~~~~~

GOODY-GOODY

WORDS and MUSIC: Johnny Mercer and Matt Malneck
INTRODUCED BY: Benny Goodman and his Orchestra,
vocal by Helen Ward, on radio

Another swing tune, "Goody-Goody" was popularized by Benny Goodman and his Orchestra, with vocal by Helen Ward, in a hit record for Victor. Also contributing to its popularity were recordings by the bands of Freddy Martin and Bob Crosby. In the fifties, Paula Kelly and the Modernaires revived it. The refrain is characterized by numerous short notes in heavy syncopation, with the melody rising each time the words of the title are pronounced. The song benefits mightily from Johnny Mercer's lyrics, which contain such striking expressions as "Hooray and hallelujah! You had it comin' to ya". As one of Goodman's signature songs, "Goody-Goody" was featured in the 1956 biographical film, *The Benny Goodman Story*.

Moderate swing tune with verse (16) and refrain (32)
PUBLISHER: Crawford Music Corporation
KEY: C maj., *STARTS*: c" (C maj.), *FORM*: ABA'C

~~~~~~~~~~~~~~~~~~~~~~

IN THE CHAPEL IN THE MOONLIGHT

WORDS and MUSIC: Billy Hill
INTRODUCED BY: Shep Fields and his Orchestra on radio

An ordinary pop tune of its day, "In the Chapel in the Moonlight" was initially popularized with a Bluebird recording by Shep Fields and his Orchestra {famous for its "rippling rhythm") and a Decca record by Ruth Etting. Richard Himber and his Orchestra had a cover record. Perhaps because of its sacred, awe-inspiring setting, the song has enjoyed periodic revivals over the years. It reached the zenith of its popularity in 1954, with a Decca record by Kitty Kallen. The Bachelors recorded it in 1965, and Dean Martin had a hit record in 1967. The song is a product of Tin Pan Alley: predictable in melody, harmony, form, and in its subject matter, love. Its only distinctive feature is the six-note pickup in eighth notes that occurs eight times in the course of the refrain.

Moderate ballad with two verses (8) and refrain (32)
PUBLISHER: Shapiro, Bernstein & Co., Inc.
KEY: C maj., *STARTS*: c' (C maj.), *FORM*: AABA

≈≈≈≈≈≈≈≈≈≈≈≈≈≈≈≈≈≈≈≈

IS IT TRUE WHAT THEY SAY ABOUT DIXIE?

WORDS and MUSIC: Irving Caesar, Sammy Lerner, and Gerald Marks
POPULARIZED BY: Al Jolson in a recording

This rollicking song, initially popularized by Al Jolson and Rudy Vallee, became grist for the swing mill. Recordings were soon made by the orchestras of Jimmy Dorsey and Ozzie Nelson. Other bands followed and the song became one of the big hits of the year. The form (ABA'C) is rather old-fashioned. The melody skips around endearingly, with some chromaticism – especially the note a-sharp', which appears eight times in the refrain. There is abundant syncopation, making the song a natural for big-band arrangements. In the movies, it was sung by Iris Adrian and Robin Raymond in *His Butler's Sister* (1943); and by Al Jolson, dubbing for Larry Parks, in *Jolson Sings Again* (1949).

Moderate swing tune with verse (16) and refrain (32)
PUBLISHER: Irving Caesar
KEY: G maj., *STARTS*: a-sharp' (G maj.), *FORM*: ABA'C

≈≈≈≈≈≈≈≈≈≈≈≈≈≈≈≈≈≈≈≈

IT'S A SIN TO TELL A LIE

WORDS AND MUSIC: Billy Mayhew
INTRODUCED: on radio by Kate Smith

The incomparable Kate Smith made this traditional waltz the surprise hit of an otherwise swinging year. Other early recordings were by young singer Bobby Breen and Russ Morgan and his Orchestra. But soon enough, it was put into 4/4 meter and jazzed up. Fats Waller had a Victor record that reached No. 1 on the charts. In 1955 it was revived by Somethin' Smith and The Redheads. And many years later Nell Carter and a chorus sang it in the Fats Waller revue *Ain't Misbehavin'*, which opened at the Longacre Theatre in New York 9 May 1978.

The refrain is a perfect blend of music and lyrics, oddly effective in spite of its obvious sentimentality. The lyrics echo with sincerity, as in "if you break my heart, I'll die". The music, too, is moving, particularly in the last section of the song, when the melody drops to a-flat', followed by a pause (fermata), and then rises to e", followed by another pause.

In the 1981 film, *Pennies from Heaven*, "It's a Sin to Tell a Lie" was sung by Dolly Dawn, with George Hall and his Orchestra.

Moderate waltz with verse (16) and refrain (32)
PUBLISHER: Bregman, Vocco &Conn, Inc.
KEY: C maj., *STARTS*: g' (C Maj.), *FORM*: ABA'C

≈≈≈≈≈≈≈≈≈≈≈≈≈≈≈≈≈≈≈

IT'S DE-LOVELY * !

WORDS and MUSIC: Cole Porter
PREMIERE: Musical comedy, *Red, Hot and Blue!*
New York: Alvin Theatre, 29 October 1936 (183 perf.)
INTRODUCED BY: Ethel Merman and Bob Hope

Following on the success of *Anything Goes* in 1934, *Red, Hot and Blue!* used the same team: Cole Porter (songs), Howard Lindsay and Russel Crouse (book), and Vinton Freedley (producer). But the show suffered from mixed reviews and never achieved as much success. Of its many songs, only one, "It's De-Lovely", has survived. Porter had first intended the song for the Metro Goldwyn Mayer film, *Born to Dance*, but it was rejected. He finally found a place for it in *Red, Hot and Blue!*, as a duet for its upcoming young stars, Ethel Merman and Bob Hope. In five refrains of the song, they trace the course of their life together. The most popular recording was on Victor, by Eddy Duchin and his Orchestra, with vocal by Jerry Cooper.

As with other Porter creations, there are several versions as to how the song came to be. In one version, it was said to have been conceived on a boat trip that Porter was taking with his wife, Linda, and his friend, Monty Wooley. At their first sight of Rio de Janeiro, Porter supposedly said "It's delightful", Linda chimed in with "It's delicious", and Wooley declared "It's de-lovely". In another version, Porter was said to have conceived the song long before, when he was on a boat trip to the South Seas, with Moss Hart, to write the show *Jubilee*.

The song offers many attractions besides the device of beginning words with "de-". Among them are its witty lyrics, its fascinating rhythm, and its melody of repeated notes, ascending in the "A" sections, at first chromatically (c', c-sharp', d') and then leaping upwards in wild syncopation. This first theme then moves a step higher in the "B" section. Following an inventive release, there is a return to the first theme, and then a frantic coda recounting all the "de-" words: "It's dilemma, it's delimit, its de luxe, its de-lovely".

Mitzi Gaynor and Donald O'Connor sang "It's De-Lovely" in the 1956 film version of *Anything Goes*. Burt Reynolds and Cybill Shepherd sang it in the 1975 film, *At Long Last Love*. With an infectious back-beat and intoxicating lyrics, "It's De-Lovely" remains a favorite, both as a show tune and a jazz standard.

Moderate foxtrot with verse (20) and refrain (36)
PUBLISHER: Chappell & Co., Inc.
KEY: F maj., *STARTS*: c" (F maj.), *FORM*: ABCA'

≈≈≈≈≈≈≈≈≈≈≈≈≈≈≈≈≈≈≈≈

I'VE GOT YOU UNDER MY SKIN ✱ ✱ ✱ !

WORDS and MUSIC: Cole Porter
PREMIERE: Film musical, *Born to Dance*. Metro Goldwyn Mayer, 1936
INTRODUCED BY: irginia Bruce

One of Cole Porter's most innovative creations, "I've Got You Under My Skin" was the other big number (along with "Easy to Love") from the film musical, *Born to Dance*, starring Eleanor Powell. It was nominated for an Academy Award. One of the most popular of standards, it has seen a host of recordings, from those of Frances Langford and the bands of Hal Kemp, Dick Jurgens, and Ray Noble in the early days, to the most popular recording of all, that of Frank Sinatra. The Four Seasons revived it in 1966.

This extraordinarily dramatic song deviates from the ordinary in many ways. It lacks a verse. It is fifty-six bars in length. It's form is most unusual; it can be diagrammed as AA'BAB'/A, with only one complete repetition of the principal theme. Replete with quarter note triplets and insistently repeated notes, it builds to a dramatic climax with an impassioned crescendo. Dynamics are very important in this song, with strong contrast between loud and soft. Harmonies are also out of the ordinary, especially the unexpected modulation from E-flat major to C major in the second "A" section. There is also word painting: the repeated notes at the words "repeats and repeats in my ear", and the powerful pause at the word "stop" – followed by "Before I begin".

In films, "I've Got You Under My Skin" was sung by Ginny Simms in the Porter biography, *Night and Day* (1946), and by Marina Koshetz in *Luxury Liner* (1948). It was featured in *This Could Be the Night* (1957), and sung by Debbie Reynolds and Tony Randall in *The Mating Game* (1959).

Moderate beguine with refrain (56)
PUBLISHER: Chappell & Co., Inc.
KEY: E-flat maj., *STARTS*: b-flat' (F min. 7), *FORM*: AA'BCB'/A

≈≈≈≈≈≈≈≈≈≈≈≈≈≈≈≈≈≈≈≈

THE ONE ROSE (THAT'S LEFT IN MY HEART)

WORDS and MUSIC: Del Lyon and Lani McIntyre
INTRODUCED BY: Bing Crosby on radio and in a Decca recording

This languid "Valse Hawaiian" was written in 1929 and languished in a trunk for years before it was published. Bing Crosby made it famous with his Decca record; other artists soon followed, most prominently Kate Smith, Ted Fio-Rito and his Orchestra, and Larry Clinton and his Orchestra. Words and music overflow with sentimentality. The refrain begins with a B-flat seventh chord at the words "You're as sweet as the red rose in June, dear". The melody is slightly chromatic and the simple harmonies change slowly, Hawaiian style, each chord lasting for two bars.

Slow waltz with verse (16) and refrain (32)
PUBLISHER: Shapiro, Bernstein & Co., Inc.
KEY: E-flat maj., *STARTS*: c" (B-flat 7)

≈≈≈≈≈≈≈≈≈≈≈≈≈≈≈≈≈≈≈≈

PENNIES FROM HEAVEN * *

WORDS: Johnny Burke, *MUSIC*: Arthur Johnston
PREMIERE: Film musical, *Pennies from Heaven*. Columbia Pictures, 1936
INTRODUCED BY: Bing Crosby

Very much a Hollywood creation, "Pennies from Heaven" originated as the title song of one movie, in 1936, and reemerged forty-five years later as the title song of another, in 1981. Bing Crosby introduced it in the first film and also popularized it on radio and in a Decca recording. The song became an instant hit and was nominated for an Academy Award; staying thirteen weeks on radio's *Your Hit Parade*. Its popularity has hardly waned to this day.

The lyrics far outshine the music. John Burke's words tell a tale in the fashion of "April Showers", saying that "Ev'ry time it rains, it rains

Pennies from Heaven". They also contain intriguing inner rhymes such as "So when you hear it thunder / Don't run under a tree". The music suffers in comparison, with a melody of many repeated notes and rather pedestrian harmony.

"Pennies from Heaven" was featured in several other films besides the one from which it originated. Dick Haymes sang it in *Cruisin' Down the River* (1953); Bing Crosby sang it again in *Pepe* (1960); and Arthur Tracy, known as The Street Singer, sang it in the 1981 *Pennies from Heaven*. Perhaps because of its predictable harmonies, it remains a favorite subject for jazz improvisation.

Moderate ballad with verse (24) and refrain (32)
PUBLISHER: Select Music Publishing, Inc.
KEY: C maj., *STARTS*: d" (C maj.), *FORM*: ABA'C

≈≈≈≈≈≈≈≈≈≈≈≈≈≈≈≈≈≈≈

POINCIANA

ENGLISH WORDS: Buddy Bernier, *MUSIC*: Nat Simon, arranged by
Helmy Kresa

Ironically, this most exotic-sounding of rumbas emanated not from Cuba or Mexico, but from composer Nat Simon, who was born in Newburgh, New York. With Spanish words by Manuel Llisa (English words by Buddy Bernier were added later), it benefited from the ongoing craze for Latin-American music. Early recordings were by David Rose and his Orchestra on Victor and Bing Crosby on Decca. The verse, which acts as both introduction and coda, consists of long-held notes centering on the dominant (d"). The delicate melody of the refrain has a modal quality caused by usage of the flatted sixth and seventh. In the key of G major, harmonies revolve about the major seventh and minor subdominant (C minor). With its wispy quality, the song is particularly effective as a flute solo.

Moderate rumba with verse (16), refrain (32), and verse (16)
PUBLISHER: Edward B. Marks Music Corporation
KEY: G maj., *STARTS*: d" (G maj. 7), *FORM*: AABA

≈≈≈≈≈≈≈≈≈≈≈≈≈≈≈≈≈≈≈

SAY "SI SI" (PARA VIGO ME VOY)

ENGLISH WORDS: Al Stillman, *MUSIC*: Ernesto Lecuona
INTRODUCED BY: Xavier Cugat and his Orchestra, vocal by Lina Romay, in a Victor recording

With music by Cuba's foremost composer, Ernesto Lecuona, this lively rumba has Spanish words by Francia Laban and English lyrics by Al Stillman. It became a hit in the United States with Xavier Cugat's 1936 Victor recording, but its real popularity began four years later, when it was recorded for Decca by The Andrews Sisters. Also in 1940, Glenn Miller recorded it for Bluebird, with singer Marion Hutton. The verse is in D minor, while the refrain is in the parallel key of D major. The bright, fast-moving melody is noted for its intense syncopation (especially in the last section of the refrain) and its Latin flavor. The song was featured in the 1948 film, *When My Baby Smiles at Me*.

Moderate rumba with verse (16) and seven refrains (32)
PUBLISHER: Edward B. Marks Music Corporation
KEY: D maj., *STARTS*: d" (A 7) ABAC/A'

≈≈≈≈≈≈≈≈≈≈≈≈≈≈≈≈≈≈≈≈

STOMPIN' AT THE SAVOY * *

WORDS: Andy Razaf, *MUSIC*: Benny Goodman, Chick Webb, and Edgar Sampson
INTRODUCED BY: Chick Webb and his Orchestra in a Columbia recording

This swing standard bears the name of the legendary Savoy Ball-room in Harlem, famous for its black performers. It was originally published as an instrumental and recorded for Columbia in 1934 by Chick Webb and his Orchestra, in an Edgar Sampson arrangement. Sampson also arranged it two years later for Benny Goodman and his Orchestra, whose Victor recording made the song a hit. It has since been recorded by many other jazz and swing artists, among them Art Tatum, Teddy Wilson, and the bands of Jimmy Dorsey and Woody Herman. The riff-like main theme is very catchy, with three call-and-response phrases in each "A" section. Of special interest are the chord changes in the release, moving enharmoni-cally through the circle of fifths from G-flat ninth to B ninth, E ninth, and A ninth, and then sliding down to A-flat ninth. Goodman also performed it with his band in his 1956 screen biography, *The Benny Goodman Story*.

Bright swing tune with refrain (32)
PUBLISHER: Robbins Music Corporation
KEY: D-flat maj., *STARTS*: f' (D-flat maj.), *FORM*: AABA

≈≈≈≈≈≈≈≈≈≈≈≈≈≈≈≈≈≈≈≈

THERE'S A SMALL HOTEL * !

WORDS: Lorenz Hart, *MUSIC*: Richard Rodgers
PREMIERE: Musical comedy, *On Your Toes*
New York: Imperial Theatre, 11 April 1936 (315 perf.)
INTRODUCED BY: Doris Carson and Ray Bolger

This winsome ballad was introduced as a duet for the characters Junior and Frankie in the Broadway musical, *On Your Toes*. However, it was written the year before, for the production of Billy Rose's *Jumbo*, but was dropped from the show before it opened. It is said that Lorenz Hart wrote the lyrics while he was in the men's room of the Shubert Theatre in Boston. The small hotel of the title still exists on the Delaware River. *On Your Toes*, which featured the outstanding ballet number "Slaughter on Tenth Avenue", was revived in New York in 1954, and again in 1983, when it ran for an impressive 505 performances.

"There's a Small Hotel" is a perfect blend of music and lyrics; each is superb and inseparable. The verse is a wonder in itself, with expressive use of dissonance (notably the note c-sharp'). and it leads into the refrain with the provocative and punning words: "One, Two, Three" and the "For" of the pickup. The refrain is charming in its simplicity, with an enchanting melody, moving stepwise. In AA'BA" form, each "A" section ends on a different note, respectively a', b', and d". A four-bar coda after the second ending – modulating briefly from G major to B-flat major, and then back again – brings the song to an unusual close on the long held-note of the dominant. Hart's magical lyrics evoke romantic images of a wishing well, a bridal suite, and a distant steeple.

The song was played as background music for the 1939 screen version of *On Your Toes*; Betty Garrett sang it in the 1948 film biography of Rodgers and Hart, *Words and Music*; and Frank Sinatra sang it in the 1957 film, *Pal Joey*

Moderate ballad with verse (16) and refrain (36)
PUBLISHER: Chappell & Co., Inc.
KEY: G maj. or A-flat maj., *STARTS*: a' (G maj. 7) or b-flat' (A-flat maj. 7),
FORM: AA'BA"

≈≈≈≈≈≈≈≈≈≈≈≈≈≈≈≈≈≈

THE WAY YOU LOOK TONIGHT * * * !

WORDS: Dorothy Fields, *MUSIC*: Jerome Kern
PREMIERE: Film musical, *Swing Time*. RKO, 1936
INTRODUCED BY: Fred Astaire

In the film, *Swing Time,* Fred Astaire sings this beautiful ballad to Ginger Rogers while her hair is lathered with shampoo. Winner of the Academy Award for Best Song of 1936, it was on radio's *Your Hit Parade* for fourteen weeks.

There is no verse. The refrain, marked "Andantino", is graced with a lovely melody featuring whole notes describing downward intervals of the fifth and octave. Accompaniment intervals are very much a part of the song; they serve as introduction, interludes, and finally are hummed at song's end, *bouche fermée.* The release is interesting harmonically, beginning in G-flat major and modulating, in Kern's magical way, back to the tonic of E-flat major. Dorothy Fields's lyrics are especially touching, emphasizing the words "lovely", "of you", and "love you", on the whole notes, and piquantly referring to "that laugh that wrinkles your nose".

Moderate ballad with refrain (68)
PUBLISHER: T. B. Harms Company
KEY: E-flat maj., *STARTS*: b-flat' (E-flat maj.), *FORM*: AABA'

≈≈≈≈≈≈≈≈≈≈≈≈≈≈≈≈≈≈≈

YOU TURNED THE TABLES ON ME

WORDS: Sidney D. Mitchell, *MUSIC*: Louis Alter
PREMIERE: Film musical, *Sing, Baby, Sing.* Twentieth Century-Fox, 1936
INTRODUCED BY: Alice Faye

This swinging song was introduced by Alice Faye in the movie, *Sing, Baby, Sing.* Benny Goodman and his Orchestra had a hit record on Victor (with vocal by Helen Ward), and Ella Fitzgerald later recorded it on Decca. The music of the refrain is heavily syncopated, beginning with a seven-note pickup of dotted eighths and sixteenths. Blue notes and a mixed bag of tied whole notes and accented quarter notes, abound. The lyrics are cute and make their point: "Just like the sting of a bee".

Moderate swing tune with verse (12) and refrain (32)
PUBLISHER: Movietone Music Corp.
KEY: F maj., *STARTS*: c, (G main. 6), *FORM*: ABA'C

≈≈≈≈≈≈≈≈≈≈≈≈≈≈≈≈≈≈≈

SWINGING AND SWAYING

1937

"Life without care – I'm broke, it's oke"

Lorenz Hart
"The Lady is a Tramp"

A somewhat subdued year for American popular song, 1937 sees the death of one of its masters, George Gershwin, who dies of complications following surgery for a brain tumor on 11 July. Gershwin has been incredibly productive in his thirty-seven years. Some of his best songs, written with his brother Ira, are introduced in films this year: "A Foggy Day", "Nice Work if You Can Get It", "They All Laughed", and "They Can't Take That Away from Me". Irving Berlin, Cole Porter, and Jerome Kern are also active in Hollywood. As for Broadway, lasting musicals are few and far between. Many theaters remain closed, and few outstanding songs are introduced, notably those of Richard Rodgers and Lorenz Hart, who do the scores for no less than three musical comedies, *Babes in Arms*, *I'd Rather Be Right*, and *I Married an Angel*, and bring forth such gems as "Have You Met Miss Jones?", "The Lady Is a Tramp", and "My Funny Valentine". The legitimate theater is enlivened only by John Steinbeck's *Of Mice and Men* (which wins the Pulitzer Prize), Clifford Odets' *Golden Boy*, and the comedy, *Room Service,* directed by George Abbott.

It is a disastrous year in other ways as well: the Depression shows no sign of abating; the Nazis are terrorizing their European neighbors; the airship, Hindenburg, explodes over New Jersey; and Amelia Earhart and her co-pilot Tom Noonan are lost near Howland Island in the Pacific.

Movies and radio fill the voids in peoples' lives. Hollywood has a banner year: Walt Disney's first animated film feature, *Snow White and the Seven Dwarfs*, brings in an unprecedented $22 million; the first Andy Hardy movie, *A Family Affair*, comes out, starring Mickey Rooney; Hedy Lamarr makes a sensational, unclad screen debut in *Ecstasy*; and The Dead End Kids show up for the first time in *Dead End*, starring Humphrey Bogart and Sylvia Sidney. Among other memorable films are *The Petrified Forest*, with Humphrey Bogart and Leslie Howard; *Lost Horizons*, starring Ronald Colman; *A Star Is Born,* with Fredric March and Janet Gaynor; and *Nothing Sacred* starring Carole Lombard and Fredric March.

Jazz is on the decline, but a new phenomenon called swing is emerging in its place, and record sales begin to improve. Clarinetist Benny Goodman dubs himself The King of Swing, while trombonist Tommy Dorsey is called That Sentimental Gentleman of Swing. A royal hierarchy is established with noblemen called Duke Ellington, Earl Hines, and Count Basie. Swing is in the air, played by big bands throughout the land, who perform in "log cabins" like Frank Daily's Meadowbrook and the Glen Island Casino. Vocalists are being pushed more and more to the forefront in these bands: singers such as Ray Eberly, Martha Tilton, Skinnay Ennis, Ella Fitzgerald, and The Andrews Sisters. The groups, sweet and hot, are heard in late-night remotes broadcast from hundreds of hotels, ballrooms, and roadhouses, and wafting through the airwaves the sounds of the bands of Glenn Miller, Artie Shaw, Duke Ellington, and innumerable others. And not to forget the immortal pronouncement: "Swing and Sway with Sammy Kaye".

So it goes in this year of ongoing Depression and saber rattling. People try to forget their troubles by turning on the radio and listening to remotes, going to the movies, buying records, and occasionally going out on the town and swinging and swaying to their favorite band.

SONGS OF 1937

Bei Mir Bist Du Schön (Means That You're Grand)
Blue Hawaii
Caravan
The Donkey Serenade
A Foggy Day * *
The Folks Who Live on the Hill * !
Gone with the Wind *
Harbor Lights *
Have You Met Miss Jones? * !
I Can Dream, Can't I?
I'll Take Romance * !
In the Still of the Night * !
I've Got My Love to Keep Me Warm
The Lady Is a Tramp * * *
Let's Call the Whole Thing Off
My Funny Valentine * * * !
The Nearness of You *
Nice Work If You Can Get It * * !
Once in a While * *
Remember Me

September in the Rain
So Rare
Some Day My Prince Will Come * *
Thanks for the Memory
That Old Feeling
They All Laughed *!
They Can't Take That Away from Me * *
Too Marvelous for Words
Where or When * *

BEI MIR BIST DU SCHÖN (MEANS THAT YOU'RE GRAND)

ENGLISH WORDS: Sammy Cahn and Saul Chaplin
MUSIC: Sholom Secunda
INTRODUCED BY: The Andrews Sisters, in a Decca recording

This swinging novelty song – which according to the sheet music, should be pronounced "By Meer Bist Du Shane" – was catapulted to fame by The Andrews Sisters, who had over a million sales of their Decca record, which reached No. 1 on the charts. The music, by Sholom Secunda, had been introduced by Aaron Lebedeff two years before in the Yiddish musical comedy, *I Would If I Could*, with Yiddish lyrics by Jacob Jacobs. The Anglicized version, maintaining the Yiddish title, took off like a rocket. Besides the sensational disk by The Andrews Sisters, who used it as their theme song, there were well-received recordings by Kate Smith, Guy Lombardo and his Royal Canadians, Eddy Duchin and his Orchestra, and Russ Morgan and his Orchestra. But the definitive swing version was by Benny Goodman and his Orchestra, and to this day the song is most often performed as a swing number. It was revived in 1959 by Louis Prima and his Orchestra, with vocal by Keely Smith.

The verse, in A minor, is melodic and heavily syncopated. It consists of two identical eight-bar sections. The refrain, also in A minor, is in conventional AABA form. Eminently singable, it has two upward jumps of the sixth in each "A" section. The release, starting with a D minor chord, brings in a touch of Russian *fraliach* rhythm.

The Andrews Sisters reprised "Bei Mir Bist Du Schön" in the 1944 film, *Take It Big*.

Moderate novelty song with verse (16) and refrain (32)
PUBLISHER: Harms, Inc., by arrangement with J.&J. Kammen Music Co.
KEY: A min., *STARTS*: e' (A min.), *FORM*: AABA

≈≈≈≈≈≈≈≈≈≈≈≈≈≈≈≈≈≈≈

BLUE HAWAII

WORDS and MUSIC: Leo Robin and Ralph Rainger
PREMIERE: Film musical, *Waikiki Wedding*. Paramount, 1937
INTRODUCED BY: Bing Crosby and Shirley Ross

"Blue Hawaii" was first performed in Hawaii by Harry Owens and his Royal Hawaiian Orchestra and then brought to the screen for the film, *Waikiki Wedding*, in which it was sung by Bing Crosby and Shirley Ross. Winner of the Academy Award for Best Song, the ballad gained renewed popularity a quarter century later, when it's title was used for the film, *Blue Hawaii* (1961), in which it was sung by Elvis Presley. Recorded by Presley for RCA, it became one of his signature songs. The simple melody is in Hawaiian style: long-held notes, a chromatic melody, and lingering harmonies. In addition to its appearance in the films, *Waikiki Wedding* and *Blue Hawaii*, Presley sang the ballad in the 1981 film, *This Is Elvis*.

Slow ballad with verse (16) and refrain (32)
PUBLISHER: Famous Music Corp.
KEY: B-flat maj., STARTS: f' (B-flat maj.), FORM: AABA

≈≈≈≈≈≈≈≈≈≈≈≈≈≈≈≈≈≈≈≈

CARAVAN   !

WORDS and MUSIC: Duke Ellington, Irving Mills, and Juan Tizol
IINTRODUCED BY: Duke Ellington and his Orchestra, in a Master recording

"Caravan" was co-written by Juan Tizol, a talented trombonist and composer, born in Puerto Rico, who was with Duke Ellington's band for nineteen years. Introduced by the Ellington band, it was also popularized by Barney Bigard and his Orchestra, Billy Eckstine in 1949, and Ralph Marterie and his Orchestra in 1953. The exotic-sounding music is marked, "Moderato quasi misterioso". And mysterious-sounding it is, capturing the Moorish influence of North Africa in its ostinato bass alternating the notes D-flat and C and in its chromatic, semi-tonal melody. The release is seldom performed as written, but arrangements maintain the underlying harmonies: four bars each of F seventh, B-flat seventh, E-flat seventh, and A-flat major modulating to C seventh. It remains a staple of big bands as well as small groups.

Moderate swing tune with refrain (64)
PUBLISHER: American Academy of Music, Inc.
KEY: F min., STARTS: c" (E dim. 7), FORM: AABA

≈≈≈≈≈≈≈≈≈≈≈≈≈≈≈≈≈≈≈≈

THE DONKEY SERENADE

WORDS: Bob Wright and Chet Forrest, *MUSIC*: Rudolf Friml and Herbert Stothart
PREMIERE: Film musical, *The Firefly*. Metro Goldwyn Mayer, 1937
INTRODUCED BY: Allan Jones

A striking novelty number, "The Donkey Serenade" was adapted from Rudolf Friml's romantic piano piece "Chanson", of 1920. In 1923, the melody of "Chanson" was transformed into a song called "Chansonette", with lyrics by Sigmund Spaeth, Dailey Paksman, and Irving Caesar, and included in Paul Whiteman's historic concert of 12 February 1924, at Aeolian Hall in New York, along with George Gershwin's *Rhapsody in Blue*. Still another transformation occurred in 1937, when "Chansonette" became "The Donkey Serenade", newly arranged by Herbert Stothart, with new lyrics by Bob Wright and Chet Forrest. Introduced by Allan Jones in the film, *The Firefly*, the song became an instant hit. It was popularized by Jones in a Victor recording and by the bands of Artie Shaw and Horace Heidt. Monte Ray used it as his theme song.

The clever lyrics tell of serenading a mule, complaining: "All that the lady can say is 'E-E-Aw!" Shuffle rhythm prevails throughout. In rondo form (AABCA'D) the broad, legato melody of the "A" section contrasts sharply with the fast-moving notes of the "B" section. In the key of C major, harmonies are mostly tonic and dominant, except for the "C" section, which introduces a new theme in A minor. The effective coda brings the song to a rip-roaring finish, with twenty-five repeated eighth notes on the high note g", at the words "Senorita, donkey-sita..."– a glorious, high-spirited way for a tenor to end with a flourish..

"The Donkey Serenade" was again featured in the Olsen and Johnson film, *Crazy House* (1945). Jose Iturbi played it on the piano in the 1945 movie, *Anchors Aweigh*. Dean Martin and Jerry Lewis sang it in *My Friend Irma* (1949). And Allan Jones reprised it in Woody Allen's 1987 film, *Radio Days*.

Moderate novelty song with two refrains (43)
PUBLISHER: G. Schirmer, Inc.
KEY: C maj., *STARTS*: e" (C maj.), *FORM*: AABCA'D

≈≈≈≈≈≈≈≈≈≈≈≈≈≈≈≈≈≈≈≈

A FOGGY DAY * *

WORDS: Ira Gershwin, MUSIC: George Gershwin
PREMIERE: Film musical, A Damsel in Distress. RKO, 1937
INTRODUCED BY: Fred Astaire

The film musical, A Damsel in Distress, had Fred Astaire without Ginger Rogers, and the omission showed; Joan Fontaine was obviously not up to the demanding dance routines. Nevertheless, the movie boasts a sparkling score by the Gershwin brothers – unfortunately, one of their last. "A Foggy Day" (often additionally denoted by its second phrase, "In London Town") is arguably one of its best numbers. According to Ira Gershwin, the refrain was written – words and music – in less than an hour. Recordings were made by Astaire (Brunswick) and the bands of Bob Crosby and Hal Kemp. Les Brown recorded it with his band in 1950.

The verse, marked to be performed "rather freely", sets the stage, with a stepwise melody and interesting harmonies. The refrain, marked "brighter, but evenly", is one of the Gershwins' most touching. The melodic line effectively combines repeated notes with skips of the minor third and fourth. Harmonies are distinctive, using for example the E-flat minor sixth chord rather than the more commonplace E-flat diminished in Bars One and Two. The highest point of the song (f") is reached at the word "suddenly", just at the beginning of the last section. Contrast between major and minor tonality throughout the song adds to it's poignancy. Played in all sorts of tempos, it remains one of the most popular of jazz standards.

Moderate ballad with verse (16) and refrain (34)
PUBLISHER: Gershwin Publishing Corporation
KEY: F maj., STARTS: c' (F maj.), FORM: ABAC

≈≈≈≈≈≈≈≈≈≈≈≈≈≈≈≈≈≈≈≈≈

THE FOLKS WHO LIVE ON THE HILL * !

WORDS: Oscar Hammerstein II, MUSIC: Jerome Kern
PREMIERE: Film Musical, High, Wide and Handsome. Paramount,
New York: Astor Theatre, 21 July 1937
INTRODUCED BY: Irene Dunne

This cheerfully melodic song was introduced by Irene Dunne in a film about pioneer days called High, Wide and Handsome. It was popularized in recordings by Bing Crosby; Guy Lombardo and his Royal Canadians; and Ozzie Nelson and his Orchestra, with vocal by Harriet Hilliard.

The lyrics by Oscar Hammerstein II, are suitably folksy and homespun, anticipating his work in the pioneer musical, *Oklahoma!*, to come six years later. Jerome Kern's music is unusual in the length of its sections: in AABA' form, they are respectively twelve, twelve, six, and fourteen bars in length. The fetching melody is one of Kern's most joyfully innocent: lightly syncopated, it contrasts long-held whole and half notes with much quicker eighth notes. The short release is in E minor, while a two-bar coda brings the song to a joyful ending at its highest point.

Moderate ballad with verse (16) and refrain (44)
PUBLISHER: T. B. Harms Company
KEY: C maj., *STARTS*: e' (C maj.), *FORM*: AABA'

≈≈≈≈≈≈≈≈≈≈≈≈≈≈≈≈≈≈≈≈

GONE WITH THE WIND *

WORDS: Herb Magidson, *MUSIC*: Allie Wrubel

"Gone with the Wind" is the most popular of a number of songs using the title of the celebrated 1939 film classic. Although never heard in the film itself, it bears this endorsement: "Based upon the greatest of all Motion Pictures, by arrangement with Selznick International Pictures, Inc". Since the song was written two years before the film was released, it is difficult to see the connection. Nevertheless, the song, "Gone with the Wind", has become a jazz classic.

Among its many recordings are those of the bands of Horace Heidt and Claude Thornhill, singers Mel Tormé and Dick Haymes, and jazz artists Art Tatum, Stan Getz, and Benny Carter. The song's chief attraction to jazz musicians lies in its interesting harmonies, moving freely between the tonal centers of E-flat and G major. Also contributing is the jagged melodic line, making the song idiosyncratic for instruments.

Moderate ballad with verse (8) and refrain (32)
PUBLISHER: Irving Berlin, Inc., (name changed to Bourne, Inc.)
KEY: E-flat maj., *STARTS*: c" (F min. 7), *FORM*: ABAC

≈≈≈≈≈≈≈≈≈≈≈≈≈≈≈≈≈≈≈≈

HARBOR LIGHTS *

WORDS and MUSIC: Jimmy Kennedy and Hugh Williams (pseud. for Will Grosz)
INTRODUCED BY: Roy Fox & his Orchestra , in the United States, in a Victor recording

Imported from Britain, this sentimental ballad was introduced to America in a Victor recording by an English orchestra, led by Roy Fox. It was popularized in the United States in recordings and radio broadcasts by Rudy Vallee and his Connecticut Yankees, Frances Langford, and Claude Thornhill and his Orchestra, and remained ten weeks on radio's *Your Hit Parade*. The song has been periodically revived. In 1950, Sammy Kaye and his Orchestra had a hit recording on Columbia, and there were Decca recordings by Bing Crosby and Guy Lombardo and his Royal Canadians. A second revival in 1960 was sparked by a Top Ten recording for Mercury by The Platters. The refrain begins with a three-note pickup outlining the E-flat major triad, leading to the major seventh, d", and B-flat dominant-seventh harmony. In traditional AA'BA form, both melody and harmonies are simple, and they are matched by the somewhat cloying lyrics.

Slow ballad with verse (8) and refrain (32)
PUBLISHER: Peter Maurice Music Co., Ltd. (London),
assigned to Chappell and Co., Inc.
KEY: E-flat maj., *STARTS*: e-flat' (B-flat 7), *FORM*: AA'BA'

≈≈≈≈≈≈≈≈≈≈≈≈≈≈≈≈≈≈≈≈

HAVE YOU MET MISS JONES? * !

WORDS: Lorenz Hart, *MUSIC*: Richard Rodgers
PREMIERE: Musical comedy, *I'd Rather Be Right*
New York: Alvin Theatre, 2 November 1937 (290 perf.)
INTRODUCED BY: Joy Hodges and Austin Marshall

A long-standing favorite with jazz instrumentalists, "Have You Met Miss Jones?" is noted chiefly for its harmonically-daring release. It was the hit song of the Broadway musical, *I'd Rather Be Right*, a spoof poking fun at the Roosevelt administration that starred veteran vaudevillian George M. Cohan. The song was interpolated in the London revue, *All Clear*, in 1939, and sung by Bobby Howes. The verse is one of Rodgers and Hart's best, with a poignant melodic line and lyrics that tell a tale of love at first sight. The refrain, in traditional AA'BA" form, has a graceful melody using the favorite Rodgers device of a rising scale (most notable in "Where or When" this year). The release acts as the climax of the refrain, both verbally and musically. Beginning with the words, "And all at once I lost my breath", harmonies diverge far from their normal parameters, with the following changes for each bar: B-flat major - D-flat seventh - G-flat major - A dominant seventh - D major - D-flat major - G-flat major - C dominant seventh. It is no wonder that jazz musicians enjoy improvising around these unusual changes. In the 1955 film, *Gentlemen Marry Brunettes*,

"Harbor Lights" was sung by a quintet comprised of Jane Russell, Anita Ellis (dubbing for Jeanne Crain), Rudy Vallee, Alan Young, and Robert Farnon (dubbing for Scott Brady).

Moderate ballad with verse (12) and refrain (32)
PUBLISHER: Chappell and Co., Inc.
KEY: F maj., *STARTS*: a' (F maj.), *FORM*: AA'BA"

≈≈≈≈≈≈≈≈≈≈≈≈≈≈≈≈≈≈≈

I CAN DREAM, CAN'T I?

WORDS: Irving Kahal, *MUSIC:* Sammy Fain
PREMIERE: Revue, *Right This Way*
New York: 46th Street Theatre, 4 January 1938 (15 perf.)
INTRODUCED BY: Tamara

This sentimental ballad was introduced in the same ill-fated revue that brought forth "I'll Be Seeing You", the short-lived *Right This Way*. Recorded on Decca by Glen Gray and The Casa Loma Orchestra and on Brunswick by Harry James and his Orchestra, it enjoyed some moderate success. But the song's popularity really soared a dozen years later, in 1949, with a hit recording on Decca by The Andrew Sisters, accompanied by Gordon Jenkins and his Orchestra. In that revival, the song stayed seventeen weeks on radio's *Your Hit Parade*. The verse is in G minor. The refrain, in E-flat major, is characterized by a smooth melodic line, moving mostly stepwise, and propelled by numerous quarter-note triplets.

Moderate ballad with verse (16) and refrain (32)
PUBLISHER: Chappell & Co., Inc.
KEY: E-flat maj., *STARTS*: e-flat', *FORM*: ABA'C

≈≈≈≈≈≈≈≈≈≈≈≈≈≈≈≈≈

I'LL TAKE ROMANCE * !

WORDS: Oscar Hammerstein II, *MUSIC*: Ben Oakland
PREMIERE: Film musical, *I'll Take Romance*. Columbia, 1937
INTRODUCED BY: Grace Moore

Opera star Grace Moore introduced this lovely waltz as the title song of the film musical, *I'll Take Romance*. It was popularized by Rudy Vallee and his Connecticut Yankees and by Eddy Duchin and his Orchestra.

Lacking a verse, the song has a refrain of sixty-eight bars, in AABA form. Melodically and harmonically, it is one of the most interesting waltzes in the repertoire. The melody is enchanting, combining skips, steps, repeated notes, and a touch of chromaticism into a tuneful whole. But it is the subtle movement between tonalities that sets this song apart, with modulations from F major to D-flat major and back in each "A" section, and from E-flat minor to C-flat major in the release. A brief coda repeats the last phrase of the song.

In addition to *I'll Take Romance*, other films that have featured the song include *Manhattan Angel* (1948, sung by Gloria Jean)), *Holiday in Havana* (1949), and *The Eddy Duchin Story* (1956). It is most often performed today as a jazz standard, in 4/4 meter and bright tempo.

Moderate waltz with refrain (68)
PUBLISHER: Irving Berlin, Inc.
KEY: F maj., *STARTS*: f' (F maj.), *FORM*: AABA

≈≈≈≈≈≈≈≈≈≈≈≈≈≈≈≈≈≈

IN THE STILL OF THE NIGHT ★ !

WORDS and MUSIC: Cole Porter
PREMIERE: Film musical, *Rosalie.* Metro Goldwyn Mayer, 1937
INTRODUCED BY: Nelson Eddy

One of Cole Porter's most dramatically evocative songs, "In the Still of the Night" was written specifically for Nelson Eddy to sing in the film version of *Rosalie*. When Eddy complained that the song was too long and too difficult for him, Porter left it for L. B. Mayer to decide whether it should be dropped from the movie. Porter performed the romantic ballad for Mayer, and the head of Metro Goldwyn Mayer was moved to tears; the song remained in the film. Among recordings were those of Tommy Dorsey and his Orches-tra on Victor and Leo Reisman's Orchestra on Brunswick.

There are a number of unusual aspects to "In the Still of the Night": it lacks a verse, has a seventy-two bar refrain, and includes a long release of twenty-four bars. In AA'BA" form, it is replete with careful performance directions, such as "mysteriously" and *piano* in the "A" sections, and "appassionato" and *forte* in the "B" section. The wide-ranging melody (an octave and a fourth) includes many sustained notes. In the key of F major, there is much contrast between major and minor, including a brief modulation to A minor at the close of the second section.

The song appeared in one other film besides *Rosalie*: Dorothy Malone, Cary Grant, and a chorus sang it in the Porter biography, *Night and Day.*

Moderate ballad with refrain (72)
PUBLISHER: Chappell & Co., Inc.
KEY: F maj., *STARTS*: c' (F maj.), *FORM*: AA'BA"

≈≈≈≈≈≈≈≈≈≈≈≈≈≈≈≈≈≈≈≈

I'VE GOT MY LOVE TO KEEP ME WARM

WORDS and MUSIC: Irving Berlin
PREMIERE: Film musical, *On the Avenue*. Twentieth Century-Fox
New York: Radio City Music Hall, February 1937
INTRODUCED BY: Dick Powell and Alice Faye

It is an established fact that Irving Berlin wrote some of his most distinctive songs for the movies, and this is one of them. It was written for the film, *On the Avenue*, which was designed to outshine the extremely popular Fred Astaire and Ginger Rogers musicals so popular at the time. Unfortunately, the movie didn't; but as Howard Barnes wrote in the *New York Herald Tribune*, "The brilliant score that Irving Berlin has composed for *On the Avenue* is the most distinctive feature of the new musical photoplay". Of that "brilliant score", only "I've Got My Love to Keep Me Warm" has survived. Recordings by Dick Powell, Alice Faye, Ray Noble and his Orchestra, The Mills Brothers, Billie Holiday, and Art Lund made it popular. In 1949, it was revived with a Columbia record by Les Brown and his Orchestra that reached No. 1 on the charts.

Lacking a verse, the refrain is in traditional AABA form, with each "A" section sixteen bars in length and an eight-bar release. The song's message is clearly presented in the lyrics, with such passages as "I can weather the storm" and "I can't remember a worse December". The broad melody has chromatic passages that ascend sequentially in each "A" section. Corresponding harmonies are pungent, modulating from E-flat major to D dominant seventh before returning to the tonic. The release starts in G minor and modulates to F minor.

The song's unusual harmonic turns have kept it popular with musicians through the years.

Moderate rhythm song with refrain (56)
PUBLISHER: Irving Berlin Music Corporation
KEY: E-flat maj., *STARTS*: b-flat' (E-flat maj.), *FORM*: AABA

≈≈≈≈≈≈≈≈≈≈≈≈≈≈≈≈≈≈≈≈

THE LADY IS A TRAMP ✳ ✳ ✳

WORDS : Lorenz Hart, *MUSIC*: Richard Rodgers
PREMIERE: Musical comedy, *Babes in Arms*
New York: Shubert Theatre, 14 April 1937 (298 perf.)
INTRODUCED BY: Mitzi Green

One of the most swinging creations of Richard Rodgers and Lorenz Hart, "The Lady Is a Tramp" was reportedly written in one day for *Babes in Arms*, a show of youthful exuberance which brought forth the talents of Mitzi Green, Ray Heatherton, Alfred Drake, and Dan Dailey, among others. Early recordings were by Sophie Tucker and Tommy Dorsey and his Orchestra, but the most popular recording of all was by Frank Sinatra.

Hart's clever lyrics detail the travails of the "lady" in the verse ("I've wined and dined on mulligan stew") and her pet likes and dislikes in the refrain ("Hate California / It's cold and it's damp"). In the verse, the music is in the style of recitative, with a plethora of repeated notes. The refrain is unusual in its asymmetry: in AABA' form, the first two sections are each sixteen bars in length, while the last two are only eight bars long. Harmonies are also out of the ordinary, moving from C major to C minor seventh and D minor seventh at the beginning of each "A" section. Also of interest is the sparkling release, with its whole notes and carefree syncopation at the words, "I'm broke, it's oke".

Babes in Arms was made into a movie in 1939, with "The Lady Is a Tramp" sung by June Preisser. Lene Horne sang it in the Rodgers and Hart screen biography, *Words and Music* (1948), and it was interpolated into the 1957 film version, *Pal Joey*, sung by Sinatra. The song is firmly entrenched both as a peppy jazz standard and a singer's showstopper.

Moderate rhythm song with verse (24) and three refrains (48)
PUBLISHER: Chappell & Co., Inc.
KEY: C maj., *STARTS*: c" (C maj.), *FORM*: AABA'

≈≈≈≈≈≈≈≈≈≈≈≈≈≈≈≈≈≈≈

LET'S CALL THE WHOLE THING OFF

WORDS: Ira Gershwin, *MUSIC*: George Gershwin
PREMIERE: Film musical, *Shall We Dance*. RKO, 1937
INTRODUCED BY: Fred Astaire and Ginger Rogers

The idea for this clever novelty song came to Ira Gershwin while he was talking to his brother-in-law, English Strunsky, who had a tomato factory in New Jersey. Strunsky complained that local farmers didn't understand him when he called a "tomato" a "to-*mah*-to". Gershwin allowed that he had the same problem with his wife over "either" and "*eye*-ther". Introduced by Fred Astaire and Ginger Rogers in the film, *Shall We Dance*, "Let's Call the Whole Thing Off" benefited from Astaire's hit Brunswick recording (accompanied by Johnny Green and his Orchestra), as well as from a Victor recording by Eddy Duchin and his Orchestra, with vocal by Jerry Cooper.

The lyrics give varying pronunciations of common words: "potato" and "po-*tah*-to", "pajamas" and "pa-*jah*-mas", and threaten to "call the whole thing off" unless this disagreement can be resolved. But a final resolution there is, with a typical Ira Gershwin twist: "Let's call the calling off off". George Gershwin's music brilliantly showcases the witty lyrics. The verse in D major leads to the refrain in G major. In the refrain, the jagged, syncopated melodic line highlights the compared pronunciations by accented notes and downward jumps of the fifth. Harmonies are of special interest in the release, progressing from E minor sixth to D seventh and then repeating the sequence. A two-bar coda caps the refrain of this charming song.

Bright novelty song with verse (18) and three refrains (34)
PUBLISHER: Gershwin Publishing Corporation
KEY: G maj., *STARTS*: g' (G maj.), *FORM*: AA'BA'

≈≈≈≈≈≈≈≈≈≈≈≈≈≈≈≈≈≈≈≈

MY FUNNY VALENTINE * * * !

WORDS: Lorenz Hart, *MUSIC*: Richard Rodgers
PREMIERE: Musical comedy, *Babes in Arms*
New York: Shubert Theatre, 14 April 1937 (298 perf.)
INTRODUCED BY: Mitzi Green

For years this wistful song was confined to cabarets and nightclubs, sung by the likes of Mabel Mercer and Bobby Short. It was only in the fifties that it attained universal popularity, with Frank Sinatra's recording. Although it is revived each Valentine's Day and the phrase "Each day is Valentine's Day" does appear at the end of the lyrics, "Valentine" was in fact the name of a boy character in the show, Babes in Arms, from which the song sprung.

It is a remarkable song, a perfect marriage of Richard Rodgers's music and Lorenz Hart's lyrics. The verse, in C minor, has no accompaniment whatsoever, and doesn't need any. The refrain, in AA'BA" form, is ambivalent in tonality, beginning in C minor, moving to E-flat major in the next two sections, returning to C minor in the last section, but ending in E-flat major. The melody is deceptively simple. Mostly stepwise in motion, it is counterpoised by a chromatically-descending line of whole notes, always performed with the song. At the climax – the words "Stay little Valentine, stay!" – the melody is a full octave higher than at its beginning. Hart's lyrics contribute mightily to the song's success, with their wonderfully-inventive rhymes of "figure less than Greek", "mouth a little week", and "open it to speak"; as well as the inner rhymes of "hair for me" and "care for me". It is altogether a most unusual song, and a most tender and appealing one.

"My Funny Valentine" was sung by Alan Young and Anita Ellis (dubbing for Jeanne Crain) in the film, *Gentlemen Marry Brunettes* (1955) and by Trudy Erwin (dubbing for Kim Novak) in the screen version of *Pal Joey* (1957).

Slow ballad with verse (16) and refrain (36)
PUBLISHER: Chappell & Co., Inc.
KEY: E-flat maj., *STARTS*: c' (C min.), *FORM*: AA'BA"

≈≈≈≈≈≈≈≈≈≈≈≈≈≈≈≈≈≈≈

THE NEARNESS OF YOU *

WORDS: Ned Washington, *MUSIC*: Hoagy Carmichael

One of Hoagy Carmichael's most touching melodies, with tender lyrics by Ned Washington, "The Nearness of You" had many recordings, including those of Glenn Miller and his Orchestra and Dinah Shore on Bluebird and Guy Lombardo and his Royal Canadians and Connee Boswell on Decca. The form is conventional enough, AA'BA", with the melody of each "A" section starting out pentatonically and then descending sequentially. A four-bar coda brings the song to its highest point. Like most other fine songs, music and lyrics are a perfect fit. One would be unimaginable without the other, as in the opening five-tone phrase at the words: "It's not the pale moon that excites me". The song was featured in the 1938 film, *Romance in the Dark*, which starred Gladys Swarthout, John Boles, and John Barrymore. Stella Stevens sang it in the 1962 film, *Girls! Girls! Girls!*

Moderate ballad with verse (8) and refrain (36)
PUBLISHER: Famous Music Corporation
KEY: F maj., *STARTS*: c' (F maj.), *FORM*: AA'BA"

≈≈≈≈≈≈≈≈≈≈≈≈≈≈≈≈≈≈≈

NICE WORK IF YOU CAN GET IT ∗∗!

WORDS: Ira Gershwin, *MUSIC*: George Gershwin
Film musical, *A Damsel in Distress*. RKO, 1937
INTRODUCED BY: Fred Astaire and the trio of Jan Duggan, Mary Dean,
and Pearl Amatore

The title of this clever song was inspired by an article that Ira Gershwin read in a British magazine. Introduced by Fred Astaire and a female trio in the film, *A Damsel in Distress*, which was released months after George Gershwin's death, the song was popularized in recordings by Astaire on Brunswick and The Andrews Sisters on Decca – the latter on the flip side of their sensational hit, "Bei Mir Bist Du Schön".

The lyrics of the verse are another variation on money-isn't-everything philosophy, stating that falling in love "is the best work of all – if you can get it". The refrain, in AA'BA" form, contrasts smooth quarter notes with fast-moving, syncopated eighths and sixteenths. In the first four bars of each "A" section, fast harmonic changes, two to the bar, go through the circle of fifths from B seventh to C seventh. The harmonies of the release are also of interest, starting in E minor and moving to D minor. There also are some inside jokes: allusions to previous Gershwin songs. The second part of the main theme is a variation of the pentatonic opening notes of "I Got Rhythm", while there are lyrical references in the release to a "cottage door" ("Soon") and "Who could ask for anything more" ("I Got Rhythm").

Georges Guetary and Oscar Levant sang this rousing and innovative number in the 1951 film musical, *An American in Paris*.

Moderate rhythm song with verse (20) and refrain (34)
PUBLISHER: Gershwin Publishing Corporation
KEY: G maj., *STARTS*: b' (B7), *FORM*: AA'BA"

≈≈≈≈≈≈≈≈≈≈≈≈≈≈≈≈≈≈≈≈

ONCE IN A WHILE ∗∗

WORDS: Bud Green, *MUSIC*: Michael Edwards
INTRODUCED BY: Tommy Dorsey and his Orchestra, vocal by Jack Leonard

One of the most popular songs of 1937, this romantic ballad appeared seven times on radio's *Your Hit Parade*. It is by far the best-known song of Michael Edwards (né Michael Slowitsky), a violinist, conductor, organist, and arranger. Among the song's many recordings were those of Tommy Dorsey and his Orchestra (Victor); Louis Armstrong (Decca);

Frances Langford; Ozzie Nelson and his Orchestra, vocal by Harriet Hilliard; and Patti Page. It was featured on Bing Crosby's last recording, made in 1977. A very traditional ballad in AA'BA' form, the broad melody of the "A" sections features repeated notes and quarter-note triplets. Harmonies, in the key of E-flat major, are straightforward, except for a diversion to G major in the release. A vocal quintet, accompanied by Harry James and his Orchestra, sang "Once in a While" in the 1950 film, *I'll Get By*. Liza Minnelli sang it in the 1977 film, *New York, New York*.

Slow ballad with verse (16) and refrain (32)
PUBLISHER: Miller MusicCorporation
KEY E-flat maj., *STARTS*: e-flat' (E-flat maj.), *FORM*: AA'BA'

≈≈≈≈≈≈≈≈≈≈≈≈≈≈≈≈≈≈≈

REMEMBER ME?

WORDS: Al Dubin, *MUSIC*: Harry Warren
PREMIERE: Film musical, *Mr. Dodds Takes the Air*. Warner Brothers, 1937
INTRODUCED BY: Kenny Baker

Written by two of the most successful songwriters contracted to Warner Brothers, Al Dubin and Harry Warren, "Remember Me?" was nominated for an Academy Award. It was popularized in a best-selling Victor recording by Hal Kemp and his Orchestra, with vocal by Skinnay Ennis. One of the most provocative of songs, it has a persistent rhythm set up by a profusion of dotted quarter and eighth notes, and is best performed in shuffle rhythm. Long-held notes appear only along with the title and in the release. It was featured in the film, *Never Say Goodbye* (1946), starring Eleanor Parker and Errol Flynn.

Moderate ballad with verse (16) and refrain (32)
PUBLISHER: M. Witmark & Sons
KEY: E-flat maj., *STARTS*: d' (E-flat maj.), *FORM*: AA'BA'

≈≈≈≈≈≈≈≈≈≈≈≈≈≈≈≈≈≈≈

SEPTEMBER IN THE RAIN

WORDS: Al Dubin, *MUSIC*: Harry Warren
PREMIERE: Film musical, *Melody for Two*. Warner Brothers, 1937
INTRODUCED BY: James Melton

James Melton, later to become lead tenor of the Metropolitan Opera in New York, introduced this sentimental ballad in the film, *Melody for Two*. The music had previously been used as background in the 1935 film, *Stars Over Broadway*, which starred Melton and Jane Froman. Early recordings were by Melton and Guy Lombardo and his Royal Canadians. But the song's popularity surged dramatically a dozen years later, with the hit Metro Goldwyn Mayer jazz recording by The George Shearing Quintet in 1949.

Continuing in the jazz tradition, Dinah Washington had a Mercury recording that reached the Top Forty in 1961. The simple melody consists of quarter notes skipping around at seemingly random intervals. The release is in reality a variation on the main theme, which then moves a whole step higher. Although first written as a romantic ballad, the song's easy-going style and slow-changing harmonies make it ideal for jazz improvisation.

Moderate ballad with verse (12) and refrain (32)
PUBLISHER: Remick Music Corp.
KEY: E-flat maj., *STARTS*: b-flat' (E-flat maj.), *FORM*: AABA

≈≈≈≈≈≈≈≈≈≈≈≈≈≈≈≈≈≈≈≈

SO RARE

WORDS: Jack Sharpe, *MUSIC*: Jerry Herst
INTRODUCED BY: Jimmy Dorsey and his Orchestra

This romantic big band standard was introduced and popularized by Jimmy Dorsey and his Orchestra in 1937, when it appeared eleven weeks on radio's *Your Hit Parade*. Dorsey used it as his closing theme thereafter. Exactly twenty years later, in 1957, Jimmy Dorsey and his band revived the song with a new arrangement that brought it back to *Your Hit Parade* for another eleven weeks, this time on television. The song lends itself well to the close harmony of reed and brass sections. The melody is disjunct and lightly syncopated, with harmonies moving briefly to and from A-flat major. In the release, the note g' is played twenty-one times and the note e' nineteen times, over changing harmonies. The lyrics are picturesque, presenting such provocative images as "Orchids in cellophane".

Moderate ballad with verse (8) and two refrain (32)
PUBLISHER: Sherman Clay & Co.
KEY: C maj., *STARTS*: g' (C maj.), *FORM*: AA'BA'

≈≈≈≈≈≈≈≈≈≈≈≈≈≈≈≈≈≈≈≈

SOME DAY MY PRINCE WILL COME (SOME DAY I'LL FIND MY LOVE)

WORDS: Larry Morey, *MUSIC*: Frank Churchill
PREMIERE: Animated film musical, *Snow White and the Seven Dwarfs*..
RKO, 1937
IINTRODUCED BY: the voice of Adriana Caselotti as Snow White

Walt Disney's first full-length animated cartoon feature, *Snow White and the Seven Dwarfs,* was an instant hit. So was its delightful score, especially this striking waltz. It eschews tradition in several ways: its unusual form (ABAC), its unusually wide range (an octave and a half), its spacious intervals (fourths and sixths), the daring descent of its melody from f-natural" to f-sharp', and the ending of its refrain on the dominant (c"). The two sets of lyrics are for male and female voice. In practice the tender waltz is most often performed as an uptempo jazz standard, either in three-quarters or common time.

Moderate waltz with verse (16) and two refrains (32)
PUBLISHER: Irving Berlin, Inc.
KEY: F maj., *STARTS*: c' (F maj.), *FORM*: ABAC

≈≈≈≈≈≈≈≈≈≈≈≈≈≈≈≈≈≈≈

THANKS FOR THE MEMORY

WORDS and MUSIC: Leo Robin and Ralph Rainger
PREMIERE: Film musical, *The Big Broadcast of 1938*. Paramount, 1938
INTRODUCED BY: Bob Hope and Shirley Ross

Bob Hope used this nostalgic song as his theme throughout his long career. In the film, *The Big Broadcast of 1938*, from which it originated, Hope and Shirley Ross sing it as a divorced couple who are still very much in love. The song was an instant hit, recorded on Decca by Hope and Ross, Mildred Bailey, and Shep Fields and his Orchestra, to name a few. Furthermore, it won the Academy Award as Best Song of 1938.

In five refrains, the lyrics are a catalogue of memories, including "gardens at Versailles", "beef and kidney pie", "candlelight and wine", "Castles on the Rhine", "sunburns at the shore", and "nights in Singapore". The music is straightforward. In AABA' form, each "A" section consists of a rising chromatic melodic line leading to the downward jump of an octave. The release begins in A-flat major, with an interesting modulation back to F major.

So popular was "Thanks for the Memory" that another movie was built around it the same year: *Thanks for the Memory*. Again, it was sung by Bob Hope and Shirley Ross.

Moderate ballad with verse (10) and five refrains (36)
PUBLISHER: Paramount Music Corporation
KEY: F maj., *STARTS*: c" (C7), *FORM*: AABA'

≈≈≈≈≈≈≈≈≈≈≈≈≈≈≈≈≈≈

THAT OLD FEELING

WORDS and MUSIC: Lew Brown and Sammy Fain
PREMIERE: Film musical, *Vogues of 1938*, later called *All This and Glamour Too*. United Artists. 1938
INTRODUCED BY: Virginia Verrill

One of the most popular songs of 1938, this rather ordinary ballad was nominated for an Academy Award. Hit recordings were made by the bands of Shep Fields and Jan Garber. The melody outlines triads and blue notes and there are many repeated notes. Jane Froman dubbed it in for Susan Hayward in the Froman screen biography, *With a Song in My Heart* (1952).

Slow ballad with verse (16) and refrain (32)
PUBLISHER: The Sun Music Publishing, Co. (London), assigned to Leo Feist, Inc.
KEY: E-flat maj., *STARTS*: g' (E-flat maj.), *FORM*: ABA'C

≈≈≈≈≈≈≈≈≈≈≈≈≈≈≈≈≈≈

THEY ALL LAUGHED * !

WORDS: Ira Gershwin, *MUSIC:* George Gershwin
PREMIERE: Film musical, *Shall We Dance*. RKO, 1937
INTRODUCED BY: Fred Astaire and Ginger Rogers

This happy-go-lucky song, introduced by Fred Astaire and Ginger Rogers in the film, *Shall We Dance*, is another tour de force by lyricist Ira Gershwin, highlighted by his brother George's delightful music. The most popular initial recordings were those of Astaire, accompanied by Johnny Green and his Orchestra on Brunswick; Tommy Dorsey and his Orchestra on Victor; and Jimmy Dorsey and his Orchestra on Decca.

Ira Gershwin got the idea from the many current advertisements in newspapers and magazines reading: "They all laughed when I sat down to play the piano" His witty lyrics catalogue a number of persons whose ideas were laughed at: Christopher Columbus, the Wright brothers, Thomas Edison, and Guglielmo Marconi, among others. Stating "they laughed at me wanting you", they end: "Who's got the last laugh now?" The refrain is in AA'BA" form. The riff-like, syncopated melody of the "A" sections describes a rising pentatonic scale. A four-bar coda rounds out the song with various types of laughs: "Ho, ho, ho!", "He, he, he!", and "Ha, ha. Ha!". The song's liveliness and syncopation have kept it alive as a jazz standard.

Moderate rhythm song with verse (20) and two refrains (36)
PUBLISHER: Gershwin Publishing Corporation
KEY: G maj., *STARTS*: d' (G maj.), *FORM*: AA'BA"

≈≈≈≈≈≈≈≈≈≈≈≈≈≈≈≈≈≈≈

THEY CAN'T TAKE THAT WAY FROM ME * *

WORDS: Ira Gershwin, *MUSIC*: George Gershwin
PREMIERE: Film musical, *Shall We Dance*. RKO, 1937
INTRODUCED BY: Fred Astaire and Ginger Rogers

In the film, *Shall We Dance*, Fred Astaire sings this touching ballad to Ginger Rogers – who is clad in a full-length fur coat – on board a ferryboat. It is the only song ever written by George Gershwin that was nominated for an Academy Award. There have been many recordings: by Astaire (accompanied by Johnny Green and his Orchestra), by Billie Holiday, by the bands of Ozzie Nelson and Tommy Dorsey, and – most popular of all – by Frank Sinatra.

It is another catalogue song – a favorite species of Ira Gershwin – this time listing adorable quirks, such as "the way you sing off key". The music of the refrain uses repeated notes with a vengeance, five at a time on the note e-flat', moving to different pitch levels: up a third, down a fourth, up a fifth. The release begins in G minor, modulating gracefully back to the tonic.

Astaire repeated his performance of the song in the film, *The Barkleys of Broadway* (1949).

Slow ballad with verse (17) and refrain (37)
PUBLISHER: Gershwin Publishing Corporation
KEY: E-flat maj., *STARTS*: e-flat' (E-flat 6), *FORM*: AA'BA"

≈≈≈≈≈≈≈≈≈≈≈≈≈≈≈≈≈≈≈

TOO MARVELOUS FOR WORDS

WORDS: Johnny Mercer, *MUSIC*: Richard A. Whiting
PREMIERE: Film musical, *Ready, Willing and Able*. Warner Brothers, 1937
INTRODUCED BY: Wini Shaw and Ross Alexander(dubbed in by James Newill); reprised by Ruby Keeler; danced to by Lee Dixon

A soulful love ballad, "Too Marvelous for Words" was given the full Hollywood treatment in the film, *Ready, Willing and Able*, especially by Ruby Keeler, who danced to it on top of a giant typewriter in her last movie for Warner Brothers. The song stands out for its marvelous lyrics by Johnny Mercer, especially the lines at the close of the release: "And just too very very! / To ever be in Webster's Dictionary". The music, by Richard A. Whiting (father of singer Margaret Whiting), features a warm melody of scalar passages interspersed by poignant skips of the fourth and fifth. There are some interesting modulations: to B major in the second section, and to C major in the release. In addition to *Ready, Willing and Able*, the song was featured in the 1947 film, *Dark Passage*, starring Humphrey Bogart and Lauren Bacall. Doris Day sang it, accompanied by Harry James and his Orchestra, in the 1950 film, *Young Man with a Horn* (known in Britain as *Young Man of Music)*; and Frankie Lane sang it in *Sunny Side of the Street* (1951).

Moderate ballad with verse (8) and refrain (32)
PUBLISHER: Harms, Inc.
KEY: G maj., *STARTS*: d' (A min. 7), *FORM*: AA'BA"

≈≈≈≈≈≈≈≈≈≈≈≈≈≈≈≈≈≈≈≈

WHERE OR WHEN? * *

WORDS: Lorenz Hart, *MUSIC*: Richard Rodgers
PREMIERE: Musical comedy, *Babes in Arms*
New York: Shubert Theatre, 14 April 1937 (298 perf.)
INTRODUCED BY: Mitzi Green and Ray Heatherton

The quintessential song of *déjà vu*, "Where or When" is a wistful expression of a commonly-known phenomenon. Introduced by Mitzi Green and Ray Heatherton in the Broadway show, *Babes in Arms*, it was an instant hit – sparked by the Brunswick recording of Hal Kemp and his Orchestra, with vocal by Skinnay Ennis. Dion and the Belmonts had a Top Ten recording in 1960.

There are several interesting aspects of Richard Rodgers's music. Repeated notes permeate both verse and refrain. But in the refrain they are used as elements of a rising diatonic scale, over pedalpoint. Although the refrain is in traditional AABA' form, each of the first two "A" sections is ten bars in length, instead of the usual eight. The final "A" section completes the rising scale by an additional two bars, bringing the song to its ultimate range of an octave and a fourth. As for Lorenz Hart's lyrics, they clearly define the phenomenon of *déjà vu* in the release: "Some things that happen for the first time / Seem to be happening again".

> Moderate ballad with verse (18) and refrain (40)
> *PUBLISHER*: Chappell & Co., Inc.
> *KEY*: E-flat maj., *STARTS*: b-flat (E-flat maj.), *FORM*: A A B A'

≈≈≈≈≈≈≈≈≈≈≈≈≈≈≈≈≈≈≈≈≈

MARTIANS AND HURRICANES

1938

Oh, the days dwindle down to a precious few

Maxwell Anderson
"September Song"

Events, rather than songs, dominate this year. Some of them are imaginary, like Orson Welles's carefully crafted depiction of an invasion from Mars. The dramatization of H. G. Wells's *War of the Worlds*, broadcast over CBS radio on *Mercury Theatre of the Air* creates a nation-wide panic, with people running for their lives in the belief that New York City is already overrun by little Martians. Other events are terribly real, however, such as the Munich Pact between Britain, France, Germany, and Italy, sanctioning Germany's takeover of Austria and Czechoslovakia in the mistaken belief it would prevent war; or the devastating hurricane that lashes Long Island and New England in late September leaving 700 dead and over 60,000 homeless.

Songs this year turn their backs on these real or imaginary events. They have their fair quotient of beautiful ballads ("Love Is Here to Stay", "Love Walked In", September Song") and big band favorites ("In the Mood", "One O'Clock Jump", "Sunrise Serenade"), but in general no correlation with the world-shaking events in progress. It is as if songwriters and the people they write for are in blissful ignorance of the tenor of the times, and couldn't care less.

And there are numerous distractions: over the airwaves, on stage, at the movies, and in the comic books. The heroic Superman (along with his alter ego, Clark Kent) makes his first appearance in *Action Comics*, bringing science fiction and the triumph of good over evil to the masses. Broadway plays include Thornton Wilder's *Our Town* (which wins the Pulitzer Prize); Robert Sherwood's *Abe Lincoln in Illinois*, starring Raymond Massie; and a six-hour-long production of *Hamlet*, starring Maurice Evans. Among hit musicals are Cole Porter's *Leave It to Me*, introducing an ingenue named Mary Martin at her sauciest in "My Heart Belongs to Daddy"; Kurt Weill and Maxwell Anderson's *Knickerbocker Holiday*, with an unforgettable performance of "September Song" by Walter Huston; and Rodgers and Hart's *The Boys from Syracuse,* containing a sparkling score which introduces the standards "Falling in Love with Love" and "This Can't Be Love".

As for Hollywood, Frank Capra wins his third Oscar for *You Can't Take It With You,* starring Jimmy Stewart and Jean Arthur; Bette Davis wins her second Oscar for *Jezebel;* and Katherine Hepburn and Cary Grant care for a pet leopard – whose favorite song is "I Can't Give You Anything but Love" (1928) – in *Bringing Up Baby.*

In short, 1938 is a puzzling year, with a fake invasion from Mars, a very real hurricane, nasty business in Europe, and songs that seem to have a mind of their own.

SONGS OF 1938

A-Tisket A-Tasket
The Breeze and I !
By Myself !
Change Partners !
Cherokee
Falling in Love with Love *
Get Out of Town !
Heart and Soul
I Let a Song Go Out of My Heart
I'll Be Seeing You ***
In the Mood*
Jeepers Creepers
Love Is Here to Stay ****!
Love Walked In **
(I'm Afraid) The Masquerade Is Over
Music, Maestro, Please!
My Heart Belongs to Daddy
My Reverie
Prelude to a Kiss !
September Song ****!
Sunrise Serenade
This Can't Be Love *
Two Sleepy People
You Go to My Head *!
You Must Have Been a Beautiful Baby *

A-TISKET A-TASKET

WORDS and MUSIC: Ella Fitzgerald and Al Feldman (Van Alexander)
PREMIERE: New York: Savoy Ballroom, 1938
INTRODUCED BY: Ella Fitzgerald, with Chick Webb and his Orchestra

The music of this children's song was first published in 1879 as "I Sent a Letter to My Love", in the *(Illustrated National) Nursery Songs and Games*. The little song remained popular with children as "Atisket, Ataskot" until 1938, when it was adapted and made into a swing tune by Ella Fitzgerald (then aged fifteen) and Al Feldman. The Decca recording by Fitzgerald, with Chick Webb and his Orchestra, was a sensational hit.

True to its derivation, "A-Tisket A-Tasket" has all the attributes of a children's song: a simple melody of quarter notes outlining intervals of the third, straightforward rhythm, and uncomplicated harmonies. The newly-composed verse and the various arrangements of the song, on the other hand, bring in an element of syncopation.

In films, it was sung by Fitzgerald in *Ride 'Em Cowboy* (1942), and by June Allyson and Gloria De Haven in *Two Girls and a Sailor* (1944).

Moderate swing tune with verse (10), refrain (32), and coda (8)
PUBLISHER: Robbins Music Corporation
KEY: E-flat maj., *STARTS*: b-flat' (E-flat maj.), *FORM*: AA'BA

≈≈≈≈≈≈≈≈≈≈≈≈≈≈≈≈≈≈≈≈≈

THE BREEZE AND I !

WORDS: Al Stillman, *MUSIC*: Ernesto Lecuona, adapted by Tutti Camerata
INTRODUCED BY: Jimmy Dorsey and his Orchestra, vocal by Bob Eberly

An exceptionally beautiful ballad, "The Breeze and I" was adapted and arranged by Tutti Camerata from *Andalucia, Suite Espanola*, by the Cuban composer, Ernesto Lecuona. The Decca recording by Jimmy Dorsey and his Orchestra, with vocal by Bob Eberly, was a hit, staying on radio's *Your Hit Parade* for thirteen weeks. Other recordings were by Xavier Cugat and his Orchestra, Vic Damone, and Caterina Valenti. Only the primary theme of *Andalucia* is used in the adaptation; the other sections are omitted. The jagged melody and sophisticated harmony (prominently featuring the chord of D-flat minor) of "The Breeze and I" is almost identical to that of the suite; only the meter is changed, from three-quarter time to four-quarter time. Ethel Smith played the song as an organ solo in the 1946 film, *Cuban Pete*, starring Desi Arnaz.

Moderate ballad with refrain (34)
PUBLISHER: Edward B. Marks Music Corporation
KEY: E-flat maj., *STARTS*: b-flat' (E-flat maj.), *FORM*: AABB'

≈≈≈≈≈≈≈≈≈≈≈≈≈≈≈≈≈≈≈

BY MYSELF !

WORDS: Howard Dietz, *MUSIC*: Arthur Schwartz
PREMIERE: Musical comedy, *Between the Devil*
New York: Imperial Theatre, 22 December 1937(93 perf.)
INTRODUCED BY: Jack Buchanan

One of the most unusual songs in the popular literature, "By Myself" has a special appeal because of its striking harmonies and unusual form: AABC, with two sixteen-bar sections followed by two eight-bar sections. Vacillating between major and minor, each "A" section begins with a G minor sixth chord, and moves to F major. There is a feeling of development in both the "B" and "C" sections. Its touch of syncopation, narrow range (only an octave), and interesting bass line also make the song a standout. In the movies, Fred Astaire sang it in *The Band Wagon* (1953) and Judy Garland in *I Could Go On Singing* (1965).

Moderate ballad with verse (16) and refrain (48)
PUBLISHER: Crawford Music Corporation
KEY: F maj., *STARTS*: g' (G min. 6), *FORM*: AABC

≈≈≈≈≈≈≈≈≈≈≈≈≈≈≈≈≈≈≈

CHANGE PARTNERS !

WORDS and MUSIC: Irving Berlin
PREMIERE: Film musical, *Carefree*. RKO, 1938
INTRODUCED BY: Fred Astaire, danced to by Fred Astaire and Ginger Rogers

This enchanting number, first sung by Fred Astaire in the movie, *Carefree*, was nominated for an Academy Award. Among recordings were those of Astaire on Brunswick, and Jimmy Dorsey and his Orchestra on Decca. One of Irving Berlin's longest songs, "Change Partners" lacks a verse. The refrain, in AA'BA' form, consists of three sixteen-bar sections and an eight-bar release. The slowly-rising melody has many sustained notes, in the style of Cole Porter's "In the Still of the Night" (1937). Perhaps its most interesting harmonic aspect is the short release, in A-flat major.

Dotted rhythms and quarter-note triplets make "Change Partners" eminently suitable for dancing, which after all was its original function.

Moderate ballad with refrain (56)
PUBLISHER: Irving Berlin, Inc.
KEY: F maj., *STARTS*: c' (F maj.), *FORM*: AA'BA"

≈≈≈≈≈≈≈≈≈≈≈≈≈≈≈≈≈≈≈≈≈

CHEROKEE

WORDS and MUSIC: Ray Noble
INTRODUCED BY: Ray Noble and his Orchestra, in a Will Hudson
arrangement, with a Brunswick recording in the United Staets

The languid, sustained melody of this swing tune was originally used in a serious composition by English composer Ray Noble called *Indian Suite*, wherein each section depicted a different American Indian tribe. Count Basie was first to discover the tune's swing potential in a recording he made with his band in 1939. But it was Billy May's arrangement for Charlie Barnet and his Orchestra, recorded for Bluebird the same year, that made "Cherokee" famous. Numerous other recordings followed, including those of the Benny Goodman Sextet and The George Shearing Trio.

Marked "Smoothly", the legato melody consists almost entirely of whole and half notes, roughly outlining the notes of the B-flat sixth chord. Harmonies are straightforward except in the release, which moves through the circle of fifths: F-sharp ninth -B major - E major - A major - D major - G major - C major - F seventh.

On screen, "Cherokee" was performed by Charlie Barnet and his Orchestra in *Jam Session* (1944), and by Gene Krupa and his Orchestra in *Drum Crazy (1959)*.

Moderate swing tune with refrain (64)
PUBLISHER: Peter Maurice Co., Ltd. (London),
assigned to Shapiro, Bernstein Company, Inc.
KEY: B-flat maj., *STARTS*: d' (B-flat maj.), *FORM*: AA'BA'

≈≈≈≈≈≈≈≈≈≈≈≈≈≈≈≈≈≈≈≈≈

FALLING IN LOVE WITH LOVE *

WORDS: Lorenz Hart, *MUSIC*: Richard Rodgers
PREMIERE: Musical comedy, *The Boys from Syracuse*
New York: Alvin Theatre, 27 November 1938 (235 perf.)
INTRODUCED BY: Muriel Angelus and chorus

One of Richard Rodgerss' loveliest waltzes, "Falling in Love with Love" attests to the composer's well-known affinity for the genre. It was introduced by Muriel Angelus in George Abbott's hilarious reworking of Shakespeare's *Comedy of Errors* as *The Boys from Syracuse*. Initially recorded by Frances Langford, it was interpolated in the London revue, *Up and Doing* in 1940, in which it was sung by Binnie Hale.

The lengthy verse recounts a spinning scene; there are many repeated notes and prominent instrumental interludes imitating a spinning wheel. In the more animated refrain – which emphasizes the character of the waltz with half notes on the strong beats – repeated notes are also very much in evidence. Lorenz Hart's lyrics carry out the premise that "Falling in love with love / Is falling for make believe". They end with the dismal words: "But love fell out with me".

In the film version of *The Boys from Syracuse*, "Falling in Love with Love" was sung by Allan Jones and Rosemary Lane. In spite of its distressing lyrics, the music has an infectious quality of gaiety that make it one of the happiest of American waltzes.

Moderate waltz with verse (52) and refrain (64)
PUBLISHER: Chappell & Co., Inc.
KEY: B-flat maj., *STARTS*: c' (B-flat maj.), *FORM*: ABAB'

≈≈≈≈≈≈≈≈≈≈≈≈≈≈≈≈≈≈≈≈

GET OUT OF TOWN !

WORDS and MUSIC: Cole Porter
PREMIERE: Musical comedy, *Leave It to Me*
New York: Imperial Theatre, 9 November 1938 (291 perf.)
INTRODUCED BY: Tamara

The musical comedy, *Leave It to Me,* was a satirical look at Communism and America's relationship with the Russians. It had a stellar cast including William Gaxton, Victor Moore, Sophie Tucker, Gene Kelly, and Mary Martin. It also had two hit songs by Cole Porter: "My Heart Belongs to Daddy" (which launched Miss Martin on a trip to stardom) and the wrenching ballad "Get Out of Town". Introduced in the show by Tamara, the song was recorded by Eddy Duchin and his Orchestra on Brunswick and by Frances Langford on Decca, but the most popular recording was by Frank Sinatra.

"Get Out of Town" vividly illustrates Porter's penchant for major-minor contrast, with a verse in G major and a refrain almost entirely in G minor, except for a turn to the relative major of B-flat at its very end. The performance direction heading the refrain reads: "in steady slow tempo, with increasing expression", and indeed this is one of Porter's most musically expressive refrains. It builds from a melody of insistently repeated notes (d's, e's, and g's) to an impassioned close employing quarter-note triplets, and ending with the pleading words, "So on your mark, get set, get out of town".

Moderate ballad with verse (16) and refrain (32)
PUBLISHER: Chappell & Co., Inc.
KEY: B-flat maj., *STARTS*: d' (G min.), *FORM*: ABAC

≈≈≈≈≈≈≈≈≈≈≈≈≈≈≈≈≈≈≈

HEART AND SOUL

WORDS and MUSIC: Frank Loesser and Hoagy Carmichael
PREMIERE: Film short, *A Song Is Born*
INTRODUCED BY: Larry Clinton and his Orchestra

A favorite of beginning students of the piano, this hardy perennial has an easy-to-learn ostinato bass progression, as in "We want Cantor": F-D-G-C. Written by two masters of songwriting, Frank Loesser (sometimes specifically credited with the lyrics) and Hoagy Carmichael (with the music), it was introduced by Larry Clinton and his Orchestra in a film short, *A Song Is Born*, starring Danny Kaye and Virginia Mayo. Clinton and his band, with singer Bea Wain, also recorded it for Victor. Over the years, "Heart and Soul" has been revived in recordings by such diverse artists as The Four Aces (1952), Johnny Maddox (1956), and The Cleftones (1961).

The refrain, in AA'BA" form, has a childlike melody, with repeated notes moving primarily stepwise. The I-VI-II-V chord and bass progression occurs four times in each "A" section. The release is slightly more sophisticated harmonically, beginning in B-flat major and moving twice through the circle of fifths: A seventh-D seventh-G seventh-C-seventh-F seventh.

"Heart and Soul" was featured in an early film, *Some Like It Hot* (1939), performed by Gene Krupa and his Orchestra.

Moderate ballad with verse (8) and refrain (32)
PUBLISHER: Famous Music Corporation
KEY: F maj., *STARTS*: f' (F maj.), *FORM*: AA'BA"

≈≈≈≈≈≈≈≈≈≈≈≈≈≈≈≈≈≈≈

I LET A SONG GO OUT OF MY HEART

WORDS: Irving Mills, Henry Nemo, and John Redmond
MUSIC: Duke Ellington
INTRODUCED BY: Duke Ellington and his Orchestra

Originally written as an instrumental piece, this perky perennial was popularized in a Vocalion record, featuring Mildred Bailey, with Red Norvo and his Orchestra. Benny Goodman and his Orchestra also had a hit recording. In instrumental style, the melody has many skips and jumps and is heavily syncopated. In the release, there is an interesting modulation to and from the B seventh chord. The catchy main theme – featuring an octave jump, eighth-note triplets, and a sharply-accented offbeat – is notably hard to sing.

Slow swing tune with verse (8) and refrain (32)
PUBLISHER: Mills Music, Inc.
KEY: E-flat maj., *STARTS*: e-flat' (E-flat maj.), *FORM*: AABC

≈≈≈≈≈≈≈≈≈≈≈≈≈≈≈≈≈≈≈≈≈

I'LL BE SEEING YOU * * *

WORDS: Irving Kahal, *MUSIC*: Sammy Fain
PREMIERE: Revue, *Right This Way*
New York: 46th Street Theatre, 4 January 1938 (15 perf.)
INTRODUCED BY: Tamara

The nostalgic ballad, "I'll Be Seeing You", has served as a good-night song at dances and social gatherings for over half a century. It made no immediate stir after it was introduced by Tamara in the short-running revue, *Right This Way*. Its real success began with the Victor recording by Tommy Dorsey and his Orchestra, with vocal by Frank Sinatra. Other recordings were made by Bing Crosby (a No. 1 Chart record), Frances Langford, and Freddy Martin and his Orchestra. During World War II, the song's theme of separation made it into something of a national anthem. Starting in the fifties, Liberace used it as his closing theme.

In the verse, beginning in E-flat minor, Irving Kahal's tender lyrics speak of Paris and the tolling of cathedral bells, while in the refrain they tell of a small café and a children's carrousel. In the refrain, Sammy Fain's plaintive melody moves mostly stepwise, with an unusual downward skip of two tritones (from c" to f-sharp', and from f-sharp' to c') just before the halfway point of the refrain, at the words "the wishing well".

A namesake movie, *I'll Be Seeing You,* featured the song in 1944. In 1973, The Five Satins sang it in the film, *Let the Good Times Roll.* It remains a favorite way to end an evening.

Slow ballad with verse (17) and refrain (32)
PUBLISHER: Williamson Music, Inc.
KEY: E-flat maj., *STARTS*: g' (E-flat maj.), *FORM*: ABA'C

≈≈≈≈≈≈≈≈≈≈≈≈≈≈≈≈≈≈≈≈

IN THE MOOD *

WORDS: Andy Razaf, *MUSIC*: Joe Garland
INTRODUCED BY: Edgar Hayes and his Orchestra, 1938, in a Decca recording

This riff-like tune, an icon of the swing era, became famous in a Billy May arrangement by Glenn Miller and his Orchestra, recorded on Bluebird 1 August 1939, featuring rival tenor sax solos by Tex Beneke and Al Klink. The music was written by arranger Joe Garland, based on an instrumental he had written with Wingy Manone in 1937 called "Tar Paper Stomp". Garland had previously submitted "In the Mood" to Artie Shaw, who turned it down, thinking it too long for a recording. Miller, on the other hand, made a few judicious cuts, and a world-famous hit was born. The Miller organization always performed the arrangement with great showmanship, with horns waving in the air, and hats acting as mutes. The closing device of fading away for three consecutive refrains, and then suddenly resuming with a loud blast of sound, invariably brought down the house. Miller used it as his theme song.

The simple melody of the refrain consists of eighth notes outlining triads of the tonic (G major), subdominant (C major), and dominant (D major), with a minimum of syncopation. The form and harmonies are consistent with twelve-bar blues form. Syncopation is more prominent in the eight-bar interlude, which also features repeated notes and the only blue note in the song: the flatted third (e-flat') at the cadence.

In films, "In the Mood" was performed by the Glenn Miller band in *Sun Valley Serenade* (1941) and again in *The Glenn Miller Story* (1954). Jennifer Holliday sang it as the title song of the movie, *In the Mood* (1987).

Moderate swing tune with refrain (12) and two interludes (8)
PUBLISHER: Shapiro, Bernstein & Co., Inc.
KEY : G or A-flat maj., *STARTS*: b' (G maj.) or c" (A-flat maj.),
OVERALL FORM: ABB

≈≈≈≈≈≈≈≈≈≈≈≈≈≈≈≈≈≈≈≈

JEEPERS CREEPERS

WORDS: Johnny Mercer, *MUSIC*: Harry Warren
PREMIERE: Film musical, *Going Places*. Warner Brothers/First National, 1938
INTRODUCED BY: Louis Armstrong and Maxine Sullivan

Louis Armstrong sang this bouncy tune to a racehorse named "Jeepers Creepers" in the film, *Going Places*. It went on to become a hit, spurred on by Armstrong's recording on Decca and a host of other recordings, including those by the bands of Al Donahue, Larry Clinton, Gene Krupa, and Stan Kenton. The song stayed five weeks on *Your Hit Parade*, and was nominated for an Academy Award.

The charm of "Jeepers Creepers" lies in its nonchalance, conveyed by Johnny Mercer's lyrical colloquialisms – "Where'd you get those peepers?" and "Gosh all git up!" – and Harry Warren's uncluttered music. The subject is, of course, eyes, but of the human variety rather than the equine. The music of each "A" section of the refrain consists of a descending scale, mostly in half notes, that is repeated.

The song was heard in several films: *Going Places* (1938), *My Dream Is Yours* (1949), *The Day of the Locust* (1975), and *The Cheap Detective* (1978). Its basic simplicity makes it attractive for jazz improvisation.

Moderate rhythm song with verse (16) and refrain (34)
PUBLISHER: M. Witmark & Sons, Inc.
KEY: B-flat maj., *STARTS*: d" (C7), *FORM*: AABA

≈≈≈≈≈≈≈≈≈≈≈≈≈≈≈≈≈≈

LOVE IS HERE TO STAY ✷ ✷ ✷ ✷ !

WORDS: Ira Gershwin, *MUSIC*: George Gershwin
PREMIERE: Film musical, *The Goldwyn Follies*. United Artists, 1938
INTRODUCED BY: Kenny Baker

It is fitting that George Gershwin's last song is also one of his best; it is also fitting that its subject is eternity. Often called "Our Love Is Here to Stay", as in the first line of the refrain, it was written for the film, *The Goldwyn Follies*: a score which Gershwin never finished (it was completed by his friends Vernon Duke and Oscar Levant). Early recordings were by Red Norvo, sung by Mildred Bailey (Vocalion); and Jimmy Dorsey and his Orchestra, sung by Bob Eberly (Decca). In the fifties, Jackie Gleason produced a famous Capitol recording, with trumpet solo by Bobby Hackett; and Gene Kelly and Leslie Caron had a hit recording for Metro Goldwyn Mayer.

George Gershwin's fondness for the pentatonic scale (see "Someone to Watch Over Me", 1926, and "I Got Rhythm", 1930) is again in evidence here. Although the opening melody of the refrain spells out the tonic chord, there is nothing stable about the accompanying harmonies, with their prevalence of seventh and ninth chords. Ira Gershwin's clever lyrics call the radio, telephone, and movies "passing fancies" that in time will go, and say that the Rockies and Gibraltar are "only made of clay".

In other films, Gene Kelly sang "Love Is Here to Stay" in the Gershwin retrospective, *An American in Paris* (1951), and Diana Ross performed it in the Billie Holiday biography, *Lady Sings the Blues* (1972). It remains one of the most popular and evocative of all love ballads.

Moderate ballad with verse (18) and refrain (32)
PUBLISHER: Gershwin Publishing Corporation
KEY: F maj., *STARTS*: c' (G 9). *FORM*: ABAB'

≈≈≈≈≈≈≈≈≈≈≈≈≈≈≈≈≈≈≈

LOVE WALKED IN * *

WORDS: Ira Gershwin, *MUSIC*: George Gershwin
PREMIERE: Film musical, *The Goldwyn Follies*. United Artists, 1938
INTRODUCED BY: Kenny Baker, Helen Jepson, and Andrea Leeds

George Gershwin considered this lovely ballad to be in the Brahmsian tradition; it does indeed have a classical feeling. Another gem from his last, uncompleted score for the film, *The Goldwyn Follies*, it was an immediate hit with recordings by Sammy Kaye and his Orchestra and Louis Armstrong, staying on *Your Hit Parade* for thirteen weeks. Prominent among later recordings are those of The Hilltoppers (1953), The Flamingos (1959), and Dinah Washington (1960).

The broad, sweeping melody outlines the E-flat major chord six times in the refrain, chiefly using whole notes and quarter notes. A touch of word painting is in evidence with the upward motion of quarter notes at the words "walked right in".

Mark Stevens sang "Love Walked In" in the George Gershwin biographical film, *Rhapsody in Blue* (1945).

Slow ballad with verse (16) and refrain (32)
PUBLISHER: Gershwin Publishing Corporation
KEY: E-flat maj., *STARTS*: g' (-flat maj.), *FORM*: ABAB'

≈≈≈≈≈≈≈≈≈≈≈≈≈≈≈≈≈≈≈

(I'M AFRAID) THE MASQUERADE IS OVER

WORDS: Herb Magidson, *MUSIC*: Allie Wrubel

A big band favorite, this wistful song was recorded by the bands of Jimmy Dorsey (Decca), Horace Heidt (Brunswick), and Larry Clinton (Victor). Although the refrain is in traditional AABA form, each "A" section is sixteen bars in length, while the release is only eight bars long, making a total of fifty-six bars in all. The song's attraction to jazz musicians lies in its intriguing harmonies, going through the circle of fifths, and its excursion to G minor in the release. The dramatic lyrics are also a contributing factor, with their reference to playing Pagliacci and getting a clown's disguise.

Moderate ballad with verse (8) and refrain (56)
PUBLISHER: Crawford Music Corporation
KEY: E-flat major, *STARTS*: b-flat' (E-flat maj.), *FORM*: AABA

≈≈≈≈≈≈≈≈≈≈≈≈≈≈≈≈≈≈≈

MUSIC, MAESTRO, PLEASE!

WORDS: Herb Magidson, *MUSIC*: Allie Wrubel
INTRODUCED BT: Frank Parker and Frances Langford

Another big band favorite, "Music, Maestro, Please!" was on *Your Hit Parade* for twelve weeks. Almost every band recorded it, including those of Tommy Dorsey (Victor), Art Kassel (Bluebird), and Kay Kyser (Brunswick). The melody of the refrain is disjunct and harmonies go through the circle of fifths. The two versions of the lyrics, male and female, tell a story of trying to assuage the pains of a broken romance through the sounds of music.

Slow ballad with verse (8) and two refrains (32)
PUBLISHER: Irving Berlin, Inc., assigned to Bourne, Inc.
KEY: G maj., *STARTS*: d' (G maj.), *FORM*: AA'BA"

≈≈≈≈≈≈≈≈≈≈≈≈≈≈≈≈≈≈≈

MY HEART BELONGS TO DADDY

WORDS and MUSIC: Cole Porter
PREMIERE: Musical comedy, *Leave It to Me*
New York: Imperial Theatre, 9 November 1938 (291 perf.)
INTRODUCED BY: Mary Martin

Mary Martin made a big splash on Broadway with this provocative song. As Dolly Winslow in the musical, *Leave It to Me*, she stopped the show at each performance while sitting on a trunk at a Siberian whistle-stop and doing an innocent little strip tease to its strains. She also recorded it on Brunswick, accompanied by Eddy Duchin and his Orchestra, and used it as her theme song thereafter. Another best-selling record was by Bea Wain, with Larry Clinton and his Orchestra (Victor).

The song's sexual innuendoes without doubt have contributed to its success, furthered along by Cole Porter's witty lyrics. They exhibit a laundry list of rhymes for "daddy": caddy, finnan haddie, laddie, paddy, and finally "Da-da-da, da-da-da, da-da-da-ad!" The music, in slow rumba tempo with a modicum of quarter-note triplets, sets off these words beautifully. The refrain is mostly in C minor, but moves briefly to C major in the last section, only to return to C minor at the end.

In the movies, Mary Martin reprised this signature song in *Love Thy Neighbor* (1940), and again in the Porter biography, *Night and Day* (1946). Marilyn Monroe sang it in *Let's Make Love* (1960).

Slow rumba with verse (20) and two refrains (32)
PUBLISHER: Chappell & Co., Inc.
KEY: C min., *STARTS*: e-flat' (C min.), *FORM*: AABB'

≈≈≈≈≈≈≈≈≈≈≈≈≈≈≈≈≈≈≈

MY REVERIE

WORDS and MUSIC: Larry Clinton, melody based on Claude Debussy's *Reverie*
INTRODUCED BY: Larry Clinton, vocal by Bea Wain, in a Victor recording

Larry Clinton adapted the haunting music of Claude Debussy's *Reverie* (composed in 1890) almost literally, under the mistaken apprehension that the work was in the public domain. However, the Debussy estate sued for copyright infringement and was awarded over $60,000. Clinton's recording for Victor with vocal by Bea Wain was a phenomenal hit, followed by the recordings of Mildred Bailey, Bing Crosby, and many big bands. The verse, in G major, is the only newly-invented part of the song; the rest is pure Debussy. The refrain, aptly marked "Dreamingly", has four sections that are nominally related to one another. Consequently, the music is almost through-composed, flowing seamlessly with a profusion of Debussian ninth chords. The lyrics fearlessly rhyme "worthless as tin to me" with "begin to be".

Slow ballad with verse (8) and refrain (36)
PUBLISHER: Robbins Music Corporation
KEY: C maj., *STARTS*: d" (G 9 alt), *FORM*: ABCA'

≈≈≈≈≈≈≈≈≈≈≈≈≈≈≈≈≈≈≈

PRELUDE TO A KISS !

WORDS and MUSIC: Duke Ellington, Irving Gordon, & Irving Mills
INTRODUCED AND RECORDED BY: Duke Ellington and his Orchestra
(Brunswick)

One of Duke Ellington's loveliest creations, "Prelude to a Kiss" was popularized by the Ellington band on a Brunswick record, as well as by Johnny Hodges's band on Vocalion. Lacking a verse, the essence of the music is melodic and harmonic chromaticism, along with impressionistic harmonies. The melodic lines in the "A" sections descend chromatically. Ninth chords predominate, going through the circle of fifths, first from D ninth to F major seventh, and then from B ninth to D minor. The release moves to the key of E major, but the song ends solidly in C major.

Moderate ballad with refrain (32)
PUBLISHER: American Academy of Music, Inc.
KEY" C maj., *STARTS*: b' (D 9), *FORM*: AA'BA'

≈≈≈≈≈≈≈≈≈≈≈≈≈≈≈≈≈≈≈

SEPTEMBER SONG * * * * !

WORDS: Maxwell Anderson, *MUSIC*: Kurt Weill
PREMIERE: Musical comedy, *Knickerbocker Holiday*
New York: Ethel Barrymore Theatre, 19 October 1938 (168 perf.)
INTRODUCED BY: Walter Huston

"September Song" was written expressly for the limited vocal capabilities and range of the great stage actor, Walter Huston, who played Peter Stuyvesant in the musical, *Knicherbocker Holiday*. Huston's half spoken, half-sung recording on the Brunswick label was a best-seller. Among a multitude of other recordings over the years, those of Bing Crosby, Frank Sinatra (1946), Stan Kenton and his Orchestra (1951), Jimmy Durante (1963), and Willie Nelson (1980) stand out.

Maxwell Anderson's poetic lyrics paint a picture of growing old with someone you love – "These precious days I'll spend with you" – and are transported by Kurt Weill's effective music in both verse and refrain. The verse, in recitative style, has a very limited range of barely an octave, and many repeated notes, suitable for Huston's voice. The refrain has a tone of sadness, underlined by the modal melody and constant alteration between major and minor. Harmonies are of special interest because of their frequent changes – from B-flat minor sixth to G-flat major and B-flat major, in the first three bars alone.

Charles Coburn sang "September Song" in the 1944 film version of *Knickerbocker Holiday*. Huston's voice was on the soundtrack of the film, *September Affair* (1951), and Maurice Chevalier sang it in *Pepe* (1960). It is one of the most beloved American songs of all time.

> Moderate ballad with two verses (15) and refrain (32)
> *PUBLISHER*: Chappell & Co., Inc.
> *KEY*: B-flat maj., *STARTS*: b-flat' (B-flat min. 6), *FORM*: A A B A'

≈≈≈≈≈≈≈≈≈≈≈≈≈≈≈≈≈≈≈≈

SUNRISE SERENADE

> *WORDS*: Jack Lawrence, *MUSIC*: Frankie Carle
> *INTRODUCED BY*: Glen Gray and The Casa Loma Orchestra in a Decca recording

The music for this romantic ballad was composed by Frankie Carle, at the time pianist with Horace Heidt's band. Carle later formed a band of his own and used "Sunrise Serenade" as his theme song. One of the biggest hits of the year, it remained fifteen weeks on *Your Hit Parade*, and was recorded by Glen Gray and The Casa Loma Orchestra on Decca, and Glenn Miller and his Orchestra on Bluebird, among many others. The verse, in C minor, prepares the way for the short refrain, in C major, by using some of the same figuration. Only sixteen bars in length, the refrain is idiosyncratic for piano, consistently using wide intervals and eighth-note triplets. In ABAC form, the melody of the "A" section is transposed to F major in the "B" section. Really an instrumental piece, the lyrics are seldom heard.

> Slow ballad with verse (8) and refrain (16)
> *PUBLISHER*: Jewel Music Publishing Co., Inc.
> *KEY*: C maj., *STARTS*: a (G 7). *FORM*: ABAC

≈≈≈≈≈≈≈≈≈≈≈≈≈≈≈≈≈≈≈≈

THIS CAN'T BE LOVE *

WORDS: Lorenz Hart, MUSIC: Richard Rodgers
PREMIERE: Musical comedy, The Boys from Syracuse
New York: Alvin Theatre, 23 November 1938 (235 perf.)
INTRODUCED BY: Eddie Albert and Marcy Westcott

The Boys from Syracuse was Broadway's first musical reworking of Shakespeare, using his Comedy of Errors as a basis. One of its songs, "This Can't Be Love" was an immediate hit. Over the years, it was featured in two London revues, Funny Side Up (1940) and Up and Doin' (1948), as well as in a 1963 off-Broadway revival of The Boys from Syracuse that ran for an astounding 502 performances.

The verse has a chromatic melodic line, while the refrain, marked "smoothly", has a stepwise melody, spiced by a few downward skips of the fifth and sixth. Added pungency comes from some light syncopation and accented notes. In the release, interesting harmonies move through the circle of fifths from F-sharp minor seventh to D seventh. The intriguing premise of the lyrics is immediately set forth at the beginning of the refrain: "This can't be love because I feel so well".

Rosemary Lane sang "This Can't Be Love" in the 1940 film version of The Boys from Syracuse. Cyd Charisse and Dee Turnell performed it in the Rodgers and Hart biographical film, Words and Music (1948); and Doris Day, Jimmy Durante, and Stephen Boyd did it in the screen treatment of Billy Rose's Jumbo (1962).

Moderate rhythm song with verse (16) and refrain (32)
PUBLISHER: Chappell & Co., Inc.
KEY: G maj., STARTS: g' (G 6), FORM: AA'BA'

≈≈≈≈≈≈≈≈≈≈≈≈≈≈≈≈≈≈≈

TWO SLEEPY PEOPLE

WORDS: Frank Loesser, MUSIC: Hoagy Carmichael
PREMIERE: Film musical, Thanks for the Memory. Paramount, 1938
INTRODUCED BY: Bob Hope and Shirley Ross

So successful was the song "Thanks for the Memory" (1937), sung by Bob Hope and Shirley Ross in the film, The Big Broadcast of 1938, that it inspired a film with the same title and same stars entitled Thanks for the Memory. Frank Loesser and Hoagy Carmichael wrote "Two Sleepy People" specifically for Hope and Ross. Among prominent recordings were those of Hope and Ross (Decca), Fats Waller (Brunswick), Hoagy Carmichael and

Ella Logan (Brunswick), and Sammy Kaye and his Orchestra (Victor). Forty years later, it was featured in the Fats Waller retrospective Broadway revue, *Ain't Misbehavin'* (1978). Carmichael's music holds few surprises, mostly moving up and down the scale, accompanied by simple harmonies. But it is Loesser's charming lyrics that captivate, telling the story of two sleepy people (husband and wife in the movie) who are "too much in love to say 'goodnight.'" They contain whimsical touches such as "out of cigarettes" and "foggy little fella / drowsy little dame", that have helped keep the song alive.

Moderate ballad with verse (9)and refrain (32)
PUBLISHER: Famous Music Corporation
KEY: E-flat maj., *STARTS*: e-flat' (E-flat maj.), *FORM*: AA'BA'

≈≈≈≈≈≈≈≈≈≈≈≈≈≈≈≈≈≈≈≈≈

YOU GO TO MY HEAD * !

WORDS: Haven Gillespie, *MUSIC*: J. Fred Coots
INTRODUCED BY: Glen Gray and The Casa Loma Orchestra, vocal by Kenny Sargent

One of the most inventive ballads to emanate from the era of the big bands, "You Go to My Head" was introduced by Glen Gray and the Casa Loma Orchestra, but had its first hit recording (Victor) with Larry Clinton and his Orchestra, sung by Bea Wain. Among other recordings were those by the bands of Glen Gray (Victor) and Mitchell Ayres (Bluebird); Ayres used the song as his theme. Singers took to the evocative ballad in droves: Frank Sinatra, Lena Horne, Marlene Dietrich, Sarah Vaughan, and many others. In 1975, John Raitt sang it in *A Musical Jubilee*.

Starting with the upward jump of an octave to repeated notes, the song goes through some remarkable chromatic harmonies; the first six bars alone navigate from E-flat major to D flat seventh to G-flat major, F seventh, B-flat seventh, and E-flat minor. Added to this is a release which modulates unexpectedly to G major, underlined by insistent quarter-note triplets on the notes d" and d'. The last section is unusual in itself, with a long coda featuring triplets at the words "Hasn't a ghost of a chance in this crazy romance". Finally, the melody ends, unusually, on repeated notes of the dominant.

Known as a musician's song *par excellence*, "You Go to My Head" is favored by vocalists and instrumentalists alike.

Slow ballad with refrain (42)
PUBLISHER: Remick Music Corp.
KEY: E-flat maj., *STARTS*: b-flat' (E-flat maj.), *FORM*: AABA'

≈≈≈≈≈≈≈≈≈≈≈≈≈≈≈≈≈≈≈≈

YOU MUST HAVE BEEN A BEAUTIFUL BABY *

WORDS: Johnny Mercer, *MUSIC*: Harry Warren
PREMIERE: Film musical, *Hard to Get*. Warner Brothers, 1938
INTRODUCED BY: Dick Powell

Introduced by Dick Powell in a forgettable film, *Hard to Get*, "You Must Have Been a Beautiful Baby" is written in an old-fashioned style, suitable for tap dancing. Nevertheless, it has been revived over the years; in 1961, with a Top Ten record by Bobby Darin, and in 1967 by the Dave Clark Five. The twenty-bar refrain goes leisurely through the circle of fifths (C seventh, F seventh, B-flat seventh, E-flat major) twice, with a profusion of dotted quarters and eighths. In other movies besides *Hard to Get*, Doris Day sang it in *My Dream Is Yours* (1949) and Eddie Cantor dubbed it in for Keefe Brasselle in *The Eddie Cantor Story* (1953).

PUBLISHER: Remick Music Corporation
KEY: E-flat maj., *STARTS*: b' (C 7), *FORM*: ABAC

≈≈≈≈≈≈≈≈≈≈≈≈≈≈≈≈≈≈≈≈

HOLLYWOOD'S FINEST YEAR

1939

Where troubles melt like lemon drops, away, above the chimney tops . . .

E. Y. Harburg
"Over the Rainbow"

The eventful year of 1939 is considered by many historians to be Hollywood's finest, producing such blockbuster hits as *Wuthering Heights*, with Laurence Olivier and Merle Oberon; *Mr. Smith Goes to Washington*, starring James Stewart; *Goodbye, Mr. Chips*, with Robert Donat and Greer Garson; *Ninotchka*, starring the elusive Greta Garbo; and the fantasy film of the year, *The Wizard of Oz*, featuring an unknown teenager named Judy Garland singing "Over the Rainbow". But all of these are dwarfed by the most wondrous film of them all: *Gone with the Wind*, starring Clark Gable, Vivien Leigh, and Leslie Howard. Produced by David Selznick at a cost of four-and-a-half million dollars, the three-hour-and-forty-two-minute dramatization of Margaret Mitchell's novel will earn $159 million by 1976, and then begin a new career in television.

But, aside from "Over the Rainbow", few songs emanate from the movies. Most of them are popularized by the big bands, which are flourishing throughout the land and wafting their strains over the airwaves from late-night remotes. This year alone sees the publication of such big-band favorites as "Moonlight Serenade", "I'll Never Smile Again", "Tuxedo Junction", "And the Angels Sing", and "Frenesi".

One of the biggest hits of the year, Irving Berlin's patriotic anthem "God Bless America", becomes terribly apposite after the first of September, when Germany invades Poland and Britain and France declare war. Still, earlier in the year there are other diversions. The New York World's Fair opens in Flushing Meadows, promising a "World of Tomorrow". Radio and recording is bringing music to the millions. During the summer, more than forty big bands broadcast over the NBC Red and Blue Networks, among them Glenn Miller, Artie Shaw, and Jimmy and Tommy Dorsey. Not to be outdone, CBS presents the bands of Benny Goodman, Sammy Kaye, and Hal Kemp. Frank Sinatra joins the Harry James band. Recording has a rebirth when Columbia Records signs Benny Goodman, Duke Ellington, and Count Basie and their bands to make new-fangled laminated disks, retailing for fifty cents each.

Broadway is also enjoying a banner year, with such plays as William Saroyan's *The Time of Your Life*, which wins the Pulitzer Prize; *The Little Foxes*, starring Talllulah Bankhead; *The Philadelphia Story*, with Katherine Hepburn; Monty Wooley as *The Man Who Came to Dinner*; and a play destined to run for seven-and-a-half years, *Life with Father*. But, as with the movies, there are few musical plays, including the disastrous *Very Warm for May*, which nevertheless gives the world one of its finest ballads, "All the Things You Are".

It is indeed a year of strange contrasts: a military invasion and a World's Fair, deadly reality and castles in the air, the shadows of war and Hollywood fantasy, World War II and *The Wizard of Oz*.

SONGS OF 1939

All the Things You Are ****!
And the Angels Sing
The Army Air Corps Song **
Beer Barrel Polka***
Brazil (Aquarela do Brasil)*!
Careless
Darn That Dream
Day In– Day Out
Deep Purple**
Don't Worry 'Bout Me
Frenesi
God Bless America ****
I Concentrate on You *!
I Didn't Know What Time it Was
I Get Along without You Very Well
If I Didn't Care
I'll Never Smile Again
Indian Summer
Moon Love
Moonlight Serenade ***
My Prayer
Our Love
Over the Rainbow ****
Perfidia
South of the Border (Down Mexico Way)
Stairway to the Stars
Tuxedo Junction
Undecided *
What's New? *

ALL THE THINGS YOU ARE ＊＊＊＊!

WORDS: Oscar Hammerstein II, *MUSIC*: Jerome Kern
PREMIERE: Musical comedy, *Very Warm for May*
New York: Alvin Theatre, 17 Nov. 1939 (59 perf.)
INTRODUCED BY: Hollace Shaw, accompanied by Frances Mercer,
Ralph Stuart, and Hiram Sherman

Two months after war erupted in Poland, the musical, *Very Warm for May*, opened on Broadway. It was a dismal failure, largely because of the book. With terrible reviews, the show lasted for only fifty-nine performances despite the eminence of its lyricist, Oscar Hammerstein II, and composer, Jerome Kern. It was Kern's last show for Broadway. Yet the doomed musical contained several fine songs, including one that in itself epitomizes the high quality of American popular song in the thirties, "All the Things You Are". The first hit recording was on Victor, by Tommy Dorsey and his Orchestra, with vocal by Jack Leonard; the song stayed eleven weeks on *Your Hit Parade*.

The ballad stands apart from other popular songs in several ways. So unusual is the harmonic meandering of the refrain (which Kern insisted on calling "burthen"), that the composer expressed strong doubts that the song could ever be a hit. Nevertheless, musicians took to it immediately. Even before *Very Warm for May* opened, "All the Things You Are" was recorded for Victor by the big band of Tommy Dorsey, with vocal by Jack Leonard. The bands of Artie Shaw and Frankie Masters soon followed suit. The song remained on radio's *Your Hit Parade* for eleven weeks. Frank Sinatra made a memorable recording.

The verse, in G major, begins simply enough in operetta style. But then, unexpectedly, Kern modulates to the F minor chord that starts the refrain. From then on the harmonic roller coaster begins, leaving the listener unaware until the end of the song that the home key is A-flat major. Most striking of all are Kern's masterly modulations, both from verse to refrain and within the refrain itself. Also notable is the enharmonic change at the close of the "B" section, reading G-sharp as A-flat. Contributing to the song's difficulty for vocalists is the melody, which is jagged and somewhat hard to sing, consisting largely of rising fourths. In contrast to all this innovative music, Hammerstein's lyrics are rather old-fashioned, bearing such archaic poetic expressions as "angel glow" and "moment divine". Nevertheless, they are effective; any words would risk being overshadowed by such brilliant music.

"All the Things You Are" was sung by Ginny Simms in the 1944 film musical, *Broadway Rhythm*; by Tony Martin in the 1946 Kern biography, *Till the Clouds Roll By*; and by Mario Lanza in the 1952 film, *Because You're*

Mine. Despite Kern's initial misgivings, it remains an American classic, one of the most beloved ballads of the twentieth century.

Moderate ballad with verse (16) and refrain (36)
PUBLISHER: T. B. Harms Company
KEY: A-flat maj., *STARTS*: a-flat' (F min.), *FORM*: AA'BA"

≈≈≈≈≈≈≈≈≈≈≈≈≈≈≈≈≈≈≈

AND THE ANGELS SING

WORDS: Johnny Mercer, *MUSIC*: Ziggy Elman
INTRODUCED BY: Ziggy Elman and his Orchestra, in a Bluebird recording

A product of the big bands, this song is unusual on several counts. Although designated as a slow love song – the opening line is "You smile and the angels sing" – it is usually performed as a moderately fast swing tune. Its music, derived from a traditional Russian *fralich*, is credited to Ziggy Elman, Benny Goodman's lead trumpeter, who had replaced Harry James when James left to form his own band in 1938. Zelman originally wrote it as a wordless instrumental called "Fralich in Swing", and initially recorded it on Bluebird, with his own band.

Johnny Mercer – who was writing special material for the prime-time radio program, *The Camel Caravan*, which featured the Goodman Band – wrote the lyrics. The song remained Elman's signature tune when he played it with his own band, and again when he performed with Tommy Dorsey. The Victor recording by Benny Goodman and his Orchesra, with vocal by Martha Tilton and Elman's trumpet solo, was a great hit. Other recordings were by Bing Crosby, Glenn Miller and his Orchestra, and Count Basie and his Orchestra. The song remained on radio's *Your Hit Parade* for twelve weeks.

The song's tripartite form (AABBAA') underlines its folk derivation. The music of the two repeated "A" sections features simple tonic-dominant harmonies and a stepwise melody in a narrow range. In contrast, the repeated "B" section introduces a note of modal exoticism to the key of C major by the use of the "foreign" notes b-flat' and f-sharp'.

The title itself was used for a 1944 film, *And the Angels Sing*, starring Betty Hutton and Fred MacMurray. The song was also featured in *The Benny Goodman Story* (1956, with Steve Allen and Donna Reed).

Moderately slow ballad with refrain (48); later, a moderately fast swing tune
PUBLISHER: Bregman, Vocco and Conn, Inc
KEY: E-flat maj., *STARTS*: g' (E-flat 6), *FORM*: AABBAA'

≈≈≈≈≈≈≈≈≈≈≈≈≈≈≈≈≈≈≈

THE ARMY AIR CORPS SONG ★ ★

WORDS and MUSIC: Robert Crawford
INTRODUCED BY: The Army Air Corps Band

In 1939, the Army Air Corps offered a prize for a song to represent that branch of the service. It was won by Robert Crawford, a former student and voice teacher from Princeton University, who later became known as "the flying baritone". With the advent of hostilities, the striking march he wrote became known throughout the world as the official song of the United States Air Corps (its title changed to "The United States Air Force Song"). In 1943, the song was the running theme of the Air Force show, *Winged Victory*, written by Moss Hart. During World War II, it became tremendously popular with both troops and civilians, sparked by the recordings of Dick Powell on Decca, Alvino Rey and his Orchestra on Bluebird, and Major Glenn Miller and the AAF Orchestra on V-disc.

The spirited march consists of three related sections in dotted rhythm, followed by a rousing climax bringing the song to its highest point. The words have much to do with the song's success, beginning with the stirring words "Off we go into the wild blue yonder", and ending, "Nothing will stop the Army Air Corps".

In the movies, the march was featured in *Ice-Capades Revue* (1942) and sung by The Bombardiers in *Follow the Band* (1943). Also, featured in the 1951 film, *The Wild Blue Yonder*, it remains one of the best-known patriotic songs.

Moderate march with three refrains (32) and trio (34)
PUBLISHER: Carl Fischer, Inc.
KEY: B-flat maj., *STARTS*: d' (B-flat maj.), *FORM*: AA'A"B

≈≈≈≈≈≈≈≈≈≈≈≈≈≈≈≈≈≈≈

BEER BARREL POLKA (ROLL OUT THE BARREL) ★ ★ ★

WORDS and MUSIC: Lew Brown, Wladimir A. Timm, Vasik Zeman, and Jaromir Vejvoda
INTRODUCED BY: Will Glahe and his Musette Orchestra, in a Victor recording, in the United States

One of the biggest song hits of the year, this famous polka was originally published in Czechoslovakia in 1934, as "Skoda Lasky". It became very popular in Europe. Five years later, Lew Brown supplied the English lyrics. The Victor recording by Will Glahe and his Musette Orchestra was a hit, but overshadowed by a highly successful recording on

Decca by The Andrews Sisters. Lawrence Welk and his Orchestra recorded it for Vocalion. It was revived in 1975 by Bobby Vinton.

A typical polka, it is in tripartite form, consisting of a verse, interlude, and trio, all of equal importance. The second and third sections are each repeated. The first two sections are in C major, while the trio is in F major. The melody is simple, moving mostly stepwise; and so are the harmonies, chiefly tonic and dominant. It is an extremely catchy tune, especially the trio, with its long notes (preceded by grace notes) at the words "Roll out the Barrel".

"Beer Barrel Polka" was first sung in the movies by Lucille Ball in *Dance, Girl, Dance* (1940). It was featured in the comedy film, *Yokel Boy* (1942); sung by The Andrews Sisters in *Follow the Boys* (1944); and was heard in the Marx Brothers film, *A Night in Casablanca* (1946). It is undeniably the most popular polka in the American repertoire.

> Fast polka with verse (16), two interludes (16), and two trios (32)
> *PUBLISHER*: Jana Hoffmanna vva., assigned to Shapiro, Bernstein & Company, Inc.
> *KEY*: C maj. (verse and interlude), F maj. (trio), *STARTS*: g' (Cmaj, verse and interlude), c" (F maj, trio), *FORM* (**Overall**):ABB'CC'

≈≈≈≈≈≈≈≈≈≈≈≈≈≈≈≈≈≈≈≈

BRAZIL (AQUARELA DO BRASIL) * !

WORDS: S. K. Russell, *MUSIC*: Ary Barroso
INTRODUCED BT: Eddy Duchin and his Orchestra in United States

This sparkling samba, the first Brazilian song to become a hit in the United States, was an early forerunner of the bossa novas imported from Brazil in the 1960s. Like them, it is highly original, rhythmic, and of superior quality. It also started a craze for the dance, the samba, that has hardly diminished to this day. Introduced in the United States by pianist Eddy Duchin and his Orchestra, "Brazil" was also successfully recorded for Decca by Jimmy Dorsey and his Orchestra, with vocals by Helen O'Connell and Bob Eberly. The song had several revivals over the years: in 1943, after it was sung by Carmen Miranda in the film *The Gang's All Here*; in 1948, in a multitrack Capitol recording by guitarist Les Paul; and in 1975, with a recording for Twentieth Century by The Ritchie Family.

The verse is immediately striking, with its commanding opening revolving around only three notes: e-flat', f', and g'. The insistent, syncopated rhythm of the samba soon takes over, in the dominant. This same rhythm, but starting now in the tonic, persists throughout the refrain. The very broad melodic line, starting with the interval of a major sixth, contains many repeated notes.

"Brazil" has been featured in several films. It was sung by Carmen Miranda's sister Aurora in Walt Disney's 1943 cartoon film, *Saludos Amigos*. The same year, it was performed by Carmen Miranda and Aloysia de Oliveira (leader of her band, the Bando da Luo), and a chorus in the 1943 film, *The Gang's All Here*. In 1944, Nan Wynn sang it in *Jam Session*. It was the title song of the 1944 film, *Brazil*. It was also featured in *The Road to Rio* (1948), and in the 1950 film biography, *The Eddy Duchin Story*, starring Tyrone Power and Kim Novak. It still remains the most popular samba ever to reach the United States.

> Moderate samba with verse (20) and refrain (56)
> *PUBLISHER*: Southern Music Publishing Co., Inc.
> *KEY*: G maj. or A-flat maj., *STARTS*: d' (G maj.) or e-flat' (A-flat maj.)

≈≈≈≈≈≈≈≈≈≈≈≈≈≈≈≈≈≈≈

CARELESS

> *WORDS and MUSIC*: Lew Quadling, Eddy Howard, and Dick Jurgens
> *INTRODUCED BY*: Dick Jurgens and his Orchestra, with vocal by Eddy Howard, in a Vocalion recording

This ballad was made to order for all three of its credited writers: Dick Jurgens, whose orchestra introduced it; his vocalist, Eddy Howard, who sang it; and Lew Quadling, who arranged it. But there was a fourth writer as well, Irving Berlin, who supplied title and lyrics, but preferred to remain uncredited. The song's popularity soared after it was performed and recorded for Bluebird by Glenn Miller and his Orchestra, with vocal by Ray Eberle.

Both music and lyrics are pedestrian. The melodic lines of both verse and refrain feature quarter-note triplets slowly descending chromatically in the "A" sections. The lyrics end with a punning punch line: "Are you just CARELESS as you seem to be / Or do you just care less for me". Despite its shortcomings, the song has survived as a romantic bit of nostalgia.

> Slow ballad with verse (8) and refrain (32)
> *PUBLISHER*: Irving Berlin, Inc.
> *KEY*: F maj., *STARTS*: b' (B7), *FORM*: ABAB'

≈≈≈≈≈≈≈≈≈≈≈≈≈≈≈≈≈≈≈

DARN THAT DREAM

WORDS: Eddie De Lange, *MUSIC*: Jimmy Van Heusen
PREMIERE: Musical comedy, *Swingin' the Dream*
New York: Center Theatre, 29 November 1939 (13 perf.)
INTRODUCED BY: Maxine Sullivan, Louis Armstrong, Bill Bailey,
The Dandridge Sisters, The Rhythmettes, and The Deep River Boys

Swingin' the Dream was a disastrous reworking of Shakespeare's comedy, *A Midsummer Night's Dream,* with a predominately black cast. Still, it provided this lovely ballad, initially recorded by Benny Goodman and his Orchestra, with vocal by Mildred Bailey (Columbia); and Tommy Dorsey and his Orchestra, with vocal by Anita Boyer (Victor). It has found staying power as an instrumental jazz standard, played by the likes of Miles Davis and Don Elliot. One of Jimmy Van Heusen's earliest hits, the melody stands out for its slowly-rising chromatic line and accompanying chromatic harmonies (the first two chords of the refrain, for example, are G major and E-flat seventh). Written in the key of G major, the tonality of the release moves abruptly to E-flat major. "Darn That Dream" is one of the first of a long line of Van Heusen ballads to be favored by jazz musicians.

Slow ballad with verse (8) and refrain (32)
PUBLISHER: Bregman, Vocco and Conn, Inc.
KEY: G maj., *STARTS*: d' (G maj.), *FORM*: A A'BA'

≈≈≈≈≈≈≈≈≈≈≈≈≈≈≈≈≈≈≈≈

DAY IN – DAY OUT   !

WORDS: Johnny Mercer, *MUSIC*: Rube Bloom
INTRODUCED BY: Bob Crosby and his Orchestra, vocal by Helen Ward, in a Decca recording

A highly unusual song, "Day In – Day Out" was written by two remarkable craftsmen, Johnny Mercer and Rube Bloom. It exhibits an emotional quality rarely found in other songs of the day. Several recordings brought it the fame it deserves (it lasted ten weeks on *Your Hit Parade*): first, that of Bob Crosby and his Orchestra, with vocal by Helen Ward (Decca); then, the Bluebird recording by Artie Shaw and his Orchestra. Tony Martin recorded it for Decca, but Frank Sinatra's recording was the most popular of all.

There are many interesting aspects to "Day In - Day Out". For one thing, it lacks a verse and has a refrain of fifty-six bars. For another, it is in modified rondo form, with seven eight-bar sections, the last of which is repeated: ABA'CA"DD'. Then there are surprising melodic and harmonic twists, most strikingly the reversion to the mixolydian mode of the Middle Ages in the "C" section at the words: "When I awake I awaken with a tingle". The song begins quietly enough, with interplay between the notes g' and a': the fifth and sixth degrees of the major scale. But as it approaches its climax in the last two sections, the ballad reaches the peak of its range and dynamic intensity to Mercer's resounding words: "the ocean's roar, a thousand drums". This is, indeed, a most evocative song.

Moderate ballad with refrain (56)
PUBLISHER: Bregman, Vocco and Conn, Inc.
KEY: C maj., *STARTS*: g' (C maj.), *FORM*: ABA'CA''DD'

≈≈≈≈≈≈≈≈≈≈≈≈≈≈≈≈≈≈≈

DEEP PURPLE * *

WORDS: Mitchell Parish, *MUSIC*: Peter De Rose

A majestic ballad, "Deep Purple" began life as part of a piano composition by Peter De Rose, published in 1934. Five years later, Mitchell Parish supplied the English lyrics (published in the sheet music with a French translation by Yvette Baruch, under the title "Sombre Demijour). Featured by violinist Joe Venuti and his Orchestra, there were many recordings, including those of Bing Crosby (Decca) and Larry Clinton and his Orchestra, sung by Bea Wain (Victor). On the sheet music, the song is dedicated to Doris Rhodes, known as "The Deep Purple Girl", who used it as the theme song in her radio show. There have been a number of revivals through the years, with recordings by Billy Ward in 1957, Nino Tempo and April Stevens in 1963, and Donny and Marie Osmond in 1976. The song was also featured in the Broadway revue of Parish songs, *Stardust* (1987).

The broad melody of the refrain, in ABAB' form, outlines the underlying harmonies in quarter notes in the "A" sections, contrasted by a descending chromatic line in the "B" sections. "Deep Purple" has an extraordinary range (an octave and a sixth) betraying its origin as an instrumental. It is a romantic song, evocative of times past.

Slow ballad with verse (16) and refrain (32)
PUBLISHER: Robbins Music Corporation
KEY: F maj., *STARTS*: c' (F maj.), *FORM*: ABAB'

≈≈≈≈≈≈≈≈≈≈≈≈≈≈≈≈≈≈≈

DON'T WORRY 'BOUT ME

WORDS: Ted Koehler, *MUSIC*: Rube Bloom
PREMIERE: Revue, *Cotton Club Parade,* World's Fair Edition.
New York: Cotton Club, 1939
INTRODUCED BY: Cab Calloway

This touching ballad was written by two talented songwriters: Ted Koehler, best known for his work with Harold Arlen; and Rube Bloom, pianist and composer of a limited number of high quality songs. Cab Calloway's introduction of this song was but the first of numerous recordings by the bands of Hal Kemp, Count Basie, Les Brown, Horace Heidt, and others. The song's greatest exposure, however, came from Frank Sinatra's recording.

The verse, with many repeated notes, is in recitative style. The refrain is immediately striking with its melodic jump of an octave to quarter note triplets, ironically underlined by an unsettling chord (an altered dominant with a flatted ninth) at the words "Worry 'Bout Me". The interplay between the poignant words, the sinuous melodic line, the octave jumps, and the quasi-dissonant harmonies makes for an extremely effective song.

Slow ballad with verse (12) and refrain (32)
PUBLISHER: Mills Music, Inc.
KEY: A-flat maj., *STARTS*: e-flat' (E-flat 7 with flatted 9th), *FORM*: ABA'C

≋≋≋≋≋≋≋≋≋≋≋≋≋≋≋≋≋≋≋

FRENESI

WORDS: Ray Charles and S. K. Russell, *MUSIC*: Alberto Dominguez
INTRODUCED BY: Artie Shaw and his Orchestra in the United States

Although this piece is called a "Cançon Tropical" on the sheet music, it became famous as a swing tune. Its Mexican composer, Alberto Dominguez, had another rousing success in 1939 with "Perfidia". Artie Shaw discovered "Frenesi" while he was on an extended vacation in Mexico. His 1940 Victor recording, reaching No. 1 on the charts, catapulted the song to success. The bands of Glenn Miller, Woody Herman, and Xavier Cugat also produced best selling records.

There are several interesting aspects to the music. First, it exploits a bipolar tonality: A-flat major and C major. The verse presents its theme twice in A-flat major and then twice in C major. The refrain, again in A-flat major, has a release in C major. Also of interest is the seven-note pickup that starts the refrain, one of the longest in popular music. The title translates as "frenzy" or "madness" in English, but according to the English lyrics "Frenesi means 'please love me'".

Moderate rumba with verse (28) and refrain (32)
PUBLISHER: Southern Music Publishing Co., Inc.
KEY: A-flat maj., *STARTS*: e-flat' (E-flat7), *FORM*: AABA

≈≈≈≈≈≈≈≈≈≈≈≈≈≈≈≈≈≈≈≈

GOD BLESS AMERICA ✶✶✶✶

WORDS AND MUSIC: Irving Berlin
INTRODUCED BY: Kate Smith, Armistice Day, 1938, on radio

The second national anthem of the United States had its origin in 1918, while Irving Berlin was putting together a soldier show, *Yip, Yip, Yaphank,* at Camp Upton in Yaphank, New York. Berlin thought that the song was too sentimental – "just a little too sticky", as he put it – for the situation, so he put it aside.

Twenty years later, with war clouds darkening, he changed a few lines of the lyrics to make them commensurate with the times and revised the melody accordingly. It happened that Ted Collins, Kate Smith's manager, was looking for a patriotic song for her Armistice Day broadcast. The song was an immediate success. It was sung at both Democratic and Republican conventions in 1940. Kate Smith used "God Bless America" as her signature song throughout her career. Bing Crosby's recording also helped popularize the song. Rather than to continue to earn royalties for such a patriotic song, Berlin established the "God Bless America" Fund. Over the years, the song's income has continued to go to the Boy and Girl Scouts of America.

Other songs entitled "God Bless America" were written as far back as George Washington's time. A piece with that title was copyrighted in 1834 and two others in 1917, the year before Berlin wrote his song. But none of them were as effective. The lyrics are heartfelt in their simplicity. The melody, in stark contrast to that of "The Star Spangled Banner", is highly singable, moving mostly stepwise, with occasional downward leaps of a fifth or sixth. The harmonies are simple, in the character of an anthem, emphasizing the tonic, dominant, and subdominant.

"God Bless America" was sung in two patriotic films of 1943: by Kate Smith in Berlin's *This Is the Army,* and by Deanna Durbin in *Hers to Hold.* It was also heard in the film, *The Big City,* sung by Lotte Lehmann and Marni Nixon, dubbing for Margaret O'Brien. The song's stature as the unofficial anthem of the United States is secure.

> Moderate patriotic anthem with verse (17) and refrain (32)
> **PUBLISHER**: Irving Berlin, Inc.
> *KEY*: F maj., *STARTS*: f' (F maj.), *FORM*: ABCD

≈≈≈≈≈≈≈≈≈≈≈≈≈≈≈≈≈≈≈

I CONCENTRATE ON YOU * !

> *WORDS AND MUSIC*: Cole Porter
> *PREMIERE*: Film musical, *Broadway Melody of 1940*. Metro Goldwyn Mayer
> *INTRODUCED BY*: Douglas McPhail, danced to by Fred Astaire and Eleanor Powell

One of Cole Porter's finest numbers, "I Concentrate on You" was buried in the film musical, *Broadway Melody of 1940*, in which it was given a lackluster performance as a ballet by Fred Astaire and Eleanor Powell. The outstanding feature of that movie was a magical production number danced by the same principals to the strains of Porter's "Begin the Beguine", which had been written four years earlier. The film's treatment of "I Concentrate on You" suffered in comparison. Nevertheless, the song became popular after it was recorded by Tommy Dorsey and his Orchestra, vocal by Anita Boyer, on Victor; and later by Eddy Duchin and his Orchestra, vocal by Stanley Worth (Columbia); and Glen Gray and the Casa Loma Orchestra, vocal by Kenny Sargent (Decca).

"I Concentrate on You" is Porter at his sophisticated best. It breaks away from tradition in many ways: its lack of a verse; its unusual length (seventy-two bars if one includes the eight-bar coda); its chromaticism; its wide range (an octave and a fourth); and, above all, the subtleness of its harmonies. Its harmonic language is encyclopedic, including chords of the major seventh, augmented seventh, minor sixth, and minor ninth. Its modulations from the home key of E-flat go to such remote areas as G-flat seventh and C-flat sixth. As in many of Porter's songs, there are hints of the rhythm of the beguine, especially in the introduction and coda. Further, as in other Porter songs, all elements build to a climax. At the words "And so when wise men say to me …" (the "C" section), instead of the expected opening notes, one hears full chords ringing out with a new melody bringing the song to the peak of its range. These extraordinary characteristics explain why "I Concentrate on You" is such a favorite with jazz musicians as a vehicle for improvisation.

Moderate ballad with refrain (72)
PUBLISHER: Chappell & Co., Inc.
KEY: E-flat maj., *STARTS*: b-flat'(E-flat maj.), *FORM*: AA'BCA

≈≈≈≈≈≈≈≈≈≈≈≈≈≈≈≈≈≈≈

I DIDN'T KNOW WHAT TIME IT WAS

WORDS: Lorenz Hart, *MUSIC*: Richard Rodgers
PREMIERE: Musical Comedy, *Too Many Girls*
New York: Imperial Theatre, 18 Oct. 1939 (249 perf.)
INTRODUCED BY: Richard Kollmar and Marcy Westcott

Too Many Girls was one of a rash of thirties musical comedies on the subject of college football. Despite a cast of young hopefuls that included Eddie Bracken, Desi Arnaz, Hal Le Roy, and Van Johnson and a score by Rodgers and Hart, only one of its many songs has survived: the haunting "I Didn't Know What Time It Was". It became generally popular after it was recorded by Benny Goodman and his Orchestra.

The lyrics exhibit Hart at his best, containing unexpected rhymes and alliterations ("never was naïve" with "imaginary sleeve"), and striking inner rhymes ("time it was" with "sublime it was"). In the release, they are passionate: "Grand to be alive, to be young, to be mad, to be yours alone!" Rodgers's music measures up, reaching the peak of its dynamic intensity and its widest range at this point. The tonality of the refrain is somewhat ambiguous. Starting with an F-sharp minor chord resolving to a B seventh, it would seem to be in the key of E minor. Only at the very end does it reveal its true tonality of G major.

"I Didn't Know What Time It Was" was featured in two films. In the cinematic version of *Too Many Girls*, it was sung by Trudy Erwin, dubbing in for Lucille Ball, along with Desi Arnaz, Eddie Bracken, and Hal Le Roy. In 1957, Frank Sinatra sang it in the film version of Rodgers and Hart's *Pal Joey*.

Slow ballad with verse (14) and refrain (36)
PUBLISHER: Chappell & Co., Inc.
KEY: G maj., *STARTS*: b' (F-sharp min. 7), *FORM*: AABA'

≈≈≈≈≈≈≈≈≈≈≈≈≈≈≈≈≈≈

I GET ALONG WITHOUT YOU VERY WELL (EXCEPT SOME-TIME)

WORDS and MUSIC: Hoagy Carmichael
INTRODUCED BT: Dick Powell, on network radio

There is an air of mystery about this lament. The sheet music bears the caption: "Inspired by a poem by J. B". Carmichael indeed based his lyrics on a poem by Jane Brown Thompson, who never lived to see the song's success. There is no doubt about the authorship of the music, however; it has all the earmarks of a Hoagy Carmichael song: striking emotional intensity and a disdain for formula. "I Get Along Without You Very Well" was not associated with any show or film. It was a child of radio, introduced by Dick Powell and popularized by the bands of Jimmy Dorsey, Red Norvo, and Larry Clinton. The song enjoyed a revival in 1967, with a recording by Karen Chandler.

The idea is wonderful. The singer obviously *isn't* getting along very well without his or her loved one. The lyrics are sentimental in their irony. The music takes a narrower road, with many repeated notes and phrases and monotonous harmonies (mostly tonic and dominant). The form is interesting in its asymmetry, with varying lengths for the four sections: 20, 14, 16, and 14 bars respectively.

Carmichael and Jane Russell sang "I Get Along Without You Very Well" in the 1952 film, *The Las Vegas Story*. It remains a most effective torch song.

Moderate torch song with refrain (64)
PUBLISHER: Famous Music Corporation
KEY: B-flat maj., *STARTS*: f' (B-flat maj.), *FORM*: AA'BA"

≈≈≈≈≈≈≈≈≈≈≈≈≈≈≈≈≈≈≈

IF I DIDN'T CARE

WORDS and MUSIC: Jack Lawrence
INTRODUCED BY: The Ink Spots in a Decca recording

A perennial favorite of vocal groups, "If I Didn't Care" lends itself well to close harmony. For this reason, it is periodically revived. It was the first hit of The Ink Spots, a group formed by four porters at the Paramount Theatre in New York, consisting of Jerry Daniels (soon replaced by Bill Kenny), Orville Jones, Ivory Watson, and Charlie Fuqua. Over the years the personnel of The Ink Spots has varied, but the group's theme song is still its first hit: "If I Didn't Care". Their 1939 Decca record of this ballad sold over a million copies and catapulted the group to international fame. Other groups have since successfully recorded it: The Hilltoppers in 1954, The Platters in 1961, and The Moments in 1970.

The song's attraction to vocal groups is not hard to understand. Its long-held harmonies moves slowly through the circle of fifths, buoyed up by a sentimental melody. This sentimentality is underlined by the chromaticism of the four-note pickups, beginning with the tones c-sharp' and f-sharp'.

The Ink Spots again performed "If I Didn't Care" in the 1941 film, *the Great American Broadcast*.

Moderate ballad with verse (8) and refrain (32)
PUBLISHER: Chappell & Co., Inc.
KEY: B-flat maj., *STARTS*: c-sharp' (B-flat 6), *FORM*: ABA'C

≈≈≈≈≈≈≈≈≈≈≈≈≈≈≈≈≈≈≈≈

I'LL NEVER SMILE AGAIN

WORDS AND MUSIC: Ruth Lowe
INTRODUCED BY: Glenn Miller and his Orchestra, February 1940, in a recording

Ruth Lowe, who had been a pianist with Ina Ray Hutton's all-girl orchestra, wrote this heartfelt ballad as a memorial to her husband who had recently passed away. The Glenn Miller recording received a tepid reaction. But three months later, the Victor recording by Tommy Dorsey and his Orchestra, with vocal by Frank Sinatra and the Pied Pipers, became an instant hit, remaining No. 1 on the charts for twelve weeks. A quiet, intimate arrangement of the song in slower tempo with Joe Bushkin playing background on the celeste, it zoomed to No. 1 on the charts. During the war years, the song's poignant lyrics became particularly appropriate. "I'll Never Smile Again" has seen several revivals: in 1953 by the Four Aces, and in 1979, when it was featured in the musical comedy, *The 1940's Radio Hour*.

The music of the refrain has a nostalgic quality, emphasized by the long-held notes (fermatas) over the three-note pickups, the opening downbeat harmony of F minor seventh, and the downward melodic leaps of a seventh (from e-flat" to f'). The harmonies in the release are intriguing, moving briefly to G major before returning to the home key of E-flat major.

Frank Sinatra and the Pied Pipers again sang it with the Dorsey band in Sinatra's first film, *Las Vegas Nights* (1941). It remains the quintessential big band ballad.

Moderate ballad with verse (5) and refrain (32)
PUBLISHER: MCA Music Publishing
KEY: E-flat maj., *STARTS*: b-flat' (F min. 7), *FORM*: ABA'C

≈≈≈≈≈≈≈≈≈≈≈≈≈≈≈≈≈≈≈

INDIAN SUMMER

WORDS: Al Dubin, *MUSIC*: Victor Herbert
INTRODUCED BY: Tommy Dorsey and his Orchestra, with vocal by Jack Leonard, in an RCA Victor recording

In 1919 the renowned operetta composer, Victor Herbert, wrote a charming piano piece called "Indian Summer". Twenty years later and fifteen years after Herbert's death, Al Dubin supplied it with words. The result was a lovely ballad with a surprisingly modern sound to it, also called "Indian Summer". The RCA Victor recording by Tommy Dorsey and his Orchestra, with vocal by Frank Sinatra, reached No. 1 on the charts. The song was also recorded on Bluebird by Glenn Miller and his Orchestra, with vocal by Ray Eberle.

There is no verse. The refrain has a flowing melodic line that seems to have a life of its own. Almost through-composed and very often in triplets, it courses through the four sections: ABAC. True to its instrumental origin, the melody has many skips and the range is wide (an octave and a half). One of the most endearing aspects of "Indian Summer" (and partly responsible for its "modern" sound) is its brief harmonic excursion to the E-flat ninth just before its final return to the home key of G major.

Slow ballad with refrain (32)
PUBLISHER: Harms, Inc.
KEY: G maj., *STARTS*: b (G maj.), *FORM*: ABAC

≈≈≈≈≈≈≈≈≈≈≈≈≈≈≈≈≈≈≈

MOON LOVE

WORDS and MUSIC: Mack David, Mack Davis, and André Kostelanetz
INTRODUCED BY: André Kostelanetz and his Orchestra, on radio

1939 was the year that Piotr Ilyich Tchaikovsky was finally recognized by Tin Pan Alley. Although songs based on Tchaikovskyan themes had long been written, it took Larry Clinton's success with "Our Love" (q.v.) to inspire other songwriters to wholesale borrowing – a love affair that eventually led to hundreds of Tchaikovsky spinoffs.

One of these was "Moon Love", based on the beautiful principal theme of the second movement of the Russian master's *Symphony No. 5.* Three collaborators had a hand in this venture: the Russian-born conductor André Kostalenetz, who introduced it with his orchestra, and two songwriters named "Mack": Mack David and Mack Davis. There's was not an original idea. As far back as 1927, a song based on the same theme had been written by Earl Burtnett and Robert Stowell; it was called "If I Should Lose You". But it never became popular. "Moon Love" did, after it was recorded on Bluebird by Glenn Miller and his Orchestra. Miller's lush arrangement of the song made it a No. 1 Chart Record and helped put the song on *Your Hit Parade* for twelve weeks. Cover recordings by Al Donahue and his Orchestra and Mildred Bailey also helped popularize the song.

Tchaikovsky's beautiful theme permeates the ballad, moving majestically forward stepwise in quarter-note triplets. The "B" section, with its downward leaps of a seventh, is also taken directly from the second movement of the symphony, although it is not repeated, as it is in the original. Unfortunately, the lyrics do not measure up to the standards of this great, uplifting melody.

Moderate ballad with verse (10) and refrain (32)
PUBLISHER: Famous Music Corporation
KEY: F maj., *STARTS*: f' (C7 sus), *FORM*: AA'BA"

≈≈≈≈≈≈≈≈≈≈≈≈≈≈≈≈≈≈

MOONLIGHT SERENADE * *

WORDS: Mitchell Parish, *MUSIC*: Glenn Miller
INTRODUCED BY: Glenn Miller and his Orchestra

Composed in 1935 as a mathematical exercise while Glenn Miller was studying arranging with Joseph Schillinger, the melody that became "Moonlight Serenade" went through several metamorphoses. It was first given a lugubriously sad set of lyrics by Eddie Heyman (lyricist of "Body and Soul"), entitled "Now I Lay Me Down to Weep". When Miller was forming his own band in 1937, he looked for lyrics in a lighter mood. The result was "Gone With the Dawn" and again, "Wind on the Trees". Finally, Mitchell Parish, who had written the lyrics to the immortal "Star Dust" in 1929, came up with a title that was perfect for the flip side of a Miller recording of Frankie Carle's "Sunrise Serenade" – "Moonlight Serenade".

His tender and romantic lyrics added a new dimension to the music. From then on, all Miller broadcasts began with this gentle song. Miller's lush arrangement, featuring his trademark clarinet-led woodwind section, helped make it a hit.

The most unusual aspect of the song is its length: forty-four bars, with three twelve-bar "A" sections and a contrasting eight-bar "B" section. The melodic line is mostly stepwise, with occasional downward leaps of the sixth. The "B" section is more forceful, featuring quarter-note triplets. One of these, at the words "valley of dreams", is always accented in performance.

"Moonlight Serenade" was sung by Ruth Hampton in the 1954 film, *The Glenn Miller Story*. It remains a favorite whenever songs of the big bands are played.

> Slow ballad with two refrains (44)
> *PUBLISHER*: Robbins Music Corporation
> *KEY*: F maj., *STARTS*: c-sharp' (F6), *FORM*: AABA

≈≈≈≈≈≈≈≈≈≈≈≈≈≈≈≈≈≈≈

MY PRAYER

> *WORDS*: Jimmy Kennedy, *MUSIC*: Georges Boulanger
> *INTRODUCED BY*: Vera Lynn

In 1926, the French composer Georges Boulanger wrote his Opus 17 for violin and piano, entitled *Avant de Mourir*. Its subject matter as well as its soulful strains helped make it a favorite throughout Europe. In 1939, British lyricist Jimmy Kennedy supplied a shortened version of Boulanger's piece with English words. The result was "My Prayer". Vera Lynn, the British singer later known as "The Forces' Sweetheart", introduced the new song. It was popularized in the United States by the bands of Glenn Miller and Sammy Kaye, as well as by The Ink Spots. Soon more of the big bands included it in their repertoires. It was revived in 1956, with a Mercury recording by the vocal group The Platters that reached No. 1 on the charts.

The cantabile melody is built around a series of notes, chiefly quarter-note triplets, skipping downward to varying degrees of the chromatic scale: d', d-flat', and c'. The release was written to order for the new song, while the four-bar coda was taken from the original strains of "Avant de Mourir".

Slow ballad with verse (14) and refrain (36)
PUBLISHER: Skidmore Music Co., Inc.
KEY: F maj., *STARTS*: c' (F maj.), *FORM*: AABA'

≈≈≈≈≈≈≈≈≈≈≈≈≈≈≈≈≈≈≈≈

OUR LOVE

WORDS and MUSIC: Larry Clinton, Buddy Bernier, and Bob Emmerich
INTRODUCED BY: Larry Clinton and his Orchestra

The craze for Piotr Ilyich Tchaikovsky in this year of borrowing began with Larry Clinton's conversion of the third theme of the Russian composer's overture-fantasy, *Romeo and Juliet,* into the romantic ballad "Our Love". Unlike "Moon Love" the same year (q. v.), the creative process involved inserting some new and non-Tchaikovskyan material into the release. The result is "Our Love". Introduced by Clinton's orchestra, the beautiful song was soon picked up and recorded by other big bands, most notably on Victor by Tommy Dorsey and his Orchestra, with vocal by Stuart Foster.

The flowing melodic line owes much of its appeal to its harmonic underpinnings. It moves through the circle of fifths: from F-sharp seventh, through B seventh, E seventh, A seventh, D seventh, and finally to G major. The release is also interesting harmonically, starting unexpectedly in the remote key of E-flat major but quickly wending its way back to G major. The soaring melody of "Our Love" makes it one of the most romantic songs in the popular literature.

Moderate ballad with verse (16) and refrain (32)
PUBLISHER: Chappell & Co., Inc.
KEY: G maj., *STARTS*: c-sharp" (A-sharp dim. 7), *FORM*: AABA

≈≈≈≈≈≈≈≈≈≈≈≈≈≈≈≈≈≈≈≈

OVER THE RAINBOW ★ ★ ★ ★

WORDS: E. Y. Harburg, *MUSIC*: Harold Arlen
PREMIERE: Film musical, *The Wizard of Oz.* Metro Goldwyn Mayer, 1939
INTRODUCED BY: Judy Garland

The film fantasy, *The Wizard of Oz,* was besieged with production problems. First, the original composer assigned to the job, Jerome Kern, suffered a heart attack and was unable to do it. So Harold Arlen took on the task, although he wasn't feeling too well himself. Then, the deal to have

Shirley Temple play the leading role of Dorothy fell through. Instead, the part went to an unknown actress named Judy Garland, who at age sixteen was supposed to play a twelve-year old. Furthermore, nobody liked the big ballad, "Over the Rainbow"; certainly not its lyricist, E. Y. (Yip) Harburg, who was convinced that its broad melody would be better sung by Nelson Eddy. In fact, the producers hated the song so much that they cut it out of the picture not once, but three times. They especially didn't like the octave leap on the opening word of the refrain "Some-where". Only Arthur Freed, the Associate Producer – himself a talented songwriter – persuaded the powers-that-be to leave the song in the final cut. Arlen claimed that the "broad, long-lined melody" came to him as his wife was driving them to see a movie at Grauman's Chinese Theater. He jotted it down in the car and wrote the release the next day. Only when Ira Gershwin put his stamp of approval on the music did Harburg write the title and lyrics.

Despite the producers' initial anguish, Judy loved "Over the Rainbow", and so did the public. It won the Academy Award for Best Song of 1939 and the hearts of people throughout the world. Best selling records were by Garland and the orchestras of Glenn Miller and Bob Crosby. On radio, it remained No. 1 on *Your Hit Parade* for seven weeks. Garland recorded it for Decca, and used it as her theme song for the rest of her career.

The song's most striking feature is, of course, the very octave jump (e-flat' to e-flat") that so upset the producers. It seems to literally propel the melodic line "somewhere over the rainbow". As a counterfoil to this sweeping legato line, the "B" section is like child's play, blithely and repetitively moving between the intervals of the minor third and major second. Most unusually, this "B" section serves as both release and coda.

"Over the Rainbow" has been featured in several films besides *The Wizard of Oz*. James Stewart sang it in *The Philadelphia Story* (1940). Eileen Farrell dubbed it in for Eleanor Parker in the 1955 film, *Interrupted Melody*, and Elizabeth Hartman hummed it in *A Patch of Blue* (1965). It has attained the rare status of a beloved American classic.

Moderate ballad with verse (20) and refrain (40)
PUBLISHER: Leo Feist, Inc.
KEY: E-flat maj., *STARTS*: e-flat' (E-flat maj.), *FORM*: AABAB'

≈≈≈≈≈≈≈≈≈≈≈≈≈≈≈≈≈≈≈≈

PERFIDIA

WORDS: Milton Leeds, *MUSIC*: Alberto Dominguez
INTRODUCED BY: Desi Arnaz

Like "Frenesi", published the same year (q.v.), this popular rumba was composed by the Mexican marimbist Alberto Dominguez. Milton Leeds supplied the English words on the subject of treachery. In 1941, when Desi Arnaz sang the song at a benefit in San Francisco, Charles Koerner, then president of RKO, was so taken with it that he bought the rights for Arnaz to sing it in the upcoming film, *Father Takes a Wife*, starring Gladys Swarthout and Adolf Menjou. But as it turned out – in true Hollywood fashion – the rumba was sung in the film as an operatic aria accompanied by a symphony orchestra. Since Arnaz had the wrong type of voice for this treatment, it was found necessary to have "Perfidia" dubbed in by an anonymous tenor. Soon thereafter, the song was recorded and popularized by the big bands of Glenn Miller, Harry James, Ozzie Nelson, Xavier Cugat, Jimmy Dorsey, Benny Goodman, and others. It remained sixteen weeks on *Your Hit Parade*. It was revived in 1952 with a recording for Decca by The Four Aces.

There are a number of interesting aspects to the music. The introduction to the refrain is in the form of a repeated, descending C major scale. The same bass line acts as on ostinato throughout the refrain. Against this, the first note after the pickup in each "A" section is held for six-and-a-half beats. Exotic touches are the verse in C minor, the cadences of the first two "A" sections in E major, and the alternate harmonies of D minor and E major in the release.

It remains one of the most popular rumbas in the repertoire.

Moderate rumba with verse (8) and refrain (32)
PUBLISHER: Peer International Corporation
KEY: C maj., *STARTS*: g' (C maj.), *FORM*: AABA

≈≈≈≈≈≈≈≈≈≈≈≈≈≈≈≈≈≈≈≈≈

SOUTH OF THE BORDER (DOWN MEXICO WAY)

WORDS and MUSIC: Jimmy Kennedy and Michael Carr
PREMIERE: Film, *South of the Border*. Republic, 1939
INTRODUCED BY: Gene Autry

Something of an international curiosity, this country-and-western song about Mexico was written in England and popularized in America. It was introduced in the United States by cowboy star Gene Autry in the film of the same name. Autry also recorded it for Okeh. Other recordings were by Shep Fields and his Orchestra (famous for its "Rippling Rhythm", actually accomplished by its leader blowing water through a straw), and singers Tony Martin, Bing Crosby, and Kate Smith, to mention a few. Frank Sinatra's recording in 1953 brought about something of a revival.

The lyrics are in the form of a narrative, telling the tale of a person who finds love in a Mexican town. The song is in modified AABA form, where each "A" section is sixteen bars and the release and coda are eight bars each: sixty-four bars in all. Like most country songs the melody is simple, outlining tonic and dominant chords to appropriate uncomplicated harmonies. The only Latin references are the rumba-like rhythm in the release and the words "Ay! Ay! Ay! Ay!" in the coda.

Bing Crosby and Cantinflas sang "South of the Border" in the 1960 film, *Pepe*, while Dean Martin revived it in *The Silencers* (1966).

Moderate serenade with refrain (64)
PUBLISHER: Peter Maurice Music Co., Ltd. (London); Shapiro Bernstein & Co., Inc. (New York)
KEY: E-flat maj., *STARTS*: b-flat' (E-flat maj.), *FORM*: AABA

≈≈≈≈≈≈≈≈≈≈≈≈≈≈≈≈≈≈≈≈

STAIRWAY TO THE STARS

WORDS: Mitchell Parish, *MUSIC*: Matt Malneck and Frank Signorelli

This expressive ballad was adapted from *Park Avenue Fantasy*, a tone-poem by Matty Malneck and Frank Signorelli, first published in 1935. With lyrics added by Mitchell Parish, it became "Stairway to the Stars". Among the many recordings were those of Glenn Miller and his Orchestra, with vocal by Ray Eberle, on Bluebird, and by the bands of Ozzie Nelson, Sammy Kaye, and Paul Whiteman. One of the biggest hits of the year, it stayed twelve weeks on *Your Hit Parade*. The majestic melody climbs two half steps and then jumps a minor third to the pervading motive of quarter-note triplets on repeated notes. Some harmonic interest is offered by the release, which starts in E minor and moves to D minor.

Slow ballad with verse (8) and refrain (32)
PUBLISHER: Robbins Music Corporation
KEY: C maj., *STARTS*: g' (C maj.), *FORM*: AA'BA'

≈≈≈≈≈≈≈≈≈≈≈≈≈≈≈≈≈≈≈≈

TUXEDO JUNCTION

WORDS: Buddy Feyne, **MUSIC**: Erskine Hawkins, William Johnson, and Julian Dash
PREMIERE: Savoy Ballroom, Harlem, New York
INTRODUCED BY: Erskine Hawkins and his Orchestra

A quintessential big band song, "Tuxedo Junction" was a cooperative effort emanating from the band of Erskine Hawkins. The music is co-credited to Hawkins as well as his tenor saxophonist, Julian Dash, while the swinging trumpet solo of Wilbur Bascomb helped make the Hawkins Bluebird recording a hit. The cover recording by Glenn Miller and his Orchestra (also on Bluebird), produced in early 1940, brought the song even more acclaim.

Tuxedo Junction is actually located near Birmingham, Alabama, not far from Hawkins's home town (His group began recording in 1936 as The Alabama State Collegians). The main theme has all the earmarks of a big-band riff: blue notes, heavy syncopation, endless repetition, frequent melodic skips; and that is probably how it originated. The song itself is simple; it was the ingenious arrangements played by both the Hawkins and Miller bands that catapulted it to fame. Played again by the Miller band (absent its leader) in the 1954 film, *The Glenn Miller Story*, "Tuxedo Junction" remains an extremely popular dance tune.

Moderate swing tune with verse (8) and refrain (32)
PUBLISHER: Lewis Music Publishing Co., Inc.
KEY: B-flat maj., **STARTS**: f' (B-flat maj.), **FORM**: AABA

≈≈≈≈≈≈≈≈≈≈≈≈≈≈≈≈≈≈≈

UNDECIDED *

WORDS: Sid Robin, **MUSIC**: Charles Shavers
INTRODUCED BY: John Kirby and "The Biggest Little Band in the Land", in a Decca recording

Bass player John Kirby called his six-piece group "The Biggest Little Band in the Land". This riff-like tune, written and arranged by the group's trumpet player, Charlie Shavers, was soon taken up by the big bands. Chick Webb and his Orchestra had a hit Decca recording with young singer, Ella Fitzgerald. Other memorable recordings were made by the bands of Benny Goodman, Red Norvo, and Fats Waller. "Undecided" was revived in 1951, with a Coral recording by The Ames Brothers, accompanied by Les Brown and his Orchestra. With one of the simplest melodies of any song, the refrain is built around a three-note riff, employing the tones a', b', and c". The song also has one of the narrowest ranges, encompassing only a flatted fifth, from a' to e-flat", with the only blue note in the piece, the e-flat", at the top of the range. Despite these apparent limitations, "Undecided" swings like few other songs.

Moderate swing tune with verse (16) and refrain (32)
PUBLISHER: Leeds Music Corporation
KEY: C maj., *STARTS*: b; (C maj. 7), *FORM*: AABA

≈≈≈≈≈≈≈≈≈≈≈≈≈≈≈≈≈≈

WHAT'S NEW? *

WORDS: Johnny Burke, *MUSIC*: Bob Haggart
INTRODUCED BY: Bob Crosby and his Orchestra

In 1938 Bob Haggart, who was Bob Crosby's bass player, wrote the music of this tender song for trumpet player Billy Butterfield as an instrumental solo, under the title "I'm Free". A year later master lyricist Johnny Burke supplied touching lyrics. The result is "What's New?" Sparked by the recordings of Bing Crosby and Benny Goodman and his Orchestra, the song was soon a hit. Over the years it has been targeted by such jazz instrumentalists as Maynard Ferguson and Stan Getz. Linda Ronstadt revived it in 1983, with a hit recording. The poignant lyrics tell the story of a romance gone astray and an ex-lover's attempt to find out "what's new". The chief attraction of the music is the inventiveness of its harmonies. The refrain, in conventional AABA form, starts with a sustained G thirteenth with flatted ninth, which resolves to a C sixth and modulates quickly to A-flat major, then to C minor, and finally back to C major, in each "A" section. The release takes the simple expedient of moving the entire harmonic sequence a fourth higher, to F major. These rich, dense harmonies, as well as the poignant lyrics, have kept the song alive.

Slow ballad with refrain (32)
PUBLISHER: M. Witmark & Sons
KEY: C maj., *STARTS*: b' (C 6), *FORM*: AABA

≈≈≈≈≈≈≈≈≈≈≈≈≈≈≈≈≈≈

1940-1945

ACT III: THE WAR YEARS

Prologue

You played it for her, you can play it for me.
If she can stand it, I can! Play it!

Humphrey Bogart to Dooley Wilson
Casablanca (1942)

World War II may have dominated the news in the years from 1940 to 1945, but it had little effect on the songs that were written. Few of them deal directly with war, Rather, they seem to reach out to other places and to other times: to take a "Chattanooga Choo Choo" (1941), or go "Deep in the Heart of Texas" (1941), or experience "Moonlight in Vermont" (1944); to take an old-fashioned ride in "The Trolley Song" (1944) or "On the Atchison, Topeka and the Santa Fe" (1945). One of Jerome Kern's last songs (written with Ira Gershwin), "Long Ago and Far Away", seems to summarize this tendency.

Love remains the subject of choice, but it is a special kind of love, addressing the subject of loneliness due to wartime separation, on the order of "I Don't Want to Walk Without You" (1941), "I'll Walk Alone" (1944), and "Don't Sit Under the Apple Tree (With Anyone Else but Me)" (1945). But the true torch song, about unrequited love, is largely relegated to the past, with the notable exception of Duke Ellington's mournful "I Got It Bad and That Ain't Good" (1941).

The big bands are very much around in the early forties, popularizing such swing tunes as "Jersey Bounce", "A String of Pearls", and "Take the "A" Train", (all of 1941). But that soon changes as the war wears on and the bands lose their leaders and their musicians. Singers come to the forefront; virtually all of them alumni of the big bands Thus, Bing Crosby started out with Paul Whiteman's Orchestra, Ella Fitzgerald came from Chick Webb's, Billie Holiday from Count Basie's, Peggy Lee from Benny Goodman's, Doris Day from Les Brown's, Dick Haymes from both Goodman's and Tommy Dorsey's, and Frank Sinatra from Tommy Dorsey's, These singers, and others, address their songs of loneliness, particularly to the millions of teenage girls whose boyfriends are away in the service. And they succeed, in the case of Sinatra, with riotous success.

As for the songs themselves, the freshness and originality of George Gershwin's music is sorely missed. Yet most of the great songwriters are still active, if less productive; they include Lorenz Hart (who dies in 1943), Jerome Kern, Cole Porter, and Irving Berlin. But two veteran songwriters take up the slack, Richard Rodgers and Oscar Hammerstein II, who bring forth a new style of musical theater that will resound through the century with their epoch-making musical plays, *Oklahoma!* (1943) and *Carousel* (1945). The songs from these musicals soon become part of the American heritage, but some of the most innovative songs of the war years come from Hollywood, written by such composers as Harold Arlen, Harry Warren, James Van Heusen, and Nacio Herb Brown, and such lyricists as the ubiquitous Johnny Mercer, Ira Gershwin, Sammy Cahn, and Mack Gordon.

For by now Hollywood has overtaken Broadway as the center of the music industry. Far more songs emanate from technicolor film musicals than from the often-darkened theaters of New York. Many of these songs are far above the ordinary, including the sparkling scores of *Meet Me in St. Louis* (1944) and *State Fair* (1945), as well as the theme extracted from the soundtrack of *Laura*.

The verse continues its downslide in importance and an increasing number of songs have no verse at all, among them "Skylark" and "That Old Black Magic" (both of 1942). Although AABA is still the favored form, there is a tendency to get away from the standard thirty-two bar refrain by the use of elaborate codas, as in "The Trolley Song" (1944) and "It Might As Well Be Spring" (1945). There also are experiments in monothematicism, using one theme at different pitch levels, as in "My Shining Hour" (1943) and "Long Ago and Far Away" (1944); in unusual phrase lengths, as in Moonlight in Vermont" (1944); and in avoidance of a tonal center, as in "How High the Moon" (1940). Also noticeable, in a trend that will become a veritable avalanche in the years to come, is the increasing number of songs from abroad: from Mexico, Brazil, Britain, France, Germany ("Lili Marlene", 1943), and even Greece ("Misirlou", 1941).

Of all the elements of music, it is melody that is dominant during the war years. Some of the most beautiful melodies come from this period, gracing such lovely songs as "My Ship" (1941), "I Remember You" (1942), "Speak Low" (1943), "It Could Happen to You" (1944), and "The More I See You" (1945). Harmony is still of major importance and great attention is still paid to the lyrics, but rhythm often resorts to formula, with few of the rhythmic experiments of the previous decades. In general, there is a definite feeling that the art of popular song has receded just a bit from its supreme eminence in the thirties.

1940

DARKENING CLOUDS

1940

No matter how they change her, I'll remember her that way.

Oscar Hammerstein II,
"The Last Time I Saw Paris"

As clouds darken over Europe, American popular songs have a lackluster year. Few of the great composers and lyricists are represented: George Gershwin is gone and Ira relatively inactive; Richard Rodgers and Lorenz Hart come out with *Pal Joey* only as the year draws to a close; Cole Porter's *Panama Hattie* produces no lasting songs; while Jerome Kern and Oscar Hammerstein II write only their wartime lament "The Last Time I Saw Paris," inspired by the German occupation of the French capital.

Germany invades Norway, Denmark, then Belgium, the Netherlands, Luxembourg, and finally France. By year's end, the Axis controls all of Europe except for Finland and Switzerland. Britain is next on the agenda, and the Battle of Britain begins with the London Blitz. Winston Churchill replaces Neville Chamberlain as Prime Minister, saying "I have nothing to offer but blood, toil, tears, and sweat." An armada of civilian boats successfully evacuates over 300,000 troops from Dunkirk.

On this side of the Atlantic, Congress passes the Selective Service Act, and the United States sees the first peacetime draft in its history. Franklin Delano Roosevelt is elected President for an unprecedented third time, handsomely defeating Wendell L. Willkie. Detective fiction becomes the rage with Raymond Chandler's *Farewell My Lovely* and Agatha Christie's *And Then There Were None* as best sellers. A new play on Broadway is Robert Sherwood's *There Shall Be No Night* with Alfred Lunt, Lynn Fontanne, and a twenty-year old newcomer, Montgomery Clift; it wins the Pulitzer Prize. Other hit shows are *Romeo and Juliet,* starring Laurence Olivier and Vivien Leigh, and *My Sister Eileen,* with Shirley Booth. Near the end of the year, three sparkling musicals brighten up the boards: *Cabin in the Sky,* with Ethel Waters; *Panama Hattie,* with Ethel Merman; and *Pal Joey,* starring a new discovery named Gene Kelly.

In addition, Hollywood has a lot to offer to help chase the clouds away. There is *The Great Dictator,* Charlie Chaplin's first talkie; *Rebecca,* directed by Alfred Hitchcock and starring Laurence Olivier and Joan Fontaine; *The Grapes of Wrath,* directed by John Ford and starring Henry

Fonda; and the first "road picture," *The Road to Singapore*, starring Bing Crosby, Bob Hope and, of course, Dorothy Lamour. Two screen classics emanate from the Disney Studios: *Fantasia,* combining classical music with cartoon characters; and *Pinocchio,* featuring Jiminy Cricket (in a voice-over by Cliff Edwards) singing "When You Wish Upon a Star."

Radio, too, is burgeoning; as the year begins, there are 743 AM stations and nine FM stations operating. Among new radio shows are *The Ed Sullivan Show, Your Hit Parade, Arthur Godfrey Time*, and *Abbott and Costello.* Many big band leaders have their own broadcasts, including Benny Goodman, Artie Shaw, and Glenn Miller. Broadcast Music, Inc. (BMI) is created by broadcasters to control their own performing rights. *Billboard* magazine issues the first record charts, with the honors for No. 1 Chart record going to two recordings of 1939 songs: "I'll Never Smile Again" (1939) by Tommy Dorsey and his Orchestra, with vocal by The Pied Pipers; and "Frenesi" (1939), by Artie Shaw and his Orchestra. With the war still far away, entertainment remains a primary consideration.

SONGS OF 1940

Because of You
Blueberry Hill *
Fools Rush In
How High the Moon *** !
I Could Write a Book *
I Hear a Rhapsody
Imagination
In a Mellow Tone
It Never Entered My Mind !
It's a Big, Wide, Wonderful World
The Last Time I Saw Paris
Polka Dots and Moonbeams
Someday (You'll Want Me To Love You)
Taking a Chance On Love *!
When You Wish Upon a Star *
You Are My Sunshine *
You Stepped Out of a Dream

BECAUSE OF YOU

WORDS: Arthur Hammerstein, *MUSIC*: Dudley Wilkinson

A rather ordinary ballad, "Because of You" was initially popularized in recordings by the bands of Horace Heidt (Columbia) and Larry Clinton (Bluebird), but reached the peak of its popularity eleven years later, with the release of the film, *I Was an American Spy*, in which it was sung by Ann Dvorak. In that same year, 1951, Tony Bennett's Columbia recording sold over a million copies and the song remained twenty-three weeks on *Your Hit Parade*. The melodic line moves in steps and skips, reaching its highest point in the last section. Here, the long-held notes bring the song to a thundering climax, making it a favorite of singers.

Slow ballad with verse (8) and refrain (32)
PUBLISHER: Broadcast Music, Inc.
KEY: E-flat maj., *STARTS*: g' (B-flat 7), *FORM*: ABA'C

≈≈≈≈≈≈≈≈≈≈≈≈≈≈≈≈≈≈≈

BLUEBERRY HILL *

WORDS and MUSIC: Al Lewis, Larry Stock, and Vincent Rose

This product of Tin Pan Alley enjoyed two lives, in 1940 and in 1956. In 1940 it was popularized in recordings by Glenn Miller and his Orchestra, with vocal by Ray Eberle (Bluebird); by the bands of Kay Kyser and Sammy Kaye; and by singer Conne Boswell. At that time it stayed fourteen weeks on *Your Hit Parade*. In 1956 it was recorded, in a more rhythmical style, by Fats Domino (Imperial). At that time, Louis Armstrong's 1949 Decca record, with Gordon Jenkins and his Orchestra, was re-released and became the most popular of all.

The refrain, in simple AA'BA' form, begins with the outlined notes of the E-flat major triad. Harmonies are also of the simple variety: two bars each of A-flat major, E-flat major, B-flat seventh, and E-flat seventh in each "A" section.

Fats Domino again sang "Blueberry Hill" in the 1973 film, *Let the Good Times Roll*.

Slow ballad with verse (16) and refrain (32)
PUBLISHER: Chappell & Co., Inc.
KEY: E-flat maj., *STARTS*: e-flat' (A-flat maj.), *FORM*: AA'BA'

≈≈≈≈≈≈≈≈≈≈≈≈≈≈≈≈≈≈≈

FOOLS RUSH IN (WHERE ANGELS FEAR TO TREAD)

WORDS: Johnny Mercer, *MUSIC*: Rube Bloom

One of the most popular ballads of the year, "Fools Rush In" is based on previously-written material. The title comes from Alexander Pope's *An Essay on Criticism, Part II*: "For fools rush in where angels fear to tread"; while the music comes from an instrumental composition by Rube Bloom called *Shangri-La*. The song was recorded by the bands of Glenn Miller, with vocal by Ray Eberle (Bluebird); Kay Kyser, with vocal by Ginny Simms (Columbia); Harry James, with vocal by Dick Haymes (Varsity); and Tommy Dorsey, with vocal by Frank Sinatra (Victor). It was revived in recordings by Brook Benton in 1960 and Ricky Nelson in 1963.

The refrain is in ABAC form. Bloom's flowing melody moves downward in sequence in the "A" sections and reaches its climactic and highest point in the "C" section. Harmonies are of special interest, opening with a D minor seventh and moving to F minor sixth (spelled out in the melody) in the "C" section. Johnny Mercer's lyrics have much to do with the song's success, with such expressions as "My heart above my head" and "So open up your heart and let this fool rush in."

> Slow ballad with verse (16) and refrain (32)
> *PUBLISHER*: Bregman, Vocco and Conn, Inc.
> *KEY*: C maj., *STARTS*: a' (D min. 7), *FORM*: ABAC

≈≈≈≈≈≈≈≈≈≈≈≈≈≈≈≈≈≈≈

HOW HIGH THE MOON * * * !

WORDS: Nancy Hamilton, *MUSIC*: Morgan Lewis
PREMIERE: Revue, *Two for the Show*
New York: Booth Theatre, 8 February 1940
INTRODUCED BY: Alfred Drake and Frances Comstock

The delight of jazz buffs for three generations, "How High the Moon" began life as a love song in a forgotten revue, sung by Alfred Drake and Frances Comstock against the backdrop of a London blackout. The song was an immediate hit, popularized in recordings by Benny Goodman and his Orchestra, with vocal by Helen Forrest (Columbia); and by Larry Clinton and his Orchestra, with vocal by Terry Allen (Victor). In a few years, it became the unofficial bebop anthem, beloved by jazz artists. Its intriguing chord changes have fascinated jazz musicians ever since; they have used them as a background for all sorts of improvisations and even as a basis for entirely new pieces. In 1951, Les Paul and Mary Ford had a No. 1

Chart Record (Capitol #1451) and used it as their theme song thereafter. Ella Fitzgerald had a hit Verve record in 1960.

The reason for the song's attraction to improvisers is its constant chord changes, modulating stepwise (rather than through the circle of fifths) from G major and G minor to F major and F minor, to E-flat major, G minor, and then back to G major in the first sixteen bars of the refrain. The same process is repeated in the second half, with no harmony lasting for more than two bars. Such avoidance of the tonal center is found in few other popular songs; "All the Things You Are," written the year before, comes to mind.

Les Paul and Mary Ford reprised their success with "How High the Moon" in the 1982 film, *My Favorite Year*. Along with "Body and Soul" and "Star Dust," it ranks as a favorite subject for improvisation.

Moderate rhythm song with verse (16) and refrain (32)
PUBLISHER: Chappell & Co., Inc.
KEY: G maj., *STARTS*: d' (G maj.), *FORM*: ABAB'

≈≈≈≈≈≈≈≈≈≈≈≈≈≈≈≈≈≈≈≈

I COULD WRITE A BOOK *

WORDS: Lorenz Hart, *MUSIC*: Richard Rodgers
PREMIERE: Musical comedy, *Pal Joey*
New York: Barrymore Theatre, 25 December 1940 (374 perf.)
INTRODUCED BY: Gene Kelly and Leila Ernst

Pal Joey differed from other musicals of its generation: its hero (played to the hilt by newcomer Gene Kelly) was a selfish, street-wise, two-timing gigolo. In this song, he articulates his line to his girl friend of the moment: "I could write a book about the way you walk and whisper and look." The song was popularized by Eddy Duchin and his Orchestra, vocal by Tony Leonard (Columbia), and by many others. It became popular all over again in 1952, with a spectacular revival of *Pal Joey*. At that time, it was recorded by Frank Sinatra (Columbia), Les Brown and his Orchestra (Columbia), and others.

The verse is in the style of recitative, with numerous repeated notes (g'), first reciting the alphabet and then counting numbers. The refrain is very simple, but very effective. It is in old-fashioned binary form, with a tender melody moving to the dominant in the first half and returning to the tonic in the second half.

Frank Sinatra, with a chorus, sang "I Could Write a Book" in the 1957 screen version of *Pal Joey*. The song is usually performed upbeat in a tempo much faster than the one in which it was originally written.

Slow ballad with verse (20) and refrain (32)
PUBLISHER: Chappell & Co., Inc.
KEY: C maj., *STARTS*: e' (C maj.), *FORM*: ABAB'

≈≈≈≈≈≈≈≈≈≈≈≈≈≈≈≈≈≈≈≈

I HEAR A RHAPSODY

WORDS and MUSIC: George Fragos, Jack Baker, and Dick Gasparre

A dramatic song with classical overtones, "I Hear a Rhapsody" was initially popularized in a Decca recording by Jimmy Dorsey and his Orchestra, vocal by Bob Eberly. Other early recordings were by Dinah Shore and Dennis Day. In 1952 Frank Sinatra had a hit recording on Columbia.

The verse, in C minor, has many repeated notes. The refrain begins broadly with three pickup chords (C minor, F-sharp diminished seventh, G seventh) leading to the on-beat chord, C minor seventh. The form is AABA, with harmonies modulating from C minor to E-flat major in each "A" section, and from G minor to B-flat major in the "B" section. Quarter-note triplets throughout serve to give the song a "classical" feel.

In the movies, "I Hear a Rhapsody" was featured in the 1951 film, *Casa Manana*, and Tony Martin sang it in *Clash By Night* (1952).

Moderate ballad with verse (10) and refrain (32)
PUBLISHER: Broadcast Music, Inc.
KEY: E-flat maj., *STARTS*: g' (C min. 7), *FORM*: AABA

≈≈≈≈≈≈≈≈≈≈≈≈≈≈≈≈≈≈≈≈

IMAGINATION

WORDS: Johnny Burke, *MUSIC*: Jimmy Van Heusen
INTRODUCED BY: Fred Waring's Pennsylvanians

Although Johnny Burke and Jimmy Van Heusen are known primarily for their work in Hollywood, "Imagination" was not written for any film. Rather, it was taken up by the big bands and by individual singers. Introduced by Fred Waring's Pennsylvanians, the song was popularized in recordings by Jan Savitt and his Orchestra and by Glenn Miller and his

Orchestra, with vocal by Ray Eberle. Cover records were made by Ella Fitzgerald and Kate Smith.

The refrain has interesting harmonies, including many diminished seventh chords, moving over a chromatic bass line. The release is especially striking, with rapidly changing harmonies; starting in A-flat major, it moves through D dominant seventh, G minor, C dominant seventh, B-flat major, and B-flat dominant seventh. It is a very romantic song, helped by Burke's charming lyrics, such as "it makes a cloudy day sunny" and "your whole perspective gets hazy." The mostly stepwise melody is rounded out by a brief coda.

Slow ballad with verse (8) and refrain (36)
PUBLISHER: Irving Berlin, Inc.
KEY: E-flat maj., *STARTS*: d' (E-flat maj.), *FORM*: AA'BA"

≈≈≈≈≈≈≈≈≈≈≈≈≈≈≈≈≈≈≈

IN A MELLOW TONE

WORDS: Milt Gabler, *MUSIC*: Duke Ellington
INTRODUCED BY: Duke Ellington and his Orchestra in a Victor recording

Initially recorded without words by Duke Ellington and his Orchestra, this rollicking swing standard was also given vocal recordings by Ella Fitzgerald and The Mills Brothers. The riff-like tune is built around the chord structure of the 1918 jazz standard, "Rose Room," composed by Art Hickman with words by Harry Williams. Ellington's instrumentally-oriented melody is entirely new, however, with a five-note motive (g', e-flat', f', g', a-flat') that is repeated almost to the point of hypnosis. The song ends with jagged upward and downward leaps of the tritone (a-flat' to d" and a-flat' to d') encompassing an octave, followed by a return to the opening motive.

Moderate swing tune with refrain (32)
PUBLISHER: Robbins Music Corporation
KEY: A-flat maj., *STARTS*: g' (B-flat 7), *FORM*: ABAC

≈≈≈≈≈≈≈≈≈≈≈≈≈≈≈≈≈≈≈

IT NEVER ENTERED MY MIND !

WORDS: Lorenz Hart, *MUSIC*: Richard Rodgers
PREMIERE: Musical comedy, *Higher and Higher*
New York: Shubert Theatre, 4 April 1940
INTRODUCED BY: Shirley Ross

The show, *Higher and Higher,* was a flop. It had an exceedingly contrived story line, with the biggest applause going to a trained seal. But one song emerged from the wreckage: "It Never Entered My Mind." Recorded by the bands of Benny Goodman, with vocal by Helen Forrest (Columbia); and Larry Clinton, with vocal by Terry Allen (Victor), the song has been kept alive by such singers as Mabel Mercer and Frank Sinatra.

Lorenz Hart's lyrics are among his most expressive, with evocative images like ordering "orange juice for one" and having to scratch one's back oneself. They illustrate the lyricist's penchant for inner rhymes, such as "warned me" against "scorned me" and "pray'r again" against "there again." Richard Rodgers's music is somber in comparison, with many repeated notes in the verse and a refrain repeatedly alternating the ostinato harmonies of F major and A minor. Like the words, they convey a feeling of world-weary urbanity.

Slow ballad with verse (16) and refrain (34)
PUBLISHER: Chappell & Co., Inc.
KEY: F maj., *STARTS*: a' (F maj.), *FORM*: AA'BA"

≈≈≈≈≈≈≈≈≈≈≈≈≈≈≈≈≈≈

IT'S A BIG WIDE WONDERFUL WORLD

WORDS AND MUSIC: John Rox
PREMIERE: Revue, *All in Fun*
New York: Majestic Theatre, 27 December 1940 (2 perf.)
INTRODUCED BY: Wynn Murray, Walter Cassell, Bill Johnson, and Marie Nash

The revue, *All in Fun*, had a lot to offer. Among other things, it had tap-dancer Bill Robinson and comedienne Imogene Coca. Nevertheless, it was a dismal failure, opening in New York on Friday, the twenty-seventh of December and closing on Saturday, the twenty-eighth. But one of its songs has survived. "It's a Big Wide Wonderful World" was popularized in 1949 in a Columbia recording by Buddy Clark, and has remained a staple of cabaret singers ever since.

It is a bright, swinging waltz with a broad, sweeping melody of thirds in downward sequence. Written in AABA form, each "A" section begins with two fermatas (held notes), at the words "It's a." The lyrics are a delight in themselves, with classical references to Nero and Apollo, as well as contemporary references to *Turkish Delights* and *The Wizard of Oz*.

The song was featured in the films *Rhythm Inn* (1951) and *Sweet Bird of Youth* (1962), and sung by Clark in *A Safe Place* (1971).

Moderate waltz with verse (14) and refrain (64)
PUBLISHER: Broadcast Music, Inc.
KEY: A-flat maj., *STARTS*: d-flat' (D flat 6), *FORM*: AABA

≈≈≈≈≈≈≈≈≈≈≈≈≈≈≈≈≈≈≈≈

THE LAST TIME I SAW PARIS

WORDS: Oscar Hammerstein II, MUSIC: Jerome Kern
INTRODUCED BY: Kate Smith

Oscar Hammerstein II wrote these poignant lyrics shortly after Paris fell to the Germans on 14 June 1940; they recall the City of Light in happier times. He asked Jerome Kern to supply the music, and the song was published independently of any show or film – the only Kern song so distinguished. Introduced and popularized by singer Kate Smith, it was interpolated in the film musical, *Lady, Be Good*, and sung by Ann Sothern. Over vigorous objections, because it was not written for the film, it won the Academy Award for best song of 1941.

"The Last Time I Saw Paris" is dedicated to Noël Coward. As indicated on the sheet music, it is to be performed "Rhythmically, not too slowly (in the manner of a simple narrative)" and "not sadly." The essence of both words and music is nostalgia: the memory of happy times past. Kern's plaintive music outlines the tonic and dominant seventh chords and emphasizes the major sixth. Hammerstein's heartfelt lyrics recall the horns of the old taxicabs he "had dodged for years." Their "squeaky horns" are emulated in the release by dissonant minor seconds.

Several film musicals besides *Lady, Be Good* have featured the song. Dinah Shore sang it in the 1946 Kern biography, *Till the Clouds Roll By*. Odette sang it in the namesake film, *The Last Time I Saw Paris* (1954). And, in 1958, Bob Hope sang it in *Paris Holiday*.

Moderate ballad with two verses (18) and refrain (34)
PUBLISHER: T. B. Harms Company
KEY: A-flat maj., *STARTS*: e-flat' (A-flat maj.), *FORM*: AABA'

≈≈≈≈≈≈≈≈≈≈≈≈≈≈≈≈≈≈≈

POLKA DOTS AND MOONBEAMS *

WORDS: Johnny Burke, *MUSIC*: Jimmy Van Heusen
INTRODUCED BY: Tommy Dorsey and his Orchestra, vocal by Frank Sinatra

This charming song was written by two songwriters who wrote primarily for the screen, Johnny Burke and Jimmy Van Heusen. Nevertheless, like "Imagination" the same year, it did not originate in any film. Rather, it was popularized by the big bands, first by Tommy Dorsey, with a vocal by Frank Sinatra, on Victor; and then by Glenn Miller, with a vocal by Ray Eberle, on Bluebird.

In traditional AABA form, the melody of the refrain is deceptively simple, running up and down the F major scale. The only departure from normality is the release, in the key of A major. Burke's imaginative lyrics have helped keep the song alive, with poetic references to "a pug-nosed dream" and "lilacs and laughter." In recent years, "Polka Dots and Moonbeams" has become popular all over again, as a subject for jazz improvisation.

Slow ballad with verse (8) and refrain (32)
PUBLISHER: ABC Music Corporation
KEY: F maj., *STARTS*: c' (F maj.), *FORM*: AABA

≈≈≈≈≈≈≈≈≈≈≈≈≈≈≈≈≈≈≈

SOMEDAY (YOU'LL WANT ME TO WANT YOU)

WORDS AND MUSIC: Jimmie Hodges
INTRODUCED BY: Elton Britt in a Victor recording

One of the few country songs to cross over to the mainstream in the forties, "Someday (You'll Want Me to Want You)" became popular only in 1949, with Vaughn Monroe's RCA Victor recording, followed by the recordings of The Mills Brothers, The Ames Brothers, and Ricky Nelson. In true country style, the song combines the simplest of harmonies (tonic, dominant, subdominant) with a stepwise melody and ordinary, but heartfelt lyrics,

Moderate country song with verse (16) and refrain (32)
PUBLISHER: Main Street Songs, Inc.
KEY: B-flat maj., *STARTS*: f' (B-flat maj.), *FORM*: ABAC

≈≈≈≈≈≈≈≈≈≈≈≈≈≈≈≈≈≈≈

TAKING A CHANCE ON LOVE * !

WORDS: John Latouche and Ted Fetter, *MUSIC*: Vernon Duke
PREMIERE: Musical play, *Cabin in the Sky*
New York: Martin Beck Theatre, 25 October 1940 (156 perf.)
INTRODUCED BY: Ethel Waters; reprised by Ethel Waters and Dooley Wilson

The first title of this swinging song was "Fooling Around with Love." Revamped as "Taking a Chance on Love" and lovingly sung by the incomparable Ethel Waters, it was interpolated in the musical, *Cabin in the Sky*, three days before its Broadway opening.

The riff-like melody is characterized by syncopation, repeated notes, and sudden upward jumps of the sixth and seventh. Contrary to much of Vernon Duke's output, harmonies are of the simple variety. It is the rhythm that shines in this song; seeming to give it a life of its own. The clever lyrics have multiple inner rhymes, such as "on the ball again," "riding for a fall again," and "gonna give my all again."

An unusually large number of films have featured "Taking a Chance on Love." Ethel Waters sang it again in the 1943 screen version of *Cabin in the Sky*." Lena Horne sang it in the 1943 film, *I Dood It!*, known in Britain as *By Hook or By Crook*. In 1950, June Haver and Gloria De Haven sang it in *I'll Get By*. Dorothy Dandridge sang it in *Remains to Be Seen* (1953). It was featured in *The Benny Goodman Story* (1956) and *This Could Be the Night* (1957). And in 1977, Liza Minnelli sang it in *New York, New York*.

Moderate rhythm song with verse (12) and three refrains (32)
PUBLISHER: Miller Music, Inc.
KEY: C maj., *STARTS*: g' (C maj. 7), *FORM*: AABA'

≈≈≈≈≈≈≈≈≈≈≈≈≈≈≈≈≈≈≈

WHEN YOU WISH UPON A STAR *

WORDS: Ned Washington, *MUSIC*: Leigh Harline
PREMIERE: Cartoon feature film, *Pinocchio*. RKO, 1940
INTRODUCED BY: Cliff Edwards as the voice of Jiminy Cricket

Walt Disney's second full-length animated feature film after *Snow White and the Seven Dwarfs* (1937) was *Pinocchio*. Many critics thought it even better than the first. It featured the voice of Cliff Edwards (Ukelele Ike) as Jiminy Cricket, Pinocchio's conscience. He sang this wistful ballad, which won the Academy Award as best original song of 1940. Almost half a century later, Ringo Starr featured it in his album, *Stay Awake* (1988).

The wistfulness stems in part from a broad, smooth melody, consisting mostly of quarter notes, and extending over a wide range (an octave and a half). It starts in the fashion of "Over the Rainbow" (written the year before) with an octave jump, but this time on the pitch of the dominant, g to g'. Four bars later, it proceeds with another octave jump a third higher (b' to b"). The same pattern is repeated in the other "A" sections. The soaring quality of the music seems appropriate in a song about wishing upon a star.

> Slow ballad with verse (8) and refrain (32)
> *PUBLISHER*: Irving Berlin, Inc.
> *KEY*: C maj., *STARTS*: g (C maj.), *FORM*: AABA

≈≈≈≈≈≈≈≈≈≈≈≈≈≈≈≈≈≈≈

YOU ARE MY SUNSHINE *

> *WORDS and MUSIC*: Jimmie Davis and Charles Mitchell
> *PREMIERE*: Film, *Take Me Back to Oklahoma*. Monogram, 1940
> *INTRODUCED BY*: Tex Ritter

Another country song that crossed over to the mainstream, "You Are My Sunshine" was used by its co-writer, Jimmie Davis, during his campaign for Governor of Louisiana; he was elected in 1944. Popularized by Tony Pastor and his Orchestra, the song became a big hit with Bing Crosby's recording on Decca and Gene Autry's on Okeh. It was revived in 1962 with a hit recording (ABC-Paramount) by Ray Charles.

In the fashion of a folk song, there are three sixteen-bar verses alternating with the same sixteen-bar refrain sung three times, giving the song an overall form of ABABAB. The melodies of verse and refrain are similar. The opening motive of the refrain spells out the F major chord, starting on c' and with an added g'. In the style of country music, there are only three chords in the entire song: F major, B-flat major, and C dominant seventh.

In addition to the film, *Take Me Back to Oklahoma*, "You Are My Sunshine" was featured in the 1942 movie, *Strictly in the Groove*; and sung by Bette Midler, Barbara Hershey, and Catherine Johnston in *Beaches* (1988).

> Moderate country song with three verses (16) and refrain (16)
> *PUBLISHER*: Southern Music Publishing Co., Inc.
> *KEY*: F maj., *STARTS*: c' (F maj.), *FORM* (Overall): ABABAB

≈≈≈≈≈≈≈≈≈≈≈≈≈≈≈≈≈≈≈

YOU STEPPED OUT OF A DREAM *

WORDS: Gus Kahn, *MUSIC*: Nacio Herb Brown
PREMIERE: Film musical, *Ziegfeld Girl*. Metro Goldwyn Mayer, 1941
INTRODUCED BY: Tony Martin and a chorus

An elegant ballad, "You Stepped Out of a Dream" was introduced by Tony Martin as a full-scale Hollywood production number, with beautiful chorus girls and an opulent set, in the Metro Goldwyn Mayer screen spectacular *Ziegfeld Girl*, which also starred Judy Garland, James Stewart, and Hedy Lamarr. The song was popularized in recordings by the bands of Glenn Miller, with vocal by The Modernaires (Bluebird); Guy Lombardo, with vocal by Carmen Lombardo (Decca); and Kay Kyser, with vocal by Harry Babbitt (Columbia).

It is a dramatic song, with a verse of repeated notes descending stepwise, followed by a refrain of repeated notes rising slowly and then skipping up and down in octaves. Harmonies are of special interest, as in the opening chords of the refrain: C major seventh, D-flat major seventh, E-flat major seventh, and A-flat major. The refrain ends, unusually, on the tone of the dominant, g'. Because of its unusual chord changes, the song is often performed as a jazz standard.

> Slow ballad with verse (8) and refrain (32)
> *PUBLISHER*: Leo Feist, Inc.
> *KEY*: C maj., *STARTS*: e' (C maj. 7), *FORM*: ABAC

≈≈≈≈≈≈≈≈≈≈≈≈≈≈≈≈≈≈≈

AMERICA AT WAR
1941

Bewitched, bothered and bewildered am I.

Lorenz Hart
"Bewitched"

War dominates the news in America this year. Even though it is still far away in Europe and the Far East, there is a growing sense of impending disaster. Songs are often subdued, reflecting the general unease. Thus, besides "Bewitched", there are such popular expressions of bewilderment as "I Don't Want to Walk Without You" and "Blues in the Night". The love ballad is still supreme, exemplified by the enchanting melodies of "I'll Remember April" and "Don't Take Your Love from Me", but the ubiquitous big bands are everywhere apparent, and some of their most swinging hits are born this year: "Chattanooga Choo Choo", "Take the "A" Train", "Jersey Bounce", and "A String of Pearls".

The war in Europe escalates with Germany's invasion of Russia on 22 June. The German armies are almost in sight of Moscow when they are forced to turn back as the weather deteriorates in the fall. Casualties on both sides are enormous. Finally, in the last weeks of the year, the United States declares war the day after the Japanese bomb Pearl Harbor on 7 December.

In their search for entertainment in this dismal year, people turn to the theater, radio, and the movies, They crave light entertainment to get away from the agonies of war. In the theater, they flock to see Noël Coward's *Private Lives*; the murderous comedy, *Arsenic and Old Lace*; or the season's one musical hit, *Let's Face It*, with a bewitching Cole Porter score. But radio is still the dominant entertainment of the masses, with big bands broadcasting throughout the land over the National Broadcasting Company's newly-established Blue and Red Networks. The largest radio audience ever, ninety million people, listens to Franklin Delano Roosevelt's address on 9 December. The increasingly popular record business reaches a new plateau when officials at RCA Victor spray some gold paint on a disk of Glenn Miller's recording of "Chattannoga Choo Choo" in order to commemorate its sale of over a million copies. And *voilà*, the first gold record is born.

As far as Hollywood is concerned, a few great films come out this year, including Orson Welles's classic, *Citizen Kane,* and Frank Capra's

Meet John Doe, starring Gary Cooper. Humphrey Bogart also has his innings in *The Maltese Falcon* and *High Sierra*. And light screen musicals, such as *Sun Valley Serenade* and *Broadway Rhythm,* offer just the right prescription to counteract the trials and tribulations America at war.

SONGS OF 1941

Amor Amor
Bewitched **!
Blues in the Night (My Mama Done Tol' Me) ***!
Chattanooga Choo Choo **
Deep in the Heart of Texas
Don't Take Your Love from Me !
Ev'rything I Love !
How About You? *!
I Don't Want to Walk Without You
I Got It Bad and That Ain't Good
I'll Remember April ***!
It's So Peaceful in the Country !
Jersey Bounce *
Miserlou
My Ship *!
A String of Pearls
Take the "A" Train ***
Time Was (Duerme)
Tonight We Love

AMOR AMOR

WORDS: Sunny Skylar, *MUSIC*: Gabriel Ruiz
PREMIERE: Film musical, *Broadway Rhythm*. Metro Goldwyn Mayer, 1944
INTRODUCED BY: Ginny Simms, with Tommy Dorsey and his Orchestra

This Mexican import was introduced to American audiences three years after it was written – sung by Ginny Simms in the 1944 film, *Broadway Rhythm*. Composed by Gabriel Ruiz, the original Spanish lyrics were by Ricardo Lopez Mendez, with Sunny Skylar supplying the English lyrics. Often performed as a rumba, the song was popularized in recordings by Bing Crosby on Decca and Xavier Cugat and his Orchestra on Columbia. It was revived in 1954 with a Decca recording by The Four Aces.

Lacking a verse, "Amor Amor" is in unusual five-part form (AA'BAA", with each section eight bars in length) and closes with a six-bar coda. Each "A" section is followed by a simple variation a step higher, first outlining the C major triad, then the D minor. The only contrast is offered by the release, with syncopated eighth notes and harmonies moving from E minor to G major.

In addition to *Broadway Rhythm*, "Amor Amor" was heard in the 1946 film, *Swing in the Saddle*.

Moderate beguine with refrain (46)
PUBLISHER: Southern Music Publishing Co.
KEY: C maj., *STARTS*: c" (C maj.), *FORM*: AA'BAA"

≈≈≈≈≈≈≈≈≈≈≈≈≈≈≈≈≈≈≈

BEWITCHED ⋆⋆!

WORDS: Lorenz Hart, *MUSIC*: Richard Rodgers
PREMIERE: Musical comedy, *Pal Joey*
New York: Ethel Barrymore Theatre, 25 December 1940 (374 perf.)
INTRODUCED BY: Vivienne Segal

Often referred to by its extended title, "Bewitched, Bothered and Bewildered", this winsome ballad was introduced by Vivienne Segal in *Pal Joey*, which starred Gene Kelly as the eponymous heel. The song created no great stir at first, but was revived after the war with a best-selling Tower record by Bill Snyder and his Orchestra in 1950. Snyder used it as his theme thereafter. Propelled by the additional recordings of Mel Tormé on Capitol and Doris Day on Columbia, "Bewitched" stayed sixteen weeks on *Your Hit Parade*. This success prompted a revival of *Pal Joey*, which ran for 542 performances, with Segal again singing "Bewitched".

Lorenz Hart's lyrics are exceptional, employing many of the devices he is famous for, including inner rhyme, word juxtaposition, and alliteration. They sometimes take self-deprecating turns, as at the close of the release when they say: "Although the laugh's on me". Richard Rodgers's tender melody is a perfect foil for these thoughts, using his favorite device of a slowly-rising scale always returning to the same two notes (See also his "Blue Room", 1927.) The AA'BA' form is conventional, although each "A" section ends on a different note. The range is narrow, barely an octave, and harmonies are simple and uncluttered.

In the 1957 screen version of *Pal Joey*, "Bewitched" was sung by Frank Sinatra and Jo Ann Greer, dubbing in for Rita Hayworth. Lloyd Nolan and Maureen O'Sullivan sang it in Woody Allen's *Hannah and Her Sisters* (1986).

Slow ballad with verse (16) and refrain (32)
PUBLISHER: Chappell & Co., Inc.
KEY: C maj., *STARTS*: g' (C maj.), *FORM*: AA'BA"

≈≈≈≈≈≈≈≈≈≈≈≈≈≈≈≈≈≈≈≈

BLUES IN THE NIGHT (MY MAMA DONE TOL' ME) * * * !

WORDS: Johnny Mercer, *MUSIC*: Harold Arlen
PREMIERE: Film musical, *Blues in the Night*. Warner Brothers., 1941
INTRODUCED BY: William Gillespie, with Jimmy Lunceford and his Orchestra

The film, *Blues in the Night*, brought about the first collaboration of two giants, composer Harold Arlen and lyricist Johnny Mercer. So it is not surprising that its title song is one of the most unusual in the literature. Nominated for an Academy Award, "Blues in the Night" was recorded, among others, by Jimmy Lunceford and his Orchestra, with vocal by Willie Smith (Decca); Dinah Shore (Bluebird); Judy Garland (Decca); the Benny Goodman Sextet; and the bands of Will Osborne, Artie Shaw, and Woody Herman. In 1952 Rosemary Clooney revived it with her recording.

The form is way out of the ordinary, ABCC'A, contrasting twelve-bar and eight-bar sections and employing, in addition to words, humming and whistling. The twelve-bar sections are, appropriately, in blues form, with an abundance of blue notes, such as the introductory flatted seventh (a-flat') and flatted third (d-flat"). Also in good supply are quarter-note triplets. The lyrics are especially homespun, with such endearing country expressions as "when I was in kneepants", "a man is a two-face", and "a woman'll sweet talk".

John Garfield did a notably poor job of singing "Blues in the Night" in the movie, *Thank Your Lucky Stars* (1943).

Slow blues with refrain (54)
PUBLISHER: Remick Music Corporation
KEY: B-flat maj., *STARTS*: f' (B-flat maj.), *FORM*: ABCC'A

≈≈≈≈≈≈≈≈≈≈≈≈≈≈≈≈≈≈

CHATTANOOGA CHOO CHOO　★ ★ ★

WORDS: Mack Gordon, *MUSIC*: Harry Warren
PREMIERE: Film musical, *Sun Valley Serenade*. Twentieth Century-Fox, 1941
INTRODUCED BY: Glenn Miller and his Orchestra, sung by Paula Kelly, Tex Beneke, and The Modernaires; danced by The Nicholas Brothers and Dorothy Dandridge

One of Glenn Miller's biggest hits, "Chattanooga Choo Choo" was recipient of the first gold record, selling over a million copies on the RCA Victor label, with vocalists Marion Hutton, Tex Beneke, and The Modernaires. Introduced in the Sonja Henie movie, *Sun Valley Serenade*, it was nominated for an Academy award and stayed thirteen weeks on *Your Hit Parade*. The song has been revived several times over the years: by Floyd Cramer in 1962, Harper's Bizarre in 1967, and Tuxedo Junction in 1978.

It is, of course, a train song, bearing all the proper accoutrements: the boogie-woogie bass, the chords simulating train whistles, the profusion of dotted eighths and sixteenths, the grace notes, the offbeat accents. But, in addition, the lyrics tell a story about going home to Chattanooga to meet "a certain party at the station", and never more to roam.

In other films besides *Sun Valley Serenade*, "Chattanooga Choo Choo" was sung by Carmen Miranda in *Springtime in the Rockies* (1942), by Dan Dailey in *You're My Everything* (1949), and played by the Glenn Miller Band (fronted by James Stewart) and sung by Frances Langford and The Modernaires in *The Glenn Miller Story* (1954).

Moderate rhythm song with refrain (56)
PUBLISHER: Twentieth Century Music Corporation
KEY: C maj., *STARTS*: e' (C maj.), *FORM*: AABB'AA"

≈≈≈≈≈≈≈≈≈≈≈≈≈≈≈≈≈≈

DEEP IN THE HEART OF TEXAS

WORDS: June Hershey, *MUSIC*: Don Swander

A novelty song with a folk-like flavor, "Deep in the Heart of Texas" was written by two urban Californians, at least one of whom had never laid eyes on Texas: the husband-and-wife team of Don Swander and June Hershey. Published on the third of December, 1941, the song became immensely popular in 1942, with many recordings including those of Bing Crosby and the bands of Alvino Rey and Horace Heidt.

It was audience participation that made the tune famous, specifically the four handclaps performed by the audience in each stanza. The music is almost simplistic, with only one theme in the refrain and a bugle-like melody that outlines the F major triad, accompanied by chords of the tonic and dominant.

As a native of California, it is no wonder that this Texas anthem found its way into a number of films. Dennis Day sang it in *I'll Get By* (1950). Wendell Corey sang it in French in *Rich, Young and Pretty* (1951). Thelma Ritter and Jane Froman (dubbing for Susan Hayward) sang it in *With a Song in My Heart* (1952). The unholy trio of Glenn Ford, Eddie Albert, and Marlin Brando did it in *The Teahouse of the August Moon* (1957). And Howard Keel and a chorus performed it in *Texas Carnival* (1959).

Moderate novelty song with verse (16) and refrain (32)
PUBLISHER: Melody Lane Publications, Inc.
KEY: F maj., *STARTS*: c' (F maj.), *FORM*: AA'AA'

≈≈≈≈≈≈≈≈≈≈≈≈≈≈≈≈≈≈≈≈

DON'T TAKE YOUR LOVE FROM ME !

WORDS and MUSIC: Henry Nemo
INTRODUCED BY: Mildred Bailey

A romantic ballad, "Don't Take Your Love from Me" is a favorite among musicians. First featured by singer Mildred Bailey, there were best-selling records by Artie Shaw, with vocal by Lena Horne; Alvino Rey, with vocal by Yvonne King; Glen Gray and The Casa Loma Orchestra, with vocal by Eugenie Baird; and The Three Suns. The graceful melody meanders up and down the scale, with occasional skips of the major seventh and, now and then, a blue note. The expressive lyrics verge on poetry, as in "Tear a petal from a rose and the rose weeps too".

Slow ballad with verse (12) and refrain (32)
PUBLISHER: M. Witmark & Sons
KEY: C maj., *STARTS*: g' (C maj.), *FORM*: ABA'C

≈≈≈≈≈≈≈≈≈≈≈≈≈≈≈≈≈≈≈

EV'RYTHING I LOVE !

WORDS AND MUSIC: Cole Porter
PREMIERE: Musical comedy, *Let's Face It*
New York: Imperial Theatre, 29 October 1941 (547 perf.)
INTRODUCED BY: Danny Kaye and Mary Jane Walsh

One of Cole Poter's most elegant ballads, "Ev'rything I Love" was written after Porter's disastrous horseback-riding accident and attendant leg operations. It was introduced in the Broadway show, *Let's Face It*, which ran for 547 performances and also enjoyed a run of 348 performances in London starting in 1942. On this side of the Atlantic, the song had best-selling records by three big bands: Glenn Miller, with vocal by Ray Eberle (Bluebird); Jimmy Dorsey, with vocal by Bob Eberly (Decca); and Benny Goodman, with vocal by Peggy Lee (Okeh).

The verse begins in E-flat minor, while the refrain is in the parallel major key. Repeated notes over changing harmonies characterize the melody of the refrain, with tonalities sometimes taking surprising turns, moving for example to G-flat major in the "B" section and G major in the second "A" section. Quarter-note triplets appear just before the end, at the alliterative words: "haven in heaven above".

The song was also featured in the 1943 screen version of *Let's Face It*, starring Bob Hope and Betty Hutton.

Slow ballad with verse (16) and refrain (32)
PUBLISHER: Chappell & Co., Inc.
KEY: E-flat maj., *STARTS*: g' (E-flat maj.), *FORM*: ABA'C

≈≈≈≈≈≈≈≈≈≈≈≈≈≈≈≈≈≈≈

HOW ABOUT YOU? * !

WORDS: Ralph Freed, *MUSIC*: Burton Lane
PREMIERE: Film musical, *Babes on Broadway*. Metro Goldwyn Mayer, 1941
INTRODUCED BY: Judy Garland and Mickey Rooney

This delectable combination of words and music was concocted for the film, *Babes on Broadway,* by Ralph Freed (producer Arthur Freed's younger brother) and composer Burton Lane. In the movie, Judy Garland

and Mickey Rooney sing it in their customary vibrant style to a scintillating arrangement by Conrad Salinger. Nominated for an Academy Award, the best-selling record was by Tommy Dorsey and his Orchestra, vocal by Frank Sinatra.

Although it belongs in the category of catalogue song, "How About You" is so charming that the listener is unaware that the lyrics are listing things, such as "New York in June" and "a Gershwin tune". The melody is especially ingratiating, moving daringly to repeated tones of f-sharp' (on harmonies of B major) at the enticing words "I like potato chips, moonlight and motor trips". Repeated notes again characterize the last section, this time on tones of g', at the words "picture show" and "lights are low".

Moderate rhythm song with verse (16) and refrain (32)
PUBLISHER: Metro Goldwyn Mayer, Inc., assigned to Leo Feist, Inc.
KEY: G maj., *STARTS*: g' (G maj.), *FORM*: ABA'C

≈≈≈≈≈≈≈≈≈≈≈≈≈≈≈≈≈≈≈

I DON'T WANT TO WALK WITHOUT YOU

WORDS: Frank Loesser, *MUSIC*: Jule Styne
PREMIERE: Film musical, *Sweater Girl*. Paramount, 1942
INTRODUCED BY: Johnny Johnston

This wartime ballad catapulted Frank Loesser and Jule Styne to the ranks of the foremost songwriters of Hollywood. The Columbia recording by Harry James and his Orchestra, with vocal by Helen Forrest, was a best-seller as were the recordings of Bing Crosby and Dinah Shore. Long after the war, the song was revived with recordings by Phyllis McGuire in 1964 and Barry Manilow in 1980.

In many respects, the verse is more interesting musically than the over-sentimental refrain, which combines outlined chords with repeated notes. Nor are the lyrics particularly distinguished, with their ubiquitous addition of "baby" to the words of the title. Nevertheless, the song was well-suited to the wartime mentality of missing a loved one.

Johnny Johnston, who introduced "I Don't Want to Walk without You" in the film, *Sweater Girl* (1942), also sang it in *You Can't Ration Love* (1944). In 1950 Lizabeth Scott sang it in *Dark City*.

Slow ballad with verse (8) and refrain (32)
PUBLISHER: Paramount Music Corporation
KEY: E-flat maj., *STARTS*: c" (F min.), *FORM*: ABAB'

≈≈≈≈≈≈≈≈≈≈≈≈≈≈≈≈≈≈≈

I GOT IT BAD AND THAT AIN'T GOOD

WORDS: Paul Francis Webster, *MUSIC*: Edward Kennedy "Duke" Ellington
PREMIERE: Revue, *Jump for Joy*. California, 1941
INTRODUCED BY: Ivy Anderson

One of Duke Ellington's most plaintive torch songs, "I Got It Bad and That Ain't Good" tells the story of a man who never treats his lady "sweet and gentle the way he should". The song was popularized on a Victor recording by the Ellington band, with vocal by Ivy Anderson and outstanding alto sax solo by Johnny Hodges. Another popular recording was on Columbia by Benny Goodman and his Orchestra with vocal by Peggy Lee. The refrain – there are in fact two, for male and female voice – is in conventional AABA form, but features an unusual upward jump of the major ninth between the second and third notes of each "A" section. Making the song especially attractive to musicians are its ever-changing harmonies, as many as four to the bar.

Slow torch song with verse (16) and two refrains (32)
PUBLISHER: Robbins Music Corp.
KEY: G maj., *STARTS*: c-sharp' (E dim.), *FORM*: AABA

≈≈≈≈≈≈≈≈≈≈≈≈≈≈≈≈≈≈≈≈

I'LL REMEMBER APRIL ✳ ✳ ✳ !

WORDS and MUSIC: Don Raye, Gene De Paul, and Patricia Johnston
PREMIERE: Film musical, *Ride 'Em Cowboy*. Universal, 1942
INTRODUCED BY: Dick Foran

A lovely and enduring ballad, "I'll Remember April" was first heard in a raucous film, starring Bud Abbott and Lou Costello, called *Ride 'Em Cowboy*. The song became an immediate hit, with Woody Herman's Decca recording the most popular. In later years, starting with a dynamic recording by The George Shearing Trio, it has enjoyed a double life as an uptempo jazz standard as well as a ballad.

It is an unusual song in several respects. Lacking a verse, the refrain is in singular three-part form (ABA), consisting of three sixteen-bar sections. Also of interest is Gene De Paul's wistful, stepwise melody, contrasting major and minor, and the often poetic lyrics, ending: "I'll remember April and I'll smile".

The song was featured in another 1942 Universal film, *Strictly in the Groove*. It also inspired a namesake film in 1945, *I'll Remember April*, in which it was sung by Gloria Jean and Kirby Grant.

Moderate ballad with refrain (48)
PUBLISHER: Leeds Music Corporation, assigned to MCA Music
KEY: G maj., *STARTS*: b' (G maj.), *FORM*: ABA

≈≈≈≈≈≈≈≈≈≈≈≈≈≈≈≈≈≈

IT'S SO PEACEFUL IN THE COUNTRY

WORDS and MUSIC: Alec Wilder
INTRODUCED BY: Mildred Bailey with The Delta Rhythm Boys, in a
Decca recording

Alec Wilder, author of *American Popular Song: The Great Innovators 1900-1950*, wrote this paean to country life as a present for singer Mildred Bailey, who was unable to go to her country home one summer because of a singing engagement. Since the subject of the song is a place rather than a loved one, few publishers were interested. Nevertheless, the song became popular, spurred on by Bailey's Decca recording with the Delta Rhythm Boys as well as a Columbia recording by Harry James and his Orchestra, with vocal by Dick Haymes. The refrain, in AA'BA" form, has a carefree quality about it, caused by melodic drops of the seventh and sixth respectively on the first beats of Bars One and Two of each "A" section. Harmonies are complex with many diminished chords as well as chords of the seventh and ninth. Of special interest is the bass line, which descends chromatically throughout the last six bars of each "A" section.

Moderate ballad with verse (14) and refrain (32)
PUBLISHER: Ludlow Music, Inc.
KEY: F maj., *STARTS*: a' (G min. 7), *FORM*: AA'BA"

≈≈≈≈≈≈≈≈≈≈≈≈≈≈≈≈≈≈

JERSEY BOUNCE *

WORDS: Robert B. Wright, *MUSIC*: Bobby Plater, Tiny Bradshaw, and
Edward Johnson

Another song that originated as a big band instrumental, "Jersey Bounce" acquired words only in 1946. However, it was popularized long before that through recordings by the bands of Benny Goodman and Glenn Miller. Lacking a verse, the song is in AA'BA" form. The melody of each "A" section outlines a harmonic progression in the circle of fifths: C major - D ninth - G ninth - C major. A quite different progression, moving stepwise rather than in fifths, rules the release: C ninth - B-flat ninth - A-flat ninth - G seventh. The Goodman band performed "Jersey Bounce" in two films:

418

Sweet and Low Down (1944) and *The Benny Goodman Story* (1955). It remains a popular jazz standard, lending itself well to easy-going, leisurely improvisation.

> Moderate swing tune with refrain (32)
> *PUBLISHER*: Lewis Music Publishing, Inc.
> *KEY*: C maj., *STARTS*: d-sharp' (C maj.), *FORM*: AA'BA'

≈≈≈≈≈≈≈≈≈≈≈≈≈≈≈≈≈≈≈≈

MISIRLOU !

> *ENGLISH WORDS*: Fred Wise, Milton Leeds, and S. K. Russell
> *MUSIC*: N. Roubanis

A rare import from Greece – with Greek words by its composer N. Roubanis – "Misirlou" was popularized in recordings by Jan August and Walter Eriksson and as an instrumental by the bands of Harry James (Columbia) and Charlie Ventura (National). Organist Leon Berry had a hit record (Dot) in 1953. One of the most unusual songs in the popular literature, the verse is of equal importance to the refrain. The entire song is built on a Middle-eastern scale of seven notes – d, e-flat, f-sharp, g, a, b-flat, c-sharp – that is more Turkish than Greek. There are only two harmonies in the verse, D major and E-flat major, while the refrain brings in the additional harmonies of G minor and A seventh. The song's exotic sound has made it a favorite of instrumentalists, particularly flutists.

> Moderate beguine with two verses (16) and refrain (36)
> *PUBLISHER*: Colonial Music Publishing Co., Inc.
> *KEY*: D maj., *STARTS*: d' (D maj.), *FORM*: ABAB'

≈≈≈≈≈≈≈≈≈≈≈≈≈≈≈≈≈≈

MY SHIP * !

> *WORDS*: Ira Gershwin, *MUSIC*: Kurt Weill
> *PREMIERE*: Musical play, *Lady in the Dark*
> New York: Alvin Theatre, 23 January 1942 (467 perf.)
> *INTRODUCED BY*: Gertrude Lawrence

Possessing one of the loveliest melodies in the popular literature, "My Ship" was the magic song that haunted Liza Elliott (originally played by Gertrude Lawrence) in Moss Hart's musical play, *Lady in the Dark*. It was part of her childhood dream, revealed gradually through psychoanalysis. Early recordings were by Lawrence, on Victor, and by Danny Kaye, who also appeared in the show, on Columbia.

Lacking a verse, the powerful song is in AA'BA" form. Kurt Weill's melody is appropriately haunting, with the main theme based on a four-note scale: c - d - f - a. The opening motive appears three times in each "A" section. Ira Gershwin's lyrics are aptly dreamlike. They tell of an imaginary ship with "decks trimmed with gold" and "a paradise in the hold". Most interesting of all is that the cadence of the first two "A" sections avoids the tonic, F major; the first cadence is on G minor seventh, the second on B-flat major. Only the third cadence is on F major, when the lyrics tell of the ship bringing in "my own true love to me". On stage, "My Ship" was performed with a most effective coda, which makes it thirty-eight bars in length. The ordinarily thirty-two bar song is usually done in that manner to this day.

In the movies, only a few bars of "My Ship" were sung by Ginger Rogers in the film version of *Lady in the Dark*. But Julie Andrews sang it in its entirety in the Lawrence 1968 screen biography, *Star!*.

Moderate ballad with refrain (38)
PUBLISHER: Chappell &Co., Inc.
KEY: F maj., *STARTS*: c' (F maj.), *FORM*: AA'BA"

≈≈≈≈≈≈≈≈≈≈≈≈≈≈≈≈≈≈≈≈

A STRING OF PEARLS

WORDS: Eddie De Lange, *MUSIC*: Jerry Gray
INTRODUCED BY: Glenn Miller and his Orchestra, in a Bluebird recording

Another swing standard that began as an instrumental band arrangement, "A String of Pearls" was composed for Glenn Miller by his arranger, Jerry Gray. The Bluebird recording became a No. 1 hit. A year later, the song was recorded by Benny Goodman and his Orchestra for Okeh, on the other side of the hit "Jersey Bounce" (q.v.). The refrain simply consists of three eight-bar sections, each of which plays the same riff three times. The riff itself consists largely of multiple repetitions of the same note, in syncopation. The only variation from this seeming monotony occurs in the middle section, which moves a fourth higher both melodically and harmonically: from g' to c", and from E-flat major to A-flat major. Eddie De Lange's seldom-heard lyrics refer to a five-and-dime store where one can buy a "string of pearls à la Woolworth".

Moderate swing tune with two refrains (24)
PUBLISHER: Mutual Music Society, Inc. assigned to Chappell & Co., Inc.
KEY: E-flat maj., *STARTS*: g' (E-flat maj.), *FORM*: ABA

≈≈≈≈≈≈≈≈≈≈≈≈≈≈≈≈≈≈≈≈

TAKE THE "A" TRAIN * * *

WORDS and MUSIC: Billy Strayhorn and The Delta Rhythm Boys
INTRODUCED BY: Duke Ellington and his Orchestra, in a Victor recording

Although this rollicking swing tune is always associated with Duke Ellington, it was not written by Ellington, but rather by his chief arranger and confidant, talented pianist and composer, Billy Strayhorn. Ellington's Victor record quickly reached the charts and the leader used the song as his theme for many years. Some thirty-five years later, it was revived for the all-black revue, *Bubbling Brown Sugar*, which opened at the Anta Theatre in New York, 2 March 1976.

The subject matter is, of course, the New York City subway system, and more specifically, the express train that runs from downtown to Harlem by way of the Independent Line, underneath Eighth Avenue and Central Park West. The distinctive theme of the AABA refrain is instrumental in nature, with jumps of the sixth in the "A" sections and of the third and fourth in the "B" section. Of special interest is the downward jump of a sixth (from c" to e-natural') accompanied by a clangorous B-flat-ninth chord, in the third bar of each "A" section. It is eminently suitable for a train song. The song's puerile lyrics, however, are no match for the exciting music.

On the screen, "Take the "A" Train" was played by the Ellington band in both *Reveille with Beverly* (1943) and *Paris Blues* (1961).

Moderate swing tune with verse (8) and refrain (32)
PUBLISHER: Tempo Music, Inc.
KEY: A-flat maj., *STARTS*: e-flat' (A-flat maj.), *FORM*: AABA

≈≈≈≈≈≈≈≈≈≈≈≈≈≈≈≈≈≈≈≈≈

TIME WAS (DUERME)

ENGLISH WORDS: S. K Russell, *MUSIC*: Miguel Prado
INTRODUCED BY: Jimmy Dorsey and his Orchestra, vocal by Bob Eberly and Helen O'Connell, in a Decca recording, in the United States

"Duerme" was the title of a Mexican song, composed by Miguel Prado, with Spanish words by Gabriel Luna. Exported to the United States and given English words by S. K. Russell, it became "Time Was". The Decca recording by Jimmy Dorsey and his Orchestra, vocal by Bob Eberly and Helen O'Connell, reached the Top Ten. The refrain, in AABA form, features a limpid melodic line of repeated notes gradually descending scalewise. The simple harmonies center about the tonic of G major in the "A" sections and move to B major in the release. Most unusual in the song is the sheer number of quarter-note triplets: some forty-five of them.

Moderate rumba with verse (8) and refrain (32)
PUBLISHER: Peer International Corporation
KEY: G maj., *STARTS*: d" (G maj.), *FORM*: AABA

≈≈≈≈≈≈≈≈≈≈≈≈≈≈≈≈≈≈

TONIGHT WE LOVE

WORDS: Bobby Worth, *MUSIC*: Ray Austin and Freddy Martin, adapted from Piotr Ilyich Tchaikovsky, *Piano Concerto No. 1 in B-Flat Minor*
INTRODUCED BY: Freddy Martin and his Orchestra, vocal by Clyde Rogers, in a Bluebird recording

One of more than one hundred American songs based on the music of Russian composer, Piotr Ilyich Tchaikovsky (1840-1893), "Tonight We Love" followed on the success of "Moon Love" and "Our Love" (see 1939). The mighty first theme of the first movement of Tchaikovsky's *Piano Concerto No. 1 in B-Flat Minor* has itself attracted at least sixteen American songs, among them "Concerto for Two" (1941) and "Alone At Last" (1960). But "Tonight We Love" became the best known, popularized with Freddy Martin's Bluebird recording, vocal by Clyde Rogers. Martin had another hit Tchaikovsky recording this year, also on Bluebird, called "Piano Concerto in B-flat", and it featured Jack Fina as piano soloist. All the derived songs change the meter from the original 3/4 to the more dance-able 4/4, and all of them maintain the massive, upward-moving piano chords of the concerto. In "Tonight We Love", except for some truncation at the end, the famous melody remains intact, heralded by its opening notes: d" - g' - a' - g'.

Moderate ballad with refrain (32)
PUBLISHER: Maestro Music Co.
KEY: G maj., *STARTS*: d" (G maj.), *FORM*: ABA'C

≈≈≈≈≈≈≈≈≈≈≈≈≈≈≈≈≈≈

MAKE BELIEVE BALLROOM
(1942)

This year's fancies are passing fancies

Johnny Mercer
"I'm Old Fashioned"

There is little room for frivolity in this year of on-going war abroad, and personal privation, blackouts, food shortages, gasoline rationing, and Victory Gardens on the home front. Popular songs this year either long for good times gone by ("Always in My Heart", "I Remember You") or dream of more precious days to come ("White Christmas", "You'd Be So Nice to Come Home To"). With musicians joining the armed forces in increasing numbers, the big bands begin to fall apart, replaced over the airwaves by a new sort of personality, the disk jockey. A leading figure in this phenomenon is Martin Block, whose radio show over Station WNEW, New York, is called *The Make Believe Ballroom* (a title that originated in the mid-thirties with Al Jarvis, over Station KWFB, Los Angeles). So powerful do these fast-talking individuals become that they can make or break a song. Bands are largely replaced by vocalists who begin a spectacular gain in popularity. Indicative of this trend is Frank Sinatra who leaves the Tommy Dorsey Band to go out on his own.

The horrors of war continue with Singapore falling to the Japanese and Stalingrad to the Germans. But, almost imperceptibly, with the invasion of North Africa, the fall of El Alamein, and the taking of Guadalcanal from the Japanese, the war begins to take a turn for the better for the Allies. So do things on the home front with improvement in the economy and the demise of the Depression.

Except for Thornton Wilder's play, *The Skin of Our Teeth,* which wins a Pulitzer Prize, Broadway has a lackluster season. The best musical by far is *By Jupiter,* which sadly is Richard Rodgers and Lorenz Hart's last collaboration (Hart dies in November 1943, only forty-seven years of age). Irving Berlin's patriotic revue, *This Is the Army,* with an all-soldier cast, opens fittingly on the fourth of July. The featured performer is Berlin himself, who wistfully sings his hit from *Yip Yip Yaphank* (1918): "Oh, How I Hate to Get Up in the Morning".

Hollywood enjoys a banner year, producing eighty movies with war themes. The immortal *Casablanca,* starring Humphrey Bogart, Ingrid Bergman, Claude Rains, and Paul Henreid is one of them, and, as an integral part of the plot, an eleven-year old song, "As Time Goes By", is sung by Dooley Wilson. Another hit war movie is *Mrs. Miniver,* which wins an Oscar for itself and for its star, Greer Garson. Escapist films are understandably in great demand. They include *Yankee Doodle Dandy,* which stars James Cagney as George M. Cohan; *Holiday Inn,* pairing Bing Crosby with Fred Astaire and introducing Berlin's perennial favorite, "White Christmas"; "You Were Never Lovelier", with the new dance team of Fred Astaire and Rita Hayworth; *Cabin in the Sky,* the third all-black film, with a wonderful score; and *For Me and My Gal,* a World War I story starring Judy Garland and her new leading man, Gene Kelly.

Symptomatic of the era of the disk jockey is the launching of Capitol Records, with a $10,000 investment by songwriters Buddy De Sylva and Johnny Mercer and record executive Glenn Wallichs. Capitol woos the songwriters, the singers, the radio stations, and the disk jockeys and is quickly successful. There is a fitting air of fantasy about this year of ongoing battles, wartime shortages, feature films starring comedians Bud Abbott and Lou Costello, Kilroy (who is here), and *The Make Believe Ballroom.*

SONGS OF 1942

Always in My Heart *
At Last
Dearly Beloved
Don't Get Around Much Anymore ***
Don't Sit Under the Apple Tree (With Anyone Else But Me)
Ev'rything I've Got
Happiness Is a Thing Called Joe !
I Remember You
I'll Be Around
I'm Old Fashioned !
I've Got a Gal in Kalamazoo
Lover Man (Oh Where Can You Be?) *
Moonlight Becomes You
Pennsylvania Polka *
Serenade in Blue *
Skylark !
Tangerine *
That Old Black Magic **!
There Will Never Be Another You **!
Wait Till You See Her !
White Christmas ****
You'd Be So Nice To Come Home To *!

ALWAYS IN MY HEART

WORDS: Kim Gannon, *MUSIC*: Ernesto Lecuona
PREMIERE: Film musical, *Always in My Heart.* Warner Brothers, 1942
INTRODUCED BY: Gloria Warren

Another hit by the brilliant Cuban composer, Ernesto Lecuona, "Always in My Heart" was written as the title song of the namesake film, starring Walter Huston and Kay Francis. Nominated for an Academy Award, the song was popularized in recordings by the bands of Glenn Miller (Bluebird) and Jimmy Dorsey (Decca). Singer Kenny Baker also recorded it for Decca.

The skipping melody of the refrain begins with a six-note pickup which leads to the tone of the major seventh (a') and then, in a similar progression, to the sixth (g'). Although nominally in ABA'C form, the refrain is in fact through-composed, since all sections are in some way related to the principal theme.

Moderate rumba with verse (16) and refrain (32)
PUBLISHER: Remick Music Corporation
KEY: B-flat maj., *STARTS*: d' (B-flat maj.), *FORM*: ABA'C

≈≈≈≈≈≈≈≈≈≈≈≈≈≈≈≈≈≈≈

AT LAST

WORDS: Mack Gordon, *MUSIC*: Harry Warren
PREMIERE: Film musical, *Orchestra Wives..* Twentieth Century-Fox, 1942
INTRODUCED BY: Ray Eberle and Pat Friday (dubbing in for Lynn Bari), with Glenn Miller and his Orchestra

This elegant staple of the big bands lent itself particularly to the full-voiced sound of the Glenn Miller Orchestra, as arranged by Bill Finegan. Introduced in the film, *Orchestra Wives*, it was popularized on a Bluebird recording by Miller, with vocal by Ray Eberle. Ray Anthony and his Orchestra revived it in 1952, with a vocal by Tommy Mercer, and Etta James had a hit recording in 1962.

The refrain's principal attraction is its use of long-held notes, coupled with blue notes of the flatted third and seventh. The short pickup (g') leads to the note c", which is held for over six beats. Etta James reprised the song in the 1988 film, *Rain Man*, starring Dustin Hoffman.

Slow ballad with verse (16) and refrain (32)
PUBLISHER: Twentieth Century Music Corp.
KEY" C maj., *STARTS*: g' (C maj.), *FORM*: AABA'

≈≈≈≈≈≈≈≈≈≈≈≈≈≈≈≈≈≈≈

DEARLY BELOVED

WORDS: Johnny Mercer, *MUSIC*: Jerome Kern
PREMIERE: Film musical, *You Were Never Lovelier*, Columbia, 1942
INTRODUCED BY: Fred Astaire and Nan Wynn (dubbing for Rita Hayworth), with Xavier Cugat and his Orchestra

This lovely ballad, enchantingly danced to by Fred Astaire and Rita Hayworth in the film, *You Were Never Lovelier,* was nominated for an

Academy Award. Leading recordings were by singer Dinah Shore on Victor and the bands of Glenn Miller (Victor) and Alvino Rey (Bluebird). In the C major refrain, which is marked "Andante cantabile, ma ben ritmato", the principal theme begins in G minor, with the descending step of a fourth (g'-d'), and then proceeds mostly stepwise, with an out-of-character injection of chromaticism at the close of the second section.

>Moderate ballad with verse (8) and refrain (32)
>*PUBLISHER*: T. B. Harms Company
>*KEY*: C maj., *STARTS*: g' (G min.), *FORM*: ABAB'

≈≈≈≈≈≈≈≈≈≈≈≈≈≈≈≈≈≈≈≈

DON'T GET AROUND MUCH ANYMORE * * *

>**WORDS AND MUSIC:** Duke Ellington and Bob Russell
>*INTRODUCED BY*: Duke Ellington and his Orchestra, vocal by Al Hibbler, in a Columbia reccording

Based on Duke Ellington's swing tune "Never No Lament", this versatile song was given a new title and lyrics by Bob Russell. It was popularized in a Columbia recording by Ellington, and also in two Decca recordings by The Ink Spots and Glen Gray and The Casa Loma Orchestra. The song is often referred to by the opening line of its refrain, "Missed the Saturday dance" (or its homophone "Mister Saturday Dance"). It has all the earmarks of swing, repeated riffs, an instrumental melody line, syncopation, and blue notes. Of special interest is the five-note pickup descending to a full octave, and then immediately repeated. With an infectious rhythmic beat, it remains an important swing standard.

>Slow swing tune with verse (8) and refrain (32)
>*PUBLISHER*: Robbins Music Corp.
>*KEY*: C maj., *STARTS*: e" (C maj.), *FORM*: AABA

≈≈≈≈≈≈≈≈≈≈≈≈≈≈≈≈≈≈≈≈

DON'T SIT UNDER THE APPLE TREE (WITH ANYONE ELSE BUT ME)

>*WORDS AND MUSIC*: Lew Brown, Sam H. Stept, and Charles Tobias
>*PREMIERE*: Film musical, *Private Buckaroo*. Universal, 1942
>*INTRODUCED BY*: The Andrews Sisters

This perky novelty song was one of the biggest hits of the year. Particularly favored by men and women of the service, it took the country by storm, propelled by two best-selling records: one by the Andrews Sisters (Decca), the other by Glenn Miller and his Orchestra with Marion Hutton, Tex Beneke, and The Modernaires (Bluebird). Introduced by The Andrews Sisters in the film, *Private Buckaroo*, the melody is merely a jazzed-up version of the English song "Long, Long Ago!" published in 1835. Written by Thomas Haynes, the words begin: "Tell me the tales that to me were so dear, / long, long ago, / long, long, ago". "Don't Sit Under the Apple Tree" uses essentially the same melody and harmonies, but with multiple repetition of some notes and an added release. There also some novelty effects, such as the offbeat setting of the words "No! No! No!" and the spelling out of "You're my L-O-V-E". The Andrews Sisters again sang "Don't Sit Under the Apple Tree" in the 1970 film, *Red Sky at Morning*. With millions of people away from home, it was a song very much in tune with its times.

> Bright novelty song with verse (16) and two refrain (48)
> *PUBLISHER*: EMI Robbins Catalog Inc. and Ched Music Corp.
> *KEY*: F maj., *STARTS*: f' (F maj.), *FORM*: AABA

≈≈≈≈≈≈≈≈≈≈≈≈≈≈≈≈≈≈≈≈

EV'RYTHING I'VE GOT

> *WORDS*: Lorenz Hart, *MUSIC*: Richard Rodgers
> *PREMIERE*: Musical comedy, *By Jupiter*
> New York: Shubert Theatre, 3 June 1942 (427 perf.)
> *INTRODUCED BY*: Ray Bolger and Benay Venuta

This sprightly tune was the hit of the show, *By Jupiter*, Richard Rodgers and Lorenz Hart's longest running show and also their last collaboration. "Ev'rything I've Got" has many of the attributes of songs of the twenties. Written in standard AABA form, the "A" sections feature a catchy rhythmic motive, first in E-flat major and then in E-flat minor. Of interest in the release is the sudden movement to B major and the artful modulation back to the tonic. As a catalogue song, Hart's clever lyrics recite all the singer's bad points, including "dirty looks", "a terrible tongue", and a "temper for two".

> Moderate rhythm song with verse (16) and refrain (32)
> *PUBLISHER*: Chappell & Co., Inc.
> *KEY*: E-flat maj., *STARTS*: g' (E-flat maj.), *FORM*: AABA

≈≈≈≈≈≈≈≈≈≈≈≈≈≈≈≈≈≈≈≈

HAPPINESS IS A THING CALLED JOE !

WORDS: E. Y. Harburg, *MUSIC*: Harold Arlen
PREMIERE: Film musical, *Cabin in the Sky*. Metro Goldwyn Mayer, 1943
INTRODUCED BY: Ethel Waters

This lovely ballad was written especially for Ethel Waters in the 1943 film version of the Broadway musical, *Cabin in the Sky* (1940). Nominated for an Academy Award, it was recorded on Decca by Woody Herman and his Orchestra, with vocal by Frances Wayne. It is a strong favorite of female vocalists, even though both verse and chorus are instrumental in nature. In the verse the melody repeatedly outlines the C major seventh chord over an ostinato bass, while in the refrain it outlines the same chord with the addition of the blue note, d-sharp'. The final cadence is unique in the literature, ending on the second degree of the scale (d') rather than on the tonic (c'). It should be noted that although the first ending, with four added measures, closes on c', almost all performers use the second ending. Susan Hayward sang this most compelling love ballad in her portrayal of Lillian Roth in the film, *I'll Cry Tomorrow*.

Slow ballad with verse (8) and refrain (36)
PUBLISHER: Metro Goldwyn Mayer, Inc.
KEY: C maj., *STARTS*: d-sharp' (C maj.), *FORM*: ABA'C

≈≈≈≈≈≈≈≈≈≈≈≈≈≈≈≈≈≈≈

I REMEMBER YOU

WORDS: Johnny Mercer, *MUSIC*: Victor Schertzinger
PREMIERE: Film musical, *The Fleet's In*. Paramount, 1942
INTRODUCED BY: Dorothy Lamour, Bob Eberly, and Jimmy Dorsey, and his Orchestra

A smoothly flowing ballad, "I Remember You" was written for the wartime film, *The Fleet's In*, with music by the film's director, Victor Schertzinger (who died before it was released), and lyrics by Johnny Mercer. The song was popularized in recordings by Jimmy Dorsey and his Orchestra, with vocal by Bob Ebely (Decca); and Harry James and his Orchestra, with vocal by Helen Forrest. In the fifties it was recorded by The George Shearing Trio. In 1962, English singer Frank Ifield had a recording that sold over two million copies. The graceful refrain, in AABA' form, revolves around a melodic line that gradually descends in half steps, and is rounded out by a four-bar coda.

Slow ballad with verse (10) and refrain (36)
PUBLISHER: Paramount Music Corporation
KEY: E-flat maj., *STARTS*: g' (A-flat maj.), *FORM*: AABA'

≈≈≈≈≈≈≈≈≈≈≈≈≈≈≈≈≈≈≈≈≈

I'LL BE AROUND

WORDS AND MUSIC: Alec Wilder
INTRODUCED BY: Cab Calloway and his Orchestra, in an Okeh recording

According to Alec Wilder, the title of this expressive song popped into his head while he was crossing the city of Baltimore in a taxi. He jotted it down on an envelope and, spotting it a few days later, wrote the music in twenty minutes, although the lyrics took much longer. Among the many recordings are those of The Mills Brothers (on Decca, on the other side of the phenomenally successful "Paper Doll"), George Shearing, and Frank Sinatra. Lacking a verse and in conventional, thirty-two bar AABA' form, "I'll Be Around" stands out for its contrapuntal interaction between melody and bass lines. The melody of each "A" section begins with an outlined C major triad accompanied by a slowly-rising bass. Also of interest are the quick-changing and complex harmonies in the release, which is marked "Broadly".

Slow ballad with refrain (32)
PUBLISHER: Ludlow Music, Inc.
KEY: C maj., *STARTS*: g' (C maj.), *FORM*: AABA

≈≈≈≈≈≈≈≈≈≈≈≈≈≈≈≈≈≈≈≈≈

I'M OLD FASHIONED !

WORDS: Johnny Mercer, *MUSIC*: Jerome Kern
PREMIERE: Film musical, *You Were Never Lovelier.* Columbia, 1942
INTRODUCED BY: Fred Astaire and Rita Hayworth (dubbed in by Nan Wynn), with Xavier Cugat and his Orchestra

This tender ballad, one of Jerome Kern's finest, is about loving such old-fashioned things as moonlight and "the sound of rain upon a window pane". Aptly, the song itself is old fashioned, spurning such "modern" devices as thirty-two bar AABA form, syncopation, and complex harmonies. Spectacularly danced to by Fred Astaire and Rita Hayworth in the film, *You Were Never Lovelier*, the song had best-selling records by Astaire (Decca), and by Xavier Cugat and his Orchestra (also in the film), on Columbia. But the biggest recording hit of all was on Decca, by Glen Gray and The Casa Loma Orchestra, with vocal by Kenny Sargent.

Length and form are unusual: forty bars in ABCA' form, consisting of three eight-bar sections and a last section extended to twelve bars. The main theme employs the time-honored device of widening intervals returning to the same note: in this case, intervals of the fourth, sixth, and seventh, all returning to middle c'. Intervals widen still further in the final section, to the octave, with repetition of the penultimate phrase as a brief coda. There is a brief modulation to A major in the "C" section, accompanied by Johnny Mercer's inspired words, "this year's fancies are passing fancies".

Moderate ballad with verse (18) and refrain (36)
PUBLISHER: T. B. Harms Company
KEY: F maj., *STARTS*: f' (F maj.), *FORM*: ABCA'

≈≈≈≈≈≈≈≈≈≈≈≈≈≈≈≈≈≈≈

I'VE GOT A GAL IN KALAMAZOO

WORDS: Mack Gordon, *MUSIC*: Harry Warren
PREMIERE: Film musical, *Orchestra Wives*. Twentieth Century-Fox, 1942
INTRODUCED BY: Glenn Miller and his Orchestra, with Marion Hutton, Tex Beneke, and The Modernaires; danced to by The Nicholas Brothers

Given a lavish production number in the film, *Orchestra Wives*, this rhythmic song became a No. 1 hit through the Victor recording by Glenn Miller's orchestra, as sung by Marion Hutton, Tex Beneke, and The Modernaires. It was nominated for an Academy Award. The clever opening gambit has eight repetitions of the note e-flat' in quarter notes, each prefaced by the grace note d'. The accompanying words recite the letters of the alphabet from "A" through "H", leading to the "I" of "I've got a gal". The remainder of the song consists of jagged, syncopated riffs (many outlining chords) in big-band, swing style.

Moderate rhythm song with refrain (38)
PUBLISHER: Twentieth Century Music Corp.
KEY: E-flat maj., *STARTS*: e-flat' (E-flat maj.), *FORM*: AABA'

≈≈≈≈≈≈≈≈≈≈≈≈≈≈≈≈≈≈≈

LOVER MAN (OH, WHERE CAN YOU BE?) *

WORDS and MUSIC: Jimmy Davis, Roger "Ram" Ramirez, and Jimmy Sherman

The quintessential song about loneliness, "Lover Man (Oh, Where Can You Be)" has always been associated with Billie Holiday, who recorded it for Decca in 1945. There have been numerous recordings over the years: some by jazz instrumentalists like Charlie Parker, Art Tatum, and Erroll Garner; who found its harmonies attractive for improvisation; some by the big bands, including those of Duke Ellington, Stan Kenton, and Claude Thornhill; and some by such singers as Sarah Vaughan. But the song's biggest success by far came in 1972, when Diana Ross sang it in the Paramount Picture, *Lady Sings the Blues*, based loosely on the life of Billie Holiday.

In a range of barely an octave, the song manages to convey a good deal of emotion through major-minor contrast and a profusion of blue notes. In the refrain, in conventional AABA form, each "A" section modulates from D minor to F major. Blue notes, especially the flatted third (a-flat'), tremendously enhance the sadness of the song. The release has attractions of its own, including a descending melodic and harmonic line: A minor - G major - G minor - F major. The underlying harmonies of the first four bars of each "A" section, alternating between D minor and G seventh, recall those of George Gershwin's "Fascinating Rhythm" of 1924 – but of course at a much slower tempo.

Slow blues song with verse (8) and refrain (32)
PUBLISHER: MCA Music Publishing, 1941
KEY: F maj., *STARTS*: d' (D min.), *FORM* AABA

≈≈≈≈≈≈≈≈≈≈≈≈≈≈≈≈≈≈≈

MOONLIGHT BECOMES YOU

WORDS: Johnny Burke, *MUSIC*: James Van Heusen
PREMIERE: Film musical, *Road to Morocco*. Paramount, 1942
INTRODUCED BY: Bing Crosby

A popular ballad of the day, "Moonlight Becomes You" was a signature song of Bing Crosby, who introduced it in the film, *Road to Morocco*, and had a No. 1 Decca recording. Other recordings of the ballad were by the bands of Glenn Miller, with vocal by Skip Nelson and The Modernaires (Victor); and Harry James, with vocal by Johnny McAfee (Columbia). The melody of the refrain features descending and ascending intervals of the sixth, a release which begins in B-flat major and moves to D minor before returning to the tonic of F major, and a short (two-bar) coda.

Moderate ballad with verse (12) and refrain (34)
PUBLISHER: Famous Music Corporation
KEY: F maj., *STARTS*: a' (F maj.), *FORM*: AA'BA'

≈≈≈≈≈≈≈≈≈≈≈≈≈≈≈≈≈

PENNSYLVANIA POLKA *

WORDS and MUSIC: Lester Lee and Zeke Manners
PREMIERE: Film musical, *Give Out, Sisters*. Universal, 1942
INTRODUCED BY: The Andrews Sisters

One of the few polkas – along with "Beer Barrel Polka" (1939) – to be regularly performed in the mainstream, this rousing song was introduced by The Andrews Sisters in their forgotten sixty-five-minute film showcase, *Give Out, Sisters*. They also popularized it on a hit Decca recording. The overall form is that of a march: ABA, with a refrain, trio, and return to the refrain. The melody of the refrain, in F major, outlines the chords of F major and C ninth. A four-bar interlude acts as an introduction to the trio in B-flat major, which is largely composed of whole and half notes moving stepwise, with occasional upward leaps to repeated notes. This is followed by a return to the F major refrain. The Andrews Sisters repeated their success with "Pennsylvania Polka" in the 1944 film, *Follow the Boys*.

Fast polka with refrain (32), interval (4), and trio (32)
PUBLISHER: Shapiro, Bernstein & Co., Inc.
KEY: F maj., *STARTS*: c" (F maj.), *FORM* (Overall): ABA

≈≈≈≈≈≈≈≈≈≈≈≈≈≈≈≈≈

SERENADE IN BLUE *

WORDS: Mack Gordon, *MUSIC*: Harry Warren
PREMIERE: Film musical, *Orchestra Wives*. Twentieth Century-Fox, 1942
INTRODUCED BY: Glenn Miller and his Orchestra, vocal by Ray Eberle and The Modernaires

One of Harry Warren's loveliest tunes, "Serenade in Blue" was introduced by the Glenn Miller band, with Ray Eberle and The Modernaires in the film, *Orchestra Wives*. The Miller organization also had a top record for Victor. There are an unusual number of notes in the refrain, many of them dotted quarters and eighths, with numerous repetitions of the notes e-flat' and f' in the release. True to its title, there are a plethora of blue notes in the often chromatic melodic line. Mack Gordon's lyrics rise to the occasion, as in: "Shall I go on whistling in the dark?"

Slow ballad with refrain (32)
PUBLISHER: Twentieth Century Music corporation, assigned to Bregman, Vocco and Conn, Inc.
KEY: E-flat maj., STARTS: d' (E-flat maj.), FORM: AA'BA'

≈≈≈≈≈≈≈≈≈≈≈≈≈≈≈≈≈≈

SKYLARK !

WORDS: Johnny Mercer, MUSIC: Hoagy Carmichael

A fanciful ballad by two veteran songwriters, Johnny Mercer and Hoagy Carmichael, "Skylark" is renowned for its extraordinary middle section. The song was popularized by the bands of Glenn Miller, with vocal by Ray Eberle (Bluebird), and Harry James, vocal by Helen Forrest (Columbia); and by singers Bing Crosby (Decca) and Dinah Shore (Bluebird). There is no verse. The refrain is conventional in form (AA'BA"), with an ornamental melody of dotted quarters and eighths (and a few triplets), moving in steps and skips. The release is noted for its quirky harmonies, from A-flat sixth to F minor, and then to G major. Mercer's lyrics are poetic, as if sung to a bird who is "sad as a gypsy serenading the moon". They end with the plea: "Won't you lead me there?"

Moderate ballad with refrain (32)
PUBLISHER: George Simon, Inc., assigned to Carmichael Music Publishers and Mercer Music
KEY: E-flat maj., STARTS: c" (E-flat 6), FORM: AA'BA"

≈≈≈≈≈≈≈≈≈≈≈≈≈≈≈≈≈≈

TANGERINE *

WORDS: Johnny Mercer, MUSIC: Victor Schertzinger
PREMIERE: Film musical, The Fleet's In. Paramount. 1942
INTRODUCED BY: Jimmy Dorsey and his Orchestra, vocal by Bob Eberly and Helen O'Connell

Another striking song – along with "I'll Remember You" – from the film, The Fleet's In, "Tangerine" was composed by the movie's director, Victor Schertzinger, who did not live to see its release, with lyrics by Johnny Mercer. The Jimmy Dorsey band, with singers Bob Eberly and

Helen O'Connell, who introduced it in the film, also had the hit record on Decca, in a famous arrangement by Toots Camarata that uses three tempos: slow for Eberly, fast for the instrumental, and moderate for O' Connell. The three-tempo arrangement was designed explicitly for a radio broadcast, sponsored by 20 Grand Cigarettes, in order to show what the band could do in only three minutes. "Tangerine" began an entirely new life as a disco standard in 1976, revived by The Salsoul Orchestra.

The music is unusual in several respects: the different keys of verse and refrain (D major and F major), the opening D seventh augmented chord, and the three consecutive statements of the main theme, in AA'AB form. The subject of the song is a lady with "lips as bright as flame, who causes toasts in ev'ry bar across the Argentine". But in the end, her heart belongs only "to Tangerine".

Moderate ballad with verse (14) and refrain (32)
PUBLISHER: Famous Music Corporation
KEY: F maj., *STARTS*: d" (D aug.), *FORM*: AA'AB

≈≈≈≈≈≈≈≈≈≈≈≈≈≈≈≈≈≈≈

THAT OLD BLACK MAGIC * * !

WORDS: Johnny Mercer, *MUSIC*: Harold Arlen
PREMIERE: Film musical, *Star Spangled Rhythm*. Paramount, 1942
INTRODUCED BY: Johnny Johnson, danced to by Vera Zorina

This magical brew of frenzied music and fiery lyrics shows the team of Johnny Mercer and Harold Arlen at its best. It was introduced in the movie, *Star Spangled Rhythm*, produced by Paramount Pictures for the entertainment of servicemen at home and abroad. Nominated for an Academy Award as Best Song of 1943, "That Old Black Magic" was originally popularized in a best-selling Victor recording by Glenn Miller and his Orchestra, with vocal by Skip Nelson and The Modernaires. But the singer most often associated with the song is Billy Daniels, who performed it regularly in nightclubs and on television, used it as his theme, and recorded it twice for Mercury. Among other hit recordings over the years were those of Sammy Davis, Jr. in 1955 (Capitol), Louis Prima and Keely Smith in 1958 (Capitol), and Bobby Rydell in 1961 (Cameo).

Lacking a verse, the song is one of the lengthiest in the literature, at seventy-two bars, and consists of five sections, AA'BA"C. The demonic flavor of Mercer's lyrics ("those icy fingers up and down my spine") is enhanced by Arlen's many jumps of the sixth, repeated notes in syncopation, occasional blue notes, and dramatic harmonic changes. All this is accompanied by an ostinato rhythm of constant eighth notes in the bass, including a lengthy pedal point (repetition of the same bass note) for fifteen consecutive bars.

"That Old Black Magic" has been featured in a remarkable number of films besides *Star Spangled Rhythm*. Bing Crosby sang it in *Here Come the Waves* (1944) and Frances Langford in *Radio Stars On Parade* (1945). Lizabeth Scott sang it in *Dark City* (1950), Billy Daniels in *When You're Smiling* (1952), and Frank Sinatra in *Meet Danny Wilson*. Marilyn Monroe performed it in *Bus Stop* (1956), and Louis Prima and Keely Smith in *Senior Prom* (1958). Les Brown and his Band of Renown performed it in Jerry Lewis' *The Nutty Professor* (1963), and Ann-Margret in *The Swinger* (1966). It also initiated a new genre of diabolic songs, later to be represented by "Old Devil Moon" (1947) and "Witchcraft" (1958).

Moderate rhythm song with refrain (72)
PUBLISHER: Famous Music Corporation
KEY: E-flat maj., *STARTS*: b-flat' (E-flat maj.), *FORM*: A A'BA"C

≈≈≈≈≈≈≈≈≈≈≈≈≈≈≈≈≈≈≈

THERE WILL NEVER BE ANOTHER YOU ＊＊！

WORDS: Mack Gordon, *MUSIC*: Harry Warren
PREMIERE: Film musical, *Iceland* (known in Britain as *Katina*).
Twentieth Century-Fox, 1942
INTRODUCED BY: Jean Merrill, accompanied by Sammy Kaye & his Orchestra

This marvelous ballad enjoys a double life as a romantic ballad and a jazz standard. Introduced by Jean Merrill in the Sonja Henie film, *Iceland*, it was recorded for Victor by Sammy Davis and his Orchestra (also in the film), with vocalist Nancy Norman. Another hit recording was by Woody Herman and his Orchestra, with vocal by Herman himself (Decca).

The song was revived in 1966, with an A & M recording by Chris Montez. In the refrain, Harry Warren's soaring melody, mostly in quarter notes, unfolds in flowing arcs of sound, accompanied by the subtle harmonic changes of sixth and seventh chords. Sung by Doris Day in the film, *I'll Get By* (1950), "There Will Never Be Another You" is a special favorite of musicians because of its beautiful melody, intriguing harmonies, and sheer musicality.

Slow ballad with verse (16) and refrain (32)
PUBLISHER: Twentieth Century Music Corp., assigned to Morley Music
KEY: E-flat maj., *STARTS*: b-flat (E-flat 6), *FORM*: ABAB'

≈≈≈≈≈≈≈≈≈≈≈≈≈≈≈≈≈≈≈

WAIT TILL YOU SEE HER !

WORDS: Lorenz Hart, *MUSIC*: Richard Rodgers
PREMIERE: Musical comedy, *By Jupiter*
New York: Shubert Theatre, 3 June 1942 (427 perf.)
INTRODUCED BY: Ronnie Graham

This enchanting waltz, one of the loveliest written by the team of Lorenz Hart and Richard Rodgers, is also one of the last songs they wrote together. Introduced by Ronnie Graham in the long-running musical comedy, *By Jupiter*, it was dropped from the show early in the run. Slow in catching on, Mabel Mercer, Bobby Short, and other cabaret performers kept the song alive over the years. The refrain, marked "in spirited tempo", has a quality of insouciance, with a melodic line that falls and then rises. The refrain is in AABA' from, with the last section (sixteen bars) twice the length of the other three. Near the close, the melody builds stepwise to a climax at the words "free her", and then brings back a reminiscence of the first two bars. Hart's tender lyrics are – in his own words: "Pensive and sweet and wise".

Moderate waltz with verse (29) and refrain (40)
PUBLISHER: Chappell & Co., Inc.
KEY: E-flat maj., *STARTS*: c" (F min. 7), *FORM*: AABA

≈≈≈≈≈≈≈≈≈≈≈≈≈≈≈≈≈≈≈

WHITE CHRISTMAS ✶ ✶ ✶ ✶

WORDS AND MUSIC: Irving Berlin
PREMIERE: Film musical, *Holiday Inn*. Paramount, 1942
INTRODUCED BY: Marjorie Reynolds and chorus

The most famous holiday song of the twentieth century, "White Christmas" was written by Irving Berlin expressly for the film, *Holiday Inn*, which highlighted a song for each holiday. Berlin wrote the song in New York, while he was remembering how he had felt spending a holiday season in Los Angeles and longing for the snow and cold weather up North. He put this longing into words and music, fully-formed, in one night, and later, with the help of his transcriber, Helmy Kresa, he polished it up. The song

437

was an immediate success. It won the Academy Award for Best Song of 1942. To servicemen separated from their families, it became an anthem of homesickness. Bing Crosby's Decca record alone sold over thirty million copies, and other recordings were made by Frank Sinatra, Perry Como, Jo Stafford, Charlie Spivak and his Orchestra, and a host of others. In its first ten years, "White Christmas" sold over three million copies of sheet music and fourteen million records.

The most unusual aspect of the refrain, in ABAB' form, is the chromatic movement in half steps of the first seven notes in each "A" section. After that, the famous melody unfolds broadly in tandem with the heartfelt words to the accompaniment of simple harmonies.

In other movies, Crosby again sang "White Christmas" in *Blue Skies* (1946) and, together with Danny Kaye, Rosematy Clooney, and Vera-Ellen, in a namesake film, *White Christmas* (1954). Translated into dozens of languages, Berlin's ballad is known worldwide, surfacing like clockwork every Christmas season.

Slow ballad with verse (16) and refrain (32)
PUBLISHER: Irving Berlin, Inc.
KEY: C maj., *STARTS*: e' (C maj.), *FORM*: ABAB'

≈≈≈≈≈≈≈≈≈≈≈≈≈≈≈≈≈≈≈

YOU'D BE SO NICE TO COME HOME TO * !

WORDS and MUSIC: Cole Porter
PREMIERE: Film musical, *Something to Shout About*. Columbia, 1943
INTRODUCED BY: Don Ameche and Janet Blair

This wistful ballad, the only surviving song from the forgotten film, *Something to Shout About*, appealed to the millions of people who were separated from their loved ones in this year of ongoing war, with such thoughts of home as "you'd be so nice by the fire". The best-selling record was by Dinah Shore, accompanied by Paul Weston and his Orchestra (Victor). The song was nominated for an Academy Award in 1943. The refrain, one of the few predominantly in minor mode, begins with a motive that is strongly reminiscent of Pablo de Sarasate's violin composition, *Zigeunerweisen* (Gypsy Airs). The resemblance quickly vanishes with the opening notes, however, and Cole Porter takes over, modulating from A minor to F major, and from there to C major, where he ends with a note of stability, at the words: "to come home to and love".

Moderate ballad with verse (16) and refrain (32)
PUBLISHER: Chappell & Co., Inc.
KEY: C maj., **STARTS**: a' (A min.), *FORM*: ABA'C

≈≈≈≈≈≈≈≈≈≈≈≈≈≈≈≈≈≈≈

1943

A CERTAIN LONGING

(1943)

I wish you'd make the music dreamy and sad

Johnny Mercer,
"One for My Baby (And One More for the Road)"

If there is one common denominator to the songs of 1943, it is a certain longing: a desire to return to happier times gone by. This pattern is evidenced in the most successful musical play of the season, *Oklahoma!*, an adoring look at bygone Americana. Enriched by five enduring songs by the newly-formed team of Richard Rodgers and Oscar Hammerstein II, this landmark show pioneers a new genre of musical theater, the folk operetta. With an initial run of 2,248 performances on Broadway, it generates the largest audience in the history of American musicals, to be superseded only by *My Fair Lady* fifteen years later. In another nostalgic look at the past, the film, *Hello, Frisco, Hello*, Alice Faye introduces the classic love song "You'll Never Know" – winner of the Academy Award. Still another type of longing, homesickness, is manifest in the G.I.'s fervent prayer, "I'll Be Home for Christmas." A sense of loss prevails even in more contemporary songs like the haunting "Speak Low," from *One Touch of Venus*, or the barfly's lament, "One for My Baby (And One More for the Road)," from the film, *The Sky's the Limit*.

Overseas, the war continues. Roosevelt and Churchill meet at conferences in Casablanca, Cairo, and Teheran, in order to plan military strategy. United States planes bomb Germany. The North Africa campaign ends, and Allied forces invade Sicily, and then Italy. Benito Mussolini resigns; Italy surrenders. United States forces land in Bougainville, one of the Solomon Islands. On the home front, civilians face rationing, shortages and long lines. The Lindy Hop, jive, and jitterbugging are popular pastimes. Teenage "hepcats" wear "Zoot Suits," featuring wide lapels and baggy pants. During a musicians' strike, all instrumental music is barred from radio and recordings; songs are often accompanied by small vocal groups rather than by instrumentalists.

Popular novels of the day include William Saroyan's *The Human Comedy* and Betty Smith's *A Tree Grows in Brooklyn*. On Broadway, Moss Hart's drama, *Winged Victory*, and the comedy, *The Voice of the Turtle*, starring Margaret Sullivan, are hits. But the musical theater loses one of its brightest stars when lyricist Lorenz Hart dies on 22 November, five days after the opening of a revival of Rodgers and Hart's *A Connecticut Yankee*. Hollywood continues with its series of escapist movies, with Irving Berlin's screening of *This Is the Army* and the second film version of George and Ira Gershwin's *Girl Crazy*, starring Mickey Rooney and Judy Garland. There are plenty of serious films as well, including Ernest Hemingway's *For Whom the Bell Tolls*, starring Gary Cooper and Ingrid Bergman; *Madame Curie*, with Greer Garson and Walter Pidgeon; *The Song of Bernadette*, starring Jennifer Jones; and *Watch on the Rhine*, with Bette Davis and Paul Lukas. But more to the point this year is Betty Grable, the G.I.'s favorite pin-up, a powerful symbol of everyone's longing for hearth, home, and happier times gone by.

SONGS OF 1943

Bésame Mucho (Kiss Me Much) *
Do Nothin' Till You Hear from Me
I Love You !
I'll Be Home for Christmas **
Lili Marlene **
(All of a Sudden) My Heart Sings
My Shining Hour !
Oh, What a Beautiful Morning ***
Oklahoma *
One for My Baby (And One More for the Road) *
Out of My Dreams
People Will Say We're in Love **
Speak Low *!
Spring Will Be a Little Late This Year
The Surrey with the Fringe On Top *
Tico-Tico
While We're Young !
You'll Never Know ***
You've Changed

BÉSAME MUCHO (KISS ME MUCH) *

ENGLISH WORDS: Sunny Skylar, *MUSIC*: Consuelo Velásquez

A Mexican import, this popular rumba was written by Consuelo Velásquez, with the composer's own Spanish lyrics. It became a hit in the United States through recordings by Andy Russell (Capitol) and by Jimmy Dorsey and his Orchestra, with vocal by Kitty Kallen and Bob Eberly (Decca). The melody of the refrain is strikingly similar to that of an aria from Enrique Granados's opera, *Goyescas,* which premiered in New York City 28 January 1916, two months before the Spanish composer lost his life when his boat was torpedoed by a German submarine. The melody is Andalusian, with a gypsy-like character of repeated notes and quarter-note triplets outlining the harmonic minor scale. The refrain, in simple song form, ABA, is comprised of two sixteen-bar outer sections surrounding an eight-bar release. Sammy Davis, Jr. sang "Bésame Mucho" in the 1988 film, *Moon Over Parador.*

Moderate rumba with refrain (40)
PUBLISHER: Peer International Corporation
KEY: D min., *STARTS*: d' (D min.), *FORM*: ABA

≈≈≈≈≈≈≈≈≈≈≈≈≈≈≈≈≈≈≈

DO NOTHIN' TILL YOU HEAR FROM ME

WORDS AND MUSIC: Duke Ellington and Bob Russell
INTRODUCED BY: by Duke Ellington and his Orchestra, in a Victor recording

In 1940, Duke Ellington wrote his classic composition, *Concerto for Cootie*, in honor of his first trumpet player, Charles Melvin (Cootie) Willams. Shortly thereafter, Williams left the Ellington band, only to rejoin in 1962. But in 1943, with the addition of lyrics and the assistance of Bob Russell, Ellington converted the main theme of *Concerto for Cootie* into the hit song "Do Nothin' Till You Hear from Me." Besides Ellington's Victor recording, the song was recorded by the bands of Stan Kenton (Capitol and Woody Herman (Decca).

True to its origins, the song has a rifflike quality about it. The principal rhythmical motive consists of seven eighth notes followed by a whole note; this motive is repeated nine times in the refrain. Harmonies, like many of Ellington's, lean heavily on major and minor sevenths. Some harmonic contrast is afforded in the "B" section, which moves briefly to E-flat major. The lyrics, with their supplication not to believe everything you hear until "you hear it from me," end with a punch line: "And you never will."

Hit recordings were made by Duke Ellington and his Orchestra, Woody Herman and his Orchestra, and Stan Kenton and his Orchestra. In the 1977 film, *New York, New York*, starring Robert De Niro and Liza Minnelli, "Do Nothin' Till You Hear from Me" was sung by Mary Kay Place.

Slow ballad with verse (7) and refrain (32)
PUBLISHER: Robbins Music Corp.
KEY: G maj., *STARTS*: c" (G maj. 7), *FORM*: AABA

≈≈≈≈≈≈≈≈≈≈≈≈≈≈≈≈≈≈≈

I LOVE YOU !

WORDS AND MUSIC: Cole Porter
PREMIERE: Musical comedy, *Mexican Hayride*
New York: Winter Garden Theatre, 28 January 1944 (481 perf.)
INTRODUCED BY: Wilbur Evans

This beguiling beguine, one of Cole Porter's finest, was written and copyrighted in 1943 but not introduced until the first month of 1944. It is the only song to have survived from Michael Todd's *Mexican Hayride*, a lavish musical extravaganza featuring Bobby Clark, June Havoc and a chorus line of attractive showgirls. With this song and others in the show, Porter demonstrated that he was coming out of his fallow period of production following his disastrous riding accident of October 1937. Popular recordings of "I Love You" were by Bing Crosby (a No. 1 Chart Record on Decca), Perry Como (Victor), and Jo Stafford (Capitol).

It is an endearing song. The lyrics in the verse declare, "just an amateur am I," but the refrain has the unmistakable mark of a professional. Like many Porter creations, there is a dichotomy between major and minor modes. The verse is in two keys: first F minor, then F major. The refrain, while clearly in F major, has minor underpinnings. The initial melodic gestures are the drops of a seventh at the words "...love you": first from c" to d-flat', then from a' to b-flat. In AA'BA" form, there is an interesting modulation to A major in the second "A" section. Another feature of the song is the six-bar coda after the second ending.

Although *Mexican Hayride* was made into a movie starring Bud Abbott, Lou Costello, and Luba Malina in 1948, "I Love You" was not featured. Yet, of the many songs with that title written over the years, it is certainly one of the most arresting.

Moderate beguine with verse (32) and refrain (32)
PUBLISHER: Chappell & Co., Inc.
KEY: F maj., *STARTS*: c" (B-flat min.6), *FORM*: AA'BA"

≈≈≈≈≈≈≈≈≈≈≈≈≈≈≈≈≈≈≈≈

I'LL BE HOME FOR CHRISTMAS ✶✶

WORDS AND MUSIC: Kim Gannon and Walter Kent
INTRODUCED BY: Bing Crosby on radio and in a Decca recording

One of a wave of Christmas songs that appeared in the forties attempting to capitalize on the overwhelming success of Irving Berlin's "White Christmas" (1942), "I'll Be Home for Christmas" echoed the sentiments of millions of servicemen and women who were far from home. It was introduced by Bing Crosby on his radio show and in a Victor recording that sold over a million copies in its first year alone. Although the song was soon taken up by numerous other singers, it is with Crosby's mellifluous baritone that it is indelibly associated.

Both music and lyrics contribute to the poignancy of the refrain. Harmonies are surprisingly rich; for example, the second chord of the refrain is identified as an A-flat diminished seventh with flatted thirteenth. The verse is in the unrelated key of D major. Also unusual is the written-out syncopation in the melodic line. The lyrics perfectly carry the wartime spirit of this warmest of holidays, ending with the punch line: "I'll be home for Christmas / If only in my dreams."

Like many other Christmas songs, "I'll Be Home for Christmas" is a perennial, returning to the airwaves each December.

Slow ballad with verse (8) and refrain (32)
PUBLISHER; Gannon & Kent Music Co., Inc.
KEY; F maj., *STARTS*: f' (F maj.), *FORM*: ABAC

≈≈≈≈≈≈≈≈≈≈≈≈≈≈≈≈≈≈≈≈

LILI MARLENE ✶✶

ENGLISH WORDS: Mack David, *MUSIC*: Norbert Schultze
INTRODUCED BY: Marlene Dietrich in the United States

Something of an international oddity, this famous little march stems from a poem written in 1915 by a German soldier named Hans Liep while he was serving on the Russian front. Originally called "Lili Marleen," the song referred to two girls, respectively named Lili and Marleen. Liep's poem was published in a 1937 anthology and set to music by composer Norbert Schultze in Berlin in 1938. In 1939, German cabaret singer Lale Anderson recorded it on Electrola, and that record became a hit when it was broadcast to German and British troops in Africa. Anne Shelton introduced an English version, with words by Tommie Connor, to British audiences. The song, also known as "My Lili of the Lamppost," was later popularized in the United States by Marlene Dietrich, who used it as her signature song on radio and in public performances. Other American recordings were made by Hildegarde (Decca) and Perry Como (Victor). "Lili Marlene" was revived in 1968, with a Capitol recording by Al Martino. The simple tune of the sixteen-bar refrain moves mostly stepwise in dotted eighths and quarters, accompanied by basic harmonies of the tonic, dominant, and subdominant.

Moderate march with four verses (8) and refrain (16)
PUBLISHER: Chappell & Co., Inc.
KEY: C maj., *STARTS*: e' (C maj.), *FORM*: ABCC'

≈≈≈≈≈≈≈≈≈≈≈≈≈≈≈≈≈≈≈

(ALL OF A SUDDEN) MY HEART SINGS

ENGLISH WORDS : Harold Rome, *MUSIC*: "Jamblan" Henri Herpin
PREMIERE: Film musical , "Anchors Aweigh" , Metro Goldwyn Mayer, 1945
INTRODUCED BY: Kathryn Grayson

Unquestionably one of the most artless songs in the literature, "(All of a Sudden) My Heart Sings" was published in France in 1941, with French words by Jean Marie Blanvillain and music by "Jamblan" Henry Herpin. Imported to the United States and given English words by Harold Rome, the song only became popular in 1945, after it was featured in the film, *Anchors Aweigh*. Popular recordings were by Hildegarde (Decca) and Guy Lombardo and his Royal Canadians (Decca). It was revived by Paul Anka in 1959 and Mel Carter in 1965.

The melody of the refrain, in two sections, simply consists of the diatonic scale with each note played eight times, rising in the first half and descending in the second half. But the changing harmonies and Rome's sensitive English words rescue the song from banality. It was featured in two other films: *Junior Prom* (1946) and *The Last Time I Saw Paris* (1954); in the latter, it was sung by Odette. Despite the song's basic simplicity, it is a curiously effective tour de force.

Moderate ballad with verse (8) and two refrains (32)
PUBLISHER: Leeds Music Corporation
KEY: C maj., *STARTS*: c' (C maj.), *FORM*: AB

≈≈≈≈≈≈≈≈≈≈≈≈≈≈≈≈≈≈≈≈

MY SHINING HOUR !

WORDS; Johnny Mercer, *MUSIC*: Harold Arlen
PREMIERE: Film musical, *The Sky's the Limit*, RKO 1943.
INTRODUCED BY: Fred Astaire and Joan Leslie (dubbed in by Sally Sweetland)

This tender ballad is one of Johnny Mercer and Harold Arlen's loveliest creations. It was first sung in *The Sky's the Limit*, an RKO film about a war hero (played by Fred Astaire) who falls in love with a girl (Joan Leslie) while pretending to be a civilian vacationing in New York. The powerful song, nominated for an Academy Award, has far outlasted the undistinguished movie. The most popular recording was by Glen Gray and The Casa Loma Orchestra, with vocal by Eugenie Baird.

The music of the verse is lovely in itself, like a lullaby, while in the refrain it has the quality of a hymn. The principal theme of the refrain is economical in its use of notes, consisting of only three tones (g', a-flat', b-flat') and the lower octave of one (b-flat). Another group of three tones (e-flat', c', and g') is prominent both in the verse and as accompaniment at the end of the refrain. The "A" sections have a range of only one octave, from b-flat' to b-flat". But the "B" section, with its repetitive phrases, goes much higher, carrying the range of the song to its full extent of an octave and a half. The lyrics are a perfect match for the music, with such à propos wartime sentiments as "Calm and happy and bright" and "Like the lights of home before me."

"My Shining Hour" was indeed a shining hour in the Mercer-Arlen collaboration.

Moderate ballad with verse (15) and refrain (32)
PUBLISHER: Harwin Music Co.
KEY: E-flat maj., *STARTS*: g' (E-flat maj.), *FORM*: AA'BA"

≈≈≈≈≈≈≈≈≈≈≈≈≈≈≈≈≈≈≈≈

OH, WHAT A BEAUTIFUL MORNIN' ✳ ✳ ✳

WORDS: Oscar Hammerstein II, *MUSIC*: Richard Rodgers
PREMIERE: Musical play, *Oklahoma!*
New York: St. James Theatre, 31 March 1943 (2,248 perf.)
INTRODUCED BY: Alfred Drake

In the very first scene of *Oklahoma!*, Curly (played by Alfred Drake) sings this folk-like number to Laurey (played by Joan Roberts). Thus the tone is set for a new era of American musical theater, concerned with everyday people and their real problems and doing away with many of the frivolous conventions of musical comedy. *Oklahoma!*, based on Lynn Riggs's 1931 play, *Green Grow the Lilacs*, had an initial run of 2,248 performances, an amount only to be surpassed fifteen years later, by *My Fair Lady*. It was almost as successful in London, where it ran for 1,548 performances at the Drury Lane Theatre, beginning 30 April 1947.

The new collaboration of Oscar Hammerstein II and Richard Rodgers, which began with this production, differed in many ways from Rodgers's previous collaboration with Lorenz Hart. An essential difference answered the proverbial question of which came first, the music or the words. With Hart, it was usually the music. But Hammerstein always conceived the words first, which were then set to music by Rodgers. In the case of "Oh, What a Beautiful Mornin'," Hammerstein took a passage from the stage directions of Riggs's play describing the morning and the stage setting – the cattle, the corn, the golden haze on the meadow – and shaped them into his own lyrics. According to Hammerstein, he first wrote that the corn was as high as "a cow-pony's eye," but later amended it to "an elephant's eye," when he noticed how high it grew in August at a neighbor's farm. The lyrics are unremittingly folksy and often turn to homespun dialect, as; "a ol' weepin' willer is laughin' at me." Best-selling recordings of "Oh, What a Beautiful Mornin'" were made by Bing Crosby (Decca) and Frank Sinatra (Columbia).

It is said that Hammerstein took three weeks to write the lyrics, while Rodgers dashed off the music in ten minutes. This seems likely, since it is a simple little waltz, far removed from the sophistication of so many Rodgers and Hart songs. It is determinately folk-like in structure, alternating three sixteen-bar verses, each set to a different lyric, with the same sixteen-bar refrain. The melody of the verse moves stepwise, while that of the refrain is chordal in nature. The only jarring note is the prominent flatted seventh (d-flat") in the third bar of the refrain. The harmonies are also characteristic of folk song: tonic, dominant, subdominant.

In the 1955 film version of *Oklahoma!*, the song was sung by Gordon MacRae. There were notable revivals of the musical play in New York at Lincoln Center in 1969 and the Palace Theatre in 1979. It as still today one of the most popular productions on the theatrical circuit. Both the landmark play and its opening number have become enduring American legends.

Slow waltz with three verses (16) and refrain (32)
PUBLISHER: Williamson Music, Inc.
KEY: E-flat maj.,STARTS: b-flat' (E-flat maj.),FORM (Overall):ABABAB

≈≈≈≈≈≈≈≈≈≈≈≈≈≈≈≈≈≈≈

OKLAHOMA *

WORDS: Oscar Hammerstein II, MUSIC: Richard Rodgers
PREMIERE: Musical play, *Oklahoma!*
New York: St. James Theatre, 31 March 1943 (2,248 perf.)
INTRODUCED BY: Alfred Drake, Joan Roberts, Betty Garde, Barry Kelley, Edwin Clay, and ensemble

With all the wonderful songs in *Oklahoma!*, one must not forget its theme song. "Oklahoma," lustily sung by the cast principals and chorus, contributed mightily to the landmark show's phenomenal success. The verse, partly in the key of F major, acts as a buildup to the refrain. An ascending scale leads to the long-sustained first note (c") of the refrain, on the syllable "O...". The form of the refrain is AABA', but since it is in 2/4 meter, each "A" section is sixteen bars in length. The "B" section, however, is only eight bars long, lending a degree of asymmetry to the structure. Especially powerful, when sung by a chorus, is the ending, with its rising sequential melody. In the 1955 film, *Oklahoma!*, the title song was sung by Gordon MacRae, Charlotte Greenwood, James Whitmore, Shirley Jones, Jay C. Flippen , and chorus.

Fast rhythm song with verse (35) and refrain (56)
PUBLISHER: Williamson Music, Inc.
KEY: C maj., STARTS: c" (C maj.), FORM: AABA'

≈≈≈≈≈≈≈≈≈≈≈≈≈≈≈≈≈≈≈

ONE FOR MY BABY (AND ONE MORE FOR THE ROAD) *

WORDS: Johnny Mercer, MUSIC: Harold Arlen
PREMIERE: Film musical, *The Sky's the Limit*, RKO 1943
INTRODUCED BY: Fred Astaire

Like "My Shining Hour," another remarkable song from the forgettable film, *The Sky's the Limit,* starring Fred Astaire and Joan Leslie, "One for My Baby (And One More for the Road)" has led a life of its own. It has been recorded by a host of vocalists over the years, most notably by Frank Sinatra (Capitol), but also by Johnny Mercer (Capitol), Lena Horne (Victor), Tony Bennett (Columbia), and Mel Tormé (Musicraft), and has been featured in a number of films. Also, because of its subject matter – booze and unrequited love – it has long been a favorite of cabaret singers.

It is a situation song; that is, it involves a talkative, lovelorn customer and a laconic bartender named Joe, who is a good listener. The stage is set with the opening line: "It's quarter to three, there's no one in the place except you and me." And the story unfolds from there. The music never gets in the way of the words, but is refreshingly original. Marked as a "slow boogie," it consists of a sixteen-bar section in E-flat major, followed by a repetition of the same, but this time in the key of G major. From then on, the song stays in G major, with an eight-bar release, a sixteen-bar recapitulation, and a two-bar coda. Blue notes are prominent, especially in the "B" section with its many B-flats.

After its introduction in *The Sky's the Limit,* "One for My Baby" was sung by Ida Lupino in *Road House* (1948), by Jane Russell in *Macao* (1952), and by Frank Sinatra in *Young at Heart* (1955). The song remains a delightful maverick, unusual in being in two keys, telling a long story, and being fifty-eight bars in length without a verse.

Slow blues song with refrain (58)
PUBLISHER: HarwinMusic Co.
KEYS: E-flat maj., G maj., *STARTS*: f-sharp' (E-flat 6), *FORM*: AA'BA'

≈≈≈≈≈≈≈≈≈≈≈≈≈≈≈≈≈≈

OUT OF MY DREAMS

WORDS: Oscar Hammerstein II, *MUSIC*: Richard Rodgers
PREMIERE:: Musical play, *Oklahoma!*
New York: St. James Theatre, 31 March 1943 (2,248 perf.)
INTRODUCED BY: Joan Roberts and The Girl's Chorus

This haunting waltz is sung by Laurey just prior to "The Dream Ballet" that closes the first act of *Oklahoma!* It is one of the best waltzes by Richard Rodgers, a specialist in the genre. The form is unusual: there is no verse, the refrain resembles a rondo, and there is an interlude in the dominant key (C major). The largely stepwise melody of the refrain is modal in character, while the "C" section brings in a new idea, characterized by chromaticism and descending skips of the major sixth. It is a romantic piece, worthy of the late nineteenth century, and Hammerstein's lyrics are appropriately poetic.

In the 1955 film version of *Oklahoma!*, "Out of My Dreams" was sung by Shirley Jones and The Girl's Chorus.

Moderate waltz with refrain (44) and interlude (36)
PUBLISHER: Williamson Music, Inc.
KEY: F maj., *STARTS*: f' (F maj.), *FORM*: ABA'CA"

≈≈≈≈≈≈≈≈≈≈≈≈≈≈≈≈≈≈≈≈

PEOPLE WILL SAY WE'RE IN LOVE * *

WORDS: Oscar Hammerstein II, *MUSIC*: Richard Rodgers
PREMIERE: Musical play, *Oklahoma!*
New York: St. James Theatre, 31 March 1943 (2,248 perf.)
INTRODUCED BY: Alfred Drake and Joan Roberts

The big ballad and most popular song from *Oklahoma!*, "People Will Say We're in Love" comes about quite naturally in the play as Laurey suggests to Curly that he not show how much he admires her or people will talk. Hammerstein's lyrics shine with such delicious passages as "Don't please my folks too much" and "Don't laugh at my jokes too much."

The melody comes from a song that Rodgers had written with Lorenz Hart a few years before. With its new lyrics, as "People Will Say We're In Love," it became the most popular song of the year. Decca released a single of the cast album, sung by Alfred Drake and Joan Roberts. The song enjoyed the longest consecutive run on the popular radio show, *Lucky Strike Hit Parade* (later *Your Hit Parade*), with thirty-eight weekly appearances between June 1943 and January 1944, including three weeks in the No. 1 position.

The verse in the key of G major leads to the refrain, in C major (in some editions, the keys are A-flat and D-flat). The form of the refrain is asymmetrical: it consists of two sixteen-bar sections followed by two eight-bar sections. The melody is broadly drawn, with many upward and downward intervals of the fifth. There are interesting harmonies in the release, which moves from F seventh to B-flat and then through the circle of fifths (A-7, D-7, G-7). The last variation of the A section acts as a coda, carrying the song to its highest point.

In the film version of *Oklahoma!*, "People Will Say We're In Love" was sung by Gordon MacRae and Shirley Jones. It remains among the best of the Rodgers and Hammerstein collaborations, a perfect mating of words and music.

> Moderate ballad with two verses (16) and two refrains (48)
> *PUBLISHER*: Williamson Music, Inc.
> *KEY*: C maj. or D-flat maj., *STARTS*: c' (C maj.) or d-flat' (D-flat maj.),
> *FORM*: AA'BA"

≈≈≈≈≈≈≈≈≈≈≈≈≈≈≈≈≈≈

SPEAK LOW * !

> *WORDS*: Ogden Nash, *MUSIC*: Kurt Weill
> *PREMIERE*:: Musical comedy, *One Touch of Venus*
> New York: Imperial Theatre, 7 October 1943 (567 perf.)
> *INTRODUCED BY*: Mary Martin, reprised by Mary Martin and Kenny Baker

This haunting beguine was one of the highlights of *One Touch of Venus*, a rollicking show that boasted Mary Martin's first starring role on Broadway. With book by S. J. Perelman and Ogden Nash, lyrics by Nash, and music by Kurt Weill, the production was blessed with superb talents. The plot, about a statue of Venus (played by Martin) that comes to life when a ring is placed on its finger, added to the show's appeal. Although *One Touch of Venus* had some wonderful numbers and enjoyed a considerable run, "Speak Low" is the only song to have survived.

Like many of Weill's songs, "Speak Low" differs from the ordinary. It uses pitches sparingly: only four appear in the first six measures (c', a', g', and d'). It lacks a verse and has a refrain with the unusual length of fifty-six bars. It is comprised of three "A" sections, each of sixteen bars, and a release of only eight bars. It resorts to repetition relentlessly: the first long-sustained note (a') is almost immediately repeated three times. The melody is disjunct, with many quarter-note triplets. The harmonies are predominantly ninths, starting with the very first chord (G minor ninth). The short release is in itself a study in harmony, modulating from F minor seventh to A-flat minor and then, enharmonically, from E-flat major seventh to E major. Nash's lyrics are at the same time poetic and philosophical, as in the release: "Time is so old and love so brief." Despite all these seemingly diverse attributes, the song as a whole has a magnificent integrity.

First to popularize "Speak Low" was the orchestra of Guy Lombardo and his Royal Canadians, with vocalist Billy Leach. In the 1948 film version of *One Touch of Venus*, it was sung by Eileen Wilson, dubbing in for Ava Gardner, and Dick Haymes. The song is understandably much beloved by musicians. Marvin Hamlisch has incorporated it into several of his film scores.

Moderate beguine with refrain (56)
PUBLISHER: Chappell & Co., Inc.
KEY: F maj., *STARTS*: c' (G min. 9), *FORM*:: A'BA"

≈≈≈≈≈≈≈≈≈≈≈≈≈≈≈≈≈≈≈

SPRING WILL BE A LITTLE LATE THIS YEAR

WORDS AND MUSIC: Frank Loesser
PREMIERE: Film musical, *Christmas Holiday*, 1944
INTRODUCED BY: Deanna Durbin

This expressive ballad is a favorite of singers. One of its earliest champions was tenor Morton Downey, but virtually all popular vocalists have embraced it. It is one of Frank Loesser's freshest ballads and was first sung by Deanna Durbin in *Christmas Holiday*, the screen version of a somewhat sad story by Somerset Maugham. Durbin also made the best-selling record (Decca). The song's chief attraction lies in its extremely disjunct melody, and especially the downward octave jump (from b-flat' to b-flat) that opens the refrain, quickly followed by two upward jumps of a major ninth (from b-flat' to c"). Also of interest are the harmonies centering around the C-flat diminished chord, and the quarter-note triplets that are prevalent in both verse and refrain. The lyrics are vintage Loesser, with such passages as "For you have left me and winter continues cold." With such words and music, it is no wonder that "Spring Will Be a Little Late This Year" is a singer's delight.

Moderate ballad with verse (10) and refrain (32)
PUBLISHER: Frank Music Corp.
KEY: E-flat maj., *STARTS*: b-flat' (E-flat maj.), *FORM*: ABAB'

≈≈≈≈≈≈≈≈≈≈≈≈≈≈≈≈≈≈≈

THE SURREY WITH THE FRINGE ON TOP *

WORDS: Oscar Hammerstein II, *MUSIC*: Richard Rodgers
PREMIERE: Musical play, *Oklahoma!*
New York: St. James Theatre, 31 March 1943 (2,248 perf.)
INTRODUCED BY: Alfred Drake, Joan Roberts, and Betty Garde

One of the highlights of the hit show, *Oklahoma!*, this perky song has all the ingredients of a novelty: cute lyrics ("Chicks and ducks and geese better scurry"), the clippity-clop rhythm of a horse pulling a surrey, a staccato melody with a plethora of repeated notes, and unexpected melodic jumps to intervals of the fourth, fifth, and sixth. The verse is interesting, with harmonic excursions a minor third apart: from G major to E major to D-flat major to B-flat major, and then back to G major. In contrast, the refrain is simple in all elements: form, melody, harmony, and rhythm. In the 1955 film version of *Oklahoma!*, "The Surrey with the Fringe On Top" was sung by Gordon MacRae, Shirley Jones, and Charlotte Greenwood.

Moderate novelty song with verse (16) and three refrains (36)
PUBLISHER: Williamson Music, Inc.
KEY: G maj. or A-flat maj., *STARTS*: d' (G maj.) or e-flat (A-flat maj.),
FORM: AABA'

≈≈≈≈≈≈≈≈≈≈≈≈≈≈≈≈≈≈≈

TICO-TICO

ENGLISH WORDS: Ervin Drake, *MUSIC*: Zequinha Abreu
PREMIERE: Cartoon film, *Saludos Amigos*, Disney, 1943
INTRODUCED BY: Aloysio Oliveira

This lively Brazilian samba is noted for its profusion of sixteenth notes and its infectious rhythm. With music by Brazilian composer Zequinha Abreu, the original Portuguese words were by Aloysio Oliveira, who introduced it in the Disney cartoon film, *Saludos Amigos*. Organist Ethel Smith is most often identified with the piece; her electrifying Decca record, with the Bando Carioca, was a best-seller. It was also recorded for Decca by singer Carmen Miranda. The refrain is in AABB' form, with the "A" sections in A minor and the "B" sections in C major. Following this is a quieter interlude in the key of A major, and then a return to the A minor-C major refrain.

"Tico-Tico" was featured in other films as well. It was danced to Maxine Barrett and Don Loper in *Thousands Cheer* (1943), played by Ethel Smith in *Bathing Beauty* (1944), heard in *Kansas City Kitty* (1944), and sung by Carmen Miranda in *Copacabana* (1947).

Bright samba with refrain (32) and interlude (16)
PUBLISHER: Peer International Corporation
KEY: A min., *STARTS*: e' (A min.), *FORM*: AABB'

≈≈≈≈≈≈≈≈≈≈≈≈≈≈≈≈≈≈≈

WHILE WE'RE YOUNG !

WORDS: William Engvick, *MUSIC*: Alec Wilder and Morty Palitz
INTRODUCED BY: Mabel Mercer

A captivating waltz, "While We're Young" was developed from a beautiful poem by William Engvick, who also supplied the musical idea for the opening motive of the refrain, which was later developed by Alec Wilder and Morty Palitz. A staple of cabaret singer Mabel Mercer, the first recording was by Fred Waring and his Pennsylvanians. Among the many other recordings are those of Peggy Lee (Capitol) and Tony Bennett (Columbia).

The sixty-four-bar refrain is marked "Moderato and expressively; not too slowly." In ABAC/A' form, it starts with a motive of five tones, soon expanded to six. The "B" section, in the key of C minor, has a feeling of modality caused by the alternate usage in the melody of both the flatted and natural forms of the interval of the sixth: a-flat' and a-natural'. The last section brings the range to its highest point of an octave and a third, and closes with a brief paraphrase of the opening motive. Engvick's lyrics demonstrate his marvelous penchant for inner rhyme: "just for today / we must while we may" and "time flies so fast / too sweet to last."

Moderate waltz with verse (10) and refrain (64)
PUBLISHER: Ludlow Music, Inc.
KEY: E-flat maj., *STARTS*: e-flat' (E-flat maj.), *FORM*: ABAC/A'

≈≈≈≈≈≈≈≈≈≈≈≈≈≈≈≈≈≈≈

YOU'LL NEVER KNOW ∗ ∗ ∗

WORDS: Mack Gordon, *MUSIC*: Harry Warren
PREMIERE: Film musical, *Hello, Frisco, Hello*, Twentieth Century Fox 1943
INTRODUCED BY: Alice Faye

Winner of the Academy Award for best song of 1943, *You'll Never Know* was a perfect expression of its time. With its opening line, "You'll never know just how much I miss you," it echoed the sentiments of millions whose loved ones were far from home.

The song was very much a creature of Hollywood. Not only was it written by two of the film industry's top songsmiths, Mack Gordon and Harry Warren, but it was featured in three movies within the first three years of its existence. Alice Faye sang it in two films a year apart: *Hello, Frisco, Hello* (1943) and *Four Jills in a Jeep* (1944). Then a year later, Betty Grable sang it in the lavish *Billy Rose's Diamond Horseshoe* (later, simply called *Diamond Horseshoe*). *Hello, Frisco, Hello* was a period musical in which Faye played a saloon singer; it featured John Payne, Jack Oakie, and June Havoc. *Four Jills in a Jeep* starred Kay Francis, Martha Raye, and Phil Silvers; while *Billy Rose's Diamond Horseshoe* enjoyed the talents of Betty Grable, Dick Haymes, and Phil Silvers. Alice Faye never lost her association with "You'll Never Know"; it became her signature song.

The song was soon taken up by the big bands and by vocalists, notably Dick Haymes, who had a No. 1 Chart Record with The Song Spinners (Decca), and Frank Sinatra, who recorded it with The Bobby Tucker Singers (Columbia). Because of the ongoing musicians' strike, the accompaniment was a cappella. Later recordings were by Rosemary Clooney, with Harry James and his Orchestra (Columbia, 1953) and The Platters (Mercury, 1956).

Much of the song's musical appeal comes from the opening notes of its refrain, which boldly outline the second inversion of the F major chord upward and downward., This idea continues with a similar outlining of the G minor chord, which eventually returns to close the refrain. In the style of the time, the notes are written out in light syncopation.

"You'll Never Know" has been featured in other films besides the initial three: Ginger Rogers sang it in *Dreamboat* in 1952 and Alice Faye reprised it in *Alice Doesn't Live Here Anymore* (1975). It remains an important piece of wartime nostalgia.

Moderate ballad with verse (8) and two refrains (32)
PUBLISHER: WB Music Corp.
KEY: F maj., *STARTS*: c' (F maj.), *FORM*: AB'AC

≈≈≈≈≈≈≈≈≈≈≈≈≈≈≈≈≈≈≈≈≈

YOU'VE CHANGED

WORDS: Bill Carey, *MUSIC*: Carl Fischer

Although published in 1943, this sentimental ballad did not become popular until 1948, when it was recorded on Columbia by Harry James and his Orchestra, with vocal by Dick Haymes. In 1954 it was recorded by Harold Mooney and his Orchestra, with vocal by Connie Russell. The refrain, in E-flat major, has a descending chromatic melodic line, starting with emphasis on the major seventh (d") and accompanied by slowly-descending chromatic harmonies. Diana Ross sang "You've Changed" in the Billie Holiday film biography, *Lady Sings the Blues* (1972).

Moderate ballad with verse (8) and refrain (32)
PUBLISHER: Melody Lane Publications, Inc., assigned to Southern Music
Publishing Co., Inc.
KEY: E-flat maj., *STARTS*: e-flat' (E-flat maj. 7), *FORM*: AA'BA'

≈≈≈≈≈≈≈≈≈≈≈≈≈≈≈≈≈≈

BOBBY SOXERS AND SINGING STARS

1944

. . . eliminate the negative, and don't mess with Mister In-Between.

Johnny Mercer,
"Ac-cent-chu-ate the Positive (Mister in-Between)"

In a nation preoccupied by war, songs tend to "Ac-cent-tchu-ate the Positive," to overlook the horrifying realties occurring in Europe and Asia, by "Swinging on a Star," taking a "Sentimental Journey," or enjoying an old-fashioned ride via "The Trolley Song." In short, they seek any time or place that is "Long Ago and Far Away." With few exceptions ("I'll Walk Alone" is one), songs about war and loneliness are taboo. The ongoing demise of the big bands due to wartime attrition brings forth such singing stars as Bing Crosby, Dinah Shore, and Judy Garland. One of them, Frank Sinatra – an alumnus of the big bands -- attracts over 30,000 fans, many of them howling teenagers known as "bobby soxers," when he appears at the Paramount Theatre in New York on Columbus Day.

The newspapers carry exciting stories about the landing of American troops in Italy in January and on the beaches of Normandy in June. A popular song of 1939 comes into its own with Operation Chattanooga Choo-Choo, which consists of air strikes in the Pas de Calais area of France, deliberately designed to deceive the Germans into thinking the invasion will occur there rather than in Normandy. With so much happening abroad, no one is surprised when Franklin D. Roosevelt is elected for an unprecedented fourth term.

In tune with the public's get-away-from-it-all mentality, the most popular play is about an imaginary rabbit named *Harvey*; starring Frank Fay, it wins the Pulitzer Prize. Among the most popular musicals are *Bloomer Girl, On the Town* (Leonard Bernstein's first), and *Song of Norway*, based on the music of Edvard Grieg.

Many of Hollwood's brightest stars are in the service, including actors Clark Gable, James Stewart, Robert Taylor, Robert Montgomery, and Mickey Rooney, and directors Frank Capra, William Wyler, John Huston, and John Ford. But enough are left to produce such films about war and religion as *Since You Went Away, Thirty Seconds to Tokyo,* and

Going My Way – the latter starring crooner Bing Crosby as a Catholic priest. Among other popular movies this year are *Laura* (with a stunning theme that will become a popular song next year), *Gaslight, Double Indemnity*, and the giant musical, *Meet Me in St.Louis*, with a magnificent score by Hugh Martin and Ralph Blaine.

Radio is more popular than ever, intermingling war news with the bobby soxers' favorite singing stars and commercials like the new one for Chiquita Banana, warning consumers to "never put bananas in the refrigerator.

SONGS OF 1944

Ac-cent-tchu-ate the Positive (Mister In-Between)
The Boy Next Door *!
Don't Fence Me In
Ev'ry Time We Say Goodbye !
Have Yourself a Merry Little Christmas *
I Fall in Love Too Easily
I Should Care
I'll Walk Alone
Is You Is or Is You Ain't (Ma' Baby)
It Could Happen to You *!
Like Someone in Love !
Long Ago (And Far Away) **
Moonlight in Vermont ***!
Sentimental Journey ***
Strange Music
Swinging on a Star
The Trolley Song !
Twilight Time
You Always Hurt the One You Love
You Belong to My Heart (Solamente Una Vez) *
You're Nobody 'Til Somebody Loves You **

AC-CEN-TCHU-ATE THE POSITIVE
(MISTER IN-BETWEEN)

WORDS: Johnny Mercer, *MUSIC*: Harold Arlen
PREMIERE: Film musical, *Here Come the Waves*, Paramount, 1944
INTRODUCED BY: Bing Crosby and Sonny Tufts

This clever novelty song was introduced by Bing Crosby and Sonny Tufts, playing two male sailors wooing two female sailors in the film, *Here Come the Waves*. The song was nominated for an Academy Award and appeared thirteen weeks on radio's *Your Hit Parade*. Best-selling records, both on Decca, were by Johnny Mercer, its lyricist, and by Bing Crosby with The Andrews Sisters. The bands of Artie Shaw and Kay Kyser also had hit recordings.

The lengthy verse starts in gospel style, with the words: "Gather 'round me, ev'rybody." It begins in the key of F minor, but moves to F major at the closing words, "Don't mess with Mister In-Between." In the much livelier refrain, Harold Arlen's melody contrasts repeated notes with dotted notes and an occasional blue note (a-flat') – aptly placed at the word "negative." The lyrics of the first and last sections are identical, except for a two-bar repetition of the last line as an abbreviated coda.

Moderate novelty song with verse (34) and refrain (34)
PUBLISHER: Edwin H. Morris & Company, Inc.
KEY: F maj., *STARTS*: c' (F maj.), *FORM*: AABA'

≈≈≈≈≈≈≈≈≈≈≈≈≈≈≈≈≈≈

THE BOY NEXT DOOR * !

WORDS AND MUSIC: Hugh Martin and Ralph Blane
PREMIERE: Film musical, *Meet Me in St. Louis*. Metro Goldwyn Mayer,1944
INTRODUCED BY: Judy Garland

This enchanting waltz always brings to mind Judy Garland, who so wistfully introduced it in the classic film musical, *Meet Me in St. Louis*. In 1989, when the movie was turned into a Broadway show, "The Boy Next Door" was sung by Donna Kane. The verse has two sets of lyrics, one for *The Girl Next Door*. There are several unusual aspects to the song. For one thing, the verse is actually lengthier than the refrain. For another, the verse is in the key of F major, while the refrain is in B-flat major. And most interesting of all, the verse ends like no other, with the note e' repeated twenty-four times at the words: "I live at fifty-one, thirty-five Kensington Avenue / And he lives at fifty-one, thirty-three." The melody of the refrain is unusual in itself, with chromatic skips, as from f' to sharp" and from e-flat' to b', accompanied by suspended dominant ninth chords. These quixotic devices and others make this lovely song of special interest to musicians.

> Slow waltz with two verses (36) and refrain (32)
> *PUBLISHER*: Leo Feist, Inc.
> *KEY*: B-flat maj., *STARTS*: d' (B-flat maj. 7), *FORM*: ABA'C

≈≈≈≈≈≈≈≈≈≈≈≈≈≈≈≈≈≈≈

DON'T FENCE ME IN *

WORDS AND MUSIC: Cole Porter
PREMIERE: Film musical, *Hollywood Canteen*. Warner Brothers, 1944
INTRODUCED BY : Roy Rogers and The Sons of the Pioneers, reprised by The Andrews Sisters

Cole Porter wrote this plaintive song for a movie planned by Fox back in 1945. It was to be called *Adios Argentina*, and Lou Brock, its producer, suggested that Porter write a cowboy lament based on a poem called "Don't Fence Me In," that had been written by a Montana mining engineer named Bob Fletcher. Porter acquired the rights to the poem for about $200, wrote his song, but the film was never produced. Finally, the song found a home nine years later in the film, *Hollywood Canteen*. Sung in the movie by cowboy star, Roy Rogers, it became one of Porter's biggest money makers, remaining sixteen weeks on *Your Hit Parade*. Among prominent recordings were those of Bing Crosby and The Andrews Sisters on Decca, Kate Smith on Columbia, and Gene Autry on Columbia.

"Don't Fence Me In" resembles a folk song, in simple ABA' form. The melody features multiple repetitions of minor seconds in the "A" sections and dotted eighths and sixteenths in the release. Harmonies, in country style, are mainly confined to tonic, dominant, and subdominant. The lyrics, as usual, demonstrate Porter's remarkable flair, as in: "Let me straddle my old saddle underneath the western skies."

Roy Rogers performed the song in two other films; the namesake mic, *Don't Fence Me In* (1945) and the Porter biography, *Night and Day* (1946). It is ironic that one of the most popular songs by this most urban of songwriters has to do with rural life.

> Moderate country song with two verses (8) and refrain (32)
> *PUBLISHER*: Harms, Inc.
> *KEY*: F maj., *STARTS*: c' (F maj.), *FORM*: ABA'

≈≈≈≈≈≈≈≈≈≈≈≈≈≈≈≈≈≈

EV'RY TIME WE SAY GOODBYE !

WORDS AND MUSIC: Cole Porter
PREMIERE: Revue, The Seven Lively Arts
New York: Ziegfeld Theatre, 7 December 1944 (183 perf.)
INTRODUCED BY: Nan Wynn

Billy Rose's lavish revue, *The Seven Lively Arts,* was a dismal flop, despite a Cole Porter score, ballet music by Igor Stravinsky, and a star-studded cast that included Beatrice Lillie, Bert Lahr, Benny Goodman, Teddy Wilson, and Red Norvo. Only one song survived, but it is one of Porter's best. In the words of Dr. Albert Sirmay (in a letter he wrote to Porter, quoted in Charles Schwartz's biography): "It chokes me whenever I hear it, it moves me to tears. This song is one of the greatest songs you ever wrote. It is a dithyramb to love, a hymn to youth, a heavenly beautiful song. It is not less a gem than any immortal song of a Schubert or Schumann." The ballad was popularized in early recordings by Hildegarde (Decca); The Benny Goodman Quintet, with Peggy Mann (Columbia); and Stan Kenton and his Orchestra, with Anita O'Day (Capitol).

"Ev'ry Time We Say Goodbye" is indeed a gem, unique in its perfect mating of words and music. In a notable example of word painting, harmonies actually change from major to minor at the words: "But how strange the change from major to minor." The refrain begins with eight repeated notes over alternating E-flat major and C minor harmonies, followed by another example of word painting: a descending figure at the words "I die a little." With the song's strong emotional appeal, it is arguably one of the most expressive in the popular literature.

Slow ballad with verse (10) and refrain (32)
PUBLISHER: Chappell & Co., Inc.
KEY: E-flat maj., *STARTS*: g' (E-flat maj.), *FORM*: ABAB'

≈≈≈≈≈≈≈≈≈≈≈≈≈≈≈≈≈≈≈

HAVE YOURSELF A MERRY LITTLE CHRISTMAS ⋆

WORDS AND MUSIC: Hugh Martin and Ralph Blane
PREMIERE: Film musical *Meet Me in St. Louis*. Metro Goldwyn Mayer, 1944
INTRODUCED BY: Judy Garland, sung to Margaret O'Brien

A tender seasonal perennial, "Have Yourself a Merry Little Christmas", originated in the blockbuster film musical, *Meet Me in St. Louis*. The story revolved about the imaginary Smith family residing in St. Louis at the time of the 1903 fair. Judy Garland, who sang it to tiny Margaret O'Brien in the film, also had a best-selling record on Decca, as did Frank Sinatra on

Columbia. In the refrain, in conventional AA'BA" form, the melody outlines the C major triad three times in each "A" section. The release, in contrast, features a series of major seventh chords descending sequentially. Garland again sang this delightful Christmas song to O'Brien in the 1976 film, *That's Entertainment, Part II*.

> Slow ballad with verse (8) and refrain (36)
> *PUBLISHER*: Leo Feist, Inc.
> *KEY*: C maj., *STARTS*: c' (C maj.), *FORM*: AA'BA"

≈≈≈≈≈≈≈≈≈≈≈≈≈≈≈≈≈≈≈

I FALL IN LOVE TOO EASILY

> *WORDS AND MUSIC*: Sammy Cahn and Jule Styne
> *PREMIERE*: Film musical, *Anchors Aweigh*. Metro Goldwyn Mayer, 1945
> *INTRODUCED BY*: Frank Sinatra

Frank Sinatra, now out on his own, sang this romantic ballad in the film, *Anchors Aweigh*, which also starred Gene Kelly, Kathryn Grayson, and concert pianist José Iturbi. With popular recordings by Sinatra and Mel Tormé, the song was nominated for an Academy Award. The melody is built around a motive of six neighbor tones, placed at varying pitch levels. Harmonies are striking, starting with an F minor seventh and moving to C minor before returning to the tonic of E-flat major.

> Slow ballad with verse (8) and refrain (16)
> *PUBLISHER*: Metro-Goldwyn-Mayer, Inc.
> *KEY*: E-flat maj., *STARTS"* c" (F min. 7), *FORM*: ABCA'

≈≈≈≈≈≈≈≈≈≈≈≈≈≈≈≈≈≈≈

I SHOULD CARE

> *WORDS AND MUSIC*: Sammy Cahn, Axel Stordahl, and Paul Weston
> *PREMIERE*: Film musical, *Thrill of a Romance*. Metro Goldwyn Mayer, 1945
> *INTRODUCED BY*: Robert Allen and Esther Williams

This ballad was popularized in two best-selling records: by Tommy Dorsey and his Orchestra, with Bonnie Lou Williams and The Sentimentalists (Victor); and by Jimmy Dorsey and his Orchestra, with vocal by Teddy Walters (Decca). The refrain, marked "tenderly," is in ABAB' form. It's most interesting aspect is the changing harmonies under the long notes of the title: D minor seventh - G ninth - C major seventh. Quarter-note triplets predominate in the "B" sections. The legato melody lazily descends in the "A" sections, only to rise again in the "B" sections. Sammy Cahn's lyrics end with a Tin-Pan-Alley twist: "But, I should care and I do."

> Slow ballad with verse (6) and refrain (32)
> *PUBLISHER*: Dorsey Brothers Music, Inc.
> *KEY*: C maj., *STARTS*: c" (D min. 7), *FORM*: ABAB'

≈≈≈≈≈≈≈≈≈≈≈≈≈≈≈≈≈≈≈

I'LL WALK ALONE

> *WORDS*: Sammy Cahn, *MUSIC*: Jule Styne
> *PREMIERE*: Film musical, *Follow the Boys*. Universal, 1944
> *INTRODUCED BY*: Dinah Shore

The quintessential song of separated lovers, "I'll Walk Alone" touched a wartime nerve with its sentiment of carrying on without a partner. Dinah Shore had the top recording (Victor), and the song was nominated for an Academy Award. It was revived in 1952, when Jane Froman dubbed it in for Susan Hayward in the Froman film biography, *With a Song in My Heart*. Froman also had a best-selling record in 1952, as did Margaret Whiting (both on Capitol).

The refrain begins with a three-note pickup, moving in half steps to the note d'. The skipping melody includes many dotted notes and some syncopation in the release. The last line accounts for the song's universal appeal: "Till you're walking beside me, I'll walk alone."

> Slow ballad with verse (8) and refrain (32)
> *PUBLISHER*: Mayfair Music Corporation
> *KEY*: G maj., *STARTS*: b (G maj.), *FORM*: AA'BA"

≈≈≈≈≈≈≈≈≈≈≈≈≈≈≈≈≈≈≈

IS YOU IS OR IS YOU AIN'T (MA' BABY)

> *WORDS AND MUSIC*: Billy Austin and Louis Jordan
> *PREMIERE*: Film musical, *Follow the Boys*. Universal, 1944
> *INTRODUCED BY*: Louis Jordan

Another hit from the film, *Follow the Boys* (along with "I'll Walk Alone"), this ungrammatical rhythm and blues song was popularized in a Decca recording by bandleader Louis Jordan, its co-writer. Bing Crosby covered it in another Decca recording. A forerunner of the rhythm-and-blues explosion to soon follow, the song was revived in 1960, by Buster Brown. The tonality vacillates between F minor and A-flat major. The

verse, in the minor key, has many blue notes, while the refrain, in AABA'
form, moves from the minor to the major in each "A" section. The many
repeated notes on the beat give a premonition of rock and roll. The song
was featured in two other 1945 films: The Andrews Sisters performed it in
Her Lucky Night, while The Delta Rhythm Boys did it in *Easy to Look At*.

Moderate rhythm song with verse (16) and refrain (36)
PUBLISHER: Leeds Music Corporation
KEY: A-flat maj., *STARTS*: c" (F min.), *FORM*: AABA'

≈≈≈≈≈≈≈≈≈≈≈≈≈≈≈≈≈≈≈

IT COULD HAPPEN TO YOU * !

WORDS: Johnny Burke, *MUSIC*: James Van Heusen
PREMIERE: Film musical, *And the Angels Sing*. Paramount, 1944
INTRODUCED BY: Dorothy Lamour and Fred MacMurray

This lovely ballad was popularized in recordings by singers Jo
Stafford, on Capitol, and Bing Crosby, on Decca. It is noted for its interesting harmonic changes, both in the verse (which is in A-flat major) and
refrain (in G major). The profusion of diminished seventh and major and
minor ninth chords is dramatically enhanced by a rising chromatic bass
line – a favorite device of composer James Van Heusen. The resulting
counterpoint between bass and treble make the song a favorite of jazz
instrumentalists and vocalists alike.

Slow ballad with verse (16) and refrain (32)
PUBLISHER: Famous Music Corporation
KEY: G maj., *STARTS*: d' (G maj.), *FORM*: ABAB'

≈≈≈≈≈≈≈≈≈≈≈≈≈≈≈≈≈≈≈

LIKE SOMEONE IN LOVE !

WORDS: Johnny Burke, *MUSIC*: James Van Heusen
PREMIERE: Film musical, *Belle of the Yukon*. International / RKO, 1945
INTRODUCED BY: Dinah Shore

Possessed of a lovely melody and intriguing modulations in the
style of Jerome Kern, this lovely ballad was introduced by Dinah Shore in
the film, *Belle of the Yukon*. The most popular recordings were by Shore on
Victor and Bing Crosby on Decca. The closely-knit melody of the refrain,
in ABAB' form, features many paired repeated notes and scalewise
passages, with occasional skips of the fourth and sixth. Interesting

modulations from C major to A major occurring in the "B" sections have made the song a favorite of extemporizing musicians.

Slow ballad with verse (16) and refrain (32)
PUBLISHER: Burke and Van Heusen, Inc. & Dorsey Brothers Music Corp.
KEY: C maj., *STARTS*: e' (C maj.), *FORM*: ABAB'

≈≈≈≈≈≈≈≈≈≈≈≈≈≈≈≈≈≈≈

LONG AGO (AND FAR AWAY) * *

WORDS: Ira Gershwin, *MUSIC*: Jerome Kern
PREMIERE: Film musical, *Cover Girl*. Columbia, 1944
INTRODUCED BY: Rita Hayworth (dubbed in by Martha Mears) & Gene Kelly

One of Jerome Kern's best-known ballads, with lyrics by Ira Gershwin, "Long Ago (And Far Away)" was introduced by Gene Kelly and Rita Hayworth (the latter dubbed in by Martha Mears) in a scene set in a seedy Brooklyn nightclub against a backdrop of chairs piled on tables. Nominated for an Academy Award, the song's most popular recordings were by Dick Haymes and Helen Forrest (Decca), Bing Crosby (Decca), Perry Como (Victor), and Guy Lombardo and his Royal Canadians, with vocal by Tony Craig (Decca).

With a typical Kern twist, the verse, of many repeated notes, modulates from F to A major, but quickly resolves to the C dominant seventh just before the refrain in F major. In the refrain, marked "cantabile," the principal theme is restated every eight bars at different pitch levels: first in F major, then A-flat major, then again in F major, and finally in both B-flat major and F major. Thus, the song is, in a sense, monothematic. The tender ballad is enriched by Gershwin's inspired lyrics in such passages as: "Chills run up and down my spine, Aladdin's lamp is mine."

Moderate ballad with verse (12) and refrain (32)
PUBLISHER: T. B. Harms Company
KEY: F maj., *STARTS*: f' (F maj,), *FORM*: ABAC

≈≈≈≈≈≈≈≈≈≈≈≈≈≈≈≈≈≈≈

MOONLIGHT IN VERMONT ★★★!

WORDS: John Blackburn, *MUSIC*: Karl Suessdorf
INTRODUCED BY: by Margaret Whiting, in a Capitol recording, with Billy
Butterfield and his Orchestra

Bearing the title of a forgotten 1943 film, *Moonlight in Vermont*,
starring Gloria Jean in which it was never heard, this striking ballad has
enjoyed a life of its own. Singer Margaret Whiting was instrumental in
popularizing it; her Capitol record, with Billy Butterfield and his Orchestra, sold over a million copies. Whiting recorded it again for Capitol in
1954, with Lou Busch and his Orchestra.

Lacking a verse, the refrain is in conventional AABA form, but
only twenty-eight bars in length. It is unusual in its use of six-bar phrases
in the "A" sections (with an added two-bar coda in the last) and an eight-
bar release. Harmonies enrich the song immeasurably, as in the E seventh
of Bar Two, the D-flat ninth of Bar Four, and the shifting chords under the
numerous repeated notes of the release: A minor, D seventh, B-flat minor
seventh, E-flat seventh. All these attributes have made the song a favorite of
vocalists as well as instrumentalists.

Slow ballad with refrain (28)
PUBLISHER: Michael H. Goldsen, Inc.
KEY: E-flat maj., *STARTS*: c" (E-flat maj.), *FORM*: AABA

≈≈≈≈≈≈≈≈≈≈≈≈≈≈≈≈≈≈≈

SENTIMENTAL JOURNEY ★★★

WORDS AND MUSIC: Bud Green, Les Brown, and Ben Homer
INTRODUCED BY: Les Brown and his Orchestra, vocal by Doris Day, in a
Columbia recording

One of the biggest hits of the war years, "Sentimental Journey" was
written because Ben Homer, the arranger for Les Brown' band, needed
some ready cash. He got an advance from Buddy Morris, a publisher
friend, and conceived the idea of the song, which he then proceeded to
work up with Brown and Bud Green. As arranged by Homer, and with a
vocal by Doris Day, the song soon became a favorite of dancers at the Café
Rouge of the Hotel Pennsylvania in New York. The Columbia recording
sold over a million copies, enabling the song to remain sixteen weeks on
Your Hit Parade – five weeks as No. 1. Later hit recordings were by Ella
Fitzgerald, with Eddie Heywood and his Orchestra (Decca) in 1947, and by
The Ames Brothers, with Les Brown and his Orchestra (Coral) in 1951.

Although "Sentimental Journey" belongs to the genre of train song, it has few of the accoutrements: only the reference to "railroad tracks" and whistle-like sounds of the release. The childlike melody, in AABA form, revolves about only two notes, c' and e', with the latter occasionally lowered to the blue note, e-flat'. The release is formulaic in its harmonies, which move from F major to C major, and then from D seventh to G seventh.

The easily-remembered song inspired, and was used in, two films called *Sentimental Journey,* one in 1946, the other in 1984.

> Very slow rhythm song with verse (8) and refrain (32)
> *PUBLISHER*: Edwin H. Morris Company, Inc.
> *KEY*: C maj., *STARTS*: e' (C maj.), *FORM*: AABA

≈≈≈≈≈≈≈≈≈≈≈≈≈≈≈≈≈≈≈≈

STRANGE MUSIC

> *WORDS AND MUSIC*: Robert Wright and George "Chet" Forrest, based on Edvard Grieg's "Nocturne" and "Wedding Day at Troldhaugen"
> *PREMIERE*: Operetta, *Song of Norway*
> New York: Imperial Theatre, 21 August 1944 (860 perf.)
> *INTRODUCED BY*: Lawrence Brooks and Helena Bliss

This mellifluous ballad is the only survivor from the operetta, *Song of Norway,* first produced in California in July, 1994, and then in New York in August. A phenomenal success, the operetta was built around the life of Norwegian composer, Edvard Grieg. The fictionalized and romanticized biography also used Grieg's music as the basis of its score. "Strange Music" was the hit song of the show, which was later produced in London (6 March 1946), where it ran for 526 performances. Early recordings were by Bing Crosby (Decca), James Melton (Victor), and Lanny Ross (Silvertone).

The music of the verse is a condensed version of Grieg's beautiful "Nocturne" transposed to the key of B-flat major. The refrain, in A-flat major, is cleverly derived from Grieg's famous piano piece, "Wedding Day at Troldhaugen", maintaining the distinctive harmonies of the opening theme, but compressing the melody from its original chordal outlining into a more lyrical line. The refrain is in four sections, ABCA', with the "B" section paraphrasing the "A" a fourth higher, the "C" section presenting new material, and the final section bringing back the principal theme with an added coda, carrying the song to its highest point. In true operetta style, the range is wide: an octave and a fourth.

Toralv Maurstad (playing Edvard Grieg) sang "Strange Music" in the 1970 film version of *Song of Norway*.

Moderate ballad with verse (19) and refrain (36)
PUBLISHER: Chappell & Co., Inc.
KEY: A-flat major, *STARTS*: c" (A-flat maj.), *FORM*: ABCA'

≈≈≈≈≈≈≈≈≈≈≈≈≈≈≈≈≈≈≈≈

SWINGING ON A STAR

WORDS: Johnny Burke, *MUSIC*: James Van Heusen
PREMIERE: Film musical, *Going My Way*. Paramount, 1944
INTRODUCED BY: Bing Crosby and The Robert Mitchell Boys' Choir

Academy-Award-winner for Best Song of 1944, "Swinging on a Star" was introduced by Bing Crosby and The Robert Mitchell Boys Choir in the film, *Going My Way*. It was popularized by Crosby, with The Williams Brothers and John Scott Trotter and his Orchestra, on a Decca record that sold over a million copies.

Written in the form of a folk song, with equal weight given to verse and refrain, Johnny Burke's lyrics present a catalogue of animals – a mule, a pig, a fish – along with words of advice, such as "If you have to go to school / You may grow up to be a mule." In James Van Heusen's catchy tune, the verse doubles as a refrain, going twice through the circle of fifths (G seventh - C seventh - F seventh - B-flat major) in each eight bars.

Besides its auspicious film début in *Going My Way*, "Swinging on a Star" was featured in two other films: sung by Crosby, Dorothy Lamour, Betty Hutton, Sonny Tufts, Diana Lynn, and Arturo De Cordova in *Duffy's Tavern* (1945); and by Frank Sinatra in *The Joker Is Wild* (1957).

Moderate novelty song with verse (8) and three refrains (20)
PUBLISHER: Burke and Van Heusen, Inc.
KEY: B-flat maj., *STARTS*: g' (B-flat maj.), *FORM* (Overall): ABABAB

≈≈≈≈≈≈≈≈≈≈≈≈≈≈≈≈≈≈≈≈

THE TROLLEY SONG !

WORDS: Hugh Martin, *MUSIC*: Ralph Blane
PREMIERE:Film musical, *Meet Me in St. Louis*. Metro Goldwyn Mayer, 1944
INTRODUCED BY: Judy Garland

This marvelous song was introduced by Judy Garland in a five-minute production number, orchestrated by Conrad Salinger, that was a highlight of the blockbuster film musical, *Meet Me in St. Louis.* Garland's Decca record was a best-seller, with other recordings by Vaughn Monroe and his Orchestra, vocal by Monroe and Marilyn Drake (Victor); Guy Lombardo and his Royal Canadians, vocal by Stuart Foster (Decca); and The Pied Pipers (Decca). The song was nominated for an Academy Award, and remained fourteen weeks on *Your Hit Parade.* Forty-five years later, it was sung by Donna Kane in the stage version of *Meet Me in St. Louis,* which opened at the Gershwin Theatre in New York, 2 November 1989.

Specifically designed as a movie production number, "The Trolley Song" is one of the longest songs in the popular repertoire: with two thirty-two bar verses and two eighty-six bar refrains. The infectious rhythm of the wheels dominates the accompaniment, with repeated notes imitating the sound of a trolley bell at the words, "Clang, clang, clang; Ding, ding, ding; and Zing, zing, zing. " The lengthy coda is virtually a song in itself, rising gradually but inexorably to the song's highest point, at the words: "To the end of the line." The wondrous momentum of the song is accomplished within a range that stays within an octave.

Bright rhythm song with two verses (32) and two refrains (86)
PUBLISHER: Leo Feist, Inc.
KEY: E-flat maj., *STARTS*: g' (E-flat 6), *FORM*: AABAC

≈≈≈≈≈≈≈≈≈≈≈≈≈≈≈≈≈≈≈≈

TWILIGHT TIME

WORDS: Buck Ram, *MUSIC*: Marty Nevins, Al Nevins, and Artie Dunn
INTRODUCED BY: The Three Suns

One of the most popular ballads of the year, "Twilight Time" was composed and introduced by the instrumental trio, The Three Suns, who recorded it for Victor and used it as a theme song thereafter. In 1945, Les Brown and his Orchestra also had a popular recording (Decca). But the song reached the peak of its popularity only in 1958, with a Mercury record by The Platters that brought it to the No. 1 spot on *Your Hit Parade.* There is no verse. The extremely ornamental melody of the refrain, which is in very slow tempo, consists of eighth-note triplets in tandem with dotted eighths and sixteenths. Harmonies of the release go through the circle of fifths: B seventh - E minor - A seventh - D seventh.

Very slow ballad with refrain (32)
PUBLISHER: Campbell-Porgie, Inc.
KEY: G maj., *STARTS*: c-sharp' (G maj.), *FORM*: AA'BA"

≈≈≈≈≈≈≈≈≈≈≈≈≈≈≈≈≈≈≈

YOU ALWAYS HURT THE ONE YOU LOVE *

WORDS AND MUSIC: Doris Fischer and Allan Roberts
INTRODUCED BY: The Mills Brothers, in a Decca recording

A sentimental little waltz, "You Always Hurt the One You Love" was introduced and popularized by The Mills Brothers, a vocal group whose Decca record sold over a million copies. It is an old-fashioned waltz in ABCA' form, with the "B" and "C" sections each paraphrasing the "A" section a step higher. Therefore, the song is, in a sense, monothematic, with a simple stepwise melody, uncomplicated harmonies, and a concept that has universal appeal.

Moderate waltz with verse (16) and refrain (32)
PUBLISHER: Sun Music co., Inc.
KEY: B-flat maj., *STARTS*: f' (B-flat maj.), *FORM*: ABCA'

≈≈≈≈≈≈≈≈≈≈≈≈≈≈≈≈≈≈≈

YOU BELONG TO MY HEART (SOLAMENTE UNA VEZ)

ENGLISH WORDS: Ray Gilbert, *MUSIC*: Agustin Lara
PREMIERE: Cartoon film, *The Three Caballeros*. Disney, 1945
INTRODUCED BY: the voice of Dora Luz

A Mexican import originally known as "Solamente Una Vez," with Spanish lyrics by its composer Agustin Lara, this lyrical melody was given English words by Ray Gilbert. Sung by the voice of Dora Luz in the Disney cartoon film The Three Caballeros – starring Donald Duck, Panchito, and José Carioca – the best-selling record was by Bing Crosby, with Xavier Cugat and his Orchestra (Decca).

The song lacks a verse. The refrain, in ABAB' form, begins with a five-note pickup leading to the long note g', which quickly moves a step higher, this time leading to c". The subtle melodies of the "B" sections alternate with a stepwise, descending line of repeated notes. Gilbert's English lyrics have a lyrical touch of their own, as in: "Now we own all the stars and a million guitars are still playing."

In other films, Tito Guizar sang "You Belong to My Heart" in *The Gay Ranchero* (1948). Ezio Pinza and The Guadalajara Trio sang it in *Mr. Imperium* (1951), known in Britain as *You Belong to My Heart*.

Moderate rumba with refrain (32)
PUBLISHER: La Salle Music Publishers, Inc.
KEY: E-flat maj., *STARTS*: b-flat' (E-flat maj.), *FORM*: ABAB'

≈≈≈≈≈≈≈≈≈≈≈≈≈≈≈≈≈≈≈≈

YOU'RE NOBODY 'TIL SOMEBODY LOVES YOU ⋆ ⋆

WORDS AND MUSIC: Russ Morgan, Larry Stock, and James Cavanagh
INTRODUCED BY: Russ Morgan and his Orchestra, in a Decca recording

The title of this song, almost a truism, has contributed mightily to its success. Originally introduced by one of its writers, Russ Morgan, the song reached its peak of popularity more than two decades after it was written, with Dean Martin's famous Reprise recording of 1965. Both music and words could have been written in the twenties. The refrain is in ABA'C form, with a simple melody outlining the obvious harmonies, which move through the circle of fifths in each "A" section: B seventh - E seventh - A minor - D seventh - G major. The lyrics sometimes stretch a point, as in: "But gold won't bring you happiness when you're growing old."

Moderate rhtythm song with verse (8) and refrain (32)
PUBLISHER: Southern Music Publishing Co., Inc.
KEY: G maj., *STARTS*: d' (G maj.), *FORM*: ABA'C

≈≈≈≈≈≈≈≈≈≈≈≈≈≈≈≈≈≈≈≈

1945

THE END OF AN ERA

1945

Kiss me once and kiss me twice, and kiss me once again

Sammy Cahn
"It's Been a Long, Long Time"

With newfound awareness that the United States does not stand alone in the world, a number of songs are imported from abroad this year, including "Beyond the Sea (La Mer)", "Symphony" from France, and "Cruising Down the River" from Britain. But by far the most à propos song of the year, at least to returning servicemen and women, is the thankful "It's Been a Long, Long Time". Although a few innovative songs are written, such as "Laura", "It Might As Well Be Spring", and "You'll Never Walk Alone", the spark of originality that characterized many of the songs of the thirties and early forties seems somewhat dissipated. Perhaps it is war weariness.

For in this momentous year, the war reaches an horrific culmination on land and sea before finally coming to an end. Newspapers are full of frightening headlines: bloody battles, devastating air raids, and catastrophic atomic bombs. People are grief-stricken by the death of Franklin Delano Roosevelt on 12 April, and wonder about his successor, Harry S. Truman. They are overjoyed by the surrender of Germany on 7 May and Japan on 14 August. But they are preoccupied with questions: When will the war be over? Will the United States invade Japan? Will troops be transferred from Europe to the Far East? There is much apprehension and much worry, but by year's end a strong feeling of relief.

And there are bright spots in the world of entertainment. In the theater, Tennessee Williams has his first hit with *The Glass Menagerie*, while Rodgers and Hammerstein have their second with *Carousel*, blessed with a remarkable score said to be Rodgers's favorite. In the movies, actor Ray Milland and director Billy Wilder both win Oscars for *The Lost Weekend*, a realistic portrayal of the horrors of alcoholism. Joan Crawford wins an Oscar for her striking acting comeback as Mildred Pierce. A wonderful film musical called *State Fair*, boasting Rodgers and Hammerstein's first and only film score, takes the country by storm.

With over 56 million radio sets throughout the land and record sales booming, popular singers continue to dominate the entertainment industry. Many are alumni of the big bands, including Frank Sinatra,

Dick Haymes, Perry Como, Jo Stafford, Doris Day, Peggy Lee, and Helen O'Connell.

There is a strong feeling that the nation has come to the end of an era. How fitting that 1945 also sees the passing of the master composer who more than any other epitomized the age of great popular songs, Jerome Kern.

SONGS OF 1945

Beyond the Sea (La Mer)
Cruising Down the River
Dream **
(I Love You) For Sentimental Reasons
If I Loved You **
It Might As Well Be Spring **!
It's a Grand Night for Singing
It's Been a Long, Long Time
June Is Bustin' Out All Over
Laura **!
Let It Snow! Let It Snow! Let It Snow! *
Love Letters
The More I See You *!
New York, New York !
On the Atchison, Topeka and the Santa Fe
Sioux City Sioux
Symphony
That's for Me
Till the End of Time
You'll Never Walk Alone **!

BEYOND THE SEA (LA MER)

WORDS: Jack Lawrence, *MUSIC*: Charles Trenet
INTRODUCED BY: Charles Trenet

Charles Trenet's majestic anthem, "La Mer", which the composer himself introduced and popularized in Paris with his own French lyrics, became tremendously popular throughout Europe in the immediate post-war years. Trenet brought it to America, where it acquired English words by Jack Lawrence. Popular recordings were by the bands of Benny Goodman (Capitol), Harry James (Columbia), and Tex Beneke (RCA Victor). But it was Bobby Darin's sensational 1947 recording on Atco that made "La Mer" a hit in North America as well as in Europe.

Lacking a verse, the music departs from the ordinary in its structure of four twelve-bar sections – forty-eight bars in all – in AABA form. The powerful, maestoso melody consists of long-held notes alternating with quarter-note triplets. The main theme also appears in the release in two 6-bar sections, the first in A major, the second in C major. Darin again sang "Beyond the Sea" in two films: *Diner* (1982) and *Tequila Sunrise* (1988).

Slow ballad with refrain (48)
PUBLISHER: Raoul Breton (Fr.), T. B. Harms Company,
Chappell & Co., Inc.,sole selling agent (USA)
KEY: F maj., *STARTS*: c' (F maj.), *FORM*: AA'BA

≈≈≈≈≈≈≈≈≈≈≈≈≈≈≈≈≈≈≈

CRUISING DOWN THE RIVER

WORDS and MUSIC: Eily Beadell and Nell Tollerton

An old-fashioned waltz, "Cruising Down the River" was the winner of the "Write a Song Contest" in England in 1945. Imported to North America, it became a hit in 1949, with two million-selling recordings: by Blue Barron and his Orchestra (Metro Goldwyn Mayer) and Russ Morgan and his Orchestra (Decca). At that time, it stayed nineteen weeks on *Your Hit Parade*, eight times as No. One. The song is one of those anachronisms that could have been written fifty years before its time. The refrain consists of four sixteen-bar sections, the melody is very reminiscent and slightly chromatic, while the harmonies are in the simple style of the popular waltzes of the 1890s. Dick Haymes and a chorus sang it in the film musical, *Cruisin' Down the River* (1953).

Moderate waltz with verse (32) and refrain (64)
PUBLISHER: Henry Spitzer Music Publishing Co., Inc.
KEY: F maj., *STARTS*: a' (F maj.), *FORM*: AA'BA"

≈≈≈≈≈≈≈≈≈≈≈≈≈≈≈≈≈≈

DREAM * *

WORDS and MUSIC: Johnny Mercer
INTRODUCED BY: Johnny Mercer

Johnny Mercer, both lyricist and entertainer, introduced this song of his own invention as the closing theme of his radio show. It has remained a closing theme ever since. Hit records were by Frank Sinatra (Columbia) and The Pied Pipers (Capitol), with the latter using it as their theme thereafter. The song was revived by The Four Aces in 1954 (Decca).

The striking main theme drifts lazily downwards in long notes: first by a half step (a chromatic touch from b-flat' to a') and then by whole steps.

"Dream" was featured in the 1945 film, *Her Highness and the Bellboy*, starring Hedy Lamarr, Robert Walker, and June Allyson. Fred Astaire performed it with a chorus in *Daddy Long Legs* (1955), and Beverly D'Angelo sang it in *In the Mood* (1987). The dreamy song also holds a secure place as a closing number of dances and other entertainments.

Slow ballad with verse (8) and refrain (32)
PUBLISHER: WB Music Corp.
KEY: B-flat maj., *STARTS*: b-flat' (B-flat 6), *FORM*: ABAB'

≈≈≈≈≈≈≈≈≈≈≈≈≈≈≈≈≈≈

(I LOVE YOU) FOR SENTIMENTAL REASONS

WORDS: Deek Watson, *MUSIC*: William Best
INTRODUCED BY: Eddy Howard and his Orchestra, on a Majestic record

A quite ordinary ballad, "(I Love You) For Sentimental Reasons" became a hit in 1947, with a No. One hit record by The King Cole Trio (Capitol). Dinah Shore followed through with a Columbia recording, as did Ella Fitzgerald with The Delta Rhythm Boys on Decca. The song was revived in 1958 with a recording by Sam Cooke (Keen).

Lacking a verse, the refrain in AABA form approaches the simplistic both in words and music. The melodic line meanders downwards, mostly stepwise, in each "A" section. Quarter-note triplets abound and harmonies are sparse. But this very simplicity makes the song a natural as a blank canvas ready for improvisation. Therefore, it is a favorite of jazz musicians to this day.

> Slow ballad with refrain (32)
> *PUBLISHER*: Duchess Music Corporation
> *KEY*: F maj., *STARTS*: d" (F maj.), *FORM*: AABA

≈≈≈≈≈≈≈≈≈≈≈≈≈≈≈≈≈≈≈

IF I LOVED YOU * *

> *WORDS*: Oscar Hammerstein II, *MUSIC*: Richard Rodgers
> *PREMIERE*: Musical play, *Carousel*
> New York: Majestic Theatre, 19 April 1945 (890 perf.)
> *INTRODUCED BY*: John Raitt and Jan Clayton, on Majestic Records

The musical play, *Carousel*, adapted from Ferenc Molnar's 1921 play, *Liliom*, was a triumphal success for the team of Rodgers and Hammerstein. It established them as the lions of the musical theater and led to even greater successes in years to come: *South Pacific*, *The King and I*, *The Sound of Music*. But *Carousel* always remained their favorite, for good reason: although it was a tragedy, it was a joyous one. In "If I Loved You", sung in Act I, carnival barker, Billy Bigelow (originally played by John Raitt), archly describes to Julie Jordan (played by Jan Clayton) how he would feel if he loved her. It is a stirring song and became the big ballad of the show as well as a hit on its own, with recordings by Perry Como (Victor), Bing Crosby (Decca), and Frank Sinatra (Columbia). It was revived by Roy Hamilton in 1954 and by Chad and Jeremy in 1965.

The verse is integral to the plot, giving the musical effect of weaving at the loom in a mill in nineteenth-century New England; it is in 2/4 meter and the key of D major. The refrain, in C major, is captioned "with great warmth and slowly". It opens with a broad melody of long notes outlining the interval of the major sixth, first based on the note c' and then on d'. The release begins in A minor, but modulates back to C major. The song reaches its highest point (f") in the final "A" section, and closes with two dramatic holds, or fermatas, on the words "if I".

Gordon MacRae and Shirley Jones sang "If I Loved You" in the 1957 film version of *Carousel*. The play, *Carousel*, itself is one of the most popular in the Rodgers and Hammerstein canon and is in a perennial state of revival. Although somewhat pretentious, "If I Loved You" remains a favorite of singers, both aspiring and established, as well as of listeners.

Slow ballad with two verses (24) and refrain (32)
PUBLISHER: Williamson Music, Inc.
KEY: C major, *STARTS*: c' (C maj.), *FORM*: AABA'

≈≈≈≈≈≈≈≈≈≈≈≈≈≈≈≈≈≈≈≈

IT MIGHT AS WELL BE SPRING * * !

WORDS: Oscar Hammerstein II, *MUSIC*: Richard Rodgers
PREMIERE: Film musical, *State Fair.* Twentieth-Century Fox, 1945
INTRODUCED BY: Louanne Hogan, dubbing for Jeanne Crain

The second of three screen versions of *State Fair* was also the most successful one because of the magnificent score by Oscar Hammerstein II and Richard Rodgers – their only original one for the movies. A highlight was this endearing ballad, which won the Academy Award for Best Song of 1945. Dick Haymes, who starred in the movie along with Jeanne Crain and Dana Andrews, had a best-selling Decca record. Margaret Whiting also had a hit recording, with Paul Weston and his Orchestra (Capitol).

It is a charming song, in a late eighteenth-century style reminiscent of Mozart and Haydn. The verse rambles up and down the scale, while the refrain consists largely of eighth notes, playing around the notes d' and e' as well as those of the G major triad: g', b', d''. Both form (AA'BA''C) and length (forty bars) are unusual, with a lengthy coda bringing in new material. Hammerstein's lyrics are particularly striking in their use of metaphor, as in "restless as a willow in a windstorm" and "jumpy as a puppet on a string".

In the 1962 remake of *State Fair*, "It Might As Well be Spring" was sung by Anita Gordon, dubbing for Pamela Tiffin.

Moderate ballad with verse (13) and refrain (40)
PUBLISHER: Williamson Music, Inc.
KEY: G maj., *STARTS*: d' (G maj.), *FORM*: AA'BA''C

≈≈≈≈≈≈≈≈≈≈≈≈≈≈≈≈≈≈≈≈

IT'S A GRAND NIGHT FOR SINGING

WORDS: Oscar Hammerstein II, *MUSIC*: Richard Rodgers
PREMIERE: Film musical, *State Fair.* Twentieth Century-Fox, 1945
INTRODUCED BY: Louann Hogan (dubbing for Jeanne Crain), Vivian Blaine, Dick Haymes, William Marshall, Dana Andrews, and chorus

A rousing waltz, "It's A Grand Night for Singing" adds much to the attractiveness of the Rodgers and Hammerstein film score of *State Fair*. The song is a lusty affirmation of joy, just the ticket for a happy family occasion like going to a midwestern state fair. As he did with other songs from the film, singer Dick Haymes had a hand in popularizing this stirring song on radio and in recording..

The song's most striking attribute is the octave jump between the words "grand" and "night", accompanied by a sparkling glissando. The refrain consists of two sixteen-bar sections, followed by an eight-bar coda in long notes, at the words: "Falling, falling in love". The song lacks a verse as well as a release. Instead, there is an interlude, playing around intervals of the second: from e' to f-sharp', from f-sharp' to g', and from g' to a'.

In the 1962 film version of *State Fair*, "It's a Grand Night for Singing" was performed by Pat Boone, Anita Gordon (dubbing for Pamela Tiffin), Bobby Darin, Bob Smart, and a chorus.

Moderate waltz with refrain (40) and interlude (32)
PUBLISHER: Williamson Music, Inc.
KEY: G maj., *STARTS*: f-sharp' (G maj.), *FORM*: ABAB'

≈≈≈≈≈≈≈≈≈≈≈≈≈≈≈≈≈≈≈≈

IT'S BEEN A LONG, LONG TIME

WORDS: Sammy Cahn, *MUSIC*: Jule Styne
INTRODUCED BY: Phil Brito

This little ditty voiced the feelings of millions of servicemen and women, happy to return to the arms of their loved ones at the end of World War II. Not surprisingly, it was the biggest hit of the year, with recordings, among others, by Bing Crosby, with The Les Paul Trio (Decca); Harry James and his Orchestra, with vocal by Kitty Kallen (Columbia); and Charlie Spivak and his Orchestra. Staying fourteen weeks on *Your Hit Parade* – five times as No. 1, it was one of two blockbuster songs (the other was "Let It Snow! Let It Snow! Let It Snow!) written this year by the dynamic duo of Sammy Cahn and Jule Styne, both of whom went on to better things in the years to come.

Music and lyrics are simple and concise, telling the tale in sixteen bars, using short, dotted notes and triplets alternating with long-held half notes at the words "long, long time".

"It's Been a Long, Long Time" was sung by Dan Dailey, June Haver, and Gloria De Haven in the 1950 film, *I'll Get By*. As an expression of its times, the song has no equal.

Slow ballad with verse (8) and refrain (16)
PUBLISHER: Edwin H. Morris & Company
KEY: F maj., *STARTS*: a' (F maj.), *FORM*: AA'BA"

≈≈≈≈≈≈≈≈≈≈≈≈≈≈≈≈≈≈

JUNE IS BUSTIN' OUT ALL OVER

WORDS: Oscar Hammerstein II, *MUSIC*: Richard Rodgers
PREMIERE: Musical play, *Carousel*
New York: Majestic Theatre,14 April 1945 (890 perf.)
INTRODUCED BY: Christine Johnson and Jean Darling, danced to by Pearl Lang and ensemble

This lively song acts as a sort of comic relief in the serious musical play, *Carousel*. The very vitality of the opening line of the refrain, "June Is Bustin' Out All Over", is captured in the melody line, rising an octave in the first three bars. In a favorite form of folk song (ABAB'C), the music features many repeated notes over harmonies that are unchanged in the first six bars of each "A" section. Cuteness prevails in the "B" sections, with childlike play on two notes, g' and e'. Finally, an eleven-bar coda plays on the notes of the octave (d' -d") at the words "June, June, June", ending the song on the tone of the dominant, d". The lyrics present Oscar Hammerstein II at his most folksy, as in "That the young Virginia creepers / Have been huggin' the be-jeepers".

Moderate rhythm song with verse (24) and three refrains (44)
PUBLISHER: Willimason Music, Inc.
KEY: G maj., *STARTS*: d' (G maj,), *FORM*: ABAB'C

≈≈≈≈≈≈≈≈≈≈≈≈≈≈≈≈≈≈

LAURA * * !

WORDS: Johnny Mercer, *MUSIC*: David Raksin
PREMIERE: Music from the film score of *Laura*. 20th Century-Fox, 1945

The mystery film, *Laura*, starred Gene Tierney as a threatened woman, Vincent Price as her southern suitor, Dana Andrews as a detective, and Clifton Webb as a cynical newspaper columnist. But the real star of the film was David Raksin's fascinating score. The main theme was soon extracted and put into the bounds of a popular song, with lyrics by Johnny Mercer. The result is "Laura", a striking ballad that started a new era of songs emanating from dramatic films. "Laura" quickly took off independently of the film, aided by the recordings of Woody Herman and his Orchestra (Columbia), Stan Kenton and his Orchestra, Freddy Martin and his Orchestra (Victor), and Dick Haymes (Decca).

The music is marvelously complex – at first glance, unsuitable for a popular song. It is replete with seventh and ninth chords and in a constant state of modulation; from the opening A minor seventh, it moves to G major, F major, and E-flat major, before returning to A minor seventh. Only at the end of the refrain is the C major tonality apparent. Happily, Johnny Mercer's poetic lyrics bring this difficult, ethereal music to life, using such expressions as "the face in the misty light" and "the laugh that floats on a summer night". And the last line says it all: "But she's only a dream".

"Laura" stands alone as one of the most harmonically complicated songs in the popular canon.

> Slow ballad with verse (16) and refrain (32)
> *PUBLISHER*: Twentieth Century Music Corporation, assigned to Robbins Music Corporation
> *KEY*: C maj., *STARTS*: b' (A min. 7), *FORM*: ABAC

≈≈≈≈≈≈≈≈≈≈≈≈≈≈≈≈≈≈≈≈

LET IT SNOW! LET IT SNOW! LET IT SNOW! *

WORDS: Sammy Cahn, *MUSIC*: Jule Styne
INTRODUCED BY: Vaughn Monroe and his Orchestra, in a Victor recording

This jolly song returns every year as part of the Christmas pantheon. It was the second big hit of the year for Sammy Cahn and Jule Styne. Among the most prominent early recordings, besides Vaughn Monroe's, were those of The Boswell Sisters, Frank Sinatra, and Woody Herman and his Orchestra. It is a happy and uncomplicated little song, starting with an octave jump and continuing with dotted notes descending stepwise. All elements are the simplest: melody, rhythm, harmony, form. But still, "Let It Snow! Let It Snow! Let It Snow! brings memories of carefree times watching the snow pile up outdoors. In that nostalgic sense, it survives as a seasonal perennial.

Moderate novelty song with verse (8) and refrain (32)
PUBLISHER: Edwin H. Morris & Company, Inc.
KEY: F maj., *STARTS*: c' (F maj.), *FORM*: AABA

≋≋≋≋≋≋≋≋≋≋≋≋≋≋≋≋≋≋≋

LOVE LETTERS

WORDS: Edward Heyman, *MUSIC*: Victor Young
PREMIERE: Developed from the soundtrack of the film, *Love Letters*. 1945

The film, *Love Letters*, starring Jennifer Jones and Joseph Cotton, is about a young woman who develops amnesia when she starts getting love letters from an unknown admirer. Victor Young's lachrymose soundtrack theme was developed into a song, "Love Letters", with lyrics by Edward Heyman, which was nominated for an Academy Award. Dick Haymes' Decca recording was a hit. The song was revived in 1962, with a million-selling record by Kitty Lester (Era), and again in 1966, by Elvis Presley (RCA). The verse is in D major, leading to the refrain in G major. The latter, in ABAC form, has a simple melody of many repeated notes in a gradually ascending melodic line. Lester again sang "Love Letters" in the 1986 film, *Blue Velvet*.

Moderate ballad with verse (16) and refrain (32)
PUBLISHER: Famous Music Corporation
KEY: G maj., *STARTS*: d' (G maj.), *FORM*: ABAC

≋≋≋≋≋≋≋≋≋≋≋≋≋≋≋≋≋≋≋

THE MORE I SEE YOU * !

WORDS: Mack Gordon, *MUSIC*: Harry Warren
PREMIERE: Film musical, *Billy Rose's Diamond Horseshoe*.20th,Century Fox, 1945
INTRODUCED BY: Dick Haymes and Betty Grable

Almost operatic in style, this lovely ballad was introduced by Dick Haymes and Betty Grable in the film musical, *Diamond Horseshoe,* originally known as *Billy Rose's Diamond Horseshoe*. Haymes had a best-selling record, with Victor Young and his Orchestra (Decca), as did Harry James and his Orchestra, with vocal by Buddy De Vito (Capitol). In 1996 Chris Montez revived the song with a hit record on A&M.

The refrain is noted for Harry Warren's lyrical melody, with long-held notes and downward leaps of the fourth. In ABA'C form, the "B" section is of particular interest for its modulations: from E-flat major to C flat major and return. In the expressive "C" section , the downward jumps extend first to an octave and then to a sixth. The beautiful singing line of this aria-like song resembles the work of Jerome Kern at his best.

Slow ballad with verse (9) and refrain (32)
PUBLISHER: Twentieth Century Music Corporation, assigned to Morley Music Co.
KEY: E-flat maj., *STARTS*: b-flat' (E-flat maj.), *FORM*: ABA'C

≈≈≈≈≈≈≈≈≈≈≈≈≈≈≈≈≈≈≈

NEW YORK, NEW YORK !

WORDS: Betty Comden and Adolph Green, *MUSIC*: Leonard Bernstein
PREMIERE: Musical comedy, *On the Town*
New York: Adelphi Theatre, 28 December 1944 (463 perf.)
INTRODUCED BY: John Battles, Cris Alexander, and Adolph Green

This rousing song – not to be confused with the much more popular "Theme from New York, New York" of 1977, by Fred Ebb and John Candor – is sometimes known by its famous line, "The Bronx Is Up but the Battery's Down".

Both verse and refrain are of equal importance, alternating three times in different keys. The verse, in E-flat major, is a twelve-bar blues, heavily syncopated, with a generous portion of blue notes. The refrain, in G major, has a catchy melody outlining chords both of G major and B-flat major. The ingenious lyrics concisely tell the story of three sailors on leave, endeavoring to see New York "from Yonkers on down to the bay", in just one day. They end with the cry: "It's a helluva town!"

Moderate rhythm song with three verses (3) and three refrains (8)
PUBLISHER: Warner Brothers, Inc.
KEY: G maj., *STARTS*: d' (G 6), *OVERALL FORM*: ABABAB'

≈≈≈≈≈≈≈≈≈≈≈≈≈≈≈≈≈≈≈

ON THE ATCHISON, TOPEKA AND THE SANTA FE

WORDS: Johnny Mercer, *MUSIC*: Harry Warren
PREMIERE: Film musical, *The Harvey Girls*. Metro Goldwyn Mayer, 1946
INTRODUCED BY: Judy Garland, Marjorie Main, Ray Bolger, Ben Carter, Margaret O'Brien, Vernon Dent, Jack Clifford, Ray Teal, and chorus

This legendary train song was the hit of the frontier film musical, *The Harvey Girls*, about a group of waitresses in the wild and woolly West.

Winner of the Academy Award for Best Song of 1946, the song had two No. 1 recordings: one by its lyricist Johnny Mercer with The Pied Pipers (Capitol); the other by Bing Crosby with Six Hits and a Miss (Decca). Other recordings were by Tommy Dorsey with The Sentimentalists (Victor), and Judy Garland with The Merry Macs and Lyn Murray's Orchestra.

There is no verse. Reminders of the railroad abound: in the ostinato, boogy-woogy beat throughout; the simulated train whistles; the word painting in the release ("Ooh, Ooh, Ooh"); the syncopation and many dotted notes; and in the folksy lyrics like "Do yuh hear that whistle down the line?", which even manage to rhyme "Santa Fe" with "Philadelphiay". Harmonic interest is afforded in the release, by the modulation from C major to A-flat major and back again.

"On the Atchison, Topeka and the Santa Fe" was reprised, with the original performers, in the 1974 retrospective film, *That's Entertainment*.

Moderate rhythm song with refrain (36)
PUBLISHER: Leo Feist, Inc.
KEY: C maj., *STARTS*: g' (C maj.), *FORM*: AABA

≋≋≋≋≋≋≋≋≋≋≋≋≋≋≋≋≋

SIOUX CITY SUE

WORDS: Ray Freedman, *MUSIC*: Dick Thomas
INTRODUCED BY: Dick Thomas, in a National recording

An aberration from other songs of the day, "Sioux City Sue" is a modest country song that was introduced by its composer, Dick Thomas, and popularized in a far-reaching recording by Bing Crosby, with The Jesters and Bob Haggart and his Orchestra (Decca). Other recordings were by Zeke Manners and Tony Pastor and his Orchestra.

In folk-song style, the three verses tell a tale about driving "a herd of cattle from old Nebraska way", while the catchy refrain chants that "There ain't no gal as true as my Sioux City Sue". In country fashion, the melody consists chiefly of broken chords; harmonies are tonic, dominant, and subdominant; and the lyrics make special use of alliteration – not to mention the homonymy of "Sioux" and "Sue".

The song was featured in the 1946 film, *Sioux City Sue*. It occupies a special place as a forerunner of the folk song revolution of the fifties and sixties.

Moderate country song with three verses (16) and refrain (16)
PUBLISHER: Edwin H. Morris & Company, Inc.
KEY: F maj., *STARTS*: c' (F maj.), *FORM*: ABAC

≈≈≈≈≈≈≈≈≈≈≈≈≈≈≈≈≈≈≈

SYMPHONY

WORDS: Jack Lawrence, *MUSIC*: Alex Alstone
INTRODUCED BY: Freddy Martin and his Orchestra, vocal by Clyde Rogers, in a Victor recording

With its broad, sweeping melody, as well as its title, "Symphony" epitomizes the classics. And, indeed, it was introduced and popularized in North America by that master of adaptation from the classics, Freddy Martin and his Orchestra (see 1941, "Tonight We Love). The music, however, is original, by French composer Alex Alstone. As "C'Est Fini (It's Over)", the French words were by André Tabet and Roger Bernstein. With the similar-sounding title, "Symphony", the music was given English words by Jack Lawrence. Other recordings were by Marlene Dietrich (Decca), Bing Crosby (Decca), Jo Stafford (Capitol), and Benny Goodman and his Orchestra, vocal by Liza Morrow (Columbia).

In conventional AABA form, the "A" sections are simple both melodically (outlining major thirds) and harmonically (employing tonic and dominant). On the other hand, the release is most interesting harmonically, modulating through the circle of fifths from A-flat seventh to D-flat major, and then from G-flat seventh to C-flat major, and finally, enharmonically to G seventh and back to C major. There is a brief coda, bringing the melody to its highest point, e", and the song to a dramatic conclusion.

Slow ballad with refrain (40)
PUBLISHER: Editions Salabert (Fr.), assigned to Chappell & Co., Inc.
KEY: C maj., *STARTS*: e' (C maj.), *FORM*: AABA

≈≈≈≈≈≈≈≈≈≈≈≈≈≈≈≈≈≈≈

THAT'S FOR ME

WORDS: Oscar Hammerstein II, *MUSIC*: Richard Rodgers
PREMIERE: Film musical, *State Fair*. 20th Century Fox, 1945
INTRODUCED BY: Louanne Hogan (dubbing for Jeanne Crain), Dana Andrews, Vivian Blaine, and Dick Haymes

Another song from the 1945 film classic, *State Fair*, "That's for Me" may not have not attained the popularity of other songs from the film, like "It Might as Well Be Spring" and "It's a Grand Night for Singing". Nevertheless, it bears some interesting qualities that lift it above the ordinary. Hit recordings were by Dick Haymes (Decca), Jo Stafford (Capitol), and Kay Kyser and his Orchestra, with vocal by Mike Douglas and The Campus Kids (Columbia).

The first two "A" sections are conventional enough, with an ascending scale given the added piquancy of the flatted sixth (e-flat"). However, the next two sections of the song are wildly original. The "B" section is only four bars in length, modulating to B-flat major, while the last "A" section returns only to the last part of the main theme, closing with a short coda. Thus, in thirty bars, did Richard Rodgers do away with the tyranny of thirty-two bar, AABA form.

Moderate ballad with verse (16) and refrain (30)
PUBLISHER: Williamson Music, Inc.
KEY: G maj., *STARTS*: d' (G maj.), *FORM*: AABA'

≈≈≈≈≈≈≈≈≈≈≈≈≈≈≈≈≈≈≈≈

TILL THE END OF TIME

WORDS and MUSIC: Buddy Kaye and Ted Mossman
INTRODUCED BY: Perry Como

One of many popular songs directly adapted from the classics, "Till the End of Time" is based on the main theme of Frederic Chopin's *Polonaise in A-Flat, Op. 53, No. 6* – a piano piece that was strongly featured in the purported Chopin film biography, *A Song to Remember*, starring Cornel Wilde, Merle Oberon, and Paul Muni, and released this year. It is rather successful, as adaptations go, but it changes a strong, martial theme into a sentimental love ballad. Like all good popular songs, its subject was appropriate to its times, when thoughts of war were turning to thoughts of love. Perry Como's Victor recording sold over two million copies. Other recordings were by Dick Haymes (Decca), and Les Brown and his Orchestra, vocal by Doris Day (Columbia). The ballad stayed nineteen weeks on *Your Hit Parade*, seven times as No. 1. Perry Como again sang the song in a 1946 film, *Till the End of Time*, a drama about three returning war veterans which starred Dorothy McGuire, Guy Madison, and Robert Mitchum.

The first two sections of the song paraphrase the main theme of the *Polonaise*; the final section is pure Tin Pan Alley.

Slow ballad with verse (8) and refrain (32)
PUBLISHER: Santly-Joy, Inc.
KEY: B-flat maj., *STARTS*: d' (B-flat maj.), *FORM*: ABAC

≈≈≈≈≈≈≈≈≈≈≈≈≈≈≈≈≈≈≈≈

YOU'LL NEVER WALK ALONE * !

WORDS: Oscar Hammerstein II, *MUSIC*: Richard Rodgers
PREMIERE: Musical play, *Carousel*
New York: Majestic Theatre, 19 April 1945(890 perf.)
INTRODUCED BY: Christine Johnson

The sheet music of "You'll Never Walk Alone" has the following performance direction: To be sung with great warmth, like a hymn". The song has, indeed, many of the attributes of a hymn: the philosophy of hope, the gradually rising melody, the spacious harmonies, the powerful climax.

Without a verse, the song is through-composed, building inexorably in long notes and grave harmonies to a stirring summit at the words "You'll never walk alone". That last line is then repeated with a melody descending in thirds, and ending, unusually, on the note of the dominant (g').

In the 1957 film version of *Carousel*, "You'll Never Walk Alone" was sung by Claramae Turner. The song stands as a symbol of carrying on in the face of adversity. A fitting end to this study, it also stands as a testament to the strength and character of a peculiarly American idiom, popular song, between the years 1920 and 1945.

Slow hymn with refrain (36)
PUBLISHER: Williamson Music, Inc.
KEY: C maj., *STARTS*: c' (C maj.), *FORM*: ABCD

≈≈≈≈≈≈≈≈≈≈≈≈≈≈≈≈≈≈≈≈

EPILOGUE

What Happened to America's Popular Songs?

After the cataclysm of World War II, the mainstream of American popular music bifurcated, forming two disparate streams. The first honored the time-honored tradition of the songs in the present book; the second all but ignored it. On the one hand were the worthy songs continuing to be written by such masters of the songwriting craft as Irving Berlin, Cole Porter, Richard Rodgers, Harold Arlen, Ira Gershwin, and Oscar Hammerstein II, and others following on the footsteps of the now-deceased Jerome Kern, George Gershwin, and Lorenz Hart. On the other hand, an entirely different concept of popular music began to arise, revolutionizing the way songs were written for the remainder of the century. So we have a dichotomy, two diverging streams of popular music, raising two paradoxical and antagonistic questions: Why *Did* Songs Continue To Sound the Way They Used To? and Why *Didn't* Songs Sound the Way They Used To?

Why Did Songs Continue to Sound The Way They Used To?

For a while after the war, the audience of returned servicemen and women and their families remained faithful to the old familiar kind of music, with songs emanating from Tin Pan Alley, Broadway, and Hollywood. By now, Tin Pan Alley was centered about the Brill Building at 1619 Broadway, near West 49th Street, in New York City, a venerable edifice which housed scores of music publishers who continued to grind out hits for a still eager audience. But, significantly, the emphasis came to be more and more on the performer rather than the matieral – the style rather than the substance. Singers, rather than big bands came to dominate the industry. Increasingly, recordings by such artists as Frank Sinatra and Nat "King" Cole far outreached sheet music in sales volume. And the songs were written for them to sing: "The Christmas Song (Chestnuts resting on an open fire)" and "Let It Snow! Let It Snow! Let Its Snow!" , both stemming from 1946, are seasonal perennials to this day.

Broadway still produced the lion's share of America's popular songs, at least for another three decades, but in significantly lesser quantity. Irving Berlin's musical comedy, *Annie Get Your Gun,* started off with a bang in 1946, introducing such songs as "The Girl That I Marry", "They Say It's Wonderful", and "There's No Business Like Show Business". Cole Porter carried the torch with the song-resplendent *Kiss Me Kate*, introducing the wryly comic "Always True to You (In My Fashion)", the soulful ballad "So In Love", and the sparkling waltz "Wunderbar". Porter again hit the jack-pot with *Can-Can* in 1953, bringing forth the songs "C'est Magnifique", "I Love Paris", and "It's All Right with Me". The splendid *Finian's Rainbow* brightened up the boards in 1947; it is remembered for its sparkling songs by E. Y Harburg and Burton Lane: "How Are Things in Glocca Morra?", "Old Devil Moon" and "When I'm Not Near the Girl I Love". Frank Loesser's *Guys and Dolls* (1950) produced a host of innovative numbers, among them "A Bushel and a Peck", "If I Were a Bell", and "Luck Be a Lady". From Stephen Sondheim and Jule Styne's *Gypsy* (1959) came the show-business songs "Everything's Coming Up Roses", and "Let Me Entertain You". Other song-worthy musical comedies included Meredith Willson's *The Music Man* (1957: "Till There Was You", "Seventy-Six Trom-bones"), Tom Jones and Harvey Schmidt's perpetually-running *The Fantasticks* (1960: "Try to Remember", "Soon It's Gonna Rain"), and Edward Kleban and Marvin Hamlisch's *A Chorus Line* (1975: "What I Did for Love", "One").

Following on the successes of their ground-breaking musical plays, *Oklahoma* (1943) and *Carousel* (1945), Richard Rodgers wrote the song-studded *South Pacific* in 1949, with a plethora of wonderful standards including "Bali Ha'i", "Younger Than Springtime", and "Some Enchanted Evening", From their memorable score for *The King and I* (1951) came "Getting to Know You", "Hello, Young Lovers", and "Shall We Dance". Rodgers and Hammerstein's last collaboration was *The Sound of Music* (1959), a resounding hit, with the songs "Climb Ev'ry Mountain", "Edelweiss", and the title song. Another songwriting team important to the development of the musical play was that of Alan Jay Lerner and Frederick Loewe. Their songs for *My Fair Lady* (1956) are legendary, including "I Could Have Danced All Night", "I've Grown Accustomed to Her Face", and "On the Street Where You Live. They followed up with *Camelot* (1960), another compelling score, including "If Ever I Would Leave You" and the title song.

One of the most important works ever produced for the American musical theater was *West Side Story* (1957), based on Shakespeare's *Romeo and Juliet*. Its outstanding score by Stephen Sondheim and Leonard Bernstein included "Maria", "Somewhere", and "Tonight". Among other song-rich musical plays were Sheldon Harnick and Jerry Bock's *Fiddler on the Roof* (1964: "If I Were a Rich Man", "Sunrise, Sunset") and Stephen Sondheim's A Little Night Music (1973, "Send in the Clowns").

The film musical, source of so many great songs of the thirties and forties, declined rapidly in the fifties, and practically disappeared by the sixties. The reasons were not hard to fathom: the emergence of television and the widening gap between the music of the movies and the music the nation was listening to: rock 'n' roll and its various offshoots. Jerome Kern's posthumous score for the film, *Centennial Summer* (1946) introduced the bittersweet ballads "All Through the Day" and "In Love In Vain".

The last gasp of the originally-scored film musical came in 1958, with Lerner and Loewe's enchanting score for *Gigi*, introducing "Thank Heavens for Little Girls", "I Remember It Well", and "The Night They Invented Champagne", among other songs. For a short while in the early fifties, retrospective film musicals enjoyed a comeback. Films like *An American in Paris* (1951) and *Singin' in the Rain* (1952) found a new audience for the songs in the present volume.

The tradition of basing independent songs on the soundtracks of non-musical films, as in "Laura" (1944), also continued, producing such hit songs as "Three Coins in the Fountain" (1954, from the picture of the same name), "Love Is a Many-Splendored Thing" (1955, from the picture of the same name), "Around the World" (1958, from *Around the World in Eighty Days*), "Moon River" (1961, from *Breakfast at Tiffany's*), "Days of Wine and Roses" (1962, from the picture of the same name), "Somewhere My Love (1965, from *Dr. Zhivago*), "The Shadow of Your Smile (1965, from *The Sandpiper*), "Born Free" (1966, from the picture of the same name), "Raindrops Keep Fallin' on My Head" (1969, from *Butch Cassidy and the Sundance Kid*), "Speak Softly Love" (1972, from *The Godfather*), "The Way We Were" (1973, from the picture of the same name), "Evergreen" (1976, from *A Star Is Born*), "(Theme from) New York, New York" (1976, from the picture of the same name), and "The Wind Beneath My Wings (1988, from *Beaches*).

And so we see that songs, many of high quality, continued to be written in the spirit of the twenties, thirties, and forties through the remainder of the century. For example, "(Theme from) New York, New York", the great hit of 1977, could just as well have been written in the 1920s as the 1970s. But now we turn to the other side of the coin.

Why Didn't Songs Sound the Way They Used To?

Beginning in the mid-1950s, there was a major sea change effecting the way many songs would be written for the rest of the century. A youthful, defiant audience demanded a new sound, a complete break from the music of the past and especially the music of their parents. Down with romantic melodies, standard forms and lengths, impressionistic harmonies, traditional instrumentation of pianos and big bands. Up with pervasive rhythm, amplication, reverberation, guitars and other electronic instruments, exaggerated showmanship, and simplication of all elements of music. Increasingly, the material became less and less important, over-shadowed by the performer. The complex web of this second stream of late twentieth-century popular music can perhaps best be comprehended by a quartet of words ending in the same suffix: idolization, importation, diversification, and commercialization. It must be emphasized that these four factors are neither carved in stone nor mutually exclusive. Interrelationships between them are the rule rather than the exception (many idols, for example, were imported). Still, the four concepts give some context and proportion to the extremely complex history of late twentieth century popular music.

Idolization

With the demise of the big bands, a younger generation needed something to fill the void. They turned to singers, many of them alumni of the big bands. And so began the practice of idolization of singers, or more accurately, performers, who came to dominate the popular music industry throughout the twentieth century. Of course, vocalists had been idolized before, as witness Frank Sinatra's swooning audience at New York's Paramount Theatre in 1944. But consummate singers such as Bing Crosby, Dinah Shore, Ella Fitzgerald, Billie Holiday, and Nat "King" Cole took second place to the songs they sang; they clearly enunciated the lyrics and did justice to the music.

Starting in the fifties, a new type of singer took precedence, one who emphasized performance over material. When Elvis Presley was elevated to the rank of pop idol, his gestures and mannered performance (Elvis the Pelvis) reflected the burgeoning rebellion of youth. It wasn't the songs he sang that mattered, but rather the gestures and gyrations of the performer. In fact, many of the songs performed by Presley were derivative, such as "Love Me Tender" (1956), taken from "Aura Lee" (1861) and "It's Now or Never" (1960), from "O Sole Mio" (1898), or else had their roots in traditional blues. This emphasis on guitar-swinging showmanship came to dominate the industry for the rest of the century, often at the expense of the quality of the songs. Beginning with The Beatles, the idolization of individual performers and groups, very often from Britain, reached out to all facets of popular entertainment.

The influence of American popular music abroad is well documented. Ragtime, jazz, the blues, and American popular songs in general have inspired a host of composers, both "serious" and popular, in Europe and throughout the world. Less well known is the steady contribution foreign nations have made to American music. Importation has always existed, but never to the extent of the last half of the twentieth century. Foremost was the British Invasion of the sixties, an invasion with two prongs: rock and theater music.

The rock invasion began with The Beatles and their often innovative music, principally by John Lennon and Paul McCartney, including "Yesterday", "Michelle" (1965), "Here, There and Everywhere" (1966), and "The Fool on the Hill" (1967). The tremendous success of The Beatles in the United States led to a host of British performers who usually sang their own songs, including Dave Clark, Barry and Robin Gibb, Mick Jagger and The Rolling Stones, Elton John, Pink Floyd, and David Bowie.

The British theater invasion started with Lionel Bart's *Oliver* (1960), and two shows by Anthony Newley and Leslie Bricusse, *Stop the World – I Want to Get Off* (1962) and *The Roar of the Greasepaint – The Smell of the Crowd* (1965); their hit songs were, respectively: "As Long As he Needs Me", "What Kind of Fool Am I", and "Who Can I Turn To?" But the most successful British shows of all were those of Andrew Lloyd Webber, especially *Evita* (1978), with "Don't Cry for Me, Argentina"; Cats (1981), with "Memory"; and *The Phantom of the Opera* (1986), with "All I Ask of You".

Brazilian music conquered North America beginning with the outstanding score for the film, *Black Orpheus* (1959), which introduced the melody that was to become "A Day in the Life of a Fool" in 1966. The extraordinary bossa novas of Antonio Carlos Jobim took the country by storm in such songs as "Quiet Night of Quiet Stars" and "Meditation" (1962), "The Girl from Ipanema" (1963), and "Wave" (1967). Jobim's music brought a new voice to American music that resounds to the present day.

A surprisingly great number of postwar hits originated in France, among them "La Vie en Rose" (1950), "Autumn Leaves" (1947), "Where Is Your Heart?" (1953), "I Wish You Love", and "Let It Be Me" (1955), "The Good Life" (1963), and the quintessential "American" song of independence, "My Way", originally "Mon Habitude" (1967). Also from France came the innovative music of Michel Legrand, who wrote the scores for well over 100 films. Among his most popular songs in the United States were "I Will Wait for You" and "Watch What Happens" from *The Umbrellas of Cherbourg* (1964); "The Windmills of Your Mind" from *The Thomas Crown Affair* (1968); and "What Are You Doing the Rest of Your Life?" from *The Happy Ending* (1970). The extremely successful quasi-opera, *Les Misérables* (1980), with a marvelous score by Claude-Michel Schönberg, contained such outstanding songs as "I Dreamed a Dream", "Master of the House", and "On My Own".

Diversification

Before World War II, one type of music prevailed, enjoyed equally by teenagers and grownups alike. After the war, this mainstream style was fragmented into a bewildering array of genres and subgenres, a veritable delta of rivulets. Some of them, like country and western and rhythm and blues, had been around since the twenties, but they were localized and generally insignificant. Country and western had evolved from "hillbilly music", while rhythm and blues were offshoots of what had been called "race records". From the mid-fifties to mid-sixties, a new style of music predominated. It was dubbed "rock 'n' roll" by Cleveland disc jockey Alan Freed, who introduced the term on his radio show, *Moondog's Rock 'n' Roll Party*. The raw style of rock 'n' roll was replaced by rock in the mid-sixties, largely through the influence of The Beatles and the British Invasion. Over the years, a plethora of subgenres of rock developed, including rockabilly, acid rock, art rock, folk rock, commercial rock, new wave, funk rock, heavy metal, motown, gospel, soul, disco, rap, and reggae. They all had in common the steady beat, the highly amplified guitars and other electronic instruments, the exaggerated showmanship, the lyrics of ambiguity and protest, and the provocative dress.

The protest movement of the fifties and sixties led to a folk song revival, with many performers who wrote their own songs, among them Bob Dylan, Joni Mitchell, Judy Collins, Phil Ochs, Tom Paxton, and Arlo Guthrie. Since the sixties, the concept of the performer-songwriter has taken root and flourished, inspired by The Beatles and coinciding with the emergence of rock and the renaissance of folk song. Among these modern-day troubadours and their hits were Bob Dylan (1962, "Blowin' in the Wind"), John Denver (1967, "Leaving on a Jet Plane"), Paul Simon (1962, "Bridge Over Troubled Water"), Paul Williams (1970, "We've Only Just Begun", 1970), Rod McKuen (1969, "Jean), James Taylor (1969, "Fire and Rain"), Don McLean (1971, "American Pie"), Jim Croce (1971, "Time in a Bottle"), Carole King (1971, "You've Got a Friend"), and Carly Simon (1971, "Anticipation").

Commercialization

The tried and true concept of the individuality of songwriter, publisher, performer, and record producer gave way to the mega-star who controlled all aspects of a song. Sales of record albums by Bruce Springsteen, Michael Jackson, and Madonna, soared into the millions. Popular music became a vast commercial enterprise, controlled by performers, who were very often also the songwriters, publishers, and record producers. On radio since the 1950s, disc jockeys could make a mediocre song into a hit by constant airplay. But the final blow to American popular song was the advent of television. In its early days, the medium had some live entertainers and even introduced some new songs. But the daily fare soon deteriorated to reruns of dreary situation comedies. Unlike radio, recordings, stage, and film, television exerted virtually no influence on American popular music. With few original American musicals on Broadway and no film musicals at all, it would seem that the main venues for the introduction of quality songs had dried up. All that was left was "bubble gum music", a plastic, commercial product that was manufactured to order and could easily be thrown away.

But all was not lost. A tremendous influx of revivals came to Broadway in the last half of the century. From the musical comedies *Oh, Kay!* (1926) to *Guys and Dolls* (1950), as well as from the musical plays *Show Boat* (1927) to *Carousel* (1945), almost every worthwhile musical had been brought back to new generations. The songs of the Roaring Twenties, Great Depression, and World War II had found new audiences. Of course, many songs had never lost their familiarity; they had been popularized through the years by jazz performers and were well-known to aficionados. But suddenly, towards the end of the millennium, there was a renaissance of the songs of long ago – swing was in, rock was out. Big bands were back on campus and the sweet songs of youth again held sway. It seemed that America's great songs had never really disappeared, after all.

APPENDICES

GLOSSARY

A

a'.

See *Pitch notation.*

"A" section.

The first theme of a *refrain.*

AABA

The predominant musical *form* used in popular song during this period. It consists of four sections: the first theme (A), a repetition of "A," the second theme (B), and a return to the first theme (A).

a cappella.

Vocal music without instrumental accompaniment.

Art song.

A song of superior quality, suitable for performance in a concert hall.

Augmented.

A raised tone, often within a *chord.*

B

"B" section.

The second theme of a *refrain.*

Ballad.

A romantic popular song in slow to moderate *tempo.*

Bar.

(1) A vertical line through the staff, dividing it into measures, (2) The measure itself.

Bass line.

The lowest-sounding part of a song. Bass lines may ascend or descend *chromatically*, stepwise, through the *circle of fifths*, or in other configurations.

Beguine.

A dance and rhythmic song in 4/4 *meter*, that accents the first, third, and fourth beats as well as the four afterbeats. It originated on the islands of Martinique and St. Lucia and was universally popularized in Cole Porter's "Begin the Beguine" (1935).

Big bands.

> Groups of ten or more musicians. The big bands reached their apogee in the late 1930s and early 1940s, when they performed, broadcast, and recorded thousands of songs. After World War II the bands gave way to singers, but gained renewed popularity towards the end of the twentieth century.

Blue note.

> A lowered note, usually a flatted third, sixth, or seventh.

Blues.

> An American musical expression of sadness and dissatisfaction that originated in the nineteenth century. It is usually in a musical form of twelve bars, with three four-bar phrases using chords of the *tonic*, *subdominant*, and *dominant*.

Boogie-woogie.

> A particular kind of *bass line*, consisting of a steady pattern of eighth notes as an *ostinato* bass.

Bridge.

> See *Release*

Broken chord.

> A melody which outlines a *triad* or *chord*, as in "Deep in the Heart of Texas" (1941).

C

"C" section.

> The third theme of a *refrain*.

Cadence.

> A harmonic and/or melodic formula that marks the end of a musical phrase, section, verse, or refrain.

Catalogue song.

> A song that lists items. A prime example is Cole Porter's "Let's Do It (Let's Fall in Love)" (1928), which catalogues animals from moths to giraffes and nationalities from Siamese to Letts, who "do it."

Chord.

> The simultaneous sounding of three or more notes of different *pitch*. Chords may be simple *triads*; named for their added notes (sixths, sevenths, ninths, elevenths, thirteenths), *diminished* (with lowered notes); or *augmented* (with raised notes).

Chordal outlining.

See *Broken chord.*

Chorus.

See *Refrain.*

Chromatic, Chromaticism.

Use of tones not in the regular diatonic scale, with frequent employment of *half steps*, as in a twelve-tone scale.

Circle of fifths.

A harmonic progression by ascending fifths, with each key adding a sharp (C, G, D, etc.); or by descending fifths, with each key adding a flat (C, F, B-flat, etc.). It is a circle because the series returns to its point of origin at its twelfth step.

Coda.

The concluding section of a song or part of a song.

Common time.

See *meter.*

D

"D" section.

The fourth theme of a *refrain.*

Diatonic.

Pertaining to a scale of eight tones in an established order; can be either *major* or *minor.*

Diminished.

A lowered tone, often within a *chord.*

Dominant.

The fifth degree of the *scale* and the chords built on it. The one most commonly used is the dominant seventh, which leads to the chord of the *tonic.*

Dotted note.

A dot written after a note increases its value by half. The jagged rhythm of a dotted quarter note followed by an eighth is characteristic of many popular songs.

Enharmonic.

> A note or chord which sounds the same but is indicated differently; for example, the notes c-sharp and d-flat and their attendant chords.

F

Fermata, or Hold.

> A symbol placed over a note indicating that it is to be held beyond its normal duration.

Fifth.

> See *Interval, Dominant.*

Film musical.

> A cinematic genre featuring lavish musical and choreographic sequences. It began with *The Jazz Singer* (1927) and had its heyday in the 1930s and '40s, introducing many fine original songs.

Flat.

> The lowering of *pitch* by a *half step.*

Form.

> The arrangement of material within a song, indicated by capital letters (AABA, ABA, ABAC, etc.). The mark ' after a letter (A') shows that the material of the first *"A" section* is altered somewhat at its repetition.

Fourth.

> See *Interval, Subdominant.*

Foxtrot.

> A dance which began in 1913 as a dance craze called "Mr. Fox's Trot." The term came to denote most American songs of the 1920s and '30s in 2/4 or 4/4 *meter.*

Half step, or Semitone.

> The smallest *interval* used in Western music. On the piano, it is the distance between any two adjacent tones, whether white or black.

Harmonic minor.

> A type of minor *scale* with a flatted sixth and raised seventh.

Harmony.

> The general succession of *chords* within a song, making up its vertical aspect, as opposed to the horizontal aspect of *melody.*

I

Improvisation.

On-the-spot creation of music by a performer; the very essence of *jazz*.

Interlude.

Music played or sung between sections of a song.

Interval.

The distance between any two *pitches*, played either simultaneously or successively. An interval is usually measured upwards by *step*; thus c-e is a third, c-f a fourth, c-g a fifth, c-a a sixth, and c-b a seventh.

J

Jazz.

An umbrella term embracing much American popular music of the twentieth century. It is linked to many other genres, including the *blues*, *ragtime*, and *swing*, and at its heart is *improvisation* around the nucleus of a song, many of which are in this volume.

Jazz standard.

A vintage popular song that is commonly used by jazz performers for *improvisation*.

K

Key.

The tonal center of a song, around which the other harmonies revolve. A key can be either *major* or *minor*. Most popular songs in this book are in the following major keys: D, G, C, F, B-flat, E-flat, A-flat, and D-flat.

L

Leitmotiv.

In opera, a musical fragment related to the drama.

Lied.

A German art song with a poem as text.

Lyrics.

The words of a song; they are of primary importance to the music, determining whether the song will be happy or sad, simple or convoluted, intelligible or inane. In fact, a perfect song is often called a "marriage of equal partners" – the lyrics and the music.

M

Maestoso.

Majestic.

Main theme.

See *Principal theme.*

Major.

A *scale, key, interval, chord,* or *triad* with a raised third.

Measure.

See *Bar.*

Melody.

A fixed succession of *pitches* moving in a horizontal direction, as opposed to *harmony.*

Meter.

The number of beats to a *bar,* The predominant meter in popular song is 4/4, also known as common time, consisting of four beats to the bar. Of lesser importance is *waltz* time (3/4), with three beats to the bar; and 2/4 time, with two beats to the bar.

Minor.

A *scale, key, interval, chord,* or *triad,* with a lowered third.

Modulation.

Harmonic movement to and from one key area and another in the course of a song.

Monothematic.

Having only one theme throughout, which may be at different *pitch* levels.

Motive.

The shortest part of a melodic idea.

Musical comedy.

The principal genre of stage musical from the 1920s to the 1950s, usually with a light-hearted plot and spoken dialogue. Many lasting *show tunes* were introduced in musical comedy.

Musical play.

A stage work that is more serious than a *musical comedy* and more dramatic than an *operetta.* The genre began with *Show Boat* (1927), continued with *Oklahoma!* (1943), and reached its zenith with *West Side Story* (1957). The last quarter century saw an invasion of musical plays from abroad, including *Les Misérables* (1980) from France and *Phantom of the Opera* (1986) from Britain.

N

Natural.

A note that is not affected by either a *sharp* or a *flat*.

Ninth.

See *Interval.*

Novelty song.

A popular song not on the subject of love. Especially, a comic song on the order of "Yes! We Have No Bananas" (1923).

O

Octave.

The interval of the eighth, as in the first two notes of the refrain of "Over the Rainbow" (1939).

Opera.

A dramatic stage work that is sung throughout. The prime American example is George Gershwin's *Porgy and Bess* (1935). Some *musical plays*, such as *Show Boat* (1927), have crossed over into the opera repertoire.

Operetta.

A musical stage work with spoken dialogue that is more substantial in plot than a *musical comedy* but not as serious as a *musical play*. Sigmund Romberg's *The New Moon* (1928) was the last American operetta in the Viennese tradition.

Ostinato.

A persistently repeated rhythmic pattern, usually in the bass, as for example *boogie-woogie*.

P

Pedal point.

A bass note or group of bass notes that is sustained under changing harmonies. Its name derives from the pedal keyboard of the organ.

Pentatonic.

Music based on a *scale* of five *pitches*.

Percussion.

Musical instruments that are struck, especially drums and cymbals.

Pickup.

The note(s) of a melody occurring before the first accented beat of a song or refrain.

Pitch, Pitch notation.

A sound determined by a tone's frequency of vibration. In this volume, Middle C of the piano keyboard is shown as c'. Notes below middle C are un-primed, those an octave and more above middle C are double-primed. Thus the full compass of notes can be shown as follows:

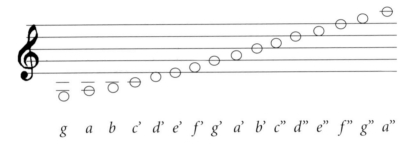

$g \quad a \quad b \quad c' \quad d' \quad e' \quad f' \quad g' \quad a' \quad b' \quad c'' \quad d'' \quad e'' \quad f'' \quad g'' \quad a''$

Polka.

A moderately fast dance, originating in Bohemia in the early nineteenth century, and its music. Prime American examples are "Beer Barrel Polka (Roll Out the Barrel)" and "Pennsylvania Polka" (1942).

Principal theme.

The central theme of a refrain, usually in the *"A" section.*

R

Ragtime.

A three- or four-part piece for piano solo, with much *syncopation,* written in the form of a march. Originating in the 1890s, the genre reached its peak in the piano rags of Scott Joplin (1869-1917).

Range.

The distance between the highest and lowest parts of a song. Popular songs are usually confined to the span of the human voice, which is generally less than two octaves. Most popular songs range from an *octave* to an octave and a half.

Recapitulation.

A return to the *principal theme.*

Recitative.

A style of vocal writing using many repeated notes, with a minimum of musical structure. Derived from *opera*, it is frequently employed in the *verse* of a popular song.

Refrain, or Chorus.

The main and usually the most important part of a song.

Release, or Bridge.

Any contrasting section of a popular song; most commonly, the *"B" section* in *AABA* form.

Revue.

A theatrical production featuring songs and skits, which may or may not have a plot. The revue developed out of *vaudeville* and reached its peak in the 1920s and 1930s.

Rhythm song.

Any song with a pronounced beat, as opposed to a *ballad.*

Riff.

In *jazz* or *swing*, a brief melodic phrase that is repeated, often over changing harmonies.

Rondo.

A form with multiple recurrence of the principal theme, such as ABACA.

Rubato.

A slight irregularity of the beat employed by a performer in the interest of musical expression.

Rumba.

A dance and song type brought to the United States from Cuba in 1930. It inspired a craze for Latin American music that lasted for two decades. There are a number of different subtypes, but all are in 4/4 meter and moderate to fast tempo, with intricate *percussion* patterns.

S

Samba.

> A Brazilian dance and song type established in the 1920s. It is usually in 2/4 meter and moderate tempo, using complex rhythms and much *percussion*. Sambas popular in the United States include "Brazil" (1939) and "Tico Tico" (1944).

Scale.

> A collection of pitches moving up or down. They are the building blocks of *melody*. The principal scales used in popular song are the *diatonic*, *chromatic*, and *pentatonic*.

Second.

> See *Interval*.

Semitone.

> See *Half step*.

Sequence.

> The repetition of a progression or phrase at differing pitch levels, as in "As Time Goes By" (1931), where the opening *motive* rises first by a *whole step*, then by a fourth, and then by another whole step.

Seventh.

> See *Interval*.

Sharp.

> The raising of *pitch* by a *half step*.

Show tune.

> A song originating either from Broadway or Hollywood.

Skip.

> A melodic leap by more than a *whole step*.

Staccato.

> Notes of short duration to be played lightly.

Standard.

> A song that has retained its popularity over the years.

Step.

> Melodic movement by either a *whole step* or a *half step*.

Subdominant.

> The fourth degree of the *scale* and the chords built on it.

Swing.

> A style of playing *jazz* with a flowing, rhythmic pulse, exemplified by the *big band* style of the 1930s and 1940s.

Syncopation.

> A displacement of rhythmic accent from a strong to a weak beat, commonly used in *ragtime*, *jazz*, and *swing*.

T

Tango.

> An Argentine dance and song type, originating in the late nineteenth century, that became a sensation in the United States in 1913. In 4/4 meter, it is characterized by a persistent, strongly-accented rhythm in slow *tempo*.

Tempo.

> The speed of performance of a song, from very slow to very fast.

Third.

> See *Interval*.

Through-composed.

> A song without repetition of the *principal theme*, in other words, with new music throughout.

Tonality.

> The central harmony or key around which a song is built.

Tone.

> A musical sound of a certain *pitch*.

Tonic.

> The first note of a *scale* and the chord built on it.

Torch song.

> An emotional *ballad* about unrequited love, as in "Bill" (1927) and "Stormy Weather" (1933).

Triad.

> A chord of three tones played simultaneously: the *tonic*, third, and fifth.

Trio.

The middle section of a march or *polka,* introducing new material in a contrasting key.

Triplet.

Three notes of equal value to be performed in the time normally occupied by two notes of the same value.

Tritone.

The interval of the augmented fourth, containing three *whole tones,* such as c to f-sharp, b-flat to e', or f to b.

U

Uptempo.

A musical *tempo* that is typically fast and in cut time (two beats to the measure). Also known as "society tempo."

V

Vamp.

A type of accompaniment that introduces a song or refrain. It may be repeated indefinitely until the performer is ready to begin; hence the expression, "Vamp till ready."

Vaudeville.

A variety show, very popular in the first two decades of the twentieth century; a prime medium for introducing and popularizing songs.

Verse.

The first part of a popular song, preceding the *refrain.* Multiple verses were the rule in the 1920s. By the thirties, single verses were the rule and a number of songs were written with no verse at all, such as "Smoke Gets In Your Eyes" (1933) and "I've Got You Under My Skin" (1936).

W

Waltz.

A dance and song type in 3/4 *meter.* It was in great favor at the turn of the century, but less so in the 1920s and thirties. It regained popularity in waltzes by Richard Rodgers, such as "Lover" (1933) and "Falling in Love with Love" (1938).

Whole step.

An *interval* consisting of two *half tones* (i.e., c to d, or b to c-sharp').

Word painting.

Illustrating the meaning of words in the music by imitation of sounds, rising or falling melodic lines, loudness or softness, or other means.

Y

Your Hit Parade.

A radio and television show that began in 1935 and continued until 1958. Each week, it ranked songs according to their current popularity. Thus, "White Christmas" (1942) appeared thirty-eight times as Number One over various holiday seasons, while "People Will Say We're in Love" (1943) had the longest consecutive run, with thirty-eight appearances from June 1943 to January 1944 – but only three times as Number One.

BIBLIOGRAPHY

Song Collections

America's Greatest Hit Songs. Edited by Lyle Kenyon Engel. New York: Grosset & Dunlap, 1962.

The Best Jazz Songs of All Time. Ojai, Ca.: Creative Concepts, n.d.

The Best of Cole Porter. Secaucus, N. J.: Warner Brothers Publications, n.d.

The Big Bands Songbook. Edited by George Simon. New York: Barnes & Noble Books, 1975.

Feist Celebrated Song Hits. New York: Leo Feist, Inc., 1936

The Genius of Kurt Weill. New York: Chappell & Co., Inc., n.d.

The Great Music of Duke Ellington. Melville, N. Y.: Belwin Mills Publishing Corp., 1973

George Gershwin, A Highlight Collection of His Best-Loved Original Works. New York: Shattinger International Music Corp.; Charles Hansen, Inc. distributor, 1977.

George Gershwin Song Album. New York: New World Music Corp., Harms Inc. distributor, 1938.

Gershwin on Broadway (From 1919 to 1933). N. Y.: Warner Bros. Publications, Inc., 1987.

Great Songs of Broadway. New York: Quadrangle / The New York Times Book Co., 1937.

The Jerome Kern Song Book. Edited by Oscar Hammerstein II. New York: Simon and Schuster and T. B. Harms Company, 1955.

Music and Lyrics by Cole Porter. New York: Chappell & Co., Inc. and Random House, n.d.

Nat "King" Cole: All-Time Greatest Hits. Ojai, Ca.: Creative Concepts, n.d.

The New York Times Nostalgic Years in Song. Edited by Irving Brown. New York: Quadrangle /The New York Times Book Co., 1974.

100 Best Songs of the '20s and '30s. New York: Harmony Books, A Division of Crown Publications, 1973.

The Rodgers and Hart Song Book. New York: Simon and Schuster, 1951.

Songs by Alec Wilder Were Made to Sing. Ft. Lauderdale, Fla.: TRO Ludlow Music, n.d.

The Songs of Richard Rodgers. New York: Williamson Music, Inc., n.d.

Too Marvelous for Words: The Magic of Johnny Mercer. Miami, Fl.: Warner Bros. Publications, Inc., 1985.

20's, 30's & 40's Showstoppers. Miami, Fl., Warner Bros. Music Publications, Inc., 1987.

Witmark Hits Through the Years. New York: M. Witmark & Sons, 1951.

The World's Most Beautiful Love Songs. Katonah, N.Y.: Ekay Music, Inc., 1995.

Books

Allen, Frederick Lewis. *Only Yesterday: An Informal History of the Nineteen-Twenties,* Harper & Row, 1931.

_____. *Since Yesterday: The 1930s in America: September 3, 1929 - September 3, 1939,* New York: Harper & Row, 1939.

ASCAP Biographical Dictionary, 4th ed. New York: R. R. Bowker Company, 1980.

ASCAP Index of Performed Compositions, 1914-1981. New York: ASCAP, 1981.

Benjamin, Ruth and Arthur Rosenblatt. *Movie Song Catalog: Performers and Supporting Crew for the Songs Sung in 1460 Musical and Nonmusical Films, 1928-1988,* Jefferson, N. C.: McFarland & Company, Inc., 1993.

Bergreen, Laurence. *As Thousands Cheer: The Life of Irving Berlin.* New York: Viking, 1990.

Boardman, Barrington. *Isaac Asimov presents From Harding to Hiroshima.* New York: Dembner Books, 1988.

Bordman, Gerald. *American Musical Comedy: From Adonis to Dreamgirls.* New York: Oxford University Press, 1982.

_____. *American Operetta: From H.M.S. Pinafore to Sweeney Todd.* New York: Oxford University Press, 1981.

_____. *American Musical Revue: From the Passing Show to Sugar Babies.* New York: Oxford University Press, 1985.

_____. *American Musical Theatre: A Chronicle.* 2nd. ed. New York: Oxford University Press, 1992.

_____. *Days to Be Happy, Years to Be Sad: The Life and Music of Vincent Youmans,* New York: Oxford University Press, 1982.

_____. *Jerome Kern: His Life and Music.* New York: Oxford University Press, 1980.

Buxton, Frank and Bill Owen. *The Big Broadcast 1920-1950*. New York: Avon Books, 1966.

Cahn, Sammy. *I Should Care*. New York: Arlington House, 1974.

Clarke, Donald. *The Rise and Fall of Popular Music*. New York: St. Martin's Griffin, 1995.

Csida, Joseph and June Bundy Csida. *American Entertainment: A Unique History of Popular Show Business*. New York: Watson-Guptill Publications, a division of Billboard Publications, 1978.

Davis, Sheila. *The Craft of Lyric Writing*. Cincinatti, Oh.: Writer's Digest Books, 1985.

DeLong, Thomas A. *Pops: Paul Whiteman, King of Jazz*. Piscataway, N. J.: New Century Publishers, 1983.

Dietz, Howard. *Dancing in the Dark*. New York: Quadrangle, 1974.

Ewen, David. *Great Men of American Popular Song*. Englewood Cliffs, N. J.: Prentice-Hall, 1972.

_____. *The Life and Death of Tin Pan Alley*. New York: Funk and Wagnalls, 1964.

_____. *Panorama of American Popular Music*. Englewood Cliffs, N. J.: Prentice-Hall, 1957.

Fordin, Hugh. *Getting to Know You: A Biography of Oscar Heammerstein II*. New York: Random House, 1977.

Friedwald, Will. *Jazz Singing: America's Great Voices from Bessie Smith to Bebop and Beyond*, New York: Charles Scribner's Sons, 1990.

Fuld, James J. *The Book of World-Famous Music: Classical, Popular and Folk*, 3rd ed., New York: Dover Publications, 1985.

Furia, Philip. *The Poets of Tin Pan Alley: A History of America's Great Lyricists*. New York: Oxford University Press, 1990.

Gammond, Peter. *The Oxford Companion to Popular Music*. New York: Oxford University Press, 1991.

Gavin, James. *Intimate Nights: The Golden Age of New York Cabaret*. New York: Limelight Editions, 1991.

Gershwin, Ira. *Lyrics on Certain Occasions*. New York: Knopf, 1959.

Gottfried, Martin. *Broadway Musicals*. New York: Harry N. Abrams, Inc., 1979.

Green, Benny. *Let's Face the Music: The Golden Age of Popular Song*. London: Pavilion Books Limited, 1989.

Green, Stanley. *Broadway Musicals Show by Show*. Milwaukee, Wis.: Hal Leonard Books, 1985.

_____. *Encyclopedia of the Musical Film*. New York: Oxford University Press, 1981,

_____. *Encyclopedia of the Musical Theatre*. Da Capo Press, 1984.

_____. *Ring Bells! Sing Songs! Broadway Musicals of the 1930's*. New York: Galahad Books, 1971.

Hamm, Charles. *Yesterdays: Popular Song in America*. New York: W. W. Norton, 1983.

Hart, Dorothy. *Thou Swell, Thou Witty*. New York: Harper & Row, 1976.

Hemming, Ray. *The Melody Lingers On: The Great Songwriters and Their Movie Musicals*, New York: Newmarket Press, 1986.

Hyland, William G. *The Song Is Ended: Songwriters and American Music, 1900-1950*, New York: Oxford University Press, 1995.

Iwaschkin, Roman. *Popular Music: A Reference Guide*. New York: Garland Publishing, Inc., 1986.

Jablonsky, Edward. *Harold Arlen: Happy with the Blues*. New York: Da Capo Press, 1986.

Jacobs, Dick. *Who Wrote That Song?* Whitehall, Va.: Betterway Publications, 1988.

Jasen, David A. *Tin Pan Alley: The Composers, The Songs, The Performers and Their Times*.

Katz, Ephraim. *The Film Encyclopedia*. New York: Thomas V. Crowell, 1979.

Kinkle, Roger D. *The Complete Encyclopedia of Popular Music and Jazz 1900-1950*. 4 vols, New Rochelle, N. Y.: Arlington House, 1974.

Lax, Roger and Frederick Smith. *The Great Song Thesaurus*. New York: Oxford University Press, 1984.

Lee, Edward. *Music of the People: A Study of Popular Music in Great Britain*, London: Barnes & Jenkins, 1970.

Lissauer, Robert. *Lissauer's Encyclopedia of Popular Music in America: 1888 to the Present*, New York: Paragon House, 1991.

Marmorstein, Gary. *Hollywood Rhapsody: Movie Music and Its Makers 1900 to 1975*, New York: Schirmer Books, 1997.

Marks, Edward B. *They All Sang: From Tony Pastor to Rudy Vallee*. New York: Viking Press, 1934.

Marx, Samuel and Jan Clayton. *Rodgers and Hart: Bewitched, Bothered and Bedeviled*, New York: Putnam's, 1976.

Mast, Gerald. *Can't Help Singin': The American Musical on Stage and Screen*. Woodstock, NY. The Overlook Press, 1987.

Paymer, Marvin E., General Editor. *Facts Behind the Songs: A Handbook of American Popular Music from the Nineties to the '90s*. New York: Garland Publishing, Inc., 1993.

Roberts, John Storm. *The Latin Tinge: The Impact of Latin American Music on the United States*. Tivoli, N. Y.: Original Music, 1985.

Rosenberg, Deena. *Fascinating Rhythm: The Collaboration of George and Ira Gershwin*, New York: Dutton, 1991.

Sanders, Ronald. *The Days Grow Short: The Life and Music of Kurt Weill*. New York: Holt, Rinehart, and Winston, 1979.

Scheuer, Steven H. *Movies on TV and Videocassette 1991-1992*. New York: Bantam Books, 1990.

Scheurer, Timothy E. *Born in the U. S. A.: The Myth of America in Popular Music from Colonial Times to the Present*. Jackson, Miss.: University Press of Mississippi, 1991.

Schwartz, Charles. *Cole Porter: A Biography*. New York: Da Capo Press, 1979.

_____. *Gershwin: His Life and Music*. New York: Da Capo Press, 1979.

Shapiro, Nat and Bruce Pollock, eds. *Popular Music: An Annotated Index of American Popular Songs (1920-1969)*. 6 vols. New York: Adrian Press, 1973.

Shaw, Arnold. *Popular Music in the 1920s*. New York: Oxford University Press, 1987.

Simon, George T. *The Big Bands*. 4th ed. New York: Schirmer Books, 1981.

Southern, Eileen. *The Music of Black Americans: A History*. New York: W. W. Norton, 1983.

Spaeth, Sigmund. *A History of Popular Music in America*. New York: Random House, 1948.

Stambler, Irwin. *Encyclopedia of Popular Music*. New York: St. Martin's Press, 1965.

Suskin. Steven. *Show Tunes (1905-1985)*. New York: Dodd, Mead, 1986.

Swain, Joseph P. *The Broadway Musical: A Critical and Musical Survey*. New York: Oxford University Press, 1990.

Taylor, Deems. *Some Enchanted Evenings: The Story of Rodgers and Hammerstein*, New York: Harper & Brothers, 1953.

Thomas, Tony. *Harry Warren and the Hollywood Musical*, Secaucus, N.J.: Citadel Press, 1975.

Tyler, Don. *Hit Parade, 1920-1955*, New York: Quill/Morrow, 1985.

Whitcomb, Ian. *After the Ball: Popular Music from Rag to Rock*, New York: Simon & Schuster,1973.

Wilder, Alec. *American Popular Song: The Great Innovators, 1900-1950.* New York: Oxford University Press, 1972.

INDEX OF COMPOSERS AND LYRICISTS

Prado, Miguel 421

Q

Quadling, Lew 372

R

Rainger, Ralph 330, 344
Raksin, David 482
Ram, Buck 471
Ramirez, Roger 432
Rapee, Erno 91, 110
Rasbach, Oscar 36
Raye, Don 417
Razaf, Andy 146, 152, 196, 323, 357
Redmond, John 356
Reynolds, Ellis 183
Richman, Harry 202
Riley, Mike 303
Rivera, E. 212
Roberts, Allan 473
Robin, Leo 111, 158, 178, 223, 330, 344
Robin, Sid 389
Robinson, J. Russel 13
Robison, Willard 184
Robledo, Julian 24
Rodgers, Richard 78, 89, 94, 96, 117, 122, 140, 166, 185, 238, 240, 241, 247, 271, 300, 302, 304, 315, 324, 334, 338, 339, 347, 353, 364, 376, 379,399, 402, 411, 428, 437, 448, 449, 450, 451, 453, 479, 480, 482, 487
Roig, Gonzalo 248
Romberg, Sigmund 55, 64, 119, 133, 136, 308
Rome, Harold 446
Ronell, Ann 247
Rose, Billy 41, 115, 150, 159, 167, 183, 215, 255
Rose, Fred 92
Rose, Vincent 9, 15, 44, 397

Roubanis, N. 419
Rox, John 402
Ruby, Harry 47, 74, 201
Ruiz, Gabriel 411
Ruskin, Harry 154
Russell, Bob 427, 443
Russell, S. K., 257, 372, 376, 419, 421
Russo, Dan 35

S

Sampson, Edgar 323
Schertzinger, Victor 429, 434
Schoebel, Elmer 46
Schonberger, John 15
Schultze, Norbert 445
Schwandt, Wilbur 211
Schwartz, Arthur 153, 199, 210, 229, 283, 352
Secunda, Sholom 329
Seiver, Bruce 245
Shapiro, Ted 131
Sharpe, Jack 343
Shavers, Charles 389
Shay, Larry 140
Sherman, Jimmy 432
Sherr, Jack 248
Signorelli, Frank 388
Silver, Frank 49
Silverman, Al, *see* Stillman, Al
Silvers, Louis 19
Simon, Nat 322
Simons, Moisés 221
Simons, Seymour 129, 208
Siras, John 237
Sissle, Noble 20
Skylar, Sunny 411, 443
Slowitsky, Michael, *see* Edwards, Michael
Smith, Dick 281
Smith, Harry B. 22, 225

Z

Zeman, Vasik 371

INDEX OF SONGS

Z